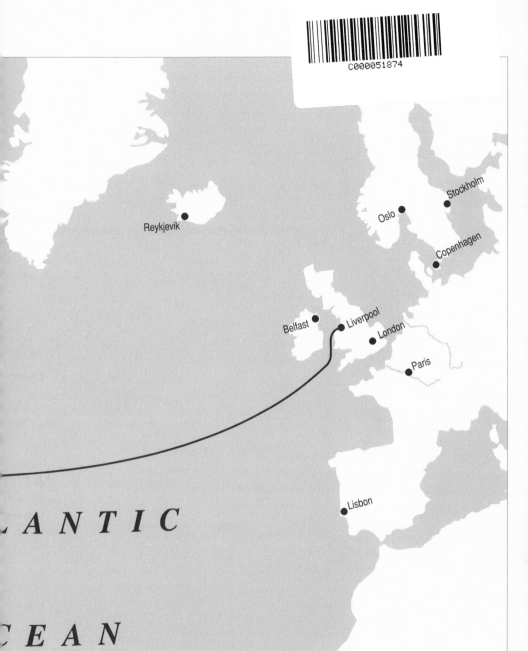

Stockholm

Oslo

Reykjevik

Copenhagen

Belfast Liverpool
London

Paris

Lisbon

LANTIC

CEAN

One inch equals 600 miles
Modified Zenithal Equidistant Projection

MEN WITH A MISSION

MEN WITH A MISSION 1837-1841

THE QUORUM OF THE TWELVE APOSTLES IN THE BRITISH ISLES ▬

JAMES B. ALLEN ▪ RONALD K. ESPLIN ▪ DAVID J. WHITTAKER

Deseret Book Company
Salt Lake City, Utah

Library of Congress Cataloging-in-Publication Data

Allen, James B.
    Men with a mission : the Quorum of the Twelve Apostles in the British Isles, 1837–1841 / James B. Allen, Ronald K. Esplin, and David J. Whittaker.
      p. cm.
    Includes bibliographical references and index.
    ISBN 0-87579-546-3
    1. Mormon Church—Missions—Great Britain—History—19th century. 2. Church of Jesus Christ of Latter-day Saints—Missions—Great Britain—History—19th century. 3. Council of the Twelve Apostles (Church of Jesus Christ of Latter-day Saints)—History—19th century. 4. Great Britain—Church history—19th century. I. Esplin, Ronald K. II. Whittaker, David J. III. Title.
BX8661.A42 1992
266'.9341'09034—dc20
          91-31542
          CIP

Printed in the United States of America

10   9   8   7   6   5   4   3   2   1

To

Kristine Allen Card; James Michael Allen;
Kathleen Allen Bellamy; Nancy Allen Black; Scott Jones Allen;

Ronda Jean Esplin Driggs; John David Esplin;
Jennifer Anne Esplin; Julie Mae Esplin; Richard Russell Esplin;
Robert Kent Esplin; Jessica Marie Esplin;

Julie Ann Whittaker; Jennifer Lyn Whittaker Patterson;
Kristen Kay Whittaker; Stephen David Whittaker:

our children, to whom we hope we have imparted our love of
our LDS heritage and our commitment to the missionary spirit

CONTENTS

List of Illustrations

LIST OF MAPS

PREFACE

The idea for this book began to form many years ago when we discovered the rich treasure trove of journals, letters, and other documents created by nine relatively young apostles and their associates as they laid the foundation for the growth of The Church of Jesus Christ of Latter-day Saints in the British Isles. If there was ever a story shouting to be told, this was it. It was a natural for the audience we were concerned with most: the general readership of the Church and especially missionary-minded young adults. But it was also a topic in which we felt our colleagues in the scholarly community would take great interest. In short, it harmonized perfectly with our continuing efforts to combine scholarship and faith in what we write.

Our yearning to complete the work, despite a myriad of other projects in which we were each involved, was enhanced when we visited the British Isles in 1987, during the sesquicentennial celebration of the opening of the British Mission. As we walked where the early apostles had walked, visited the cities and villages where they had worked, stood on the Hereford Beacon (one of the beautiful Malvern Hills) reading Wilford Woodruff's powerful meditations on that spot, and visited among the Saints in Britain, we became more determined to tell the story as completely as possible.

At first we planned to create a book of documents: the letters and journals we found were charged with religious and social drama. But as we began to write the introductory and connecting narratives, we saw that we must do more. The historical setting must be illuminated, for it added so much to our understanding of what was going on. The meaning and consequences of the mission also must be explained, for it had significance far beyond the immediate results. Consequently, after nearly fifteen years, we have produced the volume you have in your hands.

The story of the Quorum of the Twelve Apostles in the British Isles between 1837 and 1841 is a most momentous story in the history of Mormon missionary work: poignant, powerful, and inspiring. Especially with reference to the 1840–41 mission, no other single assignment has had such a profound and far-reaching effect upon the Church. The apostles and their co-workers baptized thousands of people and created a missionary system that made an extraordinary contribution to continuing Church growth. The Twelve also organized an emigration program that, within fifty years, resulted in the migration of more than 88,000 European Saints, including 55,000 Britons, to America, and they established a publication program that had a significant effect on the Church. Perhaps equally important were the far-reaching consequences of this unique shared experience of the Twelve for their quorum. During the first several years after the Church was organized, the apostles had no direct authority within the stakes where high councils were established, and neither had they functioned effectively as a quorum. The mission to England proved to be a testing ground, uniting the Twelve as they had never been before and preparing them to carry out even greater responsibilities. Shortly after their return, a delighted Prophet Joseph Smith told a special conference that henceforth the Twelve would be his right hand in conducting "the business of the church" in Nauvoo and throughout the world.[1] This new relationship with Joseph and the Saints prepared the Quorum of the Twelve to assume Church leadership at the death of the Prophet just three years later.

Students of Mormon history have long discussed the mission of the Twelve to Great Britain,[2] but the chapters of this book provide a depth and richness never before available, including detailed consideration of vital topics not explored elsewhere. First is a general discussion of the apostles as individuals and the setting in which they found themselves in Great Britain. Then comes a discussion of the organization of the Quorum and the powerful work of Elders Kimball and Hyde as they directed the opening of the mission in 1837. The book follows the apostles in 1839 and 1840 as they struggled against incredible odds to make their way from Nauvoo to New York City and then on to England for the mission of 1840–41. In Britain they discovered many devoutly religious people, some of whom were seeking a gospel message more in tune with their reading of

---

[1]Smith, *History of the Church*, 4:403.

[2]See Allen and Thorp, "Mission of the Twelve"; Evans, *Century of "Mormonism,"* 85–200; Bloxham, "Call of the Apostles" and "Apostolic Foundations."

the New Testament than what they found in the Church of England or other mainline churches. Many were already well prepared for the message of the Restoration the apostles brought them. The book also explores the missionary methods used by the apostles, as well as their success in establishing a publication program and a vast emigration system. It follows the apostles as they labored in some of England's larger cities as well as in the countryside, experiencing both success and failure. And it relates heartwarming personal stories, such as that of Willard Richards and his wife, Jennetta, whom he married while on his mission, and those of the wives and families the apostles left behind in Illinois and Iowa. The personal struggles several of the wives endured to maintain their faith, eke out a living, and give moral support to their absent husbands during the difficult early days of Nauvoo was a poignant and essential element in the story of the mission itself. This, then, is the rich and singular story of a group of remarkable men with a most remarkable mission. We hope the story you read has the same profound effect on you as it has had on us.

EDITORIAL METHOD

In an effort to capture as much as possible of the spirit of the first missionaries to Great Britain, we have quoted liberally from their letters and journals. We have attempted to preserve the integrity of the original documents and convey the style of each writer, both in the text and in Appendix B. With minor exceptions, therefore, we have transcribed the documents as faithfully as possible, including retaining original spelling and grammar. We have silently omitted inadvertent repetitions and the author's deletions, except in those few cases where the deleted material conveys useful information. Where the author added material between the lines, we have simply inserted it so that it reads as the writer intended. To improve readability, we have added a minimum of punctuation and paragraphing and have supplied capitalization, where missing, both at the beginning of sentences and for the names of people and places. Terminal dashes have been converted to periods. We have placed in brackets editorial insertions that supply missing or unintelligible text (our best guess about an illegible word). Editorial comments that are not part of the original text are italicized within brackets.

Because of the number of notes in this work, we have used short citations within the chapters and given full documentation in the Bibliography. All citations from material in the Church Archives are courtesy of the Historical Department of The Church of Jesus Christ of Latter-day Saints and are used here by permission. The first citation within each chapter to letters published in the *Millennial Star* or other such periodicals gives the inclusive pages in that publication where the entire letter is found; subsequent citations within each chapter refer only to the quotation itself. To make references to Wilford Woodruff's *Journal*, edited by Scott G. Kenney, more readily usable by the reader, we have cited the date as well as the volume and page number. In citing Joseph Fielding's diary, we have given the page number of the typescript, because the dates are sometimes obscure and difficult to ascertain. Latter-day Saint scriptural citations are from current editions.

ACKNOWLEDGMENTS

We owe a debt of gratitude to many people who have assisted us along the way. We are grateful for the valuable research assistance of John Haggarty, Warren Metcalf, Julie Hartley, and Kib Hunt. We appreciate the support of Jae R. Ballif, who, as academic vice president of Brigham Young University during the British Mission Sesquicentennial celebrations in 1987, strongly encouraged and supported us in the project. We also gratefully recognize the staff of the Historical Department of the Church, who over the years have assisted us with the valuable materials we have used, including recently donated letters. Marilyn Rish Parks, secretary at the Joseph Fielding Smith Institute for Church History at Brigham Young University, deserves a special thanks for her excellent work and remarkable patience in checking the manuscript, especially the complex notes and bibliography. We also appreciate the skills of Suzanne Brady, Richard Erickson, and their team in the publishing department of Deseret Book; refining and producing our lengthy and complex manuscript required extra effort from each of them. And finally, we must recognize with heartfelt thanks the patience of our wives and families, who have supported us so willingly even when we seemed to spend too many hours in the archives or at the office.

Chapter 1

THE MEN AND THEIR MISSION

On April 6, 1840, thirty-eight-year-old Heber C. Kimball arrived in England for the second time in three years. Eight months earlier, as a member of the Quorum of the Twelve Apostles of The Church of Jesus Christ of Latter-day Saints, he had left Nauvoo (formerly Commerce), Illinois, to fulfill a commandment of the Lord received by revelation through Joseph Smith for the Twelve to "go over the great waters, and there promulgate my gospel."[1] Ill and penniless, Heber had somehow made his way to New York City and then, with the help of friends and in the company of Brigham Young, Parley P. Pratt, Orson Pratt, and George A. Smith, on to Britain. Two other apostles, Wilford Woodruff and John Taylor, were already there, and Willard Richards was ordained on April 14, bringing to eight the number of apostles who served in England. On May 2 Heber was in the village of Clitheroe, north of Preston, Lancashire, where he took time to write to his wife, Vilate.

The letter must have taken Elder Kimball hours to finish as he poured out his loneliness as well as much of the excitement, tenderness, sorrow, and joy that were making this mission memorable. When he had arrived by train in Penwortham, he reported, Saints who had been expecting the American missionaries for months were at the railway station to meet him, and as he put his head out of the window, they raised a red flag to let the neighbors know he had arrived. It was a time of rejoicing, he wrote, reflecting the immeasurable love the Penwortham Saints felt for the apostle who had brought them the gospel nearly three years earlier. There was also anti-Mormonism in Penwortham, but that did not concern Heber for, he declared, this "is the Lords own work, and he will take care of it." He told of great missionary success, but his most ardent comments concerned the

---

[1] D&C 118:4.

goodness of the Saints toward the Twelve. "Yes if we were infants," he said, "they could not be more kind than thay are to us." He anguished, however, at the suffering he saw among the poverty-stricken members of the Church, some of whom wept because they could not provide food for him as they had done on his previous mission. "I will tell you my dear wife this is hard."[2]

THE MISSIONS OF THE TWELVE TO THE BRITISH ISLES

Heber C. Kimball's tender compassion for the Saints in England was shared by all the members of the Quorum of the Twelve who, at that moment, were engaged in a mission unique in the annals of LDS history. Soon after the Quorum of the Twelve was organized in Kirtland, Ohio, in 1835, the apostles were instructed that their central duty was to be "special witnesses of the name of Christ in all the world,"[3] but the difficulties facing the Church prevented any of them from taking the LDS message beyond the United States and Canada. Those difficulties included disagreements and apostasy among the Twelve, who for a time were anything but a united quorum. In 1837, however, Joseph Smith felt inspired to begin the task of sending the gospel overseas, and he dispatched Heber C. Kimball and Orson Hyde to lead the first mission to England. Although they remained less than a year, their remarkable success laid the foundation for even more remarkable accomplishments when, beginning in 1840, eight apostles spent a year or more in the British Isles fulfilling the commandment that the Twelve as a quorum should proclaim the gospel overseas. This is the only time in the history of the Church that the Quorum of the Twelve as a body has been called to travel outside America for such an assignment.

The message the apostles carried was one of faith, hope, love, and salvation, which they believed had profound implications for all the peoples of the world. The ancient gospel of Jesus Christ, lost through apostasy, had been restored, and new witnesses of the reality of the living Christ had appeared. Joseph Smith had seen him, along with the Father, in a vision in 1820. Later, after a series of visits from an angel named Moroni, Joseph had received and translated an ancient record, the Book of Mormon, itself another testament of Jesus Christ as well as a history of ancient inhabitants of the American continent and Christ's ministry among them. In addition,

---

[2]Heber C. Kimball to Vilate Kimball, May 2, 1840, Heber C. Kimball Collection.
[3]D&C 107:23.

the priesthood, or the authority to perform saving ordinances and otherwise act in the name of God, had been restored to the Prophet Joseph, who in 1830 had been commanded to organize the Church, the restored kingdom of God. The missionaries also told the people of Great Britain that the restoration of the gospel was one of the final heralds of the rapidly approaching Millennium. Though the world could not escape the wars and calamities that prophecy declared would precede the Millennium, those who accepted and lived the restored gospel would find spiritual salvation. Moreover, the apostles carried the message that a gathering place had been designated in America where the Saints of God would build a loving, righteous community prepared to meet and reign with the Savior when he finally came in glory. Much of the message of the Restoration was summarized in the first issue of *The Latter-day Saints' Millennial Star*, published in Manchester in May 1840:

The long night of darkness is now far spent—the truth revived in its primitive simplicity and purity. . . . It has pleased the Almighty to send forth an HOLY ANGEL, to restore the fulness of the gospel with all its attendant blessings, to bring together his wandering sheep into one fold, to restore to them "the faith which was once delivered to the saints," and to send his servants in these last days, with a special message to all the inhabitants of the earth, in order to prepare all who will hearken for the Second Advent of the Messiah, which is now near at hand.[4]

The circumstances of the time were enough to make the challenge in 1840 and 1841 overwhelming, but in addition, the apostles lacked a full quorum to discharge the most important commission they had yet received. Six of the original Twelve were gone: five had apostatized, and one, David W. Patten, had died a martyr in Missouri in October 1838. Four were replaced before the apostles left for the British Isles, and another new apostle was ordained in England, but one vacancy remained in the Quorum of the Twelve Apostles until the mission was completed. Two apostles, John E. Page and William Smith, simply never accepted the challenge to go to Britain. Both pleaded poverty and other personal difficulties. In addition, a brief period of apostasy kept Orson Hyde from going with the others. In April 1840, however, he and John E. Page were called on a special mission to Palestine; once again, Page failed to go. Elder Hyde prepared enthusiastically, and a year later he met with his brethren as he traveled through Britain on his way to Palestine. Nine apostles, therefore, served

---

[4]*Millennial Star* 1 (May 1840): 1.

on the two apostolic missions to Great Britain, but only eight represented the quorum during the momentous years of 1840 and 1841.

THOSE WHO SERVED

The nine apostles who served in the British Isles between 1837 and 1841 had much in common with each other as well as considerable diversity of personality and talent, all of which contributed to the success of their historic assignment. Their average age at the beginning of 1840 was thirty-one. Most had been reared in a rural New England or New York background, and even before they joined the Mormons, some were taking part in the early westward movement that became a vital part of the expanding and maturing of America. Although they were not frontiersmen in the sense of carving new paths and new communities in the wilderness, they were nevertheless members of young, maturing communities near the edge of the line of American settlements, and they shared in the vibrant, reforming, democratic spirit that characterized this era in American history.

Their formal education was limited. Many of their letters, like those of Heber C. Kimball, reveal a lack of modern-day sophistication in grammar and punctuation, and their spelling was usually a phonetic representation of their pronunciation. Upon reading their writings, however, we quickly become acquainted with powerful and compelling personalities. John Taylor, Orson Hyde, and the Pratt brothers showed the greatest refinement in literary style, but profound spiritual strengths are equally apparent in the writing of those who were not so proficient. It is impressive to see these faithful missionaries struggling away at numerous letters, reports, journals, and publications, and to feel the powerful spirit that comes through their writings. Extensive quotations from the apostles' writings in the chapters that follow illustrate that spirit.

Before their conversion to Mormonism, most of the early apostles were "seekers." That is, they were believers in God and Christ but were not satisfied that traditional Christian churches taught or practiced the ancient gospel of Christ in its simple purity, and they were seeking a restoration of that gospel. Their conversions, for the most part, came through reading the Book of Mormon, receiving a personal spiritual witness of its truthfulness, and becoming convinced that Joseph Smith was a prophet, chosen by God, through whom the priesthood and the ancient Church of Christ had been restored. Their own early seeking no doubt

Bingham Young   Heber C. Kimball   Orson Hyde

P. P. Pratt   Orson Pratt   John Taylor

Wilford Woodruff   Geo. A. Smith   Willard Richards

helped them empathize with many in the British Isles who were experiencing a similar quest.

The senior apostle, in age as well as position in the Quorum in 1840, was Brigham Young. He was thirty-eight when he arrived in England. Born in Vermont, he was reared there and in New York state. By profession he was a craftsman—carpenter, joiner, and glazier—and even before he became a Latter-day Saint, he was a dedicated Christian. He was converted to the Church in 1832 and soon became one of the Prophet's most avid supporters, especially during times of severe crisis and persecution. He was ordained an apostle in February 1835. Like that of Joseph Smith and other Church leaders, his formal education was minimal, but his well-rounded practical wisdom as well as his deep commitment to things spiritual could not be mistaken. As leader of the Twelve, he felt a profound responsibility to unify his quorum as well as to make the challenging overseas missionary enterprise an unqualified success for the Church.

Heber C. Kimball, also thirty-eight, grew up in Vermont, where his father was a blacksmith and where he went to school until he was about fourteen. He too learned blacksmithing and later became a potter. A hardworking tradesman, he had much in common with the people among whom he worked in England. Only three weeks after Heber and his wife, Vilate, joined the Baptist church in 1831, they encountered Mormon missionaries and, soon after, were baptized. Heber was one of the original members of the Quorum of the Twelve and, in 1837, he led the first small group of missionaries to England. A straightforward, hard-hitting preacher, he was known for never mincing words or equivocating. At the same time, he had a ready wit and a clever way with words. "Glad to hear of the prosperity of the work in that part of the Land," he wrote from London to George A. Smith in Staffordshire in December 1840. "You Say the Devle is mad. This maks me glad, and I Shall not try to pleas him. I know that your disposition is some like mine on this Subjet."[5]

Orson Hyde, a native of Connecticut, turned thirty-five in January 1840. As a fourteen-year-old youth he had walked six hundred miles to Ohio, where he worked in diverse occupations. In 1827, stirred by a revival in Kirtland, he became converted to the Methodist faith. Later, like many "seekers" and influenced by Sidney Rigdon, he joined the Campbellite

---

[5]Heber C. Kimball to George A. Smith, December 12, 1840, George A. Smith Collection (Appendix B, Document 18).

movement, which claimed to have restored the ancient order of things. He became an active and successful preacher, missionary, and pastor. Then, in the fall of 1830, he was given a copy of the Book of Mormon by missionaries passing through. Though opposed to it at first, he ultimately became convinced of its truth, and in the fall of 1831 he was baptized by Sidney Rigdon, who had joined the Church the previous December. Orson performed several missions over the next few years. He became one of the original members of the Quorum of the Twelve in 1835, continued spending nearly all his time as a missionary, wrote the first missionary tract, and in 1837 went to England with Heber C. Kimball. After his return, Elder Hyde found himself caught up in the confusion swirling around Joseph Smith in the Missouri crisis, and as a result of what he later called a period of "affliction and darkness," he was dropped from the Quorum on May 4, 1839, just when the rest of his brethren were beginning to prepare to go to England. After a time of torment, anguish, and repentance, Orson was restored to fellowship in the Church and to membership in the Quorum on June 27. He remained in America, however, until his departure for Palestine early in 1841.

Born into a poor, hard-working family in the state of New York, Parley P. Pratt was thirty-two when he arrived in England. Before his conversion to Mormonism he, too, had been a "seeker," joined the Campbellite movement, was influenced by Sidney Rigdon, made his home in Ohio, and became a preacher. He was on a self-appointed mission, preaching for the Campbellites in New York, when he met the Mormon missionaries in 1830. Converted and ordained an elder, he was soon sent on a mission for the Church. Through him Sidney Rigdon was introduced to the Book of Mormon and joined the Church. Also one of the original Twelve, Elder Pratt had a flair for writing. He produced some of the most influential early doctrinal literature of the Church, and in England he became editor and publisher of the Church's *Millennial Star*.

Parley's younger brother, Orson Pratt, was twenty-eight. One of the best-educated and literate members of the Quorum, Orson was especially interested in geography, grammar, mathematics, and surveying. Highly philosophical in nature, he argued points of doctrine with great precision. He and his brother wrote most of the literature used by the missionaries. Converted to the Church through the instrumentality of Parley, he also was one of the original Twelve.

John Taylor, age thirty-one, was a native of England, where he went to school and became a devoutly religious young man. When John was ten, his father moved the family to a farm he had inherited, and John quickly learned the rigors associated with plowing, sowing, and harvesting. Four years later he returned to Liverpool, where he became apprenticed to a cooper, but a year later, after the business failed, he went to Penrith, Cumberland, where he became skilled in woodturning. Religious in nature, John, like many other Englishmen of the time, began to question the forms and rationalism of the Church of England, and he finally joined the Methodists and became a lay preacher. In 1830 the Taylor family emigrated to Canada, where John continued to study and preach. He had long sensed that he had a special religious mission in life, but, he became convinced and confided to his wife, "this is not the work: it is something of more importance."[6] Never satisfied that the fullness of the gospel was taught by any of the churches, he anxiously looked forward to a time when there would be a restoration of the ancient order of things, and he was thus well prepared to receive the message Parley P. Pratt brought to him in 1836.[7] A year after he was baptized he visited Kirtland, only to find the Church in the midst of a severe period of trial and apostasy. Even Parley P. Pratt was wavering, and in that tense setting the recent convert bore a powerful testimony of the divine mission of Joseph Smith. John Taylor was ordained an apostle in December 1838.

Wilford Woodruff, born and reared in rural Connecticut, was thirty-two years old when he went to England. As a young man, he learned the miller's trade from his father and eventually ran his own mill. He joined the Church in 1833, became one of its most hard-working missionaries, and, in this capacity, experienced both success and great trials. Among those chosen to fill the places of fallen leaders, he was ordained an apostle at the early-morning meeting in Far West, Missouri, on April 26, 1839, when the apostles took their official leave for England. Perhaps more dedicated to effective record keeping than any other missionary, Wilford Woodruff kept a magnificent journal, which has become one of the richest sources of early LDS history, including the story of this mission.

The youngest apostle in England was George A. Smith, age twenty-two. Growing up on a farm in New York left him well acquainted with long hours and hard work. As a youth he grew rapidly, attaining his full

---

[6]As quoted in Smith, "John Taylor," 78.
[7]See, for example, Stott, "John Taylor's Religious Preparation."

growth several years earlier than most young men. That gave him the awkwardness of an overgrown boy, and he also seemed weak — partly, perhaps, because he was growing too fast. Other boys at school often made fun of him and bullied him, but that only gave him the resolve to whip every boy his age, which he eventually did, and the taunting stopped. In the letters he wrote in England, his scrawled handwriting (partly the result of poor eyesight), his deep humility, and his confidence in the ultimate success of the mission all suggest a type that has since become almost legendary in Mormon missionary stories: the overgrown, awkward farm boy, innocent in the ways of the world and not versed in fine language but possessing a spirit that could bring the more sophisticated to their knees. As a youth George A. was a seeker for religious truth, but he was skeptical of the claims of his cousin, Joseph Smith, and of the Book of Mormon, and he hoped to find his answers within the Congregational church to which he belonged. He found the Latter-day Saint message irresistible, however, and in the fall of 1832 he was baptized. It was not long before he was on his way to Kirtland, Ohio, with his family to gather with the Saints and, for the first time, to meet his relative, the Prophet Joseph. He soon proved himself an avid defender of the faith, and during the march of Zion's Camp he became Joseph Smith's armor bearer and bodyguard. He helped quarry and haul the stone for the Kirtland Temple, and he became an enthusiastic and effective missionary. In April 1839 he was ordained to the apostleship at the impressive meeting at Far West, the youngest person in the history of the Church to have become a member of the Quorum of the Twelve Apostles.

Willard Richards, age thirty-five, was born and reared in Massachusetts. He was well educated and before his conversion practiced medicine in Boston. Deeply religious in nature, he became disillusioned with the churches of the day but continued to believe that one day he would find a church that taught the full truth. In 1835 he received a copy of the Book of Mormon and, after reading it twice in ten days, he was convinced of its authenticity. After an 1836 visit by his cousins, Brigham and Joseph Young, Willard quit his practice of medicine and traveled with his brother Levi seven hundred miles to Kirtland to learn more. He was baptized by Brigham at the end of the year. After filling a mission in the eastern states, he accompanied Elders Kimball and Hyde on their 1837 mission to England. When the two apostles left England in 1838, Willard remained behind as a counselor to Joseph Fielding in the British Mission presidency. Designated by revelation to fill one of the vacancies in the Quorum of the Twelve, he was ordained after the apostles returned to England in 1840.

"Old England" As the Apostles Found It

On September 5, 1840, Brigham Young and Willard Richards wrote from England a twelve-page report to the First Presidency of the Church. They described the economic and social conditions of the people among whom the Quorum of the Twelve were laboring, mostly the working classes in the urban and industrial centers of Britain. The empathy they developed for the common people, and the importance they placed on trying to understand the society in which they worked, is nowhere more powerfully illustrated than in their report.[8]

Unlike American society, the apostles noted, English society was divided into many classes, but in general three stood out: "Lords, Tradesmen, & mechanics or laborers, or, in other words, the highest, middle, & lowest classes." They complained that because historians had traditionally written only of the upper classes, their works did nothing to help foreigners understand current conditions. They then gave their own brief account of what had happened recently, beginning with the countryside. "A few years since, and almost every family had their garden, their cow on the common & their pig in the Stye, which added greatly to the comforts of the household; but now we seldom find either Garden, Cow or Pig." As they passed through various country villages, they saw stone walls thrown down, hedges decaying, and people close to starvation. When they inquired why this was happening, they said:

We generally get but one answer.... "Our Lords & masters have become more avaricious, & are trying to get all they can themselves, & will hardly let the poor live. You see my landlord has made my garden into a meadow, & feeds his own cattle upon it; the Lord of the manner fenced in the common, so that I had no place to keep my cow & I was obliged to sell her; I killed my pig to prevent its starving."

The apostles described the multitude of beggars who filled city streets and reported that crime, drunkenness, gambling, and swearing were all commonplace and that opportunities for education among the poor were shameful. They complained of child labor, low wages, factory lockouts, and miserable living conditions, and their pained but witty observations

---

[8]Brigham Young and Willard Richards to the First Presidency of The Church of Jesus Christ of Latter-day Saints, September 5, 1840, Brigham Young Papers (Appendix B, Document 12).

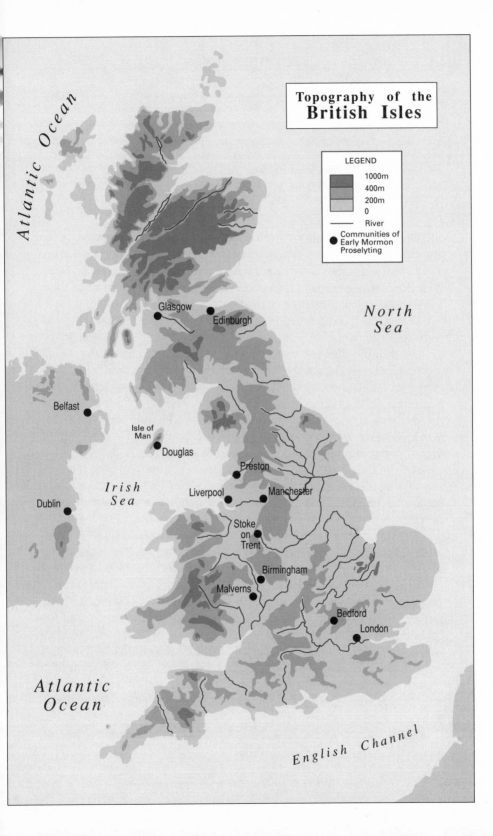

Topography of the **British Isles**

LEGEND

1000m
400m
200m
0
River
Communities of
Early Mormon
Proselyting

Atlantic Ocean

North Sea

Glasgow
Edinburgh

Belfast

Isle of Man

Douglas

Preston

Liverpool
Manchester

Dublin

Irish Sea

Stoke on Trent

Birmingham

Malverns

Bedford

London

Atlantic Ocean

English Channel

on the subject of taxes would match those of any modern tax critic. There were

taxes of *every kind*, we might say, for smoke must not go up the chimney in England without a tax, Light must not come in at the window without paying duties.... There are taxes for living & taxes for dying, insomuch that it is very difficult for the poor to get buried any how, & a man may emigrate to America & find a grave, for less money, than he can get a decent burial for in Old England. We scarce recollect an article without tax except cats, mice & fleas.

With such observations from Elders Young and Richards as background, it is important to look briefly at the political and economic setting in which the apostles found themselves, particularly in the large cities. What they discovered had much to do with the way they approached their work and is essential to understanding their mission as a whole.

The apostles could not help but compare what they found in England with what they were familiar with in America. Most of them were much in tune with the dizzying spate of political and social change that swept the United States during the Jacksonian Era (1828–48), which included increased political democracy, education, temperance, attacks on corruption in public institutions, especially government, and reform of some of the shocking conditions in America's prisons and insane asylums. In England, however, they encountered social and economic ills more severe than anything they had known in America. Not surprisingly, they identified closely with the people who were struggling to rise above those obstacles. In addition, their common interest with leaders of the temperance movement often paved the way for them to preach the message of the restored gospel.

The differences they observed in politics and social class were especially striking. It was an article of American faith that anyone could obtain wealth and that any free, white male could rise to the highest political office in the land. Moreover, all white males could vote, regardless of property-holding status. By contrast, political equality and suffrage lagged far behind in England, and political elitism and exclusion were still the general rule. Agitation for reform led to the passage of an important reform bill in 1832, but "pocket boroughs," politically controlled by powerful individuals or families, remained, and fewer than 850,000 of the six million men in the United Kingdom could vote.[9] Disdainful of such political elitism, the apostles were generally in sympathy with those demanding reform.

---

[9]Estimates vary on the exact number who could vote. Willson and Prall, *History of England,* 492,

The reigning monarch was Queen Victoria, who, at age eighteen, ascended the throne in 1837, the year the British Mission was established. She was head of state for sixty-four years.[10] When Elders Woodruff, Kimball, and Smith were in London in 1840, they visited the queen's palaces and observed all the elegance and external trappings of the monarchy—the parks, the stables, the horses and horsemen, the footmen, and the regal processions whenever the queen went out in public. On September 17, 1840, George A. Smith commented on such things when he and Elder Kimball visited the queen's stables at Buckingham Palace. The beds the horses lay on, he wryly observed, "are better than those which half the people in London sleep upon."[11]

There were other differences between Jacksonian America and early Victorian England. In America the population was mainly rural and agricultural,[12] and there was seemingly unending opportunity for agricultural expansion. In Britain, although most of the population still lived outside the cities, there was a rapid movement away from rural agriculture toward urban industrial employment.[13] This movement was directly related to the Industrial Revolution, which made England the leading industrial nation of the world. The textile industry became England's leading exporter, and the increasing demand for coal to feed the textile factories led to expansion of the coal industry and hastened the development of the railroad. The success of the railroad in reducing shipping costs created larger markets, encouraging the building of more and larger factories as well as more sophisticated machinery. These developments in turn tended to drive "cottage workers" and other artisans and small manufacturers out of business, thus contributing even more to the growth of an urban working class completely dependent upon factory owners for its livelihood. Not everyone found work, however, and unemployment in some cities was surprisingly high.[14]

---

estimates 814,000: Jackson, *England Since the Industrial Revolution*, 70, says that 840,000 could vote under the Act of 1832.

[10]For an in-depth discussion of Victorianism as a phenomenon throughout the nineteenth century, see Petrie, *Victorians.*

[11]Smith, "History," September 17, 1840.

[12]Only 8.5 percent lived in cities of more than eight thousand in 1840 and 12.5 percent by 1850. Weber, *Growth of Cities,* 22.

[13]In 1841 nearly 29 percent of the population of England and Wales lived in cities of twenty thousand or more. Ten years later this had jumped to 35 percent. By that time, however, the definition of *urban* had changed to include certain areas with less population, and on the basis of that definition half the people lived in urban districts. Ibid., 46–47.

[14]See Hobsbawm, "British Standard of Living."

Manchester, about mid century. Drawn by G. Pickering, engraved by T. Higham

The Industrial Revolution also created a new class of well-to-do factory owners, increased overall British wealth, and somewhat improved real wages,[15] though wealth increased disproportionately. It seemed to many observers that the upper classes simply ignored the pitiable conditions that became increasingly characteristic of the lives of the new working classes.[16]

Life in the poorer sections and slums was anything but pleasant or healthful. There were few parks or open areas. Often families were crowded into pathetically small rooms in row houses with neither front nor back yards and only narrow alleys separating the rows, and it was not uncommon for a family of six or eight to occupy just one room. Sanitary facilities ranged from primitive to nonexistent. In parts of Manchester, for example, one outhouse might be shared by as many as two hundred people.

Manchester, the nation's greatest textile center, symbolized the problems of industrial England.[17] In May 1840 Heber C. Kimball described for his wife what he saw there:

> I was asking some of my brethren what made the peopl look so bad. They said becaus they ware famished for the wont of food. Say they to me thare are hundreds that are starving for the wont [of] food and others things. I thought thare was misry a nough in Preston. It is nothing to compare with manchester. I asked them if they thought the brethren went hungry. Yes menny of them had not to eat. Times are so hard they cant guit [get] work. Therefore they have to go hungry. Thare has been such a change here in two years as never was known by the oldest men in this Land. . . . You may know by this that it is hard times in old England.[18]

With a population of 170,000 people, Manchester was the location of over one hundred textile factories as well as chemical works, dye works, breweries, sawmills, iron works, hat makers, and machine manufacturers. Nearly 70 percent of its workers were factory operatives. Located on the east bank of the River Irwell, and at that river's junction with the Medlock and the Irk, Manchester's factories lined a huge network of canals. The

---

[15]The question of how much real wages increased is very complex and also controversial. For an in-depth discussion see Curtis, "Economic Growth."

[16]Just how bad things were is still a matter of debate. See the various essays on this topic in Taylor, *Standard of Living.* Also, compare the optimistic treatment in a recent world history survey, McKay, Hill, and Buckler, *History of World Societies,* 1000–1008, with the highly pessimistic treatment in Pike, "Hard Times" or the analysis of Engels's view of Manchester in Marcus, "Reading the Illegible." See also Banks, "Contagion of Numbers," 1:107.

[17]The following discussion of Manchester is based on Allen and Alexander, *Manchester Mormons,* 14–20, and Girouard, *Cities and People,* 257–70.

[18]Heber C. Kimball to Vilate Kimball, May 27, 1840, Heber C. Kimball Collection.

town also boasted six railroads. The canals and railroads fed cotton and coal into the city's ever-hungry industrial plants, which in turn spewed their refuse into the water and their smoke and other pollutants into the atmosphere. Waste from the mills, dye works, tanneries, and gasworks made the rivers and canals seem more like flowing cesspools.[19] Streets were typically narrow, and workers' houses were similar to the drab, unsightly row houses or small court houses that characterized other industrial towns. With sewage running in the streets and seeping into cellars, and pigs and other animals running freely, millions of people were literally living in filth.[20] It seems little wonder that in 1840 the death rate in Manchester was extraordinarily high.[21]

In earlier years the merchants and mill owners of Manchester lived close to their warehouses or even in apartments above them, and Mosely Street was once lined with handsome brick houses owned by these entrepreneurs. By 1840, however, Mosely Street as well as other once-fine residential sections were gradually becoming crowded warehouse areas, as the "respectable inhabitants" moved out into the suburbs.

Migrants poured in more rapidly than the economy could absorb, leading to high unemployment and privation. During his first visit to Manchester Wilford Woodruff, noting these things with some alarm, recorded in his journal:

There is trouble this morning in this town of Manchester. About 3,000 souls is flung out of employ at the factories because of the pressure of times & the lowering of the wages & they are standing in every corner of the Streets in groups counciling what to do, & their are at the present time (I have been informed) thousands of Souls are almost in a State of uter starvation.[22]

Nevertheless, life in Manchester was not totally bleak, for even amid its difficulties there was a vibrant, bustling activity that tended to make the

---

[19]In 1845 the River Irk was described by Engels as "a narrow, coal-black, foul-smelling stream . . . in dry weather, a long string of the most disgusting, blackish-green slime pools are left standing . . . from the depths of which bubbles of miasmatic gas constantly arise and give forth a stench unendurable even on the bridge forty or fifty feet above the surface of the stream." As quoted in Girouard, *Cities and People,* 263–64.

[20]Marcus, "Reading the Illegible," 266. See also Hammond and Hammond, *Age of the Chartists,* chapter 7, "The State of the Towns."

[21]In 1842 it was reported that the average age of death among mechanics, laborers, and their families was seventeen; among tradesmen, farmers, and graziers and their families it was twenty; and even among the professional people and gentry it was only thirty-eight. Girouard, *Cities and People,* 268–69.

[22]Woodruff, *Journal,* January 20, 1840, 1:409.

Mosley Street, Manchester, 1843. Courtesy H. J. Dyos and Michael Wolff, eds.,
The Victorian City: Images and Realities, vol. 2; Routledge and Kegan Paul, publishers

place exciting. In addition, a number of charitable institutions helped
relieve the misery. These included several hospitals, a royal infirmary, a
royal lunatic asylum, a royal dispensary, a workhouse, a night asylum for
the destitute, and a humane society. Child labor was commonplace, but
several factories provided at least some education for young workers. There
were also schools for the children of the poor, a college, a school of
medicine and surgery, several libraries, and some literary and scientific
institutions. Manchester also had its better sections of town, which contrasted greatly with the manufacturing district and the worst living areas.
From afar, with partially-wooded, rolling countryside surrounding it, the
setting seemed almost idyllic—except for the ugly black smoke that continually hung over the city itself. Despite the problems he observed, Wilford
Woodruff once called Manchester "the metropolis of the manufacturing
Districts in England" and "a beautiful borough."[23]

The importance of all this to the work of the apostles in the British
Isles is seen in the fact that, except for the hundreds who joined the Church

---

[23]Woodruff, *Journal*, January 18, 1840, 1:407.

in Herefordshire, most Latter-day Saint converts came from the laboring classes in the industrial areas. At the general conference held in Manchester in April 1840, for example, thirty-three congregations were represented, with a total of 1517 members; 953, or 60.7 percent, of the members were from congregations in manufacturing towns and cities.[24] Manchester itself had the largest branch of the Church in England, which consisted of some 240 members. Most were young, generally in their twenties or early thirties, the majority were unmarried, and there were more women than men. Many of the women worked in the factories, and the branch probably represented a fair cross-section of the general laborers, artisans, and lower-middle-class citizenry of the town.[25] A similar pattern developed in London. During the first five years of missionary work, most male converts came from the working classes, though there were a few merchants and white collar workers, along with one professional, Dr. William Copeland. Among the female converts, 6.3 percent were white collar workers, 37.5 percent were "skilled" laborers, 25 percent were "semiskilled," and 31.3 percent were identified as household servants.[26]

Another aspect of the British setting important to the history of the Latter-day Saints was the fact that poor economic conditions contributed to the emigration of thousands of British citizens to other parts — particularly to the United States and Canada. More than 55,000 left in 1830, and by the late 1840s and early 1850s the annual figure was sometimes as high as 250,000. Emigration developed into an industry, featuring emigration agents, propaganda offices, and even shipping rebates. By holding out hope for a better future elsewhere, it functioned as a kind of safety valve that siphoned off the worst effects of economic discontent. It was not uncommon to hear emigrants sing as they left:

> Brave men are we and be it understood
> We left our country for our country's good,

---

[24]See *Millennial Star* 1 (May 1840): 20. The industrial nature of the communities listed may be ascertained by consulting Lewis, *Topographical Dictionary*. By July 1840, this profile had changed so that only about 50 percent of the members in England were living in industrial areas, but by that time a large number had emigrated. Many of them, like John Moon and his family, were probably from the cities. Most of the nonurban Mormons were in Herefordshire, where there were well over a thousand.

[25]For a fine social profile of the Manchester Mormons, see Harris, "Mormons in Victorian England," and Harris, "Mormons in Victorian Manchester." See also Allen and Alexander, *Manchester Mormons*, 20–31. For a good essay that examines a similar cross-section of Mormon converts elsewhere in England, see Fales, "Artisans."

[26]Jorgensen, "First London Mormons," 49, 55–56.

And none may doubt our emigration
Was of great value to the British nation.[27]

All this helped create an atmosphere for success when the apostles began to organize Latter-day Saint emigration, for the spirit of emigration was already there and much of the necessary machinery was in place.

Besides the problems in the cities, there were problems in the countryside, one of which was created by the enclosure movement alluded to in the report of Elders Young and Richards. Less than a century earlier the countryside boasted many open fields where small landowners and tenant farmers were allowed to graze their own cows and, perhaps, raise small gardens. As farming technology improved, however, the larger landowners began to hedge the fields and prohibit their use by anyone but themselves, thus eliminating a source of livelihood for those who once used those lands. By 1830 this enclosure movement was virtually complete.

Although they spent most of their time in the cities, working among the laboring classes, the apostles also visited the great museums and historic sites of Britain and demonstrated a sense of deep appreciation for the artistic and historic values preserved there. In addition, they spent considerable time doing missionary work and ministering to the Saints in the countryside, particularly in the picturesque villages in the vicinity of Preston and in the delightful farming communities of Herefordshire.

It was a combination of all these experiences that helped form the apostles' multifaceted images of early Victorian England. At the same time, the problems they witnessed firsthand only persuaded them more fully that judgments were about to be poured out upon the nations of the world, and particularly upon England. "The Distress of the nations is at the door in fulfillment of the word of God," wrote Elder Woodruff as he observed the unemployment and starvation in Manchester.[28] With that in mind, as well as with monumental faith and a selfless spirit of Christian service, the apostles committed themselves to bringing as many souls as possible into the restored kingdom of God.

---

[27]Briggs, *Making of Modern England,* 389.
[28]Woodruff, *Journal,* January 20, 1840, 1:409.

Chapter 2

THE FIRST MISSION TO ENGLAND, 1837 THROUGH 1838

Now behold, a marvelous work is about to come forth among the children of men.

Therefore, O ye that embark in the service of God, see that ye serve him with all your heart, might, mind and strength, that ye may stand blameless before God at the last day....

For behold the field is white already to harvest; and lo, he that thrusteth in his sickle with his might, the same layeth up in store that he perisheth not, but bringeth salvation to his soul;

And faith, hope, charity and love, with an eye single to the glory of God, qualify him for the work.[1]

With these words, given by revelation even before The Church of Jesus Christ of Latter-day Saints was organized, Joseph Smith called his father to be one of the first missionaries of Mormonism. The charge applied equally to subsequent missionaries, including members of the Quorum of the Twelve Apostles who would receive the commission to carry the Latter-day Saint message far beyond the confines of North America.

EARLY HISTORY OF THE QUORUM OF THE TWELVE

The Church was organized in Fayette, New York, on April 6, 1830, but in early 1831 Joseph Smith and most of his followers left New York for the vicinity of Kirtland, Ohio, where hundreds of other new converts welcomed them. Joseph had sent missionaries to western Missouri where, by revelation, the spot for Zion, or the "New Jerusalem," was designated, and in 1831 many Latter-day Saints began to purchase land and flock to Jackson County.

---

[1]D&C 4:1–2, 4–5.

In 1833, however, the Jackson County Saints were driven brutally from their homes. In February 1834, responding to revelation, Joseph Smith, in Ohio, began enlisting volunteers to go to Missouri and help their fellow Saints recover their lost property.[2] By June some two hundred recruits, called Zion's Camp, arrived in Missouri, only to learn that the promised help from the governor would not be forthcoming. The Prophet then disbanded the camp with a promise, given through revelation, that the Lord had prepared a special "blessing and an endowment" for those who had faithfully followed his words: "I have heard their prayers, and will accept their offering; *and it is expedient in me that they should be brought thus far for a trial of their faith.*"[3] Indeed, the arduous journey was a trial. Some grumbled, seeing little purpose to it. Others saw the trek as an unparalleled opportunity to learn at the feet of a prophet. "What have you gained by this journey?" a skeptic asked Brigham Young. "Just what we went for," Brigham shot back. "I would not exchange the knowledge I have received this season for the whole of Geauga county."[4]

On February 14, 1835, back in Ohio, the Prophet called together those who had shared the challenges of Zion's Camp and announced that the time had come for the organization of the Quorum of the Twelve Apostles, and that its members would be chosen from among their number. After a blessing from the First Presidency, and following the intent of a revelation given six years earlier, the three witnesses to the Book of Mormon made the selection.[5] Nine of those chosen were veterans of Zion's Camp, and it appeared that their success in meeting that "trial of faith" boded well for their ability to weather still greater trials in their positions as Church leaders.

The Quorum of the Twelve Apostles held a unique place in the de-

---

[2]Direct action was suggested in the parable contained in Joseph Smith's revelations of December 16, 1833, and February 24, 1834. The parable told of a nobleman and his vineyard and was given "that you may know my will concerning the redemption of Zion." The Lord of the vineyard then instructed his servant (i.e., Joseph Smith) to gather the young and middle-aged "warriors" and redeem the land that had been captured by the intruding enemy. See D&C 101:43–62; 103:15–22. See discussion of Zion's Camp and its broader setting in Church history in Allen and Leonard, *Story of the Latter-day Saints*, 84–93, and note other references in the Bibliography. See particularly Crawley and Anderson, "Realities of Zion's Camp."

[3]D&C 105:18–19; italics added.

[4]Sermon of Brigham Young, October 23, 1853, in *Journal of Discourses* 2:10.

[5]See Smith, *History of the Church* 2:186–87, and note. See also D&C 18:37, where, in a June 1829 revelation, two of the three witnesses, Oliver Cowdery and David Whitmer, were specifically designated to choose the Twelve. At this meeting, however, the third witness, Martin Harris, also participated in the selection.

veloping Church organization. A revelation the month after their ordination described them as a quorum "equal in authority and power" to the Presidency of the Church, though they would not function in that capacity until later. They were also designated "traveling councilors" and "special witnesses of the name of Christ in all the world."[6] The restored gospel was to be taken to the world, and the Twelve, as their central assignment, held the keys to lead the way.

At first the Twelve were not prepared to fill these roles. Though they shared important experiences on a mission in the East in 1835 and, after some difficulties, pulled themselves together to receive vital blessings in the Kirtland Temple in 1836, the Quorum seldom functioned unitedly. Relatively young and inexperienced as leaders, some had difficulty reconciling differences between the revealed promise of prominent position and the reality of their role in Kirtland. Their president, Thomas B. Marsh, an officious leader overly concerned with prerogative, set a tone that made it difficult for the Twelve to grow easily into their new roles.

Even in 1835, the Twelve understood their responsibility to take the gospel overseas, and England was the logical place to begin. They might well have set sail as a quorum as early as 1837, but in Kirtland the year opened with increasing disagreement about the role of Joseph as prophet-leader. By late spring, with deepening economic problems and the collapse of the charterless Kirtland bank, disagreement turned to disaffection, division, and apostasy. Of the Twelve, Lyman Johnson and John Boynton came out in open rebellion, Luke Johnson and William McLellin became disaffected, and Orson Hyde and the Pratt brothers were temporarily estranged from the Prophet after publicly criticizing his leadership. When news of the problems reached the two senior apostles in Missouri, they hastened to Ohio, hoping to unite the Twelve behind the Prophet and prepare for their foreign mission.[7] This they could not do, however, for by the time they had reached Kirtland, Joseph Smith, despite the crisis, had already dispatched the first missionaries to England.

---

[6]D&C 107:23–24. Clearly the revelation did not mean that the Twelve were "equal" with the Presidency in the sense that the Presidency could not act without them, for the Presidency presided over them. In the absence of the Presidency, however, particularly as they traveled in the world, they had authority to act in behalf of the Church. Later, as will be seen at the end of this book, the Prophet gave them additional "keys of the kingdom," and their right to succeed him in the presidency became more clear.

[7]Thomas B. Marsh and David W. Patten to Parley P. Pratt, May 10, 1837, Joseph Smith Letterbook, Joseph Smith Collection.

The Kirtland Temple and vicinity. Courtesy Utah State Historical Society

"For the Salvation of This Church": The First Call to England

To all appearances, the spring of 1837 was hardly the time to send any of his leaders abroad, but, Joseph Smith declared, "God revealed to me that something new must be done for the salvation of His Church,"[8] and this "something" was the mission to England. The announcement surprised Heber Kimball. On June 4 the Prophet approached him in the Kirtland Temple, saying, "The Spirit of the Lord has whispered to me, 'let my servant Heber go to England and proclaim my gospel and open the door of salvation to that nation.' "[9] The news astounded him. He had long thought of preaching in England, but now, with Kirtland in crisis? And alone, without others of his quorum?

Heber had expected to be part of such a mission, but he considered himself an unlikely candidate to lead out. With his lack of formal education

---

[8]Smith, *History of the Church* 2:489.
[9]Kimball, "Synopsis," *Deseret News*, April 14, 1858.

and limited experience as a leader, the idea of leading a mission to sophisticated England "was almost more than I could bear up under."[10] He asked the Prophet if Brigham Young could accompany him, but needing "Brother Brigham" in Kirtland, Joseph would not consider it. One disaffected colleague chided Heber for being such a fool as to listen "to Joseph Smith, the fallen Prophet" and leave for England at such a time. Another also thought it foolish but, seeing his determination, gave him a cloak to help him on his way. Brigham Young urged him to go, promising "in the name of Israel's God you shall be blessed."[11] In preparation, Heber daily retreated to the attic story of the temple and poured out his soul.

In the light of this call, previous experiences and premonitions held new meaning. Three months earlier Heber had told Brigham Young and Parley Pratt that he felt "deeply impressed and exercised about a foreign mission," believing the time "nearer than many knew or thought."[12] The year before Heber had blessed Parley, encouraging him to go to Canada on a mission despite his debts and a sick wife. His wife would be healed, Kimball promised, the Lord would supply him with means, and "from the things growing out of this mission, shall the fulness of the gospel spread into England."[13]

Parley P. Pratt's mission to Canada resulted in the conversion of John Taylor, the Fielding family, and other recent English immigrants who, anxious that their relatives should hear the message of the Restoration,[14] would provide the vital link across the Atlantic. Joseph Fielding, for example, had in England a brother who was a minister and two sisters married to ministers. He and his two sisters in Canada had already written these family members about the Restoration. One sister, Ann, cautiously responded that "my mind seemed alternately to rejoice and mourn," and even her more skeptical minister husband, Timothy Matthews, desired to hear more.[15] In June 1837, Fielding was already in Kirtland, ready to ac-

---

[10]Kimball, *Journal*, 10.

[11]Sermon by Heber C. Kimball, November 22, 1857, *Journal of Discourses* 6:65. Kimball later said that Hyrum Smith, "seeing the condition of the Church . . . wept like a little child" when he talked about the mission. Hyrum continually blessed and encouraged Kimball, "pouring out his soul in prophecies upon my head" and promising Heber that "you shall prosper as not many have prospered" (Whitney, *Life of Heber C. Kimball*, 105).

[12]Kimball, Autobiography, ms.

[13]P. Pratt, *Autobiography*, 130–31.

[14]John Taylor, another transplanted Englishman in Canada, had also written at the Fieldings' request to explain more. See *Journal of Discourses* 23:31.

[15]Ann [Fielding] Matthews to "Dear Brother & Sisters," January 18, 1837. Joseph Fielding Collection. This includes a letter from the Reverend Mr. Timothy R. Matthews.

company Heber to England, while three other Canadian converts, John Goodson, Isaac Russell, and John Snyder, were preparing to meet them in New York and sail with them.[16]

Elder Kimball met with the First Presidency on June 11 to be set apart for his mission. As they laid their hands upon him, Orson Hyde entered the room, begged forgiveness, and asked if he could accompany Heber to England. After blessing Heber, the First Presidency then set apart Elder Hyde as well as Joseph Fielding, a priest.[17]

Some time earlier Heber's close friend Willard Richards had made a covenant with him that he would be among the first to carry the gospel abroad. Although Willard was on a mission in the East when Heber received his call, he suddenly felt "a strong desire to start for Kirtland immediatly." He arrived a week later, in time to accompany Brigham Young to the home of Joseph Smith on June 11 while the Prophet was giving final instructions to the departing missionaries. As Willard listened to all that went on, he later wrote in his journal, "I felt my heart burn within me strongly desiring that I might be one" of them, but he sadly concluded that it would be impossible because of the heavy responsibilities he had for the "temporal affairs" of the Church in Kirtland. The next day Elder Kimball surprised him on the street: "Elder Richards I am now ready to fulfil my engagement with you. You recollect it dont you. I start for England Tomorrow & you May go with me." At first Willard saw no way to extricate himself from his Kirtland responsibilities or to raise the money to go. Nevertheless, at 5 o'clock that afternoon, after Brigham agreed to handle his business, Willard Richards was set apart for the mission under the hands of Sidney Rigdon and Hyrum Smith. The next day, June 13, he said farewell to his friends, and at nine that morning left Kirtland in the company of Elders Kimball, Hyde, and Fielding.[18]

With the help of donations from faithful Saints, the four traveled by steamboat, canal boat, and rail, arriving in New York City June 22. It took them a week to gather enough money for their passage to England but

---

[16]John Taylor, Fielding's friend and religious mentor, had earlier "prophesied with . . . great Power" that the Spirit of God would be upon Brother Fielding "and he should lift up his voice in his native land." Though timid and unsure of himself, Fielding "began to believe that the Lord had called me to go to England" (Fielding, Diary, 4).

[17]Kimball, Diary, June 1837.

[18]Richards, Diary, June 5–13, 1837. Before departing, Heber also gathered his family about him and with full emotions blessed each of them and commended them to God. See Kimball, *Journal*, pp. v–vi, and Kimball, "Synopsis."

The packet ship *Garrick*, which carried the first missionaries to Great Britain in 1837
Courtesy Peabody Museum of Salem

finally, now seven strong with the addition of the Canadian contingent, the missionaries boarded the sailing ship *Garrick* June 29 and headed out to sea July 1. The missionaries provided their own provisions and slept on buffalo robes rather than beds, but their "second cabin" accommodations proved comfortable enough.[19]

A new vessel of some nine hundred tons and the largest ship sailing to Liverpool, the *Garrick* was the pride of the famed E. K. Collins Line of fast Atlantic packets and the "noblest" ship Heber had ever seen. Passage was safe and rapid.[20] Though it sometimes took five or six weeks for sailing ships—thirty-one days even for fast packets,—spurred on by a substantial wager with the rival Black Ball Line's *South America* and blessed by good weather, the *Garrick* crossed the Atlantic in eighteen days. Both ships had

---

[19]Heber C. Kimball to Vilate Kimball, June 27, 1837, Heber C. Kimball Collection; S. Kimball, *Heber C. Kimball*, 42.

[20]"We were not becalmed o[n]ce," Orson Hyde reported to his wife, Marinda, "neither had we any heavy storms." Orson Hyde to Marinda Hyde, July 18, 1837; *Messenger and Advocate* 3 (August 1837): 550–52.

Liverpool, from the River Mersey. Contemporary engraving,
Samuel Austin, Robert Brandard

every inch of canvas spread as the *Garrick* reached Liverpool only minutes
ahead of its rival. "Truly a more splendid sight is not often seen," reported
Hyde.[21] Unwilling to wait for a steamer to shuttle passengers ashore, the
eager missionaries found space on a small boat that came alongside. Still
several feet from the pier, Elder Kimball leaped out and waded ashore,
followed immediately by Elders Hyde, Richards, and Goodson. The first
Mormon missionaries had arrived in England.[22]

Liverpool was England's chief port and also the port of embarkation
through which practically every emigrant from England passed. Situated
on the east bank of the Mersey River, it was the exporting harbor for all
the rest of Lancashire, the center of British manufacturing. It had a population of approximately 223,000 people. On the east side, wide streets
and squares boasted elegant houses, often built of brick with slate roofs;
on the west side, near the docks and warehouses, stood poorer houses
on narrow, busy streets. The city was well paved and lighted, and it had
several libraries and news rooms as well as the Royal Institution, which
housed a library, various lecture and committee rooms, a museum, a
schoolroom, and a scientific laboratory. The art gallery, the zoological

[21]Ibid.
[22]Richards, Diary, July 19, 1837; Kimball, *Journal*, 15.

garden, the botanical garden, and several other public institutions provided educational and cultural activities.

The apostles' first impressions of their new mission field were not reassuring. Immediately they noticed the striking distinction between rich and poor. "Having no means, poor and penniless," Elder Kimball later wrote, "we wandered in the streets of that great city, where wealth and luxury, penury and want abound. I there met the rich attired in the most costly dresses, and the next moment was saluted with the cries of the poor, without covering sufficient to screne them from the weather; such a distinction I never saw before."[23] His early fears about proclaiming the gospel in a land "so much extolled for religion" were not dispelled. "I was led to cry mightily to the Lord for wisdom and for that comfort and support which I so much needed."[24]

The missionaries arranged lodging with a kind widow, offered a prayer of thanksgiving, and settled in. It took three days for the Custom House, swamped with business, to clear their trunks, and this time was spent mostly in prayer and council.[25] As soon as possible, without even preaching in Liverpool, they left for Preston, where Joseph Fielding's family appeared to offer the best opening.

"TRUTH WILL PREVAIL": THE ENGLISH FOUNDATION IN PRESTON

In Preston the apostles experienced their first real glimpse of the new industrial civilization that made England so profoundly different from anything they had seen before. Their initial impressions were a mixture of marvel at the ingeniousness of the factory system and shock at the social conditions prevalent among the common people. The city had grown unusually rapidly: by 1837 it was burgeoning at a rate of approximately eighteen thousand newcomers annually, producing crowded conditions described by one historian as not bad enough to produce rebellion but not good enough to promote happiness.[26] By the 1840s Preston had no fewer than thirty-eight cotton factories, which employed sixteen thousand workers.

Preston, nevertheless, was attractively situated on the banks of the River Ribble, and from a distance it had a pleasant appearance. Within the

---

[23]Kimball, *President Heber C. Kimball's Journal*, 16.
[24]Kimball, *Journal*, 15.
[25]Richards, Diary, July 19, 1837; Kimball, Diary, July 1837.
[26]Hoskins, *English Landscape*, 228.

Preston, from Penwortham Hill. Contemporary engraving, J. Hardwood, R. Winkles

city there were lovely homes, handsome public buildings, and elegant churches. Avenham Walk, which included a stretch along the banks of the Ribble, provided a relaxing atmosphere for an enjoyable Sunday stroll. As one city historian wrote in 1857: "Few towns, manufacturing or otherwise, of the size of Preston, possess so agreeable a promenade, within five minutes' walk from the business centre of the borough."[27]

The missionaries arrived in Preston on Saturday, July 22, a "public day" or holiday before a Monday parliamentary election. Streets were thronged with factory hands released from work, bands played, and various groups marched, political banners flying. After unloading their trunks from the coach, the elders looked up and saw flying before them a large flag bearing the gilded motto: "Truth Will Prevail." With one voice they responded, "Amen, and amen." This they took as a sign from heaven of good things to come.[28]

While crossing the ocean Joseph Fielding had prayed fervently that the Lord would prepare the hearts of his brother and other relatives. While the other missionaries found lodging for themselves, Joseph looked up his brother, the Reverend James Fielding, who immediately made him welcome, invited him to stay at his house, and sent him back to the others

---

[27]Hardwick, *Borough of Preston*, 436.
[28]Kimball, Diary, July 22, 1837; Fielding, Diary, 6.

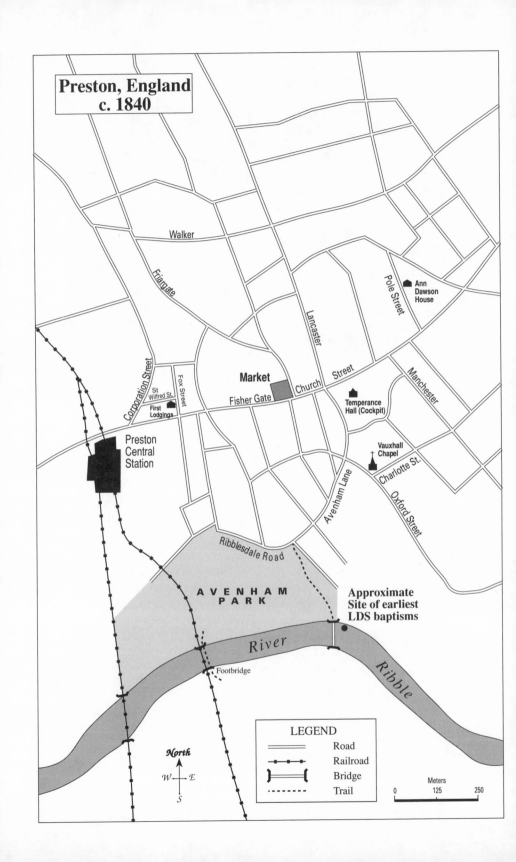

Preston Market Place. Contemporary engraving, J. Harwood, R. Winkles

with the happy news that he would like to see them that night. Accordingly, Elders Kimball, Hyde, and Goodson met with the Fielding brothers and a Reverend Watson, a brother-in-law. Everyone seemed friendly, and James even offered the elders his pulpit on Sunday afternoon. Joseph promised his brother that they would not abuse the privilege and that they would be cautious "so that he might judge of it before he repeated that favour." Earlier James had shared with his congregation the letters from Canada, prompting some to petition the Lord to send them his authorized servants. "Thus you see," Joseph wrote to his sister, "they prayed us here, no wonder that we should come." All this had created interest not just among Fielding's flock but "through the town, so that when the news was circulated that the Elders were come many were ready to hear."[29]

The Reverend Fielding's Sunday morning announcement that one of the Latter-day Saint elders would preach in the afternoon packed Vauxhall Chapel. Heber Kimball experienced "peculiar feelings" as he began his first sermon in England. The people were excited "to hear the strang[e] thing" from America, and he did not disappoint them. Declaring that an angel had committed the Everlasting Gospel to man, he called on them to repent, urged them to prepare for Christ's coming, and explained how

---

[29]Joseph Fielding to Mary Fielding, October 2, 1837, Joseph Fielding Collection; Fielding, Diary, 6.

Vauxhall Chapel, Preston. Courtesy LDS Church Archives

they might "Enter I[n]to his Rest." Elder Hyde then bore testimony. The response was astounding, according to Elder Kimball's diary, and the people began to praise God for sending his servants to them. At Reverend Fielding's invitation the missionaries held another meeting that evening, where Elder Goodson preached and Joseph Fielding bore his testimony.[30]

Many people received their message favorably, and the missionaries were delighted when James Fielding let it be known that his chapel would be open to them again Wednesday night. Joseph was concerned, however, because his brother "did not seem to receive our Testimony himself." Indeed, before Wednesday, as James began to see how the message had taken hold of his people, "he began to wish he had not been so liberal."[31]

Wednesday evening the chapel again was full. Elder Hyde preached and, Heber noted, the "power of god rested down on the congr[eg]ation

---

[30]Kimball, Diary, July 1837. Willard Richards noted simply: "Brother Heber opened the Mission (in Mr James Fieldings Meeting house) followed by O. Hyde" (Richards, Diary, July 23, 1837). This was the pattern for the mission: almost always, when there were two elders, one would preach and the other would bear testimony.

[31]Fielding, Diary, 6.

32

and manny pricked to the hart."[32] Too many for the Reverend Mr. Fielding. "The people began to believe more & more," Joseph wrote to his sister Mary, which "made Bro James begin to fear" and "to object." The baptism the following Sunday of nine people, including George D. Watt, one of James Fielding's "leading men," and others of his congregation, "had a great effect on his mind, and he began to oppose."[33]

While those who left James Fielding had no particular quarrel with him, observed Joseph, "the way seemd so plain that they could not but see it and . . . could not rest without doing it."[34] By the time the Reverend Fielding closed his chapel to the elders, seeds had been planted not only in Fielding's congregation but throughout Preston. Private homes were opened, and the missionaries began to hold two or three meetings each night. Conversions continued.

Even while the elders felt blessed by the power of God, they were also keenly aware of the powers of darkness arrayed against them. One encounter came the night before their first baptisms. The two apostles occupied a tiny room on the top floor of a Saint Wilfred Street lodging house, and Elders Goodson, Russell, Snyder, and Richards occupied the floor below. The missionaries knew that Isaac Russell had long been troubled by what he thought were devils, though Heber Kimball, at least, did not fully believe all Russell had said about his difficulties.[35] Tormented again during the early morning of Sunday, July 30, Russell went upstairs and awakened Elders Kimball and Hyde, asking for a blessing. Heber stood up and Orson sat on the bed while the two apostles laid their hands on Russell, prayed, and rebuked the spirits. As Heber later wrote:

> While thus engaged, I was struck with great force by some invisible power and fell senseless on the floor as if I had been shot, and the first thing that I recollected was, that I was supported by Brothers Hyde and Russell, who were beseeching a throne of grace in my behalf. They then laid me on the bed, but my agony was so great that I could not endure, and I was obliged to get out, and fell on my knees and began to pray. I then sat on the bed and could distinctly see the evil spirits, who foamed and gnashed their teeth upon us. We gazed upon them about an hour and a half, and I shall never forget the horror and malignity depicted on the countenances of these foul spirits, and any attempt to paint the scene which then presented itself, or portray the malice and enmity depicted in their countenances would be vain.

---

[32]Kimball, Diary, July 1837.
[33]Joseph Fielding to Mary Fielding, October 2, 1837; Fielding, Diary, 6.
[34]Joseph Fielding to Mary Fielding, October 2, 1837. See also Kimball, Diary, July 1837.
[35]Fielding, Diary, 7.

Saint Wilfred Street lodgings in Preston. © LDS Church

I perspired exceedingly, and my clothes were as wet as if I had been taken out of the river. I felt exquisite pain, and was in the greatest distress for some time. However, I learned by it the power of the adversary, his enmity against the servants of God and got some understanding of the invisible world.[36]

Any doubts Heber had about the reality of Isaac Russell's confrontations with the powers of darkness were erased. Joseph Fielding, who also had doubted some of Russell's claims, was not present, but after he heard of the experience, he summarized in his diary the lessons of the night:

Upon the whole we got considerable Instruction from the Maneuvers of the Devil. The Spirit of the Devil produces Confusion, Disorder and Misery; the Spirit of God produces Calmness, Order and Happiness. If we never before knew that there were evil Spirits, we did now. We also knew how [to] feel for dear Bro. Russel.[37]

It was only natural for Heber to conclude in his diary that "it seames

---

[36]Kimball, *President Heber C. Kimball's Journal*, 20. For a later recollection of the event by Orson Hyde, see Whitney, *Life of Heber C. Kimball*, 131. Whitney's account also quotes a few additional details from Heber, but we have been unable to find the original material apparently used by Whitney. See also Kimball, *Journal*, 19; Kimball, Diary, July 1837.

[37]Fielding, Diary, 8. Fielding's description of this event varies in some detail from Kimball's description. Fielding also records two experiences, one early Sunday morning and the other on Sunday night. Kimball, on the other hand, here mentions only one experience.

View from Avenham Walks, Preston

that the devels ar determined to distroy us and prevent the truth from being declared in England." When Joseph Smith later heard of it he rejoiced for, he said, "I then knew that the work of God had taken root in that land."[38]

Exhausted from the experience of the night, the elders nevertheless met at the River Ribble early Sunday morning, just a week after their initial meeting with Reverend Fielding's congregation, to perform the first baptisms in Great Britain. Thousands of people were out taking their usual Sunday morning strolls in Avenham Park, along the banks of the river, and when they learned that the elders from America were going to hold a baptismal service, many stopped in curiosity.

Among the nine ready for baptism that day were two especially eager candidates who raced to the river to see who could be first. The winner was George D. Watt.[39] The last of the nine was Elizabeth Ann Walmsley, a frail consumptive not expected to live, who was carried to the water by her husband. Elder Kimball had promised her that if she would repent

---

[38]Kimball, Diary, July-August 1837; Whitney, *Life of Heber C. Kimball*, 131–32.

[39]See Jones, "Who Came in Second?" Watt later became a clerk and scribe for both Joseph Smith and Brigham Young.

and be baptized, she would be healed. She began to improve immediately, later emigrated to Utah, and died among the Saints at the age of eighty-two.[40] Another of those baptized that day was Ann Dawson, who invited the missionaries to move to her boarding house, on Pole Street. There they found not only warm hospitality but also a room where they could begin to hold Church services.

The seven missionaries were delighted with their success and tireless in their continuing efforts. On Sunday afternoon Elder Russell stood on a pedestal in the marketplace preaching to a large crowd, several of whom were "pricked to the heart." The next day they decided to extend their reach by dividing up, and on Tuesday, August 1, Russell and Snyder left for Alston and Richards and Goodson for Bedford. Kimball, Hyde, and Fielding continued in Preston and its surrounding villages.[41]

The missionaries experienced almost every reaction possible to their message: from immediate acceptance and joy to bitter confrontation. Perhaps the most difficult experience to bear, however, was the divisive effect it sometimes had on families, and there was no more touching example of this division than in the family of Joseph Fielding. Although he continued to live at his brother's home, James became increasingly bitter against the missionaries. On the morning of August 5, at the breakfast table, James sharply attacked the Book of Mormon. Joseph arose from the table, took the book in his hand, and declared as forcefully as he could that it was the word of God and that James must repent. He then left the house, seldom to return.[42]

The effect on Joseph himself was devastating. His sister Ann, married to the Reverend Timothy Matthews of Bedford, later wrote him a sorrowful letter explaining her understanding that he had pronounced an anathema on James and confirming that she and Timothy had rejected the message of the missionaries. "I am now as a Stranger in my Native land, and almost to my Father's house," he wrote in a touching, bittersweet reflection. "I am something like Joseph when sold by his Brethren. The Devil would suggest perhaps I am wrong, but it cannot be. I have too much Evidence of the Truth to give way to such a thought. May the Lord help me to stand fast

---

[40]Whitney, *Life of Heber C. Kimball*, 135–36.

[41]Kimball, "Synopsis," *Deseret News*, April 21, 1858, 37.

[42]Fielding, Diary, 8. James Fielding's bitterness was fed by the anti-Mormon writings and sermons of Richard Livesey, a Methodist Episcopal minister from Massachusetts. James Fielding to Joseph Fielding, August 15, 1838, Fielding Collection.

in the Liberty of the Gospel and my Calling." James later told Joseph that coming from America to oppose him within his own congregation had made religion "stink in the Noses of the sensible and intelligent," to which Joseph could only reply that he was content to suffer in the cause. Nevertheless, he admitted to himself, "I must not wonder that he is not friendly with me."[43]

EXPANSION: PRESTON AND BEYOND

In Bedford, as in Preston, Elders Richards and Goodson began their missionary work with members of Joseph Fielding's family, who had learned of their message by letter from Canada in 1836. Ann Matthews, though cautious lest she be deluded, at first affirmed that she was looking for "a revival of primitive Power." The Reverend Timothy Matthews received the elders cordially, apparently believed what they had to say, and admonished his followers also to believe. Before long, however, he was vacillating: though convinced by the elders of the necessity of baptism by immersion, he sought out another minister to baptize him and his congregation. This strange conduct caused some of his parishioners to leave him. Many were baptized by the Latter-day Saint elders, including his "best member" and, eventually, most of his church.[44] Thus it was that Reverend Matthews became the second of three ministers instrumental in opening important fields of labor for the first Latter-day Saint missionaries to England and whose congregation helped provide a nucleus of Latter-day Saint converts in their communities.

In Preston, meanwhile, success continued: Fielding baptized eight on Monday, July 31, Kimball baptized three on Thursday, one on Friday, and another on Saturday, and Hyde baptized six on Sunday.[45]

The Friday baptism was a young woman, the daughter of a minister from the nearby village of Walkerfold. After meeting Elder Kimball and discussing the principles of the gospel with him at length, she twice went to hear him preach, believed his message, and asked to be baptized. Kimball immediately took her to the River Ribble and fulfilled her request. In addition, since she was leaving for her home village, he decided to confirm her a member of the Church there and then. This was the first confirmation

---

[43]Fielding, Diary, 10.
[44]See Joseph Fielding to Mary Fielding, October 2, 1837, and Kimball, *Journal*, 24.
[45]Kimball, Diary.

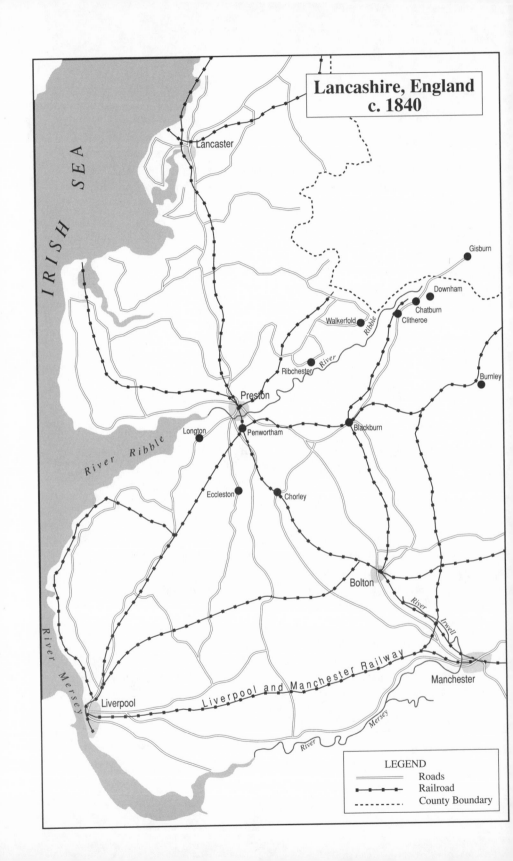

Lancashire, England c. 1840

IRISH SEA

Lancaster

Gisburn

Downham

Walkerfold

Chatburn

Clitheroe

Ribble

Ribchester

River

Burnley

Preston

Blackburn

Longton

Penwortham

River Ribble

Eccleston

Chorley

Bolton

River Irwell

Liverpool and Manchester Railway

River Mersey

Manchester

Liverpool

River Mersey

LEGEND

——— Roads

▪—▪—▪ Railroad

- - - - County Boundary

in England.[46] It was also Heber's introduction to Jennetta Richards, the woman who one year later married bachelor Willard Richards.[47] It was through Jennetta, moreover, that Elder Kimball met the third minister (and congregation) of importance to the success of the mission.

The following Sunday evening, August 6, the elders gathered the new converts together at Ann Dawson's home to confirm them members of the Church. After administering the sacrament, the missionaries explained in detail the ordinance of laying on of hands for the gift of the Holy Ghost and then confirmed twenty-six people. This was the first official meeting of The Church of Jesus Christ of Latter-day Saints anywhere outside North America. "The spirit of the Lord rested down upon us in a powerful manner," Kimball wrote of this historic occasion, "which caused us to rejoice excedingly; thus the work of the Lord spread and prevailed."[48]

Jennetta Richards, meanwhile, returned to Walkerfold, while Heber and his companions prayed earnestly that her father, the Reverend John Richards, would not only accept her decision to be baptized but also open his chapel to them. Though apprehensive that her father might find fault with her, Jennetta prayed for the same thing, and the following week Heber was delighted to receive a letter from the Reverend Richards requesting his presence and informing him that arrangements had been made for him to preach three times the following Sunday.[49]

Heber gladly walked the fifteen miles to Walkerfold, where Richards received him cordially. There he preached in the reverend's chapel, not just on Sunday but on Monday and Wednesday as well. Doors were opened to private homes, and in the next two weeks he preached thirteen times, baptized eight people, and found "menny more that believed on my words."[50] This was the first of many villages near Preston that Kimball worked in during his eight months in Lancashire.

---

[46]The exact date of this baptism and confirmation is difficult to determine, for the chronology in both Kimball's and Fielding's diary is difficult to follow. In addition, Kimball, especially, often made mistakes in his diary. It appears from the Fielding diary, however, that Kimball first met Jennetta on Tuesday, August 1. If this is accurate, then her baptism took place on Friday, August 4. All the others who had been baptized were confirmed the following Sunday.

The name of Jennetta Richards's village is spelled both "Walker Fold" and "Walkerfold" in the early sources. For consistency, we have standardized the spelling as "Walkerfold."

[47]Kimball, Diary; Kimball, "Synopsis," *Deseret News*, April 21, 1858; and Kimball, *Journal*, 21–22.

[48]Kimball, *Journal*, 21. See also Kimball, Diary, August 1837. The 1840 dictated account says "between forty and fifty," but Kimball did not have his diary with him when he dictated this account. Evidently he remembered that there had been "many" baptized and misremembered the exact number.

[49]Kimball, Diary, August 1837.

[50]Ibid.

Heber's first trip away from Preston was cut short by a vision in which he was told that he must return to Preston immediately.[51] When he arrived there, he found that Orson Hyde and Joseph Fielding were preaching and baptizing every day, and that there was considerable business for him to attend to.

Converts poured in from James Fielding's congregation, and eventually most of his church joined with the Saints. The Reverend Fielding, on the other hand, rued the day that he had invited the elders to preach in his chapel, for he now saw it as the "ruin" of his flock. "Kimball bored the holes, Goodson drove the nails, and Hyde clinched them,"[52] Fielding concluded, speaking of the first three sermons in his chapel. Little wonder that he and other ministers were soon accusing the missionaries of sheep stealing, and led out in organizing an intense opposition. "With regard to your robbing me of my flock," James wrote to his brother a year later, "I do not believe at all that you were sent of God to rend my little church to pieces. Were I to speak as 'plain' as you do I should boldly declare that it was not God but Satan as an angel of light sent you here."[53]

Heber and Orson continued to work together in and around Preston until, early in September, the Spirit spoke to Heber again, telling him to visit the little branch he had left in Walkerfold.[54] Like Jennetta, most of those who accepted Kimball's message in Walkerfold were young people, and when he returned he found several of them persecuted by their parents, some even driven from their homes. His presence seemed to revive their spirits, and his heart went out to them for what they were being called upon to endure.

Jennetta's father, meanwhile, fearing the loss of members as well as salary, closed his chapel to the American missionary, but Heber quickly found new places to preach. For the time being John Richards remained friendly and frequently listened to the apostle preach, but he, like James Fielding, ultimately complained that Kimball had "ruined his church, and

---

[51]Ibid; Heber C. Kimball to Vilate Kimball, September 2, 1837, Heber C. Kimball Collection: "The Lord warned me in a vision to go back to Preston for I was wanted there; the Lord is with me, and warns me of almost every thing before hand."

[52]Kimball, *Journal*, 18. On September 11 Fielding noted in his diary that "almost all my Bro. James" people were baptized.

[53]James Fielding to Joseph Fielding, August 27, 1838, Joseph Fielding Collection.

[54]As in so many instances, the chronology here is confusing when Kimball's diary is compared with his 1840 published journal. As nearly as we can, however, we reconstruct the chronology from the diary, adding to it the insights provided by the expanded, though chronologically questionable, 1840 journal.

had taken away all his young members."[55] Heber worked for several days, adding still more people to the Church, but he was also frustrated at times by the fact that most of those he met simply refused to listen. "O the darkness that covers the Earth," he lamented, for the priests had lulled the people to sleep, and it was like breaking through bars of iron to get to their hearts.[56]

The work of the Lord in Preston was "going on in power," Kimball wrote with satisfaction in his diary,[57] and by mid-September some ninety Latter-day Saints lived in that area, including a small branch of nineteen in Bedford. While Orson Hyde usually stayed close to Preston, Heber often went farther out into the countryside, visiting such places as Ribchester, Longridge, and Walkerfold, and then back to Preston for several days before returning again to the villages. "The Standard is planted in the Land and they can't Root it up for it has become so powerfull, and it is spreding," he wrote to his wife.[58] His early doubts and fears about his own ability had fled, for "perfect love casts out all fear, I feel firm in the Lord, I never enjoyed myself better than I do now."[59]

When Ann Dawson's home became too small for the meetings of the Saints in Preston, they began to hold early-morning Sabbath meetings in the open air. Growing numbers and the approach of cold weather, however, made this increasingly impractical. In September the elders arranged to use the large and centrally located "Cock Pit," which could hold nearly eight hundred people. Originally an arena for cock fighting, its use for that grisly sport ended in 1830, and it was fitted out as a meeting hall for temperance gatherings and preaching. The seating was still arranged in the round, looking down on a bare earth center, but the elders were delighted with their new, gas-lighted facilities.

Nevertheless, there were some inconveniences. Located in the center of town, the hall stood near a church, perhaps the oldest in Lancashire, which boasted twelve bells. Rung before every service, the bells made so much noise that if the Saints were meeting next door, they had to pause until the ringing stopped. More serious, however, was the disturbance of a meeting by some Methodist ministers, but after the missionaries obtained

[55]Kimball, *Journal*, 52. See also p. 23.
[56]Kimball, Diary, August-September 1837.
[57]Kimball, Diary, September 1837; see Fielding, Diary, 10, for numbers in Preston.
[58]Heber C. Kimball to Vilate Kimball, November 12, 1837, Heber C. Kimball Collection.
[59]Heber C. Kimball to Vilate Kimball, September 2, 1837, *Elders' Journal* 1 (October 1837): 4–7.

preaching licenses, two local constables volunteered to protect them from any further such incidents.[60]

On October 8, Elders Kimball and Hyde held a special conference in Preston. Nearly one hundred fifty Saints attended. Several men were ordained to the Aaronic Priesthood, and the Saints were divided into five branches. From then on, each branch held its own prayer meetings each Thursday, and on Sundays all would assemble in the Cock Pit for the sacrament and for preaching. It was a "refreshing time," Joseph Fielding noted in his diary, and the two apostles seemed "to act in perfect unison and as led by the Spirit of God."[61]

Not in perfect unison, however, were Elders Goodson and Snyder. Each for his own reasons decided to return to North America, much against the wishes of the apostles, leaving the mission severely shorthanded. Kimball remained optimistic, however, even concluding that the Lord was "giving us more power than we had before."[62]

By October a number of Preston ministers were concerned enough about inroads made by the American missionaries that they united to oppose them. Far from letting this discourage them, however, the apostles welcomed it, confident that God would turn it to good. As Orson Hyde noted earlier in a letter to his wife: though they had not spoken a "hard word against the priests" or against the sects, "yet they say all manner of evil against us." The people, in fact, "have discovered this difference between us . . . and it gives us unbounded influence." Indeed, as Heber Kimball observed, the priests helped fill the Cock Pit weekly by warning the people that it was "sure de[a]th" for them to hear the American elders preach, "for they will surely be caut in the Snare."[63] The result, according to Elder Kimball, was that they baptized fifty people in eight days. On Sunday, October 15, they administered the sacrament to about two hundred people (apparently including some who were not yet Church members) and confirmed thirty-five.[64]

---

[60]Kimball, *Journal*, 26.

[61]Fielding, Diary, 12. See also Kimball, Diary, October 1837.

[62]Kimball, Diary, October 1837. See also Fielding's comments. "I think they should not have gone and Elders Kimball and Hyde believe so too. They left on the 5th. Bro. G. [Goodson] has some old Enemies in London, but he wanted to go home. Bro. Snyder has some business at home but not pressing. He had never spoken much in public, had not much liberty, and was discouraged. May the Lord yet bless them and make them useful in his Church" (Fielding, Diary, 12).

[63]Orson Hyde to Marinda Hyde, September 14, 1837, *Elders' Journal* 1 (November 1837): 19–22 (Appendix B, Document 1); Heber C. Kimball to Vilate Kimball, November 12, 1837, Heber C. Kimball Collection.

[64]Kimball, Diary, October 1837.

The "Cock Pit," Preston

Interior of the "Cock Pit"
Courtesy LDS Church Archives

In mid October the elders went before the Court of Quarter Sessions in Preston and obtained licenses to preach. At first they had not thought it necessary, but after consulting with friends, they realized that it was at least wisdom, for it was actually a requirement under the law. One of these friends, an attorney, was the son of the Reverend John Richards of Walkerfold, and it was he who helped them get their licenses. Heber later discovered, to his surprise, that there were few licensed preachers in Preston, a fact that he turned to his advantage. "When they abused me I told them if they did not cease their abuse I would see the laws put in force . . . and this generally silenced them."[65]

The Church grew remarkably during the nine months the two apostles remained in England. Interest became so great in Preston that they could hardly fill one in ten of the calls that came to them. It was in the villages, however, that Elder Kimball found his greatest success. In many cases he went to particular "country towns" because someone had sent for him. In one instance he arrived to find a large congregation waiting. He preached and then went two miles farther to preach again. At the next stop, even before the people gathered, five presented themselves for baptism. He preached three sermons and baptized ten people, including two Methodist preachers. At Walkerfold he baptized another nine. In another town he baptized four members of the Thomas Benson family who, as soon as he entered the house, declared that he was a servant of God and announced they were ready for baptism. He also felt constrained to visit another home where he found that the family had been praying for him to come. He stayed with them half a day and baptized six. The first time he preached south of Preston he baptized twelve. And so it continued.[66] During one four-week period Heber baptized more than a hundred people and was instrumental in building up churches in Eccleston, Wrightington, Askin, Exton, Daubers Lane, Chorley, Whittle, and Leyland Moss. "More loving and affectionate saints I never saw before," he wrote of the new converts. They were "patterns of humility."[67]

The hearts of the first missionaries went out to the early converts in the Preston area. "They are nearly all poor," Joseph Fielding noted. "If others come in it appears the poor will be first. They have the least to sacrifice." Orson Hyde observed that they were "mostly manufacturers and

[65]Whitney, *Life of Heber C. Kimball*, 160–61.
[66]Kimball, Diary, October-December 1837.
[67]Kimball, *Journal*, 28.

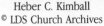

Heber C. Kimball
© LDS Church Archives

Orson Hyde
© LDS Church Archives

some other mechanics," men and women of "open hearts and strong faith," but also "extremely poor, most of them not having a change of clothes decent to be baptized in." "It is as much as they can do to live," Heber C. Kimball wrote to his wife. "There is not more than one or two that could lodge us over night if they should try; and in fact, there are some that have not a bed to sleep on themselves." What they had, however, they shared willingly: "The brethren will frequently divide the last loaf with us, and will do all in their power for us," testified Elder Hyde.[68]

At the end of October Joseph Fielding was ordained an elder, and the next month he accompanied Elder Kimball on a trip northeast of Preston. They preached and baptized in Ribchester, Thomly, Stoney Gate Lane, Waddington, Downham, and at the large market town of Clitheroe. In Clitheroe Kimball baptized a preacher and six members of the Methodist church following his first sermon.[69]

---

[68]Fielding, Diary, 10; Orson Hyde to Marina Hyde, September 14, 1837, *Elder's Journal* 1 (November 1837): 19–21 (Appendix B, Document 1); and Heber C. Kimball to Vilate Kimball, September 2, 1837, *Elder's Journal* 1 (October 1837): 4–7.

[69]Kimball, *Journal*, 28.

The educated and polished Orson Hyde was especially impressive in the city. According to Joseph Fielding, he was "very faithful and diligent" and had "great power in his preaching." On Sunday, December 3, 1837, Fielding heard him preach "with extraordinary Power. I think I never heard anything to equal it. He was filled with the Spirit, as I never before saw any man."[70] Elder Hyde had earlier written to his wife of his surprise at his own effectiveness. "I never before preached with that power and Spirit that I have since I come to this place," he confided to her.[71] His writing was also important. His powerful *A Prophetic Warning*, reprinted as a broadside entitled *A Timely Warning to the People of England*, became the missionaries' basic tract.

What seemed to set Heber C. Kimball apart was his spiritual power. Joseph Fielding called him "mighty in Tongues and in Prophesying" and "mighty in Faith and also in Preaching," while Orson Hyde wrote to his wife simply that "the Lord is with him."[72] Elder Kimball himself noted the spiritual promptings that frequently guided his travels. "The Lord . . . warns me of almost every thing before hand," he wrote to Vilate in September, and in November he told her that God was "teaching me the things of the kingdom both in dreams and in vissions and so it is with Brother Hide."[73] The combination of these gifts with his common, homespun approach proved especially effective. His sermons were very short, but he later recalled, "the Holy Ghost spake through me, and it was like melted lead to those who received."[74] Brigham Young once described the warm, comfortable way Kimball put people at ease so he could teach them. "Come, my friend, sit down," he would say; "do not be in a hurry." Then he preached the Gospel in "a plain, familiar manner" that made his hearers

---

[70]Fielding, Diary, September-December 7, 1837, 10, 14.

[71]Orson Hyde to Marinda Hyde, September 14, 1837 (Appendix B, Document 1).

[72]Fielding, Diary, 10 and 13; Orson Hyde to Marinda Hyde, September 14, 1837 (Appendix B, Document 1).

[73]Heber C. Kimball to Vilate Kimball, September 2, 1837; and Heber C. Kimball to Vilate Kimball, November 12, 1837, Kimball Collection. Twenty-five years later he wrote his sons who were in England as missionaries, recalling that "I was humble, knew nothing else but to trust in God alone . . . and his angels truly went with me" (Heber C. Kimball to David and Charles Kimball, July 27, 1863, *Millennial Star* 25 [October 17, 1863]: 669). Looking back in later years for the key, Heber thought in terms of the scriptural image of the weak made strong in the Lord. See sermon by Heber C. Kimball, November 22, 1857, *Journal of Discourses* 6:65. He also wrote to his sons that "I could not discover in all of this that it was me — I know that it was an invisible power and that it was of God" (Heber C. Kimball to David and Charles Kimball, November 10, 1863, *Millennial Star* 26 [February 6, 1864]: 91–92).

[74]Heber C. Kimball to David and Charles Kimball, July 27, 1863, *Millennial Star* 25 (October 17, 1863): 669.

believe what he said. Some stayed with him all day; some were converted after one sermon. He gently led them: "You see how plain the Gospel is? Come along now," and at the right moment he put his arm around them saying, "Come, let us go down to the water."[75]

Elder Kimball's personality and approach exactly suited the common folk with whom he worked. He was easily accepted by workman and villager. "The Lord appointed me to that work because I was willing to be the simplest," he concluded later.[76] Among Heber's converts were William and Ruth Clayton, a young couple in Penwortham, just across the River Ribble from Preston, where William was a factory clerk. Ruth believed first, but Heber's effect on William was more dramatic. When he was finally converted on October 21, he allowed Heber to take him out to the river and baptize him at 11 o'clock that night.[77] William took to the gospel wholeheartedly and soon became one of the most successful missionaries in England. Ruth's relatives, the Moons, were also part of Heber's harvest, and through them more than thirty family members and friends were baptized.[78] In 1840 her cousin, John Moon, led the first organized group of Saints to leave England for the United States.

WINTER MONTHS: THE CHILL OF THE AIR AND THE WARMTH OF THE SPIRIT

Christmas Day 1837 was celebrated in a special way by the British Saints. Early that morning, five people were baptized; then, at 10 A.M., Elders Kimball, Hyde, and Fielding conducted the first general conference of the Church in England. More than three hundred Saints, including those from Preston and representatives from branches throughout Lancashire, gathered in the Cock Pit. The elders blessed a hundred children, confirmed fourteen new members of the Church, ordained ten men to the office of priest, and seven, including William Clayton, to the office of teacher. It was also at that conference that the guide to health known as the "Word of Wisdom" was first publicly taught in England.[79]

Immediately after the conference Elders Kimball and Hyde visited Longton, a few miles southwest of Preston and close to the sea. Though

---

[75]Remarks by Brigham Young, April 6, 1857; *Journal of Discourses* 4:305.
[76]Discourse by Heber C. Kimball, March 19, 1854, *Journal of Discourses* 3:113.
[77]Allen, *Trials of Discipleship*, 17.
[78]Moss, "Gospel Restored," 87.
[79]Kimball, Diary, Christmas 1837; Fielding, Diary, 15.

Hyde had preached there earlier, no one had been baptized. This time ten people asked for baptism. The weather was so cold, however, that the River Ribble was frozen over, so they all went down to the seashore and the new converts were baptized in the frigid ocean.[80]

The two apostles planned to leave for America in the early spring, which made the next few months especially pivotal. In addition to continuing their missionary work, they had to organize and strengthen existing churches in preparation for their departure. Shortly after the conference Heber took Joseph Fielding as a companion on his village circuit to "regulate the churches,"[81] probably with an eye toward his remaining behind to preside over the mission.

They went north, up the Ribble Valley, where they preached regularly, blessed children, baptized and confirmed new converts, and instructed the Saints in their duties. Perhaps no visit pleased Elder Kimball more than their unusually long stay with the little branch at Walkerfold.[82] Members there "have gone through much Persecution, but remain very firm," noted Fielding. Their meeting did not break up until two in the morning, and at that point the missionaries realized they had no place to spend the rest of the night. Evidently the families and friends of the young converts simply were not willing to entertain the American intruders. Their only option was to cross the frozen River Hodder into Yorkshire where, they believed, they could stay at the home of James Smithies, a member. The two missionaries were nevertheless overwhelmed with gratitude, and they stopped long enough on the ice for Heber to pray for the Saints at Walkerfold and to "give glory to God for we felt as though all heaven was pleas[ed] with what we had don that night." When they finally arrived at the Smithies home they had to rouse the family, but they were welcomed in and finally got to bed around four that morning.[83]

Being continually on the move and having little sleep tested their endurance to the utmost, but the opportunities seemed almost endless. "We could not fill the calls we had from day to day," Kimball later recalled,

---

[80]Kimball, Diary; Kimball, *Journal*, 30. In the latter source, Kimball says they baptized fifteen, but since that account is based partly on reminiscence, we rely on the diary.

[81]Kimball, Diary, January 1838.

[82]Kimball's diary indicates that this meeting took place at Chaigley, while Fielding indicates that it was at Walkerfold. The two villages are so close together, however, that it is apparent that the Saints in both were all part of the same group.

[83]Fielding, Diary, January 23, 1838, 16; Kimball, Diary, January 1838.

Chatburn-Downham, England, by Al Rounds. Courtesy Robert Pratt

"for the work kept spreading." From every direction around Preston came invitations and urgent pleas for their presence.[84]

Many people thought the cold of winter would stop the missionaries, but they could not have been more wrong.[85] "We would baptize as many as fifty in Preston in a week, exclusive of those in the country," Kimball later recalled, and with respect to the country he wrote in his diary that he had not preached once in a place but what he had baptized people and built up a church.[86]

Few experiences, however, surpassed those of Elder Kimball in March in the villages of Downham and Chatburn, some sixteen miles upriver from Preston. When earlier he had expressed his desire to visit them, some of the brethren from nearby branches tried to dissuade him. For thirty years, he was told, various ministers had attempted without success to establish churches in those towns, but they were wicked places and the people were hardened against the gospel. Nevertheless, Kimball said, he

---

[84]Kimball, *Journal,* 36.
[85]Fielding, Diary, February 14, 1838, 17.
[86]Kimball, *Journal,* 30; Kimball, Diary, 13.

wanted to go, for "it was my busines, 'to call not the righteous, but sinners to repentance.' "[87]

Accompanied by Joseph Fielding, Heber went first to Downham[88] where, in a scene just the opposite of what he had been led to expect, he preached in a large barn and then baptized several people. As he prepared to leave Downham for an evening appointment in Clitheroe, a very pressing invitation reached him from Chatburn. So urgent was the plea that he finally sent Fielding to Clitheroe alone and walked to Chatburn. Someone had already obtained a large barn for him to preach in and there, surrounded by villagers, he proceeded to speak about the condition of the world, the blessings of embracing the truth, and the resurrection. "My remarks were accompanied by the spirit of the Lord and were received with joy," he noted. The so-called "obdurate" were "melted down into tenderness and love, and such a feeling was produced as I never saw before." As he concluded he felt someone pulling at his coat, and as he turned he heard Mrs. Elizabeth Partington earnestly asking, " 'Please, sir, will you baptize me,' 'And me,' 'And me,' exclaimed more than a dozen voices." It took him until after midnight to baptize and confirm some twenty-five new converts.[89]

"These towns seemed to be affected from one end to the other," Kimball later recalled. "Parents called their children together, spoke to them of the subjects which I had preached, and warned them against swearing and all other evil practices. . . . Such a scene I presume was never witnessed in this place before—the hearts of the people appeared to be broken." As Kimball and Fielding began to leave the two towns, doors were crowded and villagers lined the streets, weeping as they said their farewells. The whole experience was an overwhelming spiritual highlight for the apostle from America, and it moved him to tears. His feelings can best be described in his own words:

> While contemplating this scene we were induced to take off our hats, for we felt as if the place was holy ground—the Spirit of the Lord rested down upon us, and I was

---

[87]Kimball, *Journal*, 33.

[88]The exact chronology of these events, as well as others in February and March, is impossible to obtain from the sources extant. Some writers indicate that Kimball visited Chatburn first, then Downham. Our interpretation of the Fielding diary, coupled with some things written by Kimball, suggests that it was the other way around. Fielding's references to these events, however, are separated, sketchy, and chronologically confusing, while Kimball's references are separated, sometimes detailed, but still chronologically confusing.

[89]Kimball, *Journal*, 33–34.

constrained to bless that whole region of country, we were followed by a great number, a considerable distance from the villages who could hardly seperate themselves from us. My heart was like unto theirs, and I thought my head was a fountain of tears, for I wept for several miles after I bid them adieu.[90]

Fielding, too, was moved. "There is a wonderful Work in Downham and Chatburn," he wrote. "It appears as though the whole of the Inhabitants were turning to the Lord from 10 to 90 years old. . . . They are full of Love."[91]

THE APOSTLES SAY GOOD-BYE

With only a short time remaining before their return to America, word spread that the apostles would be leaving, and great numbers flocked to hear them. They also went from house to house in Preston, calling upon people to repent and baptizing as many as twenty in a day. The faith of the Saints was rewarded when the apostles were able to heal many of their sick.[92]

In the villages, too, the Spirit continued strong. In a Baptist church in Barnaldwick, Elders Kimball and Hyde preached to several hundred people, and their message touched the hearts not only of the congregation but also of the minister. Even after the meeting finally broke up, conversations continued until nearly dawn. They could scarcely tear themselves away, and when they did so, the villagers "wept like little children."[93]

On April 2 Elders Kimball and Fielding walked to Chatburn and Downham for a last farewell. As soon as they were seen in Chatburn, the people left their work and flocked to the streets to greet them. Children followed them from place to place, singing. "Some of them said that if they could but touch us they seem better. They evidently believe that there is Virtue in Brother Kimball's Cloake," wrote Fielding. "Such gratitude, I never witnessed before," concluded Heber.[94] Just before leaving England, he sent a warm letter to the Saints of these two remarkable villages, giving them tender pastoral advice and expressing his heartfelt gratitude for their many kindnesses.[95]

On Sunday, April 8, 1838, more than six hundred Saints from Preston

[90]Kimball, *Journal*, 34.
[91]Fielding, Diary, 18.
[92]Kimball, *Journal*, 35–36.
[93]Kimball, *Journal*, 32–33.
[94]Fielding, Diary, 18; Kimball, *Journal*, 49.
[95]Heber C. Kimball to the Church of Latter-day Saints in Chatburn and Downham, April 15, 1838, *Millennial Star* 1 (August 1840): 103–4. In the *Star* the letter is dated 1840, but that is obviously an error.

The interim British Mission presidency: Joseph Fielding, president (center);
Willard Richards, first counselor (left); William Clayton, second counselor
© LDS Church

and the surrounding villages assembled in the Cock Pit at 9 in the morning
for a mission conference that lasted nearly eight hours. Perhaps the most
important business was the selection of Joseph Fielding to be the mission
president and Willard Richards and William Clayton to be his counselors.[96]
Joseph Fielding shuddered at the thought of having the full responsibility
laid on his shoulders. "This work seems far too great for me," he wrote
with trepidation. "My heart is ready to sink at the Thought, and nothing
but a full belief that it is the Will of God could ever have induced me to
take it upon me, but I know that my Strength is in the Lord, and I intend
to be faithful, if I die under it."[97]

Much more business was conducted at the conference: forty confirmations, more than one hundred children blessed, eight new elders ordained and others given the lesser priesthood, and hours of singing and
instruction.[98] Immediately after the public meeting, all the officers of the
Church (nearly eighty had now been ordained) met in a private home to
be instructed. Toward the end of the meeting President Joseph Fielding,
on behalf of all the English Saints, thanked Elders Kimball and Hyde for
their sacrifice in leaving their families, for their faithfulness and diligence
in preaching the gospel, and for their kindness and instruction. Elder
Kimball, in turn, on behalf of the Church in America, extended the hand

---

[96]Kimball, *Journal*, 37–38; Fielding, Diary, 19. The apostles ordained each member of the new
presidency to the office of high priest.

[97]Fielding, Diary, 19.

[98]Kimball, *Journal*, 37–38.

of fellowship to the presidency in England "in token of Union or oneness." He then blessed each member of the new presidency. This "delightful yet an affecting time" ended some time after midnight.[99]

As a final gesture of their love for the apostles, the English Saints raised enough money to pay their passage home. They donated bedding and provisions for the voyage back to America and gave them other presents.[100] Elders Kimball, Hyde, and Russell left Preston on Tuesday, April 10, with the expectation of sailing the following Monday on the *Garrick*, the same ship that had brought them from America the year before. The press of well-wishers, meanwhile, prevented the apostles from giving more private instruction to Joseph Fielding and Willard Richards, but on Thursday these two joined them in Liverpool. By then word had spread that contrary winds were delaying the sailing, and other Saints from Preston soon arrived for the final farewell. The delay also prevented Elders Fielding and Richards from seeing their brethren sail for, after absorbing whatever additional counsel they could obtain and feeling the heavy weight of their new responsibilities, they departed to begin their ceaseless rounds of visiting members and branches.[101]

When the *Garrick* finally sailed on April 20, it was into a storm that damaged the ship and left everyone ill. Even so, the well-built vessel made up lost time, and conveyed the returning missionaries to New York City, where they landed on May 12.

The first apostles in England left more than fifteen hundred members in Preston and the surrounding villages[102] and a strong presidency to direct the work. But all this was only prelude, so far as the apostles were concerned, for they assured the Saints that they fully expected to return, this time with their entire quorum. What they did not anticipate was the months of hardship they would face before any of the Twelve would again set foot on English soil.

---

[99]Fielding, Diary, 19.

[100]Kimball, *Journal*, 40–41.

[101]Kimball, *Journal*, 40–41; Fielding, Diary, 19–20. See also Richards, Diary, 10–12 April 1838.

[102]Kimball, *Journal*, 41. Fielding noted in his diary (April 10, p. 19) that there were nearly one thousand members organized into twenty branches. No doubt hundreds of others baptized during the hurried mission were not so organized. Total baptisms in England during this period numbered between fifteen hundred and two thousand, but all did not remain in the Church. The numbers of nearly thirteen hundred members and twenty-six branches have also been used. See Evans, *Century of "Mormonism,"* 244. Among the number was Alexander Neibaur, the first Jewish Latter-day Saint. See S. Kimball, *Heber C. Kimball*, 51.

Chapter 3

BETWEEN THE MISSIONS: PREPARATION AND TRIALS

When Heber C. Kimball arrived in Kirtland on May 22, 1838, he found that dissension and persecution had forced Joseph Smith, Brigham Young, and many others to flee Ohio and join the Saints in Missouri. Soon he, too, was on the way, arriving at Far West on July 25. Just two weeks earlier the Prophet had received the revelation that would send him back to England.[1] "Let the Twelve be organized," it said, "and let men be appointed to supply the place of those who are fallen." The new appointees were specifically named: John Taylor, John E. Page, Wilford Woodruff, and Willard Richards. The revelation assured the apostles that their families would be cared for in their absence and even specified the exact date and place of their official leave-taking: "And next spring let them depart to go over the great waters, and there promulgate my gospel . . . and bear record of my name. Let them take leave of my saints in the city of Far West, on the twenty-sixth day of April next, on the building-spot of my house, saith the Lord."

This revelation could hardly have come at a less opportune time. Apostasy continued to plague the Church, and even the Quorum of the Twelve Apostles was still riddled with dissent. Four apostles had apostatized in the aftermath of the Kirtland difficulties, and by the end of the year Quorum president Thomas B. Marsh turned against the Church, and apostle David W. Patten was killed as a result of renewed mob activity. Also in 1838, Missouri Governor Lilburn W. Boggs issued his infamous "extermination order," brutalities such as the Haun's Mill massacre were perpetrated against the Saints, Joseph Smith along with some members of the Twelve and other Church leaders were jailed, and the Missouri Saints began another tragic exodus, this time to Illinois.

---

[1]See D&C 118.

Joseph Smith
© LDS Church

It would seem that Joseph Smith was singularly optimistic in sending the Quorum of the Twelve away in such trying times, for despite its lack of unity there were still within its ranks men who could be most helpful in the giant task of building a new gathering place for the Saints. Nevertheless, the commandment had been given. Perhaps the future well-being of the Church was directly related to the strengthening of the Twelve, both as individuals and as a quorum, that would result from this mission.

After the departure of Thomas B. Marsh and the death of David W. Patten, Brigham Young became the senior member of the Twelve. With the entire First Presidency imprisoned in Liberty, Missouri, it fell upon him and a few of his quorum to direct the Saints in their exodus from the state. On December 19 they ordained John Taylor and John E. Page to the apostleship. At his urging the Saints entered into a covenant that, regardless of means, none would be left behind, and because of his firm and energetic direction during this time of crisis, Elder Young began to emerge in the eyes of the Saints as a strong and effective leader.

The unfortunate image some still had of the Twelve, however, was emphasized on April 17, 1839, at a conference in Quincy, Illinois, when

Brigham presented the name of George A. Smith, whom Joseph Smith had named from Liberty jail, to be sustained as one of the Twelve. The vote was in the affirmative, but not without a remark from Reynolds Cahoon that "there had been so much apostacy among the Twelve that he hoped the Saints would exercise faith to keep this one from flying [off] the track."[2]

In Quincy, the Twelve held a council with other Church officials about returning to Missouri to fulfill the commandment to leave on their mission from Far West. Some present, believing that the Lord would take the will for the deed, did not expect the Twelve really to carry it through. "But I felt differently," Brigham later reported, "& so did the Twelve who were with me."[3] He knew that anti-Mormons had boasted that the revelation could not be fulfilled, thus proving, they declared, that Joseph Smith was not a prophet. Brigham was determined never to let that happen. After each of the Twelve expressed his own feelings, Brigham announced that "the Lord God had spoke & it was our business to obey, & the Lord would take care of us." All present agreed to go and fulfill the revelation.[4] The next day Elders Young, Pratt, Taylor, Woodruff, and Smith, accompanied by Alpheus Cutler, set out for Missouri. En route they encountered John E. Page, just leaving Missouri, and turned him around. Heber C. Kimball, directing the last few of the faithful still in Missouri, awaited them near Far West.

Because some of the Twelve were wanted men in Missouri—men whose enemies had sworn to kill them—some Saints found it hard to believe that the Lord would require them to return to the spot from which they had recently been driven just to fulfill the letter of the revelation. Theodore Turley, who was on the Far West committee on removal, thought otherwise. On April 5 eight men, including John Whitmer and Captain Bogart, who had led the mob forces in the Battle of Crooked River, confronted Turley in his office. Bogart taunted him with a copy of the revelation, reminding him that the Twelve were "scattered all over creation." They dare not come, he chided, for if they did they would be murdered, and since the revelation could not be fulfilled, Turley must give up his faith.

---

[2]Smith, "History," April 17, 1839; see also Young, "History of Brigham Young," *Deseret News*, February 17, 1858, p. 394.

[3]Young, "History," ms. For a reminiscent account of this meeting, see discourse by Elder Wilford Woodruff, December 12, 1869, *Journal of Discourses* 13:159.

[4]Young, "History," ms.

Temple site at Far West, Missouri
© LDS Church

"In the name of God that revelation will be fulfilled," Turley responded with the unwavering conviction that later resulted in his selection as one of the missionaries to accompany the Twelve to England.[5]

Despite the dangers, some time before dawn on the morning of April 26, Brigham Young, Heber C. Kimball, Orson Pratt, John E. Page, John Taylor, Wilford Woodruff, George A. Smith, and eighteen other Church members met at the designated spot. During a short service, Wilford Woodruff and George A. Smith were ordained to the apostleship, other ordinations took place, several dissidents were excommunicated from the Church, the apostles each prayed, a song was sung, and a cornerstone was symbolically placed for the temple. Those present then quickly took leave of the place and made their way to Commerce, Illinois. On the way, however, Theodore Turley could not resist a quick stop at the home of Isaac Russell, whom he awakened and presented with the astonishing news that the Twelve had just left the temple site. Russell had baptized Turley in 1836, but he had returned early from the 1837 mission to England, and

---

[5]Smith, *History of the Church* 3:306–7.

he was among those who had just been excommunicated during the meeting of the Twelve.[6]

Although that was their official leave-taking, it was several months before any of the apostles were actually on their way to England. Like the other Saints so recently driven from Missouri, they too had to find places to settle their families either in western Illinois or across the Mississippi in Iowa Territory. With food and other provisions in short supply and poor living conditions in the swampy, malaria-infested river bottoms, suffering and death were commonplace among the Saints. Several miraculous healings rewarded their faith, but continuing hardships complicated preparations for the forthcoming mission.

Late in July young George A. Smith left his parents, brother, and sister at Green Plains, Illinois, and went to Commerce, expecting soon to accompany the rest of the Twelve to England. Instead, he wrote in his journal, "I found great numbers of the brethren lying sick. Joseph told me and Don Carlos [Joseph's brother] to begin at his house and lay hands on every sick person, rebuke their diseases and command them in the name of the Lord Jesus Christ to arise and walk and not leave a single person on their bed." They spent all of July 23 administering to the sick, "a great number of whom were instantly healed, and gave glory to God." Over the next several weeks George A. attended council meetings with Joseph, Hyrum, and the Twelve, and spent his nights "watching with the sick, and going from cabin to cabin, and camp to camp, frequently watching with half a dozen families at once."[7]

While disease devastated the weakened Saints, the apostles were urgently concerned with leaving their families prepared for a long separation. Buildings of any sort were scarce around the swampy lowlands of Commerce, and the Saints were living in tents, wagons, and other temporary structures. Brigham Young, John Taylor, Wilford Woodruff, and Orson Pratt all moved their families into the old log barracks of an abandoned military post, Fort Des Moines, in Montrose, Iowa. Heber C. Kimball moved his wife and four children from temporary locations into a fourteen- by sixteen-foot log cabin he had built in Commerce. Parley P. Pratt had joined with Elder Kimball in purchasing some wooded land, and he began clearing it

---

[6]Turley, "Mission Journal," 5, 12–13.
[7]Smith, "History."

and building a cabin. He soon sold his holdings, however, and took his family with him when he left for his mission. His brother Orson, meanwhile, moved his wife and two children into one of the shanties on the Kimball property. George A. Smith took his father and brother John to Commerce, where they created a house for the family by moving a twelve-foot-square log stable to a better location, putting a new shake roof on it, and then moving in, even though it still had no chinking between the logs. Almost immediately the three of them became ill, and they remained so until George started for England.

Providing for their families was vital, but the spiritual preparation the apostles received before they left was even more critical to the success of their mission. The hectic summer of 1839 thus also became a period of intensive training for the Twelve. Joseph Smith met with them frequently and instructed them in spiritual affairs, doctrine, and practical leadership. The apostles, filled with anticipation of the coming mission, drank eagerly from the fountain of knowledge and inspiration that came from the Prophet in these private sessions. Foreshadowing some of their trying experiences with the powers of evil, for example, he gave them a "key" by which they could detect the devil if he were to appear as a man. This same instruction was later placed in the Doctrine and Covenants as a revelation to the entire Church.[8]

The afternoon of Tuesday, July 2, was especially memorable. The apostles and others preparing to accompany them to England met with the First Presidency at the temporary quarters of Brigham Young in Iowa. The Presidency gave special blessings to the two newest apostles, Elders Woodruff and Smith, to Theodore Turley, and to the wives of some of the missionaries. Hyrum Smith then talked to the Twelve about their mission, after which Joseph Smith arose and gave them what Wilford Woodruff described as "some precious things of the kingdom . . . yea precious principles that ought to be engraven upon our hearts & practiced in our lives."[9] He talked to the apostles of prudence, love, and humility in exercising their priesthood authority, and of guarding against "self-sufficiency, self-righteousness, and self-importance." He urged the apostles to "be humble,

---

[8]See Woodruff, *Journal*, June 27, 1839, 1:341; compare with D&C 129:4–8. Even though Joseph Smith gave this information privately to the apostles in 1839, it was not recorded as a revelation until 1843. In the Church Archives is a manuscript by Willard Richards called "Pocket Companion" that contains many of these teachings. Richards may well have created this from notes shared with him by the apostles when they arrived in 1840.

[9]Woodruff, *Journal*, July 2, 1839, 1:342–44.

and not be exalted, and beware of pride, and not seek to excel one above another, but act for each other's good, and pray for one another, and honor our brother or make honorable mention of his name, and not backbite and devour our brother." Remembering those who had fallen, he called for the Twelve to fortify themselves against a repetition of such apostasy. Would the new members "exalt themselves so high that they will soon tumble over and have a great fall . . . as several of the quorum have done," he wondered aloud, or "will they learn wisdom and be wise? O God! give them wisdom, and keep them humble, I pray."[10]

On Sunday, July 7, several members of the Twelve met with the First Presidency and others in Commerce and gave their farewell addresses. According to Wilford Woodruff, President Rigdon's address "was of such a nature in appealing to our affections, in parting with our wives, and children, & the peculiarity of our mission, the perils we might meet with, & the blessings that we should receive, &c. that tears was brought from many eyes." "May the Lord enable us the Twelve ever to be meek & humble to lie passive in his hands as the clay is in the hands of the potter," he reflected in his diary that night.

In addition to receiving such vital counsel from the First Presidency, the apostles studied the scriptures and frequently met together to discuss their mission and its significance. This along with their preparations for leaving took them through the spring and early summer of 1839. The spirit of the times could have been expressed no more tenderly than in the way Wilford Woodruff did it in his journal the day before he left:

> [August 7, 1839] I spent the day in preparing to leave home to go on my long mission to England. I make a sacrifice of my all for Christ sake to do his work. It is no small trial of faith to leave my family & my all & to start on a mission of four thousand miles to preach the gospel to the nations of the earth & that to without money purs or scrip with the power of desease resting upon me even a shock of the fever & ague every other day but yet I do this freely for Christ Sake trusting in him for the recompence of reward. May the Lord give me grace according [to] my day & a safe return to my family which favor I ask in the name of JESUS CHRIST.[11]

WILLARD RICHARDS AND THE INTERREGNUM

In England, meanwhile, the new mission presidency succeeded not only in preserving the fledgling flock but also in strengthening it. Though

---

[10]Smith, *History of the Church* 3:383–84 (Appendix B, Document 2).
[11]Woodruff, *Journal*, August 7, 1839, 1:349.

disappointed that he and his colleagues could not maintain the momentum established by Elders Kimball and Hyde, Joseph Fielding could take satisfaction that they continued to attract new people to replace those who drifted away or were cut off. In addition, Willard Richards went through a trial by fire that, in its own way, tested his mettle as much as Zion's Camp had tested that of his future colleagues in the Quorum of the Twelve Apostles.

Joseph Fielding and Willard Richards traveled widely, doing missionary work, setting in order the affairs of the various branches, and working with local missionaries. William Clayton spent most of his time in Manchester, where he built up a branch of the church numbering about 240 people.[12] All three suffered financial hardships, and Richards was troubled with illness. On the other hand, the two unmarried members of the presidency found new happiness, for each married a young woman he met while doing missionary work: Joseph Fielding married Hannah Greenwood of Preston, and Willard Richards married Jennetta Richards of Walkerfold.

The courtship and marriage of Willard and Jennetta Richards is of special interest here, not just because Willard became one of the Twelve but also because of what it reveals about the problems of the Saints during the interregnum.[13] On Friday, August 4, 1837, the day he baptized Jennetta, Heber C. Kimball wrote to Willard, who was working in Bedford, saying, "I baptized your wife today."[14] Willard was no doubt bemused, but the letter also aroused a compelling interest in meeting this young woman who already shared his surname.

Willard did not return to Preston until the following March, and a few days later he set out with Joseph Fielding to visit nearby towns. On March 22 he was in the home of Brother James Mercer of Thornley when Jennetta walked into the room. Apparently Heber had continued to press the idea of marriage, and perhaps both Willard and Jennetta were well prepared for their immediate mutual attraction. Accompanied by one of the Saints, they set out to attend a meeting. Somewhere along the way Willard remarked that "Richards" was a good name. "I never want to change it," he

---

[12]See Allen and Alexander, *Manchester Mormons,* and Allen, *Trials of Discipleship,* for details of this remarkable story.

[13]The account here draws slightly on Noall, *Intimate Disciple.* This work is highly fictionalized, but its historical chronology and basic factual material seem reasonably accurate. See also Evans, *Century of "Mormonism,"* 71–72.

[14]Whitney, *Life of Heber C. Kimball,* 143.

continued. "Do you?" "No, I do not," Jennetta replied without hesitation, and Willard noted in his journal that "I think she never will."[15]

The courtship began immediately. Jennetta went to Preston and, for a few days at least, stayed in the home of Ann Dawson, though during the next several months she intermittently spent time in Preston, at home in Walkerfold, or with friends in nearby towns. The visits from Willard were also intermittent, since his pastoral duties continued, but on June 29 he gave her a ring. "We acknowledged each other as husband and wife," he wrote in his journal that night, "& sealed it with our mutual kisses."[16]

Willard and Jennetta's happiness was tempered, however, by their certainty that her parents would never approve, and they even kept the engagement secret until after she came of age on her twenty-first birthday, a little less than two months later.[17] Her life, meanwhile, was filled with frustration, for she knew her parents sensed her attraction to the American missionary. She had planned to leave home, but her mother was ill and, despite her parents' opposition to Willard and the Church, she could not tear herself away. She wrote on July 22, "I should like you my dearest love to let me know your mind upon my leaving home at the time appointed for I cannot think of leaving my poor mother in the delicate state of health she is in now with the little one without giving her time to get a servant." Besides, she said, her leaving might give her parents reason to suspect something, "which may cause both you my dearest love and I some trouble." In addition, she felt obligated to take care of other family responsibilities, including cleaning her father's chapel, and also to do considerable sewing for herself.

Jennetta received nothing but criticism from her parents about the Church and Willard. "What a thing it [is] to be married and be poor," her mother chided her, to which Jennetta defiantly replied that Willard might be poor in worldly property but he was rich in grace. Her mother even threatened her with what amounted to exile, saying that if she went to Preston "I shall never look upon you again." "Well," replied the distraught Jennetta, "if Father and Mother forsake a child for serving the Lord as well as she is able with all her might the Lord will not forsake her but take her

---

[15]Richards, Diary, March 22, 1838.
[16]Ibid., June 29, 1838. He also wrote a prayer: "My heavenly father sanction it in heaven & bless our union to the fulfillment of the design for which marriage was instituted for Christs sake *Amen* & amen."
[17]Fielding, Diary, 27.

in." Finally, on the night of Friday, July 27, her mother told her she must leave home — the tension between them had become too great.[18]

Jennetta did not leave, however, and two weeks later she wrote to Willard again, describing the same kinds of problems along with a new objection. Willard was about to die of consumption, her mother told her, and was therefore just trying to cheat her. Jennetta did not believe it, but she knew of his recent illness, and she pleaded with him to carry an umbrella and take care of himself. "I hope my Dear Love you will be more careful of getting wet if not for your own sake do it because it is the earnest request of your Jennetta who loves you most dearly."[19]

Several days later Jennetta went to Preston, and on August 21 she turned twenty-one. The two spent her birthday together, and on September 1 they officially registered their intent to marry. After that Jennetta went to Kirkham, where she stayed with her brother. In the meantime, she heard still another accusation against Willard. He was deceiving her, said her mother, for he was actually a widower and had said as much to people in England. Someone even suggested that he had a wife and family in America. Both stories were false, and Jennetta wrote to Willard: "I can as soon believe that the gospel you preach is false . . . for if you will deceive in one thing you will in another." Her brother, meantime, still wanted to investigate, and asked her to wait until he had done so. "He loves me as a Sister and wishes to be satisfied," she told Willard, but "I told him I was satisfied." If her brother found the story to be false he said he would withdraw his objections to their marriage.[20]

Jennetta's romance was also troubled by the opposition of some of the Saints, who were not happy with the prospective union between the American missionary, whom they were supporting, and the daughter of the relatively well-off minister from Walkerfold.[21] In September, for example, Jennetta had to return to Kirkham because no one in Preston was willing to let her stay with them, even though Willard was ill and needed nursing.[22] In another instance, Thomas Webster and other dissidents charged that Willard had said that he would not marry until the coming of Christ. When, somehow, the dissidents heard he was about to wed, they

[18]Jennetta Richards to Willard Richards, July 22–27, 1838, typescript, Willard Richards Collection.

[19]Jennetta Richards to Willard Richards, August 11, 1838, Willard Richards Collection.

[20]Jennetta Richards to Willard Richards, September 7, 1838, Willard Richards Collection.

[21]See Richards, Diary (expanded), August 6, 1838,

[22]Richards, Diary, September 7, 1838.

Willard, Jennetta, and Heber
John Richards, Nauvoo, 1845
Courtesy LDS Church

began to say that a "prophecy" had failed. Willard was both startled and chagrined at the accusation. That was not what he said, he told Joseph Fielding, but if he said anything like it at all, it was after he became engaged and people had begun to press him about the rumors. Wishing to keep the engagement secret, he felt that his private affairs were no one else's business and said whatever he said only to "put them off."[23]

Despite the problems, at 8 A.M. on September 24, 1838, only six months after their first meeting, Willard, age thirty-four, and Jennetta, age twenty-one, were married in the registrar's office in Preston. Joseph Fielding and his wife, Hannah, who had also received petty criticism for their recent marriage, signed the certificate as witnesses. "Most truly do I praise my Heavenly Father for his great kindness in providing me a partner according to his promise," the grateful Willard wrote that night. "I receive her from the Lord & hold her at his disposal. I pray my heavenly father he will bless us forever."[24]

---

[23]Fielding, Diary, 27. Webster continued to bring ridiculous charges against the Church leaders, including a completely irrational accusation that Richards had helped Jane Dawson kill her daughter, Alice. On October 3 Willard and Jane were even hauled into court on that charge but were quickly released. Webster, meanwhile, left the Church and was officially excommunicated on September 30. Fielding, Diary, 18; Richards, Diary, September 30 and October 3, 1838.

[24]Noall, *Intimate Disciple*, 230; Richards, Diary, September 24, 1838.

Willard and Jennetta had a six-day honeymoon near the sea and then returned to the rigors of missionary life. Jane Dawson allowed them to board at her house, along with the Fieldings, and from there the two mission leaders continued their work. Both Willard and Jennetta were frequently ill, however, and when both couples moved out of the Dawson home on December 20 they had to carry Jennetta in a chair. "I cannot but wonder at the Dealing of God with them," Joseph Fielding wrote. "Brother R[ichards] has been surprisingly patient in his Afflictions."[25]

Life did not become easier, for Willard and Jennetta continued to struggle with ill health and with criticism from Preston Saints. For one thing, Jennetta still wore fine clothes that, to some Saints, seemed inconsistent with the life-style expected of her husband, who was being supported by the Church and had only the most austere wardrobe. In mid December Joseph Fielding observed that Willard had "gone in his old Coat as long as he is fit to be seen."[26] In March Jennetta bought a muff to guard her frail health against the cold weather, but even that antagonized some. As Joseph Fielding observed, nothing she wore was purchased by other Church members, but that hardly satisfied the critics. They also censured her for not attending meetings often enough and even criticized Willard for staying home too much to take care of her when she was ailing.

Joseph Fielding admired Willard and continued to support him fully, believing that the Lord had a special reason for keeping him in Preston, but he also observed privately that perhaps Elder Richards was himself a bit too harsh in his judgment of others.[27] The criticism and petty bickering within the Church disturbed Joseph greatly. "The Saints would not do in Zion," he opined to himself one day in March, "yet I have told them the Lord will perhaps keep them here some time to try them, as they wouldn't agree together."[28]

Despite the difficulties, Joseph and Willard also recorded times of spiritual uplift, their joy in missionary work, and the love of the faithful Saints, especially those outside Preston. In addition, on June 27, 1839, Hannah Fielding delivered a baby girl. Three weeks later, on July 17, Jennetta Richards gave birth to a boy. He was named Heber John, the first name in honor of Heber C. Kimball and the second after Jennetta's father.

[25]Fielding, Diary, 30.
[26]Ibid., 29.
[27]Ibid., 33.
[28]Ibid., 34.

To please the grandfather, they called him John. Five months later, however, the previously healthy baby contracted smallpox and, on December 28, he died. When the distraught Willard saw that the child's breath was gone, he threw himself to the floor in prayer, believing for a moment that this simply could not happen. But then, he wrote in his diary, "in an instant I felt to exclaim, the Lord gave & the Lord hath taken away & blessed be the name of the Lord."[29]

Meanwhile, the mission leaders had to deal with an unfortunate problem created by Isaac Russell, who had returned to America against the wishes of the apostles in 1837. Russell wrote a secret letter to his converts in Alston in which he claimed that great judgments were to befall the Church, that it must be purified, and that he was being sent by God into the wilderness to prepare a way for them. It was only with great difficulty that Willard Richards convinced the Saints in Alston that Russell had misled them.[30]

The mission presidency kept in touch with Elder Kimball, and he continued to comfort and encourage them through the mail. "Feed the hungry, clothe the naked, and visit the widow and the fatherless, and turn not the stranger away empty, feed thine enemy, do good to them that revile you and say all manner of evil if it be false great is your reward in heaven," he wrote in July 1839,[31] and it was, indeed, in that spirit that they carried out their work.

Although the mission presidency and their associates had considerable success in missionary work, that was almost counterbalanced by apostasy. When the apostles returned to Britain in 1840, the total membership of the Church in England was about sixteen hundred—the same number that Elders Kimball and Hyde had left behind in 1838. That was enough, however, to provide a firm foundation for the remarkable work the Twelve would soon commence.

---

[29]Ibid., 38–39, 47; Richards, Diary, July 17, December 17 and 28, 1839. Richards added "& no murmuring thought has risen in my bosom." Compare the expanded version, where he said, "And no murmuring thought has since been felt in my bosom."

[30]Willard Richards to Joseph Fielding and William Clayton, Alston, May 7, 1839, Willard Richards Collection.

[31]Heber C. Kimball to Fielding, Richards, and Clayton, Commerce, Illinois, July 25, 1839, Joseph Fielding Collection.

Chapter 4

PATHWAYS TO LIVERPOOL

Circumstances could not have been less encouraging as the seven apostles prepared for their departure from Commerce, Illinois. Under-nourished and ill as they were, it seemed doubtful that some would make it even to New York, let alone across the ocean. But Church members far outside Commerce, aware of what was happening, were anxious to provide whatever assistance they could. Everywhere the apostles went, from the Mississippi to New York City, sympathetic Latter-day Saints cared for them in illness, provided lodging and transportation, and gave whatever financial aid they could. There seemed to be a spirit in the Church affirming that this mission was of unique importance, and even the poorest among the Saints were eager to support it.[1] The story of their journeys from Commerce to New York City, which took from two to more than four months, and then on to Liverpool is a story of remarkable faith in the face of incredible hardships.

TO NEW YORK CITY BY ANY MEANS POSSIBLE

Wilford Woodruff and John Taylor were the first to start out. Wilford, in Montrose, had been suffering for days from chills and fever. His infant daughter, Sarah Emma, also seriously ill, was being cared for by friends with more suitable accommodations. On August 8 he finally bade Phoebe a tender farewell and walked to the banks of the Mississippi. Brigham Young paddled him across the river in a canoe. When Joseph Smith found

---

[1]In May 1840, for example, after all the apostles had arrived in England, a missionary in Philadelphia wrote to Church headquarters commenting on the generosity of the Saints in that area in helping them: "I must say with feelings of gratitude and respect to the brethren and friends in Chester county, that they have manifested a spirit of generosity, and liberality, worthy of imitation, in assisting the Twelve in their mission to Europe, and also in the late mission to Washington city" (Lorenzo Barnes to Bro's Smith & Robinson, May 5, 1840, in *Times and Seasons* [June 1, 1840]: 117).

him resting by the post office, Wilford told the Prophet that he felt and looked more like a subject for the dissecting room than a missionary.[2]

John Taylor left Montrose the same day, his family also in pathetic circumstances and living in a single room. He lamented "the prevalence of disease, the poverty of the brethren, their insecurity from mobs, together with the uncertainty of what might take place during my absence." But despite the difficulties, he said, "the thought of going forth at the command of the God of Israel to revisit my native land, to unfold the principles of eternal truth and make known the things that God had revealed for the salvation of the world, overcame every other feeling."[3]

It took Elders Woodruff and Taylor, traveling together, the rest of the month to make it as far as Germantown, Indiana. They frequently stopped with Church members, preached the gospel, conducted Church business, and received assistance from the Saints. On August 13 they were near Macomb, Illinois, at the home of John Coltrin, who was going to visit his family in Ohio and who invited them to accompany him in his wagon.[4] George Miller gave them a horse. On August 16 they were in Springfield, where John Taylor arranged to have printed some two thousand copies of a pamphlet on the persecutions of the Saints in Missouri. He paid for it, in part, by selling the horse they had just been given.[5] They took some of the pamphlets with them and left others with the Coltrins, asking them to send the proceeds to Leonora and Phoebe.

By the time they arrived at Germantown John Taylor was so desperately ill that it was impossible for him to continue. Wilford Woodruff was also ill, but at Taylor's urging he reluctantly went on with Coltrin on September 2, leaving his companion "in the hands of a merciful God & a kind &

---

[2]Cowley, *Wilford Woodruff*, 109.

[3]As quoted in Roberts, *Life of John Taylor*, 67–68. Roberts does not document his quotations, and those cited here are found only in his book. It is known, however, that Roberts had access to John Taylor's journals, but their whereabouts today are apparently not known.

[4]Ibid., 68–69, says that it was Zebedee Coltrin who took them to Ohio. Woodruff, however, wrote in his journal that they were at "Father John Coltrins" on August 11, and that two days later they decided "to accompany father Coltrin" to Ohio. They did spend some time, however, with Zebedee Coltrin, who was John's son. Woodruff, *Journal*, August 11–13, 1839, 1:350–51.

[5]Wilford Woodruff's journal says that fifteen hundred pamphlets were printed, but Roberts says there were two thousand. See Woodruff, *Journal*, August 16, 1839, 1:351; Roberts, *Life of John Taylor*, 69. This pamphlet, *A Short Account* . . . was especially significant to what was going on elsewhere in the Church, for in November Joseph Smith would be in Washington, D.C., seeking redress for the wrongs suffered by the Saints in Missouri, and already the Saints were preparing hundreds of petitions to support the Prophet's case. See D&C 123:1–6 for the revelation that told the Saints to compile the petitions.

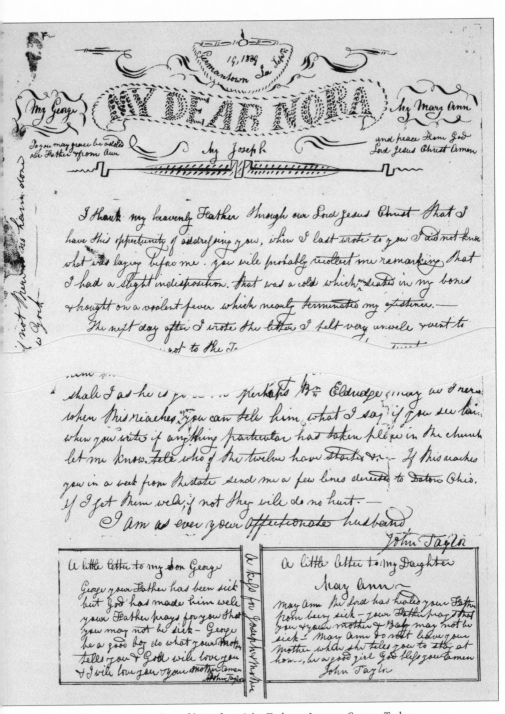

Beginning and ending of letter from John Taylor to Leonora Cannon Taylor,
September 19, 1839 (see Appendix B, Document 3). Courtesy LDS Church Archives

benevolent family, who promised to do evry thing in their power to make him Comfortable untill his recovery."[6]

It was another month before Wilford reached his destination. He crossed Lake Erie in a severe snow storm, by steamer, took a boat down the Erie Canal, and then made his way to Farmington, Connecticut, where he spent about two weeks with his family. From there he took a stage to Hartford and then a steamer to New York City, where he arrived at 6 A.M. on October 6.

John Taylor remained ill, sometimes near death, for about three weeks. His optimism was tenacious, however, as suggested in a tender letter to Leonora, dated September 19:

> You may ask me how I am going to prosecute my journey, with my trunk a distance of 300 miles or upwards by land, without means. I do not know but one thing I do know, that there is a being who clothes the lillies of the valley & feeds the ravens & he has given me to understand that all these things shall be added & that is all I want to know. He laid me on a bed of sickness & I was satisfied, he has raised me from it again & I am thankful. He stopped me on my road & I am content.... If he took me I felt that it would be well. He has spared me, & it is better.[7]

As he began to recover, Elder Taylor could not refrain from preaching. He obtained the use of a courthouse and began holding meetings, even though weakness forced him to remain seated part of the time while delivering his sermons.

As soon as he was able, Taylor went on to Dayton, Ohio, where, about November 1, he met George A. Smith, who had left Commerce more than six weeks after he did. On November 3, they both joined up with Brigham Young and Heber C. Kimball in Cleveland.

Elders Young and Kimball were the third and fourth apostles to strike out for New York City. On September 14 Brigham crossed the river from Montrose to Commerce, leaving his little family so ill that none could go to the well for a pail of water, and so destitute that they had no change of clothes. He, too, was sick, and immediately went to bed at the home of Heber C. Kimball. On September 17 his wife, Mary Ann, arrived to nurse and comfort him, and the next day the two apostles, both deathly ill and practically penniless, left Commerce in a wagon: "I was determined to go

---

[6]Woodruff, *Journal*, September 2, 1839, 1:357.

[7]John Taylor to Leonora Taylor, September 19, 1839, John Taylor Collection (Appendix B, Document 3).

to England or to die trying," Brigham recalled later.[8] Heber's wife, Vilate, and two of their three children were in bed with the ague and, he said, "It seemed to me as though my very inmost parts would melt within me at the thought of leaving my family in such a condition." On impulse he told the teamster to stop and, turning to Brigham, proposed that they give a cheer to those they were leaving behind. The two apostles stood up in the wagon and swung their hats over their heads three times, crying, "Hurrah, hurrah, hurrah for Israel!" The shout brought Vilate from her bed, and the two wives stood in the doorway bravely crying back to their husbands, "Good bye; God bless you!"[9] The men returned the heartfelt prayer and continued on. By the second day they had gone only as far as Quincy, where, too feeble to continue, they stayed with helpful Saints for five more days.

On September 21 George A. Smith, still not recovered from his illness, started out on horseback for New York. Stopping at Joseph Smith's home to rest, he walked into the room where his uncle, Joseph Smith, Sr., lay sick, propped up in a huge chair with pillows. His uncle immediately burst out laughing. "Who has been robbing the burying yard?" he asked. He then gave the young apostle a blessing, promising that he should not only go on his mission but also be restored to health, accomplish a great deal of good, and return safely home.[10] He continued on his way, accompanied by Theodore Turley and Reuben Hedlock. The trio survived an overturned wagon without serious injury and arrived in Quincy two days later. By then George A.'s illness had so affected his eyes that he was nearly blind, unable even to distinguish colors. He continued to have eye trouble through most of his mission.

Elders Young and Kimball were also in Quincy, but after spending a short time preaching and recuperating, the two parties continued on separately. Elder Smith and his group reached Springfield on October 2, followed by Young and Kimball three days later.

The five missionaries had made it that far only by the generous, though meager, support of faithful Saints. As they considered how they might continue, they and Elder Kimball's father-in-law, Roswell Murray, "put our mites together," as George A. Smith described it, "and rigged up a two-horse wagon and attached three horses to it." The wagon was donated by

[8]Discourse by Brigham Young, July 17, 1870, *Journal of Discourses* 13:211.
[9]Kimball, *President Heber C. Kimball's Journal*, 84.
[10]Smith, "History."

the Saints, who had paid fifty-five dollars for it and who also gave the missionaries another thirty-five dollars in cash. The women prepared a bed in the wagon for Brigham Young, the most seriously ill, and on October 11, the missionaries left the city.[11]

Even while the Saints were giving of their means to help the missionaries along the way, some were also scrutinizing them. Eight miles out of Springfield, for example, they stopped for the night at the home of a Father Draper. Some Saints in Springfield had prepared "tonic bitters" for George A. Smith. This bitter, aromatic, sometimes alcoholic solution concocted from various plant products was a popular folk medicine for the feverish illness plaguing him. As he stooped to warm himself by the fire, Elder Smith's flask of bitters slipped out of his pocket and broke on the hearth. "You are a pretty set of Apostles," exclaimed the astonished Father Draper, "to be carrying a bottle of whisky with you!" The elders quickly explained who had prepared it and what it was for and, reported Elder Kimball, "this appeased his righteous soul, so that he consented to allow us to stay through the night."[12]

On the evening of October 17 the sickly group arrived in Terre Haute, Indiana. Heber C. Kimball and Brigham Young spent the night at the home of a Church member who was also a physician. Heber's report of the evening was less than complimentary to the doctor who, he said, after visiting George A. Smith and company, wept at their circumstances but "did not have quite sympathy enough to buy them a chicken to make them some broth or even give them a shilling," although he was relatively wealthy.[13] Perhaps Elder Kimball had a right to be cynical, for that evening when his own illness intensified, the doctor, by this time drunk, overdosed him with morphine. Heber spent the night in nauseated agony, with Brigham sitting up all night to nurse him.

The next morning the other missionaries came to the house and blessed Elder Kimball. Elders Young and Kimball then urged them to go on to Kirtland, Ohio. They complied only after Heber chided them by predicting that he and Brigham would arrive in Kirtland before they did. About an hour later, Heber was able to get out of bed. He and Brigham arrived in Cleveland on the night of November 2, having passed a tavern

[11]Smith, "History," October 11, 1839; Kimball, *President Heber C. Kimball's Journal*, 86–87.
[12]Kimball, *President Heber C. Kimball's Journal*, 87.
[13]Ibid., 88.

in Strongsville, about twenty miles from Cleveland, where George A. Smith's party and Elder John Taylor were spending the night.

On the afternoon of November 3, Elders Young, Kimball, Taylor, and Hedlock reached Kirtland, followed the next day by Elders Smith and Turley. George A. Smith, meanwhile, had found cause for celebration when he discovered that by putting his nose close to the paper he was able to read an advertisement in large print—the first words he had been able to read since the onset of his illness.

At this point Heber noted one of the many financial miracles that kept them solvent as they made their way toward New York City. Examining their record of expenditures, they found that they had spent "over eighty-seven dollars out of the thirteen dollars and fifty cents we had at Pleasant Garden." They had traveled four hundred miles by stage, paid eight to ten cents per mile, eaten three meals per day at fifty cents per meal, and paid fifty cents a day for lodging. Brigham Young suspected that Heber had a secret purse of money but, noted Heber, "this was not so; the money could only have been put in the trunk by some heavenly messenger, who thus administered to our necessities daily as he knew we needed."[14]

Kirtland, Ohio, held a special place in the hearts of the Latter-day Saints, and the missionaries must have been filled with nostalgia as they rode into town and gazed upon their beloved temple and recalled both the trials and the spiritual highlights associated with it. But as the memories flowed through the visitors' minds, they must have been accompanied by a depressing realization that Kirtland would never again be the prominent Mormon center they had loved.[15]

Neither could the apostles resist commenting on their discouragement with some of the Saints who were still in Kirtland. When Heber Kimball preached at a meeting in the temple on Sunday, November 10, he ruffled the feathers of several by comparing them "to a parcel of old earthen pots that were cracked in burning, for they were mostly apostates who were living there." The Saints in Kirtland seemed much less willing to help than those elsewhere, and George A. Smith noted that before they could be on their way they had to sell their horse and wagon for "what little we could get."[16]

---

[14]Ibid., 91–92.

[15]For an examination of Kirtland in the years after Joseph Smith's departure, see Bitton, "Waning of Mormon Kirtland."

[16]Kimball, *President Heber C. Kimball's Journal*, 92; Smith, "History."

The Kirtland Temple. Courtesy Utah State Historical Society

The apostles nevertheless enjoyed a spiritual uplift as they revisited the Kirtland Temple, and on the evening of Sunday, November 17, they held a deeply moving meeting with some of the local elders. They no doubt remembered that it had been less than four years since the Savior, Elijah, Elias, and Moses had appeared in that sacred hall to restore certain ancient keys and authority to Joseph Smith.[17] Toward the end of the meeting, some "pure sweet oil" was consecrated by Elders Young, Kimball, and Smith, then Brigham Young anointed John Taylor and gave him a special blessing. He was the only member of the Quorum who had not previously received such a blessing in the temple. After that Theodore Turley received a similar anointing at the hands of Daniel S. Miles, and Taylor and Turley each poured out the desires of their hearts in special prayers. The congregation then "sealed" the anointings with shouts of "hosannah!" All this was followed by the simple ordinance often performed in those early days

[17]See D&C 110.

to promote humility and unity: Brigham Young washed the feet of John Taylor, and Daniel Miles washed Turley's. John Taylor then delivered a prophecy, and Brigham Young closed the meeting with prayer.[18] Despite their concerns about the Saints in Kirtland, that day the apostles and their companions were spiritually rejuvenated.

The group left Kirtland on November 22 but was detained for four days at Fairport, on Lake Erie, by a heavy snowstorm. The delay provided time for intimate discussions, and Brigham Young gave George A. Smith some pointed suggestions about a few things he had observed in his young colleague during the past two months. As George A. himself reported it: "President Young reproved me for some of my unwise speeches in which I had hurt the feelings of some of my brethren previous to leaving Nauvoo, upon which I made satisfaction and felt thankful for the timely reproof."[19]

When the snow subsided, the group took a lake steamer to Buffalo and then, on November 27, a train to Batavia, New York. The next day most of the missionaries took the train to Rochester, but Heber C. Kimball left the others to do missionary work among family members and friends in and around his home town of Mendon, New York. On New Year's Day 1840, he baptized Vilate's brother, William Murray, and his wife. On February 10, he left for New York City, traveling some distance by sleigh, but by the time he reached Jersey City, he had no money for a ticket to cross the river into New York City. An unknown passenger heard him discussing the problem with the captain of the ferry and simply gave him the necessary twenty-five cents.

The other members of the group arrived in New York City ahead of Elder Kimball, but not without continuing difficulties. By the time they reached Auburn, Brigham Young and George A. Smith were out of funds, so they persuaded John Taylor and Theodore Turley to go on while they worked their way more slowly. Reuben Hedlock remained for a time in Batavia. After taking a boat down the Hudson River, Taylor and Turley arrived in New York City on December 13.

Elders Young and Smith preached in the Auburn area, walked to Moravia, where they stayed among the Saints for about a week, and then went to East Hamilton with a Church member who offered to take them in his wagon. The weather was cold, there was considerable snow, and by

---

[18]Smith, "History," not dated, but entries for November 1839; Kimball, *President Heber C. Kimball's Journal*, 92–93; Turley, "Mission Journal," 22.

[19]Smith, "History," November 27, 1839.

this time George A. was ill again. For seventeen days he lay in bed at the Joseph Murdock home, being nursed with great care by Hannah Tinkam. Even in severe illness, however, he retained his sense of humor. "I vomited phlegm by the wholesale," he wrote, "and it altogether reduced me to a more reasonable size."[20]

On January 7 the two apostles took a stage for West Stockbridge, Massachusetts. Elder Smith's eyesight was so impaired by the new illness that he could not distinguish one dish from another when they were eating, and Brigham Young had to select his food and put it on his plate for him. It probably made the twenty-two-year-old apostle feel even worse when he heard someone ask who that old gentleman was who was being waited on by the young man!

They arrived at West Stockbridge later that day, and Brigham went on to Richmond alone and sent a horse and sleigh back for Elder Smith. They preached in the area for a while, even though George A. continued to suffer from the fever and shakes. "Slow[?] going to England," he wrote laboriously. "Sick [and] poor but good courage. Truth will Prevail. Lord Remember thy servant. Give him wisdom."[21] But his good humor never failed him. As he preached on January 9, for example, the mischievous sons of some local sectarians threw sulphur on the stove, disrupting the meeting. After things calmed down, Elder Smith lectured his listeners on their lack of etiquette. His first impression, he told them, was that some sectarian preacher, "a wholesale dealer in fire and brimstone," had got so near hell that he had been unable to take all the brimstone away with him. But at least, he said, knowing that sulphur was considered a cure for the itch, he considered himself in no danger of catching that malady in Massachusetts.[22]

On January 27 a Brother French took the two apostles in his sleigh to New Haven, Connecticut, where, four days later, they caught a boat bound for New York City. They had to land at Frog Point because of the icy weather and take a stage the rest of the way, but by this time they were again out of money and could not pay the fare. Taking the same stage, however, was the captain of the steamer they had just left, and when Brigham Young boldly asked him if he would pay their fare, the good captain obliged! The

[20]Ibid., not dated, but entry covering December 1839.
[21]Smith, Journal, January 15, 1840; see Smith, "History," January 15, 1840.
[22]Smith, "History," January 9, 1840.

two apostles then found their way to 58 Mott Street, where Parley P. Pratt and his wife, Mary Ann, welcomed them.

THE PRATT BROTHERS

Parley P. and Orson Pratt were not in as desperate financial straits as the other five apostles, nor did they suffer the same problems with ill health. Nevertheless, they had their share of distress before they left Illinois. The malaria plague that ravaged the settlers along the swampy Mississippi river bottoms did not bypass them, but, "by the power of God," the two brothers were able to arise and accompany Joseph Smith as he went among the Saints, laying on hands and healing many. One of the casualties, however, was Orson's eight-month-old daughter, Lydia, who died on August 18.[23]

Eleven days later the two brothers drove away from Commerce, accompanied by Parley's wife and three children[24] as well as Hiram Clark, another missionary called to England. They traveled in a private carriage, visited with various Church members along the way, preached frequently and, after five enjoyable weeks, arrived at the home of their parents in Detroit. There they found their father, Jared, nearly seventy, on his death-bed, and visited with him one last time. He died shortly after they went on to New York.

In Detroit the brothers did missionary work, and Parley spent time working on publications. They sold the horse and carriage, at some sacrifice, to raise funds to continue, and Orson, accompanied by Hiram Clark, left earlier than Parley to do more preaching in Ohio and New York. After about two weeks Parley and his family took a Lake Erie steamer to Buffalo, a boat down the Erie Canal, the railroad to Albany, and a steamer down the Hudson to New York City. They arrived on October 25, nearly three weeks before Orson, who arrived about November 13.[25] Nearly two years earlier Parley had been instrumental in establishing a branch of the Church in that city. "We were received by the Saints in New York almost as one of the old saints risen from the dead," he later recalled.

---

[23]England, *Orson Pratt*, 59–60.

[24]Mary Ann Frost, widow of Nathan Stearns, was Parley P. Pratt's second wife, and she brought one daughter to the marriage. The other children were Parley Parker Pratt, son of Thankful Halsey Pratt, who had died in childbirth on March 25, 1837, and Nathan Pratt, the son of Parley and Mary Ann. P. Pratt, *Autobiography*, 172, 462. The following story is based on ibid., 294–301; O. Pratt, *Journals*, 105–7, 513; Woodruff, *Journal*, November 13, 1839, 1:368–69.

[25]See Woodruff, *Journal*, October 25 and November 13, 1839, 1:365, 368–69.

New York City in the 1840s. Courtesy I. N. Phelps Stokes Collection;
Miriam & Ira D. Wallach Division of Art, Prints and Photographs;
The New York Public Library; Aster, Lenox and Tilden Foundations

ON TO ENGLAND: WILFORD AND JOHN

After Wilford Woodruff arrived in New York on October 8, he spent
the next several weeks preaching and trying to decide what to do about
sailing for England. He had heard nothing from the rest of the Twelve,
but other missionaries waiting to go to England booked passage for three,
including Elder Woodruff, on the packet ship *Tarolinta*. When Parley P.
Pratt arrived with word that the others were expected soon, Wilford decided
to wait so the Twelve could hold a council meeting before any of them
left. Hiram Clark took Wilford's place on the packet, which sailed for
England on November 1.[26]

Wilford Woodruff spent the next month and a half doing missionary
work and trying to raise enough money to pay his way to England. On
December 13 John Taylor and Theodore Turley arrived, both completely
without means. Elder Woodruff, however, had raised the fifteen dollars
necessary to book passage in the steerage compartment of the ship *Oxford*,
and on December 16 he did so. He was impatient to be on his way, even
though all his colleagues were still not there.

---

[26]Woodruff, *Journal*, October 8-November 1, 1839, 1:363–67; O. Pratt, *Journals*, 106 (citing
Hiram Clark in *Millennial Star* 4:145). Clark adds the detail concerning Parley P. Pratt's influence on Wilford
Woodruff's decision to remain in New York.

John Taylor arrived in New York penniless but optimistic. He stayed in Parley P. Pratt's home, and when anyone asked him about his financial situation, he simply replied that he had plenty of money. Elder Pratt, who needed money to publish his *Voice of Warning* and several other items, asked him for two or three hundred dollars to help with publication. "You are welcome to all I have," Elder Taylor responded, reaching into his pocket and handing Parley a copper cent. When Parley reminded him of his statements that he had "plenty of money," Taylor simply replied that he did, for he was well clothed, Parley was providing him with good lodging and plenty to eat and drink, and "with all these things and a penny over, as I owe nothing, is not that plenty?" When Wilford Woodruff later insisted that Taylor should sail with him on the *Oxford*, he simply replied, "Well, Brother Woodruff, if you think it best for me to go, I will accompany you," assuring him that there would be no difficulty with money. Overhearing all this and assuming that Elder Taylor had some hidden resources, Theodore Turley urged the two apostles to take him along, too, and let him cook and do other tasks for them. Taylor confidently told Wilford to arrange passage for both himself and Turley, and it was not long before unsolicited, voluntary donations resulted in enough money to secure passage for both of them.[27]

On December 20 the *Oxford* sailed from New York harbor carrying sixty-four passengers in steerage (including the two apostles and Turley), fifteen in cabins, and thirty crewmen. The unfortunate steerage passengers soon found that they were victims not only of the usual discomforts of that less-than-desirable compartment (crowded bunks, no ventilation, no privacy, etc.), but also of overbooking. Agents had sold tickets with berth numbers marked, saying that there would be two people in each berth. The passengers discovered, however, that as many as five people had been promised the same bunk and some had no berth at all. The crew put up a few extra bunks in a storage compartment, but even at that there were sometimes four people to a bunk and at least two ended up sleeping on boxes and on the floor.[28]

The passage itself was fairly rough. The ship rolled and pitched so badly on the night of December 30, for example, that "trunks, Boxes &

---

[27]Roberts, *Life of John Taylor*, 72–74.

[28]John Taylor to Leonora Taylor, January 30, 1840, John Taylor Collection (Appendix B, Document 6). John Taylor indicates that there were sixty-three people in steerage, and Wilford Woodruff says there were sixty-four.

barrels were tumbling about the cabin," and it was only with great difficulty that the passengers stayed in their bunks. The missionaries arrived in Liverpool on January 11, 1840, and began proselyting nearly three weeks before Brigham Young, Heber C. Kimball, and George A. Smith reached New York City.[29]

THE REMAINING FIVE JOIN THEIR BRETHREN

The rest of the apostles remained in New York City and vicinity until their departure as a group on March 9. The Pratt brothers spent most of their time preaching in the area and baptized several new converts. Parley also published several items that became important doctrinal expositions and missionary tools. On December 21 Orson went to Philadelphia, encountered Joseph Smith there, and immediately sent for his brother. The two spent several days with the Prophet and received instruction from him in important and far-reaching new doctrines, including the principles of eternal marriage and eternal family relationships, as well as an enhanced understanding of the "true dignity and destiny" of men and women.

Parley later went to Washington, D.C., apparently at the request of Joseph Smith, where he did considerable preaching. This excursion depleted his resources so much that it put his ability to depart for England with the others in serious doubt. Nonetheless, the apostles felt gratified that he had preached in Washington, "for by so doing we can go from America feeling our duty to this Government for the present more fully done."[30]

The other three apostles also preached in the New York area while gathering sufficient means to cross the ocean. Still suffering from chills and fevers, early in February George A. Smith went to Philadelphia, accompanied by Benjamin Winchester. There he was invited to preach at a seminary in Yellow Springs, Chester County, and when he had finished, the people, mostly non-Mormons, gave him twenty-six dollars toward his forthcoming trip, in addition to his travel expenses from Philadelphia.[31] On February 24 Elder Smith returned to New York City, where Elders Young and Kimball finally booked steerage passage on the *Patrick Henry*,

---

[29]For accounts of the voyage, see Roberts, *Life of John Taylor*, 72–74; Woodruff, *Journal*, December 16, 1839–January 11, 1840, 373–403; Turley, "Mission Journal," 28–29.

[30]P. Pratt, *Autobiography*, 297–98; O. Pratt, *Journals*, 108–10.

[31]Smith, "History."

at the rate of eighteen dollars apiece. George A. Smith, it turned out, had enough money to pay the fare for two of them.[32]

The five apostles held a conference on March 4 with the New York Saints, many of whom had made donations to help them. Parley P. Pratt had written a song especially for the occasion, and it must have touched everyone deeply as they sang:

> When shall we all meet again?
> When shall we our rest obtain?
> When our pilgrimage be o'er—
> Parting sighs be known no more;
> When Mount Zion we regain,
> There may we all meet again.
>
> We to foreign climes repair;
> Truth, the message which we bear;
> Truth, which angels oft have borne;
> Truth to comfort those who mourn.
> Truth eternal will remain,
> On its rock we'll meet again.
>
> Now the bright and morning star
> Spreads its glorious light afar,
> Kindles up the rising dawn
> Of that bright Millennial morn;
> When the Saints shall rise and reign,
> Then may we all meet again.[33]

Shortly before 11:00 A.M. on Monday, March 9, 1840, Brigham Young, Heber C. Kimball, the Pratt brothers, George A. Smith, and Reuben Hedlock climbed into a small boat that took them out to the *Patrick Henry*, a packet ship of the Black Ball Line, lying at anchor a short distance offshore. They carried with them straw beds, pillows, and blankets, all donated by the New York Saints, for the Black Ball Line provided no such comforts with the plain wooden bunks in steerage. In addition, as Heber wrote to his wife, "The brethren put up evry thing that was good to eat. I will tell you what we had. Potatoes gren Aples, dried Aples, dride Prunes dried Plumes; Preserves quince, Plum, Peach; dride Beef, Ham, Pork, Cod fish, swet bread, bakers Bread, common bread, Crackers, Wrice, Chogar [sugar], Buter, Pe-

---

[32]Heber C. Kimball to Vilate Kimball, February 19, 1840, and March 5, 1840, Heber C. Kimball Collection.
[33]P. Pratt, *Autobiography*, 300.

The Prince's Dock, Liverpool. Contemporary engraving, J. Hardwood, F. R. Hay

per, mustard Salt, Horsh Redish Pickles lemmons Rasons, Pies."[34] As the boat moved out into the water, the missionaries returned the farewells of the Saints, many of whom, in tears, were waving with hats and handkerchiefs. Saints on ship and shore joined in singing "The Gallant Ship Is under Way" until the sounds of each other's voices were lost in the distance. About noon the *Patrick Henry* was towed out to sea, where its sails were unfurled before a fair Atlantic breeze. The last of the apostles were finally on their way.

Unlike the smooth passage enjoyed by Heber C. Kimball three years earlier, and as if to underscore the difficulties associated with this mission, the crossing of the *Patrick Henry* was rough and difficult. Brigham Young was sick and confined to his bunk for nearly the whole twenty-eight days. In addition to his ague and malaria, George A. Smith was so seasick much of the time that he could not eat. As Heber later described the voyage to his wife, the waves rolled "mountains high" making it seem as if the sea "would swallow us up some times." They experienced rain, hail, snow, thunder, and lightening worse than the crew had seen in fifteen years, and there were few days that the sea did not beat over the bulwarks and run in torrents down the hatch into the steerage compartment where the

---

[34]Heber C. Kimball to Vilate Kimball, April 3, 1840, Kimball Collection (Appendix B, Document 8).

missionaries lay on their bunks. On one occasion Orson Pratt was sitting on a bale of cotton when a huge wave swept over the deck and threw the cotton "S[w]iming with him on it." The trip seemed twice as long to Heber as it had on his first ocean crossing. "We could not have gon in a worse time in the whole year for head winds."[35]

Finally, on April 6, 1840, the missionaries celebrated the tenth anniversary of the organization of the Church by setting foot on the docks at Liverpool. It had been eight long, arduous months since the first apostles left Commerce, and the emotions of Heber and his companions ran high. Brigham Young later recalled that after he got both feet firmly planted, "I gave a loud shout of hosannah . . . I felt that the chains were broken, and the bands that were upon me were burst asunder." They found lodging at No. 8 Union Street and that evening held a prayer meeting, blessed each other, partook of the sacrament of the Lord's Supper, and thanked their Heavenly Father for preserving them.[36] Their mission was about to begin.

---

[35]Ibid.

[36]P. Pratt, *Autobiography*, 301; Smith, "History"; Arrington, *Brigham Young*, 78.

Chapter 5

WHAT IT MEANT TO BE MISSIONARIES

The apostles' enthusiasm seemed boundless as they looked forward to sharing with the people of Britain their vision of God's plan for the salvation of the world. They believed their task was to bring as many as possible to Christ and to lay the foundation for the gathering of Zion. In seeking to accomplish this they became exemplary missionaries, both individually and as a united quorum.

WITHOUT PURSE OR SCRIP

The missionary apostles in early Victorian Britain subsisted in much the same way as their New Testament predecessors, who were sent out carrying "neither purse, nor scrip."[1] Though they had some luggage with them, they generally lacked means to sustain themselves, and they relied largely on financial donations and other help from faithful Saints and friends. Small cash contributions mounted up to help pay for living quarters, though the apostles often slept at the homes of Church members and others, ate with them, and wore clothes donated by them. Many of the Saints were eager to help — so eager, in fact, that at times the missionaries simply could not refuse the proffered aid, even if they wanted to. John Taylor and Joseph Fielding, for example, spent their first several months in Liverpool living with Taylor's brother-in-law, George Cannon. On one occasion they were sitting in their upstairs room discussing how they could pay the Cannons for their hospitality when George came in and presented a sovereign to Elder Taylor. The apostle objected, but Cannon insisted, telling him that his old hat was getting shabby and he needed a new one. Taylor had no choice but to accept the money graciously.[2]

---

[1]Luke 10:4. The word *scrip,* in the scriptural context, refers to a small bag or satchel used for carrying personal provisions.

[2]Fielding, Diary, 54.

At times, however, it became necessary to remind the Saints of their duty to help. On Sunday, March 1, for example, James Whitehead preached to the Preston congregation on the need to take care of the wives and children of the local missionaries. Some, he said, were in want, and if the Saints allowed that situation to continue they would lose the blessings of the Lord. Mission president Joseph Fielding assured the Saints that such a request for funds was not "priestcraft," for he knew the temporal circumstances of the elders and they clearly needed help. Thomas Walmsley then spoke briefly, reminding the group that it was not only the missionaries who had come from America who needed help but also that more local missionaries were ready to go out and their families must be taken care of. Fielding noted that a good collection was taken up that day.[3]

The missionaries were acutely aware that most of the Saints could hardly meet their own needs, and they were reluctant to accept more than absolute necessities. Joseph Fielding refused to take any of the money raised by the March 1 collection, telling the deacons that it should be used instead to care for the children of the other missionaries. He confided in his journal that his purpose was to free his conscience as he pleaded the cause of others. The result, however, was that sometimes his wife did not have enough food and, though she never complained, he believed that was the cause of her illness.[4]

Something of what it meant to the missionaries to rely on the Saints for sustenance is revealed in a January 1841 letter from Reuben Hedlock to George A. Smith. It was the coldest time of the year, and, working in Glasgow, Scotland, Hedlock had not been well. His destitution, along with that of the recent converts, only made matters worse. "I know how to Pity you," he wrote to his friend, who had also been ill.

I know what it is to be very Sick with Sore lungs and be obliged to preach and travel from place to place Among the poor [brethren] to get my food. Some times I got very Cours food I'll assure you but it was the best the Saints could give me and I partook with them with a thankfull hart. I have some times walked a mile and a half when I was Sick to get my breakfast but through the Blesings of God I was able to Eduer it and my health is some better.[5]

Despite such problems and privations, the apostles bore witness that

---

[3]Ibid., 60.
[4]Ibid.
[5]Reuben Hedlock to George A. Smith, January 12, 1841, George A. Smith Collection.

relying on the Lord and on the Saints for all their needs was a blessing. As John Taylor noted in his final communication to the Saints in England before his departure in April 1841:

I feel to rejoice before God that he has blessed my humble endeavours to promote his cause and kingdom and for all the blessings that I have received from this island; for although I have travelled 5,000 miles without purse or scrip, besides travelling so far in this country on railroads, coaches, steamboats, waggons, on horseback, and almost every way, and been amongst strangers and in strange lands, I have never for once been at a loss for either money, clothes, friends, or a home, from that day until now; neither have I ever asked a person for a farthing. Thus I have proved the Lord, and I know that he is according to his word.[6]

THE MILLENNIAL MESSAGE

The imminence of the Millennium weighed heavily upon the early Latter-day Saints. For them the Restoration itself was a sign that they lived in the last days, adding urgency to the task of taking their message to the world.[7] All the "signs of the times," and particularly natural disasters, were often interpreted as foreshadowing the calamities that would befall the nations before the Second Coming. The apostles, then, felt responsible not only to gather the honest in heart into the gospel fold but also to warn all others of the impending apocalypse. In a letter to the *Times and Seasons*, Wilford Woodruff noted the outstanding missionary success in Hereford-shire and then, reflecting the millennial expectations of all the apostles, observed:

If any one asks why these things are so, I answer because the Lord is about to make a short work in England, and not only in England, but upon the face of the whole earth, for the wickedness of the earth is great, and the cry of the widow, the orphan, and the poor, and oppressed, are entering into the care of the Lord of Saboaoth, who is about to call down his indignation upon the heads of the Gentile world.[8]

The *Millennial Star* amply lived up to its name by regularly reporting the "signs of the times" and calling upon the world to repent. Four pages of the August 1840 issue, for example, were devoted to describing disasters in America and Europe, including the results of the devastating potato famine in Ireland. The editor then cried:

[6]John Taylor to the Editor, n.d., *Millennial Star* 2 (May 1841): 12–16.

[7]For a discussion of early Mormon millennialism and its broader context, see Underwood, "Millenarian World."

[8]Wilford Woodruff to the Editors, October 7, 1840, *Times and Seasons* 2 (February 15, 1841): 311–14 and (March 1, 1841): 327–31.

O ye inhabitants of the earth, when will ye learn wisdom? Now that the judgments of the Most High are going forth in the midst of the nations, and by earthquake, and volcano, and tornado, and whirlwind, and floods, and hail, and devouring fire, and plague, and pestilence, and famine, God is pleading with all flesh, will you not awake from your long night of sleep, and put your sins far from you by repenting of your iniquities, and seeking forgiveness for your multiplied transgressions . . . through the blood of Jesus, and by *obedience* to *all* his *commandments*.[9]

These millennial expectations weighed heavily on Elder Woodruff. He pondered his prophetic responsibility, while he was in London, and he cried out for help in delivering the warning and bringing the "honest in heart" out of Babylon. "O Mighty God of Jacob," he prayed, "cloth us with thy power. Let the power of the Priesthood rest upon us . . . & enable us to warn the inhabitants of this city in such manner that our garments will be clean of their Blood & that we may seek out the honest in heart & the meek from among men & have many souls as seals of our ministry."[10] The last phrase of that heartfelt prayer suggests another element of the apostles' view of their ministry. Like a crest, emblem, or stamp, each new convert served as both a symbol of the missionaries' dedication and a sign of God's acceptance of their labor.[11]

The apostles believed that one prelude to the Millennium was the process of gathering the Saints from the nations of the earth to the center of Zion, in North America, and it was not long before they began to preach and implement that doctrine throughout the British mission. The importance of this idea was reinforced in the mind of Parley P. Pratt when he returned to New York in August 1840 to pick up his family and he learned that Joseph Smith had defined Zion as "all of North and South America." This announcement was so momentous to Parley that when he wrote Orson about it, he punctuated the sentence with seven exclamation points. Parley also reported that Joseph Smith had said the American government was "guilty of Blood" (apparently for failing to protect the rights and lives of the Latter-day Saints in Missouri) and therefore needed redeeming. "The government," he said, "cannot stand as it now is but will come so near

---

[9]*Millennial Star* 1 (August 1840): 100.

[10]Woodruff, *Journal*, August 18, 1840, 1:493–94.

[11]Woodruff used a similar expression in writing about Willard Richards in Herefordshire in May and June 1840: "Elder Richards laboured in this part of the vineyard about two months, during which time he travelled extensively, preached night and day, gave much instruction to the Saints generally, and had many souls as seals of his ministry" (Wilford Woodruff to the Editor, July 9, 1840, *Millennial Star* 1 [July 1840]: 71–72 and [August 1840]:81–84).

dessolation as to hang as it were by a single hair!!!!!!" However, the servants of the God would go to the nations of the earth and gather the strength of the Lord's house, "a mighty army!!!!!!" That would be the redemption of Zion, making America "an asylum for the remnant of all nations. . . . Hence you see it brings the saints continually in unison with the *constitution*, & their enemies are against it, & [their enemies] will be traitors to the *constitution*. Glory!!!"[12]

Much of this information came to Parley secondhand, and no doubt it was colored also by his personal interpretation, but clearly he saw it as giving an added dimension to the doctrine of the gathering and the gravity of the mission of the Twelve.

British converts shared the apostles' apocalyptic fervor and saw the gospel as a preparation for what was to come. When Wilford Woodruff first visited Manchester, for example, he heard one Latter-day Saint declare that she had seen a vision of "Jesus pleading with the Father to spare England one year more that the reapers might gather the grain for the harvest was fully ripe."[13]

Because the mission of the apostles was to preach and to warn, if people rejected their warning after having ample opportunity to understand and accept it, the missionaries sometimes bore witness against them before the Lord. Whether they shook the dust off their feet against a city or a household or washed their feet as a testimony against offenders, such actions symbolized their belief that they had done their duty and the fate of the unbelievers was now in the hands of the Lord.

The Apostles Organize and Direct the Missionary Work

The apostles set the tone and generally directed the activities of all the missionaries, but they worked closely with those who were more experienced in the country, and they supported and built up local leaders. Wilford Woodruff and John Taylor were the first to arrive, and instead of assuming the direction of everything immediately, they worked in cooperation with the mission presidency that had been functioning since Heber C. Kimball left in 1838.

In their first quorum meeting in England, in April 1840, the Twelve

---

[12]Orson Pratt, giving excerpts from a letter received from Parley, to George A. Smith, January 21, 1841, George A. Smith Collection. See also Jessee, "Joseph Smith's 19 July 1840 Discourses."

[13]Woodruff, *Journal*, January 19, 1840, 1:408–9.

formally and unanimously sustained Brigham Young as their president, though he had assumed that role in the fall of 1838. Final decisions on assignments were up to him, policy matters were referred to him, and through correspondence he was constantly aware of what each of them was doing. He did not dictate, however, but conscientiously made decisions in council with the others, and when a council was not possible, he at least kept his colleagues informed. He received regular reports from them, and spent much of his administrative time writing to them. He exercised his authority with both firmness and kindness as he strove to build unity in his quorum.

Working under Brigham's direction, the apostles became extremely close. Usually separated by many miles, they communicated frequently by mail, and their letters reveal mutual love and support that would be exemplary under any conditions. They were even comfortable opening each other's mail, particularly if they felt the messages inside would be of value to all of them. "I thought I would do as I would be done unto," Willard Richards wrote to Brigham Young and Heber C. Kimball, who were in Preston, just after he opened some letters for them that had arrived in Manchester. He summarized the news and promised the letters would be waiting for them when they returned.[14]

WAYS OF MAKING CONTACT

Since nearly everywhere the Twelve went was unworked territory, they tried to find the best and fastest way possible to share their message with large groups of people. They sought out local ministers, attempted to secure speaking engagements before their congregations, and often succeeded in doing so. In 1837, as we have seen, Heber C. Kimball opened missionary work in England by preaching in the Reverend James Fielding's chapel. They also sought out special groups, particularly temperance societies, to preach to. If a temperance society platform was extended to them, they would preach on temperance, a comfortable topic for believers in the Word of Wisdom, and then invite the audience to come listen to a gospel message later, usually in the same hall. Other times they simply hired whatever halls they could and put out notices that missionaries from America would be preaching at a certain time. In Preston it was the Cock

---

[14]Willard Richards to Brigham Young and Heber C. Kimball, October 24, 1840, Brigham Young Papers.

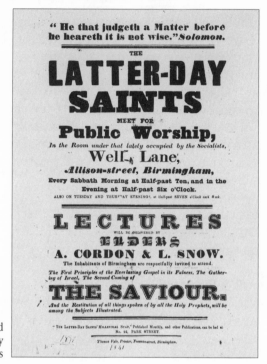

"He that judgeth a Matter before he heareth it is not wise." *Solomon.*

THE

LATTER-DAY SAINTS

MEET FOR

Public Worship,

In the Room under that lately occupied by the Socialists,

Well Lane,

Allison-street, Birmingham,

Every Sabbath Morning at Half-past Ten, and in the Evening at Half-past Six o'Clock.

ALSO ON TUESDAY AND THURSDAY EVENINGS, at Half-past SEVEN o'Clock each Week.

LECTURES

WILL BE DELIVERED BY

ELDERS

A. CORDON & L. SNOW.

The Inhabitants of Birmingham are respectfully invited to attend.

The First Principles of the Everlasting Gospel in its Fulness, The Gathering of Israel, The Second Coming of

THE SAVIOUR.

And the Restitution of all things spoken of by all the Holy Prophets, will be among the Subjects Illustrated.

"THE LATTER-DAY SAINTS' MILLENNIAL STAR," Published Monthly, and other Publications, can be had at No. 24, PARK STREET.

Thomas Vale, Printer, Freeman-street, Birmingham.

1841

Missionary handbill distributed in Birmingham, 1841. Courtesy LDS Church Archives

Pit, in Manchester it was Carpenter's Hall, and in Liverpool it was the Music Hall.

The elders also used all available means to advertise meetings, including making announcements in other churches, posting handbills, and sending the message by word of mouth through Church members and friends. In Leek, on Saturday, May 2, 1840, for example, George A. Smith hired the town criers to announce that he would preach at 4:00 P.M. on Sunday.

The missionaries also preached regularly in private homes. Members and nonmembers alike invited friends and neighbors into their homes to hear the messengers from America. In the Staffordshire Potteries, for example, on February 17, 1840, Wilford Woodruff, William Hume, and William Mumford spent several hours looking for a place to hold a meeting. They called first on Joseph Harding, a shoemaker, and then on Widow Welch, and, finally, on Widow Gilbert. When Widow Gilbert told them they could preach in her house, they sent out the word, and at seven in the evening a "small congregation" gathered to hear Elder Woodruff preach the first Latter-day Saint sermon in the town of Stone.[15]

Referrals from members and friends were their most important missionary tool. No matter where they went, they first contacted people with whom they were acquainted or to whom they had some kind of introduction. When Wilford Woodruff and Theodore Turley arrived in the Potteries, they immediately made contact with faithful members already there: William Benbow, George Simpson, William Hume, and others. On the night of January 24 William Hume opened his home to the two missionaries for preaching, and after the meeting two people applied for baptism. Alfred Cordon obliged them the following day. Not long afterwards, on February 11, Wilford Woodruff was preaching in Burslem when a woman whose husband was already a member asked to be baptized. As they went to baptize her they called on her sister, who was also married to a Church member, and she, too, accepted the gospel and joined the procession. Before they got to the water they called on the wife of still another Church member who said she wanted to be baptized but could not do so right then for she had a dead child in the house. "I told her to let the dead bury the Dead," Wilford Woodruff wrote, "but rise & follow Christ & she did & we walked two miles & I baptized the 3 females."[16] On the other hand, one reason for the early lack of success in London was that Elders Woodruff, Smith, and Kimball simply did not know anyone there. They had to go out "cold," so to speak, and it was a long, hard road even to moderate acceptance.

When they were not preaching in chapels, rented halls, or homes, the apostles might be found preaching in the streets, a most acceptable practice of the time. In October 1840, Orson Pratt wrote that he was preaching every night in the streets of Edinburgh where, when weather permitted, "large congregations gather round us eager to hear."[17] In London, after spending twelve fruitless days trying to find places to preach and people to listen, even going from door to door, Wilford Woodruff, Heber C. Kimball, and George A. Smith finally went to Tabernacle Square, where street meetings were regularly held and preached. The result was the first conversion to the Church in London.[18]

---

[15]Woodruff, *Journal*, February 17, 1840, 1:419.

[16]Ibid., February 11, 1840, 1:418.

[17]Orson Pratt to Parley P. Pratt, October 17, 1840, *Millennial Star* 1 (December 1840): 214.

[18]Woodruff, *Journal*, August 30, 1840, 1:502–4.

GIFTS OF THE SPIRIT

Gifts of the Spirit were abundant during the apostles' mission to England. They were viewed as sacred and deeply personal, not to be touted as part of the missionary message or used as evidence for unbelievers, but diaries and letters recorded many, including miraculous healings in connection with priesthood blessings. When Wilford Woodruff visited Manchester for the first time, he was asked to call on three sick persons and to give them blessings. That same night he administered to six more individuals, and the following day, Sunday, he did the same for twenty people who, he reported, were all healed. "The Saints in England have great Confidence in God & his Servents," he wrote, and so many were applying for the laying on of hands that "we need as much faith as St. Paul had that at the touch of our garments or hankerchefs that they might be healed."[19]

The apostles tried to avoid making a public show of things they considered sacred. They refused to give blessings if it appeared that the request was some kind of test for the curious or unbelieving. Wilford Woodruff was forcefully reminded of this principle when, in Manchester, he accompanied William Clayton to visit a woman who seemed possessed of a devil. When they arrived at her home, she was raging terribly, trying to tear off her clothes. Among those present were several non-Mormon skeptics who had come to see whether a miracle could be wrought. "Had I acted upon my own judgment," Elder Woodruff recalled later, "I should have refrained from administering to her in the company of those present." He nevertheless deferred to the local leaders and joined Clayton in administering to the woman, but to no avail. Her raging only increased. Elder Woodruff quickly ordered the room cleared. The administration was performed again, and this time "the devil left, and she was entirely healed and fell asleep." The next day, Sunday, she bore testimony of her healing before a large congregation.[20] Woodruff continued to perform healings but not as spectacles for unbelievers.[21]

---

[19]Ibid., January 19, 1840, 1:408–9.

[20]Cowley, *Wilford Woodruff*, 115. See also Allen and Alexander, *Manchester Mormons*, 71.

[21]On June 23, 1840, for example, while Woodruff was visiting a church member in West Bromich, two men suddenly burst into the house, "full of wrath & anger," bringing with them a blind girl and demanding that Woodruff perform a miracle and heal her, as a sign to make them believe. He informed the intruders of "the character of those that sought signs," but the anger continued and his testimony was rejected. Woodruff, *Journal*, June 23, 1840, 1:470–71.

The same was true of speaking in tongues. Most of the apostles had witnessed or experienced this gift, and it was not uncommon among the British Saints. There is no evidence, however, that they encouraged the missionaries to pray for it or use it as a conversion tool. It was a sign that followed belief, not an evidence for unbelievers.[22]

Gifts of the Spirit, nevertheless, abounded both with the apostles and among the Saints generally. In July 1840 Joseph Fielding noted that the gift of tongues and the gift of the interpretation of tongues were common among the Saints in Manchester.[23] On February 8, 1841, Elder Levi Richards wrote of the missionaries' continuing success in Herefordshire and Gloucester, telling the readers of the *Millennial Star* that the gift of healing was manifest extensively and that the gift of tongues was received in most of the branches.[24]

The gifts of the Spirit enjoyed by the Saints included dreams, visions, and prophesying. On March 12, 1840, for example, Anne Booth, a Manchester Saint, saw a recently martyred American apostle preaching to spirits in prison (those in the spirit world who had not heard the gospel in mortality) and was beginning to baptize them. John Wesley, the eighteenth-century British reformer and founder of Methodism, was among those spirits, and after the apostle baptized him, Wesley proceeded to baptize others. Latter-day Saint doctrine does not suggest that the dead themselves will baptize or be baptized in the spirit world, but Ann Booth's vision clearly anticipated the forthcoming doctrine and practice of baptism in behalf of the dead. Significantly, the apostles had not yet even heard of

---

[22]On occasion, it appears, the enemies of the Church attempted to discredit it by circulating stories of failed attempts at speaking in tongues. James Mahon, a young priest in the Manchester branch, was apparently one of those who seemed especially receptive to the gift. On June 14, 1840, he and five other people spoke in tongues at a Sunday evening meeting (Allen and Alexander, *Manchester Mormons*, 162). On October 12, according to Wilford Woodruff, some of the opponents of the Church sent for Mahon to come and speak to them in Hebrew, and "if he did not speak to them correctly in Hebrew they would rise up against the work & try to overthrow it. They are watching for iniquity & trying to stir up the people against the work of God" (Woodruff, *Journal*, October 12, 1840, 1:527–28). Woodruff said nothing more about the incident in his journal, but it may be that the whole affair proved embarrassing. According to a non-Mormon report, Mahon accepted the challenge and went to the meeting. There someone read some Hebrew to him, but he could not understand it. Then he spoke in what he said was the Hebrew language, but none of the teachers of Hebrew in the audience recognized any Hebrew in what he said (Axon, *Annals of Manchester*, 211). Whether the meeting was rigged, the report distorted, or Mahon and his critics simply misunderstood the gift may never be known. But certainly the publication and circulation of such stories could be used as evidence by the Saints that the Lord would not allow them to flaunt spiritual gifts simply as a means of persuading the unconverted.

[23]Fielding, Diary, 80.

[24]He also reported, however, that there were not many interpretations. *Millennial Star* 1 (March 1841): 283.

the doctrine from Joseph Smith, but Wilford Woodruff was so impressed when he heard about the vision that he wrote a full report of it in his journal.[25] No doubt the description of the martyred American apostle brought to his mind memories of David W. Patten, one of the original members of the Quorum of the Twelve, who was killed in Missouri at the Battle of Crooked River on October 25, 1838.

The gifts of the Spirit did not encompass folk magic. The practice of magic received the apostles' clear denunciation and was prohibited within the Church. On March 27, 1841, Wilford Woodruff met in council with Church leaders in Hanley, where a Brother Mumford had been engaged in magic and fortune-telling. When he was practicing his priesthood properly, Woodruff noted, Mumford was unable to perform with his so-called "magic glasses," but because he persisted in his magical practices even after the council tried to persuade him to stop, his Church fellowship was withdrawn. At a conference in Hanley the next day, that decision was confirmed, and a resolution was passed that the Church would not fellowship "any individual who Practiced Magic fortune Telling, Black art &c for it was not of God."[26]

SERVICE AND RECIPROCATED LOVE

All these perspectives, techniques, and policies might well have amounted to little, however, if the apostles themselves had not exemplified the qualifications essential for the success of any missionary as described in an early revelation on missionary work: "And faith, hope, charity and love, with an eye single to the glory of God, qualify him for the work. Remember faith, virtue, knowledge, temperance, patience, brotherly kindness, godliness, charity, humility, diligence."[27] The journals and correspondence of the eight apostles in Great Britain demonstrate that these were the qualities that served them best. Their uncommon love for the people seemed to know no bounds. They willingly sacrificed personal comforts for the greater cause of the mission, and, though not timid, they demonstrated a deep humility that helped many feel the genuineness of their convictions.

Even at a distance Joseph Smith sensed what was happening in England

---

[25]Woodruff, *Journal*, July 2, 1840, 1:475–77.

[26]Ibid., March 27 and 28, 1841, 2:73–76. See also Cordon, Journal; George A. Smith to D. C. Smith, March 29, 1841, *Times and Seasons* 2 (June 1, 1841): 434.

[27]D&C 4:1–2, 5–6.

and, especially, the love of the apostles. In a long epistle, which they received early in 1841, he expounded on this trait with eloquence:

Love is one of the leading characteristics of Deity, and ou[gh]t to be manifested by those who aspire to be the sons of God. A man filled with the love of God, is not content with blessing his family alone but ranges through the world, anxious to bless the whole of the human family. This has been your feelings and caused you to forego the pleasures of home, that you might be a blessing to others, who are candidates for immortality but who were strangers to the principals of truth and for so doing I pray that Heavens' choicest blessings may rest upon you.[28]

The apostles' readily apparent love for the people was just as readily reciprocated. Heber C. Kimball told his wife that he had never before seen a more loving people than the Saints at Ribchester, commenting that he thought if he should ask them even to pluck out their eyes and give them to him they would do so.[29] The experience of George A. Smith was a striking example of reciprocated love. In Staffordshire he felt totally inadequate before the better-educated people he was trying to teach, but through his deep concern for their spiritual well-being, along with his dedication and humble demeanor, he found his way into the hearts of many who were much older and clearly more sophisticated than he. They sought and took counsel from him, rejoiced whenever he was with them, and loved and revered him as highly as they could any religious leader.[30]

THE POWER OF THE SPIRIT

Above all, the apostles attributed the success they found to their willingness to follow the dictates of the Spirit. Wilford Woodruff, for example, began a summary of his memorable Herefordshire experiences with the words "I Willford Woodruff being led by the spirit," and he concluded by writing "I feel thankful to God for all his mercy & kindness unto me & all the Saints in opening so many doors."[31] Indeed, the story of their entire mission suggests that they profited from the counsel of Joseph Smith:

---

[28]Joseph Smith to the Twelve, December 15, 1840, Joseph Smith Collection (Appendix B, Document 21). The letter was mistakenly printed in Joseph Smith's history (which was not actually published until some years later) as if it had been written on October 19, 1840. Smith, *History of the Church* 4:226–32. A long extract was printed in the *Times and Seasons* 2 (January 1, 1841): 258–61 and reprinted in the *Millennial Star* 1 (March 1841): 265–69 without an exact date. The best version is the transcription from the original in Jessee, *Personal Writings of Joseph Smith*, 480–87. Our quotations are based on that source.

[29]Heber C. Kimball to Vilate Kimball, May 27, 1840, Heber C. Kimball Collection.

[30]See George A. Smith to Lyman Smith, January 8[?], 1841, George A. Smith Collection, for the young apostle's comments on his own inadequacies (Appendix B, Document 22).

[31]Woodruff, *Journal*, April 16, 1840, 1:439–40.

When the Twelve or any other witnesses stand before the congregations of the earth, and they preach in the power and demonstration of the Spirit of God, and the people are astonished and confounded at the doctrine, and say, "That man has preached a powerful discourse, a great sermon," then let that man or those men take care that they do not ascribe the glory unto themselves, but be careful that they are humble, and ascribe the praise and glory to God and the Lamb; for it is by the power of the Holy Priesthood and the Holy Ghost that they have power thus to speak.[32]

OBSERVERS OF THE WORLD AROUND THEM

The Twelve had a healthy interest in the things around them, and considered it one of their responsibilities as Latter-day Saints to learn everything they could, even if occasionally doing so meant taking some time away from preaching. They took seriously an 1833 revelation through Joseph Smith that concluded, "It is my will that you should hasten to translate my scriptures, and to obtain a knowledge of history, and of countries, and of kingdoms, of laws of God and man, and all this for the salvation of Zion."[33] As if to demonstrate the practical effect of this revelation, on October 29, 1840, Heber C. Kimball, Wilford Woodruff, and George A. Smith wrote a long letter to the *Times and Seasons* in Nauvoo with detailed extracts from Elder Woodruff's journal concerning the historic sites and monuments they had recently visited:

As we consider it perfectly consistant with our calling, with reason and revelation, that we should form a knowledge of kingdoms and countries, whether it be at home or abroad, whether it be ancient or modern, or whether it be of things past present or to come, whether it be in heaven, earth or hell, air or seas; or whether we obtain this knowledge by being local or travelling, by study or by faith, by dreams or by visions, by revelation or by prophecy, it mattereth not unto us; if we can but obtain a correct principle and knowledge of things as they are, in their true light, past, present, and to come. It is under such a view of things that we are endeavoring to avail ourselves of every opportunity in our travels among the nations of the earth, to record an account of things as they pass under our observation.[34]

Joseph Smith agreed. The statement, he said, "refers to the liberty the Elders of the Church incidentally enjoyed while engaged in the ministry; and . . . it breathes that spirit of liberty in the pursuit of knowledge characteristic of the work of God in the last days."[35]

---

[32]The Prophet's address to the Twelve, July 2, 1839, Smith, *History of the Church* 3:383–85 (Appendix B, Document 2).

[33]D&C 93:53.

[34]Heber C. Kimball, Wilford Woodruff, and George A. Smith to Brothers Robinson & Smith, October 28, 1840, *Times and Seasons* 2 (January 1841): 261–64.

[35]Smith, *History of the Church* 4:234.

Several years later, Brigham Young expressed the same feelings to his missionary sons in England. He wrote to Joseph A., who was in Manchester in 1855:

I wish you to lose no opportunity of making yourself familiar with all that is useful and likely to benefit you, for to be able to combat with the world we must make ourselves acquainted with the ways of the world. This can only be done by keeping your mind constantly on the alert and when in society never allow anything to escape your notice. Listen attentively, and observe minutely the manners, customs, and remarks of all, for from the most humble of our fellow creatures an observing man can learn something that will be useful to him in after life. Such has been my course and, from daily and hourly experience of its benefits, I recommend you to pursue the same.

There are many things you can inform your mind upon, the laws of England, her form of government; lose no opportunity in your travels of visiting her manufactures, her works of art, her grand and spacious buildings, and all that is worthy of note, not from a mere idle curiosity but to store your mind with that which will benefit yourself and your brethren in after years.[36]

In 1862 he advised Brigham, Jr., who was in Liverpool, to "improve yourself to the utmost in studying good books and in associating with, and listening to, and profiting by, the conversation and experience of good persons," and later he complimented his son on taking such advice seriously.

I am also pleased that you have been privileged to visit the Exhibition and other instructive places you mention, and approve of your plan of buying books descriptive of the noted places you visit, so far as they are to be had, that you may not only learn all you can at the time, but also have the means of refreshing your memory and learning still more when leisure moments permit after your return home.[37]

As missionaries, then, the Twelve were not reluctant to take time out occasionally to study and enjoy the history, arts, and culture of Great Britain. Wilford Woodruff's journal especially is replete with notes of visits to historic sites and museums, including detailed descriptions of everything he saw. Many of these visits, as well as those of his colleagues, are noted elsewhere in this volume.

The missionaries were interested in public affairs, as well. On March 13, 1840, John Taylor went with Joseph Fielding to hear a lecture on the so-called Opium War with China. The war had begun as a result of China's

---

[36]Brigham Young to Joseph A. Young, February 3, 1855, in Jessee, *Brigham Young to His Sons*, 14.

[37]Brigham Young to Brigham Young, Jr., August 6, 1862, October 11, 1862, in Jessee, *Brigham Young to His Sons*, 28, 31.

The Thames and the City of London

efforts to keep opium out of the country and to expel British merchants who persisted in importing it. Fiercely opposed to the war, the irate speaker proclaimed that China had a right to keep the drug out and that the British were guilty of all manner of corruption. Fielding and Taylor were "well satisfied with the Lecture." The spirit of the address, wrote Fielding, "is that the Pagan Chinese have far more noble Principles than the Christians, so called, who will grow or sell anything, even [the] Souls of Men for Gain. . . . The Americans have protested against the Conduct of the British in attempting to blockade, etc. I pray God to turn all these things to his own Glory & that Truth may triumph."[38] Three weeks later the two missionaries went to hear a lecture on socialism, another controversial topic of the day.

The apostles also appreciated the skills of the English in arts and crafts. Some of them had portraits painted before they left for home, and Brigham Young, himself a fine craftsman, ordered a handmade watch from Henry Connor, a watchmaker and the first LDS convert in London. He had the

---

[38]Fielding, Diary, 63. The eventual outcome of the war was a treaty, signed in 1842 and ratified in 1843, in which China was forced to cede Hong Kong to the British, to pay an indemnity of $21,000,000, and to open certain additional ports for trade.

twelve letters of his name placed around the face of the watch instead of the twelve numerals.[39]

EXTERNAL CONCERNS: FAMILIES

Amidst all their concerns and acitvities as missionaries, the apostles did not forget their families. Brigham Young, Heber C. Kimball, Wilford Woodruff, and John Taylor left their wives and children in pitiable conditions, and they could do little but worry, pray, and trust in the fulfillment of Joseph Smith's promise that they would be cared for. The families bore their burdens with extraordinary faith,[40] as seen in the letters the wives wrote to their far-off missionary husbands.

The apostles' poignant letters show that they longed for home as much as they longed for success as emissaries of the Lord. Two letters written by Heber C. Kimball to Vilate in May 1840, for example, reflect his deep concerns, especially with where she would be living while he was gone. At first it seemed as if she would move to Kirtland, but he was relieved to find that she had decided to stay in Commerce. Friends were watching out for her, and he reminded her that the Lord had said that she would be blessed with friends as well as with the good things of the earth. He remembered her in all his prayers, and he was so delighted with her letters that he read them to the Saints with whom he met and even had one read in a public meeting. It made the people both laugh and cry, he said.[41]

On June 12, 1840, Brigham Young wrote to his wife from Manchester and, in a choice expression of his values and mixed emotions, he said: "my soul says sweet home sweet home. . . . You might think that I am verry anxious to get home, but it is not so. When the Brethern [emigrant Saints] started from Liverpool I tried myself to see if I wanted to goe. I could not bare the thought of going, but when the time has fully com, and the Lord says goe home my hart then will leap for joy."[42]

---

[39]Heber C. Kimball and Brigham Young to George A. Smith, October 14, 1840, George A. Smith Collection.

[40]See chapter 11 for a more detailed discussion of what was happening to the wives and families in Illinois.

[41]Heber C. Kimball to Vilate Kimball, May 2, 1840 and May 27, 1840, Heber C. Kimball Collection. Kimball and his wife each longed so much to hear from the other that they became a bit impatient when the letters did not come regularly enough. After hearing from Vilate that she thought he had forgotten his family, he good-naturedly chided her that "you must have been quite out of your head I think," for it was really the other way around.

[42]Brigham Young to Mary Ann Young, June 12, 1840, Brigham Young Papers.

When they could, the apostles sent presents home and sometimes even a little money. When the John Moon company left for America in June, Brigham Young sent along a little box containing a few small presents and two letters.[43] In September he sent some money with Theodore Turley, who, he later wrote Mary Ann, would pay her thirty dollars whenever she wanted it. "Glory to God in the highest for his goodness to me in putting it in my power to help my poor wife and Children to a little to by them a morsel of bread," he wrote with deep emotion. "It is not me but the Lord that has don it th[r]ough me." He hoped he could send even more soon, and he instructed his wife to purchase a "first rate" cow so they would have plenty of milk and butter when he got home so they could feed the poor, "for I shall have a grate menny to visit me."[44] Such a request must have astounded Mary Ann, who was still wondering where *her* next meal was coming from.

George A. Smith, the only unmarried apostle, left behind a young woman, Bathsheba W. Bigler, with whom he corresponded regularly. On December 5, 1840, for example, he wrote longingly:

I keep you Still in Memory and the Pleasante hours which I have Spent in your Society are also Remembered. . . . And the Lord willing We Shall See Each other again & talk Over Matters. I am Determined Never to take another Mission across the Ocean without Leaveing a *Rib* at home unless the Lord So orders it.

On January 18, just three days before they had originally been scheduled to be married, he wrote her from Staffordshire, saying: "I am thinking the time will come When We Shall be One. The Lord knows and Will mak known in Due time. . . . if I could Enjoy your Society I Should be Well Satisfied but the Lord called and I have to Obey."[45] He also confided his loneliness to Orson Pratt, his colleague and friend with whom he had much good-natured correspondence, who replied with a realistic though tough kind of comfort. "She will get a little annured to disappointments," he wrote, "so that it will not be entirely new for you to leave her thereafter."[46]

George A. worked as hard as any of his colleagues, made many friends,

---

[43]Brigham Young to Mary Ann Young, June 2, 1840, Phillip Blair Collection.

[44]Brigham Young to Mary Ann Young, January 15, 1841, Brigham Young Papers.

[45]George A. Smith to Bathsheba W. Bigler, December 5, 1840, and January 14, 18, 1841, George A. Smith Collection (Appendix B, Documents 19 and 20).

[46]Orson Pratt to George A. Smith, January 21, 1841, George A. Smith Collection.

and had outstanding success as a missionary, but Bathsheba never left his mind. In March 1841, as he prepared to return home, he penned a love poem:

> While I am abroad I spend my Breath
> in Prayer for her I Love in truth
> In a Distant Land I call to Mind
> my true and faithful friend So kind
> When I Return From this Distant Land
> I will take her by the Lovely hand
> and Raise my voice in Humble Prayer
> that God Would Make us A Heavenly Pair.[47]

A Note on Church Policy and Practice

In many ways the Church of 1840 was different from the Church today, and those familiar with present policies, practices, and perspectives should not be surprised to find that some things have changed.

Doctrinal essentials were the same as those taught today: the "first principles," the atonement of Christ, the apostasy and restoration, modern revelation, priesthood authority, the Second Coming and the Millennium, and so on. Joseph Smith's Articles of Faith were not yet written, but most of the ideas in them were fairly widely taught. In addition, the idea that the Saints were a "covenant people" and that in being baptized, they had accepted a "new and an everlasting covenant,"[48] was very much on their minds. For example, many of the early Saints closed their letters with a phrase such as "Yours in the Everlasting Covenant," or "Yours in the E.C."[49]

What was not being taught in Great Britain by the missionary apostles was the wide range of doctrine opened up by Joseph Smith during the pivotal four years in Nauvoo, including "eternal progression," salvation for the dead, eternal marriage, and all the doctrines and practices relating to the temple ordinances. These and other refinements would come "line upon line" as the Saints were better prepared to receive them and as the

---

[47]This document, titled simply "Lines," is in the George A. Smith Collection. There are two slightly different versions; the one quoted here is the second.

[48]See D&C 22:1.

[49]Examples from the George A. Smith Collection: "Yours in the new Covenant" (James Blakely to George A. Smith, December 5, 1840); "Yours in the N. E. L. C. [New and Ever Lasting Covenant]" (Reuben Hedlock to George A. Smith, December 4, 1840); "I Remain your Br. in the E C" (Edwin Mitchell to George A. Smith, November 31, 1840. This letter is dated November 31, but since there are only thirty days in that month, it may have been written December 1. It was postmarked December 2, 1840). There are many such examples in this and other collections in the Church Archives.

need for additional light became apparent.[50] The doctrine of baptism for the dead, for example, was introduced in Nauvoo while the apostles were in England. Joseph Smith first preached it on August 15, 1840, at the funeral of Seymor Brunson and elaborated on it again at a conference on October 4.[51] Word of the new doctrine did not reach England until November or December, when Vilate Kimball reported the October sermon in a letter to her husband, who in turn wrote about it to Joseph Fielding.[52]

Some aspects of Church organization were also different. The stake was the basic unit, but there were no "wards" until later in Nauvoo. In England there was a mission presidency, and each local "church," or "branch," had a president. Several branches were organized into "conferences." Whenever the organized conferences met, their meetings were also called conferences, and usually a member of the Twelve was present. It was the practice for the senior apostle present to call the meeting to order and then nominate someone else to be the president of that particular conference gathering. That president would then conduct the rest of the conference sessions. The same pattern was followed at the general conferences of the Church in England.[53]

In addition to these minor differences in organization, there were some interesting differences in Church practice. There were no regular sacrament meetings as Latter-day Saints know them today. Rather, there were prayer or preaching meetings, sometimes in homes and sometimes in rented halls or chapels, where the sacrament of the Lord's Supper was often administered. Collection boxes frequently were passed in such Church meetings to raise money for the poor or for missionaries, a practice unheard of in Latter-day Saint services today. There were also public preaching meetings, scheduled by the missionaries strictly for missionary purposes. In these gatherings the elders were not reluctant to take up col-

---

[50]For discussions on some aspects of changing doctrine and practice in the Church, see Alexander, "Reconstruction of Mormon Doctrine"; Alexander, "Mormon Religious Experience"; Allen, "Line upon Line"; Whittaker, "'Articles of Faith'."

[51]Ehat and Cook, *Words of Joseph Smith*, 49; Smith, *History of the Church* 4:206.

[52]Fielding, Diary, 99.

[53]For example, see the minutes of the Bran Green and Gadfield Elm Conference, September 14, 1840, where Brigham Young called the meeting together and then Thomas Kington, who was already president of this organized conference, was chosen, by nomination and vote, to be president of the immediate conference (i.e., meeting) (Woodruff, *Journal*, September 14, 1840, 1:513–15). See also minutes of the general conference in Manchester, October 6, 1840, in which Brigham Young called the conference to order and then Orson Pratt was chosen to be conference president (*Millennial Star* 1 [October 1840]: 165–68). A misprint in the *Star* identifies this as the July conference, but it is clearly the October conference minutes that are being reported.

lections, partly because money was needed to pay for hired halls.[54] When illness struck, the elders were called upon, as they are today, to administer to the sick by anointing them with oil as part of a priesthood blessing. What may seem peculiar to us, however, is that often the consecrated oil was applied to the affected part of the body, rather than simply to the crown of the head, and sometimes it was even taken internally. Church discipline was often more public, as members were asked to confess their transgressions in open meeting, and disciplinary actions were decided upon and announced in the conferences as well as in local branch meetings. Today such matters are taken care of in very private disciplinary councils.

An interesting variation between the attitudes of Church members in 1840 and those of today relates to the Word of Wisdom. Today this revelation enjoins upon Latter-day Saints the obligation not only to eat wisely and generally take care of their health but specifically to abstain from tea, coffee, alcohol, and tobacco. In the 1840s, however, total abstinence was not yet required. The Word of Wisdom, revealed through Joseph Smith in 1833, came "not by commandment or constraint, but by revelation and the word of wisdom, showing forth the order and will of God in the temporal salvation of all saints."[55] Adherence was always encouraged, and drunkenness was forbidden, but it took many years for the present interpretation and practice to mature.[56]

The apostles, nevertheless, preached the Word of Wisdom strongly, and because of their reputation for opposing the use of alcoholic beverages, they were regularly invited to speak at temperance meetings. They were most concerned with the avoidance of excess, and particularly drunkenness, and it seems that they personally avoided hard liquors of any sort, but they were not teetotalers. An occasional glass of wine on a special occasion was deemed appropriate, and at times they drank porter (a light beer) with their meals.[57] In January 1841, on one of their frequent sight-

---

[54]See, for example, Orson Pratt to George A. Smith, October 7, 1841, George A. Smith Collection. Here Orson tells George A. about the hall he had hired in Edinburgh, where he was preaching regularly but to very small congregations. The contributions at first scarcely averaged enough to pay the rent, though by the time the letter was written they were becoming more substantial.

[55]D&C 89:2.

[56]See Alexander, "Word of Wisdom"; Bush, "Word of Wisdom in Early Nineteenth-Century Perspective"; Peterson, "Historical Analysis of the Word of Wisdom." In the twentieth century the Word of Wisdom has taken on added significance as a test of faithfulness and obedience. In the nineteenth century, plural marriage and standing steadfast against persecution served a similar role.

[57]On the morning of May 27, 1840, for example, Heber C. Kimball ordered a quart of porter, and on Christmas eve of that year Elders Kimball and Woodruff, in London, made themselves a supper of bread

seeing tours, Wilford Woodruff and Heber Kimball visited what was said to be the largest wine vault in the world. They participated in the traditional tasting ritual, "found the wine a good article," but thought it "dreadful to see such vast sums of mony expended for intoxicating drinks when there are thousands nearly starving for bread in the streets."[58] The missionaries also took tea, an important British tradition, when invited by gracious hosts and hostesses.[59]

Finally, there were other subtle differences between missionary work today and missionary work in the 1840s. Modern missionary work is highly structured and closely supervised, complete with detailed weekly reports. In 1840 the Twelve only loosely supervised the missionaries under them. Even though they regularly received reports through the mail, there were no forms to fill out or report meetings to attend. Modern missionaries must remain within their assigned areas, but the missionaries of the 1840s paid little attention to boundaries.

Missionaries today usually get from one place to another by bicycle, automobile, or public conveyance, but the Twelve in Britain thought nothing of walking many miles a day to meet their various appointments. This fact suggests that their pace and timing, perhaps even their sense of time, were significantly different from those of missionaries in today's fast-paced world. In the countryside, especially, they spent literally hours, and sometimes all day, walking from one appointment to another, yet they usually seemed unhurried and unharried as they methodically went about their work. Heber C. Kimball, for example, spent the second week of May 1840 with Joseph Fielding walking from town to town outside Preston. On Sunday he preached to a full house in a large barn in Chatburn, and the next evening he preached at nearby Clitheroe, where five people were baptized. From there the two missionaries hiked to Waddington for an evening preaching engagement, and the next day, Wednesday, they crossed the river to the village of Chaigley. There they visited Jennetta Richards,

---

and cheese and a pint of beer (probably porter). Allen and Alexander, *Manchester Mormons*, 157; Woodruff, *Journal*, December 24, 1840, 1:582. See also Smith, "History," September 2, 1840, where a Campbellite minister invited Elder Smith to take some bread and cheese and beer with him, "the only minister that ever had good feelings enough to ask me to eat or drink with him in London."

[58]Woodruff, *Journal*, January 23, 1841, 2:31–32; Kimball, *Journal*, January 23, 1841.

[59]For example, see Woodruff, *Journal*, February 16, 1841, 2:47–48. Unfortunately for accurate historical perceptions, later summaries of the mission tended to recall incidents in light of later interpretations of the Word of Wisdom. One, for example, commented that "as soon as they obeyed the Gospel they abandoned their excess drinking; none of us drank any kind of spirits, porter, small beer, or even wine, neither did we drink tea, coffee, or chocolate" (Whitney, *Life of Heber C. Kimball*, 152).

heard her read a letter from Willard, and conducted a preaching meeting. Two days later they walked to Ribchester and then to Preston. By modern standards, spending so many hours simply walking between towns might seem wasteful of precious time, but they knew how to turn it into time well spent. As Joseph Fielding wrote, "our Hearts burned within us while we talked by the Way."[60]

[60]Fielding, Diary, 73–74.

Chapter 6

LIKE FIRE IN THEIR BONES: THE FIRST CONTINGENT BEGINS WORK

The enthusiasm for missionary work could hardly have been greater than it was among the first contingent of apostles who set foot in England in 1840. "I feel the word of the Lord like fire in my bones," John Taylor told a group of interested listeners in Liverpool,[1] and with that fervor the apostles were ready to make any sacrifice to deliver their message.

John Taylor, Wilford Woodruff, and Theodore Turley arrived in Liverpool on January 11, 1840. They landed at the Prince's Dock and found lodging at the Birmingham Arms, a most distasteful inn on Church Street. "May the Lord henceforth deliver me from such a place," Wilford Woodruff wrote in his journal.

The next day was the Sabbath, and the three missionaries attended religious services at two different Anglican churches. John Taylor began his mission by seeking out his wife's brother, George Cannon. Much surprised to see him, the Cannons invited him to dinner, treated him most cordially and, inevitably, made him homesick for Leonora. He briefly unfolded the gospel to them and left a copy of the Book of Mormon and Parley P. Pratt's *Voice of Warning*. Cannon was soon convinced that the Lord had a hand in sending his brother-in-law to England to show him the "dangerous state I lived in without even the form of religion."[2]

On Monday, after clearing customs, the missionaries took their trunks and boxes to the Cannon home, left some of their belongings there, and about 6:00 in the evening departed for Preston. When they arrived two

---

[1]John Taylor to Leonora Taylor, January 30, 1840, John Taylor Collection (Appendix B, Document 6). See the context of this statement in the discussion below. Although dated January 30, this letter was finished several days later.

[2]See ibid., and note from George Cannon to Leonora Taylor penned at the end of this letter.

John Taylor
© LDS Church

hours later, they found several Saints eagerly waiting at the station. Wilford Woodruff enjoyed an especially satisfying reunion with Willard Richards, whom he had last seen in Kirtland in 1837. They went to Richards's home and conversed late into the night. John Taylor, meeting Willard Richards for the first time, was warmly impressed with him and with the rest of the Saints who crowded around to see them. Their kindness and love as well as "their simple unadorned manner" appealed to him.

Though John Taylor had lived in England from the time of his birth in 1808 until 1830, economic conditions were far worse in 1840 than anything he remembered. On his first night in Preston, he had dinner at the home of John Parkman, a member of the Church and a shoemaker, but immediately afterward Mrs. Parkman had to leave home to go to work in a factory. Taylor wrote to Leonora that he was dismayed at seeing Mrs. Parkman leave her husband and the children to go to work, "thus breaking up those social endearments that unite the family. It makes my heart bleed to see these things. When will the earth cease to mourn?"[3] Wilford Woodruff, too, was appalled at the general poverty and privation he observed, noting

---

[3]John Taylor to Leonora Taylor, January 30, 1840 (Appendix B, Document 6).

that the streets were crowded with the poor, both male and female, going to and from the factories in their wooden shoes and making "a great ratling over the pavement." It seemed to him that "the poor are in as great Bondage as the children of Israel in Egypt."[4]

As in Liverpool, John Taylor's arrival in Preston was also a time of reunion, this time with old friends as well as family. One of the first people he met was Canadian Hiram Clark, who had been serving as a missionary in England since December. "He rejoiced to see me & I to see him," he reported to Leonora. "It gives us peculiar feelings to meet our friends in another country." He also had two uncles in Preston, George and James Hodgson. George and his son John were partners in a plumbing, painting, and glazing firm, and James's son, Robert, was their foreman. The first thing Taylor did was look them up and tell them of his mission. Before leaving he promised George and his family that if they would gather all his friends together when he returned, he would preach the gospel to them.[5]

John Taylor's reunion with Joseph Fielding, on January 16, was especially warmhearted. The two were close because of their earlier experiences together in Canada, where they were both converted. "I thank God that he has preserved him & given him wisdom for the arduous duties devolving upon him," Taylor wrote to his wife. "We felt something like Jonathan & David after an absence of 3 years."[6]

On Friday, January 17, the missionaries held a special council meeting at the Richards home. Interestingly enough, in light of later Church protocol, no one found it unusual for Joseph Fielding, president of the mission, to preside at the council meeting, even though two apostles were present. The apostles received the respect due their office, but Wilford Woodruff and John Taylor deferred to the authority of the mission president. They continued to do so until the Quorum of the Twelve itself assumed the mission presidency nearly six months later.

During the meeting, it was decided that John Taylor and Joseph Fielding would open missionary work in Liverpool, Hiram Clark would go to Manchester, and Wilford Woodruff and Theodore Turley would go to the Staffordshire Potteries and there seek the mind of the Lord about their going to Birmingham. Willard Richards was to go where the Spirit directed

---

[4]Woodruff, *Journal*, January 14, 1840, 1:405.
[5]John Taylor to Leonora Taylor, January 30, 1840 (Appendix B, Document 6).
[6]Ibid.

him. The next day they met again at the Richards home for "a season of prayer & fasting"[7] and to give blessings to each other, after which Elders Woodruff, Turley, and Clark left by rail for Manchester.[8]

JOHN TAYLOR IN LIVERPOOL

John Taylor, working with Joseph Fielding, had a busy four days even before he got to Liverpool. Sunday morning began with a street meeting in Preston, which somewhat surprised Elder Taylor, but he was assured that the Saints had been holding such meetings for some time. He and Joseph Fielding also attended several other meetings that day, and at one of them a group from Longton persuaded them to stop there on Wednesday, on their way to Liverpool.

On Monday Elders Fielding and Richards took Elder Taylor across the river to Penwortham, where several people from surrounding towns were gathered to hear him. That evening he obliged them, taking as his text Romans 1:16: "For I am not ashamed of the gospel of Christ: for it is the power of God unto salvation to every one that believeth." Finally, on Wednesday, Taylor and Fielding left for Liverpool, stopping, as promised, in Longton, where they enjoyed an evening filled with spiritual delight. At a meeting in the home of William Blackhurst, John Taylor preached on the restoration of the gospel, taking as his text Revelation 14:6. The audience, including some who had begun to belittle the Church, was very attentive. Afterwards, during a visit with the Blackhurst family, Elder Taylor spoke in tongues, and still later, at the home of Deacon Rawcliff, he did so again. His message, upon interpretation, told Joseph Fielding that he had been faithful in his office, that the Lord would continue to bless him in ways he had not even imagined, and that he would bring many to Zion. Such a blessing left the steadfast mission president weeping for joy.[9]

The next day the missionaries walked thirteen miles to Ormskirk, failed to find an opportunity to preach, hired a gig (a light, two-wheeled, two-passenger, one-horse carriage) to carry them the next five miles, and then took a coach to Liverpool. Fielding spent the night at a tavern, while

---

[7]Woodruff, *Journal*, January 18, 1840, 1:407–8.

[8]The chronology for these few days, and the days immediately following, is found in John Taylor to Leonora Taylor, January 30, 1840 (Appendix B, Document 6); Fielding, Diary; Woodruff, *Journal*. The dates, however, are one day wrong in both Taylor and Fielding, for the day they list as Sunday is dated wrong; Woodruff's dating corresponds correctly with the calendar.

[9]Fielding, Diary, 50. Curiously, in his letter to Leonora, John Taylor made no mention of speaking in tongues.

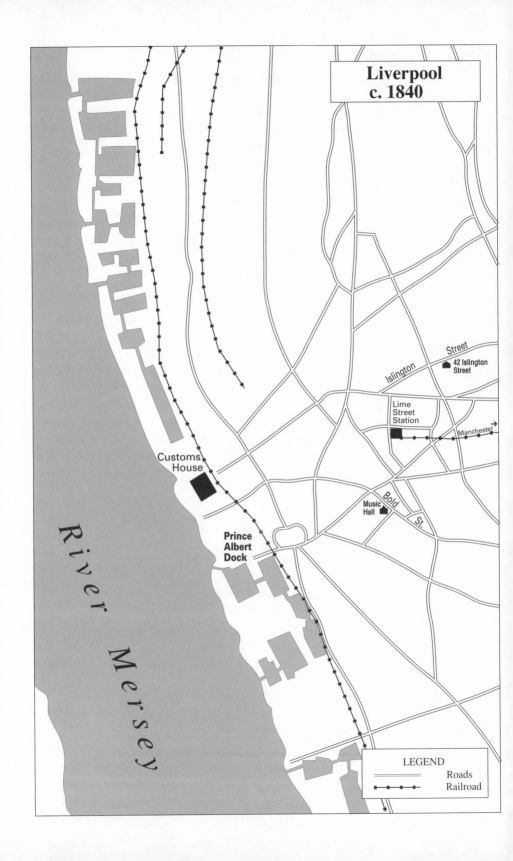

Liverpool in 1847. Courtesy Eric Midwinter, *Old Liverpool,*
David & Charles (Publishers), Ltd.

John Taylor went again to the Cannon home, which soon became the permanent Liverpool residence for both missionaries.

On their first day in Liverpool, the elders found themselves in an ardent discussion with two learned religious leaders. One, a Mr. Kent, seemed at first to consider their message seriously, but then a Mr. Stewart arrived. Once a priest in the Church of England, Stewart now led a dissenting Staffordshire congregation. He rejected their testimony outright, apparently after hardly listening, whereupon the missionaries warned him in a straightforward manner that if he persisted in this way, he would lose whatever light he had and his own work would never prosper.

As early as 1831 a revelation instructed missionaries that if the "congregations of the wicked" rejected them, they should "shake off the dust of thy feet against those who receive thee not, not in their presence, lest thou provoke them, but in secret; and wash thy feet, as a testimony against them in the day of judgment."[10] Stewart's blunt rejection was so harsh that the two elders felt duty-bound to do what the revelation said. Accordingly, they found a private place and washed their feet against their antagonist

---

[10]D&C 60:15; see also D&C 99:4.

to symbolize that they believed they had done all they could to warn him of the consequences of rejecting their message. As they "bore testimony before the Lord," they also uttered a prayer in Stewart's behalf, asking their Father in Heaven that he be forgiven and led to the truth. They felt better about Mr. Kent and had some hope that he would continue to listen. So ended John Taylor's first full day of missionary work in Liverpool.[11]

The next day, Sunday, was especially notable because it marked the beginning of missionary success among the Aitkenites.[12] The missionaries began the day by attending services at an Aitkenite chapel where Timothy R. Matthews, Joseph Fielding's brother-in-law, was the minister. The brethren were probably relieved that Matthews, who had already rejected the gospel, was not there, especially when they heard a sermon by a devout young preacher who deplored the state of the existing church, prayed for the Holy Ghost, and looked forward to the establishment of the kingdom of Christ. That this kingdom had been established was John Taylor's message, and he longed to proclaim it to the congregation. Afterward, he and Joseph Fielding met in the vestry with several class leaders and preachers, who immediately began to inquire about their beliefs. Elder Taylor complimented them on their many correct principles and practices, including baptism by immersion and the laying on of hands, and then announced to his listeners that he and Fielding had traveled two thousand miles without purse or scrip to testify to them that the Lord had revealed himself from heaven and restored the things for which they were so anxiously looking and praying. "Glory be to God," he heard several people shout in great emotion. "Brethren & Friends," he continued, "I feel an anxious desire to deliver this testimony. I feel the word of the Lord like fire in my bones," and he asked for further opportunity to present his entire message.

John Taylor's impromptu sermon was followed by considerable discussion. Some of his hearers were delighted, but others were upset. They asked if the two were Mormons. No, Taylor explained, they belonged to The Church of Jesus Christ of Latter-day Saints, sometimes known by the term Mormons. "We have heard an unfavorable opinion of you by our Pastor Mr. Matthews & Aitken," commented one listener. "Mr. Matthews says that the thing is from Hell." The missionaries then asked for an appointment to come back and preach to them, but even though some

---

[11]John Taylor to Leonora Taylor, January 30, 1840 (Appendix B, Document 6); Fielding, Diary, 50–51.
[12]See the discussion of the Aitkenites in Appendix A.

apparently were disposed to agree, the group decided that that would not be proper without permission from the Reverend Timothy Matthews. They parted, though, with friendly handshakes.

Next they went to a Baptist meeting at the Music Hall, apparently still looking for an opportunity to preach. The Baptist gathering was only a prayer meeting, however, so preaching was not appropriate, but the leader, Mr. Bennett, invited them to his home. Bennett told them that even if they were allowed to preach, the people were so unyielding that they would not hear them out. "I am afraid that the religion of this Generation will sink them to hell," John Taylor wrote to his wife. "They have so much religion that they have no time to listen to the truths of God."[13]

That evening they were back at the Aitkenite chapel. After the sermon William Mitchell, one of the preachers, invited them to spend the night at his home. There, late into the night, they taught the gospel to Mitchell and his wife, who were delighted with their message. "This was just what we hoped for," Fielding noted in his journal, "that the Lord [would] open the heart of one or 2 to converse with us."[14]

When the elders got up the next morning, Monday, Mitchell had gone to work, but they were invited to come back on Tuesday evening. When they arrived, they found that their host had taken a great deal of criticism from his fellow preachers, who had even made him promise that he would not allow missionaries to preach in his home. He told them, however, that they could not stop him from talking with the Mormons. His wife, meanwhile, had invited several friends and neighbors to hear the missionaries preach, but because of Mitchell's promise she had to tell them not to come. Nevertheless, about a dozen people showed up at the house, anxious to hear what the elders had to say. Taylor and Fielding talked with them, carefully trying to avoid the charge that they were preaching, and by the end of the evening several accepted an invitation to hear them preach on Sunday evening. Mitchell was so pleased that he got no sleep that night. Both he and his wife had decided to become Latter-day Saints.

Church responsibilities, meanwhile, included more than missionary work, and Joseph Fielding, still president of the mission, was burdened with other concerns. During this week, for example, he received letters from his counselors William Clayton in Manchester and Willard Richards

---

[13]John Taylor to Leonora Taylor, January 30, 1840 (Appendix B, Document 6).
[14]Fielding, Diary, 52.

in Preston, both detailing problems within their branches. Fielding thus had to take considerable time from missionary work to write to his co-workers with suggestions and instructions.

On February 2 Taylor and Fielding began holding regular Sunday evening preaching meetings in a rented hall on Preston Street that held more than three hundred people. That night John Taylor preached the first public LDS sermon in Liverpool to a near capacity crowd. Taking as his text Jude 3, "It was needful for me to . . . exhort you, that ye should earnestly contend for the faith," he gave a powerful sermon on the restoration of the gospel. He concluded by saying, "This is glorious intelligence & asked is it not. Yes was responded by many & praise the Lord." After Joseph Fielding bore testimony of the truth of what Elder Taylor had said, Taylor told the congregation that the Lord had sent them there to baptize and invited any who wanted to repent and be baptized to make it known. "The spirit of the Lord indeed was with us," he reported to Leonora, and several weeping and rejoicing people gathered round and told of their conversions and of special spiritual manifestations that had come to them.[15] William Mitchell testified to several of his Aitkenite class members that these things were of God and told them of his own decision to be baptized.

The following Tuesday, February 4, at 3:00 in the afternoon at the seashore was the time and place set for the first baptisms in Liverpool. Even then, questions continued to plague some who had been baptized by the Reverend Mr. Matthews in the same spot not long before and whose friends among the Aitkenites were still trying to dissuade them by telling them that there was no need for rebaptism. Not yet fully comprehending the principle of priesthood authority, they worried that being baptized again would be an affront to their friends. William Mitchell, on the other hand, had no such reservations. Ten people, including the Mitchells, were baptized that day in the chilly waters of the Irish Sea, and by the end of the service, all reservations had disappeared. "We left them rejoicing," said Joseph Fielding, and as they returned to their homes, the warmth of the Spirit abundantly compensated for the cold of the atmosphere.[16]

More people soon were baptized, among them George and Ann Cannon. George had read the Book of Mormon twice, and concluded that "no wicked man could write such a book as this; and no good man would

---

[15]John Taylor to Leonora Taylor, January 30, 1840 (Appendix B, Document 6).
[16]Fielding, Diary, 53–54.

Lord Street, Liverpool. Courtesy Francis E. Hyde, *Liverpool and the Mersey,*
David & Charles (Publishers), Ltd.

write it, unless it were true and he were commanded of God to do so."[17]
Leonora was overwhelmed with joy when she heard the news.[18]

These converts became the seed of the Church in Liverpool as they
broadcast their conversion to friends and neighbors. "I hope that more
of your friends may yet embrace the gospel," John wrote to Leonora. "Your
sister [i.e., sister-in-law] Ann has introduced us to many of them. She is a
complete missionary & happy in the Lord."[19]

Elders Taylor and Fielding, meanwhile, continued to contend with the
Aitkenites. On the evening of February 11, for instance, Timothy Matthews
visited the Mitchell home, evidently trying to persuade the newly baptized
converts that they had made a mistake. Several other people also were

---

[17]As quoted in Evans, *Century of "Mormonism,"* 101.

[18]As she wrote to her husband: "I went over the river yesterday, and I got a letter from you, dated
15th Feb.; I never received a letter that gave me so much real comfort as it has done. I do rejoice, and
praise God for what he has done in bringing my dear brother George, and sister Ann, into the Church,
(the only Church with which the Lord is well pleased.) I do hope that the rest of our dear scattered ones
may yet be gathered into the fold, and yet live and reign with our blessed Lord and Saviour." This was
penned on April 14. See Leonora Taylor to John Taylor, April 12, 1840, and continued on April 14, *Millennial Star* 1 (July 1840): 63–65.

[19]John Taylor to Leonora Taylor, January 30, 1840 (Appendix B, Document 6). See also Fielding, Diary,
53, and Roberts, *Life of John Taylor,* 79–80.

there, including the two missionaries, and the sometimes heated exchange included discussions of the Book of Mormon, the Holy Ghost, and authority in the ministry. Matthews commented that he and Aitken had been wrong when they once said that they had no authority, for, he believed, they were called of God, by the Spirit, to preach the gospel, and that was authority enough. The debate continued until 10:00 that night, after which Taylor and Fielding remained for a while to visit with the Mitchells. Suddenly, perhaps as a faith-bolstering sign to the dedicated new converts, Elder Taylor began speaking in tongues. When interpreted, the message was another blessing to Joseph Fielding for his faithfulness.[20]

The two missionaries were deeply concerned with the continuing activities of the Reverend Mr. Matthews and his colleague, a Mr. Bradford, and, because Matthews and Bradford had been given ample opportunity to accept the gospel as well as their warnings, the missionaries felt they must now bear witness against them. Consequently, the next day they found a private spot, washed their feet as a testimony against their antagonists and, kneeling down in the cleft of a rock, "bore witness of it unto the Lord, according to the Commandment." As Joseph Fielding explained in his journal, "We felt that we had done as God would have us do."[21]

Their worries about the possible effect of their Aitkenite adversaries seemed confirmed when they visited William Mitchell that afternoon and found him greatly troubled, "almost in the Dust," because of the pressures received from his former colleagues. "There is a mighty Struggle against the Work here & we need great Power to resist it; Lord grant it for Christ's sake," the anxious Fielding wrote in his journal. Matthews continued his intensive efforts to get his flock back, and the missionaries unhappily saw some of them begin to waver.[22]

Though Fielding occasionally went to Preston or Manchester on Church business, he continued to work closely with John Taylor in Liverpool. They worked through Church members, relatives, and other acquaintances, and slowly the message spread. By the end of February, William Mitchell's brother and sister-in-law were listening, and on March 17 both of them were baptized.[23]

The newly baptized Saints were as generous in helping the two mis-

[20]Fielding, Diary, 55–56.
[21]Ibid., 56.
[22]Ibid., 56.
[23]Ibid., 59, 64.

sionaries as their poor circumstances would permit. The Saints mended their clothes, gave them food and money, and provided lodging. Just as Joseph Fielding was leaving Liverpool on February 27, for example, George Cannon insisted that he take a sovereign, as a loan to be repaid whenever he could do it. Sister Chandler, who often fed the missionaries, also gave him money. A Sister Arrington let them use her home as a place to hold preaching services and often gave them other assistance. The grateful Fielding expressed his feelings in his journal on March 31:

> The Saints are very kind; we want for nothing temporal. Sis. Arrington in particular has been so always even when most others were cast down, almost like the Disciples at the time our Lord was betrayed, she still stood by us, believed our Words, gave us Money in time of need & fed us liberally at all times. Her Sister Mary Dixon is of the same Stamp, or much like her; not that we find fault with any of them. I feel to love the Saints.[24]

Various preachers, including Aitkenites, continued to be their greatest antagonists. On February 21 John Taylor attempted to convince one of them that rebaptism with proper authority was necessary, but the preacher became quite insulting. Though combative in nature, Elder Taylor held his temper well. Fielding, however, had to utter a silent prayer to God for patience.[25] Perhaps it was preachers such as these who led John Taylor to comment scornfully to Joseph Smith that some ministers in Liverpool "were so good in general, and so pure, that they had no room for the gospel, they were too holy to be righteous, too good to be pure, and had too much religion to enter into the kingdom of heaven."[26]

Taylor and Fielding continued preaching on Sunday evenings in the hall on Preston Street, in addition to holding regular meetings in the homes of the Saints, until the end of March, when they moved to a hall on Renshaw Street, closer to the center of town. The new hall cost them four shillings per week, but it also held between three and four hundred people, and there they were able to hold two meetings a day.[27]

By the time the other apostles arrived, there were twenty-eight members of the Church in Liverpool. That was a modest number for three months' work, but John Taylor nevertheless felt elated at the progress. He

---

[24]Ibid., March 31, 1840, 68.
[25]Ibid., 58, 67.
[26]John Taylor to Joseph Smith, February 3, 1841, *Times and Seasons* 2 (May 1, 1841): 400–402.
[27]Fielding, Diary, March 31, 1840, 68.

had baptized several of Leonora's relatives, they had begun to make inroads into the Aitkenite stronghold, and large crowds were gathering to hear him preach. "The little stone is rolling forth," he wrote to Leonora on March 16. "One of the brethren dreamed he saw two men come to Liverpool, they cast a net into the Sea and pulled it out full of fishes, he was surprised to see them pick the small fish out first and then the large; well if we get all the fish I shall be satisfied."[28]

WILFORD WOODRUFF IN THE POTTERIES

On January 18 Wilford Woodruff, Theodore Turley, and Hiram Clark set out from Preston for the Staffordshire Potteries. They stopped that night at Manchester, where they found the Saints eager to greet them and quick to seek healing and other blessings from Elder Woodruff. Before the day was over, he had cast the devil from one sister and administered to five people who were ill. Three days later he and Turley went to Burslem, in the heart of the Potteries, but on January 29, evidently believing that Elder Turley could be especially effective in his old hometown, Woodruff sent him on to Birmingham, about fifty miles further south. "We are determind by the assistance of God to open a Door in every town from the Potteries to Birmingham & erect a Standard in it," he wrote Willard Richards. Reflecting the urgency felt by all the apostles, he added, "I feel as though it will be a day of warning & not of many words to England. I think that what we do we shall do quickly."[29]

Located some thirty miles south of Manchester, the Potteries centered on six towns: Tunstall, Burslem, Hanley, Stoke-on-Trent, Fenton, and Longton (also known as Lane End). The towns were dominated by the famous bottle ovens where the precious earthenware and stoneware were fired. Mixing, molding, decorating, glazing, and firing all required special skills, and the products of the Potteries became known the world over. By the 1840s the towns were becoming crowded as out-of-work migrants from the countryside sought employment, and children were often employed for long hours in the factories. As in Manchester, the smoke from the bottle ovens darkened the air. The pollution was local, however, and the rolling countryside around the towns still provided delightful, unspoiled scenery for those passing through.

---

[28]As extracted in *Times and Seasons* 1 (May 1840): 110.
[29]Wilford Woodruff to Willard Richards, February 3, 1840, Willard Richards Collection.

Wilford Woodruff
Courtesy LDS Church Archives

Wilford Woodruff remained in the Potteries for about six weeks, work-ing with Alfred Cordon and other local Church members. He walked from village to village, getting to know the Saints. He became especially well acquainted with two recent converts in Hanley: William Benbow, a grocer, and his wife, Ann.

As in Preston and Manchester, the Saints in the Potteries were both honored and awed at the presence of a modern apostle. On January 26, for example, a sister in Burslem wanted to wash his feet, evidently as a sign of her own humility and sense of service, and Elder Woodruff con-sented. Then, he noted in his journal, the spirit of prophecy came over him, and he delivered to her a comforting message about the future in the gospel of her sons and daughters.

In the Potteries, as elsewhere, Mormonism had its adversaries, and it was not long before Wilford Woodruff met some of them. One confron-tation came on the night of February 6, while he was preaching to ap-proximately four hundred people in Hanley. He described the encounter to Willard Richards in words that conveyed his image of himself as a warrior in the cause of truth. While he was preaching, he said, several priests arrived,

A potbank yard, Staffordshire
Potteries, about 1845
Courtesy David Sekers, *The
Potteries,* Shire Publications, Ltd.

armed with i[n]visible weapons to give me dreadful battle upon the Book of Mormon. The Lord showed it to me & I preached to them upon the Book of Mormon & disarmed them of every weapon that they had chosen to fight me with & it flung them into confusion & they did not wish to leave without doing sumthing & so they jumped upon a Bench & roared & hallowed like mad men untill they were not only checked up but pulled off from the Bench by the people.

Elder Woodruff answered questions as long as he thought proper and then left the hall "all in an uproar." Such opposition pleased him, for, he said, "I like to see some excitement & things are working about right now in the potteries to have the people hear the word whether they embrace it or not. The priests are quite mad because we are getting a hold in Hanly."[30]

He was encouraged by his work in the Potteries, for in a short time he had baptized about forty converts. Apparently he had planned to stay much longer, but a combination of circumstances, including the strong impression of the Spirit, sent him elsewhere.

WILFORD WOODRUFF AND THE HEREFORDSHIRE CONVERSIONS

Herefordshire, a beautiful farming country dominated by the lovely Malvern Hills, lies about seventy miles south of the Potteries. In contrast

---

[30]Wilford Woodruff to Willard Richards, February 8, 1840, Willard Richards Collection.

to the crowded poverty of the cities, the region offered the missionaries exceptionally pleasant conditions, and they found it delightful to wander through the unpolluted countryside. There were, of course, both rich and poor among the Herefordshire farmers, and some were landowners whereas others were tenants, but in general life was good for those fortunate enough to be able to stay on the farm during these trying times.[31] More importantly, however, in Herefordshire Wilford Woodruff found a people singularly well prepared to receive the gospel.

The remarkable story of Wilford Woodruff's Herefordshire mission actually began in Staffordshire with William Benbow.[32] Elder Woodruff worked closely with Benbow, preached in his home, and spent at least thirteen nights there. William told him about his brother, John, a prosperous farmer in Herefordshire, and his wife, Jane, who were members of the United Brethren and openly seeking for a restoration of the ancient gospel.

Theodore Turley, meanwhile, returned from Birmingham on February 28 and began urging Wilford Woodruff to take up missionary work in that city. Elder Woodruff seemed persuaded and decided to leave Turley in charge of the work in the Potteries, presumably so he himself could go to Birmingham, not far distant. But on Sunday, March 1, during the opening hymn at a meeting of the Saints in Hanley, the Spirit whispered to Elder Woodruff, "This is the last meeting that you will hold with this people for many days." Though surprised, he was so sure of what he felt that he made the announcement to the congregation.[33] He also discussed his impression with William Benbow, who immediately offered to take him to meet John and Jane Benbow in Herefordshire and even to pay his way there.[34]

The next morning Elder Woodruff "went in secret before the Lord" to seek His will. "As I asked," he later reported, "the Lord gave, and showed me that it was his will that I should go immediately to the south of En-

---

[31]For insight into the lives of at least some farmers in this era, see Fussell and Fussell, *English Countrywoman*, chapter 6, "Regency and Early Victorian Countrywomen," and Fussell and Fussell, *English Countryman*, chapter 6, "The Victorian Farmer."

[32]There are several slightly differing accounts of what happened. The traditional one is found in Cowley, *Wilford Woodruff*, 116. Much of this work, including the part dealing with this episode, is based on Woodruff, *Leaves*, originally published in 1881. In preparing *Leaves*, Wilford Woodruff added details and interpretations not included in the original journal. The quotation above is often cited as the "most traditional" account because Cowley's work is the most well known and widely distributed book to date on Wilford Woodruff.

[33]Cowley, *Wilford Woodruff*, 116.

[34]Wilford Woodruff to Elders Robinson and Smith, October 7, 1840.

The Malvern Hills. Courtesy James B. Allen

gland."[35] Birmingham, to be sure, was south of the Potteries, but it was clear that he was not to stop there. About forty miles beyond was Herefordshire, where, though they did not yet know it, William Benbow's brother and a host of friends were waiting for what Wilford Woodruff would bring.

On Tuesday, accompanied by William Benbow and William's eight-year-old son, Wilford was on his way by omnibus. They spent the night at Wolverhampton and the following day took a coach as far as Worcester and then walked about fourteen miles to John Benbow's farm at Castle Froome, Ledbury, Herefordshire. They were immediately welcomed and

[35]Wilford Woodruff to Elders Robinson and Smith, October 7, 1840, *Times and Seasons* 2 (February 15, 1841): 311–14 and (March 1, 1841): 327–31. Although the various accounts of this story are not consistent with each other, we have here put together what seems to be the most reasonable synthesis. See also Wilford Woodruff to Willard Richards, March 11, 1840, Willard Richards Collection; "Manuscript History of the British Mission;" Cowley, *Wilford Woodruff*, 116; Woodruff, *Leaves*, 77–78; Woodruff, *Journal*, March 2–4, 1840, 1:423. He noted in his diary on March 2 simply that "the Lord warned me to go to the South." Woodruff, *Journal*, March 2, 1840, 1:423.

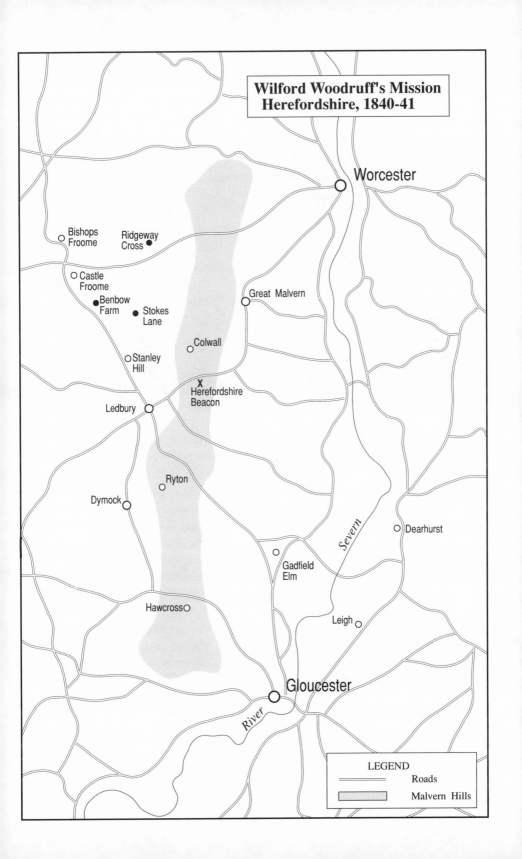

Wilford Woodruff's Mission Herefordshire, 1840-41

Worcester

Bishops Froome

Ridgeway Cross

Castle Froome

Benbow Farm

Stokes Lane

Great Malvern

Colwall

Stanley Hill

X
Herefordshire Beacon

Ledbury

Ryton

Dymock

Severn

Dearhurst

Gadfield Elm

Hawcross

Leigh

Gloucester

River

LEGEND

——————— Roads

▨ Malvern Hills

The John Benbow farmhouse. Courtesy W. Dee Halverson

invited to spend the night, though it was two o'clock in the morning, after a lengthy discussion of the gospel, before anyone retired.

John and Jane Benbow immediately opened their home for friends and neighbors to hear Elder Woodruff, and within a few days he began to reap a harvest that he had scarcely dared dream of. On the evenings of March 5 and 6, Benbow invited the people of the neighborhood to meet at his home, in which there was a room licensed for preaching, to hear the American missionary, and on the second day, the Benbows and four friends were baptized. Woodruff spent most of the following day, Saturday, clearing out a pond on the Benbow farm in preparation for more anticipated baptisms on Sunday. On the Sabbath he preached three sermons in three different locations to an estimated one thousand people. (The local Anglican parish church reportedly had a congregation of only fifteen that day.) The last sermon of the day was at the Benbow farm, where one of the audience turned out to be a constable sent by the local parish rector with a warrant for Woodruff's arrest. The American missionary pointed out that he, like the rector, had a license to preach, but that if the constable would wait until after the meeting he would talk with him. "The power of God rested upon me, the spirit filled the house, and the people were

124

Wilford Woodruff Prepares for Baptisms at Benbow Farm,
by Richard Murray. Courtesy LDS Church Museum

convinced," Elder Woodruff later recalled. When the meeting was over, seven people asked for baptism, including, ironically, the constable and four preachers. After being immersed in the newly prepared pond, these seven, along with the six previously baptized, were all confirmed members of the Church. Wilford Woodruff administered the sacrament of the Lord's supper, and the rest of the evening was spent rejoicing. "I praise God for his goodness in opening my way,"[36] he wrote in his journal that night.

The parish rector, however, was not through with Elder Woodruff. He sent two people to listen to his next sermon, but they, too, were "pricked in their hearts," believed what they heard, and were baptized. Understandably alarmed, the rector stopped sending people to hear the Mormon preacher. Several months later ministers in the area petitioned the Archbishop of Canterbury to request of Parliament a law prohibiting the Mormons from preaching for, they said, in seven months they had baptized

---

[36]Cowley, *Wilford Woodruff,* 118; Woodruff, *Journal,* March 8, 1840, 1:424.

fifteen hundred people. The archbishop and his council rejected the request, and, according to Wilford Woodruff, even chided the ministers by telling them that "if they had the worth of souls at heart as much as they valued ground where hares, foxes, and hounds ran, they would not lose so many of their flock."[37]

One March 11, a very pleased William Benbow left for home,[38] after two weeks that had demonstrated some important elements of successful missionary work. William had fulfilled an obligation as a Church member by being concerned for his family and leading Elder Woodruff to a people primed for baptism. Wilford, at the same time, had listened to William, prayed for guidance, and followed the dictates of divine inspiration. The result was the beginning of a most dramatic harvest in LDS missionary history.

Wilford Woodruff continued to preach daily and to baptize almost as often. By the time he left for the mid-April conference in Preston, he had baptized 158 people, including forty-eight United Brethren preachers, a clerk of the Church of England, a constable, and "a number of wealthy farmers." In addition, another two hundred people were ready to be baptized. These converts brought with them forty-two places already legally licensed for preaching, including one chapel. "This," Woodruff wrote with enthusiasm as well as thanksgiving, "has opened the largest field for labour & increase of numbers of any door that has been opened in the same length of time since the Church of Jesus Christ of Latter Day Saints has been esstablished. . . . I feel thankful to God for all his mercy & kindness unto me & all the Saints in opening so many doors that the kingdom of God may roll forth that there may be a people prepared for the coming of Jesus Christ."[39]

Especially important among the newly baptized converts was Thomas Kington, superintendent of the United Brethren organization, who, with his wife, Hannah, was baptized on March 21. Ordained to the office of elder the following day, this effective leader was called within three months to preside over the Gadfield Elm Conference, which consisted of twelve

---

[37]Ibid., 118–19.

[38]Wilford Woodruff, however, referred to this in his journal as a dark and sorrowful day for both of them, evidently because they enjoyed each other's company so much they hated to part.

[39]Woodruff, *Journal*, April 16, 1840, 1:440. The statistics given here differ slightly from those in Cowley, *Wilford Woodruff*, 119, where he says that he had baptized forty-five preachers and 160 members of the United Brethren and had obtained one chapel and forty-five houses. Also, in the journal entry, he says forty-eight preachers in one place but forty-six in the next paragraph.

UNITED BRETHREN PREACHERS' PLAN
OF THE FROOMS HILL CIRCUIT, 1840.

BEST OF ALL, GOD IS WITH US.

But the Lord said unto me, Say not, I am a child: for thou shalt go to all I shall send thee, and whatsoever I command thee thou shalt speak. Be not afraid of their faces: for I am with thee to deliver thee.—JEREMIAH i. 7, 8.

PREACHERS' NAMES.

1 J Gailey
2 C. Price
3 T. Clark
4 J. James
5 M. Rowberry
6 J. Parry
7 J. Morgan
8 J. Pullin
9 J. Hill
10 A. Perkins
11 W. Jenkins
12 P. Holt
13 M. Possons
14 S. Badham
15 T. Jones
16 W. Possons
17 E. Lambert
18 J. Burns
19 J. Meeks
20 M. Jenkins
21 M. Halard
22 M. Powell
23 G. Davies
24 J. Gailey
25 M. Preece
26 T. Jenkins
27 M. Badham
28 J. Lucy
29 A. Graves
30 P. Green
31 M. Wall
32 J. Pullin
33 E. Phillips
34 S. Tomkins
35 J. Green

ON TRIAL.

36 J. Powell
37 T. H.
38 W. W.
39 ‡

LORD'S DAY PLAN.

PLACES AND TIME.		APRIL 12	19	26	MAY 3	10	17	24	31	JUNE 7	14	21	28	JULY 5
Frooms Hill	10	3 s	9	20	38	‡ P	1 c	11	18	6	5	4	30	16
Hill	2	3	9	20	38 P	2 c	1 r	11	18	6	6	7	36	5
M Stanley Hill ...... 10 and	6	1 P	3 c	5	9	20	34	23	38	33	11	6	4	7
Ridgeway Cross	10	10	24 P	12 c	3 s	38	13 P	1 r	28	22	14	19	6	2
M Greenyeal	2	10	31	12 P	3 c	38	20	1	28	13	14	19	6	2
M Moorend Cross	6	8	13	26	12	3 s	28	26	33	17	21	15	19	14
Colwall	10	15 P	8 c	21	24	12	3 s	20	32	28	33	2	38	1
M Pale House	2	15	8	21	31 P	12 c	3	20	32	28	33	2	38	1
M Ledbury ...... 2 and	6	16 P	15 c	8	26	21	9	3 s	25	2	22	17	23	24-31
M Malvern Hill	6	19	16	15	28	8 P	21 c	12	3 s	38	1	26	18	17
Keysend Street •s	10	18	21 P	1 c	15	16	8	2	12	3 s	32	38	28	6
M Wind Point	2	18	21 P	1 c	15	16	8	2	12	3	32	38	28	6
M Woferwood	2	4	10	19	27	26	16 P	33 c	19	20	12	10	34	15
M Hope Rough	2	7	14	10	30-36r	5 c	24	16	34	26	29-35	37	27	
Rough Leasowe •	2	22	4	33	14 P	18 c	33	27	1	16	20	12	‡	3
Dunns Close	2	22 P	7 c	33	14	18	33	27	1	16	20	12	‡	3 s
M Ashfield	6	6	22 P	4 c	19	10	14	15	21	‡	3 s	16	20	12
Crowcutt	2	6	22 P	7 c	19	10	14	15	21	‡	3	16	20	12
Old Starridge	10	28 P	1 c	6	22	4	19	18	10	14	27	21	16	20
M Birchwood	2	28	1 P	6 c	22	7	19	18	10	14	27	21	16	20
M Alfrick	2	12	15	28	33 P	6 c	22	19	26	17	7	14	1	33
M Shucknell Hill •s	10	17	2	29 P	1 c	23	4	24	8	35	30	32	3 s	26
M Lugwardine	2	17	2	29	1	23	4	24	8	35	37	32	3	60
M Marden	10	23	31	20	2	35 P	6 c	7	30	24	8	34	36	37
M Stokes Lane •s ... 10 and	6	30-36	23	34	6	32 P	6 c	8 c	4	1	24-31	4	8	37
M Ashperton	6	2	30	23	34	17	32 P	37 c	6	7	9	1	34	8
Mission	2	2	36	23	34	17	32	37	6	4	9	1	31	8

WEEK DAY PLAN.

PLACES AND NIGHTS.		APRIL 13	20	27	MAY 4	11	18	25	JUNE 1	8	15	22	29	JU. 6
Frooms Hill ......M.		1 P		1 r		1 L		1		1		1		1
Ledbury ....T.		1 P		1 r		1		1		1		1		1
Lugwardine ......W.		1 P		1 r		1		1 L		1		1		1
Marden ....Th.		1 P		1 r		1		1		1 L		1		1
Shucknell ....F.		1 P		1 r		1		1		1		1 L		1
Ashfield ....M.			1 P			1 r		1 L			1			1	
Crowcutt ....T.			1			1 L			1		1				1
Tenbridge ....T.			1			1 r			1		1				1
Duffsclose ....W.			1						1					1	
Birchwood ....W.		1 P			1 r		1		1 L			1			1
Colwall ....Th.		1 P		1 r		1		1		1 L		1		1
Malvern Hill .....F.		1 P		1 r		1		1		1		1 L		1
Stanley Hill ....M.		PM		PM		PM		PM		PM		PM		PM
Hope Rough ....T.		PM		PM		PM		PM		PM		PM		PM
Green Yeal ....W.		PM		PM		PM		PM		PM		PM		PM
Old Starridge ...Th.		PM		PM		PM		PM		PM		PM		PM
Moorend Cross ...F.		PM		PM		PM		PM		PM		PM		PM

COMMITTEE—J. Benbow, J. James, J. Hill, J. Parry, T. Clark, J. Morgan, A. Perkins, P. Holt, T. Jenkins, W. Possons.—To meet at the Hill, or wheresoever the Elders may appoint, the First Wednesday in each Month.

QUARTER DAY June 1st, at KEYSEND STREET, to commence at 9 o'clock, M.

REFERENCES—L. *Stanley Hill*; P. Publish, T. T ets, C. Collection, S. Sacrament, M. Preachers to me t the Classes.

Every Preacher who loves the Lord and souls, will be punctual to attend his or her appointments, or get them supplied by one that do love the Lord.

BRANGREEN AND GADFIELD ELM BRANCH OF THE FROOMS HILL CIRCUIT.

PLACES AND TIME.		12	19	26	3	10	17	24	31	7	14	21	28	5
M Bran Green	10	1	6	13 P	4 P	2 c		17	8	18	3	10	15	2
Haw Cross	2	1 s	6	13	4 P	2 c		17	8	18	3	10	16	2
M Ryton	10	2		5 P		15		1	6		18	3		3
	2		1 s		13 c			17		8		2		
M Red Marley	6	2	1	5	13	38	‡ c	6	8	18	2	3		
M Gadfields Elm ... 10 and	2	10	7 c	1 s	6	3		2	13	14	3	9		15-16
M Lime Street .... 10 and	6	3 P	10 c	8	1 s	9		2	14	8	13	9	18	6
✠ M Windbrook	2	6	13 P	15-16c	18	6		13	9	2	7	13	14	
M Drmock	3	8 P	3 c	17	32	1 s		2	6	‡	M	18	13	10
M Deerhurst	6	13	14	9 P	10 c	5	15	3	18	12	2	17	1	18
M Apperly	2	13	14	9	10	5	16 P	3 c	18	12	2	17	1	18
M Norton	2	15	12	18 P	2 c	14	9	7	10	6	16	5		8
Leigh	6	16	12 P	18 c	2	14	9	1	7	10	6	15	5	8
M Twigworth ...... 2 and	6	17	2	7	18 P	3 c	10	16-15	3	1 s	2	8	13	
M Killcott	10	8	3	17	32 P	1 c	2	6	‡	M	18	13	10	9
M Ashleyworth Missions	2	9	2	3	8 P	10 c	13	14	5	16-15	9	1	17	10

BRANCH COMMITTEE—Wm. Coleman T. Oakey, D. Browett, J. Hill, T. Brookes.
QUARTER DAY at *Apperly*, May 5th, to commence at 10, M.

PLACES AND TIME.		13	20	27	4	11	18	25	1	8	15	22	29	6
Killcott ....M.		2 P		1 r		2			2		1		2	
Brangreen ....T.		2 P		1 r		2			2		1		2	
Windbrook ....W.		2 P		1 r		2			2		1		2	
Keysend Street ...Th.		2 P		1 r		2		1 L		2		1		2
Dymock ....F.		2 P		1 r		2		1 L		2		1		2
Lime Street ......M.			2 P		1 r		2		13		2		1 L	
Apperly ....T.			2 P		1 r		2 L		12		2		1	
Leigh ....W.			2 P		1 r		2		17		2		1	
Haw Cross ....Th.			2 P		1		2		18		2 L		1	
Killcott ....F.			2 P		1		2			2		1		
Deerhurst ....M.		1 P		2 r		1 L			2		1		2	
Mission ....T.		1 P		2 r		1			2		1		2	
Norton ....W.		1 P		2 r		1			2		1		2	
Twigworth ....Th.		1 P		2 r		1 r		2 L		1		2		
Gadfields Elm ...•.		1 P		2 r		1		2		1		2		
Mission ....M.			1		2		1		2		1		2	
Mission ....T.			1		2		1		2		1		2	
Mission ....W.			1		2		1		2		1		2	
Mission ....Th.			1		2		1		2		1		2	
Mission ....F.			1		2		1		2		1		2	

Preachers' Names.

1 T. Kington
2 E. Arkell
3 W. Jenkins.
4 W. Coleman
5 A. Oakey
6 T. Oakey
7 E. Jenkins
8 D. Browett
9 C. Hayes
10 J. Hill
11
12 E. Browett
13 J. Spires. T. B.

ON TRIAL.

15 A. Robings
16 W. B.
17 H. P.
18 J. P.

14 J. Vernam
16 W. B.
17 H. P.
18 J. P.

HYMN.

As I gladly bid adieu
To the world's fanci'd pleasures,
You pity my weakness;
But, ah! did you know
The joys of religion,
That best hidden treasure;
Would you have me forsake them,
Ah never! ah no!

You ought to rejoice
When I say, I've received
The only true pleasures
Attained below;
I know by experience
In whom I've believed;
Shall I give up my treasure,
Ah never! ah no!

I the gay scenes of life,
I was happiness wooing;
But, ah! in her stead,
I encountered a woe:
I found I was only
A phantom persuing;
Never once did I find her,
Ah never! ah no!

But in the bright paths,
Which you call melancholy,
I've found the delight
The world does not know:
And did you partake them,
You'd then see your folly,
Nor, again, bid me slight them,
Ah never! ah no!

F. AND A. MERRICK, PRINTERS, HIGH STREET, HEREFORD.

branches.[40] "Glory Hallaluyah the work of God rolls on," Wilford Woodruff wrote in his journal the day Kington was baptized, and little wonder. With Benbow, Kington, and fifteen other preachers already in the Church, the harvest in Herefordshire could hardly fail to continue.

Wilford Woodruff received another unexpected boon with the conversion of Kington and other United Brethren preachers. They gave him their Preacher's Plan, a printed schedule of meetings to be held during the next three months for all their congregations in Herefordshire, Glousershire, and Worcestershire. With all the baptisms, most of the names on the March 1840 plan could simply be left in place and the converted preachers could be sent out to preach as Latter-day Saints to the same congregations.

Woodruff's success and the potential that lay ahead so overwhelmed him that he pleaded with Willard Richards to leave his wife, Jennetta, with friends so that he could come and help. "I cannot do the work alone," he wrote on March 31. "I am called to Baptize 4 or 5 times a day. I want no better man than yourself to council and labor with me here & help me reep this mighty harvest."[41] Three days later he wrote again, still pleading with him to come to Herefordshire. "Their is no field at present in England, where your labour & council is more needed or would be of more benefit than to join me in this field a season."

Success itself presented problems, including the possibility that the recently converted preachers would soon find the doors of their former congregations closed to Mormon preaching. Woodruff told them to continue to meet their appointments and prepare the people for the gospel but not to administer any gospel ordinances until he could get some help in organizing the Church and ordaining "such persons as God shall call." "It has put me at times to my wits end," he explained to Willard Richards, "to know what to do with so many places of preaching & preachers." Then he added, in wistful frustration, "I wonder why the Twelve do not come from America."[42]

Anglican ministers warned their congregations against Wilford Woodruff and his followers. Other people also were wrought up, including rowdies who did what they could to stop the continuing baptisms. On Sunday, April 5, for example, Wilford Woodruff obtained permission from

---

[40]Woodruff, *Journal*, March 21, 22, and June 14, 1840, 1:426–27, 457–60.

[41]Wilford Woodruff to Willard Richards, March 31, 1840, Willard Richards Collection.

[42]Wilford Woodruff to Willard Richards, April 3, 1840, Willard Richards Collection.

Daniel Browetts, a member of the Church, to use his pool in the village of Leigh to baptize ten people. But, as the preparatory services came to a close, a mob of about one hundred people gathered, and the owner, fearing what might happen to his property, withdrew permission. "You American whare are you going to wash your sheep?" the rowdies jeered as they followed the missionary while he searched for another place. Late in the afternoon, the crowd finally dispersed, Browetts renewed his permission, and Woodruff began the baptisms. The mob showed up again, but amid the jeers he was able to baptize nine with no injury except, perhaps, to the pride of a dog thrown into the pool.[43] Four days later a similar mob broke up a preaching service, preventing several people from being baptized. Some wanted baptism so badly that they waited until midnight, but when they went back to the pool, the troublemakers were still there. Nevertheless, Woodruff went into the water and baptized five people while the mob showered them with stones. One stone hit him on the top of the head, nearly knocking him under the water. Concentrating on the work at hand was difficult, to say the least, but, wrote the apostle, "the Lord saved me from falling & I continued untill I had closed my Baptizing & my mind was stayed on God."[44]

That same day, April 9, Wilford Woodruff received the news he had been waiting for since January: the five other apostles had arrived in England and a conference had been called for the fifteenth in Preston. The next afternoon he spent several hours with John Benbow, and then, with two pounds in his pocket—Benbow's gift to take care of his expenses to and from the conference—he set out for Preston.

On the way he stopped in Staffordshire to visit the Saints and Elder Turley, who had been jailed on March 16. Seventeen years earlier Turley had emigrated to Canada, but he allegedly still owed money in England that, because of financial misdealings by his business partner, he simply could not pay. John Jones claimed to be one of Turley's long-standing creditors, but he was also a bitter enemy of the Church, and it was Jones who swore out the warrant that landed Turley in jail, where he languished until May 8. All his colleagues believed, and apparently with good cause, that he was in jail unlawfully and that the primary reason for the warrant was to hinder the missionaries.[45]

---

[43]Woodruff, *Journal*, April 5, 1840, 1:431–32.

[44]Ibid., April 9, 1840, 1:433.

[45]See Turley, "Mission Journal," 40–49, for the story of Turley's time in jail. This excellent reproduction of the Turley journal, edited by Richard E. Turley, Jr., includes some carefully researched notes and excerpts from various diaries that relate to parts of Turley's experience.

With no funds of his own, Turley could hardly have survived in jail without the largess of the local Saints, who provided him with food and other necessities. When Wilford Woodruff was pleading by mail with Willard Richards to come to Herefordshire, he also asked him to help collect what funds he could from Preston, Manchester, and the Potteries and deliver them to Elder Turley.[46] Woodruff also took him some provisions when he stopped by on April 11. He visited for an hour and then traveled on, arriving in Preston on the night of April 13 for what he termed a "happy interview" with some of the Twelve.

WILLARD RICHARDS: THREE MONTHS OF TRIAL AND PREPARATION

The first quarter of 1840 was a time of heavy trial for Willard Richards, the thirty-five-year-old counselor in the British Mission presidency. First, he was assigned at the January council to correspond regularly with all the brethren laboring as missionaries in both England and Scotland. That alone took a substantial amount of time. In addition, he had the affairs of the branch in Preston to deal with, including a number of heart-wrenching problems among the Saints and the need, at times, to conduct Church disciplinary action. He further kept himself busy visiting Church members in Preston and surrounding towns, preaching and setting the affairs of the Church in order. He also had his own financial problems, his father-in-law still rejected him, and the frail Jennetta, pregnant with their second son, was almost constantly ill. These three months were a time of testing for the man who would soon be ordained to the apostleship.

One particularly difficult challenge came his way on February 21, when he made his first visit to the town of Burnley. There he discovered some unfortunate difficulties among the members so serious that they had held no meetings for several weeks. On Sunday, February 23, he called them together, somehow settled their problems, and got them to promise they would henceforth hold and attend their meetings. Then, after preaching a sermon, he returned to Preston.[47]

Richards corresponded regularly with the missionaries in Great Britain, giving them both comfort and advice. On April 6, for example, Elder Alexander Wright reported on the work in Scotland, and he thanked Rich-

---

[46]Wilford Woodruff to Willard Richards, March 31, 1840, and April 3, 1840. Richards noted on April 5 that he received a letter from Woodruff "desiring me to come down to Hereford immediately. & call for collections for bro Turley." Richards, Diary, expanded version, April 5, 1840.

[47]Richards, Diary, February 21–23, 1840.

ards for the "fatherly advice" that helped remove the "downcast" feelings of his companion, Samuel Mulliner. Wright and Mulliner, converts from Canada, were the first two Mormon missionaries in Scotland, having arrived in Glasgow on December 20, 1839. By the end of March, they had baptized only ten people[48] and were discouraged. "We feil our selves but children," Wright wrote to Richards, "and feil the need of some of our fathers to be with us yet we have no need to complain for our hevenly father is with us and through our meek instrumentality the work is moving on in this place." He reported on their latest baptism and indicated that he hoped to baptize two preachers from Paisley—a Baptist and a Methodist—both of whom had stopped preaching and were coming to Mormon meetings. "The wheel is now started in Scotland and t[h]rough the prayers and asistance of our brethren and the lord being our helpers we are determened to keep it roling."[49] Such letters must have returned comfort to Elder Richards.

Though he spent precious little time with her, Richards's deepest concern was always with Jennetta. Her father still did not accept him, but the relationship seemed to improve a little and he was received somewhat kindly when he visited Walkerfold on February 17.[50] Jennetta's pregnancy was hard on her naturally frail body, and her continual illness was a constant worry to her husband. All her hardships affected her feelings, too, and at times they caused her faith to waver, which also worried Willard. On March 12 she received a blessing through the laying on of hands and, Willard gratefully noted in his journal, "her faith began to revive." Her sickness continued, however, and finally, on March 15, she left Preston with her sister to go to her father's place in Walkerfold. Willard hoped that this would lead to an improvement of her health and also, as he put it, "that she might be released from the grasp of the power of evil which had long been striving to overcome her & me."[51]

During the next two weeks Jennetta kept in touch with her husband by mail. On April 7, and again the following day, he stopped at Walkerfold to visit her. Exhausted when he arrived on April 8, he was delighted when, for the first time since their marriage, Jennetta's father invited him to spend the night. The weary missionary gratefully accepted. He was also grateful

48Buchanan, "Church in Scotland," 10.
49Alexander Wright to Willard Richards, April 6, 1840, Willard Richards Collection.
50Richards, Diary (expanded), February 17, 1840.
51Richards, Diary, March 25, 1840.

for another blessing that day: the brethren of the Church had given him money to buy some clothes.[52]

The following day, refreshed after his stay at Walkerfold, Willard returned to a stunning surprise in Preston. As he walked into his room about 4:00 P.M., he found waiting for him none other than his old friends and mentors, Brigham Young and Heber C. Kimball. The rest of the apostles had arrived from America on April 6, 1840, and were ready to take up the work as a quorum. Five days later Willard would be counted among their number.

---

[52]Ibid., April 8, 1840.

Chapter 7

"OF ONE HEART AND ONE MIND": APRIL THROUGH JULY 1840

Even before Elders Brigham Young, Heber C. Kimball, George A. Smith, and Parley and Orson Pratt heard of Wilford Woodruff's amazing harvest in Herefordshire, possibilities for their own success seemed limitless. Parley P. Pratt was convinced that the work would keep him there for years: "Here is a boundless harvest for the next 15 or 20 years," he wrote to Mary Ann the day he landed in Liverpool, "and here if the Lord will I expect to spend five or ten years at least." But he could not be apart from his family that long, and "time . . . is to precious, money to scarce, and comfort to dear, to be thrown away in crossing the ocean every few months." He told her, therefore, to sell everything except their clothes and bedding, fill two chests and a trunk, and come to England at the first opportunity.[1]

On their first day in England George A. Smith and Heber C. Kimball walked through a Liverpool marketplace filled with numerous varieties of fruits and vegetables from many parts of the world. George A. had never seen anything like it, and Heber offered to buy him whatever he wanted. "No accounting for taste," George A. later noted, for he chose a large onion, which he ate "with a craving appetite" and "shed many tears over it." The apostles also celebrated their arrival by each purchasing a new black hat.[2]

The other apostles did not expect to remain in England as long as Parley did, but they were equally enthusiastic about the prospects of their

---

[1]Parley P. Pratt to Mary Ann Pratt, April 6, 1840, Parley P. Pratt Collection (Appendix B, Document 9). Pratt had left his wife in charge of his book business to collect all the current debts, sell as many books as she could, and then leave the business in charge of a friend who, Pratt promised, would be given a good percentage of the profits for his trouble.

[2]Smith, Journal, April 6, 1840.

mission. That evening they held a prayer meeting in which they partook of the sacrament, thanked God for his protection on the high seas, gave each other blessings, and prayed "that our way might be opened before us to accomplish our missions successfully."[3]

The next day the new arrivals had a happy reunion with John Taylor, and the following day, April 8, 1840, they went by rail to Preston, where they planned to hold an all-important conference. Aware that they were coming, the Saints turned out in force to meet them. They were especially anxious to greet Heber C. Kimball, to whom they had grown close two years earlier. As the train pulled in at the Penwortham station, across the River Ribble from Preston, he put his head out the window and waved his hat. The delighted crowd raised a red flag announcing his arrival, and it was an emotional, affectionate reunion for all of them.[4]

On Sunday, April 12, they preached in Preston's Temperance Hall, often still called the Cock Pit, to some seven hundred people who had come as far as sixty miles to hear them. They "bore testimony to the work, and spoke with power, for the Lord was with them."[5] The following day Wilford Woodruff arrived from Herefordshire.

APRIL CONFERENCE

On Tuesday, April 14, all the apostles were in Preston, and the Quorum of the Twelve held its first official council meeting in England. The first order of business was to ordain Willard Richards to the apostleship and receive him into the Quorum. Coming on the heels of so many personal and family problems, the weight of his new responsibilities pierced Willard's soul deeply. "O my God," he prayed, "I ask Thee to enable me to execute the duties of this office in righteousness even unto the end, with my Brethren the Twelve, that we may even be of one heart and one mind in all things to be formed of thee in thy kingdom, in the name of Jesus Christ, Amen."[6] At the same meeting, the apostles formally sustained Brigham Young as their president. They also agreed to send to America for at least twenty additional missionaries.

---

[3]Young, *Manuscript History*, 69; Smith, Journal, April 6, 1840.

[4]Heber C. Kimball to Vilate Kimball, May 2, 1840, Heber C. Kimball Collection. In this letter Kimball indicates that the date was April 9, but the journals of George A. Smith and Brigham Young both make it clear that it was on Wednesday, April 8, that they all went to Preston by rail.

[5]Heber C. Kimball and Joseph Fielding to the Editors, May 6, 1840, *Times and Seasons* 1 (July 1840): 138–39.

[6]Richards, Diary (expanded), April 14, 1840.

The next day was devoted to a general conference of the Church, held in the Temperance Hall. The apostles chose Hiram Clark to replace Willard Richards in the mission presidency, made some important decisions with regard to forthcoming Church publications in Britain, performed various priesthood ordinations, and agreed to choose and ordain a patriarch "to bestow patriarchal Blessings on the fatherless."[7] On April 16, in a private quorum meeting, they selected Peter Melling, a native of Preston, to be the patriarch, made more decisions regarding Church publications, and discussed in some detail the all-important subject of emigration.

At the end of the conference, Brigham Young sent a copy of the minutes to Joseph Smith. "If you see anything in or about the whole affair that is not right," he wrote, "I ask, in the name of the Lord Jesus Christ, that you would make known unto us the mind of the Lord and his will concerning us."[8] He had little need to worry, however. Sometime after the Prophet received the report, he told Mary Ann Young that he approved of all they were doing. "J. Smith said he received nothing in [the] letter you had written that he disapproved of. But he wanted you to *go ahead, he gloried in your resolutions to go ahead.*"[9]

ANNOUNCING THE GATHERING

One matter of far-reaching consequence, both for the Saints in Europe and for the destiny of the Church in America, was the gathering to Zion. Creating a desire to emigrate was not difficult, for many Saints were suffering the same economic privations that had already persuaded tens of thousands of other Britons to migrate. Even more important to them, however, were the spiritual attractions of Nauvoo, Illinois. America, after all, was identified by revelation as the land of Zion, where the New Jerusalem would be built, and from where Christ himself would soon conduct his millennial reign. In addition, the Prophet was there, and under his direction the Saints were building a new city in the American West. The British converts could think of nothing more desirable than joining with them.

---

[7]Woodruff, *Journal*, April 15, 1840, 1:435–38.

[8]Young, *Manuscript History*, 71.

[9]As cited in Willard Richards to Brigham Young, August 22, 1840, Brigham Young Papers. Brigham was in Preston when the letter arrived in Manchester. Willard Richards decided not to send it on and chance losing it in the mails, for Brigham was returning to Manchester soon anyway. He opened it, however, reported that it was a "very affectionate letter," and quoted this much. Mary Ann had begun the letter in April but did not get it finished or mailed until July 10.

The British Mission presidency understood all this, but they were reluctant to allow emigration without authorization from the Twelve. Joseph Fielding feared that approving even one request could touch off a rash of hasty and premature efforts to leave. Equally important in Fielding's mind was the need to maintain a strong presence in Britain, rather than decimating the Church population through emigration just when the apostles were arriving to build it up. In March 1840, for example, Francis Moon, who had been in the Church approximately two years, wrote to Fielding asking for his consent to emigrate. The mission president reminded Moon of the sacrifices the American missionaries, including the apostles, were making to preach the gospel in England and asked if the Saints should run away and leave them to bear the burden and heat of the day themselves. "No! No!" he exclaimed. The field was widening, laborers were wanted, and now that they had reinforcements from America, surely it was no time to quit the work.[10] As he explained in a letter to Willard Richards, until clearly instructed otherwise "*I will not be responsible for any thing that is or may be done about it.* If any go they will not Say that Brother or President Fielding gave his Sanction to it."[11]

Technically, of course, no one needed permission to emigrate, but the British Saints recognized the Quorum of the Twelve Apostles as their divinely appointed leaders and looked to them for guidance. Thus it was that emigration became one of the first items of business in their April 16 meeting. No doubt aware of the difficulty of stemming the eager tide, they decided that the Saints who were ready could leave, though they should do it with as little public notice as possible.[12] In addition, they established the policy that those who wished to go should first receive recommends to the Church in America, and no one with means should leave without also assisting the poor. Two days later, at Preston, Parley P. Pratt gave what was probably the first general discussion of the gathering to a group of Saints. He talked for about an hour, telling them about America, how they should act there, and of the need for those who had means to help those who did not. Joseph Fielding could not have been more pleased with the policy once it was announced.

This, then, was the official beginning of Mormon emigration, and in

---

[10]Fielding, Diary, 65.

[11]Joseph Fielding to Willard Richards, March 25, 1840, Joseph Fielding Collection.

[12]This decision is not noted in the minutes but it is noted in Fielding, Diary, 71.

June, John Moon led the first organized group to the New World.[13] In August the First Presidency of the Church issued a general address inviting all Saints everywhere to participate in the gathering,[14] but the decision of the apostles in April first opened the door to what eventually became a torrent of migration.

THE GATHERERS SCATTER

On April 17, Good Friday, the apostles spent one more day together before scattering to their assignments. This time they met at the home of Alice Moon, in Penwortham, who was so thrilled that she produced a bottle of wine she had kept for forty years. She had first planned to serve it on her wedding day, she explained, but in the rush of things it was forgotten, just as it was on several subsequent special occasions. There must have been "something providential in its preservation," she said, for now she had the privilege of presenting it to the members of the Quorum of the Twelve. The apostles blessed and and drank it,[15] and then spent the day discussing the affairs of the kingdom. In the evening they met again in the Moon home and ordained Peter Melling to the office of patriarch.

The next day the apostles separated for their various assignments: Heber C. Kimball to visit the branches he had founded in 1837–38, Orson Pratt to proselyte in Scotland, John Taylor to continue his work in Liverpool, Parley P. Pratt to begin work on publications in Manchester, George A. Smith to preach in the Staffordshire Potteries, and Brigham Young and Willard Richards to join Wilford Woodruff in Herefordshire. Their next official quorum meeting would be in Manchester in July.

Already the British mission was having a marked effect upon the Twelve as a quorum. In England, their assignment required them to work more closely as a unit than they had ever done before. In these first few days together in April, 1840, they not only made decisions that would affect the future of the Church but also began the process that would mold them into a smoothly working administrative unit. They felt themselves growing in unity and confidence almost daily, as Heber C. Kimball explained to his wife in May: "Thare never was beter feelings among the twelve then at

---

[13]For an account of the Moon emigration, see Allen, " 'We Had a Very Hard Voyage,' " 339–41.

[14]*Times and Seasons* 1 (October 1840): 177–79. See also Smith, *History of the Church* 4:185–86. In the *History of the Church* the letter appears under the date of August 31, 1840, whereas the *Times and Seasons* dates it "Sept. 1840." We have followed the dating in the *History of the Church.*

[15]Young, *Manuscript History*, 71–72.

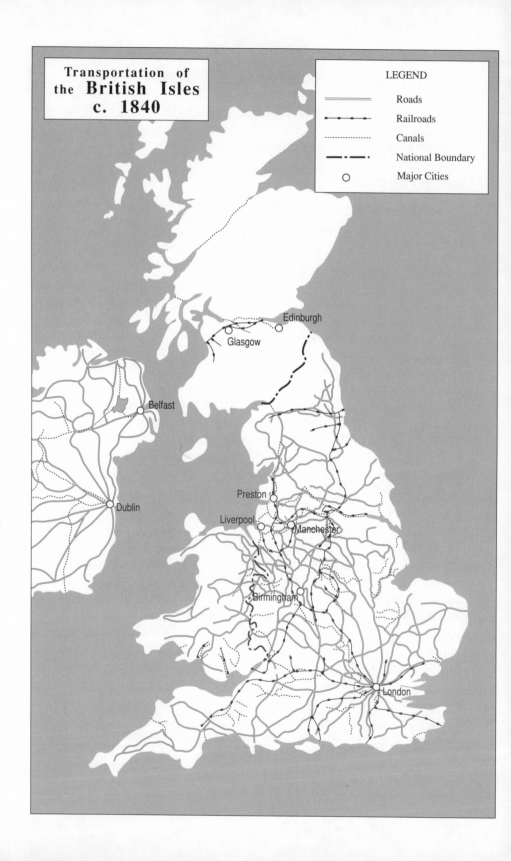

Transportation of
the **British Isles**
c. 1840

LEGEND

Roads

Railroads

Canals

National Boundary

○ Major Cities

Edinburgh
Glasgow
Belfast
Dublin
Preston
Liverpool
Manchester
Birmingham
London

this time. All things go on well. We are some what feeble as yet. We are increasing in strength fast."[16]

As the Twelve prepared to go their various ways, most needed means for travel and necessities. On Sunday, April 19, at the urging of Willard Richards, Joseph Fielding made a special appeal during a meeting at the Cock Pit. After the regular collection was taken up, Fielding stood and reminded the Saints that the brethren were going on long journeys, and if anyone had anything more to contribute to their expenses, please give it to the deacons. Those who were able contributed again, and, said Fielding, "I think Preston is honored by sending out the Servants of God to all Parts, though it be at some little Expense." All the apostles were supplied with means, and funds were raised also to help Elder Theodore Turley, who was still in jail. As it turned out, however, Turley had received help from other sources, and so that money, too, was given to the Twelve.[17]

Willard Richards had a most difficult time leaving Preston, for Jennetta was still suffering from illness and pain. On Sunday, April 19, he asked Heber C. Kimball to join him in giving her a blessing. Her pain subsided, but she remained ill. The next day Willard anointed her with consecrated oil, also with spirits and myrrh; Heber sealed the anointing and gave her a blessing. The next morning she was better than she had been for years. "Praise the Lord, O my soul, for Thou hast wrought wonders in my home," the grateful apostle exclaimed.[18] Jennetta's ordeal was not over, but Willard could put off fulfilling his assignment no longer, and by the weekend he was on his way to Herefordshire. He arrived penniless at a Sister Pullen's home in Ledbury on the evening of April 29.[19] The next day he went on to Thomas Kington's home in Dymock, where he was joined by Brigham Young and Wilford Woodruff, who had left Preston several days earlier.[20]

HEBER C. KIMBALL

Heber C. Kimball could not have been more pleased with his assignment to build up the branches he had established in 1837–38, and he spent

---

[16]Heber C. Kimball to Vilate Kimball, May 27, 1840, Heber C. Kimball Collection.

[17]Fielding, Diary, 71–72.

[18]Richards, Diary (expanded), April 20, 1840.

[19]Richards, Diary (expanded), implies that he arrived at 8:00 the following morning, but the smaller holograph diary indicates that he arrived at 8:00 in the evening. Because of the distances involved, the latter seems correct, and we assume that whoever prepared the expanded diary simply made an error.

[20]Again, there is some discrepancy in the record. Richards, Diary, May 1, 1840, leaves the impression that Young and Woodruff did not arrive until the evening of May 1, but Woodruff, *Journal*, April 30, 1840, 1:444, indicates that they were there on the night of April 30. We suspect, however, that Richards actually meant to say that they arrived the evening before.

Heber C. Kimball
© LDS Church

most of the next three months doing just that. Following the pattern of his earlier mission, he worked out of Preston, preaching and baptizing there and in such nearby communities as Chatburn, Downham, Clitheroe, Waddington, Ribchester, Longton, Southport, and Churchtown, frequently accompanied by Joseph Fielding.[21] The two got along famously, and Fielding wrote an account of their mission together for the *Star*.[22] They often baptized several people each day, and after the first two weeks Heber was convinced that their preaching was causing a great stir among both the people and the ministers.[23]

Depending upon the Saints for his livelihood, however, was emotionally draining, and Heber cried inwardly at the poverty he saw among his

---

[21]Whitney, *Life of Heber C. Kimball*, 280–83; Fielding, Diary, 72–76; Heber C. Kimball to the Editor, June 6, 1840, *Millennial Star* 1 (June 1840): 37–40; Heber C. Kimball to Vilate Kimball, May 27, 1840.

[22]Heber C. Kimball to the Editor, *Millennial Star* 1 (June 1840): 37–40; Fielding, Diary, 76. It is only from Fielding's journal entry dated June 7 that we learn who actually composed this letter.

[23]Heber C. Kimball to Vilate Kimball, May 2, 1840.

friends. His heart melted when those who treated him so well on his first mission felt hurt because now they could not even feed him.[24]

He also continued to show concern for Jennetta Richards, whose illness lingered and whose father was still angry with the Mormons. When Heber visited the family at Walkerfold on May 1, the Reverend Mr. Richards ordered him out of the house, and as he walked down the road he could hear Jennetta and her mother crying.[25] According to Jennetta, her mother was so distraught that she was "not right" for several days. Her father, however, was also ill, and the gentle Jennetta blamed his outburst on that as well as on the fact that he could not hear well and therefore probably did not understand much of what Heber said.[26]

Heber and Joseph held meetings everywhere—in public buildings, in private homes, even in barns,[27]—and interest ran high. On Sunday, May 10, at Chatburn, they could not find a house large enough for the crowd, so Heber preached in a barn. Many wanted to be baptized, including some who had joined the Church earlier but had fallen away. Just as in 1837, Heber felt a special spirit in Chatburn. "There appears to be something peculiar in the people of this place," he wrote to the *Millennial Star*. "We have never received any thing like an insult all the time we visited the place, and we feel bound to bless them."[28]

On May 20 Kimball and Fielding received an unusual display of kindness as Robert Roscough accompanied them from Longton to Southport, a resort town on the coast. To get there they either had to ford the River Aston, and thus get wet, or walk several extra miles to find a bridge. They were saved the trouble of doing either, however, when Roscough volunteered to carry them across the river on his shoulders.[29]

At Southport they met people with all sorts of debilitating diseases and handicaps who came to this famous bathing area for relief, but they also noted how pleasant a place it was for the rich and noble. They held a meeting with the small branch of the Church and met a sister who was not expected to live. Through faith she was healed, and the next day she walked two miles with them. Such experiences were commonplace, but

---

[24]Ibid.

[25]Ibid.

[26]Jennetta Richards to Willard Richards, May 15, 1840, Willard Richards Collection.

[27]Fielding, Diary, 73, 74. One barn was in Downham, and another was a Brother Blackhurst's barn in Longton.

[28]Heber C. Kimball to the Editor, *Millennial Star* 1 (June 1840): 37–40; Fielding, Diary, 73–74.

[29]Ibid.; Fielding, Diary, 74.

The River Ribble Valley, from Preston
From Hardwick, *History of the Borough of Preston,* 1857

so were times like those in Churchtown, where the missionaries found that the Saints had too little faith and were having trouble among themselves. "But we hope to preserve a few," Fielding noted. "We were plain with them."[30]

As an apostle, Elder Kimball was responsible to encourage and instruct many newly called Church leaders. A particularly important opportunity came on Monday, May 25, during a meeting at Thomas Moon's home in Penwortham. For the first time in the history of the Church outside America, a group of Saints met to receive patriarchal blessings, and there Peter Melling gave his first blessings. To encourage and support the new patriarch, Elder Kimball stood with him and laid his hands, too, on the heads of Thomas Moon and his wife, Lydia, the first English converts to receive such blessings. Then, in accord with the principle that the father is the patriarch of his family, Thomas Moon gave blessings to his children, as well as to his son-in-law, William Clayton, who had come from Manchester. Melling then blessed Joseph Fielding's wife, Hannah, after which Elder Kimball gave further instruction.[31]

---

[30]Heber C. Kimball to Vilate Kimball, May 27, 1840; Fielding, Diary, 74–75.

[31]Fielding, Diary, 75; Allen and Alexander, *Manchester Mormons,* 156; Heber C. Kimball to the Editor, June 6, 1840.

Downham, 1987. Courtesy Paul Anderson

Heber C. Kimball was also part of the publications committee, and on Wednesday, May 27, he accompanied William Clayton back to Manchester to work on the new hymnal with Brigham Young, John Taylor, and Parley P. Pratt. He spent his nights at the Hardman boarding house, where Clayton lived, and on Friday evening, during a visit by Brigham Young, they all joined in singing and had the experience of speaking in tongues.[32]

While in Manchester, Heber was overwhelmed again with the scope of what they were doing collectively as missionaries. There were around three hundred Saints in this city, and their numbers were growing rapidly. He heard from Brigham of the success in Herefordshire, he learned that there were sixty or seventy members in Scotland, and he thought of his own successes in Preston and vicinity. Oh that the Lord would send more faithful laborers into the field, he lamented, for the wheat was falling to the ground for want of harvesting. The new converts were among the

---

[32]Whitney, *Life of Heber C. Kimball*, 283; Allen and Alexander, *Manchester Mormons*, 157.

choice people of England, he wrote Vilate, and the gathering to Zion would never stop until the salt was drained out of the nations. He also observed that the rich among the Saints loved the poor so well they could not leave them behind. "This is a Celestial Spirrit," he wrote. "I would to God that all the Saints had it."[33]

On June 1 Heber and Brigham organized the first official company of emigrating Saints, and on June 6 they joined John Taylor at the dock in Liverpool to see the beginning of the gathering. That afternoon they blessed and said farewell to the group, under the leadership of John Moon, as the emigrants set sail aboard the ship *Britannia*.[34] It was a momentous symbol of what was to come.

Monday, June 8, was a holiday, Whit Monday, commemorating the day of Pentecost. Joseph Fielding was offended at the way it was celebrated, however, for it appeared to be a day of revelry, vanity, and folly, punctuated by drunkenness, rather than a day of piety. By contrast, the Saints met together in an open-air meeting and then went to the Melling home in Penwortham for an afternoon meeting and for blessings. There Elder Kimball spoke in tongues and baptized two people. "So," noted Fielding at the end of Whit Monday, "we had our Pleasure as well as Babylon."[35]

Heber C. Kimball and Joseph Fielding worked well together, and on June 26 Heber fulfilled an earlier promise to give Joseph a special blessing. It was both tender and powerful, as he promised him success as a missionary, power to heal the sick and the handicapped, and the blessing of bringing kinfolk into the kingdom. Heber also promised him that his wife would share all his blessings and that he would "become a Prophet, a Priest and a King, to administer for ever and ever." Joseph was told, further, that he and his family would soon go to America where, if he were faithful, he would "see the Saints that have been driven restored to their own Lands and their Enemies brought Low." The blessing concluded with a gentle admonition that elegantly reflected the advice Kimball frequently gave: sup-

---

[33]Heber C. Kimball to Vilate Kimball, May 27, 1840.

[34]Heber C. Kimball to the Editor, *Millennial Star* 1 (June 1840): 37–40. Back in Herefordshire, curiously, Willard Richards was not so sure that it was right for Moon to leave. Not fully aware that the company had already gone, he wrote Brigham Young on June 8 of his impression that the Lord wanted Elder Moon to be a missionary in Herefordshire. When Willard finally heard that Moon had left, he wrote: "I am sorry to hear that John Moon has gone to America. He has lost a blessing." Willard Richards to Brigham Young, June 8, 1840, Brigham Young Papers; Willard Richards to Brigham Young, June 15, 1840, Brigham Young Papers (Appendix B, Document 10).

[35]Fielding, Diary, 76.

The packet ship *Britannia*. Courtesy The Mariner's Museum, Newport News, Virginia

port and honor the brethren, resist the temptations of the devil, and you will be blessed. "Hold the Character of thy Brethren sacred . . . and nothing shall be withheld from thee, and thou shalt see greater things than have entered into thy Heart. Satan has tempted thee to be rebellious, but the Spirit of God has said Be still, and thou shalt overcome all evil Propensities and become pure. All these blessings I seal upon thee in the Name of Jesus Christ, Amen and Amen."[36]

In contrast to Heber C. Kimball's ability to give inspiring, tender blessings, his capacity to show righteous indignation was demonstrated two days later while he presided at a conference in Thornley. There he scolded a congregation of about 150 people for shirking their responsibilities as Saints. Shaking his cloak at them, he told them he would preach no more

---

[36]Curiously, no one recorded this blessing at the time, so three weeks later, on July 17, Elder Kimball repeated it while Fielding wrote it down, then laid his hands on Fielding's head again in order to confirm it. Fielding, meanwhile, had left room to insert it in his journal on the correct day. Fielding, Diary, 79, 82.

in that area and declared himself free of their blood. "It affected the Saints much," observed Fielding.[37]

Willard Richards was also at the Thornley conference, for he had returned to the Preston area several days earlier than planned because of the illness of Jennetta. That night he walked back to Preston with Kimball and Fielding, and the next day they went on to Penwortham, where several Saints spent another deeply spiritual evening at the home of Thomas Moon. About fifteen spoke in tongues, others interpreted, and many had the gift of prophecy. The next day the two apostles took the train to Manchester, looking forward to the forthcoming conference with their colleagues.

JOHN TAYLOR STAYS IN LIVERPOOL

John Taylor returned to Liverpool immediately after the April conference to find himself faced with an emotional crisis. There could have been many reasons: seeing the brethren from home, knowing that Parley P. Pratt had already sent for his wife and children, his own overwhelming loneliness after eight months away from his family, and the reception of a long letter written by Leonora on March 12. The letter itself must have created in him feelings of both exhilaration and despondency as he learned not only of what was happening among the Saints but also of Leonora's continuing economic trials, and, most of all, of her longing for him.[38] Perhaps it was a combination of all these things that caused him suddenly to write to Brigham Young on April 19 asking for permission to send for his family. Leonora was in delicate health, he wrote, but she desperately wanted to see her family and friends in England, and they were anxious that she should come. Apparently he felt that they could nurse her back to health, but he also asked Brigham Young to send him the name and address of someone in Albany who might allow her to rest there after the fatiguing trip from Nauvoo. Like Parley P. Pratt, he reasoned that having his wife with him would keep him from frequently leaving England and then returning, and, also like Pratt, he hoped that one of the missionaries for whom Brigham Young was sending would take charge of getting Leonora across the ocean. He was optimistic enough to believe that she could somehow obtain her own financing, so he assured Brigham that bringing

---

[37]Ibid., 80.
[38]See chapter 11 for a summary of this letter.

her would be no burden on the Saints.[39] The records reveal no action on this ardent request, but presumably the practical-minded Brigham Young simply turned it down as gently as he could.

John Taylor's loneliness was partly palliated, however, as he found increased opportunities for preaching the gospel. People listened, baptisms came frequently, and the members were anxious to help spread the word. In May he ordained several priests and elders, who in turn took to the streets, the parks, and the fields proclaiming the message of the Restoration. When opposition increased and antagonists began disturbing their meetings, Taylor simply sent his co-workers out into the major thoroughfares of Liverpool just before preaching meetings, where they announced the time and place that a discourse would be delivered. The result, despite the opposition, was more interest among the people and well-attended meetings.[40]

John Taylor also helped select and arrange the hymns for the new hymnal and read proofs of the Book of Mormon. Since he was not in Manchester, on May 4 he wrote to Willard Richards expressing concern that the final selection not be made without him. Three weeks later he went to Manchester to assist in the work and stayed there four days.[41] For the most part, however, Elder Taylor's time between the April and July conferences was spent preaching and working with the Saints in and around Liverpool.

THREE APOSTLES GO TO HEREFORDSHIRE

Wilford Woodruff was pleased with the assignments made at the conference in Preston, for both Willard Richards and Brigham Young were to work with him in Herefordshire. Wilford and Brigham left Preston on Saturday, April 18, and spent Easter Sunday with the Saints in the Potteries. They arrived in Ledbury on the night of April 21 and the next day went to Froome's Hill, where Wilford introduced the president of the Twelve to John Benbow and Thomas Kington. They attended an important meeting

---

[39]John Taylor to Brigham Young, April 19, 1840, Brigham Young Papers. Note that the letter is actually dated April 19, 1839, but this would have been impossible because Taylor did not arrive in Liverpool until 1840. The only logical year is 1840, but the mere fact that he made such a mistake in dating his letter suggests that John Taylor had a lot of other things on his mind, including his longing for Leonora and the children.

[40]Roberts, *Life of John Taylor*, 83–84.

[41]John Taylor to Willard Richards, May 4, 1841, Willard Richards Papers; Evans, *Century of "Mormonism,"* 133; Bloxham, "Apostolic Foundations," 127.

that day, during which Benbow was ordained to the office of teacher in the Aaronic Priesthood.

The two apostles immediately began to build on Wilford Woodruff's earlier success. On April 26, for example, Wilford baptized ten individuals, including one minister, and Brigham baptized four. On April 30 they were joined by Willard Richards.

Wilford was delighted with the work of his new companions. The hearts of the Saints were "made glad with the teaching and instruction by Elder Young," he later wrote to the *Millennial Star*. "I also obtained much benefit myself by enjoying his society, sitting under his instruction, and sharing in his council."[42] Richards, he observed, "was a great Blessing unto me as well as many Saints for he has passed through a great school of experiance and learned much wisdom & sound Judjment which is readily manifest in all Councils & conferences in which we have set together."[43]

Even as the Church continued to grow in Herefordshire, Brigham was somewhat critical of religious leaders who refused to listen. On one occasion he had an interview with two ministers, one a Baptist and the other a Methodist. They impressed him as "jest like the rest of the Priest[s]. They have jest relegon enough to damb them," but no inclination to inquire after the truth. "This is a wicked place," he opined, "but there is a fue that want to be saved."[44]

Converts poured in, however, and Wilford Woodruff continued to be humbled by it. Given to introspection anyway, he frequently retreated to the heights of the Malvern Hills to meditate and pray. On May 9 he hiked to the top of one of them and was awed at the grand panorama below: Worcester on the north, the village of Gloucester on the south, Ledbury and other villages to the west, and "a fine beautiful cultivated vale upon evry hand." As he stood there exulting in the view, clouds rolled in below him, thunder rumbled, and lightning danced through the clouds beneath his feet. To him it was a wondrous and awe-inspiring scene that provided "a grand survey of the works of nature & the power of God."[45]

---

[42]Wilford Woodruff to the Editor, July 9, 1840, *Millennial Star* 1 (July 1840): 71–72 and (August 1840): 81–84.

[43]Woodruff, *Journal*, June 22, 1840, 1:469–70.

[44]Brigham Young to George A. Smith, May 4, 1840, Brigham Young Papers.

[45]Woodruff, *Journal*, May 9, 1840, 1:445–46. The hill he climbed that day could have been the Malvern Beacon, though he identified it in his journal simply as Malvern Hill. Technically, the major range in the area is referred to as the Malvern Hills, and there are several prominences, each with its own name. It is often not clear from Woodruff's account just which hill he climbed.

Two days later, on May 11, he decided to hike to the top of Herefordshire Beacon, one of the most prominent of the Malvern Hills, for a
time of solitary contemplation. After preparing his mind "for a lonely walk
& meditation" by reading Parley P. Pratt's remarks on the " 'eternal duration
of matter,' " he began his climb. On the way he noted several entrench-
ments, which he surmised were artifacts of Roman activities more than a
thousand years before. Standing atop the hill with its magnificent view of
the surrounding countryside, he could not help but reflect upon where he
stood, in time as well as in space, and what it all meant for him. He also
knelt in a private prayer of thanksgiving. He wrote later in his journal:

> But I soon drew my thoughts from the busy rabit, sheep, & asses to the solumn
> reflections which the ravages of time presented before me. O! Malvern thy lofty Hill
> bares up my feet while mine eyes take a survey of thy deep intrenchments. Thy mighty
> bulwarks, which have trembled by the roar of cannon, the clash of arms, & din of war
> has reeched around thy brow & died away in the vale beneath, while the blood of
> many a roman & Englishman to, have washed thy brow & soaked thy soil while they
> have fallen to rise no more. They sleep in death & time has earth'd them all & they
> are forgotten & blotted from the history & memory of man. Notwithstanding O! Malvern
> thou hast been the Ark or refuge for thousands in the time of trouble or war.
>
> Yet Willford is the ownly solitary soul that treads thy soil this day & he alone bends
> his knee upon [thee] on the highth of thy summer in the midst of the Clouds to offer
> up the gratitude of his heart unto that God who will soon level all hills exhalt all valies
> & redeem the earth from the curse of sin & prepare it for the abode of the Saints of
> the MOST HIGH.
>
> I retired from the hill into the vale reflecting upon the rise, progress, decline, &
> fall of the empires of the earth, & the revolutions which must still transpire before the
> winding up scene & the comeing of Christ.[46]

The next day Wilford baptized three women, each of whom was converted after only one discussion, but such spontaneity disquieted him.
Could it be himself more than the Spirit, he worried, that was affecting
the people? "It seemed as though some would worship me while they
cried out here is a man of Zion the man of God that we have so long
looked for. Who is worthy to receive him into our house? I told them to
worship God for I was ownly a servant of God."[47]

Willard Richards spent his first two weeks in Herefordshire working
with Thomas Kington, and by May 15 the two of them had baptized fifty

---

[46]Ibid., May 11, 1840, 1:446–48. See photograph, p. 122.
[47]Ibid., May 12, 1840, 1:448.

people and confirmed one hundred as members of the Church.[48] The new apostle's own reaction to what he found in Herefordshire was much like Wilford Woodruff's earlier emotions: delight at their success but an overwhelming sense of urgency at the need for more laborers in the field. All the elders, he wrote to the *Millennial Star*, were "preaching daily, talking night and day, and administering the ordinances of the gospel as directed by the Spirit." Nevertheless, he said,

The branches are small, the brethren much scattered, consequently the field is so large that the reapers cannot call to each other from side to side; neither can they often see each other without a telescope. There are many doors open which we cannot fill; calls for preaching on almost every hand which we cannot answer. Oh! that the saints would pray to the Lord of the harvest to send forth labourers.[49]

On May 17 the three apostles met with the Saints at the Gadfield Elm chapel, where Brigham Young demonstrated his refusal to be intimidated no matter what the distraction. As he preached in the afternoon, several antagonists, including some preachers, began making loud disturbances, determined to break up the meeting. Brigham, however, rising to full stature in both body and authority, commanded peace and order in the name of the Lord. Willard Richards and another man then went to the door, and peace was restored.[50]

The next day must have been especially interesting for the American elders. A traditional United Brethren feast day, it began for them at 5:00 in the morning at Joseph Hill's home in Dymock with the baptism of two Anglican churchmen and a Wesleyan. The missionaries and their friends then walked to William Hart's home where Thomas Kington baptized seven people, Wilford Woodruff baptized five, and Brigham Young and Willard Richards confirmed them as they came out of the water. Then, while on the way to Kington's home, a woman met them on the road, insisting that she be baptized, and Thomas Kington readily obliged.

About 2:00 in the afternoon nearly one hundred former United Brethren gathered at Thomas Kington's home to partake of the feast he had prepared. After a powerful sermon from Brigham Young, which he concluded with a blessing on the food, they all sat down at the table and, with "glad hearts & cheerful Countenances," ate and drank and enjoyed each

---

[48]Ibid., May 15, 1840, 1:449.
[49]Willard Richards to the Editor, May 15, 1840, *Millennial Star* 1 (May 1840): 23.
[50]Young, *Manuscript History*, 75; Woodruff, *Journal*, May 17, 1840, 1:449-50.

other's company to their heart's content. Brigham then gave another short sermon, three people were confirmed, several men were ordained to priesthood offices, and the Saints witnessed one of the miraculous healings that frequently rewarded their faith. Because of problems in her spine, Mary Pitt had been confined to her bed for six years and had not walked without crutches for eleven. The three apostles laid hands on her, rebuked the infirmity, and she was healed.[51] After this meeting James Morgan, who had been baptized and ordained a priest just that day, baptized three more converts.[52] There could hardly have been a more exhilarating day for the missionaries.

On May 20 Wilford took his colleagues to the top of Herefordshire Beacon for quiet meditation, prayer, and counsel. There they felt inspired that it was God's will that Brigham Young should leave immediately for Manchester to work on publishing the Book of Mormon and the new hymnbook. Already they had collected a substantial amount of money toward publication, including £100 from Thomas and Hannah Kington and £250 from John and Jane Benbow. As soon as they hiked down from the hill, Brigham was on his way, carrying the precious funds with him.[53] It was the end of one of his most memorable months as a missionary. "I shall never forget my little mision in that contry with Brother Woodruff and with Br Richards," he wrote back to Willard.[54]

Wilford and Willard remained in Herefordshire until it was time to leave for the July conference in Manchester, working at times with Thomas Kington, who was also spending full time in the ministry. Wilford was ecstatic about their continued success and wrote in his journal that "new doors were opening on every hand—a multiplicity of calls constantly reached our ears, many of which we could not answer for the want of laborers."[55] On June 18, for example, they baptized and confirmed six people, blessed thirteen children, healed two people who were ill, ordained two men to the office of priest, and preached at the home of a Church member. Elder Woodruff noted that almost everyone he conversed with that day expressed a desire to be baptized.[56]

---

[51]More than two weeks later, Elder Woodruff noted in his journal, she was still walking "without the aid of crutch or staff" (Woodruff, *Journal*, May 18, 1840, 1:450–51, and June 3, 1840, 1:455).

[52]Ibid., May 18, 1840, 1:450–51.

[53]Ibid., May 19, 20, 1840, 1:451; Young, *Manuscript History*, 76.

[54]Brigham Young to Willard Richards, June 17, 1840, Brigham Young Papers (Appendix B, Document 11).

[55]Wilford Woodruff to the Editor, July 9, 1840, *Millennial Star* 1 (August 1840): 82.

[56]Woodruff, *Journal*, June 18, 1840, 1:461.

Wilford Woodruff's journal, May 20, 1840
Courtesy LDS Church Archives

On May 30, amidst all his success, Wilford Woodruff received good news. "Glory Hallelujah," he exulted in his journal, "I have now got a letter from *Phebe*." It was the first he had received from her since his arrival in England, and it announced the birth of a son, Wilford Woodruff, Jr., on March 20.[57]

During the first part of June, Willard Richards went for several days to the southern part of Herefordshire, where he baptized eleven people and ordained one of them to the office of teacher.[58] With such rapid growth, clearly the Church required further organization, and the apostles decided to arrange all the new groups into branches and conferences. Among other things, this improved administrative structure would allow the branches

[57]Ibid., May 30, 1840, 1:454.
[58]Ibid., June 12, 1840, 1:457.

152

Herefordshire Beacon, by Al Rounds. Courtesy LDS Church Museum

to be properly represented at the coming general conference in Manchester. Therefore, at a conference held on June 14 in the Gadfield Elm Chapel, Worcestershire, twelve former United Brethren congregations were organized into the Bran Green and Gadfield Elm Conference of The Church of Jesus Christ of Latter-day Saints, with Thomas Kington as the presiding elder. A week later at Stanley Hill, the Froome's Hill Circuit of the United Brethren became the Froome's Hill Conference of the LDS Church. Thomas Kington also became presiding elder over that conference, which included twenty branches. The organization of these two conferences was a significant milestone in the progress of the Church, for they represented a grand culmination of all Wilford Woodruff had begun in February. Within four months, he noted with a sense of fulfillment, the Church had grown in that area from nothing to thirty-three congregations (including one small congregation not attached to either conference) and 534 members: proof, he declared, "that God is beginning to make a short work in these last days."[59]

Not unexpectedly, the missionaries continued to be challenged by

[59]Ibid., June 14, 1840, 1:457–60 and June 21, 1840, 1:463–69. See also Wilford Woodruff to the Editor, *Millennial Star* 1 (August 1840): 82.

boisterous and sometimes violent opposition. Two days before the Froome's Hill conference, Wilford Woodruff rose early in the morning for a baptism and confirmation, and soon several more people came asking for the same thing. As they walked to the river looking for a suitable place, suddenly a mob led by an angry man named Pitt began to threaten them. Boldly, but to no avail, Willard Richards warned Pitt to repent and be baptized himself, but when the ugly threats continued, the missionaries decided that the better part of valor was to retire. Pitt and his mob followed, jeering and yelling, said Woodruff, "as though a part of hell at least had broke loose." Later the elders made a point of stopping along the way to wash their feet "as a testimony against Mr Pitt for rejecting our testimony, & forbiding, & hindering, others from Entering into the kingdom of God."[60]

Willard Richards's two months in Herefordshire were troubled by his continuing worry over the frail and ailing Jennetta, who was staying with her parents in Walkerfold. Sensitive to such things, Brigham Young wrote to him on May 24, suggesting that he cut his work a little short and have his wife meet him in Manchester. Willard readily agreed and wrote to Jennetta that she should meet him in Manchester on June 29 or 30. He also wrote to Brigham on June 2 that "you must help us with all the faith you can to get her out." He felt a pressing need, apparently, to get her away from the chiding of her father, who still could not accept her conversion to the LDS Church. Adding to his consternation was the fact that his former landlady in Preston had been turned out of the house by her husband, and Willard's belongings left in her keeping had been moved out of the apartment.[61]

Willard nevertheless continued faithfully to toil away in Herefordshire. On Sunday, June 14, he attended the Gadfield Elm conference where, he said, the chapel was full of "men women & Devils." Apparently he gave an unusually exhilarating sermon, for, he reported, "the Lord helped me to scare the Devil pretty well till after conference." In the middle of the meeting, however, he received a letter from Jennetta, dated June 9, and when he read it he was devastated. She was doing very poorly, she wrote, "never free from pain a moment. No not one moment. I can assure you that Death would be a friend at present. Would my heavenly father take

---

[60]Woodruff, *Journal*, June 19, 1840, 1:461–62.
[61]Brigham Young to Willard Richards and Wilford Woodruff, May 24, 1840, Brigham Young Papers; Willard Richards to Brigham Young, June 2, 1840, Brigham Young Papers.

me to himself. But his will be done." With respect to going to Manchester, she said, it was almost impossible, but she sent her love to Brigham with thanks for his "kind invitation."

Shocked and distraught, Willard wrote immediately to Brigham Young. He reminded him of all that must be done before the Manchester conference, but he was bewildered about his own situation and what course of action he should take. "Now is not the Lord willing to hear prayers in her behalf," he asked, "& let me stay in the vineyard till conference?" Although Willard and his brethren in Herefordshire had prayed mightily, no dream, vision, or revelation had given them an answer. Why must her life be a continual burden, and why must he be taken from the vineyard to care for her? "The heavens are brass here," he said in frustration, and "I wish you would get an answer from the Lord to these things & write me at Ledbury. . . . What the Lord says I will do."[62]

Willard's perplexity was a serious matter to the senior apostle, and in a letter of June 17 he responded with his typical wisdom and good-natured pragmatism:

Now as to the other question about Jennet, thus saith the scripter[:] he that provideth not fore his own house hold[63] has—but perhaps he has no hous, well has he got a famely[?] Yes, he has got a wife. Then let him see that she is taken care of and her hart comforted. But stop say som, why doe you not takcare of your famely[?] I doe when circumstances doe not renderit otherwise. There is a difference betwene 3 months jorny and afue [h]ours ride. Now I say to ancer my own feelings com as soon as you can leve things there. This is not by revelation nor by commandment so put it not with the anapistles of the new testament but Brigham sayes come and see your wife.[64]

Six days later Willard was on the train.[65]

Wilford Woodruff also left Herefordshire the same day as Willard in order to attend the July conference in Manchester. "We felt constrained to offer up the gratitude of our hearts unto our heavenly Father for so abundantly blessing our labours in the vineyard of the Lord," he wrote of the harvest he and Richards had shared.[66] On July 1 he arrived in Manchester in the company of George A. Smith and Theodore Turley.

---

[62]Willard Richards to Brigham Young, June 2, 1840, Brigham Young Papers.
[63]See 1 Timothy 5:8.
[64]Brigham Young to Willard Richards, June 17, 1840 (Appendix B, Document 11).
[65]Richards, Diary, June 29, 1840.
[66]Wilford Woodruff to the Editor, *Millennial Star* 1 (August 1840): 83.

now as to the other question about Jennet — thus saith the scripter he, that provideth not fore his own house hold — has — but perhaps he has no house. well has he got a family yes he has got a wife then let him see that she is taken care of and her heart comforted — but stop say som why dos you not take care of your family. I doe when circumstances doe not render it otherwise there is a Difference between 3 months jorny and a fue rods ride. now I say is mens my own feelings I can as son as you can tell things there this is no by revelation nor by commandment so put it not with the epistles of the new testament but Brigam says come and see your wife — To Mr Richards I am yours in the N.C. Brigam yours

excuse errors and mestakes you must remember its from me Elizabeth Haven is married to I. Barlow

BRIGHAM BEARS THE ADMINISTRATIVE BURDEN

At this time, Manchester was the headquarters of the Church in England. The apostles decided to locate the office of the *Millennial Star* on Oldham Road, one of the city's wider thoroughfares, in a building that would also serve as Parley P. Pratt's home. Though the rent was expensive, Elder Pratt found the building to his liking.[67]

Brigham Young arrived in Manchester on May 23, and from that time on, as leader of the Twelve, he was so involved in publishing and general administrative work that, compared to the other apostles, he had little time for extended preaching. He worked largely in the Manchester and Liverpool areas, where he preached, visited the Saints, and wrote letters to keep in touch with the rest of the Twelve. He rented Carpenter's Hall for the use of the Church, and on June 14 he preached there for the first time. As frequently as possible he visited and worked briefly with his brethren in other parts of Britain, but long, sustained periods of missionary work in one place necessarily eluded him. He traveled so much that he told Mary Ann to direct his mail to John Taylor in Liverpool, who would always know his whereabouts.[68]

Brigham also worked closely with Parley P. Pratt, who spent nearly all his time in Manchester working on the *Millennial Star* and other publications. After the hymnal was published in mid June, Brigham told his wife that he had done most of the work himself, for John Taylor had been ill and Pratt had as much as he could do to publish the *Star* and read proof for both the *Star* and the hymnbook. But Brigham, too, was ailing, and he told Mary Ann that his work was so hard that it seemed impossible that he would ever regain his health. The climate would agree with him, he said, if there were good air, but there was so much black coal dust in the atmosphere that when it settled it made "the waters look like strong sut tea." He emphasized, nonetheless, that he was as happy in this country as he could be any place in the world, for the people were as loving as he had ever seen, even more than in America.[69]

It is interesting to contemplate Brigham Young as editor and publisher, for he was very much aware of his weaknesses, including his meager "book

---

[67]Parley P. Pratt to Brigham Young, May 4, 1840, in "Manuscript History of the British Mission."

[68]Brigham Young to Mary Ann Young, June 12–24, 1840, typescript, Brigham Young Papers. The Letter was begun on June 12 but was continued on several later dates.

[69]Ibid.

Early photograph, thought to be
of Brigham Young. © LDS Church Archives

George A. Smith
© LDS Church Archives

learning" and phonetic spelling, and recognized them with good humor. "Now my Dear Brother," he once wrote to Willard Richards, "you must forgive all my noncense and over look erours." A week later he wrote: "excuse erours and mestakes you must remember its from me." His sense of humor carried even further, as he realized that his letters to the other apostles might well be preserved for posterity. "Be careful not to lay this letter with the new testament wrightings," he told Willard Richards, for "if you doe som body will take it for a text after the Malineum a[nd] contend about it."[70]

[70]Brigham Young to Willard Richards, June 10, 1840; June 17, 1840 (Appendix B, Document 11); Brigham Young Papers.

The Youngest Apostle Ministers in Staffordshire

On April 18 George A. Smith took the train from Preston to Manchester, where he stopped for a few days on his way to Staffordshire. There he had an experience that not only tested his sense of humor but also revealed a potential problem. Several Church members met him at the station and took him to Alice Hardman's boardinghouse. Blithely unaware that the Saints in Manchester took literally Paul's biblical comments about greeting one another "with an holy kiss,"[71] he seated himself comfortably on a sofa. Almost immediately several young ladies filled the room, evidently anxious to see the only bachelor among the apostles. One of them, "decidedly a little beauty," he reported, suddenly shocked him by saying, "Brother Smith, we want a kiss of you!" while the eyes of the others flashed like "stars on a clear night." "I never felt so foolish in my life," he wrote later, but he summoned up resolution enough to tell them that kissing was no part of his mission to England. The young women were obviously disappointed, and thereafter he was regarded in Manchester as no lady's man. The idea that there was no harm in such a greeting was being perpetuated by some of the elders in Manchester and, wrote the apostle, "it required a very decided course, both in Manchester and other places to prevent evil corruption growing out of this custom, which might have been firmly established had not the Twelve put it down."[72]

Five days later George A. Smith was in the Potteries, where he was met in Burslem by Alfred Cordon, and immediately went to work. Before long he had completely won the hearts of the hundred or so members in the area. During the next ten weeks, his main place of residence was the home of one of them, Samuel Johnson, but he frequently walked to other towns, spending his nights with Saints and prospective Saints. On his first day he preached at a flea-infested building, evidently recently used as a chicken house but rented by the Saints in Hanley for their meetings. Later he also preached in the homes of the Saints, in public buildings, in marketplaces, in a temperance hall in Longton, in a field near Stoke-upon-Trent, in a silk-twisting shed in Leek, and in any other place where he could find an audience. On the evening of April 29, Mrs. Elizabeth Allblasters became the first person in England to be baptized by Elder Smith.

Willard Richards, en route to Herefordshire, spent a few days with

---

[71]Romans 16:16; 1 Corinthians 16:20; 2 Corinthians 13:12; 1 Thessalonians 5:26.
[72]Smith, "History," April 18, 1840.

George A. Smith, and on April 29 the two visited Theodore Turley in the Stafford jail, warmly shaking hands through a large iron grate. It seemed to George that this was a fulfillment of a prophecy by Joseph Smith, who had blessed them as they were leaving Nauvoo, saying, "Keep up good courage, boys, some of you will look through the grates before you come back."[73]

The two apostles visited with Turley for about an hour and learned from him about the charity of the Saints of Staffordshire. The state did not provide food for prisoners like Turley, and, having no money of his own, he had fasted for about four days. When the sisters in the Potteries learned of his plight, several walked fourteen miles to take him some money. Johnathan Locket, an elderly and poverty-stricken Saint from Hanley, walked to Stafford several times, using a staff, to take Elder Turley some food.

Slightly over a month later, Johnathan Locket was dead, leaving behind not even sufficient means to bury his body. Dismayed at the thought of this poor but generous Saint suffering the indignity of burial in a pauper's grave, George A. Smith made a contribution and then enlisted others to do the same in order to give him a respectable burial. On June 4 some twenty Saints, including Elder Smith, followed Brother Locket's body to the grave, where, according to custom, a clergyman of the Church of England gave a sermon. It created a great deal of interest on the part of onlookers that "so poor a man should have so many friends."[74]

Walking from town to town, preaching wherever and whenever he could, sometimes hiring town criers to announce his meetings, holding conversations with preachers, and baptizing people regularly: these were the things that took up Elder Smith's time. On Sunday, May 31, he preached at one place in the morning, at another in the afternoon, confirmed seven people after the afternoon meeting, and walked back to where he had been earlier to baptize two people. Then, still wet because he had no change of clothes, he preached in the evening and, clothes still drying on his body, walked ten miles to Burslem to spend the night. "I did not stay at Leek fearing the army of fleas which would attack me in every house where I stayed," he commented wryly in his history.[75] He became so

[73]Ibid., April 29, 1840.
[74]Ibid., June 4, 1840.
[75]Ibid., May 31, 1840.

involved in his work that for two and a half weeks he did not even write in his journal. He finally described his hectic schedule on June 26:

For the last twenty days I have been so busy with preaching, counselling, baptizing, confirming, and teaching the people that I had not time to journalize any; and have seldom gone to bed before 2 o'clock in the morning, as people were constantly in my room enquiring about the work of the Lord.[76]

Perhaps he took a few minutes out that day to write in his journal because it was his birthday: he was twenty-three years old.

While in the Potteries George A. Smith experienced a rude awakening to the difficulties of working men and women. He was much impressed with the earthenware industry as such, but he noticed immediately that large numbers of people were out of work. He saw more beggars than he had seen in all his life and was dismayed when he observed "delicate females" gathering manure as a way of earning a living for their starving children. He was also amazed at the high cost of living. "I never before realized the value of American institutions," he wrote to a cousin in Ohio.[77] But it was his keen sensitivity to the problems of those around him that helped endear George A. to the people of Staffordshire.

He also possessed a kind of practical wisdom that may have helped, as suggested by an assignment he gave to Daniel Bowers. Bowers, a large, strong man living in Hanley, attended one of George A.'s preaching meetings that was rudely interrupted by John Jones, a Methodist preacher who was in the habit of disturbing Mormon meetings. The indignant Bowers picked up Jones bodily and carried him out of the house, saying, "These people pay the rent here, and you must not disturb them." He was baptized not long after that, whereupon George A. ordained him a deacon and assigned him to keep order in the meetings.[78]

William W. Player, a Methodist preacher in Longton, was profoundly affected by the apostle's humility and lack of pretension. He first visited Elder Smith on May 18 and asked him to explain such things as the beast in the book of Revelation and "leviathan" in Job. "What?" he responded when the missionary told him he did not know. "Do you profess to be a preacher of the Gospel and not understand the Bible?" Never one to avoid

---

[76]Ibid., June 26, 1840.
[77]George A. Smith to Cousin C. C. Walker, June 6, 1840, *Times and Seasons* 1 (October 1840): 223–24.
[78]Smith, "History," May 10, 1840.

a challenge, George A. answered with his characteristic, if not always diplomatic, directness. "That's the difficulty with you preachers; you are not willing to acknowledge your ignorance, and consequently undertake to explain to the people things which you do not understand yourselves, and as blind leaders of the blind, you lead the blind, giving your own ignorant opinions instead of teaching the principles of truth." George A. went on to inform him that "I teach what I do know. What I do not know, I let alone,"[79] and that if Player would obey the first principles of the gospel and let the Holy Spirit guide, he would understand the passages in question as the men who wrote them did. Touched by the spirit Elder Smith carried, Player invited him to give a lecture on total abstinence in the Temperance Society's hall. Smith consented, the meeting was advertised by town criers, and after he gave an address that greatly pleased the audience, the Mormons were able to use the hall for three meetings each Sunday and three meetings during the week merely for the cost of cleaning. Player was soon baptized and became the presiding elder of a branch of one hundred Saints in Longton.

ORSON PRATT IN SCOTLAND

Immediately after the April 1840, conference, Orson Pratt and Reuben Hedlock, who had accompanied the last group of apostles to England, went north to Alston, in Northumberland just south of the Scottish border. A branch of some forty Saints was already established there, and Hedlock remained for about a month.[80] After a few days, however, Elder Pratt moved on to Scotland and there spent his entire mission cultivating the gospel seeds already planted by two Scottish-born Latter-day Saints from Canada.[81]

In 1839, while Orson was making his own way to New York and preparing to cross the Atlantic, Alexander Wright and Samuel Mulliner, who had emigrated to Canada and been converted, were on their way back to their homeland as missionaries. They arrived in Glasgow on De-

---

[79]Ibid., May 18, 1840.

[80]Reubin Hedlock to the Editor, n.d., *Millennial Star* 2 (October 1841): 90–93.

[81]Unfortunately, the record of Orson Pratt's activities in Britain is sketchy, because his personal journals are not extant, but there is enough to provide an extensive outline. We have used what documents are available in the Church Archives, as well as O. Pratt, *Journals*, which is a compilation of various original sources related to Pratt. See also England, *Orson Pratt*, 61–71; England, "Gospel Seeds"; Buchanan, "Church in Scotland"; Buchanan, "Mormonism in Scotland"; Orson Pratt to Parley P. Pratt, April 16, 1841, *Millennial Star* 2 (May 1841): 10–12, where Orson briefly summarizes the mission and his attitude toward it.

Orson Pratt
© LDS Church

cember 20 and began working among friends and relatives in nearby cities. The first baptisms came at Bishopton on January 9, 1840, when Mulliner took Jessie and Alexander Hay into the icy waters of the River Clyde. They attracted a great deal of attention, including criticism and rock-throwing persecution, but by the time Orson Pratt arrived on May 3, they had baptized eighty new Latter-day Saints. Five days later the American apostle organized the first Scottish branch of the church at Paisley.[82] At Pratt's invitation, Reuben Hedlock soon joined the modest missionary force in Scotland.

On May 18 Orson Pratt and Samuel Mulliner made their way to Edinburgh, sometimes called the "Athens of the North," and Elder Pratt quickly fell in love with it. At the end of his mission, he extolled this city, inhabited by the gentry and the nobility and known for the splendor and magnificence of its buildings, as "one of the most renouned cities of the world." His description was as much as any modern-day chamber of commerce could ask for:

Its streets, gardens, and walks are extremely beautiful and pleasant, while the surround-

---

[82]Buchanan, "Church in Scotland," 269–70.

View of Edinburgh from Arthur's Seat. Courtesy James B. Allen

ing country, for the most part, presents an aspect delightfully variegated with gently rising hills and pleasant vales. As you emerge from the city on the east, the mountains or hills rise suddenly to the height of several hundred feet, which throws a romantic and sublime appearance over the whole scenery. From their summits there is a beautiful prospect, not only of the city but for miles around.[83]

One of the summits was Arthur's Seat, a particularly prominent rocky peak that provides an extraordinary view of the city and of the sea. Frequently Orson climbed to its top, where he contemplated the magnificent scene before him and "lifted my desires to heaven in behalf of the people of the city."[84] Since then this spot has been known among the Latter-day Saints as "Pratt's Hill." On his first climb, it is said, he pleaded with the Lord for two hundred converts.[85] By the time he left Scotland, that prayer had been more than answered.

<hr />

[83]Orson Pratt to Parley P. Pratt, April 16, 1841.

[84]Ibid.

[85]Buchanan, "Church in Scotland," 270. We have found no evidence to support the popular assumptions that Pratt here dedicated Scotland for the preaching of the gospel.

Like the other apostles, Orson preached wherever and to whomever he could, at times held public debates, and, with his co-workers, labored long and hard. He immediately hired a public hall, Whitfield Chapel, for six months, and there, on Sunday, May 24, he preached the first public Latter-day Saint discourse in Edinburgh. He continued to preach there three times every Sabbath and at eight o'clock on Tuesday and Friday evenings. To advertise his meetings he had a thousand handbills printed. The first week he posted two hundred at various places around the city, and then, for the next few weeks, about a hundred a week, after which he tapered off to a dozen or so. He also had flyers posted on heavy pasteboard, which he hung in conspicuous places, including two in front of the chapel every Sunday. The results were discouraging, for even though the first meeting was well attended, he attracted fewer than twenty people after that. For weeks, he wrote to George A. Smith, "I had to preach almost to empty walls."[86] A few, however, began to listen, and before long some were baptized, including Samuel Mulliner's parents, with whom the apostle lived at first. By the end of July, there were still only eighteen members in Edinburgh, though the Church was growing rapidly elsewhere. Orson wrote to Reuben Hedlock that he had "not given up all hopes of that place yet," and by fall the Edinburgh Conference was organized.[87]

Among the delights of Edinburgh was that some of the great philosophical contributions to the western world had come from there, and important work in philosophy, physics, and astronomy was still going on. Such an intellectual climate was made to order for Orson Pratt, who later became an accomplished mathematician and philosopher, and the ideas he came across there had important influence on his later publications.[88] The intellectual climate may also have provided incentive for his own writing. Sometime in 1840, possibly during those discouraging early months, he began to prepare for publication his important thirty-one-page pamphlet, *Interesting Account of Several Remarkable Visions.*

PARLEY P. PRATT IN MANCHESTER

Appointed editor of the *Millennial Star*, Parley P. Pratt remained in Manchester and immediately went to work. Though he did considerable

---

[86]Orson Pratt to George A. Smith, October 17, 1840, George A. Smith Collection. See also Reuben Hedlock to George A. Smith, June 15, 1840, George A. Smith Collection.

[87]Orson Pratt to Brigham Young, August 28, 1840, Brigham Young Papers; excerpts of letter from Reuben Hedlock in *Millennial Star* 1 (August 1840): 92; O. Pratt, *Journals*, 487.

[88]England, *Orson Pratt*, 66–67.

Edinburgh. Courtesy David Daiches, *Edinburgh:
A Traveller's Companion,* Constable Publishers

preaching in and around the city, he spent most of his time publishing. It was a natural assignment, for he exulted in writing in defense of the kingdom. He also loved to compose hymns, and on the wrapper of the first issue of the *Star* was printed one he wrote especially for the occasion.[89] Portraying in powerful verse the spirit of what the apostles were doing, it was placed first in their new hymnbook and soon became one of Mormonism's best-loved anthems.

> The morning breaks, the shadows flee;
> Lo! Zion's standard is unfurled!
> The dawning of a brighter day
> Majestic rises on the world.
> The clouds of error disappear
> Before the rays of truth divine;
> The glory, bursting from afar,
> Wide o'er the nations soon will shine.

[89]P. Pratt, *Autobiography,* 303.

Calton Hill, Edinburgh, with Nelson Monument. Courtesy David Daiches,
Edinburgh: A Traveller's Companion, Constable Publishers

The Gentile fulness now comes in,
    And Israel's blessings are at hand;
Lo! Judah's remnant, cleans'd from sin,
    Shall in their promised Canaan stand.
Jehovah speaks! Let earth give ear,
    And Gentile nations turn and live!
His mighty arm is making bare,
    His covenant people to receive.
Angels from heaven, and truth from earth
    Have met, and both have record borne;
Thus Zion's light is bursting forth,
    To bring her ransomed children home.

Some fifty of his hymns were included in the hymnbook he and his colleagues published in England.

Parley expressed lofty hopes for the *Star* in the first issue:

We trust this paper will prove a welcome visitor to the palaces of the noble, the
mansions of the rich, the towers of the brave, and the cottages of the poor: that the
sublimity of its truths, the splendour of its light, and the easy simplicity of its style and

THE

LATTER-DAY SAINTS
MILLENNIAL STAR,
EDITED BY PARLEY P. PRATT.

No. 1. Vol. 1.   **MAY, 1840.**   **Price 6d.**

PROSPECTUS.

THE long night of darkness is now far spent—the truth revived in its primitive simplicity and purity, like the day-star of the horizon, lights up the dawn of that effulgent morn when the knowledge of God will cover the earth as the waters cover the sea. It has pleased the Almighty to send forth an HOLY ANGEL, to restore the fulness of the gospel with all its attendant blessings, to bring together his wandering sheep into one fold, to restore to them "the faith which was once delivered to the saints," and to send his servants in these last days, with a special message to all the nations of the earth, in order to prepare all who will hearken for the Second Advent of Messiah, which is now near at hand.

By this means, the Church of Jesus Christ of Latter-Day Saints, (being first organized in 1830) has spread throughout many parts of America and Europe; and has caused many tens of thousands to rejoice above measure, while they are enabled to walk in the light of truth.

And feeling very desirous that others should be made partakers of the same blessings by being made acquainted with the same truths, they have thought

proper to order the publication of a Periodical devoted entirely to the great work of the spread of truth, sincerely praying that men may be led to carefully examine the subject, and to discern between truth and error, and act accordingly.

"THE MILLENNIAL STAR" will stand aloof from the common political and commercial news of the day.—Its columns will be devoted to the spread of the fulness of the gospel—the restoration of the ancient principles of Christianity—the gathering of Israel—the rolling forth of the kingdom of God among the nations—the signs of the times—the fulfilment of prophecy—recording the judgments of God as they befal the nations, whether signs in the heavens or in the earth "blood, fire, or vapour of smoke"—in short, whatever is shown forth indicative of the coming of the "Son of Man," and the ushering in of his universal reign on the earth. It will also contain letters from our numerous elders who are abroad, preaching the word both in America and Europe, containing news of their success in ministering the blessings of the glorious gospel.

As an Ancient Record has lately been discovered in America, unfolding

B

Millennial Star, volume 1, number 1, page 1. Courtesy LDS Church Archives

language, may, at once, interest and edify the learned, and instruct and enlighten those in the humbler walks of life.

No doubt his readers included more people in the "cottages of the poor" than in the heights he described. The *Star* proved invaluable to the Saints, but it was not long before the hard-working apostle found himself in deep financial difficulty. The "cottages of the poor" could provide little money for the support of the *Star* and it survived as a shoestring operation. Parley's remarkable achievement in keeping the *Millennial Star* in print and managing other LDS publications in Britain will be considered in more detail later.

THE MANCHESTER CONFERENCE, JULY 6–7

During the first week in July, all the apostles except Orson Pratt, who remained in Scotland, arrived in Manchester for the second general conference of the Church in England. It was held in Carpenter's Hall at 10:00 A.M. on Sunday, July 6. Reports from the various branches revealed that

842 Saints had been added to the Church since the last conference and that there were forty-one congregations in England and Scotland with a membership of 2,513, including 256 priesthood holders. The apostles presented the new hymnbook, which the conference unanimously accepted, and several people were approved for ordination to priesthood offices. One of them was Thomas Kington, to be ordained to the office of high priest. It was also agreed to release the British Mission presidency, so Fielding, Clayton, and Clark could "have the privilege of more fully entering into the field of labour."[90] The practical result of this move was that the Twelve, and particularly Brigham Young, were even more directly involved in managing the affairs of the Church in the British Isles.

The Twelve selected Parley P. Pratt to preside at this all-day conference, but between the morning and afternoon sessions, he received a shock that so dazed him that he could hardly function. During the morning meeting a letter arrived from his wife, who, he thought, was in New York, planning to sail to England. This was the first word from home since he had sailed four months earlier, so he put the letter in his pocket, planning to read it during the noon hour. When the rest of the Twelve went to dine, he shut himself in a private room, eagerly anticipating that the letter would give him some idea of when Mary Ann would arrive. He read, instead, that she was ill and could not travel. Stunned, he went back to the conference fasting, stayed in meetings until 7:00 P.M., and then walked two miles home, still without eating. "My feelings are Such that my Stomach will not bear it," he noted as he sat down that same night and wrote a heartbroken letter back to Mary Ann. How could he go on without her, he wondered, especially since he did not expect to leave England for years. Besides, he thought, the family would be of considerable help in the office, and it would be less costly if they were with him.[91] In a private council late Monday afternoon, the Quorum agreed that he could return to New York City to bring his family back to England. He left almost immediately.

In a Monday council with other Church officers at the *Star* office, the apostles assigned several full-time missionaries to new fields of labor. Joseph Fielding, for example, was sent to Bedford, Charles Price was told to "give up his business" and work under the direction of Thomas Kington, and John Parkinson was given "a roving commission, so long as he keeps busy, and doing good."[92]

[90]*Millennial Star* 1 (July 1840): 67–71.
[91]Parley P. Pratt to Mary Ann Pratt, July 6, 1840, Parley P. Pratt Collection.
[92]*Millennial Star* 1 (July 1840): 71.

At the same council meeting, Brigham Young discussed the custom of greeting by kissing, which, despite George A. Smith's effort in April, still had not been rooted out from among the Manchester Mormons. Brigham condemned no one but urged again that the habit be set aside before it led to evil.[93]

Later in the day the Twelve visited the warehouse where the paper for five thousand copies of the Book of Mormon was stored. They watched it being weighed and paid for it. They also decided to open new areas for missionary work and agreed that Heber C. Kimball, Wilford Woodruff, and George A. Smith should go to London.[94]

After the Twelve separated again, Wilford Woodruff reflected upon his six months in England and wrote for publication a long epistle on what had happened in Herefordshire. His conclusion capsulized the message of all the missionaries and set the tone for what they would be doing for the next six months:

I now take the liberty, through the channel of the press, to invite all . . . into whose hands these lines may fall, that have not already obeyed the fulness of the gospel of Jesus Christ, to repent of all their sins, and be baptized in water for the remission of their sins, that they may receive the gift of the Holy Ghost by the laying on of hands, – that they may have upon them the wedding garment, that their lamps may be trimmed and burning, and be prepared to go forth and meet the Bridegroom, who is at the door – for the day when the Lord Jesus shall cleanse the earth, by the spirit of judgment and the spirit of burning, from sin, wickedness, and pollution, until it becomes a fit abode for the Saviour to dwell upon, and reign one thousand years with his Saints.[95]

---

[93]Fielding, Diary, 81.

[94]Woodruff, *Journal*, July 7, 1840, 1:482; Smith, "History," July 8, 1840. It is unclear whether the decision to go to London was made on the seventh or the eighth. Wilford Woodruff's journal lists a meeting on July 7 where the decision regarding Pratt was made, though it does not mention the London decision. Smith's history for July 8 mentions both decisions. We tend to accept Woodruff's dating of the meeting, though it could have happened on the eighth when he was also in Manchester. Later, Woodruff wrote that the decision to go to London was made just by the three of them, but it seems unlikely that such a decision would be made without the consent of the rest of his quorum. Wilford Woodruff to the Editor, October 7, 1840, *Times and Seasons* 2 (March 1, 1841): 330.

[95]Wilford Woodruff to the Editor, July 9, 1840, *Millennial Star* 1 (August 1840): 84.

Chapter 8

EXPANDING THE HARVEST: JULY THROUGH OCTOBER 1840

Rejuvenated by the conference, the apostles eagerly returned to their work. All, that is, except Parley P. Pratt, who lost no time in taking a ship for America. Brigham Young and Willard Richards remained in Manchester, taking over Parley's publishing duties, preaching when they could, and visiting other places. John Taylor went back to Liverpool and from there expanded his activity to Ireland and the Isle of Man. Heber C. Kimball, Wilford Woodruff, and George A. Smith repaired to London, where they became the first LDS missionaries in England's greatest metropolis. The harvest was enlarging geographically, though none of the newly opened fields produced the abundance of converts the missionaries had enjoyed elsewhere.

BRIGHAM AND WILLARD: MORE TIME IN MANCHESTER

Willard's family problems persisted, and Jennetta's chronic illness was complicated by pregnancy. Because her husband would be in Manchester more or less permanently, it was not difficult for her to decide to move there with him. She arrived from Walkerfold on July 5 and, during the next ten days, Willard went to Walkerfold, packed her belongings, and moved them to Manchester. He also moved his own possessions that had been stored in Preston. By July 21 they had somehow obtained enough money to pay three months' advance rent on a house on Chapman Street,[1] where they continued living until they moved to Regent Road the following December.

In September Brigham and Willard wrote to the First Presidency of

---

[1]Richards, Diary, July 5–21, 1840.

the Church, asking a number of specific questions, including whether they were doing right in printing the Book of Mormon and the hymnbook and how long they were expected to stay in England. During all this time they had received no direct communication from the Prophet, and they had no choice but to proceed on the assumption that he would either approve all they did or let them know if he thought they were wrong. "We desire not to council you in any, but to be counseled by you," they said with deference, "for it is the desire of our hearts to do the will of God in all things, & we feel our own weekness & insufficiency for the great work which is committed to us." Until such direction came they were determined to go ahead without hesitation: "Our motto is *go ahead.* Go ahead—& *ahead* we are determined to go—till we have conquered every foe. So come life or come death we'll go ahead, but tell us if we are going wrong & we will right it."[2]

On September 5, the same day their letter was dated, the two apostles traveled to Liverpool and organized the second official company of Saints, two hundred strong, to sail for America. They handed the letter to one of the emigrants, probably either Theodore Turley, who was in charge of the group, or John Benbow, with instructions to deliver it to Joseph Smith when they arrived in Nauvoo.[3]

Brigham and Willard spent the night of September 7 aboard the ship *North America* and the next day, along with John Taylor, accompanied the departing Saints fifteen or twenty miles out to sea.[4] The gathering was seriously underway, for with these Saints, the Moon company that had left in June, some fifty Scottish Saints who went in October, and a few who went on their own, more than three hundred British converts sailed in 1840.

Just before the *North America* departed, the generosity of the Benbows was demonstrated once again. For months Brigham Young had worried about repaying the 250 pounds borrowed from the Benbows for printing the Book of Mormon. "Tell Br. John and Sister Jane Benbow all is well and the Lord will bless them. Nothing shall fall to the ground unnot[i]sed,"

---

[2]Brigham Young and Willard Richards to the First Presidency, September 5, 1840, Brigham Young Papers (Appendix B, Document 12).

[3]The address side of this letter to Joseph Smith included the note "By Turly or Benbow."

[4]Smith, *History of the Church* 4:188; Young, *Manuscript History*, 79; Allen and Alexander, *Manchester Mormons*, 43, 172–73.

he had written to Elders Richards and Woodruff in May.[5] But he remained concerned, for the Benbows were planning to emigrate and apparently expected to be repaid before they left. In June Brigham asked Willard to talk to them about the possibility of going to America without all their money and whether the balance could be sent later after they had time to sell books. "If Brother and Sister Benbow are amind to doe so, it would favor us for we can not get the Hym Book out till in to July and then they will have to be bound before they can be sold."[6] By September there was still no money available, but on September 7, the day before sailing, John Benbow signed an agreement relinquishing all claim to the debt, except for that needed to assist certain family members and friends the next season. The agreement left all the remaining money as well as any money realized from the sale of the Gadfield Elm chapel at the disposal of Brigham Young, Wilford Woodruff, and Willard Richards.[7]

JOHN TAYLOR: LIVERPOOL, IRELAND, AND THE ISLE OF MAN

John Taylor remained in Liverpool, still longing for Leonora but reconciled to the fact that she would not be joining him. He compensated with hard work, and particularly delighted in giving public lectures to large audiences. In July he arranged to give a series of lectures in the Music Hall, on Bold Street, which held some fifteen hundred people. Before he gave them, however, he took a whirlwind preaching tour of Ireland.

With one in every seven people in Liverpool an Irish emigrant, it was only natural that several Mormon converts there were Irish. One of these was James McGuffie, an elder, who introduced Elder Taylor to Thomas Tait, a friend visiting from Ireland. The apostle felt impressed to prophesy that Tait would become the first person to be baptized there. William Black, also a native Irishman, was officially called as a missionary to Ireland on July 7 during the Manchester conference. On July 27, John Taylor, James McGuffie, and William Black set sail together for the Emerald Isle.

The next day the missionaries arrived at the beautiful little village of

---

[5]Brigham Young to Willard Richards and Wilford Woodruff, May 24, 1840.

[6]Brigham Young to Willard Richards, June 10, 1840, and June 17, 1840 (Appendix B, Document 11), Brigham Young Papers.

[7]The agreement, signed by Brigham Young, Willard Richards, Wilford Woodruff, and John Benbow, is in the Brigham Young Papers. See also Young, *Manuscript History*, 79–80.

The Music Hall on Bold Street, Liverpool
© LDS Church

Newry where McGuffie, who had once resided there, arranged for the use of the Session House for a meeting. There, before six or seven hundred people, John Taylor preached the first Latter-day Saint sermon in Ireland. The effect, however, was not great, for only a handful of people came to the follow-up meeting the next evening, which turned into a rather informal question-and-answer session.[8]

McGuffie remained in Newry, while John Taylor and Black went on to the Four Towns of Bellinacrat, accompanied by Thomas Tait, who was showing interest in the Mormon message. There John Taylor preached in a large barn, though again with little apparent effect, and the next morning, with Tait helping to carry their luggage, the missionaries started walking toward the town of Lisburn. Along the way Taylor preached to Tait from the scriptures, and, when they came to Loch Brickland, the believing farmer asked, in a manner reminiscent of that of the eunuch in the book of Acts, "See, here is water; what doth hinder me to be baptized?" (Acts 8:36.) The

---

[8]One source says that the reason the reception was poor was that McGuffie, in a misguided effort to show his good feelings toward his former friends and neighbors, began drinking with them and became intoxicated. The situation deeply embarrassed John Taylor, but he made the best of it; see "Missionary Sketches," *Juvenile Instructor* 5 (October 15, 1870): 166–67.

group stopped, Taylor took him down into the water, and Thomas Tait became the first person baptized in Ireland.[9]

In Lisburn John Taylor preached four times to large crowds in the marketplace and then wound down his trip by going to Belfast where, on August 6, he caught a steamer for Glasgow, Scotland, leaving behind another new field opened by an apostle. McGuffie and Black remained in Ireland as missionaries and soon began harvesting a few souls.

After meeting briefly with the missionaries in Glasgow, Elder Taylor went on to Paisley. The Saints recognized the apostleship as something of remarkable value and took every opportunity to benefit from the presence of an apostle in their midst. He ended his ten-day trip with the Saints flocking about him for his blessing, not allowing him to retire until early in the morning.[10]

Back in Liverpool, John Taylor delivered his series of lectures in the Music Hall, where he attracted large crowds as well as continuing opposition, particularly from Timothy Matthews and his followers. Because local Church leaders and missionaries seemed capable of dealing with the situation, however, the apostle saw no reason why he should not carry on with his plan of opening up missionary work on the Isle of Man.

Elder Taylor had been thinking for months of going to the Isle of Man, and let it be known at least as early as March 25. That day he and Joseph Fielding were visiting with a Mr. Radcliff, a Bible Society agent, and a Miss Brannon, a resident of the Isle and an old acquaintance of Leonora Taylor's. Radcliff was deeply interested in what Taylor had to say, but not Miss Brannon, who expressed concerns when he announced that he was thinking of going to the Isle. He was going there anyway, he told her.[11] Nearly six months later, on September 16, accompanied by Hiram Clark and William Mitchell, he sailed from Liverpool. They arrived in Douglas the following day.

As he set foot on the Isle of Man, John Taylor's lonesomeness for Leonora came flooding back, for it was here, he knew, that she had spent

[9]Ibid.; Roberts, *Life of John Taylor*, 84–87; Barlow, "Irish Experience," 300–2; John Taylor to Editor, n.d., *Millennial Star* 2 (May 1841): 12–16. There are slightly different versions of the details of the baptism of Tait. Roberts says that John Taylor suggested to Tait that since they had come to water there was nothing to keep him from being baptized, while the *Instructor*, in a piece presumably based on an interview with John Taylor, gives the version reported here. Unfortunately, no primary sources are extant to help resolve the conflict.

[10]Roberts, *Life of John Taylor*, 87.

[11]Ibid., 81–82; Fielding, Diary, 66–67.

Douglas, Isle of Man, about 1850. Photograph from imprinted cloth
Courtesy A. C. Anderson family

her youth. He allowed himself to think also of her privations and suffering and the ordeal of separation they both endured, but he comforted himself by crying inwardly: "A few more struggles and the battle will be fought, the victory will be ours."[12]

While his companions went on to the town of Ramsey, Taylor remained in Douglas, where he began work by contacting some of Leonora's girlhood friends, visiting a local Primitive Methodist preacher, and hiring the largest hall in town, the Wellington Rooms, capable of holding a thousand people. There he began giving lectures which, as usual, generated both interest and opposition.

On Friday, September 25, one of John Taylor's lectures was interrupted by a disorderly party of Primitive Methodist preachers and others. They were so furious at him that, according to the *Manx Liberal*, they seemed ready to fight. The disorder subsided when the person in charge proposed that if they believed Taylor had said anything contrary to the word of God, they should agree to a public debate with him. The intruders readily accepted the idea, and the next day one of their number, Thomas Hamilton, challenged him to a debate, charging him with misquoting, mutilating, taking from, and adding to the Bible. The apostle accepted the challenge, he later reported, not because he felt he could teach Hamilton anything but "merely to remove public prejudice, and to let it be known that I

---

[12]As quoted in Roberts, *Life of John Taylor*, 90.

courted publicity and light, and was not afraid of bringing my principles to the touchstone of truth."[13]

The debate was held the following Monday, September 28. Each side was given an hour to present its case, and then each had another half-hour for final responses. Speaking first, Thomas Hamilton conducted himself so irresponsibly that the *Manx Liberal* described him as "a mere braggadocia, possessing no qualifications save ignorance and presumption." His arguments were so far from responsible, in fact, that John Taylor had nothing to refute, so he spent his hour giving his regular missionary message. During the rebuttal period Hamilton performed much as he had previously, whereupon John Taylor, as the *Liberal* described it, inflicted

deserved chastisement on the arrogant simpleton, who had given the challenge without being able to utter a single sentence against his opponent; and this he did right well, for while poor Mr. Hamilton writhed beneath his heavy flagellation, it was truly heart-rending to see his (Mr. H.'s) agony. There he sat biting his lips, and shaking his head, and every muscle of his distorted countenance seemed to implore the mercy of the meeting.

At the end, Elder Taylor "affectionately" urged Hamilton to repent and be baptized for the remission of his sins.

Time finally expired and the meeting was ready to vote, as was customary in public debates, on the proposition that Hamilton had proved none of his charges. According to the *Liberal*, the vote would have gone overwhelmingly against him, but suddenly some of his boisterous supporters began again to make charges against Taylor and demand time to prove them. The audience, however, hissed, groaned, and shouted them down. Finally, John Taylor himself gave the doxology and a closing prayer, and the meeting was over. His summary of the whole affair to Brigham Young was no more terse than it deserved: "I have had a controversy with a Primitive Methodest Preacher but of all the lame attempts to oppose the truth that ever I heard I think his was the weakest & the worst & the people were disgusted with him."[14]

---

[13]John Taylor's account of the debate is found in his letter to the Editor, February 27, 1841, *Millennial Star* 1 (March 1841): 276–80. See also Roberts, *Life of John Taylor*, 93. Roberts's account is apparently based partly on sources not presently available. In the Church Archives there is also a scrapbook of newspaper clippings relating to this mission. An account by a non-Mormon, G. W. Gee, was printed in the *Manx Liberal* [Douglas, Isle of Man], October 4, 1840; also in *Times and Seasons* 2 (March 1, 1841): 331–32. This was reprinted as "Public Discussion on the Isle of Man," *Millennial Star* 1 (November 1840): 178–80. For an account of John Taylor's work on the Isle of Man by convert Ann Pitchforth, see *Millennial Star* 8 (July 15, 1846): 12–15.

[14]John Taylor to Brigham Young, October 2, 1840, Brigham Young Papers.

Victoria Street, Douglas, Isle of Man. Photograph from imprinted cloth
Courtesy A. C. Anderson family

As Elder Taylor reported to the *Millennial Star*, Mr. Hamilton was so well acquainted with history that he could declare

that in some countries where there was no water they baptized with oil!!! about which opinion I had the hardihood to be a little sceptical despite of his great proficiency in historical lore; for I was foolish enough to wonder (as any old woman would do who did not possess the same knowledge of history as himself,) what they made use of as a beverage in that country!! as oil would not be very palatable to drink at all times, and also what they cooked their victuals with. It was the same individual, sir, who on being asked his authority to preach answered "I sent myself," I was led to tell him that I was of that opinion before, but that he had confirmed my impressions; that I had thought from the beginning that God had nothing to do with sending him out. Yet foolish, ignorant, and untaught as he was, there are those, sir, (who think that because the Scriptures says "*God has chosen* the weak things of this world to confound the wise," that any and every person is qualified to preach the gospel merely because they are fools, whether *God calls* them or not;) who had it not been for this exposure, might have mistaken him for a wise man, and have thought that he was called of God.[15]

---

[15]John Taylor to the Editor, February 27, 1841, *Millennial Star* 1 (March 1841): 277–80.

The dauntless Taylor confronted every challenge head on. He replied in print to a series of newspaper articles against the Mormons by a Mr. J. Curran, and to each of three pamphlets published by the Reverend Robert Heys, a Wesleyan minister.[16] So important was his battle with Heys, in fact, that he missed the October conference because of it. On October 2, 1840, he wrote Brigham Young: "A methodist publication has come out in opposition to [the gospel] & the fire is begenning to rage & I do not wish to leave the field untill my enemies & the enemies of God lay down their arms or till there is a sufficient army to contend with theirs." Four days later Taylor reported to Young that he had "got into the wars" and that as "I have got into the scrape I shall have to fight through."[17] His fellow apostles followed his war of words with delight. "Elder Taylor's letters in the 'Manx Liberal' are superlative, Methodist Priests stand no chance at all," exulted Orson Pratt to Wilford Woodruff and George A. Smith, and later he laughed that "Taylor [in his 2nd address] has cut Hey into fine fodder.... Taylor understands weilding the weapons of truth to a very good advantage & he has a very good good opportunity of doing it. I presume we could do more good in Edinburgh & London if we could bring the enemy into open combat."[18]

John Taylor gathered around him a small and faithful nucleus for his army of Saints. Once he went into the countryside, sat in a chimney corner talking to a few neighbors who came into the house where he was, and baptized and confirmed eight people the same night. They simply would not wait until morning.[19] This "country place" may have been the home of Charles Cowley, who lived near the village of Kirk German and who, according to his own account, had been "seeking and praying for correct information concerning the Will of God." He and his wife, Ann, read in the newspaper about the minister from America who was to preach in Douglas, and Ann's brother-in-law, John Quayle, went to hear him. Deeply impressed, he brought Elder Taylor to Cowley's farmhouse where, in the

[16]See chapter 10 for a discussion of these publications.

[17]John Taylor to Brigham Young, October 2, 1840, and October 6, 1840, Brigham Young Papers.

[18]Orson Pratt to George A. Smith and Wilford Woodruff, November 2, 1840, George A. Smith Collection. "The Editor of the Manx Liberal has published several lengthy communications for Elder Taylor in defense of the truth" (George A. Smith to the Editor, November 18, 1840, *Times and Seasons* 2 [February 1, 1841]: 307–8); and "Er Taylor is writing a reply to Mr. Hey's 'Third Address.' He says Mr. Hey is on his last legs." (Orson Pratt to George A. Smith, November 23, 1840, George A. Smith Collection.)

[19]John Taylor to Joseph Smith, February 3, 1841, *Times and Seasons* 2 (May 1, 1841): 400–2.

course of the evening, Quayle and his wife, Catherine, along with the Cowleys, were convinced that the apostle's message was the truth.[20]

John Taylor soon organized a branch of the Church on the Isle of Man and left it in good hands when he departed in mid November.[21] He spent the rest of his mission mostly in and around Liverpool, preaching, working with publications, and helping to organize the emigration program. He also visited Manchester, Birmingham, Sheffield, and several other cities and briefly returned to the Isle of Man in March.

ON THE WAY TO LONDON

One of the decisions made at the Manchester conference was that Elders Kimball, Woodruff, and Smith should introduce the gospel in London. First, however, Woodruff and Smith spent more than three weeks in the Staffordshire Potteries before going on to Herefordshire. During his brief return to the Potteries, Elder Smith continued to be rewarded for his missionary zeal and to experience the unfeigned love of the Saints. He baptized several people, including, on July 19, Richard Rushton, Sr., a sixty-year-old silk manufacturer in Leek who considered the unsophisticated young man from America a spiritual giant. Elder Smith stayed at the home of the Samuel Johnson family, where his room was constantly crowded with "Saints and strangers," all seeking instruction. Nearly every night someone would be baptized after leaving his room, and George A. seldom could retire before 2:00 A.M. When it came time to leave, he poured out his heart in thanksgiving. "Sister Johnson," he said, "attended me with all the care and kindness of a mother," taking pains to keep him in good health and to keep his clothes in order. As he left, she cried as if her only son were departing.[22] The continuing affection between the Johnsons and Elder Smith was exemplified in the first letter Samuel Johnson ever wrote, which was addressed to George A. Smith and Heber C. Kimball in London.[23]

In Herefordshire Wilford Woodruff found many things to warm his

---

[20]Bloxham, "Apostolic Foundations," 130. According to this account, however, the Cowleys and Quayles were baptized the next day, so there is some question as to whether they were the same people who could not wait until morning about whom John Taylor was writing.

[21]Roberts, *Life of John Taylor*, 95. Young, *Manuscript History*, 83, indicates that he was in Manchester November 16–20, when, presumably, he went back to Liverpool.

[22]Smith, "History," July 20, 1840.

[23]Samuel Johnson to George A. Smith and Heber C. Kimball, September 17, 1840, George A. Smith Collection.

soul, but at least two stood out. For one thing, missionary work continued unabated, and, with the forty baptized on Sunday, August 2, approximately 250 people had joined the Church since the July conference. "Elder Kington is labouring constantly in this wide field which is under his care," he wrote to the readers of the *Star*, "and he, with the Elders and Priests generally through this region, are blessed with many souls as seals of their ministry."[24]

The other source of satisfaction was the continuing faith of John and Jane Benbow. True to the admonition of the apostles that those with means should help the poor to emigrate to Zion, the Benbows were "willing to make every sacrifice in their power for the gathering of the Saints" before they themselves departed in September. About fifty Herefordshire converts were preparing to go to America with several other Saints, and the generous Benbows willingly paid the way of forty, at a total cost of about one hundred pounds. On August 11 Woodruff warmly shook hands with Theodore Turley, who would lead this company to America, and the Benbows, "to see them No more untill I meet them in NAUVOO *U.S.A.*" "Let the blessings of Almighty God rest upon [John Benbow] forever & ever," he prayed. The faithful and generous Benbows had also given Wilford Woodruff fifteen pounds to help him and his companions on their mission to London.[25]

Heber C. Kimball finally arrived in the Herefordshire village of Ledbury on August 11 but had difficulty locating the Latter-day Saints. Finally some of the Saints discovered his identity and, delighted with his presence, escorted him to the home of Thomas Kington in nearby Dymock. The next morning Heber was joined there by the other two apostles, and during the next few days they baptized several people.[26] On Sunday, August 16, they held their final meetings, outdoors in a field at Leigh. A large crowd attended and four people were baptized, including two men who had walked twelve miles for the occasion and who were also ordained to the office of priest that same afternoon.

LONDON: "WHAT AM I AND MY BRETHREN HERE FOR?"

On August 17 the three apostles set out by train for London, arriving at Paddington Station, some five miles northwest of the City of London,

---

[24]Wilford Woodruff to the Editor, August 5, 1840, *Millennial Star* 1 (August 1840): 93; Woodruff, *Journal*, August 11, 1840, 1:490–91.

[25]Woodruff, *Journal*, August 2, 1840, 1:488–89 and August 11, 1840, 1:490–91.

[26]Heber C. Kimball said in his letter to Vilate, August 19, 1840, Heber C. Kimball Collection, that they baptized fifteen. The total recorded in Wilford Woodruff's diary during those few days was eleven.

Shillibeer's Omnibus, 1839. Courtesy of the London Transport Museum

about 4:00 P.M. the next day. They knew no one in this giant metropolis,[27] but Theodore Turley had suggested that they begin by contacting Mrs. Mary Ann Allgood, his wife's sister. They took an omnibus[28] into the City, walked south across London Bridge, and found Mrs. Allgood at her home, 19 King Street.[29] She received them kindly, gave them some refreshment, and directed them to the nearby Kings Arms Inn where they spent their first two nights in London. But the Kings Arms was in one of London's busiest districts. The constant singing and yelling in the streets and the noisy passing of horses and carts was hardly conducive to sleep, and they soon moved elsewhere.[30]

The missionaries were struck, perhaps even awed, with the size of London, its teeming population, its many magnificent homes and public buildings, and its poverty. The spectacle also seemed to give them a re-

[27]On August 28 and 29, however, they visited with a "Brother" John Hulme, but he must have been a member of the Church who was just visiting London, for he brought them some papers and a letter from Willard Richards. Woodruff, *Journal*, August 28 and 29, 1840, 1:501–2.

[28]Omnibuses ran from Paddington to the Bank of England. These box-like vehicles, drawn by three horses, held twenty passengers facing each other on two parallel benches, and the fare ranged from sixpence for an intermediate journey to a shilling for a trip to one of the outlying areas. Sheppard, *London*, 120–21. In 1841 the Blackwall line was able to extend the railroad into the city, with a permanent terminus at Fenchurch Church. Ibid., 128.

[29]Now known as Newcombe Street. Bloxham, "Apostolic Foundations," 151.

[30]Woodruff, *Journal*, August 19, 1840, 1:494–95; Smith, "History," August 19, 1840.

Omnibus Life in London, 1859, by William Maw Egley
Courtesy Tate Gallery, London / Art Resource, N.Y.

newed sense of solemnity as they thought of the challenges ahead. "O London," Wilford Woodruff soliloquized,

as I walk thy street & behold the mass of human beings passing through thee & view thy mighty pallaces, thy splended mansions, the costly merchantdize wharewith thou art adorned even as the capital of great Babylon, I am ready to ask myself, what am I & my Brethren here for? & as the spirit answers to warn thee of thine abominations & to exhort the[e] to repent of thy wickedness & prepare for the day of thy visitation thy mourning thy calamity & thy wo, I am ready to cry out Lord who is sufficient for these things?[31]

He ended his musing with a fervent prayer for success.

Metropolitan London had a growing population of around two million people[32] and boasted the most elegant architecture and lavish life-style in

---

[31]Woodruff, *Journal,* August 18, 1840, 1:493–94.

[32]Mitchell, *British Historical Statistics,* 20 lists the 1841 population as 2,073,000. In his journal entry of August 18, 1840, Wilford Woodruff estimated the London population at 1,500,000.

all of England. The River Thames meandered through the middle of this sprawling urban complex, and on the east side a series of huge docks made the Port of London larger even than that of Liverpool.[33] Several major thoroughfares ran in every direction, but most of London's streets were short, narrow, and crowded. Dotted with lovely parks, both public and private, the city was also becoming soiled by industrial discharge. The increasing number of gasworks, the furnaces of the ever-growing coal-burning factories, and the coal-burning locomotives of the rapidly proliferating railroad lines belched black, tar-filled smoke into the air. In cold weather, the chimneys of the coal-burning fireplaces that heated almost every house must have doubled the pall.[34]

Four days after their arrival, Heber C. Kimball, Wilford Woodruff, and George A. Smith climbed to the top of Sir Christopher Wren's magnificent monument commemorating the great London fire of 1666. It was a clear day and, standing two hundred feet above the street, they had an extraordinary view of what Wilford Woodruff described as

the largest most noted, populous & splendid City upon the face of the whole earth. . . . & such a splendid prospect & grand scenery I never before beheld. . . .

East of us lay the splended tower of London & the Mint, North the Mansion of the Lord Mayor of London, North West St Pauls Church West, Westminster Abbey & the house of Parliment. South lies the river Thames with five large arched bridges acrossed it in full view, & another which is not seen from the pillar making six. . . .

South of the River lies London Borough & in addition to this were hundreds of Churches, chapels, & Spires standing in the midst of one universal dens mass of brick & Stone buildings, covering about six miles squair of ground.

While viewing this scenery in a Clear day we were conversing with a Prussian traveller (citizen of Berlin) who had traveled much over Europe & Asia & other parts of the world, & he declaired we could not find another spot upon the face of the earth that would present to our view as grand a scenery as the one before us.[35]

Closer acquaintance with London, however, modified this initial idyllic image. Five months later, in the midst of a bitterly cold winter, Wilford Woodruff found himself in a London so filled with smoke that he could

---

[33]Petrie, *Victorians*, 71.

[34]London, in fact, consumed 25 percent of all the coal produced in Britain, and it took some seven hundred colliers sailing regularly between that city and the coal fields to keep the vast metropolitan area supplied. Sheppard, *London*, 193.

[35]Woodruff, *Journal*, August 21, 1840, 1:496–97.

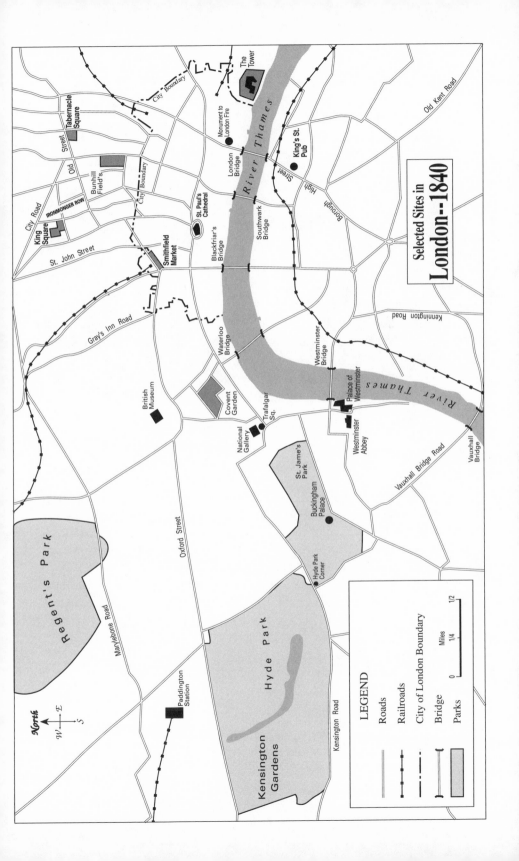

Selected Sites in
London--1840

North

LEGEND

Roads
Railroads
City of London Boundary
Bridge
Parks

Miles
0   1/4   1/2

River Thames

The Tower
Monument to London Fire
London Bridge
King's St. Pub
St. Paul's Cathedral
Southwark Bridge
Blackfriar's Bridge
Smithfield Market
Borough High Street
Tabernacle Square
Old Street
City Boundary
City Road
Bunhill Field's
IRONMONGER ROW
King Square
St. John Street
Gray's Inn Road
Waterloo Bridge
British Museum
Covent Garden
National Gallery
Trafalgar Sq.
Westminster Bridge
Palace of Westminster
Westminster Abbey
Kennington Road
Vauxhall Bridge
Vauxhall Bridge Road
St. James's Park
Buckingham Palace
Hyde Park Corner
Oxford Street
Marylebone Road
Regent's Park
Hyde Park
Paddington Station
Kensington Gardens
Kensington Road
Old Kent Road

London, 1842. Courtesy The Illustrated London News Picture Library

see no more than a few yards.[36] The apostles were concerned also with more than the atmosphere, and not long after they arrived they characterized the giant metropolis as a place of sin and corruption, "full of evry thing but righteousness."[37]

There was a clear distinction between metropolitan London and the central, mile-square City of London, located on the north bank of the Thames. Ruled by a city corporation, with the Lord Mayor at its head, the City had a population of fewer than 130,000 and was politically independent from the rest of the metropolis. At its heart was the Bank of England, standing like a fortress within high, windowless walls, and the Mansion House, official residence of the Lord Mayor. The City was the financial center of London and most of its residents were shopkeepers and tradesmen.[38] It was a tightly knit community whose economic and political influence extended far beyond its bounds.

At the same time, the City had serious problems: almost no sewers; one hundred fifty slaughterhouses, most of them underground; and the

[36]Ibid., January 8, 1841, 2:25.
[37]Ibid., September 2, 1840, 1:506.
[38]Sheppard, *London*, 46.

worst prisons in all of England. A most distressing area was the Smithfield meat market on the north side. This "vile nuisance," as one historian has called it,[39] was the location of several slaughterhouses, and was often filled with an odious milieu of livestock and raucous human beings. On September 4, Wilford Woodruff visited the market during a fair. He wrote in his journal not only of the cattle headed for slaughter but also of the numerous exotic animals exhibited and the vast array of goods and sideshows crammed into the tight space: "men women, & children of almost evry grade & rank," prostitutes, a giant woman exhibiting a seven-foot high sheep weighing six hundred pounds, and a female snake charmer. Disgusted with such an amazing mass of beasts and revelling humanity, the American apostle could not help but compare it with something more familiar to him:

Should a Missourian from the western wiles of America whose knowledge extends ownly to his gun, Corn Crib & hog pen behold such a Scenery he would think he was in another world. What affect it would have upon him I know not but one thing is certain that any man that loved virtue peace & retirement would turn from such a

---

[39]Ibid., 22.

The Smithfield Market, London

scenery with his heart sicken within him knowing that virtue peace nor righteousness
Could not long dwell in such a sink of confusion & iniquity.[40]

Economically and socially, London's population was a study in remarkable contrasts. At the top was the landed aristocracy, consisting of
slightly more than three hundred families. With annual incomes of £5,000,
such a family often owned a mansion in the countryside in addition to a
mansion, or large townhouse, in one of London's exclusive residential
areas. Next on the social scale were another seven thousand people who
belonged to almost equally wealthy families and who, in combination with
the aristocracy, owned 80 percent of all the land in Britain. Then came
the rest of the upper class: bankers, merchants, and the most successful
businessmen whose living was extremely comfortable.

Next came the vast middle class, with its wide range of gradations in
wealth and living standards, including almost anyone with an annual income of £150 or more. The more affluent could often afford servants and
enjoy a profusion of activities and pleasures that bespoke a good life,
including grand shopping boulevards and bazaars, gardens and parks, art

---

[40]Woodruff, *Journal*, September 4, 1840, 1:507.

188

A Thaw in the Streets of London. Courtesy The Illustrated London News Picture Library

galleries, museums, concerts, and theaters. The shops were closed on Sunday, which became the day for family excursions to such places as Kensington Gardens, Hyde Park, and Regent's Park.[41] There were not many such open spaces left, however, and by the 1840s private pleasure gardens, open to the public for an admission fee and catering to the tastes of the middle class, were becoming popular. Often these parks offered such entertainment as fireworks, acrobatics, and balloon rides. London had much to offer those who had the time and money to take advantage of it.

Finally there was the "sunken sixth," as contemporaries dubbed London's lower classes: the poverty stricken who constituted some 16 percent of the population. Their growing numbers were largely a result of immigration from other parts of Britain, and many of the immigrants found nothing but unemployment, poverty, and squalor almost unheard of even in Manchester. Children born in the slums seemingly had no chance to learn about the world beyond them and seek a better life. With little opportunity for education and needing some way to help their families

---

[41]Sheppard, *London*, 356. For a comment on when these and other parks were opened to the public, see Hammond and Hammond, *Age of the Chartists*, 346n.

obtain the necessities of life, they turned to the trades of the streets: shoe-blacking, sweeping, and, at the very bottom of the scale of respectability, collecting from the streets cigar butts and animal manure, which they sold by the bucketful to tanneries.[42] Too often, they also turned to crime.

The contrast between rich and poor in London of the 1840s was incredible to the American Henry Coleman, who observed it with stunned disbelief: "In the midst of the most extraordinary abundance, here are men, women, and children dying of starvation; and running alongside of the splendid chariot, with its gilded equipages, its silken linings, and its liveried footmen, are poor, forlorn, friendless, almost naked wretches, looking like the mere fragments of humanity."[43] The American apostles had similar reactions. "It gave me pain," wrote Wilford Woodruff on February 2, 1841, "while passing through the streets of London this cold day to see poor women & esspecially children freezing nearly to death without food, fire, & but little cloathing but begging for a morsel to eat."[44]

London's masses were not as ready for the Mormon message as were the people of Herefordshire, Staffordshire, or Lancashire, and the three apostles found their time in London to be the most frustrating of their entire mission. When Wilford Woodruff later said that the London experience was "as profitable a school to me as any I have met with in my travels,"[45] he probably had in mind not only all he learned at the museums and historic sites but also what he learned about patience in the face of indifference, adversity, and relatively meager success.

For ten days the missionaries walked the streets of London, sometimes together and sometimes separately. They contacted individuals, visited established churches, talked to preachers, and spoke at temperance meetings, all in an effort to find someone who would listen to their message. On the first Sunday, August 23, they went twice to hear the celebrated Robert Aitken, who, George A. Smith said, "preached a regularly built hell-fire and damnation sermon" comparable to those of American revivalists Charles G. Finney and Jedediah Burchard.[46] Wilford Woodruff was impressed with some of the "sublime truths" he heard from Aitken and also

[42]Sheppard, *London*, 366.
[43]As quoted in ibid., 348.
[44]Woodruff, *Journal*, February 2, 1841, 2:36.
[45]Wilford Woodruff to the Editor, October 7, 1840, *Times and Seasons* 2 (February 15, 1841): 311–14; and (March 1, 1841): 327–31.
[46]Smith, "History," August 23, 1840.

with the way he lashed out at the ministers of the day. Nevertheless, he observed, Aitken was building a house with no foundation, for he rejected the first principles of the gospel.[47]

During all that week and a half the apostles were neither invited into a home nor given an opportunity to preach, except when George A. Smith lectured at a temperance meeting on August 25. They carried with them Parley P. Pratt's *Address . . . to the People of England*, sometimes leaving copies with people they visited, but they found no serious interest anywhere. Such total indifference was a new experience for all of them.

On August 28 they saw a small ray of hope when, after "we all started out in the morning to go through the city of London to see if we could find any man that had the spirit of God," they came across a Mr. Manning, who seemed to have a "good spirit" and was actually willing to talk to them. They soon discovered that Manning had recently lost a child and another lay near death, whereupon Heber C. Kimball felt inspired to tell him that his child should live. Manning gave them some information on where they might preach. That afternoon they stopped by his home and found that the child had recovered, but that was apparently the last they saw of Manning or his family.[48]

Finally, on August 29, they were invited into the home of Henry Connor, a watchmaker, on Ironmonger Row. He was so receptive that Woodruff was impressed that he would be baptized soon. He opened his house for preaching, and the delighted missionaries set up a meeting for the following evening, a Sunday.

On Sunday morning what they had been working and praying for finally began to happen. In the morning they went to the Smithfield Market, intending to hold a street meeting, but they were soon notified by the police that the Lord Mayor had prohibited street preaching within the City. Henry Connor immediately took them to Tabernacle Square, on Old Street, not far from his home and just outside the Lord Mayor's jurisdiction. There they found an Aitkenite standing on a chair preaching to about four hundred people. When he finished, another preacher arose, but Heber C. Kimball interrupted, pointing to George A. Smith and telling the first evangelist that an American was there who would like to preach. Interested in what an American would have to say, the preacher invited George A. to speak,

---

[47]Woodruff, *Journal*, August 23, 1840, 1:498.
[48]Ibid., August 28, 1840, 1:501–2.

which he gladly did for twenty minutes. His subject was the first principles of the gospel, though he did not specifically identify himself as a Latter-day Saint. The missionaries then tried to make an appointment to preach that afternoon, but when the man in charge suddenly discovered what church they represented, he immediately began to berate them. "We have got the gospel," he shouted to his listeners, "and we can save this people, without infidelity, socialism, or Latter-day Saints." Elder Kimball asked to stand on the chair and make an appointment with the people himself, but the irate preacher shouted at him again, jerked the chair from his hands, and ran away. Undaunted, Kimball simply told the people they would be back at 3:00 that afternoon, and when they arrived a large crowd was there. Kimball and Woodruff both spoke, and their listeners included not only the gathered crowd but also people living in buildings around the square who opened their windows, some as high as the fourth floor, to hear.

Elated at this turn of events, when the meeting was over the elders retired to Henry Connor's home. Kimball, however, suddenly felt impressed to go back, and when he did so, he found a large group of people talking about what they had heard. He spoke to them again, and several invited him to their homes. At the Connor home, meanwhile, Woodruff and Smith taught the gospel to Connor and others, and Connor offered himself for baptism. Thus ended their most satisfying day yet, for the three apostles had finally preached to the people of London and had "one soul as a seal of our ministry."[49] On Monday, August 31, they repaired to a nearby public bath, and, at the hands of Heber C. Kimball, Henry Connor became the first person to be baptized in London.[50]

Nevertheless, the three apostles were still far from satisfied. Each of them had recently enjoyed extraordinary success elsewhere, and they wondered why it was not so here. Impatience, however, was not discouragement. "London is the hardest place I ever visited for esstablishing the gospel," Wilford Woodruff wrote two days after Henry Connor's baptism. "It is full of evry thing but righteousness, but we do not feel discouraged in the least. We are determined in the name of the Lord to set up the Standard of truth in this city & to seek out the honest in heart & the meek from among men & warn all as far as in our power that the world may be left without excuse."[51]

---

[49]Ibid., August 30, 1840, 1:502–4. See also Smith, *History of the Church*, 4:183–84.

[50]Woodruff, *Journal*, August 31, 1840, 1:505; Smith, "History," August 31, 1840.

[51]Woodruff, *Journal*, September 2, 1840, 1:506.

In some ways the three apostles hardly seemed interesting to Londoners. All the dissenting sects were represented somewhere in the city, including such unusual groups as the Southcottians and the Irvingites. Southcottians believed that Joanna Southcott (1750–1814) was chosen by God to be, in a spiritual sense, the bride of Christ, that the Holy Spirit revealed to her things to come, that they should observe the Jewish Sabbath and certain Jewish dietary laws, and that believers could become "sealed" as "Heirs of God and Joint-Heirs with Jesus Christ."[52] The Irvingites, or the Catholic Apostolic Church, initially based their teachings on those of Edward Irving (1792–1834). They had strong millennial expectations, believed in the exercise of spiritual gifts, emphasized prophetic authority, had twelve apostles at their head (though the body of twelve was not perpetuated), and believed in a lay ministry.[53]

In a letter to the *Times and Seasons*, the three apostles observed how London's diversity of ideas and profusion of religious societies affected them. "We have never before found a people, from whose minds we have had to remove a greater multiplicity of objections, or combination of obstacles," they said. To many Londoners everything they taught seemed but an echo of something else. When they preached baptism, they were accused of being Baptists; when they spoke of the body of Christ being made up of apostles and prophets, they were called Irvingites; when they said that "the testimony of Jesus is the Spirit of prophecy," they were called Southcottians; if they preached the second coming of Christ, they were confused with the Aitkenites; if they talked of the priesthood, they were called Catholics; and when they told of the ministering of angels, their detractors replied that even the Duke of Normandy would swear that he had the administration of angels every night. Then, in a humorous summary of their own reaction, the missionaries said:

These salutations in connexion with a multitude of others, of a similar nature, continued to salute our ears from day to day, until we were about ready to conclude that London had been such a perfect depot of the systems of the nineteenth century, that it contained six hundred three score and six[54] different Gods, gospels, Redeemers, plans of salvations,

---

[52]Hastings, *Encyclopedia* 9:756. See also Hopkins, *Woman to Deliver Her People,* for a biography of Southcott.

[53]Hastings, *Encyclopedia* 7:423–27; Eliade, *Encyclopedia of Religion* 7:287. See also Lively, "Catholic Apostolic Church."

[54]Note the clever play on the number "six hundred three score and six" which, according to Revelation 13:18, was the number of the Beast.

Robert Aitken, nonconformist
British preacher. Courtesy
Charlotte E. Woods, *Memoirs
and Letters of Canon Hay
Aitken,* C. W. Daniel Co., Ltd.

religions, churches, commandments, essential and non essential, orders of preaching, roads to heaven and to hell; and that this order of things had so affected the minds of the people, that it almost required a *trump* to be blown from the highest heavens, in order to awaken the attention of the people, and prepare their minds to candidly hear and receive the doctrine of one gospel, one faith, one baptism, one Holy Ghost, one God, and one plan of salvation and that such as Christ and the Apostles preached.[55]

On September 7 Heber C. Kimball and George A. Smith visited the Reverend Robert Aitken, who remembered meeting Kimball and Orson Hyde during their previous mission to England.[56] He received them cordially and, after a conversation on gospel principles, even acknowledged that much of what they had to say was valid. By that time Aitken, who had left the movement that bore his name, was doing a great deal of soul searching about what course he should take. "Your doctrines are so near to those of the Gospel that it is impossible to detect you," he told the missionaries, evidently fearing that Mormonism was nothing more than a

---

[55]Heber C. Kimball, Wilford Woodruff, and George A. Smith to the Editors, October 12, 1840, *Times and Seasons* 2 (December 15, 1840): 257.

[56]Heber C. Kimball to Edward Martin, typescript, September 11, 1840, Heber C. Kimball Collection.

clever approximation of the truth inspired by the devil. After more conversation he began wringing his hands in agony. "I am sorry that I ever left the Church of England," he said and expressed remorse that he had preached and published so many hard things against it.[57]

London was first and foremost a mission field for the apostles, but it was also one of the richest historical and cultural spots on earth. The apostles believed that they would have been remiss in their responsibilities if they ignored the important attractions unique to London, and they took the time to see what they could. They visited London Bridge; many famous streets and byways, such as Regent Street, which Woodruff dubbed "one of the most splendid streets in the world," and Picadilly Circus; several cathedrals, including St. Paul's Cathedral and Westminster Abbey, both of which Woodruff described in detail in his journal; historic monuments; the markets; the tunnel under the River Thames; the Tower of London; the houses of Parliament; the parks of London; royal mansions; Buckingham Palace, where, on September 8, Wilford Woodruff saw young Prince Albert; and the National Gallery, with its famous collection of paintings from around the world. "A visit to this ABBEY," wrote Elder Woodruff after they had spent most of a day at Westminster Abbey, "is not ownly worthy of the Attention of all travellors but to occupy A place in the Journal of any Historian fond of British ANTIQUITY."[58]

On September 9 the missionaries moved to No. 40 Ironmonger Row, about a mile and a half north of the Thames. The move seemed natural, for whatever interest they had received came mostly from this area, Saint Luke's Parish, and the place they moved to was just across the street from Henry Connor's home. The streets were wide and clean, the houses, as George A. Smith described them, "retired and quiet," and the rooms nice though plainly furnished. Elders Kimball and Woodruff shared one bedroom, while George A. slept alone in a room in the back. This choice location remained the permanent headquarters for the London missionaries for the next two and a half years.[59]

The first night on Ironmonger Row provided Elder Smith with a fright-

[57]Smith, "History," September 7, 1840. See also Heber C. Kimball to Edward Martin, September 11, 1840.

[58]Woodruff, *Journal*, September 6, 1840, 1:508. Many of the historical sites they visited at this time and later were described in detail in a letter to the *Times and Seasons*. See Heber C. Kimball, Wilford Woodruff, and George A. Smith to the Editors, October 28, 1840, *Times and Seasons* 2 (January 1, 1841): 261–64.

[59]Woodruff, *Journal*, September 9, 1840, 1:511–12; Bloxham, "Apostolic Foundations," 155.

ening experience that made him realize that his previous skepticism on the reported experiences of others might have been misplaced. During the night, he wrote, he was "constantly annoyed by visitations from the spirit of darkness, which required all my faith and energy of mind to resist." He said little about it to his companions, however, for he had always felt "somewhat sceptical" with regard to the appearances of evil spirits to Heber C. Kimball and Orson Hyde in Preston three years earlier. He suffered his own bouts with the forces of evil alone and perhaps learned an important lesson.[60]

The next day Wilford Woodruff left to attend conferences in Herefordshire and Staffordshire and then go to Manchester for the general conference of October 6. There had been no more baptisms in London, but Woodruff felt a little encouraged because Connor had been ordained a priest, six people had agreed to be baptized, and, he believed, there was a possibility that Robert Aitken might join the Church.[61] The last, however, proved to be a fruitless hope. Unwilling to risk being deceived, Aitken eventually returned to the Anglican fold.

It was not just missionary work that suffered in London but also the apostles' health, and Elders Kimball and Smith, especially, suffered continuing illness. Shortly after Woodruff left, Kimball had a bout with what he believed to be cholera, with terrible cramps in his legs and bowels. In his pain he thought of home, for, he told Vilate, "I was in a strange place and no one to assist me." Chills came on him so severely that he thought he was freezing to death, so he climbed into bed with George A. Smith just to keep warm. The next day he could hardly walk, and he remained that way for three days.[62]

The apostles in London were not forgotten by the Saints elsewhere, though they could do little more than encourage them. On September 21, Alexander Neibaur, a Jewish convert living in Preston who later became Joseph Smith's Hebrew teacher, wrote a few words of consolation and advice to Elders Kimball and Smith after he had heard of their continuing struggles and sickness:

Our Dear Brother Kimball said many times that there are no big Men or little men in the Kingdom of our God. This embold[e]nes me to give a Word of consolation to you

---

[60]Smith, "History," September 9, 1840.
[61]Woodruff, *Journal*, September 10, 1840, 1:512.
[62]Heber C. Kimball to Vilate Kimball, September 19, 1840, Heber C. Kimball Collection.

Respecting London. I feel dear Br. that it is a hard Work for you. Nevertheless I know by the Spirit of our God that a Glorious Work will be wrought there. You know weeping may endure for a Night but joy comet[h] in the Morning, it only wants labourers. . . . My Wife sends her kind love to you, all the Saints greet you. Again I say in the Name of Jesus Christ cheer up and you shall Rejoice yea we will Rejoice in our fathers Kingdom.[63]

By the time Heber C. Kimball and George A. Smith left for Manchester, a total of eleven people had been baptized in London. In a rather humorous incident, one prospective member backed out. On September 19 a man called Father Biggs came to their rooms asking for baptism. They all repaired to the public bath, paid their entrance fee, and went in. The water, however, was so cold that it scared Biggs off. "Oh," he said as he stepped in, "it will take my breath! I feel it going!" and he refused to be immersed. Not willing to waste their money, however, Elders Kimball and Smith took the occasion to go in swimming. Six days later Father Biggs was finally baptized.[64]

Despite the comparatively meager harvest in London, Heber C. Kimball refused to be discouraged. He wrote to his wife that the ice was broken and the Church finally was getting such a hold that

the Devle cannot Root it out. But he is verry mad and I am glad. I never Shall try to pleas him. . . . You may think I feel discouradg my dear Vilate. I will say unto you I never have Seen the first moment as yet fore I dow not See anny thing to discourag me but Evry thing to the Reverse. I know that I am built on the foundation of Jesus Christ and the Apostles. . . . It maters not to me whather I die or live if I dow the will of my Father which is in heaven.[65]

George A. Smith left for Manchester on September 29 and Kimball followed a few days later. En route, George A. traveled through the Potteries where he was warmly received by the Saints, who "brought in their mites to furnish me money to pay my passage to Manchester."[66]

WILFORD WOODRUFF: BACK TO HEREFORDSHIRE

Wilford Woodruff left London on September 10 and arrived among the Saints in Herefordshire about 4:00 P.M. that day. He was delighted to find missionary work in good hands and, in marked contrast with London,

---

[63]Alexander Neibaur to George A. Smith and Heber C. Kimball, September 21, 1840, George A. Smith Collection.
[64]Smith, "History," September 19 and 27, 1840.
[65]Heber C. Kimball to Vilate Kimball, September 19, 1840.
[66]Smith, "History," October 5, 1840.

Gadfield Elm Chapel, by Al Rounds. Courtesy Mr. and Mrs. Jack Emery

the Church growing steadily. "I rejoice," he exclaimed, "to find the work universally progressing with great rapidity upon evry hand. . . . Yea the Lord is making a spedy work & short in the Earth."[67]

He spent the next several days visiting the Saints, working with local leaders, and, in connection with Thomas Kington and his assistants, conducting two conferences: one at the Gadfield Elm chapel on September 14 and another a week later at Stanley Hill. As he shook hands with the Saints at the end of that day, he was filled "with no ordinary feelings" and silently gave thanks that more than a thousand people had accepted the Gospel within a half year in "one field which God has enabled me to open." That night he summarized in his diary one of the busiest days he had ever spent in Herefordshire. "After standing upon my feet 8 hours in Conference, Conversing much of the time, Ordaining about 30, confirming some, healing many that were Sick, Shaking hands with about 400 Saints,

---

[67]Woodruff, *Journal,* September 10, 1840, 1:512.

wa[l]king 2 miles, & Preaching 4 hours in the Chimney Corner, I then lay down & dreamed of Ketching fish."[68]

Woodruff was especially pleased with Thomas Kington, who presided in the area and had built up a congregation of about fifty Saints in his hometown of Dymock. When the apostle visited Dymock on September 16, he also found that there was no let-up in opposition. When the Saints assembled to hear him preach, a mob gathered outside the house, beating drums, pails, pans, and sticks and generally trying to disrupt the meeting. The Saints closed the doors and shutters, but the rowdies threw eggs, bricks, rocks, and anything else they could grab, breaking glass and roof tile. The Saints took it all in stride, however, apparently without bitterness, though after the mob drifted away, they had the task of clearing the rooms of the debris.[69]

On September 26 Woodruff went to Staffordshire, where he was joined on October 1 by Smith and Kimball, who had just arrived from London. Four days later they and three other apostles were in Manchester.

Orson Pratt: Slightly Discouraged

Pushing slowly but doggedly toward his goal of two hundred converts in Edinburgh, by mid September Orson Pratt had built up a congregation of forty.[70] He showed signs of discouragement, though, especially when he heard of the success of others. "I was not as much favored as you for I could not get the Priests out to hear as you have done," he wrote to George A. Smith, but "I keep hammering & pounding away perhaps the stone will break by and by." He also tried to encourage George A., whose work in London was suffering the same fate as his own. "Hold on to the Londonites for it is an important station. . . . If you cannot turn the London world upside down perhaps you can weaken its foundations."[71]

The work was prospering a little better elsewhere in Scotland, and by the time Orson Pratt and Samuel Mulliner went to the Manchester conference, there were 193 members in the Glasgow region and 43 in Edinburgh.[72]

---

[68]Ibid., September 21, 1840, 1:517–20.

[69]Ibid., September 16, 1840, 1:516–17.

[70]Reuben Hedlock to George A. Smith, September 17, 1840, George A. Smith Collection.

[71]Orson Pratt to George A. Smith, September 24, 1840, George A. Smith Collection (Appendix B, Document 13). He repeated the admonition in another letter: Orson Pratt to George A. Smith, October 17, 1840, George A. Smith Collection.

[72]"Minutes of the General Conference," *Millennial Star* 1 (October 1840): 166. Note that these minutes are identified in the *Star* as the minutes of the July conference, but this is clearly a misprint.

THE MANCHESTER CONFERENCE, OCTOBER 6 AND 7

Taking stock midway through their mission, the Twelve had reason to be pleased—indeed amazed—at what had been accomplished. But the challenge still ahead weighed heavily on their minds, particularly in the face of the calamities they expected soon to come. Perhaps thoughts such as these caused Wilford Woodruff and Heber C. Kimball to awaken on the morning of October 2 feeling that the power of God was resting upon them. "Yea," Wilford wrote, using a familiar metaphor, "the spirit of God is like fire shut up in my bones." Why was this happening, he wondered, and why were his eyes a fountain of tears? "What art thou about to do O my God that causes this thing?" In response, the missionary-apostle received a revelation that forcefully reconfirmed all his feelings about the importance of what he and his brethren were doing:

> Thus Saith the Lord God unto thee my servant Willford. This is my spirit that resteth upon thee to enlighten thy mind to show the things to cum not ownly upon thee but upon all my faithful servants upon the face of the whole earth. Therefore lift up thy voice & spare not for I am about to perform a great work upon the face of the earth Saith the Lord. Mine indignation is about to be poured out without mixture upon the heads of this nation & all the nations of the earth & they shall not escape. The cry of the poor, the widow & orphan is assending into mine ears Saith the Lord & I am about to avenge the cry of mine elect by laying low the oppresser & executing the decree of mine heart upon all the ungodly from among men.
>
> Therefore I put my spirit upon the[e] & say unto thee lift up thy voice & spare not & Call upon all men to repent that cume within the sound of thy voice & many souls shall be given unto the[e] & great shall be thy reward & eternal shall be thy glory Saith the Lord.[73]

No doubt the revelation only added to the fire in Wilford Woodruff's bones, and it was with similar fire in all their bones that six of the eight apostles met for a general conference in Manchester.

The Twelve had originally planned to hold a conference every three months, but as October approached, it appeared difficult to get even a majority of the quorum back to Manchester. Parley P. Pratt was still somewhere on the high seas, accompanying his family to England. John Taylor, on the Isle of Man in the midst of his public debates with the Reverend Heys, felt that he could not leave the field of battle.[74] Orson Pratt, in Scotland,

---

[73]Woodruff, *Journal*, October 2, 1840, 1:524–25.

[74]"I am very sory that I am prevented from coming but think that it would not be prudent at the present time," he explained to Brigham Young (John Taylor to Brigham Young, October 2, 1840, Brigham Young Papers).

was also debating whether to attend, and, in London, Heber C. Kimball and George A. Smith considered the possibility that only one of them should leave. Brigham Young and Willard Richards bluntly reminded them that there was business the Twelve should handle collectively and that "we barely have a quorum in Europe." They had written Orson Pratt and left the decision up to him, "as we now leave it with you. *We should be glad to see you.*"[75] In the end, only John Taylor stayed away, and because Parley had not yet returned to England, six members of the Quorum of the Twelve were in Manchester for the conference that began on October 6.

Brigham Young carried with him a list of problems that he thought should be discussed. Where should the Book of Mormon be published? Who will take charge of the *Star* if Parley P. Pratt does not return? Should some of the Twelve go home in the fall and come back the next season? When should the next company of emigrants go to America, and how should it be organized? Who should have authority to ordain officers in the Church? Would the Church help Brother Richards financially? Who should make and prepare the index of the Book of Mormon? Not all these issues were aired, but the list suggests the myriad of administrative concerns that occupied the thoughts of the president of the Quorum of the Twelve as he prepared for this conference.[76]

The first item of business was a membership report from each of the conferences, or branches, represented. The figures showed a total of 3,626 members in Britain—an increase of 1,113, or 44 percent, in just three months. The numbers were satisfying, but rapid growth also brought unexpected irregularities and administrative problems, and it was clear to the Twelve that a few things must be checked before they got out of hand. For one thing, it appeared that there had been some irregularity in ordaining priesthood officers. Perhaps the Twelve discovered that their own practice of ordaining selected men to the priesthood and giving them leadership responsibilities almost overnight had been followed too hastily by some local leaders. In any case, it was decided that henceforth all ordinations would take place by or under the direction of one of the Twelve. It also appeared that local conferences were being held too often,

[75]They also said that if they decided not to have another conference for six months, and then meet in London, this would be the last Manchester conference, but, they added, "we say 'if,' which costs nothing" (Brigham Young and Willard Richards to Heber C. Kimball and George A. Smith, September 28, 1840, Brigham Young Papers).

[76]Notes, October 6, 1840, Brigham Young Papers.

Confrence - Oct-6-1840

Whare shall the Book of
Mormon be bound what
stile shall it be bound in
Shall we despose of it —

Who shall take Charge of the
Malennal Star- if P. Pratt dos not com

is it best for som of the 12 to goe
home this fall and com back next
seson

what time shall the next
Company goe to america and how
shall they be organized to goe

Bisness of the confrence
on the 6 of oct-
Represent the Churches

Sarah Perkins lives
in Gommet St No 15 —

Thomas Miller lives in
Edward St No 2 or 3 - —

Shall we rase a sum of money
and send a Delagate with it to
america for the printing the new
translation of the bible

Brothers Mellen &
whitehead recive pay

Who shall have authority
to ordane officers in the
Churches

will the Church help
Brother Richards

Who shall make or prepare
the endex to the Book of Mormon

Brigham Young's notes for the conference of October 6, 1840
Courtesy LDS Church Archives

and the time and extra expense incurred by members in order to attend was becoming too heavy. Brigham Young suggested that henceforth they be held only when necessary, as determined by the Twelve. The conference also took care of some disciplinary action.

Ten high priests were in attendance at the conference (including the six apostles), thirteen elders and nineteen priests, all of whom were spending their full time in the ministry. In the evening meeting, several missionaries were assigned to new places of labor, after which Brigham Young, Orson Pratt, Willard Richards, and Heber C. Kimball all spoke on one of the most pressing needs of the moment: providing support and clothing for those missionaries whose circumstances required such help. Orson Pratt made it clear that theirs was nothing like a paid ministry: the missionaries did not make a living from it, but there were certain necessities that had to be taken care of while they were called to labor "without taking thought for the morrow." It was agreed, finally, that two members would be appointed in every branch of the Church to receive weekly voluntary contributions from the members for promoting the spread of the gospel, and that the funds collected would be dispensed by the vote of the Church, in council with the traveling high council (the Twelve).[77]

The next day the Twelve met with other Church officers, and that night most of them were among the fifteen hundred people who attended a public debate in Carpenter's Hall. A month earlier Brigham Young had signed an agreement for the debate to take place between John Berry, a Methodist preacher, and an elder of Brigham Young's choosing. Berry agreed to "prove" that the Book of Mormon was false and that baptism by immersion was not essential to salvation. The Mormon elder, on the other hand, was to "prove" the opposite. Berry arranged for the hall and for advertising but both sides shared the expense.[78] Brigham Young chose Alfred Cordon, one of the most energetic missionaries from the Potteries, to represent the Church, and the debate lasted well over two hours. How non-Mormons reacted is not known, but George A. Smith thought that Cordon defended the doctrine of baptism "so clearly that no honest man could go away and say it was not a scriptural doctrine."[79] "Much good was done," he said, though it does not appear that such public debates usually resulted in many immediate conversions.

[77]*Millennial Star* 1 (October 1840): 165–68.
[78]Memorandum of intent to hold a debate, September 4, 1840, Brigham Young Papers.
[79]Smith, "History," October 7, 1840; Woodruff, *Journal*, October 7, 1840, 1:526–27.

The Twelve remained in Manchester for a few days, counseling with each other, writing, preaching, and buying clothing. Wilford Woodruff bought a traveling bag and a hat, and five of the apostles each purchased a broadcloth cloak, all of them just alike. More important, Wilford Woodruff, Willard Richards, and Jennetta Richards each received patriarchal blessings from Peter Melling.[80]

---

[80]Woodruff, *Journal*, October 7–12, 1841, 1:526–28. The cloaks were purchased on October 12, and the apostles who bought them, according to this account, were Elders Young, Kimball, Richards, Woodruff, and Smith. The latter, however, was already back in London, so the others must have purchased it for him.

Chapter 9

CONSOLIDATION:
OCTOBER 1840 THROUGH MARCH 1841

The apostles opened no new fields during the final six months of their mission. Instead they worked in familiar places, gleaning all they could to add to the harvest and continuing to direct the gathering. By the first of the year they were planning their return to America, and they spent the next three months organizing the churches, building up the Saints, and winding down their activities.

THE MANCHESTER-LIVERPOOL CONNECTION: BRIGHAM, PARLEY, WILLARD, AND JOHN

Because Manchester and Liverpool were the administrative hubs of the Church in England, Brigham Young spent considerable time in both cities. On October 19 Parley P. Pratt arrived in Manchester with his family. There he resumed editing the *Millennial Star,* preached when he could, and sometimes entered into public debates.[1] There, too, lived Willard and Jennetta Richards. Willard assisted Brigham Young, wrote for the *Star*, counseled with the Saints, and preached. After returning from the Isle of Man on November 16, John Taylor once again made Liverpool his headquarters. Heber C. Kimball also worked closely with his brethren in these cities, especially in Manchester, until he left for London in November.

As Brigham and Heber continued to bring in converts, their success also helped stir up continued opposition in Manchester. "The Devle Rages here most powerfully," Heber wrote to George A. Smith on October 14. "Those five persons that I baptised on Fridy night has Raised the Devle in

---

[1]Brigham Young to Mary Ann Young, November 12, 1840, Phillip Blair Collection, wherein Brigham briefly describes one such debate.

Model of engine and car of the Liverpool and Manchester Railway,
the first major railroad to be completed. Copyright National Railway Museum, York

this place," and the Wesleyans had been meeting every night to try to persuade them to come back.[2] In the same spirit, Brigham wrote to his wife: "Sence we have ben in Manchester We have don all that we posably could to spead this work. We have succeeded in makeing the priest mad, so that they rave like demonds. We keepe Baptiseing every weak which causes much per[se]cution."[3] One manifestation of the persecution, as Brigham Young observed in November, was that "Menny of the Bretherin are turned out of worke because of their religion, and those that are instrementle in throwing them out generaly get turned out them selves." The Rigby family, for example, with whom he had lived most of the summer, suffered when Brother Rigby was "turned out of work about 2 or 3 weaks agoe on account of his religon, but the factory stoped in a fue days after, and has not started yet."[4]

Such problems, along with the general poverty of the members, tore at Brigham's heart and heightened his appreciation for all the Saints did for him. As he told Mary Ann, despite feeling unwell and longing for a

[2]Heber C. Kimball and Brigham Young to George A. Smith, October 14, 1840, George A. Smith Collection.
[3]Brigham Young to Mary Ann Young, October 16, 1840 (Appendix B, Document 15).
[4]Brigham Young to Mary Ann Young, November 12, 1840.

warmer climate, "I am duing as well as I can and fare as well as I can ask. The Brotherin and Sisters would pluck out there eyes for me if it ware ne[ce]ssary. They due all they can for my comfort. They feed me and give me close and monny. They wash my feet and wate upon me as they would a little child, and may the Lord bless them for it and he will."[5]

On the last day of October, Brigham and Heber took a short trip to Harwardin, Wales, where they both preached on Sunday, November 1. They healed a young man with a fever and a woman with bad eyesight, but it was their preaching that created the most interest. "They say," Brigham reported to Mary Ann, "that Elder Kimball has such sharp eyes that he can look wright through them, and Elder Young Preashes so that every Body that heres him must beleve he preaches so plane and powerful."[6]

Brigham organized the priesthood holders to do missionary work in Manchester similar to the way John Taylor had done in Liverpool. Every Sunday morning they scattered to various parts of the city, preached in the streets at nearly forty different locations, and invited their listeners to the regular meetings at Carpenter's Hall. In November irate sectarian preachers complained to the mayor, who then ordered all street preachers arrested. When Brigham went to priesthood meeting on the morning of November 8, however, he felt impressed to tell the brethren to return to their homes rather than preach. That day the police arrested some twenty Methodist street preachers, but when it was discovered that there were no Mormons among them, they were quickly released.[7]

Brigham Young had hoped to spend the winter and spring in London,[8] but administrative responsibilities made that impossible and ultimately he could find time only for a short stay. He left Manchester with Heber C. Kimball on November 25, and after eleven days in London and a quick visit to missionaries in other places, he was back in Manchester the day after Christmas. A few days later he went on to Liverpool, where he remained through most of January and February and where, in January, he completed indexing and publishing the Book of Mormon.

In early January Brigham Young, Parley P. Pratt, and Willard Richards held conferences in Liverpool and Preston. One of their concerns was to

---

[5]Brigham Young to Mary Ann Young, October 16, 1840 (Appendix B, Document 15).
[6]Brigham Young to Mary Ann Young, November 12, 1840.
[7]Young, *Manuscript History*, 82–83.
[8]Brigham Young to Mary Ann Young, October 16, 1840 (Appendix B, Document 15).

be sure that local leadership was functioning well before they left. At Preston, for example, they made it clear that new ordinations to the priesthood were the responsibility of the local presidency. In view of the October prohibition on new ordinations without apostolic approval, this step was an important one, for if the Twelve could now trust such matters to local leaders, a great portion of their mission was accomplished.

The three apostles also preached on the subject of the gathering. Parley P. Pratt underscored how reasonable it was for a "dense and hungry" population to look for better conditions elsewhere. The other two apostles provided practical details on how to act when traveling and how much money was needed, even advising the Saints to borrow if they could. "This set the Saints on the move," Joseph Fielding reported, and many were determined to get ready for the first ship to New Orleans.[9]

By this time England was experiencing the coldest part of the year, and the frigid weather discouraged some prospective Saints from being baptized. Others gritted their teeth and went into the water anyway, and the Church continued to grow. In February, the editor of the *Star* noted favorable missionary reports from Edinburgh, Glasgow, London, Birmingham, Stockport, Bolton, Oldham, Ashton, Herefordshire, Staffordshire, Wales, and many other places.

Scores are bringing forth fruits of repentance, and are uniting with the Saints in baptism, notwithstanding the weather is so severe. This is a matter of astonishment to the public: some threaten our lives, thinking it will kill those who go into the cold water, and others exclaim that it must be the work of God, or they would die, by being thus exposed in such cold weather. In the mean time the Sectarian priests are raging and lying as usual, and the editors of newspapers are helping them to publish lies against the truth. But all to no purpose; for God works and none can hinder.[10]

The cold weather, however, brought its share of misery, and in Manchester it was accompanied by scarlet fever and other illnesses. One family of Saints buried three children at the same time.[11]

Most of Parley P. Pratt's time was consumed by the *Millennial Star*. He relished the work, for he saw the *Star* as a vehicle for disseminating

---

[9]Fielding, Diary, 100–101.

[10]*Millennial Star* 1 (February 1841): 263. In the Potteries, George A. Smith noted that the number of baptisms in January was less than the previous month for "Some have had A Disposition to let of[f] Baptism on account of the cold Weather." (George A. Smith to his Father and Mother, in letter to George Gee, January 28, 1841, George A. Smith Collection).

[11]Parley P. Pratt to Sidney Rigdon, January 8, 1841, *Times and Seasons* 2 (April 1, 1841): 364–65.

Church news and doctrine and also for defending the Church against attack. Anti-Mormon pamphlets seemed to be flooding the country, he wrote to Sidney Rigdon, and "John Bull" was more ingenious even than the Americans when it came to inventing lies.[12] A master of witty and often biting sarcasm, he frequently used his skill in rapierlike counterattacks. In February 1841, for example, he answered a series of doctrinal questions submitted by Joseph Fielding, the last of which was, "What is meant by that common and popular saying, 'The Canon of scripture is full?' " He simply did not know the meaning of this "sectarian logic," Parley feigned, but if he must venture an opinion on the statement,

we suppose it to apply to some false system, where the people worship a DUMB AND CHANGEABLE GOD; whom they suppose to have been in the habit of talking with man, in olden times; but who has long since lost his SPEECH, either by old age or some other means, so that they should never hear from him any more. At any rate, we are sure of one thing, viz., that the text cannot apply to the true and living God, nor to the HOLY Scriptures, for they every where hold forth the principle of continued REVELATION.[13]

On April 7, 1840, the *Edinburgh Intelligencer* published a long attack on the Book of Mormon, which gave Parley another chance to whet his pen and do battle. At the end of an extended reply, he caustically inquired of the editors of the *Intelligencer*: "Gentlemen will any of you venture to give your readers both sides of the question, by publishing the foregoing reply? We fear you will not."[14]

Parley also found opportunity for more direct missionary work. On one occasion two Campbellite ministers traveled seventy miles to attend a Latter-day Saint meeting in Manchester. The next morning they called at the office of the *Star*. One bought a copy of Parley P. Pratt's *Voice of Warning*, and the other remained in town for three days, asking questions. Parley expressed his delight to Sidney Rigdon, who had been his own pastor when both were Campbellites more than ten years earlier: "Tell friend Campbell to go ahead and prepare the way, the Saints will follow him up and gather the fruits."[15]

On January 20, while preaching to a small religious group in Bolton,

---

[12]Ibid.

[13]*Millennial Star* 1 (February 1841): 259.

[14]Ibid., 2 (May 1841): 1–4.

[15]Parley P. Pratt to Sidney Rigdon, January 8, 1841 (Appendix B, Document 23). See also D&C 35:3–5, in which Sidney Rigdon was told that he had been sent to prepare the way for Joseph Smith.

Parley was furiously interrupted by two preachers who demanded that he "prove" the truth of his new doctrine. When the meeting became a near riot the police came, handcuffed the two men, and marched them away. At least one of them, James Pendlebury, was found guilty of breach of the peace, fined ten pounds, and required to pay for damages to the building.[16]

Willard and Jennetta Richards, meanwhile, continued on in Manchester, and on Sunday, October 11, Jennetta gave birth to a baby boy. They named him Heber John, the same as their first child, who had died only ten months earlier. Both mother and child suffered recurring illnesses of one sort or another almost until the day they left for America.

Twelve days after the baby was born, Willard received what must have seemed a mixed blessing. Susannah Liptrot, his former Preston landlady who had been driven out by her husband, was living with them as their housekeeper. On the evening of October 23, her husband, John, unexpectedly showed up at the house and asked for baptism. "He thinks he has served the Devil long enough," Willard observed, and even though it was "raining like pitchforks," he baptized the repentant husband about 9:00 P.M., confirmed him a member of the Church, and took him home to Susannah. Willard and Jennetta were happy for the reunited couple, but Willard again had the care of his not very healthy family all to himself. With his mission responsibilities already consuming nearly all of his time, that only intensified his long-standing perplexity at trying to find a balance between two competing obligations.[17]

Sometime in late November or early December Willard spent ten days in Bolton, and upon his return discovered that both Jennetta and the baby were seriously ill. He spent three days and nights almost without sleep, nursing them the best he could, until finally a Sister Muir relieved him for two days. After that a friend by the name of Catherine assisted occasionally, as Willard alternated between Church duties and his family. He tried to get more help, but other people had their own problems. One sister, for example, was "very kind and would be glad to do for us but she has twice too much work of her own for any woman."[18] Disheartened, he wondered if he would ever find the time he desperately needed to fulfill his apostolic duties: "God knows whether I will ever have the priv-

[16]*Millennial Star* 1 (February 1841): 255–56.

[17]Willard Richards to Brigham Young and Heber C. Kimball, October 24, 1840, Brigham Young Papers.

[18]Willard Richards to Heber C. Kimball and Wilford Woodruff, December 21, 1840, Helen Bourne Fleming Collection.

ilege of going into the vineyard or not," he wrote to Brigham Young on December 10. "He knows I desire it."[19] The apostle and his wife patiently endured their trials. In a poignant letter to George A. Smith, Willard laid bare both his troubles and his faith:

I had half proposed in my heart to have met Brother Young at Conference on the 25th But I see no prospect. I am confined night and day with a Sick family. & I believe few expect the life of Heber John. I want your faith & prayer that the promises & prophecies of his life & his posterity on the earth may be realized—for I have nearly to stand alone in this matter. Sister Richards sends her love, fell down stairs yesterday & is very sore yet God is Kind.[20]

John Taylor, meanwhile, carried on with his ambitious preaching schedule in Liverpool's Music Hall, the "largest & best hall" in town. He continued to labor closely with Brigham Young on publications and in organizing emigration,[21] but he also visited other places, including Wales and the Isle of Man. He may have gone to the Isle in January,[22] but he was also there in March. After a preaching meeting in Douglas on March 17, he baptized twelve people. The next day he baptized another, and several more were ready to join the Church.[23] He was back in Liverpool by March 23.

"THE PEOPLE HERE WILL GET WAKED UP AFTER AWHILE": ORSON PRATT CONTINUES HIS MISSION IN EDINBURGH

After the October conference, Orson Pratt went directly back to Edinburgh, where he continued to work toward his goal of two hundred converts. More people than ever came to hear him, especially on Sundays,

---

[19]Willard Richards to Brigham Young, December 10, 1840, as quoted in Noall, *Intimate Disciple*, 266–67. While this work cannot be relied upon for either its manufactured dialogue or its interpretations, it is nevertheless generally accurate with respect to specific people and locations, and quotations from letters.

[20]Willard Richards to George A. Smith, December 21, 1840, George A. Smith Collection. See also Willard Richards to Heber C. Kimball and Wilford Woodruff, December 21, 1840.

[21]"Er Young and myself have been very busy lately preparing passengers & ships for Zion" (John Taylor to Leonora Taylor, February 13, 1841, John Taylor Collection).

[22]John Taylor to George A. Smith, January 14, 1841, George A. Smith Collection, wherein Taylor writes that he has been ill but is somewhat better and will "start to day for the Isle of Man for a few days."

[23]John Taylor to Mr. Greenow, March 23, 1841, typescript, John Taylor Collection. Apparently he wanted to return in February, rather than March, and tried to persuade Joseph Fielding to accompany him. Fielding was afraid to leave his wife who had just given birth to a baby girl and was still in great pain. "I am still afraid to leave my Wife," Fielding wrote on February 20, "yet I hope to be at liberty soon. I feel thankful that I and my Wife have the good will of the Saints and of the Elders" (Fielding, Diary, 103).

and he baptized a few each week. By the end of October the membership was over seventy.[24] He reported to the *Star* on October 17:

We preach about seven times on every Sabbath, and we also preach every night, in the streets. When the weather will permit, large congregations gather round us eager to hear. During our last three meetings in the streets we disposed of something like eighty printed addresses. The people here will get waked up after awhile, and begin to oppose. The work will go ahead, however, opposition or no opposition.[25]

In the intellectual milieu of Edinburgh, the interest exhibited was often merely a sign of tolerant curiosity, whereas elsewhere confrontation seemed to both attract attention and kindle a desire to know more. Orson longed for the same kind of opportunity in Edinburgh. "I presume we could do more good in Edinburgh & London if we could bring the enemy into open combat but in this place I can hardly get a dog to move his tongue."[26]

Orson did everything he could, however, to increase the Church's visibility. In Leith, about a mile from Edinburgh, he hired a hall for two Sundays and preached in the streets as well. He also hired a second hall in Edinburgh that held nearly fifty people and also had a good fireplace and a bedroom for the missionaries. There the Saints began to hold their prayer meetings. They wanted to hire a larger hall, but "our means are limited & the saints all poor," Orson observed.[27] Nonetheless, he wrote to Wilford Woodruff on November 16, "[I] am thankful that I have been enabled to lay the foundation of a church in Edinburgh."[28]

About the first of November, George D. Watt, the first person baptized in England, arrived in Edinburgh to assist Elder Pratt. He left a family in Preston and, like the other missionaries, relied on the people for his sustenance. Perhaps his wife sent a little money, but she was struggling even to support the family. When he visited her in January he found her

---

[24]In Orson Pratt to Parley P. Pratt, October 17, 1840, excerpted in *Millennial Star* 1 (December 1840): 214, Pratt said there were seventy-four members. There is a discrepancy here, however, for in letters to George A. Smith on October 17 and 24, he reported forty-eight and fifty-four members, respectively. A possible explanation could be that he reported to Smith on Edinburgh alone, while to the *Star* he was including the larger area around Edinburgh. Orson Pratt to George A. Smith, October 17, 1840, George A. Smith Collection; Orson Pratt to George A. Smith, October 24, 1840, George A. Smith Collection.

[25]*Millennial Star* 1 (December 1840): 214.

[26]Orson Pratt to George A. Smith and Wilford Woodruff, November 2, 1840, George A. Smith Collection (Appendix B, Document 16).

[27]Orson Pratt to Wilford Woodruff and George A. Smith, November 6, 1840, Wilford Woodruff Collection.

[28]Quotation included in Wilford Woodruff to George A. Smith, November 21, 1840, Wilford Woodruff Collection.

unwell, "almost worked to death in those *abominable Factories.*"[29] Watt persisted in his mission, however, and was left in charge of the work in Scotland when Orson returned to America.

The two preached in the streets every evening, weather permitting,[30] and by December they finally attracted some of the opposition Orson craved. Their meetings were interrupted almost every night, they wrote with delight to George A. Smith. "The priests are begining to get mad, and warn their congregations not to come and hear us, as it is dangerous to hear us. This we hope will do good, for when ever the *priests* begin to *Bark* the sheep gets terrified and runs into the fold, that is kept by the true shephard."[31] On December 4 and 5 Pratt participated in a debate with an angry Methodist priest, who apparently did little but embarrass himself, and as a result at least three people were baptized and several others began to show serious interest.[32]

At the end of the year Orson went to Glasgow, where he spent a little over two weeks helping Reuben Hedlock, who was ill. He also visited the Saints in Paisley, Johnston, and Bridge of the Weir.[33] In his absence, Watt baptized ten people in the icy waters of the North Sea, bringing Edinburgh's membership to 122, and they added fifteen more by the end of the month.[34] The apostle's goal of two hundred seemed within reach.

BACK TO LONDON: GEORGE A. SMITH AND WILFORD WOODRUFF

George A. Smith went directly to London from the October conference, and Wilford Woodruff followed him about a week later. On the way, however, Wilford felt a heavy foreboding that remained with him for days. Convinced that terrible persecution and trials were about to come upon the Saints in Europe and in America, his trepidation intensified when other Saints told of having similar apprehensions.[35] He arrived in London on Saturday, October 17, and by Sunday night he felt well enough in his mind that he was able to sleep comfortably until midnight. Then he awoke and

[29]Orson Pratt to George A. Smith, February 1, 1841, George A. Smith Collection.

[30]Orson Pratt to George A. Smith, November 23, 1840, George A. Smith Collection.

[31]George D. Watt and Orson Pratt to George A. Smith, December 4, 1840, George A. Smith Collection.

[32]George D. Watt and Orson Pratt to George A. Smith, December 11, 1840, George A. Smith Collection.

[33]Reuben Hedlock to George A. Smith, January 12, 1841, George A. Smith Collection; George D. Watt to George A. Smith, January 16, 1841, George A. Smith Collection.

[34]George D. Watt to George A. Smith, January 16, 1841, George A. Smith Collection; Orson Pratt to George A. Smith, February 1, 1841.

[35]Woodruff, *Journal*, October 14 and 15, 1840, 1:528–31.

for three hours meditated upon his mission, renewing his determination to overcome the powers of darkness that seemed to be bridling the work in England's capital city. Suddenly the apprehension of the last several days came to a head when, he said, a person whom he considered the Prince of Darkness appeared to him, fought with him, and nearly choked him to death. "As he was about to overcome me I prayed to the father in the name of Jesus for help. I then had power over him & he left me though much wounded." At that point three more persons appeared, all dressed in white, and "prayed with me & I was immediately healed & delivered me from all my troubles."[36]

The days of presentiment were over and Wilford Woodruff was soon back to preaching in the streets of London, as optimistic as ever. The days of anguish were not over, however, for just four days later he learned through George A. Smith of the death of his two-year old daughter, Sarah Emma Woodruff, more than three months earlier. It was four more days before he received Phoebe's heartrending letter telling the sad details but also expressing her deep, abiding faith.[37] The distressing news strengthened Wilford's determination to beat the devil at his own game and find success in London.

On October 24 the missionaries hired a hall, known as Barrett's Academy, at 57 King Square, where they began to hold preaching meetings each Sunday and to give lectures each Tuesday and Thursday. They posted handbills announcing the meetings, each carrying the quotation: "He that judgeth a matter before he heareth is not wise."

They began preaching at the academy on Sunday, October 25, but the turnout was disappointing (about fifty people in the afternoon, a handful in the evening), and no one seemed interested in what they said. Following a five-mile walk, Elder Woodruff finally got a good night's rest and dreamed, as he often did, of catching fish. Such dreams probably had a double meaning for him: a reminder of one of his greatest recreational pleasures and an obvious analogy to missionary work.[38] They kept the academy open four days a week, but their meetings continued to be sparsely attended.[39]

---

[36]Ibid., October 18, 1840, 1:532. George A. Smith evidently shared the experience, though he did not write about it in his journal. See Bloxham, "Apostolic Foundations," 156–57, citing *Deseret News.*

[37]Woodruff, *Journal*, October 22, 1840, 1:537–40 and October 26, 1840, 1:541–42.

[38]Ibid., October 25, 1840, 1:540–41. See Matthew 13:47–50.

[39]George A. Smith to D. C. Smith, November 18, 1840, in *Times and Seasons* 2 (February 1, 1841): 307–8.

That hardly meant, however, that the Mormons were unknown in London. Opposition dogged them everywhere, and even the handbills they posted were torn down. As Wilford wrote to Willard Richards, "for some cause or other the *devil* is dreadful fraid the work will get set up in *London*."[40]

An angry article published in the *London Dispatch* on November 8, 1840 demonstrated the nature of the opposition. It told of twelve Latter-day Saints "or Mormonites" from America who had "pitched their tents" in Gloucester "for the purpose of plundering the innocent people in the neighborhood." They were said to have "a new bible of their own, in which it is declared that they are the apostles and prophets of the . . . only true and living church on the face of the earth," and they preached to the people of Gloucester and Bristol the horrifying notion that "God has not revealed in the bible all that is sufficient to salvation." The missionaries were also charged with plundering three families in Herefordshire and leaving them in poverty, obtaining in their perfidy something between two and three hundred pounds. Wilford Woodruff spent a good part of November 12 writing a reply to the *Dispatch*.

Parley P. Pratt reprinted the offending article in the *Star*, and added his own response. After demonstrating how ridiculous the charges had to be, he also chided the comparatively well-off ministry of the established church. "But again to this plundering business," he wrote sarcastically,

the Bishop with two or three palaces and £9000 a year, is a humble shepherd of the true fold, is he not? His scores of non-resident clergy and others, all supported by a salary, are not plunderers, are they? . . . No, — no, — it is this two or three hundred pounds, divided to twelve pernurious missionaries (and this is a falsehood) that is the only plundering known in England, is it not?[41]

The critics had no idea of what was really happening to the Mormon missionaries who continued to live on faith and whatever the Saints could provide. Expenses were especially high in London, and it was only "with the greatest prudence," Wilford Woodruff noted in October, that they could "get along much short of a pound per week each person & what few saints there are at present in this city are vary poor & not able to assist us at Present."[42] Most of their support came from Saints elsewhere, particularly in the Potteries and Herefordshire, but many in the Potteries were nearly

[40]Wilford Woodruff to Willard Richards, November 1, 1840, Willard Richards Collection.

[41]*Millennial Star* 1 (November 1840): 188–90.

[42]Woodruff, *Journal*, October 17, 1840, 1:531–32.

destitute themselves. "We are extremely sorry to hear of your hard living in London," Richard Rushton, Sr., wrote to George A. Smith on October 27, "but what to say to you with respect to money we do not know as many of the Saints at Leek are destitute of work and others are very poor indeed but we will do all that we possibly can to collect you a little."[43] Only a money order for £1 received from Willard Richards at the end of October enabled them to pay their month-end bills.[44] The next month a letter from Thomas Kington containing a donation of £2 was lost in the mail or, as Wilford suspected, stolen.[45]

The apostles were painfully aware that some struggling Saints, especially those in the Potteries, were doing more than they could afford. "You speak of the poverty of the Saints in the potteries," Wilford Woodruff wrote to George A. Smith after the younger apostle had returned to Staffordshire. "I dont want them to *starve* or *clam* [feel pinched inside, as one does in fasting][46] themselves, to try to keep me from *clamming* or to send me money. If any body has got to *clam* it may as well be me as ... the Lord hath provided for me this far & I have no fears but what he will do it." If they had anything to spare, he said, "let them give it to you."[47]

The apostles maintained surprisingly good contact with the Saints by mail. While in London, for example, George A. Smith cemented a close relationship with the Richard Rushton family of Staffordshire. In July he baptized Richard Rushton, Sr., a silk merchant in Leek, a town about fifteen miles from Burslem and a center for silk manufacturing. Rushton's wife, Lettie, and one son, Richard, Jr., soon followed him into the Church.[48] Richard, Jr., quickly took up missionary work himself, probably at the urging of George A., and the apostle kept in close contact by mail with both father and son. Elder Smith wrote first on August 17 and then again ten days after he got to London. Richard, Jr., meanwhile, proselyted throughout the Potteries, where he baptized a young woman at Lane's End but also had dogs turned on him in the Leek Market Place.[49]

---

[43]Richard Rushton, Sr., to George A. Smith, October 27, 1840, George A. Smith Collection.

[44]Wilford Woodruff to Willard Richards, November 1, 1840.

[45]Woodruff, *Journal*, November 9, 1840, 1:546–47 and November 25, 1840, 1:551; Wilford Woodruff to Elder D. Browett, November 13, 1840, Wilford Woodruff Collection.

[46]The term *clam* was in common usage in the nineteenth century as a derivative of the word *clem*, meaning to "pinch with hunger." It was a very apt term for Woodruff to use under these circumstances. Simpson and Weiner, *Oxford English Dictionary* 3:264, 308–9.

[47]Wilford Woodruff to George A. Smith, November 21, 1840, Wilford Woodruff Collection.

[48]Perkes, *History of Richard Rushton Sr.*, 7–10.

[49]Richard Rushton [Jr.] to George A. Smith, September 9, 1840, George A. Smith Collection.

George A. Smith soon found himself giving considerable advice to Richard, Jr., who was four years older than he but who, like many, felt inadequate as a missionary. In one letter Elder Smith counseled him that the more often he stood before the people to warn them, the greater the blessings he would receive. Rushton took the advice seriously, and he wrote to his mentor that "you[r] words have been verified for I receive greater blessings and Power every time I get up to Speak even so as to astonish myself."[50] Then, in an ardent outpouring of his soul, he again suggested the powerful effect Elder Smith had on the people of the Potteries: "Dear Brother I cannot discribe the Love and gratitude I feel towards you for the great Blessings you have been instrumental in the hands of God of bringing upon our Family and Neibourhood. We can never repay your kindness towards us. But God will Bless you for your Labour. Dear Brother we Should be happy to see you again soon."[51]

On October 12 George A. wrote, reporting on his own success and improving health, and Richard, Jr., read the letter aloud to the Staffordshire Saints. In his response of October 15, Rushton again poured out a heartfelt expression of gratitude for the great example the apostle was to him: "Dear Brother your kind Letter give me great Encouragement for when I think of your Labours your persecutions your trials your Sufferings in your journeyings . . . it spurs me on to fresh Exertions and makes me every day more diligent in warning the people and exhorting my Brethren to do the same."[52] Richard, Sr., wrote several days later and commented gratefully on how much his son had improved in preaching, just as Elder Smith had promised. Moreover, the father said, "many come to him to be healed of their sicknesses and thay all return home healed rejoicing in the Lord, praise be unto his Holy name for this great blessing added to the church."[53]

The final Rushton letter in George A. Smith's papers was written by Richard, Jr., on November 6. It contained the usual report of activities among the Staffordshire Saints and also a profound expression of humility: "Dear Brother your kind advice and instruction is very acceptable to me as I have often needed it since I saw you Last For I feel that when I am strong in myself then am I weak in the Lord and when I am weak in myself

---

[50]Richard Rushton [Jr.] to George A. Smith, September 25, 1840, George A. Smith Collection (Appendix B, Document 14).

[51]Ibid.

[52]Richard Rushton [Jr.] to George A. Smith, October 15, 1840, George A. Smith Collection.

[53]Richard Rushton, Sr., to George A. Smith, October 27, 1840, George A. Smith Collection.

then I am strong in the Lord for when I Exalt myself then I am sure to be abased But when I humble myself then do I get Exalted."[54]

George A., meanwhile, was in poor health, and shortly after his return to London he began suffering with cold and ague. A thick fog on October 14 affected his lungs, and on October 23 he spat blood. On October 27 another cold in his head caused his face to swell so badly that one of his eyes almost closed. He stubbornly continued working until, on November 9, instructions came in a letter from Willard Richards that he should return immediately to the Potteries. His health was a major factor in this decision, but Brigham and the group in Manchester suggested that there was work enough for only one in London anyway.[55]

As George A. reflected on his time in London, he was not sure he wanted to leave, but he accepted the inevitable:

> From the time I continued laboring in London to the present, I used every exertion consistent with my health and strength to plant the Gospel standard; every visit I made, or call, or association was one continued effort to bear testimony; to teach, to warn the people, and thereby fulfill my calling; and, I believe, I can truly testify before the Lord, that my garments are clean of the blood of the inhabitants of the British metropolis, and I can also testify the same of the labors of Elder Kimball, and Woodruff.... I regret having to leave Brother Woodruff, but necessity seems to require it.[56]

George A.'s departure on December 10 was a blow to Henry Connor, Jr., son of the first London convert. The two had spent considerable time together discussing the scriptures and became close friends, even though Connor could not accept Latter-day Saint teachings. The day after George A. left, Henry, Jr., wrote him a poignant letter expressing both his disappointment and his admiration. "I must confess that I was loath to part with you for I feel for you all the affection of A brother," he affirmed. He also said that if George A. was right and he was wrong, he hoped he would soon be convinced.[57] A little more than a month later young Connor was baptized.

---

[54]Richard Rushton, Jr., to George A. Smith, November 6, 1840, George A. Smith Collection.

[55]George A. Smith to the Editor, April 11, 1841, *Millennial Star* 1 (April 1841): 306; Woodruff, *Journal*, November 9, 1840, 1:546–47. Smith, *History of the Church* 4:236 assigns George A.'s health as the main reason for his leaving. "Elder George A. Smith received counsel to leave London and go to Staffordshire for his health, as he had injured his lungs by preaching in the streets, so that he discharged considerable blood from them."

[56]Smith, "History," November 9, 1840.

[57]Henry Connor, Jr., to George A. Smith, November 11, 1840, George A. Smith Collection (Appendix B, Document 17).

Losing the companionship of George A. Smith was also a shock to Wilford Woodruff, who had no desire to work alone. Even though William Pitt, from Dymock, spent five days with him,[58] he quickly became extremely lonesome.

Wilford spent the next few weeks visiting the Saints, preaching to small groups, writing letters, and sometimes holding discussions with members of other religious groups, including Southcottians and Irvingites.[59] Finally, on November 22, four more people offered themselves for baptism. Although the next Sunday he baptized three of these new converts, Woodruff could not help but comment that he and his co-workers had "laboured vary hard & with much expens to accomplish little in London."[60]

Elder Woodruff kept looking forward to the arrival of Heber C. Kimball, for several people were anxiously waiting for him to return and baptize them.[61] On November 30, after spending a day with Dr. William Copeland touring the facilities of the College of Surgeons, he returned home to find both Brigham Young and Heber C. Kimball. He could not have been more delighted.

BRIGHAM YOUNG'S ELEVEN DAYS IN LONDON

Brigham Young's first full day in London consisted of a visit to the City in the company of Wilford Woodruff and Heber C. Kimball, and a meeting with the Saints. Then began several days of sightseeing. On December 3 the three visited the Tower of London, where they seemed especially struck with the magnificent crown jewels as well as the spacious Horse Armory. They also went to the Thames Tunnel, Buckingham Palace, Westminster Abbey, St. Paul's Church (where they attended services on December 6), the College of Surgeons, the National Gallery, the Royal Theater at Covent Garden, St. James Park, and the Queen's stables. On the last day of sightseeing, December 9, they visited the magnificent St. Paul's Cathedral,[62] climbed to the top of the 202-foot-high monument commemorating the 1666 London fire, walked across London Bridge and then up to and across the elegant cast-iron Southwark Bridge, stopped for a meal, took a ride to

---

[58]Woodruff, *Journal*, November 12, 1840, 1:547–48 and November 17, 1840, 1:550.

[59]Wilford Woodruff to George A. Smith, November 21, 1840.

[60]Woodruff, *Journal*, November 22, 1840, 1:551.

[61]Wilford Woodruff to George A. Smith, November 21, 1840.

[62]Some architectural historians have suggested that there is a possible connection between the towers in the front of the cathedral and Brigham Young's ideas for the spires on the Salt Lake Temple.

The Tower of London

the British Museum, which Wilford estimated covered about five acres, and walked through every room. That day they traveled twelve miles, walked up and down 1,200 steps, and by bedtime were "weary," "sumwhat sore," and more than ready for a good night's rest.

Even more than usual, Woodruff spent long hours writing about their activities in his journal — ten pages on the Tower of London alone — to the point that Brigham, who wrote little, wondered briefly if too much journalizing was interfering with missionary work.[63]

During his eleven days in London, Brigham spent time with members of the Church, preached a few times, and, on December 7, witnessed a baptism.[64] As he recalled later, when he arrived, the meetings were sparsely attended but "I preached as well as I could, though it was pretty hard work

---

[63]Many years later, and clearly with good-natured exaggeration, he chided Wilford Woodruff for all his writing: "When we found them in London, Brother Woodruff was busily engaged in writing his history from morning until evening; and, if a sister called on him, he would say, 'How do you do? take a chair,' and keep on writing and labouring to bring up [to date] the history of the Church and his own. . . . and that was the sum of the conversation. If a brother came it would be the same" (Sermon of Brigham Young, April 6, 1857, *Journal of Discourses* 4:305).

[64]Brigham Young to the Editor, December 30, 1840, *Millennial Star* 1 (January 1841): 239.

to pump when there was no water in the well." He credited Heber's warm, friendly way with the people for infusing a new spirit into the branch. "When I left the little meeting-house was crowded to overflowing."[65]

COLD DAYS, WARM HEARTS: HEBER'S AND WILLARD'S LAST TWO MONTHS IN LONDON

None of the apostles found London conducive to good health, and in December Heber C. Kimball had such a severe cold, along with congestion in his lungs, that he could hardly speak. The weather was frigid, and the thick, black smoke from all the coal-burning stoves, fireplaces, and factories made the air so dense they could hardly see. Lamps were lit even in the daytime, Heber reported, "and we have to write by candle some times in the midle of the day. It makes me like a hors that has got the Heaves."[66]

Heber and Wilford nevertheless found a few more people wanting to be baptized. On a snowy December 16 they baptized Henry Connor, Jr., and Christopher Smith, both apprentice watchmakers, as well as Benjamin Morgan, a bricklayer, and his wife, Elizabeth, whose occupation was listed as a hostess.[67] They also met frequently with the Reverend James Albion, pastor of an independent church, and Dr. William Copeland, both of whom proved receptive. On December 20 Albion not only offered them his chapel for preaching but also informed the congregation that he was a Latter-day Saint. He was going to be baptized, he said, and they should no longer consider him a member of their body unless they, too, were baptized. Neither Albion nor Copeland was baptized immediately, but the apostles continued to work closely with them. Copeland also delighted in taking them to see the sights of London.

Both Heber C. Kimball and Wilford Woodruff gradually became more optimistic, and both continued to have dreams of catching fish. "I hope we may soon realize it by Baptizing many Souls," Wilford wrote on De-

---

[65]Sermon of Brigham Young, April 6, 1857, *Journal of Discourses* 4:304. Brigham also recalled that "thirty had been baptized, but brothers Kimball, Woodruff, and Geo. A., the man who owned the small room that we had hired, and, I think, two other persons, comprised the congregation." The reason the congregation enlarged, he went on to explain, was because of the congenial, familiar way Kimball treated the people. Young might have been prone to some slight exaggeration as he recounted such stories nearly seventeen years after they happened. His estimate that thirty people had been baptized, for example, was in error, for when he arrived in London there were actually fewer than twenty members there.

[66]Heber C. Kimball to George A. Smith, December 12, 1840, George A. Smith Collection.

[67]Woodruff, *Journal*, December 16, 1840, 1:578–79. Information on occupations is found in Jorgenson, "First London Mormons," Appendix IX.

cember 20, "for we have laboured hard in this City for many weeks & with great expens & baptized as yet ownly 19 souls. But we will not despise the Day of Small things but hope for more."[68] On Sunday, December 27, Wilford preached at Albion's Independent chapel to the largest audience yet in London. When he finished, a Wesleyan minister began to berate his doctrine, at which time most of the people walked out and those who remained became so disgusted with the minister's deportment that their sympathy turned toward the Mormons. Some even invited the apostles to visit them and tell them more.[69]

When the year-end holidays arrived the missionaries took time to enjoy themselves with the Saints. On December 23 they spent the evening with Dr. Copeland and his wife at the theater, where they saw Shakespeare's *A Midsummer Night's Dream.* On Christmas morning they met with the Saints at Henry Connor's home to teach them "plain principles" and then had dinner with the Morgans. The menu was probably one of the best they had enjoyed in England: baked mutton, goose, rabbit pie, mince pie, plum pudding, bread, cheese, porter, and water. They then spent the evening at James Albion's home, discussing the "things of God."[70] New Year's Eve found them preaching and taking supper with the Copelands.

This was also an occasion to reflect on a year that must have seemed to them both the best of times and the worst of times. Heber wrote a poignant prayer thanking his God for his increase in knowledge, recovery from illness, prosperity in the ministry, sustenance, and for never forsaking him in time of trouble. He also prayed mightily for the welfare of his family.[71] Wilford Woodruff recalled that twelve months earlier he was on the Atlantic, practically penniless, but since landing in England he had traveled 4,469 miles, held 230 meetings, established fifty-three places of preaching, planted forty-seven branches of the Church numbering 1,500 Saints, attended fourteen conferences, personally baptized 336 people (including fifty-seven preachers), confirmed 420 people, ordained eighteen elders, ninety-seven priests, thirty-four teachers, and one deacon, blessed 120 children, and administered to 120 sick persons. In many instances,

---

[68]Woodruff, *Journal,* December 20, 1840, 1:580; Heber C. Kimball to the Editor, December 28, 1840, *Millennial Star* 1 (January 1841): 240.

[69]Heber C. Kimball to the Editor, December 28, 1840, *Millennial Star* 1 (January 1841): 240; Woodruff, *Journal,* December 27, 1840, 1:583–84.

[70]Woodruff, *Journal,* December 25, 1840, 1:582–83.

[71]Kimball, Diary, 1 January 1841.

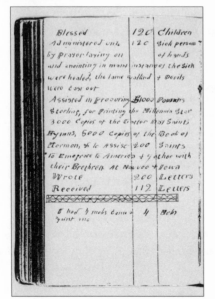
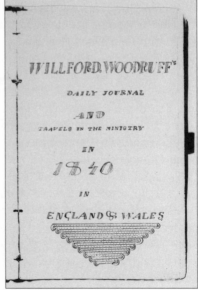

Year-end synopsis and title page of Wilford Woodruff's 1840 journal
Courtesy LDS Church Archives

"the sick were healed, the lame walked & Devils were cast out." He had also raised money for Church publications, assisted two hundred Saints to emigrate, and visited numerous historic sites and other places of interest. These were among the blessings he counted. There were also tribulations: being away from home and family, the loss of his baby daughter, financial sacrifice, rejection, persecution, public humiliation, and all the other challenges related to missionary work, especially in London. Two terse sentences from his summary were full of meaning: "Never have I spent a year with more Interest than 1840. Never have I been called to make greater Sacrifices or enjoyed greater Blessings."[72]

In January, despite the bitter cold, the frequency of baptisms slowly increased. On Saturday, January 9, moved by the Spirit, Heber C. Kimball went to Woolwich, a few miles down the Thames, and the following day four people asked for baptism. They searched up and down the Thames until 9:00 P.M. trying to find a suitable place, but the ice and mud made it impossible. On Tuesday, therefore, Elder Kimball and his four eager converts showed up in London, picked up Wilford Woodruff, and proceeded to the pool at Tabernacle Square, which they were using so often that Woodruff dubbed it their "private bath."

Kimball also sent for William Copeland, convinced that he could finally persuade the good doctor to go into the water. Just as he finished baptizing the four from Woolwich, Copeland arrived and the persistent Kimball asked him if he was ready. He had not come prepared, the doctor objected, but Heber replied that he could put on the clothes the previously baptized brethren had just taken off. The moment of decision at hand, Copeland resolutely donned the wet clothing, went in to the freezing water, and was baptized. "I must confess it was a cold job," Kimball quipped later. They all then returned to the apartment on Ironmonger Row for tea, confirmed the new members of the Church, and, in the evening, had a prayer meeting. It was, said Kimball, a "glorious time."[73] Eleven days later Wilford Woodruff baptized the Reverend James Albion.

As elsewhere, the London converts called upon the apostles not only for spiritual sustenance but also for a variety of nonecclesiastical services. Wilford Woodruff spent most of January 27, for example, going from one government office to another, trying unsuccessfully to help a member

[72]Woodruff, *Journal*, December 31, 1840, 1:586–87.
[73]Heber C. Kimball to George A. Smith, January 14, 1841, George A. Smith Collection; Kimball, Diary, January 9–12, 1841; Woodruff, *Journal*, January 9–12, 1841, 2:25–28.

Lorenzo Snow
Courtesy LDS Church Archives

make arrangements for a military pension. Two days later he spent the evening copying a will for another.[74] In their minds, no doubt, whatever help they could provide was small recompense for the love and support that came their way from the Saints.

TRANSITION: LORENZO SNOW TAKES THE REINS IN LONDON

On the afternoon of February 14 the apostles organized the London Conference, which comprised the London branch and small branches in Bedford, Ipswich, and Woolwich. After seven months of missionary work, there were forty-six members in London. During the evening meeting, attended by the largest number of people yet to be at a Latter-day Saint gathering in the capital city, one more person asked for baptism. Wilford Woodruff's early pessimism was abated, as he wrote in his journal:

This is a day I have long desired to see, for we have laboured exceding hard to esstablished the work in this city, & in several instances it seemed as though we should have to give it up but by claiming the promises of God & holding on to the word of God, the rod of Iron we have been enabled to overcome, & plant a church & esstablish

---

[74]Woodruff, *Journal*, January 25, 1841, 2:32; January 27, 1841, 2:33–34; and January 29, 1841, 2:34.

225

a conference which we are enabled through the grace of God to leave in a Prosperous Situation which has the appearance of a great increase.[75]

President of the new London Conference was twenty-four-year-old Lorenzo Snow, who had arrived in Liverpool from America on October 22, carrying with him a letter to the Twelve from Joseph Smith.[76] He reached London on February 11, but he probably knew at least two months earlier that he was going there. On December 10, while working in Birmingham, he opined to George A. Smith that "I think you exhibited much wisdom in leaving that seat of Satan" but then suggested with good-natured apprehension that he knew what was in store for him:

I suppose you intend keeping me preaching to the *spirits* in *prison* untill I have been properly prepared then send me to the *great seat* of his black Majesty from whence you have so fortunately escaped. Elder Young writes in a letter which I just received from Elder Woodruff "we do not know but we shall be glad for Elder Snow to come to London if he can be spared there and we can provide a place for him here." I wonder where you will send me next.[77]

Elder Snow's introduction to the work in London began immediately. The day after he arrived, Heber C. Kimball took him on a tour of the city and then to visit the little branch at Woolwich. Humbled at the thought of taking over from the apostles in this vast metropolis, he wrote to George A. Smith: "I want your prayers for the powers of darkness are great in this city; and I shall soon be left alone being assisted only by those who are infants in the kingdom, and at the same time, I can scarcely say that I yet have hardly arived at the state of childhood."[78] In 1849 Lorenzo became a member of the Quorum of the Twelve himself, and in 1898 he succeeded Wilford Woodruff as president of the Church.

GEORGE A. SMITH'S LAST DAYS IN STAFFORDSHIRE

George A. Smith arrived back in Staffordshire on November 17 and that night held a meeting with the Saints. He preached whenever and wherever possible, including a December 2 meeting in Burslem, where

---

[75]Ibid., February 14, 1841, 2:45–47.

[76]Snow arrived in Liverpool on October 22, and from there apparently went to Preston briefly and then on to Manchester. He was in Manchester when Brigham returned there from his trip to Wales on November 2. See Lorenzo Snow to Charlotte Granger, February 25, 1841, in Lorenzo Snow, Notebook; Brigham Young to Mary Ann Young, October 16, 1840, where Brigham says that he had received a letter from Willard Richards in Preston telling him of Snow's arrival with Joseph's letter; Young, *Manuscript History*, 82.

[77]Lorenzo Snow to George A. Smith, December 10, 1840, George A. Smith Collection.

[78]Lorenzo Snow to George A. Smith, February 17, 1841, George A. Smith Collection.

he spoke to "as vile a set of ruffians as I ever saw anywhere."[79] His health continued intermittently poor, and as winter settled in he continually had serious coughing spells, but there was no let-up in his efforts. "Preached three times today and broke bread," he wrote in his journal on December 20. "My cough is much better today. I confirmed four persons. The Lord seems to have given me strength today, for I have not performed a day's labor so easily for some weeks."[80] But that night he took cold again, and the next day his lungs were so painful and his throat so sore he could hardly speak. He spent most of that day in bed.

His personal discomfort, however, was almost inconsequential compared to his pain for the Saints, as he sadly observed that there was even less employment among them than when he was there earlier.[81] He estimated that only a third of the 450 Saints in Staffordshire were fully employed, others worked only two or three days per week, and some worked not at all. He saw Church members suffering from want of food, and was furious when he discovered that some had been fired from their jobs simply because they were Latter-day Saints. Such persecution was little better than murder, he thought. "Hard times for these poor people. I pray daily for the Lord to gather them up and send them to Zion."[82] There was little he could do personally, however, for he was still dependent upon them, even in their poverty.

Christmas Day 1840 was devoted to a conference of the Saints in Hanley, attended by both George A. Smith and Brigham Young, who was passing through on his way to Manchester. George A. felt better that day, and the two apostles spent an enjoyable evening at the home of a recent convert, John Taylor, a tailor by trade. Three days later George A. went to a holiday "tea meeting" with the Hanley Saints and then attended a preaching service. By New Year's Eve, however, he was ill again.

Like his colleagues elsewhere, the youngest apostle was involved not only in missionary work but also in constantly giving advice and counsel to the many Saints who sought him out. He seldom went to bed before midnight and sometimes lay awake until 2:00 A.M., pondering how it was that such a young, untutored person as he should be called upon to teach

---

[79]Smith, "History," December 2, 1840.
[80]Ibid., December 20, 1840.
[81]Ibid.
[82]Ibid., December 12, 1840; George A. Smith to Josiah Flemming, December 5, 1840, George A. Smith Collection.

so many people with much more learning and experience. He wrote to his younger brother:

you cannot think how foolish it makes me feel to Be Looked up to with So much Earnestness by Persons Who have been Professers of Religion and Preachers of the Different Sects. I thank the Lord for the Wisdom he has given me and the Success I have had in the teaching thes Men for thire is Now in this District No less than 88 official Members in the Church and they all Look to me for instruction as Children to A Father and this Makes me feel vary Small indeed and Causes me to cry unto my father Who is in heaven for Wisdom and Paetence to do my fathers Work and Sound his gospel to the World Which may the Lord grant.[83]

His health was poor, with severe colds plaguing him continually, and in February he was bothered with rheumatism in his shoulder. His eyesight had improved enough that he could write by a strong light, but not by candlelight, and he could not do much reading.[84] Nonetheless, he preached and worked with the Saints and helped conduct official Church business.

Heber C. Kimball arrived in Staffordshire from London on March 3 and spent a little time working with George A. before going on to Manchester on March 6. Elder Kimball was also suffering from a bad cold, and for a few days the Saints in Staffordshire cared for two ailing apostles.

Inevitably, as the Church grew, differences in perspective, along with human weaknesses such as envy or jealousy, occasionally caused tension, and at times not even the apostles were immune to criticism. In Hanley, for example, a man named Mason, claiming to have talked with God, began to curse George A., and accused him of lying and hypocrisy. On January 26 Elder Smith received a letter from Mason, accusing him of being no more than a pretending priest and charging that his God was really gold. It seems incredible that anyone who knew George A. could believe such charges. Not that he or his associates were free of failings, but the motives ascribed by Mason were so far from anything of which George A. could have been guilty as he labored among the poverty-stricken Saints that the accusations seemed laughable. In any case, the Saints at Hanley would have none of it and immediately withdrew fellowship from the "non-prophet," as Elder Smith labeled him.[85]

---

[83]George A. Smith to Lyman Smith, January 8, 1841, George A. Smith Collection (Appendix B, Document 22).

[84]Ibid.

[85]George A. Smith to Father and Mother, in letter to George Gee, January 28, 1841; Smith, "History," January 26 and 27, 1841; George A. Smith to Brigham Young, January 24, 1841, George A. Smith Collection. The day after Mason's fellowship was withdrawn, Elder Smith received another abusive letter from him.

In another instance, personal jealousy among the Saints also resulted in an attack on Elder Smith. During a conference at Leek on March 18, the apostles proposed that Steven Nixon be ordained an elder. A Brother Jackson objected, registering several complaints that may seem trivial but were serious to this recent convert: Jackson himself was the oldest priest and therefore he should have the office; Elder Smith had never visited him at his home; it had been given in tongues that Nixon should be ordained, but tongues did not govern the Church; and he had been offended by Richard Rushton, who was pressing him about the rent money for the room in which they met. George A. Smith reminded Jackson that, according to the scriptures, he should have taken his grievances first to the brothers who had offended him, and after considerable discussion it was decided that Jackson should be suspended until he publicly acknowledged his error. The next day, however, when they met to perform the ordinations that had been approved, a Brother Clowes also objected, accusing Elder Smith of partiality. "Brother Nixon has taken you to his house, fed and treated you like a gentleman," he said, and "that is the reason you have called him to be an Elder and his calling was not by the spirit of God." At that point the rest of the council unanimously rallied around their young leader, and Alfred Cordon moved that Clowes be suspended for "publicly and falsely" accusing him. The motion carried.[86] Such unfortunate tensions among the Saints illustrated both the youthfulness of the Church in Britain and the way human foibles inevitably affect any organization, no matter how inspired its principles.

THE GATHERING CONTINUES

One of Brigham Young's chief concerns was the gathering, and he, along with John Taylor and Willard Richards, did much of the work of organizing the emigration. Even before the John Moon company left in June 1840, formally launching the gathering, many Saints were looking ahead to emigrating in 1841. On May 22, for example, Heber C. Kimball was delighted to find that the Saints of Longton were planning to leave the following spring, not just as individuals but as churches. "The Rich love the poor so well that they cant leave them behind," he wrote to his wife, and this, he said, was the celestial spirit.[87]

---

[86]Smith, "History," March 19, 1841.
[87]Heber C. Kimball to Vilate Kimball, May 27, 1840, Heber C. Kimball Collection; Fielding, Diary, 75.

Though the yearning to escape poverty was one motivation in their decision to migrate, a more important factor was the Saints' eagerness to participate in building up the kingdom of God in the last days. It was this that the First Presidency stressed when they officially announced the policy in August 1840:

The work which has to be accomplished in the last days is one of vast importance, and will call into action the energy, skill, talent, and ability of the Saints, so that it may roll forth with that glory and majesty described by the prophet; and will consequently require the concentration of the Saints, to accomplish works of such magnitude and grandeur.

The work of the gathering spoken of in the Scriptures will be necessary to bring about the glories of the last dispensation. It is probably unnecessary to press this subject on the Saints, as we believe the spirit of it is manifest, and its necessity obvious.[88]

It was not enough that this family or that decided to emigrate: the gathering must be organized in such a way that the rich would help the poor, that unskilled workers would not overwhelm skilled workers in the early stages of building up Nauvoo, and that the torrent of emigrants could find passage across the Atlantic with some efficiency and order. In his December letter Joseph Smith cautioned the Twelve on the difficulties that might be faced by the extremely poor, especially those not used to farm work, if they emigrated too soon. He encouraged them to get people who had manufacturing skills as well as those with substance to emigrate first, so they could build factories, foundries, potteries, etc., and prepare the way for the poor to come and have work.

After the initial 1840 emigration, the *Star* published several pieces designed to encourage the Saints to prepare for the coming season. One was a report from Nauvoo, dated July 28, 1840, of a committee selected to pick a suitable spot in Iowa Territory for establishing a stake of Zion. The committee enthusiastically recommended an area between the Des Moines River and the northern boundary of Missouri, but the real significance of the report was that it opened the eyes of the British Saints to the vision that the Kingdom was indeed expanding in the new world and that they should be a part of it.[89]

The February *Star* contained a long letter from Francis Moon, a member of the initial emigrant company. "I know what it is to bid farewell to my native land," he said in an effort to sway those who may hesitate,

---

[88]"An Address by the First Presidency of the Church," in *Times and Seasons* 1 (October 1840): 177–79.

[89]*Millennial Star* 1 (January 1841): 231–33.

Emigrant ship leaving Liverpool. Engraving by Frederick Piercy
Courtesy LDS Church Archives

to receive the parting tear of my friends, and with a heart heaving with inexpressible emotion, turn my back upon the nearest and dearest relations in this life.... But in all these sacrifices and troubles ... the Lord has helped me and brought me safely through; and now I have the privilege of being acquainted with the mysteries of the kingdom of God, and these things causes me to forget as it were the things that are past.

After giving a radiant description of the Nauvoo area, he told his readers the prices they could expect to pay for goods in America, and advised them to delay no longer. He also told them of Joseph Smith: "I have been acquainted with him for some time, and as far as I can see he is a good man, and I find him to be a prophet of the Lord, and the more I speak with him and the more I hear him, the more I am convinced of the truth of these things."[90]

Few British Saints needed Moon's encouragement, however, for, as Brigham Young wrote to his brother in October, they were eager to go, no matter what.

---

[90]Francis Moon to the Editor, November 4, 1840, *Millennial Star* 1 (February 1841): 254.

On the deck of an emigrant ship. Courtesy Peabody Museum of Salem

The Saints have got a start for to gether to America and goe they will, and nothing can stop them. . . . They have so much of the spirit of gethering that they would goe if they knew they would die as soon as they got there or if they knew that the mob would be upon and drive them as so[o]n as they got there. They have the spirit of the times here as well as the Church there.[91]

On February 6 Brigham Young, John Taylor, and Willard Richards organized a company of 235 Saints and placed Hiram Clark in charge. The next day they saw them off on the ship *Sheffield*. Two days later the same three apostles organized a company of 109 Saints under the leadership of Daniel Browett, who sailed on the *Echo* on the sixteenth. As the February issue of the *Star* characterized it, they were on their way to "the colonies of the Saints" in a country that "God has provided for a refuge for all nations."[92] On March 17 another fifty-four Saints, led by Thomas Smith and William Moss, sailed on the *Alesto*.

Moving from their homes in England to new homes across the waters was no simple task for the Saints, and it took faith, courage, planning, and preparation. Those who went before wrote back with detailed suggestions about what to bring, what not to bring, and what to expect when they got to the promised land.[93] In addition, the Twelve tried to follow Joseph

[91]Brigham Young to Joseph Young, as part of his letter to Mary Ann Young, October 16, 1840 (Appendix B, Document 15).

[92]*Millennial Star* 1 (February 1841): 263.

[93]See Francis Moon to the Editor, November 4, 1840; William Clayton to Edward Martin, November

The steerage compartment of an emigrant ship. Courtesy Peabody Museum of Salem

Smith's pragmatic advice to send skilled workers first in order to prepare the way for the poor. Their final epistle to the Saints in England explained that "men of capital" should go first and purchase land, erect mills, and produce machinery and manufactured goods "so that the poor who go from this country can find employment." It was not wise, they said, for the poor to flock to Nauvoo until the necessary preparations were made. "Neither is it wisdom for those who feel a spirit of benevolence to expend all their means in helping others to emigrate, and thus all arrive in a new country empty handed." The Saints were admonished not to go in haste but to prepare well and to settle their debts and other affairs before they left.[94] Finding that delicate balance between the desire to go quickly versus the need for planning, or Christian generosity versus pragmatic saving for necessary investments in Nauvoo, was indeed a complex challenge.

According to Joseph Fielding, most of the Saints who departed in February were poor and began their momentous transatlantic voyage with no more than £4 each. His wife's brother, G. Greenwood, helped many of them, but, Fielding remarked, "times are bad for the Poor, and we have to live by Faith." The exodus did not make it easy for those who stayed behind, either, for helping the migrants left less money to help the poor who remained or to assist the missionaries. Fielding himself was still trying

---

29, 1840, in Carter, *Heart Throbs of the West* 5:373–80; William Clayton to the Saints at Manchester, December 10, 1840, William Clayton Collection.

[94]"An Epistle of the Twelve," *Millennial Star* 1 (April 1841): 309–12 (Appendix B, Document 25).

to prune the vineyard without purse or scrip, and when the emigrants left he was in debt. "I never lived so sparingly in my life," he said, "yet we do not complain of want while so many of even the Saints are lacking."[95]

Coordinating the migration was complex. Elders Young, Taylor, and Richards contracted for ships, purchased provisions, and arranged for ship's stores. Passengers, especially those in steerage, were furnished nothing but water during the voyage and had to arrange for their own food. Before the February migration, the apostles negotiated contracts with ship owners that allowed the Saints to cross the ocean for £5 each.[96] They organized each company of emigrants as a Church unit and set apart a presidency. In order to bring together emigrants, money, supplies, and ships all at the correct moment, they also coordinated by mail with the other apostles. On February 13, for example, Brigham wrote to George A. Smith, who was working in Staffordshire:

We wish you to Call the Churches together in your part and ascertaine emeditly how meny of the Bretherin can be reddy to sale by the 10 of March next, as we shall fit out another Company then. . . . Let us know by the 25 of this month. Let us have the names of all, and the ages of all children under 14 years. Children from one to 14 will goe 2 for one. Under one year they goe free.

George A. was also told to appoint an agent to handle the money and he was promised that

as soon as we find out the name of the Ship and the day of Saling we shall wright and let you know what time to send your agent and also what day your famelies must be here. . . . Our advice is for all to goe that can in March, as they will goe by New Orleans. . . . [much cheaper than] by New York—and such as cannot goe then had better stay till the last of August or September and then sale for New Orleans.[97]

Unfortunately, George A. discovered that the Saints of Leek were so poor that all "were willing but none able to gather at present," and he so reported.[98] Brigham Young's understanding response to such concerns was simply that the apostles' instructions were not law but advice in anticipation of greater expense in the future. The ships were overflowing already, and cost of passage would be higher later on, "but we say to the Bretherin goe when you can."[99]

---

[95]Fielding, Diary, 102.

[96]George D. Watt to George A. Smith, January 16, 1841, George A. Smith Collection.

[97]Brigham Young to George A. Smith, February 13, 1841, as cited in Arrington, *Brigham Young*, 94.

[98]Smith, "History," February 18, 1841.

[99]Brigham Young to Levi Richards, March 13, 1841, as cited in Arrington, *Brigham Young*, 95.

The apostles appointed Amos Fielding as Church emigration agent in Liverpool. His responsibility was to superintend the outfitting of the Saints for the voyage and particularly to help the inexperienced Saints avoid the "pick-pockets" who hovered at the port of embarkation to "take every possible advantage of strangers, in Liverpool." Emigrants were advised that the first thing they should do after arriving in Liverpool was to consult Fielding about the voyage. Some, they were warned, had tried to take care of matters themselves, only to be "robbed and cheated out of nearly all they had." They were also advised to travel in companies rather than alone.[100] This was the beginning of an emigration system — greatly enhanced as time went on — that would transport tens of thousands of Saints to America.[101]

[100]"An Epistle of the Twelve," *Millennial Star* 1 (April 1841): 310–11.

[101]For a discussion of the long-range organization of emigration, see Taylor, *Expectations Westward*, chapter 6, "Planning the Migration"; Jensen, "British Gathering."

Chapter 10

TO "HURL TRUTH THROUGH THE LAND": PUBLICATIONS OF THE TWELVE

"It hath truly been a miricle what God hath wrought by our hands in this land since we have been here & I am asstonished when I look at it," wrote Wilford Woodruff as he prepared to leave England. He included on his list of miraculous accomplishments the fact that the Twelve had printed five thousand copies of the Book of Mormon, three thousand hymnbooks, 2,500 volumes of the *Millennial Star,* and around fifty thousand tracts.[1] He could have dwelt longer on that topic, for their publications were among their most remarkable achievements. Through printed matter they spread the gospel, defended the faith, communicated with the Saints, and left a vital historical record of much of what they thought and did. The literature they produced, moreover, had a lasting impact on the spiritual and intellectual heritage of Mormonism, and it affected for generations to come the way many doctrines and ideas would be presented.

BEGINNINGS

In 1837 the first missionaries to England had few printed items to share with prospective Saints. The Book of Mormon appeared in March 1830, just three weeks before the Church was organized, and several other items were issued over the next few years, but no missionary tracts or pamphlets appeared until 1836.[2] There were, however, other developments

---

[1] Woodruff, *Journal,* April 16, 1841, 2:89–90.
[2] A good introduction to early Church literature is Crawley, "Bibliography of the Church." We have also benefited from access to Crawley's unpublished "Descriptive Bibliography."

before 1840 that are important to understanding the significance of what the Twelve did during their time in Britain.

Early Church leaders recognized the potential power of the press as they encountered attacks against their faith in books and in newspaper articles. Their first reaction to these attacks was to send individuals on special preaching missions so that a response could be given one-to-one. Such an approach was appropriate as long as the missionaries remained in smaller villages, but by 1836 they were beginning to enter the larger cities of the United States and Canada.[3] To reach a larger audience in urban and cosmopolitan settings, the elders turned more and more to the press, which provided opportunity for a more systematic and sophisticated presentation of their message.

The first Church newspaper, *The Evening and the Morning Star*, was established in Independence, Missouri. Its pages announced the message of the Restoration, carried revelations received by the Prophet, and provided a forum for communication among the Saints. The press was operated by William W. Phelps, who, as "Printer to the Church," set editorial policy and infused the paper with his own millennial fervor.

Several general precedents for early Mormon publishing were established in Missouri.[4] The first was the practice of publishing two newspapers: one religious and one secular. Thus, in Missouri, the Saints issued the *Star* and the *Upper Missouri Advertiser*; in Ohio, they published both the *Latter Day Saints' Messenger and Advocate* and the *Northern Times*; and in Nauvoo, Illinois, they published the *Times and Seasons* and the *Nauvoo Neighbor*. In England, however, the Twelve published just one periodical, *The Latter-Day Saints' Millennial Star*.

The second pattern was a group approach to publishing that combined a business venture with the economic philosophy of consecration. In its fullest expression this effort was called the Literary Firm. Established by revelation in November 1831, the Firm was to supply the Church with a variety of published materials, including a collection of revelations, a hymnal, newspapers, an almanac, the New Translation of the Bible, and some items intended for children, all from a printing house in Missouri.[5] The Firm also issued the *The Evening and the Morning Star* and was near to finishing the Book of Commandments when a mob destroyed the press

---

[3]See Ellsworth, "History of Mormon Missions."
[4]A useful introduction is Moore, "History of Mormon Periodicals."
[5]See the summary in Cook, *Law of Consecration*, 45–55.

in July 1833. Thereafter the publishing business was moved to Kirtland, Ohio, where the Firm issued *The Latter-day Saints' Messenger and Advocate*. It also continued to publish the *Star*, retitling it simply *Evening and Morning Star*.[6] In addition, in 1835 it issued the hymnbook compiled by Emma Smith. The Firm was discontinued in 1836, the same year the first clearly identifiable Mormon tract appeared.

In Toronto, Canada, in August 1836 Orson Hyde first published *A Prophetic Warning to all the churches, of every sect and denomination, and to every individual into whose hands it may fall*.[7] The next year Parley P. Pratt's *Voice of Warning* was published in New York City.[8] *A Prophetic Warning* was merely a short broadside which, in the first edition, failed even to mention the name of the Church, but *Voice of Warning* was a small book that examined in detail the basic beliefs of the Church, whose identity was clear on almost every page.

Other items were issued by early Mormon authors. About 1835 someone published a four-page *References to the Book of Mormon*, which was really an extended table of contents for the first edition.[9] In the same year Parley P. Pratt published the first volume of Mormon poetry[10] and *A Short Account of a Shameful Outrage*, which told of his treatment at the hands of troublemakers when he was preaching in Mentor, Ohio, in April 1835.[11] Also about this time a broadside printing of Joseph Smith's translation of Matthew, chapter 24, appeared. Other broadsides were issued within the next year, among which were several revelations to Joseph Smith, the dedicatory prayer for the Kirtland Temple (D&C 109), and a handbill published by Parley P. Pratt explaining Mormonism while responding to an anti-Mormon preacher.[12]

THE 1837–38 MISSION

The first missionaries in England, then, could have taken a variety of things with them but, beyond the Bible, the Book of Mormon, and the

---

[6]In addition, it reprinted earlier editions, making some textual changes.

[7]This broadside was dated August 1836. Its text was published in the *Messenger and Advocate* 2 (July 1836): 342–46, where it is dated June 16, 1836.

[8]P. Pratt, *Voice of Warning*. It appeared in an edition of three thousand about September 1837.

[9]See Crawley, "Bibliography," 505.

[10]P. Pratt, *Millennium*.

[11]See Crawley, "Bibliography," 497–98.

[12]Broadsides of D&C 101 and 88 (probably published in 1834) are located in the Archives, Harold B. Lee Library, Brigham Young University, Provo, Utah. A broadside of D&C 59 can be found in the Church Archives.

A TIMELY WARNING

TO THE PEOPLE OF ENGLAND,

Of every Sect and Denomination, and to every Individual into whose hands it may fall.

BY AN ELDER OF THE CHURCH OF LATTER DAY SAINTS, LATE FROM AMERICA.

PRESTON, 19th August, 1837.

FORASMUCH as many have taken in hand to set forth in order a declaration of those things which are most assuredly believed among us, and which must shortly come to pass: It seemeth good unto me, and also unto the Holy Spirit, to write unto you, that you may know of a certainty your standing and relation to God; and also of the times and seasons of the fulfilment of the words of his servants the Prophets.

After our Lord had completed the work which his Father had given him to do, he led forth his disciples as far as Bethany, and lifted his hands towards heaven and blessed them. While in the act of performing this kind office upon his disciples, he was received up to heaven in a cloud. As the disciples stood gazing upon his exit, two men, (angels) stood by them, clad in white apparel, and said: "Ye men of Galilee, why stand ye gazing up into heaven? This same Jesus who is taken up from you into heaven, shall so come in like manner as you have seen him go into heaven."

Some have laboured to show that this promise of Christ's second coming was fulfilled at the destruction of Jerusalem; but such was not the fact. Jerusalem was destroyed during the reign of Vespasian, the Roman Emperor, by Titus, his son. Vespasian began to reign in the 70th year of the christian æra, and reigned nine years. He was then succeeded by his son, Titus, who reigned two years; and Titus was succeeded by his younger brother, Domitian, in whose reign, and by whose order, the Apostle John was banished upon the Isle of Patmos, in the 95th year of the Christian æra; being somewhere between sixteen and twenty-five years after the destruction of that city. The Saviour, who appeared to John while in banishment, said unto him: "Behold I come quickly, and my reward is with me to give unto every man according as his works shall be." It is plain, therefore, that Christ represented to John, that his coming was yet in the future, even sixteen or twenty-five years after Jerusalem was destroyed. Therefore, so far from that promise being fulfilled at that time, it yet remains to be fulfilled. And we may look with certainty for the Son of God yet to appear in the clouds of heaven with great power and glory. The question now arises; Is the Christian world prepared to behold the day of the coming of the Lord from heaven? The day that shall burn as an oven, when all the proud, and they that do wickedly, shall be as stubble. This is a question of no ordinary moment.

The Jews rejected the Messiah when he came to them, and the Gentiles received him; but when he comes the second time, the Gentiles will be entirely unprepared to enjoy his glory; but the Jews will be brought in by virtue of the promise and covenant which God made with their fathers, which I shall attempt to prove from the Scriptures.

There was a cause of the Jews rejecting the Redeemer; and what was that cause? It was their previous departure from the law which God gave to them by Moses. The law was given them as a school master to bring them to Christ; and had they not made it void through the tradition of their Elders they would not have disowned their King. The Lord said to them, himself, "If you had believed Moses, you would have believed me, for Moses wrote of me. But if you believe not his writings, how can you believe my words?" The fate which this people met some thirty years after they rejected the counsel of God, is entirely without a parallel in the history of the world. The wretched few that escaped destruction at that time, only seem to have been spared to perpetuate their shame and misery until the day of their redemption, which now is near at hand.

The Gospel was committed to the Gentiles for the express purpose of preparing them for the second coming of Christ, as the law was given to the Jews to prepare them for his first coming, But the Gentiles have made void the gospel through the tradition of their Elders, which now becomes my painful duty to show; and may the great Shepherd of Israel inspire my heart with a clear view of the fallen state of the Christian world at this period, and enable me to declare it with all that sympathy, plainness and christian love which, ever were the characteristics of a servant of the MOST HIGH.

In the first place, let me ask: Have the founders of the christian system foretold an apostacy of the church from the true order of worship? They certainly have. Paul says, 2 Thess. 2. 3. "Let no man deceive you by any means; for *that day* shall not come except there come a falling away first, and that man of sin be revealed, the son of perdition, &c." Again, 1. Tim. 4, 1. "Now the Spirit speaketh expressly, that in the latter times some shall depart from the faith, giving heed to seducing spirits and doctrines of devils." Also 2 Tim. 4, 3, and 4. "For the time will come when they will not endure sound doctrine, but after their own lusts shall they heap to themselves teachers having itching ears; and they shall turn away their ears from the truth, and be turned unto fables." These passages clearly show what the churches would do when left to act upon their agency, viz: that they would forsake the truths of God and be turned unto fables and traditions of men.

I will now present the Gentile churches before the glass of the holy scriptures, and see if they possess the same form and beauty now that they did eighteen hundred years ago. When Jesus gave his disciples their last commission to go forth into all the world to preach the gospel, he said unto them: "These signs shall follow them that believe. In my name shall they cast out devils; they shall speak with new tongues; they shall take up serpents: and if they drink any deadly thing, it shall not hurt them; they shall lay their hands upon the sick, and they shall recover." It appears that this miraculous power did, and ever will continue with true believers: for the same Being who said, "These signs shall follow them that believe:" also said, "Though the heavens and the earth pass away, yet my words shall not fail." It is very readily discovered why the above signs do not follow pretended believers; because Jesus never said they should. There is a difference between the spurious and true coin; although, the spurious contains some genuine silver, yet it will not lawfully pass; and is, comparatively speaking, of no real value. By a chemical process, we can very readily discover the difference between the pure and the base: so, by an application of the word of God to any religious body, we may soon determine whether they are believers in the scriptural sense of the word; or according to the notions and opinions of uninspired men. Some pretend to say that the promise of Christ to his disciples, that miraculous signs shall follow them that believe, was limited to the apostles. But I think that no honest man who understands the English language sufficiently to tell the difference between the second and third person, will contend for any such thing. For Jesus did not say, these signs shall follow you, (Apostles) but he said: "These signs shall follow them that believe."

Again: Paul said, God set some in the church, first apostles; secondly, prophets; thirdly, teachers; after that, miracles; then gifts of healing, helps, governments, diversities of tongues. To one is given by the spirit, the word of wisdom; to another, faith by the same spirit; to another the word of knowledge, by the same spirit; to another the gifts of healing; to another the working of miracles; to another prophecy; to another discerning of spirits; to another divers kinds of tongues; and to another the interpretation of tongues." This seems to have been the gospel and order of worship which Paul advocated and established; and said: "Though we, or an angel from heaven, preach any other gospel unto you than that which we have preached unto you, let him be accursed." Do the Gentile churches, of this day, preach and practice the above order? or have they lost it? They certainly have lost it. And have they not great reason to fear that a curse instead of a blessing will rest upon them. If the Jews were broken off because of unbelief, what must the Gentiles expect, who have not continued in the goodness of the Lord? It really appears to me that every person who is not biased by most unhallowed prejudice, can see that the churches of this day bear but a faint resemblance to those which existed in the days of the Apostles. Whence arises this difference? Do we live under a different dispensation from what they did? If we do, when was the dispensation changed, and by whose authority? If we do not, why not preach and practise the same things which they did? Because thou are fallen! fallen! from thy first love. But those who are determined to support their peculiar creeds at the expence of truth, and the most plain declaration of holy writ, which are found written, as with a sun-beam upon almost every page, will deny the possibility of these precious and heavenly blessings being enjoyed by mortals now. But let me ask: Has God changed so much during the last eighteen hundred years? The language of the Bible is, "I am the Lord, I change not; therefore, ye sons of Jacob are not consumed."

I am aware that there are many who preach for hire, and love to be called of men, Rabbi, &c. who will seek refuge from the arrows of truth behind the bulwarks of affected sanctity, and put the unhallowed influence in operation which they exercise over the hearts and consciences of their deluded followers, to prevent them from hearing, investigating or receiving the truth. Such hiding places may screen iniquity for a time. But when the trump of God shall sound, such bulwarks shall fall to the earth like the walls of Jericho, leaving those who have taken shelter behind them, exposed to the sword of God's indignation which will proceed out of his mouth, saying: Depart ye cursed, &c.

How plain it is, therefore, that a great apostacy from the true apostolic order of Worship, has taken place; and it now becomes my duty to show the awful consequences of this apostacy, however painful may be the task. But

Shall I behold the nations doomed
To sword and famine, blood and fire?
And not the least exertion make
But from the scene in peace retire?
No. While kind heaven shall lend me breath
I'll sound repentance far and broad;
And tell the nations to prepare
For Jesus Christ, their coming Lord.

The Jews were the natural branches of the good olive tree, but were broken off in consequence of unbelief. The Gentiles were the branches of a wild olive; but were grafted in where the natural branches had been broken off, and received of the root and fatness of the pure stock. The apostle, Paul, gave the Gentiles a very solemn warning after they had been grafted into the good olive. See Romans 11 and 22. Behold the goodness and severity of God; on them which fell, severity: but towards thee, goodness, if thou continue in his goodness; otherwise thou shalt be cut off." Nothing is more plain than that the Gentiles have not continued in the goodness of God; but have departed from the faith and purity of the gospel. Query: Must they now be cut off? Jer. 4, 7, will answer this question. "The lion is come up from his thicket; and the destroyer of the Gentiles is on his way: he is gone forth from his place to make thy land desolate; and thy cities shall be laid waste without an inhabitant. Also, Isa. 24th chap., is a striking exhibition of the fate of the Gentiles in the last days. But the Jews will be grafted back into their own olive tree. Read Rom. 11, 23—28th.

Many are flattering themselves with the expectation that all the world is going to be converted and brought into the ark of safety. Thus the great milennium, in their opinion, is to be established. Vain, delusive expectation! The Saviour said to his disciples; that, "As it was in the days of Noah, so shall it be also in the days of the coming of the Son of Man." Again, he said: "As it was in the days of Lot, so shall it be in the days of the coming of the Son of Man." Query. Were all people converted in the days of Noah, or mostly destroyed? Were the cities of Sodom and Gomorrah saved or destroyed in the days of Lot? The answers to these questions are familiar to almost every person, and further comment is unnecessary.

God will soon begin to manifest his sore displeasure to this generation, and to your own country by distressing famine; for the season will hence forth be more irregular and uncertain in causing the earth to yield her bounty for the sustenance of her inhabitants. The trade and commerce of nations which have hitherto been a source of great wealth and pride, already begin to feel the withering touch of the Almighty, and must fade and sink to rise no more. Your nation is now, probably, at peace; and so are most nations. The sun of prosperity has shone upon them for some length of time, with scarcely a cloud to obstruct its rays. But the golden luminary of peace is now fast reclining behind the western waters; and then comes a night darkened by war-clouds, arising from almost every quarter and filling the political horizon with terror and dismay. The hearts of kings, rulers, and nobles, will then faint because they know not the time of their visitation; and will know not what measures to adopt to avert the calamities of war.

O ye shepherds! ye teachers! ye rulers in Israel! hear the word of the Lord concerning you—The Lord who shall suddenly come to his temple—The Lord who shall come down upon the world with a curse to judgment, and upon all the ungodly among you. Wo! Wo!! unto them, saith the Lord, who preach for hire and *pervert* the ways of *truth*. Wo! unto them who suffer themselves to be led by the precepts of men contrary to that which they know to be written in the oracles of truth, for they shall perish. Wo! unto him who drinketh strong drink and taketh the name of his God in vain! Wo! be unto all the wicked ones of the earth; for the fire of God's jealousy will consume them, root and branch, except they speedily repent.

Earthquakes, strange things and fearful sights, together with the waves of the sea heaving themselves beyond their bounds, will cause men's hearts to fail them for fear. This is the Lord's recompence for the controversy of Zion, whose innocent blood, unavenged, cries to him from the ground. The Lord has looked down from heaven and beheld all your scenes of revelling and drunkenness. He has seen all your frauds—all your evil designs, and all the snares you have laid to take advantage of your neighbour. He has, also, seen the sterling virtues of many of the fairest portion of his creation sacrificed upon the altar of infamy and prostitution: all of which have a tendency to increase the displeasure of the Almighty, and draw down upon the world the storm of his indignation.

The apostacy of the church is the prime cause of the earth being visited by the judgments of God. Had the church remained in a steadfast, upright and righteous course, it would have saved the nations from destruction. But, alas! the salt has lost its savor. "They have transgressed the laws, changed the ordinances, and broken the everlasting covenant."

The wicked will behold these judgements; and know not what they mean; yet the servants of God will view them as tokens of the coming of the Son of Man, as messengers sent before his face to execute vengeance. They will continue the work of destruction until the Saviour comes; for,

Lo! he comes with truth and vengeance,
With his garments dyed in blood;
To redeem his chosen people,
Favour'd Children, sons of God.

When Jesus appears in the clouds of heaven, the saints who have slept, will arise from their graves; and those who are living will be changed speedily, and all be caught up to meet the Lord in the air. Then shall all the wicked who have escaped the former judgments, be consumed root and branch. Then shall the earth be cleansed from pollution; and the Lord descend upon it, and all the saints with him, to reign a thousand years while satan is bound. Then will the saints inherit this promise: "Blessed are the meek, for they shall inherit the earth." Then one need not say to the other, Know ye the Lord? For they shall all know him, from the least to the greatest. Then the earth shall be full of the knowledge of God, as the waters cover the great deep. Then shall the saints unite in singing this new song: saying,

'The Lord hath brought again Zion
The Lord hath redeemed his people, Israel,
According to the election of grace.
Which was brought to pass by the faith
And covenant of their fathers.
The Lord hath redeemed his people;
And Satan is bound, and time is no longer.
The Lord hath gathered all things in one:
The Lord hath brought down Zion from above:
The Lord hath brought up Zion from beneath:
The earth hath traveled and brought forth her strength,
And truth is established in her bowels;
And the heavens have smiled upon her;
And she is clothed with the glory of her God:
For he stands in the midst of his people.
Glory, and honour, and power, and might,
Be ascribed to our God, for he is full of mercy,
Justice, grace, and truth and peace,
For ever and ever——————Amen.'

I am unwilling to dismiss this subject without telling you what the Lord has done for his creatures in these latter times, and, also, what he requires of you, that my garments may be clean of your blood in a coming day. The Lord has been pleased to send his holy angel from heaven to announce the joyful tidings to witnesses now living, that the time has come for him to set his hand the second and last time to gather in the remnants of Israel; and with them the fulness of the Gentiles—to establish permanent peace on Earth for One Thousand Years. The everlasting Gospel must go forth to the nations once more, to seal up the righteous, and to prepare them for the hour of judgment and desolation that awaiteth the inhabitants of the Earth: and, also, for the coming of the Son of Man, which will be witnessed by this generation, according to the testimony of the Angel of the Lord.

As John was sent before the face of the Lord to prepare the way for his first coming, even so has the Lord now sent forth his servants for the last time, to labour in his vineyard at the eleventh hour, to prepare the way for his second coming, by the preaching of repentance and baptism for the remission of sins, that they may be ready to go forth to meet the Bridegroom.

I am quite surprised that the clergy of this day pursue the course which they do in relation to this messuage which God has sent to man. They appear to feel themselves perfectly justifiable in raising the cry of false teachers and false prophets against the servants of God; but have no fears whatever that they may offend the Lord by so doing. Christ once said that offences must come: but wo! unto him by whom they come, &c. They are very ready to close their doors against what they are pleased to call delusion and deception: but they have no fears that they may close their doors against good by so doing, and shut out Christ and his servants from them.

Jesus was once grieved and wounded in the house of his friends because he testified against their iniquities, corruptions, and gross departure from the truth of heaven; so when he sends forth his servants to do the same they may ever expect to meet with a similar reception. If we had come to you declaring that an angel had come from heaven and testified that your works and your ways were all accepted of the Lord; and that he had pronounced his benediction upon you: you, no doubt, would have acknowledged that the ministration of angels, in these days, was a scriptural doctrine: but because he testified against your departure from the truth, your errors and your traditions, you are now ready to cry, "False prophets, and false teachers."

But we are determined to preach the doctrine of Jesus Christ and to contend for the faith once delivered to the saints: Tho' every priest on Babel's towers should oppose us.

Therefore, go forth, little sheet, and tell the people of England, and all people into whose hands you may fall, that the Lord has spoken from the heavens—that he hath sent forth his servants to them, preaching repentance, and baptizing for the remission of sins, to prepare them for the coming of the Son of Man, which is drawing near.

MAY, 4TH, 1839.

REPRINTED BY W. R. THOMAS, SPRING-GARDENS, MANCHESTER.

An 1837 broadside by Orson Hyde, the first LDS imprint in England
Courtesy LDS Church Archives

Doctrine and Covenants, it appears that only one item was commonly used. Titled *A Timely Warning to the People of England*, it was actually a reprint, done in Preston in August 1837, of Orson Hyde's *A Prophetic Warning*, which had been printed earlier in Toronto, Canada, and had been distributed as part of their missionary labors in New York City prior to departing for England.[13] After Elders Kimball and Hyde left England, another edition was printed in Manchester in May 1839.[14] Significantly, this edition eliminated many of the more grim references to the predicted events of the last days, toned down the negative references to the sectarian clergy, and, unlike the American editions, clearly identified itself as a Latter-day Saint tract. At least two other English editions appeared, the first in Manchester in 1840.[15]

It may seem strange that no other pamphlets appeared during the first British mission, for the missionaries felt that the "Lord was troubling the people's minds," and printed matter would have strengthened the work immensely.[16] Elder Kimball, however, was not likely to publish anything by himself, for he had neither the skills nor the interest. Orson Hyde, on the other hand, was a writer. But given the shortness of the mission and the fact that they were so short-handed they could not meet all their speaking opportunities, publishing was not a high priority. Nor did they have the financial support that was forthcoming in 1840 from several more prosperous converts.

Such practical considerations aside, two other factors may also have discouraged them from publishing. For one, they may have wanted to avoid a pamphlet war, as might have been implied in Joseph Fielding's comment in June 1838 about two small anti-Mormon pamphlets that had recently appeared. They were, he said,

full of lies and Slander, the last in particular called an exposure of Mormonism, etc. Its motto is "Let no Man deceive you." This must bring a signal Curse on the Author. It

---

[13]See Heber C. Kimball to Vilate Kimball, June 27, 1837, Heber C. Kimball Collection: "We did up about one hundred and fifty in letter form and directed to evry priest of evry profession in the city." See also *Millennial Star* 1 (April 1841): 290.

[14]This actually may have been the third edition, and the second with the new title. The bibliographical details are presented in Crawley and Whittaker, *Mormon Imprints*, 15–16.

[15]The other was an eight-page pamphlet published in Oxford-Hill in the later 1840s. All the previous editions apparently were broadsides.

[16]Early Mormon concern for the printed word is discussed in Whittaker, "Early Mormon Pamphleteering," 1–92. The quotation comes from Joseph Fielding to Hannah Fielding, March 27, 1839, Manchester, photocopy, Joseph Fielding Collection, Brigham Young University.

appears they want to provoke us to Controversy, but we have washed our feet against them all, so they may talk and write until they are tired, or till the Lord puts a stop to them.[17]

As they had done in America, the early missionaries relied mostly on the spoken word to address both investigators and critics. The rest would be left to the Lord, on whose errand they were.

In a curious way, another inhibition to publishing may have grown from the charge, given focus in two unfortunate episodes, that the American missionaries harbored secret teachings. The first episode grew out of John Goodson's reading publicly to investigators in Bedford, contrary to the counsel of Joseph Smith, what is now section 76 of the Doctrine and Covenants, then simply called "The Vision." The doctrines therein about three degrees of glory, modifying the traditional view of heaven and hell, greatly disturbed some new members as well as potential converts who had no background for understanding it.[18] Related to this was another episode, which led to apostasy and to the first published attack by a former Church member in England. Concerned with the implications of the law of consecration, Thomas Webster, a recent convert, challenged and then attacked the Church. He disapproved of both "The Vision" and the revelations in the Doctrine and Covenants that spoke of money and other temporal things. He convinced himself and several others that the missionaries were interested only in money, and he used the scarcity of printed copies of the Doctrine and Covenants to bolster his arguments that it was a secret book and that Mormonism had many doctrines and secrets which the missionaries withheld from the public. In his pamphlet, *Some Extracts from the Book of Doctrine and Covenants . . .* , he attempted to warn others of what he thought was the real message of Mormonism. Even had they considered a publications program, problems such as these might well have left the first missionaries uncertain about just what they should or should not print.[19]

---

[17]See Fielding, Diary, 21.

[18]A number of early LDS sources refer to this. See letter of Orson Hyde to Willard Richards, October 12, 1837, and February 14, 1838; Fielding, Diary, January 1838; and "Manuscript History of the British Mission," August 15 and October 5, 1837. On June 11, 1837, Joseph Smith had counseled departing English missionaries Heber C. Kimball and Joseph Fielding not to preach on "The Vision" and other doctrines until the new converts were more grounded in the basics. See Smith, *History of the Church* 2:492.

[19]The best source on the Thomas Webster episode is the diary of Joseph Fielding. Webster was the first British convert to apostatize and write against the Church. He was baptized in October 1837 by Orson Hyde and then excommunicated on September 30, 1838. Webster's main objections can be seen in Webster,

Parley P. Pratt
© Courtesy LDS Church Archives

THE SIGNIFICANCE OF PUBLICATIONS BETWEEN THE MISSIONS

Before the Quorum went to England in 1840, several important publishing developments occurred in America. To begin with, Parley P. Pratt issued his classic *Voice of Warning* in New York City in 1837. Outside of the standard works,[20] this was the first and for a long time the most important LDS book of the nineteenth century, and it was an ideal missionary tract. It was the first publication to detail the differences between Mormonism and traditional Christianity, and it established the basic formulas for describing the fundamental doctrines of the Church. It

Some Extracts. This work probably appeared in December 1838. Other references to Webster and his anti-Mormon activities include letter of Heber C. Kimball to Saints at Liverpool, April 13, 1838, *Millennial Star* 2 (May 1841): 8; Thomas Webster to Nehemiah Greenhalgh, October 2, 1838; and entry for October 7, 1838, all in "Manuscript History of the British Mission."

Charges that the Doctrine and Covenants was a "secret" book continued to plague LDS missionaries in England. See, for example, *Millennial Star* 2 (May 1841): 3 and 2 (July 1841): 36. Parley P. Pratt, responding to the same charges in Rollo, *Mormonism Exposed*, wrote, "He complains bitterly of our not keeping the commandments given us in the Book of Covenants to publish it to the world. To which we reply that it has been published to the world till out of print. Mr. R., be patient; three printing establishments have been destroyed for us in ten years, by the cruelty and violence of men who were inspired by such misrepresentations as you have published" (*Millennial Star* 2 [July 1841]: 47).

[20]The Bible, Book of Mormon, Doctrine and Covenants, and, after 1880, the Pearl of Great Price.

would have an important influence on missionary work for more than a century.

In April 1838 Parley also published in New York the first tract by an LDS author to respond specifically to an anti-Mormon work. His *Mormonism Unveiled: Zion's Watchman Unmasked, and its editor, Mr. L. R. Sunderland, exposed: The Devil mad, and priestcraft in danger!* was a response to a tract repeating anti-Mormon arguments that had appeared in 1834 in E. D. Howe's *Mormonism Unvailed,* which at that time, had been almost ignored by the Church.

The printed material growing out of the Saints' last months in Missouri was also important to the second British mission. Most significant was the effort to publish accounts of their persecutions.[21] John Taylor's first pamphlet, published in 1839 in Springfield, Illinois, was titled *A Short Account of the Murders, roberies, burnings, thefts, and other outrages committed by the mob and militia of the state of Missouri, upon the Latter Day Saints.*[22] The most influential such work, however, came from Parley P. Pratt, who had traveled north into Michigan after his escape from a Missouri jail in July 1839. In Detroit he published *History of the Late Persecution . . . ,*[23] the history he had written while imprisoned. In New York City, before leaving for England, he reissued this work, adding an introduction that included a summary of the basic beliefs of the Church.[24] In February 1840 in Washington, D.C., he slightly reworked that summary and issued it as a separate pamphlet, *An Address . . . to the Citizens of Washington.*[25] This concise statement of faith became a significant Latter-day Saint work and, among other things, clearly influenced the "Articles of Faith" Joseph Smith appended to his Wentworth letter of 1842.[26] It was reprinted at least six times in both the United States and England, often with just a changed title. Parley himself reissued it at least twice within a few months of arriving in England.

Another factor helped change the attitude toward publishing in the

---

[21]D&C 123 specifically commanded members to gather and publish accounts of their Missouri persecutions.

[22]See Woodruff, *Journal,* August 16, 1839, 1:351; August 20, 1839, 1:352–53; and August 30, 1839, 1:356.

[23]Parley provided a short summary of his early publishing activities in *Millennial Star* 1 (July 1840): 50–51. P. Pratt's *History of the Late Persecution* appeared in October 1839 per Parley's October 12, 1839, letter to the Editor, *Times and Seasons* 1 (January 1840): 43.

[24]P. Pratt, *History of the Late Persecution.*

[25]P. Pratt, *Judge Higbee and Parley P. Pratt.* Reprinted in *Times and Seasons* 1 (March 1840): 68–70.

[26]See Whittaker, " 'Articles of Faith'."

second mission. In the winter of 1839–40, during his unsuccessful trip to the nation's capital seeking redress for the Missouri difficulties, Joseph Smith met in a series of conferences and other gatherings with Latter-day Saints along the east coast. Judging from the pamphlet literature that soon emerged from individuals who heard the Prophet speak, it appears that on this trip he began to introduce publicly certain doctrines that had not been clearly defined previously but that gradually became central to LDS thought. The Pratt brothers were among those who heard him, and not long afterwards Parley published a work that denied the traditional Christian notion of *ex nihilo* creation and argued for belief in a finitistic God.[27] In the spring of 1840, Samuel Bennett published a pamphlet that asserted the LDS belief in a corporeal, anthropomorphic God,[28] and Benjamin Winchester, in a reply to a critic of the Church, referred to the idea of the premortal existence of spirits.[29]

It is significant that all these doctrinal tracts were printed *outside* Church headquarters, away from the direct control of Joseph Smith. Usually these individual efforts were attempts to reach larger and more sophisticated urban audiences with the message of the Restoration. That pattern was continued in the British Isles, where many of the new teachings of Joseph Smith found their way into print. Orson Pratt's Edinburgh pamphlet, for example, contained the first public account of Joseph Smith's 1820 First Vision.

By the time the Quorum of the Twelve headed for England, both the content and the direction of LDS imprints had clearly changed. Parley Pratt, the individual most active in the change, also became the key figure in England. Little wonder that he is referred to as the father of Mormon pamphleteering.[30]

THE TWELVE AS PUBLISHERS

The arrival of the Twelve in Britain in 1840 gave renewed vitality and direction to LDS publications, just as it did to missionary work. The apostles took three approaches; first, they used material recently published in America; second, individuals, for various reasons, issued their own works; third, in a more corporate approach, they collected or borrowed the necessary

---

[27]P. Pratt, *Millennium*.
[28]Bennett, *Few Remarks*.
[29]Winchester, *Examination of a Lecture*.
[30]For a full development of this, see Crawley, "Parley P. Pratt."

funds and coordinated larger publishing projects. As we have seen, Brigham Young, Heber C. Kimball, and Parley P. Pratt, functioning as a publishing committee, quickly raised money for three initial projects: a hymnal, a periodical, and an edition of the Book of Mormon. In a strikingly different attitude from that of the 1837 mission, the apostles considered their publication program an essential element of their missionary work.

Even before leaving America, and throughout their early months in Britain, the apostles sought to obtain authorization from the Prophet to publish abroad. Before departing from New York with others of the Twelve, Parley P. Pratt had written to Joseph Smith, seeking permission to publish another American edition of the Book of Mormon.[31] In Joseph's absence, Hyrum Smith replied that he thought the Twelve could publish what they wanted, though the Book of Mormon ought to be published in Nauvoo, and he thought it best to wait for Joseph's personal response before they did anything.[32]

Apostles Orson Hyde and John E. Page also wrote from Columbus, Ohio, to the Prophet in May 1840, asking if the Twelve were at liberty to publish abroad any book that they felt necessary.[33] Joseph Smith responded by giving them full authorization to publish, expressing reservations only about the hymnbook.[34] Brigham, being in England, was of course unaware of that response, and on May 7 he wrote from Herefordshire, seeking both permission and counsel with respect to publishing the Book of Mormon and the Doctrine and Covenants in England.[35]

Brigham heard nothing directly from Joseph, but he moved ahead with the publications anyway because they seemed so urgent. Not until early in November did he receive the letter the Prophet had sent to the Twelve with Lorenzo Snow. It was smudged and difficult to read, but as near as he could make out, Joseph seemed displeased with the decision

---

[31]Parley P. Pratt to Joseph Smith, November 22, 1839, Joseph Smith Collection. This letter is important as it foreshadows most of the developments in England relating to publishing. Parley was also publishing a second edition of his *Voice of Warning* as well as his *Millennium*.

[32]For Hyrum Smith's letter to Parley P. Pratt, December 22, 1839, see Smith, *History of the Church* 4:47–48. Hyrum reported this to Joseph Smith on January 3, 1840. See ibid., 4:51.

[33]Orson Hyde and John E. Page to Joseph Smith, May 1, 1840, Joseph Smith Collection. Also in Smith, *History of the Church* 4:123–25. This letter focuses on plans for publishing in Germany.

[34]See Joseph Smith to "Dear Brethren," [Hyde and Page] May 14, 1840, Joseph Smith Collection. See also Smith, *History of the Church* 4:128–29

[35]Brigham Young to Joseph Smith, May 7, 1840, Joseph Smith Collection, reproduced in Smith, *History of the Church* 4:125–27. This letter clearly implies that they had discussed this matter before and had probably concluded then to import books once they were established in England.

to print the hymnbook and the Book of Mormon before clearing it with him. Convinced that Joseph did not fully understand the pressures they were under, Brigham poured out his feelings to Mary Ann. He said they would have gladly written to Joseph again, but they could not delay for the many months a reply would require. "All I have to say about the matter . . . ," Brigham explained, "is I have don all that I could to doe good and promote the cause that we are in. I have don the verry best that I knew how. . . . You may read this letter to Br Joseph or not, jest as you please, but tell him at ennyrate to say what he wants me to doe and I will try and doe it the Lord will."[36]

Clearly, Brigham tried to keep Joseph informed of their decisions, and his letters suggest a sense of caution even as he moved forward.[37] Happily, the next letter from the Prophet ratified everything the Twelve had done, and by then both the hymnbook and the Book of Mormon were at press. Joseph was delighted. His later decision to place the Quorum of the Twelve Apostles in charge of publishing in Nauvoo was surely an outgrowth of their work in England.[38]

A NEW HYMNBOOK

From the first, publishing a hymnbook was a high priority, for nothing was available to the British Saints but Protestant hymnals.[39] Even in America, as Parley wrote Joseph Smith from New York, there was "a great call for Hymn Books, but none to be had."[40] On the eve of their departure, the apostles who left New York in March noted that "a good Hymn book is very much wanted abroad."[41] When they arrived in Britain, Brigham later

---

[36]Brigham Young to Mary Ann Young, November 12, 1840.

[37]Brigham Young and Willard Richards to First Presidency, September 5, 1840, Joseph Smith Collection (Appendix B, Document 12). "Have we done right in Printing a hymn book? Are we doing right in Printing the book of Mormon? . . . Shall we print the Doctrine & Covenants?" Young asked. But with his characteristic pragmatism, he concluded, "Our motto is *go ahead*."

[38]See Joseph Smith to the Twelve, December 15, 1840. For information on the Quorum of the Twelve Apostles taking over LDS publications, including information on the revelation justifying such, see Whittaker, "Early Mormon Pamphleteering," 63–65. Compare Woodruff, *Journal*, February 8, 1842, 2:154 (re: revelation dated January 4, 1842).

[39]See, for example, Kimball, *Journal*, 32.

[40]"I wish Sister Smith would add to the old collection such New ones as is best and republish them immediately." Parley P. Pratt to Joseph Smith, November 22, 1839, Joseph Smith Collection. Parley even offered to oversee the publishing project on the east coast. He had published the first volume of Mormon poems several months before Emma's 1835 hymnal was available. See P. Pratt, *Millennium*. This volume contained eleven hymns (pp. 31–52), and he included them in his 1840 *Millennium*.

[41]Parley P. Pratt, Brigham Young, Heber C. Kimball, and Orson Pratt to the "Church of the Latter Day Saints in Commerce, Illinois," February 19, 1840, *Times and Seasons* 1 (March 1840): 71.

A COLLECTION

OF

SACRED HYMNS,

FOR THE

CHURCH OF JESUS CHRIST

OF

LATTER-DAY SAINTS,

IN EUROPE.

SELECTED BY
BRIGHAM YOUNG, PARLEY P. PRATT, AND
JOHN TAYLOR.

PUBLISHED BY ORDER OF A GENERAL CONFERENCE,
AND FOR SALE AT 149, OLDHAM ROAD, MANCHESTER,
AND BY AGENTS THROUGHOUT ENGLAND.

Manchester:
PRINTED BY W. R. THOMAS, SPRING GARDENS,
1840.

Sacred Hymns.

PUBLIC WORSHIP.

HYMN 1. L. M.

The morning breaks the shadows flee,
Lo! Zion's standard is unfurled!
The dawning of a brighter day
Majestic rises on the world.

The clouds of error disappear
Before the rays of truth divine—
The glory bursting from afar,
Wide o'er the nations soon will shine.

The Gentile fulness now comes in,
And Israel's blessings are at hand:
Lo! Judah's remnant, cleansed from sin,
Shall in their promised Canaan stand.
A 3

Title page of the first LDS hymnbook in Great Britain. Courtesy LDS Church Archives

First page of the Manchester hymnal Courtesy LDS Church Archives

wrote, "we found the brethren had laid by their old hymn books, and they wanted new ones; for the Bible, religion and all is new to them."[42] Not surprisingly, the apostles decided to publish one without delay, a decision that was ratified at the April 1840 conference in Preston. Brigham Young, Parley P. Pratt, and John Taylor were assigned to choose the hymns.[43]

They moved quickly. By May the apostles had granted a printing contract for three thousand copies to W. R. Thomas.[44] Writing to Brigham Young on May 4, Parley said that he wrote new hymns every day and hoped

---

[42]Brigham Young, *Manuscript History of Brigham Young*, 71. See also Brigham Young to Joseph Smith and Counselors, April 15–16, 1840, *Times and Seasons* 1 (June 1840): 122.

[43]See Journal History of the Church, April 17, 1840; see also "History of Brigham Young," *Millennial Star* 25 (November 14, 1863): 727.

[44]Before receiving the contract, Thomas gave them a written bid. A printing estimate is noted in Parley P. Pratt to Brigham Young, May 4, 1840, Brigham Young Papers. It did not include binding. A series of bills from Winstanley of Manchester (81 Fountain Street) to Brigham Young indicated that he did the lettering. These are in Brigham Young Papers, Church Archives, as are the receipts for payment to W. R. Thomas for printing.

to contribute one hundred to the new book. "There is indeed a great call for Him[n] Books Suited to our worship," he added.[45]

Brigham Young, meanwhile, went with Wilford Woodruff south to Herefordshire, where, in addition to doing missionary work, he set about raising funds for publishing the hymnbook and the Book of Mormon. A month later he was on his way back to Manchester with the borrowed money.[46] Immediately Brigham, Parley P. Pratt, and John Taylor, who had come from Liverpool, began selecting hymns. By June 29, the day they prepared the index, the volume of hymns was ready for the press.[47] A week later enough copies were ready so that Parley P. Pratt could present the new hymnal to the conference in Manchester, where it was officially accepted, and two days later all three thousand copies were available.[48] By the end of July, they were being distributed throughout Great Britain.[49] Within a year the first edition was exhausted, and on April 3, 1841, Parley P. Pratt was authorized to reprint it without alteration (except for typographical errors), which he did in November 1841.[50]

This first British hymnal was of far-reaching significance, for it became the basis for all other LDS hymnbooks published in the nineteenth century.

---

[45]Parley P. Pratt to Brigham Young, May 4, 1840.

[46]The money, £250 from the Benbows (part of Jane Benbow's inheritance) and £100 from the Kingtons, was secured by notes signed by Wilford Woodruff and Willard Richards on May 20, 1840, located in the Brigham Young Papers. Brigham Young to Willard Richards, June 10, 1840, Willard Richards Collection, suggested the possibility of borrowing more money from the Benbows. They were to be paid back through the sales of the two volumes, and existing records reveal Brigham Young's concerns to fulfill these obligations. See, for example, Brigham Young to Willard Richards, June 17, 1840, Brigham Young Papers. In September 1840 the Benbows forgave the debt. The Mormons were accused by critics of stealing money later that year, but Parley P. Pratt made it plain they just borrowed money to publish and would repay it through the sale of the works produced. See *Millennial Star* 1 (November 1840): 189.

[47]On June 17, 1840, Brigham Young wrote to Willard Richards that "we are getting along finely with the hym Book thou[gh] my labor has been such that I am quite unwell, but I keepe doing with all my might" (Willard Richards Papers). Three days later Brigham Young wrote to his wife Mary Ann that "I have now got through with the hy[m]nbook, I have had prety much the whole of it to doe myself. Brother J. Taylor has been sick, Brother P. P. P[ratt] has had as much as he could doe to attend to the Star preparing matter, reading proof for Star and hyms" (Brigham Young to Mary Ann Young, June 20, 1840, Brigham Young Papers).

[48]See *Millennial Star* 1 (July 1840): 69; Wilford Woodruff to Phoebe Woodruff, July 8, 1840, *Times and Seasons* 1 (September 1840): 169.

[49]See, for example, John Taylor to Brigham Young, July 23, 1840, Brigham Young Papers, wherein, on the eve of his departure to Ireland, he ordered one hundred hymnbooks to take with him. In the same letter John Taylor complains of the many typographical errors in the hymnbook. Later John Taylor ordered more when he was on the Isle of Man. (John Taylor to Brigham Young, October 2, 1840, Brigham Young Collection.) Joseph Smith's approval of the British hymnbook was conveyed in his epistle, "To the Elders in England," *Times and Seasons* 2 (January 1, 1841): 259; reprinted in *Millennial Star* 1 (March 1841): 266–67.

[50]See *Millennial Star* 25 (December 26, 1863): 819.

It included seventy-eight of the ninety selections in Emma Smith's 1835 hymnal and added 193 others. Forty-four of the new hymns were by Parley P. Pratt, and seventeen of those came from the 1840 New York edition of *The Millennium and Other Poems*. Thirteen editions were printed before 1871.[51]

THE BOOK OF MORMON

In 1837 John Goodson took several copies, possibly as many as two hundred, of the 1837 Kirtland edition of the Book of Mormon to England, but his eventual apostasy, along with other problems, seems to have prevented many of them from being distributed.[52] Parley P. Pratt's November 1839 letter to Joseph Smith, no doubt anticipating the mission to England, suggested "that the publication of the Book of Mormon in Europe in English, French, German, and other languages be committed to the Twelve, . . . whose duty it shall be to secure to you the Copy rights in the several governments, and to render strict account from time to time to the first Presidency."[53]

The need for a British edition of the Book of Mormon was abundantly clear. Parley told Brigham Young in May 1840 that it was "verry much wanted and it is all important to print immediately for why withhold the fulness of the Gospel, in the face of all the prophesies that it Shall go to

---

[51]Crawley and Whittaker, *Mormon Imprints*, 18–19. For the best study of the history of Mormon music to date, see Hicks, *Mormonism and Music*.

[52]Extant records indicate that Goodson had either twenty or two hundred copies of the Book of Mormon in England in October 1837. These seem to have been his share for his role in the production of the five thousand copies of the Kirtland edition. The "Manuscript History of the British Mission" reports for October 5, 1837 that Goodson and John Snyder had left their English mission for America, taking "over two hundred copies of the Book of Mormon and Doctrine and Covenants," which they refused to sell to Heber C. Kimball, and that Goodson later burned his books.

Given the value of these books it seems unlikely Goodson would have destroyed them. Goodson did leave about twenty copies of the Book of Mormon with Willard Richards, which Heber C. Kimball instructed him to sell "either to saint or sinner" to obtain money to purchase some clothes. See Orson Hyde to Willard Richards, October 12, 1837, Willard Richards Collection; Heber C. Kimball to Willard Richards, November 12, 1837, as cited in Whitney, *Life of Heber C. Kimball*, 174. That Goodson did sell a few copies to his fellow missionaries prior to his departure is evident in an entry in the diary of Joseph Fielding in January 1838, reporting a letter from Heber C. Kimball: "We kept as many as we could by any means pay him for; the rest [he] took back" (Fielding, Diary, 31). As late as February 1838 Goodson's books were a topic of discussion among the first group of missionaries. See Orson Hyde to Willard Richards, February 14, 1838, Willard Richards Collection. "Bring the Books with you that were left by bro. Goodson."

[53]Parley P. Pratt to Joseph Smith, November 22, 1839. The book, he observed, was "not to be had in this part of the vineyard for love or money. Hundreds are waiting in various parts here about but there is truly a famine in that respect."

THE

BOOK OF MORMON:

AN ACCOUNT WRITTEN BY THE HAND OF MORMON
UPON PLATES TAKEN FROM THE
PLATES OF NEPHI.

Wherefore it is an abridgment of the record of the people of Nephi,
and also of the Lamanites; written to the Lamanites, who are a
remnant of the house of Israel; and also to Jew and Gentile:
written by way of commandment, and also by the spirit of prophecy
and of revelation.   Written, and sealed up, and hid up unto the
LORD, that they might not be destroyed; to come forth by the gift
and power of GOD unto the interpretation thereof: sealed by the
hand of Moroni, and hid up unto the LORD, to come forth in due
time by the way of Gentile; the interpretation thereof by the gift
of GOD:

An abridgment taken from the book of Ether: also, which is a record of the people of Jared; who were scattered at the time the
LORD confounded the language of the people when they were
building a tower to get to heaven; which is to shew unto the remnant of the house of Israel what great things the LORD hath done
for their fathers; and that they may know the covenants of the
LORD, that they are not cast off for ever: and also to the convincing
of the Jew and Gentile that JESUS is the CHRIST, the ETERNAL
GOD, manifesting himself unto all nations. And now if there are
faults, they are the mistakes of men; wherefore condemn not the
things of GOD, that ye may be found spotless at the judgment-seat
of CHRIST.

TRANSLATED BY
JOSEPH SMITH, Jun.

First European, from the Second American Edition.

PRINTED BY J. TOMPKINS,
Liverpool, England:
FOR BRIGHAM YOUNG, HEBER C. KIMBALL
AND PARLEY P. PRATT.
By order of the Translator.

1841.

Title page of the first British
edition of the Book of Mormon
Courtesy LDS Church Archives

all nations?"[54] Brigham, in turn, reported to Joseph Smith that "they beg and plead for the Book of Mormon."[55]

Brigham Young was determined to make the book available to the British Saints, and the project was approved by the same conference that approved the hymnal. Brigham Young, Heber C. Kimball, and Parley P. Pratt were appointed as the publishing committee,[56] and after Brigham returned from Manchester with the funds obtained from the Benbows and the Kingtons, they at first decided to publish three thousand copies with an index.[57] Brigham immediately sought bids for the printing. On June 7, 1840, after visiting almost every printer in Manchester and Liverpool,[58] he obtained a bid from John Tompkins & Company that was low enough to

[54]Parley P. Pratt to Brigham Young, May 4, 1840.

[55]Brigham Young to Joseph Smith, May 7, 1840.

[56]See Young, *Manuscript History*, April 16, 1840; Woodruff, *Journal*, April 2, 1841, 2:77, and April 5, 1841, 2:78.

[57]See Woodruff, *Journal*, May 14, 1840, 1:449; May 19, 1840, 1:451; and May 20, 1840, 1:451. See also Esplin, "Emergence of Brigham Young," 439–40.

[58]Many of the original bids are in the Brigham Young Papers.

allow them to contract for printing five thousand copies for £210.[59] The contracts were signed on June 17, and Brigham expected the printing to be finished in about twelve weeks.[60]

The work progressed slowly, however,[61] due partly to Tompkins's changing the width and length of the page, even though he was simply reprinting the 1837 Kirtland edition. After this change was approved by the apostles, they were told that the volume would be ready in about two months. The lengthy job of proofreading was underway by the middle of October, but not until January was a complete set of galleys available to Brigham Young and Willard Richards from which they could compile their index.[62] Wilford Woodruff reported five hundred copies off the press and in the bindery on January 8, and the *Millennial Star* announced to its February 1841 readers that the Book of Mormon was ready for sale.[63] Unfortunately, Tompkins delivered only 4,050 of the 5,000 copies agreed upon, but he promised to make up the difference at his own expense. His company failed, however, and the additional copies were never produced.

The new volume itself was a faithful reprint of the 1837 Kirtland edition, and except for two more editions that would appear in Nauvoo, it is from this Liverpool edition that all other LDS editions of the Book of Mormon descended.[64] Heber C. Kimball and Wilford Woodruff secured the English copyright in Joseph Smith's name at Stationers Hall, London, on February 8, 1841.[65]

The Book of Mormon was publicized and sold in many ways, including

---

[59]The bid, in Brigham Young Papers, Church Archives, estimated the cost for three thousand copies to be £148 and for five thousand copies £210. In a letter to Willard Richards dated June 10, 1840, Brigham Young said Tompkins's bid was £40 less than the next closest bid. (Brigham Young Papers.) Young was to supply the paper for the job as well as make separate arrangements for the binding.

[60]The contract is in Brigham Young Papers, Church Archives. Receipts in the Brigham Young Papers from J. Tompkins indicated the amount paid (£110) for printing was paid in installments beginning July 24, 1840, and ending February 12, 1841. The paper was obtained on July 7, 1840, for £107. See Woodruff, *Journal*, July 7, 1840, 1:482.

[61]By July 23 three forms were available for proofing, but the work had not moved much further a month later. John Taylor to Brigham Young, July 23, 1840, and John Taylor to Parley P. Pratt and Brigham Young, August 29, 1840, Brigham Young Papers.

[62]The index (really an extended table of contents) was compiled between January 18 and January 21, 1841; it was the first index to be published as part of the book and was used until the 1920 edition.

[63]Woodruff, *Journal*, January 8, 1841, 2:25. *Millennial Star* 1 (January 1841): 263.

[64]Brigham Young learned of the first Nauvoo edition in a letter from Ebenezer Robinson dated December 27, 1840, Brigham Young Papers. The information on the offer of J. Tompkins to print another edition is presented in Stock, "Book of Mormon, 1830–1879," 73–74.

[65]See Woodruff, *Journal*, February 8, 1841, 2:40–41. Their report was made to a meeting of the Quorum of the Twelve Apostles on April 2, 1841, in Manchester. See Young, *Manuscript History*, 93. A copy of the English copyright is reproduced in *Millennial Star* 25 (December 26, 1863): 819.

the use of three hundred placards printed by J. Tompkins.[66] The most important means of distribution, however, was obtaining subscriptions from members throughout the British Isles, and the committee spent much of March 1841 packaging and sending off copies to those who had subscribed or lent them money for printing the book.[67]

THE MILLENNIAL STAR

The April 1840 conference also voted to publish "a monthly periodical in pamphlet form,"[68] and that became the apostles' third major publishing project. Parley P. Pratt, who was already the most prolific writer among the Twelve and who, according to Brigham Young, "craved the privilege of editing it," was the natural choice for editor.[69] His enthusiasm and literary skills were essential to the new publication, and he lost no time in preparing a prospectus for it. The beautifully printed broadside, received from the printer in Manchester on April 25, provided a fitting introduction to what its name, *The Latter-Day Saints' Millennial Star*, implied. The Almighty had sent forth a holy angel, Parley announced with all his millennial fervor, to restore the fulness of the gospel, to bring his wandering sheep into one fold, and to prepare all who would hearken for the second advent of the Messiah, "which is now near at hand."[70] He said the forthcoming periodical would be "devoted entirely to the great work of the spread of truth" and would stand aloof from the common political and commercial news of the day. Its pages would carry information on the Restoration, the gathering, and the signs of the times and also contain extracts from the Book of Mormon and "from some remarkable visions and revelations which have been given to the saints in this age." As a harbinger of the millennium, it would announce to its readers that the slumber of ages was now broken, that the long night of darkness was ending.

---

[66]The receipt for one placard dated February 11, 1841, is in the Brigham Young Papers.

[67]See *Millennial Star* 25 (December 19 1863): 808, and also the letter of Thomas Kington to Brigham Young, March 26, 1841, complaining of mistakes in the edition, particularly as it related to the binding. Brigham Young took these complaints to the J. Tompkins Company but was told they could do nothing about missing pages. See their letter to Brigham Young, Heber C. Kimball, and Parley P. Pratt, April 8, 1841, Brigham Young Papers.

[68]See Young, "History of Brigham Young," April 15 and 16, 1840.

[69]See discourse by Brigham Young, August 31, 1856, *Journal of Discourses* 4:35. Earlier, in 1839, Pratt had wanted to begin a periodical in New York City and had written to Joseph Smith asking for permission to do so. Parley P. Pratt to Joseph Smith, November 22, 1839.

[70]P. Pratt, *Prospectus*. The only known copy is in Church Archives. Most of the *Prospectus* was reprinted in the first issue of the *Star*.

PROSPECTUS
OF THE
LATTER-DAY SAINTS
MILLENNIAL STAR.

THE long night of darkness is now far spent—the truth revived in its primitive simplicity and purity, like the day-star of the horizon, lights up the dawn of that effulgent morn when the knowledge of God will cover the earth as the waters cover the sea. It has pleased the Almighty to send forth an HOLY ANGEL, to restore the fulness of the gospel with all its attendant blessings, to bring together his wandering sheep into one fold, to restore to them " the faith which was once delivered to the saints," and to send his servants in these last days, with a special message to all the nations of the earth, in order to prepare all who will hearken for the Second Advent of Messiah, which is now near at hand.

By this means, the Church of Jesus Christ of Latter-Day Saints, (being first organized in 1830) has spread throughout many parts of America and Europe ; and has caused many tens of thousands to rejoice above measure, while they are enabled to walk in the light of truth.

And feeling very desirous that others should be made partakers of the same blessings by being made acquainted with the same truths, they have thought proper to order the publication of a Periodical devoted entirely to the great work of the spread of truth, sincerely praying that men may be led to carefully examine the subject, and to discern between truth and error, and act accordingly.

"THE MILLENNIAL STAR" will stand aloof from the common political and commercial news of the day.—Its columns will be devoted to the spread of the fulness of the gospel—the restoration of the ancient principles of Christianity—the gathering of Israel—the rolling forth of the kingdom of God among the nations—the signs of the times—the fulfilment of prophecy—recording the judgments of God as they befal the nations, whether signs in the heavens or in the earth " blood, fire, or vapour of smoke"—in short, whatever is shown forth indicative of the coming of the " Son of Man," and the ushering in of his universal reign on the earth. It will also contain letters from our numerous elders who are abroad, preaching the word both in America and Europe, containing news of their success in ministering the blessings of the glorious gospel.

As an Ancient Record has lately been discovered in America, unfolding the history of that continent and its inhabitants, as far back as its first peopling after the flood, and containing much historical, prophetical, and doctrinal knowledge, which is of the utmost importance to the present age, we shall give such extracts from time to time as will be most interesting to the lovers of truth.

From this source we shall be able to pour a flood of light upon the world on subjects before concealed—upon the history of a nation whose remnants have long since dwindled to insignificance in midnight darkness, and whose former greatness was lost in oblivion, or only known by the remains of cities, palaces, temples, aqueducts, monuments, towers, fortifications, unintelligible inscriptions, sepulchres, and bones.

The slumber of ages has now been broken. The dark curtain of the past has been rolled up. The veil of obscurity has been removed, as it regards the world called new.—This discovery will yet be hailed among all nations, as among the most glorious events of latter times, and as one of the principal means of overwhelming the earth with knowledge.

This paper will also contain extracts from some remarkable visions and revelations which have been given to the saints in this age, unfolding the mysteries of the kingdom of God from days of old and for ages to come ; for truly some of the wonders of eternity have been opened to our view, and things to come have been shown to us, even the things of many generations.

CONDITIONS.

The " MILLENNIAL STAR" will be published monthly, at Manchester, by P. P. Pratt, in numbers suitable for binding at the end of the year. It will be neatly executed on good paper, each No. containing 24 demy 8vo. pages, double columns, with a neat cover. It will be forwarded to subscribers throughout the kingdom with as little delay as possible, price 6d. each No. Subscriptions are to be paid quarterly or yearly in advance, as may best suit the circumstances of the subscribers. Our elders and other church officers throughout the kingdom, are respectfully invited to act as agents. They can take the names of those who wish the paper, together with the advance-money, and forward the same to us, with orders for as many papers as they wish. The first No. to be issued as soon as a sufficient number of subscribers are obtained. All letters and orders should be addressed to the Editor, P. P. PRATT, 4, Chapel Court, Jersey-st., Gt. Ancoats, Manchester.

Manchester, April, 1840.   P. P. PRATT.

W. R. Thomas, Printer, 61, Spring Gardens. Manchester.

Prospectus for the *Millennial Star.* Courtesy LDS Church Archives

Parley concluded his prospectus by addressing several more mundane but essential matters. The *Star* would be published monthly, as a twenty-four-page pamphlet with double columns printed on good paper suitable for binding at the end of the year. Each issue was to cost six pence, with subscriptions payable quarterly or yearly in advance. Missionaries and Church leaders throughout the British Isles were invited to act as agents for the *Star*, and the first issue was to appear as soon as a sufficient number of subscribers was obtained. Parley immediately set about sending copies of the prospectus to the elders, encouraging them to act as agents.[71]

Brigham Young and Parley disagreed on how many copies of the first issue should be printed. Parley, reluctant to print more than subscriptions would pay for, suggested printing only one thousand copies, but Brigham told him he was thinking too small.[72] They finally decided on two thousand copies, and the agreement with the printer, W. R. Thomas, was signed on May 13. By May 24 the first issue was off the press.[73]

Even before coming to England, Parley had anticipated the establishment of a printing enterprise "in some stake of Zion according to the word of the Lord and the pattern given."[74] In Manchester he found a "good House and Shop" on Oldham Road, which he rented for £17 annually. His home thus became the quasi headquarters, printing office, and book depot for the apostolic mission, and even though it was short-lived as a headquarters, the initial activity there laid a broad foundation for most all LDS publishing in the nineteenth century.[75]

In a preface to the first bound volume of the *Millennial Star*, dated April 17, 1841, Parley noted that his aim was not just to benefit his age "but to hand down to posterity a journal" of the events of the developing movement. He accomplished that objective well, for the *Star* remains one of the essential sources of early Mormon history. In its pages are letters,

---

[71]Joseph Fielding reported in his diary for May 2, 1840: "On Tuesday I received a Packet of the Prospectus of the Millennial Star from Bro. P. P. Pratt, Manchester, which I have distributed, and have now about 45 Subscribers." Fielding, Diary, 73.

[72]Brigham Young to George A. Smith, May 4, 1840, Brigham Young Papers.

[73]See also letter of Brigham Young to Willard Richards and Wilford Woodruff, May 24, 1840. Young noted: "The Star is out and about 1300 copies are already gon[e]. If we had on[e] thousand only we should come short of our object."

[74]Parley P. Pratt to Joseph Smith, November 22, 1839. No doubt Parley was thinking of D&C 72:20–23.

[75]In his May 4, 1840, letter to Brigham Young, Parley wrote of his finding "a good House and Shop, on the great Oldham Road" in Manchester for £20 per year. "I think I shall take it for our office and Book Establishment." The memo of agreement signed by Parley P. Pratt for the house and shop at No. 149 Oldham for twelve months for £17 and signed May 6, 1840, is in the Brigham Young Papers.

conference reports, editorials, missionary reports, and other material that preserve the fabric of the British Latter-day Saint experience. In addition, the *Star* provided British readers with a variety of material that had appeared in earlier American LDS publications, including excerpts from the *Elders' Journal*, the *Messenger and Advocate*, the *Times and Seasons*, and LDS scriptures.[76]

The *Star* was also a vehicle for responding to critics. In an editorial at the conclusion of the first volume, Parley noted that "Lies, Slanders, Misrepresentations, &c., in all their varied forms, have been heralded forth from the press and pulpit, and have come in upon the world like a flood of water out of the mouth of the dragon, to stop the progress of truth, but all in vain."[77] Anti-Mormon publishing had troubled the first group of elders that came to England when Richard Livesey, in 1838, summarized in twelve pages the arguments of E. D. Howe's 1834 *Mormonism Unvailed*, the first anti-Mormon book.[78] This "nefarious merchandize," as the first missionaries later called it, for a time had a damaging effect on missionary work in the Preston area[79] and it was still plaguing the elders in 1840.[80] In other major cities, such as Birmingham and Manchester, large numbers of anti-Mormon handbills and pamphlets also circulated.[81]

PARLEY P. PRATT'S RESPONSES AND EXPOSITIONS

For Parley Pratt, issuing a Mormon periodical and responding to critics went hand in hand. He offered missionaries practical advice on dealing with anti-Mormon works. "Look at Both Sides of the Question," he counseled in one editorial, and, in another, he suggested ways of "answering

---

[76]See, for example, *Millennial Star* 1 (July–September 1840): 76, 113, 119, 123, 129.

[77]Ibid., 1 (April 1841): 312.

[78]Livesey, *Exposure of Mormonism*. A testimonial at the end was dated July 24, 1838. The publisher, Joseph Livesey (1794–1884), was not a close relation of the author. A second edition of Richard Livesey's tract was published in Manchester by Wm. Shackleton and Sons in 1840.

[79]The comments are in a report entitled "Mission to England, or the First Foreign Mission of the Latter-day Saints," by Heber C. Kimball, Orson Hyde, and Willard Richards dated March 24, 1841, Preston, in *Millennial Star* 1 (April 1841): 288–96. The best source on the initial impact is Fielding, Diary, 24–26 (July-August 1838) and 55 (February 11, 1840).

[80]As earlier noted, Livesey's anti-Mormon work was a factor in the opposition of the Reverend James Fielding, Joseph Fielding's brother, in Preston. Parley P. Pratt responded to Livesey's charges that the Mormon missionaries were destroying families in "Falsehood Refuted," *Millennial Star* 1 (November 1840): 187; and more fully to the 1840 edition of Livesey's pamphlet in *Reply to Mr. Thomas Taylor*, 4–8. Livesey was a Methodist Episcopal minister in Winchendon, Massachusetts.

[81]For Birmingham in early 1841, see Cotterill, "Midland Saints," 224. Parley wrote from Manchester in January 1841: "The country is flooded with pamphlets, tracts, papers, etc. published against us" (Parley P. Pratt to Sidney Rigdon, January 8, 1841 in *Times and Seasons* 2 [April 1, 1841]: 364–65).

objections" and "correcting misrepresentations."[82] More important, Parley published his own replies to selected attacks as they appeared in various areas of the country.

The first reply to a British anti-Mormon tract was Parley Pratt's *Plain Facts, Showing the Falsehood and Folly of The Rev. C. S. Bush*.[83] C. S. Bush, a minister of the Parish of Peover, had published *Plain Facts, Showing the Falsehood and Folly of the Mormonites . . .* in early 1840, presenting the Spaulding theory of the origins of the Book of Mormon.[84] Parley's response, probably appearing in July 1840, provided a strong rebuttal to the charges that critics were making against Mormonism's claims to new revelation.[85]

Parley's second reply to critics addressed attacks made in two different tracts printed in the Preston and Manchester areas, one by Thomas Taylor and another by Richard Livesey.[86] He had briefly responded in the *Millennial Star* to the reissuing of Livesey's tract, but a separate pamphlet allowed him to express his thoughts on it more extensively.[87]

Parley's third reply to an anti-Mormon work, published in December 1840, was a critique of a tract written by William Hewitt of the Potteries. Hewitt had attacked both Joseph Smith and George A. Smith, and in his preface he mentioned challenging George A. to a debate.[88] Pratt responded,

---

[82]In P. Pratt, "Look at Both Sides," *Millennial Star* 1 (October 1840): 156–58, he suggested ways of reading tracts against the Church and specifically requested that these works be sent to his office. In his "Editors Address to his Patrons," *Millennial Star* 1 (May 1840): 2–3, he gave advice to those who would be "entering into the field of controversy."

[83]While no author is identified in the pamphlet, it is clear it was Parley. He so identifies himself in his later *Reply to Thomas Taylor's "Complete Failure,"* 6.

[84]The Bush pamphlet is dated February 5, 1840. Copies are in the Church Archives and the Mitchell Library, Glasgow, Scotland.

The Spaulding Theory basically argued that Joseph Smith had created the Book of Mormon by copying an earlier, unpublished work written by Solomon Spaulding. This theory was presented in Howe's *Mormonism Unvailed*. Sidney Rigdon was said to have been the link as pertains to the manuscript. Since Parley P. Pratt had helped convert Rigdon after he himself had read the Book of Mormon, he knew Rigdon had no connection with the Book of Mormon until Pratt himself brought it to him. This theory had been refuted by these early converts, but in 1839 a letter supposedly written by Spaulding's widow had been introduced publicly. Parley had responded in America to this theory. See P. Pratt, *Mormonism Unveiled*, and his letter to the *New Era* [New York City] dated November 27, 1839, in *Times and Seasons* 1 (January 1840): 45–46. A scholarly study of the history of this explanation is in Bush, "Spaulding Theory."

[85]Parley's tract was advertised on the back wrapper of the August 1840 issue of the *Millennial Star*. Since he left for America to get his family in August, we must conclude the tract appeared prior to his departure. Copies were still on hand in May 1841, per *Millennial Star* 2 (May 1841): 5–6.

[86]See Taylor, *Complete Failure*.

[87]See P. Pratt, "Falsehood Refuted," *Millennial Star* 1 (November 1840): 187. Parley's pamphlet was titled *Reply to Mr. Thomas Taylor's "Complete Failure."* It would seem that this pamphlet appeared in November 1840.

[88]Hewitt, *Errors and Fallacies*. The preface is dated October 1840. George A. Smith reports receiving

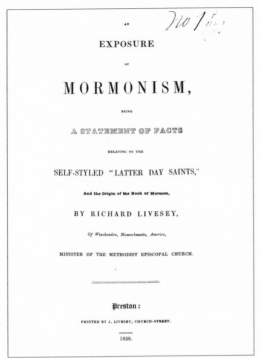

AN *Ño / 5…*

EXPOSURE

OF

MORMONISM,

BEING

A STATEMENT OF FACTS

RELATING TO THE

SELF-STYLED "LATTER DAY SAINTS,"

And the Origin of the Book of Mormon,

BY RICHARD LIVESEY,

Of Winchendon, Massachusetts, America,

MINISTER OF THE METHODIST EPISCOPAL CHURCH.

Preston:

PRINTED BY J. LIVESEY, CHURCH-STREET.

1838.

Title page of the first
anti-Mormon tract in England
Courtesy LDS Church Archives

point by point, using some of the same logic he had used in earlier replies.[89] His fourth and last reply to specific anti-Mormon works during this British mission consisted of two articles appearing in the *Star* in July 1841 and quickly republished in pamphlet form.[90]

By that time Elder Pratt had apparently grown tired of responding to arguments he had already addressed in his other works. No doubt some

---

a copy in London on November 7, 1840. See Smith, "History" and also Woodruff, *Journal*, November 7, 1840, 1:546. The tone of Parley's February 18, 1840, letter to George A. Smith suggests Smith had earlier requested help in responding to this tract. A copy of Hewitt's tract, with marginal notes by George A. Smith, is in Church Archives. Hewitt's letters to George A. Smith, dated June 2 and 13, 1840, suggesting an ongoing discussion between them, are in the George A. Smith Collection. It is possible that the "Reverend Hewitt" of England mentioned in the April 21, 1835, letter of Thomas Shaw is the same person. See *Messenger and Advocate* 1 (May 1836): 316–17. This letter says Hewitt was an Irvingite.

[89]See P. Pratt, *Answer to Mr. William Hewitt's Tract*. No doubt this tract, issued in an edition of a thousand copies, appeared in December 1840. Parley apparently expected some payment for his work as he so hinted in his February 1841 letter to George A. Smith. Parley P. Pratt to George A. Smith, February 18, 1841, Parley P. Pratt Collection. "I have never Rec'd one *penney* for the 1,000 replies to Hewitt which I got printed allmost entirely for the poteries."

[90]See P. Pratt, *Truth Defended*. These responses had appeared in the *Millennial Star* 2 (July 1841): 43–48.

frustration was behind the broadside he issued in Manchester in December 1840: *An Epistle of Demetrius, Junior, The Silversmith, to their workmen of like occupation, and all others whom it may concern, — greeting: showing the best way to preserve our craft, and put down the Latter Day Saints.* This work is a finely crafted satire modeled after the story of Demetrius, an Ephesian metalworker who opposed Paul (see Acts 19) because Paul's message would affect the income he and his fellow artisans received through making idols. Parley portrayed the English sectarian clergy, in their opposition to the Latter-day Saints, as the modern equivalent of the ancient Demetrius.[91] About a year later he issued the first LDS pamphlet to attack other religions without replying to a specific anti-Mormon work.[92]

Elder Pratt also published several pamphlets dealing with the main messages of Mormonism and reprinted several of his works that had appeared in America. *An Address . . . to the Citizens of Washington* was retitled *An Address . . . to the People of England*, and ten thousand copies from at least two printings were circulating shortly after his arrival.[93] Five thousand copies had sold out within four weeks of the first printing in May 1840.[94] Its influence was even more widely felt in Britain than in America because it provided the basis for the summary of the Latter-day Saint faith that Orson Pratt included in his *Interesting Account of Several Remarkable Visions* and because it was the model for the tract Heber C. Kimball and Wilford Woodruff issued in London in 1841.[95]

Another effective and popular pamphlet was Parley's *A Letter to the Queen*, ten thousand copies of which were printed.[96] Like his other works,

---

[91]The bibliographical information is in Crawley and Whittaker, *Mormon Imprints*, 22.

[92]See P. Pratt, *Dialogue*. This item first appeared in the *Millennial Star* 2 (January 1, 1842): 129–32. Parley added a letter of Thomas Smith dated December 30, 1841. Together these pieces attack Methodism, Roman Catholicism, and the Church of England and specifically the evils of infant baptism. Smith's letter describes his conversion from Methodism to Mormonism. Parley had earlier responded to a circular of the Church of England. See *Millennial Star* 1 (May 1840): 17–18.

[93]P. Pratt, *Address by a Minister*. Bibliographical information is in Crawley and Whittaker, *Mormon Imprints*, 17–18.

[94]The first address was dated May 18, 1840. The second printing was dated May 28. Orson Pratt told his brother of giving out about eighty copies during one street meeting in Scotland in October 1840. Orson Pratt to Parley P. Pratt, October 17, 1840 in *Millennial Star* 2 (December 1840): 214.

[95][Wilford Woodruff and Heber C. Kimball], *Word of the Lord*. See Woodruff, *Journal*, 9, 17, 20, 24 February 1841, 2:41–51. Three thousand copies were printed.

[96]P. Pratt, *Letter to the Queen*. There were three editions issued, totaling ten thousand copies. These were issued in June and July 1841. The tract was dated May 28, 1841 and first advertised in the *Millennial Star* 2 (July 1841): 48. The text was reprinted in the *Times and Seasons* 3 (November 15, 1841): 593–96 under the slightly modified title *Letter to the Queen of England*. Peter Crawley suggests that this text was probably taken from a New York imprint and that it is the source for Adams, *Letter to His Excellency John Tyler* (1844). See Crawley, "Parley P. Pratt."

it stressed the core of the early Latter-day Saint message. It used Daniel 2 to predict the triumph of the Kingdom of God, the millennial government the Saints expected to establish.

In September 1841, several months after his colleagues returned to America, Parley issued the first European edition of his most famous work, *A Voice of Warning*. Although copies of the earlier American edition had circulated in England, constant requests for additional copies undoubtedly led him to reprint the work.[97] He issued at least two other items in 1842. *The True God and His Worship Contrasted with Idolatry* was a reprint of material that appeared in the *Millennial Star* in April 1842.[98] It attacked various religions in England and Scotland, with particular emphasis on the Protestant view of a God "without body, parts or passions." This view, the tract argued, was atheism, that is, a belief in a God who does not exist.[99] It concluded with some practical rules on prayer. The second work, appearing about the same time, also republished parts of an early work. *The World Turned Upside Down, or Heaven on Earth*... reprinted his earlier essay "The Regeneration and Eternal Duration of Matter."[100]

JOHN TAYLOR'S DEFENSES OF THE FAITH

John Taylor was also active in responding to anti-Mormon attacks. Arriving on the Isle of Man on September 16, 1840, he was soon debating Thomas Hamilton. This confrontation lead to a challenge from J. Curran, which was also covered in the local papers.[101] Taylor then began a more extended discussion with Robert Heys, a "Weslyan Methodist Superintendent Preacher." Early in October, Heys published his *Address to the Members of the Wesleyan Societies and Congregations in Douglas and its*

---

[97]George A. Smith, for example, had said that there was a great call for copies of the *Voice of Warning* in the Potteries in 1840; see *Millennial Star* 1 (June 1840): 44. This first European edition was taken from the second American edition, published in New York in 1839, and consisted of an edition of 2,500 copies.

[98]Though no author is listed, it is presumed that this pamphlet was by Parley P. Pratt. It clearly reads like his writing, and he was editor of the *Star* at the time it appeared.

[99]This line of thought was more fully developed later by Parley's brother Orson Pratt, in his *Absurdities of Immaterialism*.

[100]The essay had first appeared in his 1840 *Millennium*. This English tract was published in an edition of 3,000 and first advertised in the *Millennial Star* 3 (May 1842): 16.

[101]The *Manx Liberal* issue for 17 October 1840 was reprinted in *Millennial Star* 1 (November 1840): 180–83 as "Elder Taylor's Reply to Mr. J. Curran." In the same issue Parley P. Pratt editorialized (pp. 185–87) on Curran's attack on John Taylor and the idea of continual revelation. The *Manx Sun* issue for October 30, 1840 was reprinted in the *Millennial Star* 1 (December 1840): 197–202 as "Elder J. Taylor's Closing Reply to Mr. Curran." In a letter to Parley P. Pratt, dated February 27, 1841, John Taylor refers to these debates. See *Millennial Star* 1 (March 1841): 276–78.

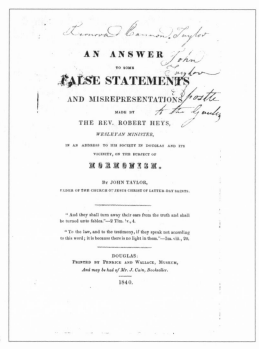

AN ANSWER

TO SOME

FALSE STATEMENTS

AND MISREPRESENTATIONS

MADE BY

THE REV. ROBERT HEYS,

WESLEYAN MINISTER,

IN AN ADDRESS TO HIS SOCIETY IN DOUGLAS AND ITS
VICINITY, ON THE SUBJECT OF

MORMONISM.

BY JOHN TAYLOR,
ELDER OF THE CHURCH OF JESUS CHRIST OF LATTER-DAY SAINTS.

" And they shall turn away their ears from the truth and shall
be turned unto fables."—2 Tim. iv., 4.

" To the law, and to the testimony, if they speak not according
to this word; it is because there is no light in them."—Isa. viii., 20.

DOUGLAS:
PRINTED BY PENRICE AND WALLACE, MUSEUM,
And may be had of Mr. J. Cain, Bookseller.

1840.

Courtesy LDS Church Archives

vicinity, on the Subject of Mormonism,[102] and Taylor responded with *An Answer to Some False Statements and Misrepresentations,* which answered Heys's attack on the origin of the Book of Mormon and challenged Heys to a debate.[103] One of Taylor's arguments that Heys had quoted contradictory accounts regarding the origin of the Book of Mormon from anti-Mormon literature was picked up and used by Parley P. Pratt in one of his own replies to critics.[104]

Taylor's second reply, *Calumny Refuted and the Truth Defended; Being a Reply to the Second Address of the Rev. Robert Heys . . .* , dated October

---

[102]Although copies of two other pamphlets by Heys have survived, no copies of any of the three he published against the Latter-day Saints are known to exist. The title to his first is given in Taylor, *Answer to Some False Statements,* 3.

[103]The first reply, dated October 7, 1840, and was printed in Douglas. Copies of the Douglas newspapers' accounts are in a scrapbook kept by John Taylor, John Taylor Collection. See also Roberts, *Life of John Taylor,* 74–95. In John Taylor to Brigham Young, October 6, 1840, Brigham Young Papers, Taylor offered to send copies of his pamphlet to Manchester "if you think these pamphlets will sell well and be of any use." He said he had paid 5 shillings per each hundred printed.

[104]See P. Pratt, *Reply to Mr. Thomas Taylor's "Complete Failure,"* 11.

29, 1840, was printed twice, once in Douglas and once in Liverpool.[105] In this pamphlet Taylor responded in more detail to Heys's uncritical rehearsing of anti-Mormon explanations of LDS origins. He also defended various Mormon doctrines Heys had attacked. His third reply, *Truth Defined and Methodism Weighed in the Balances and Found Wanting*, dated December 7, 1840, apparently prepared after he left the Isle of Man, was a patchwork of various early works written by Parley P. Pratt.

John Taylor's pamphlets hardly quelled the opposition, but all the commotion seemed to benefit the Church, for by February 1841 the Mormon congregation there had reached seventy. Parley, meanwhile, kept the readers of the *Star* informed of the developments on the Isle of Man, and assured them that "our readers will see that the truth is completely triumphant on the Isle of Man; and that the gainsayers are confounded."[106]

After Taylor's departure, Samuel Haining, a schoolteacher and author of a popular guidebook to the Isle of Man, published a sixty-six-page attack on the Church entitled *Mormonism Weighed in the Balances*, and the LDS response came from both John Taylor and Parley Pratt in pages of the *Star*.[107] The same printer who issued Haining's work published another diatribe against the Mormons in 1841.[108]

THE TWO ORSONS

Next to his brother Parley, Orson Pratt became the most prolific LDS author in the nineteenth century. In Edinburgh he distributed copies of Parley's *Address . . . to the People of England*,[109] but his own major works lay in the future.[110] The two exceptions were a handbill, of which he printed a thousand copies to be posted weekly throughout Edinburgh, and his *Interesting Account of Several Remarkable Visions*, which appeared late in September. It appears that a copy of the handbill sent to London influenced

---

[105]It was printed in Douglas probably in November 1840, and in Liverpool probably in December 1840.

[106]Editorial comments in *Millennial Star* 1 (November 1840): 192.

[107]Haining, *Mormonism Weighed in the Balances*. Parley's response was "Mr. Samuel Haining's Unjust Balances," *Millennial Star* 1 (February 1841): 259–60. John Taylor's response took the form of a detailed letter to the Editor, dated February 27, 1841, in *Millennial Star* 1 (March 1841): 276–80. Haining was being refuted as late as November 1841 by LDS missionaries. See letter of Joseph Fielding to [P. P. Pratt], May 26, 1841, Isle of Man, in *Millennial Star* 2 (June 1841): 30–31; and editorial comments of Parley P. Pratt in *Millennial Star* 2 (December 1841): 113.

[108]See *Imposture Unmasked*.

[109]See excerpt of letter from Orson Pratt, October 17, 1840 in *Millennial Star* 1 (December 1840): 213–14 and his November 21, 1840 letter in "Manuscript History of the British Mission."

[110]For an overview of Orson Pratt's writings, see Whittaker, "Orson Pratt, Prolific Pamphleteer."

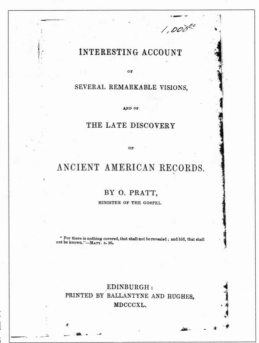

INTERESTING ACCOUNT

OF

SEVERAL REMARKABLE VISIONS,

AND OF

THE LATE DISCOVERY

OF

ANCIENT AMERICAN RECORDS.

BY O. PRATT,
MINISTER OF THE GOSPEL.

" For there is nothing covered, that shall not be revealed ; and hid, that shall not be known."—MATT. x. 26.

EDINBURGH :
PRINTED BY BALLANTYNE AND HUGHES,
MDCCCXL.

Title page of the first LDS tract
published in Scotland
Courtesy LDS Church Archives

a similar production there by Elders Woodruff and Kimball, which in turn served as a model in Birmingham in 1841.[111]

Orson's *Interesting Account* was especially important, for it included the most detailed account of early Mormon history issued by the apostolic mission.[112] Of particular significance was the first account ever to be published of Joseph Smith's First Vision of 1820. Before that time, Mormon

[111]Orson Pratt to George A. Smith, October 17, 1840, George A. Smith Collection, discussed his own handbills and recommended the same to his colleagues in London. On October 22, just after receiving Orson's letter, Wilford Woodruff engaged a printer in London (Doudney and Scrymgour) to print five hundred handbills to advertise their meetings. See Woodruff, *Journal*, October 22, 1840, 1:537. No copy of the London handbill exists, but the text was copied into Woodruff's *Journal*, October 24, 1840, 1: 540. The next year, in Birmingham, Alfred Cordon and Lorenzo Snow used the text of the London handbill to issue one of their own. The only known copy of this Birmingham broadside is in the Church Archives. There is a copy of a missionary handbill that circulated in Scotland in the early 1840s in the Robert Campbell Collection, Church Archives. Most likely this is the handbill Orson Pratt had printed.

[112]This imprint, published in Edinburgh by Ballantyne and Hughes, exists in two states: with and without the "A" at the beginning of the title. Orson's letter implies the correct title began with "An," but as the printing process was underway when the single "A" was discovered, it was decided it was easier to eliminate it than add the "n." The wording of sections of this pamphlet bears a close resemblance to the manuscript of Joseph Smith's 1832 account of his early visions. Compare the relevant portions of the 1840 pamphlet with the 1832 account in Jessee, *Personal Writings of Joseph Smith*, 5–7.

missionary literature and historical essays had emphasized the Book of Mormon, and even though Joseph Smith had previously discussed the all-important vision with selected friends and acquaintances, he had chosen not to publish it to the world. Only in 1838, in an effort to put down "the many reports which have been put into circulation by evil-disposed and designing persons, in relation to the rise and progress of the Church," did he begin to prepare his own account for publication. Orson Pratt surely had heard an account of the vision from Joseph. He told the story elegantly and even included many details not recorded elsewhere by the Prophet. Although the apostles and other contemporary missionaries continued to emphasize the Book of Mormon and the preparation for the millennium as their central message, in later years the First Vision emerged to hold a prime place in Latter-day Saint teaching and missionary work.[113]

Drawing upon his own memory of what Joseph Smith had taught plus Parley's tracts, Orson crafted a valuable work that was at once historical and doctrinal. In addition to the vision, *Interesting Account* contained a notable discussion of the faith and doctrine of the Church that, along with his brother's writings, was probably one source for the "Articles of Faith" written later by Joseph Smith. The title was apparently taken from similar wording in the prospectus for the *LDS Millennial Star*, and Orson expanded Parley's *Address . . . to the People of England* in structuring his list of basic beliefs.[114]

Orson Pratt used his thirty-one-page tract extensively in his missionary work, apparently even peddling it while he was preaching in the streets, and he also made it available to other missionaries. While it was in press, he wrote to George A. Smith that he would take two thousand copies to the October conference in Manchester.[115] Surely the growth of the Church in Edinburgh was enhanced by his use of the press, especially in combination with public debates where both the oral and written messages could be disseminated.

Orson Pratt's pamphlet was the model for another work written in England but published in Germany: Orson Hyde's *A Cry from the Wilder-*

---

[113]For information on the emergence of the First Vision in Mormon thought, and on the various accounts of the vision, see Allen, "Significance of Joseph Smith's 'First Vision'," and "Emergence of a Fundamental"; Backman, "Joseph Smith's Recitals," and *Joseph Smith's First Vision*; Jessee, "Early Accounts of Joseph Smith's First Vision."

[114]For more detail see Whittaker, " 'Articles of Faith'."

[115]Orson Pratt to George A. Smith, September 24, 1840, George A. Smith Collection (Appendix B, Document 13).

ness: A Voice from the Dust of the Earth. It was written just outside London between April and June 1841, before Elder Hyde went on to Europe.[116] Another pamphlet by Hyde, *A Voice from Jerusalem*, which consisted of letters giving an account of his mission to Palestine, was published in April 1842 by Parley P. Pratt in Liverpool.[117]

CONCLUSION

After his colleagues returned to America, Parley P. Pratt remained for more than a year to continue editing the *Star* and to lead the mission. During this period another notable missionary, Lorenzo Snow, published an important sequel to the publications of the Twelve. In November 1841 he issued in London *The Only Way to be Saved*, a work that became one of the most widely distributed LDS tracts in the nineteenth century.[118] Reflecting his concerns that missionaries stick to the basic principles of the gospel, he examined the fundamental Mormon beliefs of faith in Jesus Christ, repentance, baptism by immersion, and the gift of the Holy Ghost. He carefully anchored each doctrine in biblical references and at the end invited interested persons to hear more from official representatives of the Church.

Lorenzo Snow's pamphlet seems to have been an expansion of the earlier London tract by Heber C. Kimball and Wilford Woodruff, *The Word of the Lord to the Citizens of London*. This shorter tract, based on Parley

---

[116]Titled in German, *Ein Ruf aus der Wüste, eine Stimme aus dem Schoose der Erde*, Hyde's pamphlet was published in Frankfurt in August 1842. He discussed this work in Orson Hyde to Joseph Smith, June 15, 1841, in *Times and Seasons* 2 (October 1, 1841): 551. "I have written a book to publish in the German language setting forth our doctrine and principles in as clear and concise a manner as I possibly could. After giving the history of the rise of the church, in something the manner that Br. O. Pratt did, I have written a snug little article upon every point of doctrine believed by the saints."

[117]In January 1842 Hyde sent Parley P. Pratt a long letter from Trieste, Italy, with a note asking Pratt to publish the letter in pamphlet form. Two weeks later Hyde wrote again asking that both letters be published. Pratt published Hyde's two letters together with a third letter from Alexandria (which contained Hyde's prayer offered on the Mount of Olives), a fourth letter from Jaffe, plus the two earlier notes from Hyde together with an introduction in an edition of three thousand copies in March/April 1842. George J. Adams republished it in Boston later in 1842, and a third printing was issued in Salt Lake City in 1869.

[118]While an exact publishing date is not known, it would seem the item did not appear until November. Snow wrote to Heber C. Kimball, November 10, 1841 indicating that he had been using "The books that you left here" (*Times and Seasons* 3 [March 15, 1842]: 712–13). It would thus seem that as long as copies of *The Word of the Lord to the Citizens of London* were available, Snow had no need to publish his own work. In a letter to his parents dated November 11, 1841 he wrote: "I have sent you a tract I have written and got published. I have published four thousand copies. It is expected that another Edition will be wanted. Tho they have been out of the press only a week or two yet they have been mostly spoken for" (Snow, Journal, 109). From various references it would seem the first printing of four thousand copies appeared about the first of November 1841 and another thousand copies were printed early in 1842.

P. Pratt's *Address*, was published on the eve of their departure from London, just as Lorenzo Snow assumed the presidency there.[119] Later it was reprinted in Bristol as *The Word of the Lord to the Citizens of Bristol* and also in the Nauvoo *Times and Seasons*.[120]

In these printed works, many pieces of Mormon history and doctrine, including some that had not previously been published in America, received their first widespread airing in Britain. Later missionaries followed this precedent and issued their own publications. In a real sense, the appearance of tracts and books after 1837 parallels the movement of Mormonism into more urban, cosmopolitan settings, where the printed word became an important vehicle for building the Church.

From the beginning, the apostle-writers sensed the value of the press in helping to address the "great spirit of inquiry" they found in the British Isles. Parley P. Pratt, who probably saw that more clearly than anyone, was convinced that truth would triumph wherever it was *published*.[121] His efforts during this mission established the basis for an extensive publishing and distribution system of Latter-day Saint literature in the years that followed. But his fellow apostles also knew the power of the press. Wilford Woodruff felt he had really begun his work in London when the newspapers began to report the missionaries' presence, and Brigham Young noted with interest the teetotalers he saw in a parade who "had two printing presses in large carts, so they could strike off hand bills as they marched through the streets and give them out to the people."[122] Years later Elder Young remembered approvingly their extensive publication program, including the printing and distribution of sixty thousand tracts, and the important role it played in the success of the mission.[123]

In his February 18, 1841, letter to George A. Smith, Parley told his

---

[119]According to Wilford Woodruff, on February 9, 1841, "Elder Kimball and myself spent the day in preparing a pi[e]ce or small tract for the press to present to the citizens of London before we leave it showing in plainness the first principles of the gospel and the commission given by Jesus to his Ancient Apostles" (*Journal*, February 9, 1841, 2:41). Woodruff reported they finished the work on February 11, corrected the proof sheet of their "Address to the Citizens of London" on February 17 (2:49), and received three thousand copies on February 20 (2:49). Woodruff's reference to the work in his journal as the "Address to the citizens of London" shows the influence of Parley P. Pratt's *Address by a Minister*.

[120]The London edition also appeared in *Times and Seasons* 2 (September 15, 1841): 535–39. Wilford Woodruff worked in Bristol with Thomas Kington (from February 26 to March 4) after leaving London. He surely left copies of the London tract there, which were then reprinted with just a title change when these copies were exhausted.

[121]*Millennial Star* 1 (March 1841): 286.

[122]Wilford Woodruff to Willard Richards, November 1, 1840, Willard Richards Collection; and Brigham Young to Mary Ann Young, June 12, 1840, Phillip Blair Collection.

[123]Discourse of August 31, 1856, by Brigham Young, *Journal of Discourses* 4:35–6.

colleague that their great mission was to "hurl truth through the land." In their publications as in their preachings they "hurled" the truth very well indeed.

Chapter 11

MEANWHILE, IN NAUVOO

In July 1839, illness stalked the swampy river bottoms of Commerce, soon to be renamed Nauvoo, where the Saints were gathering. Heber C. Kimball's wife, Vilate, about eight months pregnant, and their children were among the sick, and Heber had moved them into a crude log hut he had built onto the back of another Church member's home, about a mile from Commerce. There was no floor and no chinking between the logs. The roof and walls leaked so badly that during a rainstorm, water stood nearly ankle deep on the ground inside. With the help of a few friends and neighbors who were not ill, Heber was anxiously working on a new log home on a five-acre wooded lot, and he hoped to finish it in time for the new baby to be born there. It was not long, however, before he and Vilate were both prostrate with chills and fever, and he could not complete the house. David Patten Kimball was born in the leaky old cabin on the night of August 23, during a heavy thunderstorm. A week or so later the Kimballs moved into the new fourteen- by sixteen-foot cabin where Vilate and the four children would live while her husband was on his mission to England.

Such experiences were commonplace among the Saints during that difficult year of 1839, and as Vilate and the wives of the other apostles looked toward the future, they foresaw not only their loneliness but also the continuing hard work and difficulties they must endure. Their husbands would suffer considerable hardship and privation, but the women who remained behind would face challenges often much more trying than those of the missionaries. Rear the children, earn a livelihood, help build the new community, care for those less fortunate than they, buoy up their husbands through the mails and keep them informed of what was happening at home, and prepare for their eventual return: all that and more would fall on the lonely shoulders of the women while the apostles were out seeking converts to gather to the new community.

Vilate might have complained, but instead she wrote a poem to her husband that exemplified her love, faith, courage, and hope for the future:

> Dear Heber, you and I must part,
> It seems as though it would brake my heart
> But in Gods grace I will confide
> Praying him to waft you safely oer the tide.
>
> And when you land on Europes shore,
> Where you have labored once before;
> May you find favor in the eyes
> Of rich and poor, both great and wise.
>
> And when you with your brethren meet,
> May all your joys, then be compleet,
> And when your labors there are done
> May you be wafted swiftly home.
>
> And when our labors all are oer,
> And we shall meet to part no more;
> May we together in heaven reign,
> Where there's nomore sorrow, death nor pain.
>
> There we shall see our children dear,
> Who've gone before in infant years,[1]
> And with our children that remain
> We'll praise God in the highest strain.
>
> And with our brethren all unite,
> To praise Gods son, his souls delight;
> While we shall look upon the scenes,
> That's brought us to this glorious end.
>
> Now my dear husband, I bid adieu,
> To earthly joys while gone from you,
> But when we come to meet again,
> Our joys will surely be the same.

Heber quickly responded in kind:

> My dear Vilate, you are my wife,
> The choice companion of my life,

---

[1] Two Kimball children had died in infancy. Their first child, Judith Marvin, was born July 29, 1823, and died May 20, 1824. The fifth child to be born to them, Roswell Heber, was born June 10, 1830, and died five days later. Altogether Vilate gave birth to ten children, one more of whom died in infancy. S. Kimball, *Heber C. Kimball*, 311.

But with you I am called to part
Which sorely grieves my akiing heart.

But I will leave you in God's care,
And pray his blessings you may share
While I am gone acrost the Main,
The gospel tidings to proclaim.

While you are here, and I am there;
Remember me in all your prayers
That I may there, successful prove
In winning souls to truth and love.

And every chance that I can see,
I'll fall upon my bended knee,
And there implore the God of heaven
To protect the wife, to me he's given.

For be assured my dearest girl,
That while I'm in this lower world
I never can forgetful be,
Of the family God has given to me.

Nor neither in the world to come;
For there we ever shall be one:
And our dear saviour we shall see,
With all of our posterity.

May they be numerous as the sand
And dwell upon mount Zions land
When the saviour comes to reign,
And not be found among the slain.

For by the Prophets, we understand
That Zion will be a blessed land,
When from it the curs is moved,
And souls are filled with celestial love.

But cease, my mind, off from this strain
Til you and I shall meet again;
And then we'll talk of what is past
And dwell in Zion with the blesst.

And now Vilate, I can say with you,
To earthly joys I bid adieu;
While you and I are called to part
But when we meet I'll rejoice in heart.

My children all, I bid farewell.
We must be parted for a while
But when we meet to part nomore
Our troubles then, will all be oer.[2]

---

[2]Both poems are found in the Helen Bourne Fleming Papers.

No doubt the other apostles had similar feelings, and, even though the focus of this book is on the Quorum of the Twelve, it would be incomplete without some insight into the lives of those the apostles left behind. The records are sketchy at best, and for some, almost nonexistent, which accounts for the unevenness of the following discussion. Those records that remain, however, provide important insights into what the mission meant to the apostles' wives and families back in America.

MARY ANN ANGELL YOUNG

Mary Ann Angell Young and her family were desperately ill when Brigham left, and their economic situation in Iowa was precarious, to say the least. Though the apostles had received a general assurance that their families would be cared for,[3] neither Joseph Smith himself nor the church could provide much help. From time to time the Nauvoo bishops were able to give Mary Ann, as well as other needy households, a few such provisions as meat, potatoes, and flour, but she was reluctant to accept charity. She worked hard to obtain whatever she could for herself and family, and did not complain to Brigham. For the most part he heard about her difficulties not from her but from others.[4]

Brigham Young left his family on the Iowa side of the river because there were a few rooms in a deserted military post. Both food and money were scarce, and on several occasions during the winter of 1839–40 Mary Ann's resources were so exhausted that she had to cross the river to see if she could obtain help from friends or from the Church. Though she left the children to be tended by the older girls, she could not leave the baby. On one bitter, cold day in November, she bundled little Emma as warmly as she could and took her across the Mississippi in an open boat. "I shall never forget how she looked," a friend recalled years later, "shivering with cold and thinly clad." Mary Ann left the baby with her friend while she went to the tithing office and was able to obtain a few potatoes and some

---

[3]"I, the Lord, give unto them a promise that I will provide for their families," said D&C 118:3, the revelation that called them on the mission in the first place. In addition, on April 6, 1839, Heber C. Kimball had received what he took to be a binding personal promise from the Lord: "Trouble not thyself about thy family, for they are in my hands; I will feed them and clothe them and make unto them friends. They never shall want for food nor raiment, houses nor lands, fathers nor mothers, brothers nor sisters; and peace shall rest upon them forever, if thou wilt be faithful and go forth and preach my gospel to the nations of the earth" (Kimball, *President Heber C. Kimball's Journal*, 70–71).

[4]Brigham Young to Mary Ann Young, June 12, 1840, and November 12, 1840, Brigham Young Papers.

Mary Ann Angell Young
© LDS Church

flour. Then, still suffering from ague and fever, she took the baby and made her way back to the cold and uninviting river.[5]

Sometime during the summer of 1840 Mary Ann managed to move her family across the river into Nauvoo. Their means were still meager, but they would be closer to friends and other assistance. Brigham forced himself not to worry about them for, he told Mary Ann, "the Lord said by the mouth of Brother Joseph, that they should be provided for, and I believed it." Nevertheless, he let them know in no uncertain terms he longed deeply for them. Also, from time to time, he was able to send them a little money and a few presents. At least some of what he sent arrived. Mary Ann's good friend Vilate Kimball observed in June: "I am glad Brother Brigham has sent some assistance to his family for they are needy."[6]

Mary Ann resolved to have a house built while her husband was gone and also began to keep a garden. Their lot was in the low, swampy section

---

[5]Wells, "Mary Ann Angell Young," 56–57.
[6]Brigham Young to Mary Ann Young, October 16–30, 1840, Luna Young Thatcher Collection (Appendix B, Document 15); Vilate Kimball to Heber C. Kimball, June 6, 1840, Heber C. Kimball Collection. See also S. Kimball, "Heber C. Kimball and Family," 451–53.

of Nauvoo. By June 1840 the house was begun. Vilate Kimball wrote Heber that "their house could hardly be called a shelter," but added the expectation that "they will soon have it fixed nice."[7] Brigham was delighted when he heard that it was begun, and he wrote Mary Ann that he would be glad if she could have it finished by the time he returned home, though she was not to trouble herself if she could not.[8] When he arrived home on July 1, 1841, it was not complete. As he later described it: "On my return from England I found my family living in a small unfinished log-cabin, situated on a low, wet lot, so swampy that when the first attempt was made to plow it the oxen mired; but after the city was drained it became a very valuable garden spot."[9]

Toward the end of 1840, Mary Ann wrote a long letter to Brigham, describing her hard work and telling him she had been ill. The family was lonesome for him, and one night little Mary began to cry, saying she did not want to go to bed until she knelt down and prayed for her father. All the children felt the same except for Emma, born only ten days before Brigham left on his mission, who did not know him at all. After reviewing these and other troubles, Mary Ann hastened to add that she hoped her husband would not think her ungrateful. Brigham responded with exemplary love and tenderness. He prayed for her and the children continually, he said, but that was all he could do. He knew how well she supported him in this difficult assignment and thanked her for it. After loving admonitions to the children about helping their mother and each other, like any typical father, he promised them presents upon his return.[10]

VILATE MURRAY KIMBALL

On September 18, 1839, Vilate Murray Kimball was shaking so severely with the ague that she could do little more than weakly shake hands with her husband, who was also ill, when he came to her sickbed to say good-bye. Tenderly, Heber embraced her and the children and then painfully climbed into the wagon that would take him and Brigham from Nauvoo. No one knows what thoughts ran through Vilate's mind as she watched him go out the doorway, but, in addition to the loneliness she already felt,

---

[7]Vilate Kimball to Heber C. Kimball, June 6, 1840.

[8]Brigham Young to Mary Ann Young, January 15, 1841, Brigham Young Papers.

[9]Young, *Manuscript History*, 109.

[10]Brigham Young to Mary Ann Young, January 15, 1841. Mary Ann's letter is not extant, but in replying, Brigham summarized parts of it.

Vilate Murray Kimball
Courtesy LDS Church Archives

she must have wondered how she and four children would survive the coming months. Little David was less than four weeks old and only one child, four-year-old Heber Parley, was well enough even to carry water for the ailing family. She was thankful for the little log shanty just completed by her husband, for at least they would have a roof over their heads. Suddenly she heard an unexpected shout, "Hurrah, hurrah, hurrah for Israel," and dragged herself from her sickbed to the door. There she and Mary Ann Young, who had crossed the river for a farewell, saw their ailing husbands standing in the wagon waving their hats. A warm smile came to Vilate's face as she and Mary Ann cried out as strongly as they could, "Good bye! God bless you!" That smile reflected not just her love for Heber but also her determined faith that, despite hardships, the family would survive.

The smile did not reflect how she felt physically. What happened over the next three days might have made Heber wonder if he should have left at all. She was "perfectly reconciled" to his going, she wrote on September 21, "But I must say I have got a trial of my faith as I never had before." The day he left home the pain in her head and back, made worse by her weeping before he left, was nearly intolerable. Young William, also severely ill, cried all day and took a chill in the evening. The only person who could stay with them during the day, a Sister Bently, who was also ill, did all she could, and another friend stayed the night. For a while, however, Vilate was alone, so she crawled out of bed, knelt before the Lord, and prayed for a good night's rest. The next morning she was free from pain, though she could not walk without staggering, and the older children, William and Helen, were too sick to assist. With the help of Heber Parley, Vilate crawled about the house doing her chores, including some washing, but she overdid it and relapsed with chills and fever. Sick all afternoon, she did not rest that night and was unable to do anything the following day. "I was taken early this morning with a shake, and shook about an hour and a half as hard as I ever saw any body in my life," she wrote that night, "and then weltered under a fever and extream pain until almost night." William, too, continued having severe chills, and the medicine left by a friend seemed to do no good. Helen also continued ill but could do a few chores.

As she wrote the letter listing all these troubles, Vilate must have wondered how it would affect Heber, and she hastened to try to comfort him. "I have given you a statement of our situation," she wrote, "not to make you feel bad, but because you requested it of me. . . . But all that I can ask of you is to pray that I may have patience to endure to the end whether it be long or short." The next morning she added her final lines:

Dear Heber we are all alive and tolerable comfortable this morning. Would to God we could remain so through the day. We will hope for the best. Mother Bemon stayed with me last night. She said I [must] tell you she had slept with your little Prophet. I must draw to a close for Br George is waiting. Unless my health should improve I shall not be able to write next week as you requested, for im groing weak every day. You had better enquire for a letter at New York, perhaps I shall direct there. So fare you well my dear Heber. I pray that it may be well with you.[11]

Though she did improve, like many of the Saints afflicted with "river sickness" Vilate apparently alternated between seasons of illness and health. In May 1840 she was again suffering from the ague and fever.[12]

Heber left his family with only nine dollars, barely enough for Vilate to pay a debt, leaving nothing for food or shoes needed by their daughter Helen. Like Mary Ann Young, she depended upon the bishops for at least

---

[11]Vilate Kimball to Heber C. Kimball, September 21, 1839, Heber C. Kimball Collection (Appendix B, Document 4). Vilate actually began the letter on the evening of Friday, September 20, and finished it the next morning.

[12]Phebe [Phoebe] W. Woodruff to Wilford Woodruff, May 4 and 24, 1840, *Millennial Star* 1 (August 1840): 90.

a few provisions during the winter, but by June of 1840 she had a garden and was growing potatoes, turnips, and other produce. She also had a pig, given to her by a Brother Hubbard, and Joseph Young had obtained a cow for the family. "I hope I shal not have to call on the Bishop again while you are gone," she wrote to Heber.[13]

Vilate was elated when, from time to time, she and the children received presents from her husband. It seemed as if the Spirit had directed him in everything he sent, she wrote gratefully in June 1840, except for the worsted. It was too expensive for her tastes, she reminded him, and she could do with factory cloth or any kind of clothing. "You know I can never enjoy any unnecessary thing while I see so much poverty around me," she wrote. But she stopped short of scolding him. The cloth was beautiful and she knew he was trying to please her, "therefore I thank you for it." He had also made another, less serious mistake: the boots he sent were a size too small for her, but they fit young Heber exactly.[14]

From time to time other gifts arrived. Brigham Young sent Heber's older children copies of the British edition of the Book of Mormon, with their names printed in gold on the cover, and Heber sent the same gift to Brigham's daughters. Helen, Heber's daughter, also received handkerchiefs, toy china, and dolls. She was a bit perturbed, however, when Joseph Smith called by the house one day and accidentally broke a doll, excusing himself only by saying, "As that has fallen, so shall the heathen gods fall." This was a "rather weak apology for breaking my doll's head off," Helen commented several years later.[15]

Vilate's life in Nauvoo ran the gamut of experience from the spiritually exhilarating to the depths of economic and physical distress. At one point, early in 1840, Vilate considered selling their property in Nauvoo and moving to Kirtland, where some members of her family were still located, but Heber discouraged her from that.[16] She was uplifted when she heard the doctrine of baptism for the dead preached for the first time in the summer of 1840, and she was baptized for her mother. She also enjoyed

---

[13]Vilate Kimball to Heber C. Kimball, June 6, 1840.

[14]Ibid.

[15]Whitney, "Scenes in Nauvoo," *Woman's Exponent* 10 (August 1, 1881): 34.

[16]Vilate Kimball to Heber C. Kimball, February 2, 1840, and Heber C. Kimball to Vilate Kimball, March 5, 1840, Heber C. Kimball Collection. See also in the same collection Heber C. Kimball to Vilate Kimball, May 27, 1840, where Heber recalls that he even prayed that Vilate might move to Kirtland but could not get much faith for this prayer. He was later sorry that he had even prayed that way, and he felt it providential that one letter (apparently one that might have persuaded her to go to Kirtland) was misdirected.

frequent visits with some of the sisters who had come from England and who, no doubt, told her of her husband. On the other hand, expenses were high, she did not have enough money to make regular payments to Hiram Kimball, Heber's distant cousin from whom they were buying their lot, and she had no regular income. To top it off, her father died just as he was planning to come to Nauvoo. "But alass," she wrote on December 8, "how are my fond anticipations blasted? and my joy is turned to mourning."

In the same letter Vilate let Heber know how troubled she was to hear of his illnesses. "O that I could fly to your relief," she wrote, and she penned a touching poem that captured the mixed feelings of love, sorrow, and faith flowing through her heart:

> My husband's gone, my Father's dead
> But my ever living head;
> Always hears my souls complaint
> And ever comforts me when faint.
>
> If I could fly to you I would,
> But the Lord is very good;
> He will care for him that's dead
> And you who from your family's fled.
>
> I, here with four children dear,
> But I know I need not fear;
> For the Lord is always nigh,
> And will all my wants supply.
>
> O Lord it is my souls desire
> That thou would my heart inspire
> With a fore knowledge of thy will,
> That I may all thy laws fulfill.

No doubt these lines affected Heber deeply, as did the end of the letter. The children were all impatient to have him come home, she wrote, but, more to the point,

you are losing all the most interesting part of David's life, a child is never so pretty as when they first begin to walk and talk. He goes prattleing about the house, and you may be assured that we think he is cunning. Elizabeth [*Young*] calls him Heber altogether, and every one that sees him says that ought to be his name, he looks so much like you.[17]

---

[17]Vilate Kimball to Heber C. Kimball, December 8, 1840, as cited in S. Kimball, "Heber C. Kimball and Family," 452–53.

Mary Ann Frost Pratt
Courtesy LDS Church Archives

Sarah Marinda Bates Pratt
Courtesy Daughters of Utah Pioneers

MARY ANN FROST PRATT

Mary Ann Frost Pratt did not stay in Commerce when her husband, Parley, left. She and her three children traveled with Parley to New York and lived there in relative comfort after he embarked for England on March 9, 1840, though, at one point they all became seriously ill with scarlet fever. Less than six months after he left, Parley was back in New York to take them to England with him. Because she was away from the poverty and sickness of emerging Nauvoo, when compared with the other wives, Mary Ann had a relatively easy time.

SARAH MARINDA BATES PRATT

None of the wives had a more troubled and spiritually confusing time than twenty-two-year-old Sarah Marinda Bates Pratt, wife of Orson Pratt.[18] She endured poverty, like the others, but she also struggled with the consequences of a twisted interpretation of a new doctrine.

Like her sister-in-law, Sarah could have gone to New York City with

---

[18]Sources are sparse on Sarah's life during this period, but we have relied on two important secondary sources: England, *Life and Thought of Orson Pratt*, 77–86; Van Wagoner, "Sarah M. Pratt."

277

Parley and Orson. She chose to remain behind, however, because Orson, Jr., was only two years old, and because of her resolve to support the Church leaders in gathering to Nauvoo. When she said her tearful farewells to Orson on August 29, Sarah was grief stricken over the loss of their baby daughter just eleven days earlier. Moreover, her husband left her nearly impoverished, living in a hastily built log shack on Heber C. Kimball's property. The Church helped some, and she took in sewing to eke out a livelihood. She eventually went to live in the home of Stephen H. and Zeruiah Goddard and, later, the home of Robert D. Foster.

Among those who provided sewing for Sarah were Joseph Smith and John C. Bennett. It was her relationship with these two Nauvoo leaders that eventually resulted in her distress. Joseph was the man she revered as prophet, whose teachings had brought them to this Illinois frontier in the first place, and who had sent her husband on a mission. Bennett, former quartermaster general of Illinois, arrived in Nauvoo in the fall of 1840. Although he quickly became one of its leading citizens, sometime in 1841 Joseph became aware that he was also a charlatan who had joined the Church under false pretenses. Bennett, estranged from his wife and family in Ohio because of adultery, was guilty of additional improper behavior in Nauvoo, including plotting against the Prophet. Following his excommunication from the Church in 1842, he immediately began to publish bitter anti-Mormon exposés.

Just at that time Joseph Smith began introducing some of the far-reaching doctrines that further distinguished Mormonism from contemporary Protestantism. These doctrines included an expanded understanding of God as well as of man's eternal potential, salvation for the dead, eternal marriage, and plural marriage. Understandably, Joseph told those to whom he taught the principle of plural marriage that for the time being it must be a private doctrine, though eventually, when the Church had extracted itself from the problems swirling around it at the time, it would be taught openly and plural wives would be publicly acknowledged. Prematurely and unofficially, John C. Bennett learned of the doctrine of plural marriage and apparently saw in it a way to justify his personal immoral tendencies. Without authorization, he soon began to teach a distorted version, which he used to try to seduce several Nauvoo women. That, in fact, was one of the things that led to his excommunication.

Exactly what happened among Sarah, Joseph Smith, and John C. Bennett may never be clear, for there are numerous conflicting versions. In a society where the doctrine of plural marriage was not yet openly taught and practiced, any woman could have been confused when presented with it. The problem was compounded by Bennett's selfish and distorted interpretation. Bennett later spread the story that Joseph Smith was smitten with Sarah and urged her not only to become one of his "spiritual wives" but also to share his bed. According to Bennett, Sarah angrily refused and threatened to tell her husband if Joseph ever again approached her. More than forty years later Sarah said that she had been so enraged by the proposal that she refused to accept any further help from the tithing house.[19]

Bennett's charges were countered not only by Joseph Smith but by numerous affidavits from prominent citizens who were disgusted with Bennett himself and who were also witnesses of what was going on between him and several women. From their perspective, the treacherous Bennett made his charges in an attempt to hide his own sins as well as to overthrow the Prophet. If Sarah seemed to agree with him, then she, too, was dishonest. Stephen and Zeruiah Goddard, for example, both said that it was Bennett, not Joseph, who made advances to her. She was living in their home at the time, and they both testified that on several occasions they had found her in compromising situations with Bennett. When Mrs. Goddard confronted Bennett, asking him what Orson would think, he only replied that he could "pull the wool" over Orson's eyes.

It was not until 1842, some months after his return, that Orson learned details of the accusations against his wife, and the discovery threw him into a turmoil. His unrest and confusion eventually led to an estrangement from Joseph and his excommunication from the Church in August 1842. That did not last long, however, for when Bennett tried to enlist his support in an effort to have Joseph arrested, Orson became irate at Bennett's actions and presumptions and made it clear that he and Sarah were still loyal to the Church. He was rebaptized in the icy waters of the Mississippi in January 1843 and was reinstated in the Quorum of the Twelve. At the same time, even though Sarah had not been cut off from the Church, she was rebaptized along with her husband as a symbol of her renewed commitment.

After all his doubts and intense suffering, Orson accepted the doctrine of plural marriage fully, as did all the members of the Twelve who had

---

[19]Although the details are simply not known, if Joseph Smith did speak to Sarah about plural marriage, he probably did so to test the Pratts as he tested Heber and Vilate Kimball and others. For the Kimball's test, see S. Kimball, *Heber C. Kimball*, 93.

Leonora Cannon Taylor
Courtesy LDS Church Archives

gone to England. In 1852 he preached the first public sermon in its support and became, in print, its most visible advocate and defender.[20]

LEONORA CANNON TAYLOR

Leonora Cannon Taylor and her three small children were still living in an abandoned, broken-down barracks in Montrose, Iowa, when John left on August 8. Each child had a birthday the following January: Joseph turned two, Mary Ann four, and George six. So far as their physical circumstances were concerned, their birthdays could hardly have been happy ones, but given the tenderness and remarkable faith of their mother, they likely counted their blessings more than their hardships.

Sickness and death were all around them when Elder Taylor left, and young Joseph and George were both afflicted. The distraught Leonora fully expected Joseph to die on August 19, the day after Sarah Pratt's baby died. Neither was she well, she wrote to her husband, but "I keep upon my Feet *grunting about*."[21] Within a few more days, however, they felt better.

---

[20]See Whittaker, "Bone in the Throat."

[21]Leonora Taylor to John Taylor, September 9, 1839, John Taylor Collection. This letter was begun on September 9 but was written over a period of a month. Most of what follows is based on this letter. See published version in Esplin, "Sickness and Faith."

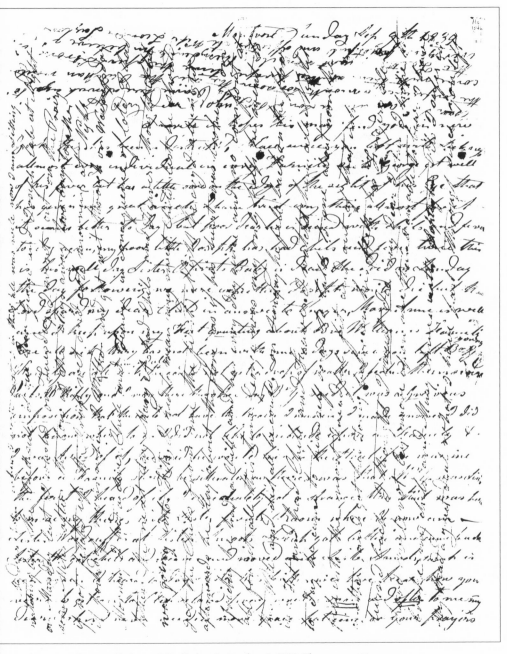

Leonora Taylor to John Taylor, September 9, 1839. The cross-writing was a
common practice to save paper and postage. Courtesy LDS Church Archives

At first Leonora lived in the same barracks as Brigham Young's wife and children, who were so ill they could not even go for water and she had to fetch it for them. When crowded conditions, sickness, and poverty led to stress between the two families, Leonora moved in briefly with Sarah Pratt. She had been promised that a house would be built for her, but she planned to move into the Smoot house until it was ready. If not, she said, she would live with Phoebe Woodruff, whose house was also not ready, and "we can *croak* togather."[22]

"I never needed more grace patience or your prayers than I do at pressent," she wrote, but, she added, "I do feel thankfull to the Lord my health is as good as it is." She also let her husband know what she needed, in case he could send her anything: red and yellow flannel, a little lace, checked or plain muslin, a little black silk for an apron, a few yards of cheap calico for children's frocks, and some low-priced diaper cloth. Most of all she wanted letters. "Dear John," she wrote, "dont let me have cause to complain for *want* of *them*." One night as she walked out with a neighbor looking for a cow, she realized that they were on the same path she and John used to take. Suddenly she felt profoundly alone. "But if we suffer to promote the cause of our Blessed Lord it will end in J[oy] which no Man taketh from us," she wrote. "We are seperated for a short time but I hope we shall yet meet to part no more for ever."[23] Few lines could capture more poignantly the depth of both her faith and her loneliness.

A few weeks later Leonora, baby Joseph, and George were again afflicted with chills and fever, and again Leonora feared that Joseph was dying. During the first week in October she heard from someone that John, too, had been seriously ill. This news troubled her, because she had not yet received a letter from him. When he recovered, he wrote her a moving description of his sickness as well as his determination and faith to proceed.

On March 12, 1840, Leonora wrote a poignant letter to John that reveals much about her life on the Iowa side of the river during that first desperate winter.[24] The most immediate problem was that she had to move, for the room she was living in had just been given to a non-Mormon as a result of a lawsuit. She had a lot in Commerce, and Joseph Smith had promised that a house would be built on it without delay, but for the moment she had no idea where she would live.

---

[22]Ibid.
[23]Ibid.
[24]Leonora Taylor to John Taylor, March 12, 1840, John Taylor Collection.

Still struggling to make ends meet, she had sold one of her two cows during the winter. The other, "Old Bopsy," had calved on March 1, and that would eventually be some help, but at the moment she had to scratch even to find food for the cow, and she was anxiously awaiting the spring grass. Her winter expenses included medical bills, and she had to buy some of her household supplies on credit. She had kept an account of everything she spent, but most of her funds were gone. The bishop had promised to find her money for bread and meat, but at the moment he had none to give her. A friend, a Dr. Patten, kept her supplied with wood and water. With all her privations, however, Leonora confessed to an extravagance: she had purchased six teaspoons made of German silver which, she hastily reminded John, was much cheaper than pewter!

The letter also contains glimpses of what was going on among the Saints. Joseph Smith had returned from his disappointing trip to Washington, D.C., where he was unable to enlist the aid of the national government in getting redress for the losses of the Saints in Missouri, and on Sunday Leonora had gone across the river to hear him tell of his experiences. The name Commerce had been changed to Nauvoo, and the town was growing rapidly, with houses springing up like mushrooms.

There was also news of the children. The family was well again, though little Joseph was teething, five teeth at once. He was also sitting on his mother's lap as she wrote. George and Mary Ann, going to school each day and "learning fast," each sent a hundred kisses to their father. Three marks at the bottom of the last page were each labeled as a kiss from one of the children. Leonora also asked longingly about her family and relatives in England.

Though Leonora's letter is generally optimistic, her loneliness for John is abundantly clear. "I want to hear from you very bad in deed," she said. "I hope you will write often the letters are so long on the way. Wont you come back in the fall. I cant have you stay away longer, do try. I miss you more and more. When I tell Joseph you are coming home he gets vext he has been told so, so often and you never come." "Pray for me my dear John," she wrote as she came to the end of the letter, " . . . that I may have wisdom to walk so as to please my Heavenly Father. . . . this is a trying World . . . but I have a Freind who will neaver leave or forsake me. . . . I hope I shall not Murmer." Almost as a final desperate effort to hold on to thoughts of her absent husband as long as possible, she wrote sideways on the page: "I feel as if I want to get into this Letter and go too."

283

Phoebe Carter Woodruff
Courtesy LDS Church Archives

On July 1, 1841, John Taylor arrived in Nauvoo to find the patient, steadfast Leonora near death. Immediately he called in twenty elders to be sure that all the faith possible was there to heal her. They prayed, anointed her with oil, laid hands on her, and blessed her. Their faith and Leonora's was rewarded, and once again her health was restored.[25]

PHOEBE CARTER WOODRUFF

Phoebe Carter Woodruff tenderly embraced her husband on the morning of August 8, 1839, and then watched him begin to row across the Mississippi to Commerce. She was about two months pregnant, still living in the uncomfortable abandoned barracks in Montrose, and she had no idea when she would see her husband again. Clearly, however, he would not be there when the new baby was born. She did not even have the comfort of cuddling her little daughter, Sarah Emma, who had been sickly since birth, for Sarah was four miles west with the Abraham O. Smoot family, who had volunteered to take her to try to improve her health. Phoebe was nearly destitute, but as she watched her husband disappear

[25]Roberts, *Life of John Taylor*, 98.

across the river, she no doubt comforted herself for the thousandth time with the assurance that he was on God's errand and that ultimately his mission would be a blessing to them. Wilford understood her pain: "She parted with me with that fortitude that becometh a Saint realizing the call & responsibility of her companion," he wrote in his journal.[26]

Phoebe did not escape the malarial plague that immobilized so many people that fall. Her chills and fever were severe, and the old barracks were hardly comfortable quarters. Finally, early in September, she moved in with the Smoot family.[27]

How long Phoebe remained with the Smoots and what she did during the next several months is not clear from the available records. Undoubtedly, she happily watched the settlers pour into Commerce and across into Iowa as the Saints continued to gather. She cared for little Sarah, prepared for the new baby, and hoped for news from Wilford, which usually came at least once a month. Often his letters contained a bit of money to help her.

In mid March 1840 Phoebe was at last ready to deliver the baby. Across the ocean, Wilford realized that her time was near, and prayed mightily for her. On March 20 he wrote in his journal, "Oh Lord comfort Phebe thy handmaid this day in her distress," and the next day he pleaded "Oh Lord bless Phebe this day in need in every time of need I pray."[28] The next day, at six o'clock in the morning, Phoebe gave birth to a son, Wilford Woodruff, Jr. She wrote her husband as quickly as she could, and he received the letter on May 30. "Yes glory Hallelujah," he exulted, "I have now got a letter from *Phebe*. It is the first letter I have received from her since I have been in England. . . . She informed me that she was blessed with the birth of a Son. . . . May he be preserved blameless unto the comeing of the Lord Jesus Christ for which I will ever Pray."[29]

Phoebe crossed the river to attend church services whenever she could, and in April 1840, on the tenth anniversary of the organization of the Church, she was at the conference meeting at which Elders Orson Hyde and John E. Page were set apart for their missions to Palestine.[30]

---

[26]Woodruff, *Journal*, August 8, 1839, 1:349–50.

[27]Leonora Taylor to John Taylor, September 9, 1839.

[28]Woodruff, *Journal*, March 20 and 21, 1840, 1:426. Curiously, these entries were written in Woodruff's shorthand, which most people could not decipher. He often made entries such as this for items that were particularly personal or sacred to him.

[29]Ibid., May 30, 1840, 1:454.

[30]Ibid., June 24, 1840, 1:471.

On May 4 Phoebe began an especially newsy letter to her husband, though she did not complete it until May 24. Commerce was building up surprisingly fast, she reported, and immigration seemed much greater than it had ever been in Caldwell County, Missouri. The children were in good health, as were the families of Sisters Young, Taylor, and Pratt, but Vilate Kimball was suffering from the ague and fever and so, at times, was Phoebe. She then expressed her anxiety for Wilford and added her usual steadfast feeling of reconciliation with hard reality:

I know that it is the will of God that you should labour in his vineyard; therefore, I feel reconciled to his will in these things. I have not been left to murmur or complain since you left me, but am looking forward to the day when you shall return home once more to the bosom of your family, having fulfilled your mission in the love and fear of God. You are always present with me when I go before the throne of grace, and when I am asking for protection and blessings upon myself and children, I claim the same for my dear companion, who has gone far from me, even to a foreign nation, to preach the fulness of the gospel of Jesus Christ.[31]

From time to time Wilford sent packages to his family, containing presents of various sorts, and Phoebe told him of the things she needed. In one letter she asked for some calico dresses as well as some linen to make an everyday dress, for hers were worn out. She also wanted some red flannel for making children's clothes and a muslin cape for herself.[32]

Great sorrow struck on July 17 when two-year-old Sarah Emma died.[33] The next day the heartsick Phoebe wrote an anguished and tender letter to the absent father. Its words eloquently reveal the pain and pathos as well as the remarkable faith of these stalwart women who lived without their husbands on the edge of civilization, helping to build a new gathering place for the Saints of God:

My dear Willford, what will be your feelings, when I say that yesterday I was called to

---

[31]Phebe [Phoebe] W. Woodruff to Wilford Woodruff, May 4, 1840, in *Millennial Star* 1 (August 1840): 89–90.

[32]When he received the letter, Wilford wrote to Brigham Young and Willard Richards, asking them to buy the material for him. Normally, he commented, he did not like to take time to worry about such things, but the tone of Phoebe's letter convinced him that under the circumstances, alone, poor, and without means, she was doing her best and he was obliged to help. Wilford Woodruff to Brigham Young and Willard Richards, n.d., [but clearly 1840], Brigham Young Papers.

[33]Nearly seven months earlier, on November 28, 1839, Wilford had a premonition of this calamity. He saw Phoebe in a dream and asked her where Sarah Emma was. Weeping and kissing him, she told him that the baby was dead. Wilford woke wondering if the dream was true. Later he inserted another entry into his journal on this same date, indicating when Sarah died. He said, "This dream was a warning of what was to come" (Woodruff, *Journal*, November 28, 1839, 1:371).

witness the departure of our little Sarah Emma from this world. Yes she is gone. The relentless hand of death has snatched her from my embrace. But Ah! She was two lovely, to kind, to affectionate, to live in this wicked world. When looking on her I have often thought how I Should feel to part with her. I thought I could not live without her esspecially in the Absence of my companion. But she has gone. The Lord hath taken her home to himself for some wise purpose.

It is a trial to me, but the Lord hath stood by me in a wonderful manner. I can see & feel & [know] that he has taken her home & will take better care of her than I possibly Could for a little while untill I shall go & meet her. Yes Willford we have one little Angel in heaven & I think it likely her spirit has visited you before this time.

It is hard living without her. She used to call her poor Pa Pa & putty papa many times in a day. She left a kiss for her papa with me just before she died. She eat her dinner as well as usual thursday. Was taken about 4 oclock with a prestness for breath. The Elders lade hands upon her & anointed her a number of times, but the next day her Spirit took its flight from this to another world without a groan.

To day Willford & I with quite a number of friends accompaning us came over to Commerce to pay our last respects to our little darling in seeing her decently buried. She had no relative to follow her to the grave or to Shed a tear for her but her Ma & little Willford. . . . I have just been to take a pleasing melancholy walk to Sarah's grave; She lies alone in peace. I can say that the Lord gave & the Lord hath taken away & blessed be the name of the *LORD*.[34]

Margaret Smoot also wrote a letter to Wilford that day, in which she enclosed a poem about Sarah and asked him to accept it "from one who had evry feeling but that of a parent for your departed Sarah."[35] With the aid of many good friends, Phoebe endured the loss of Sarah Emma.

Her financial situation improved. By the end of the summer, she had moved across the river into the home of William Clark, who wrote to her husband, assuring him that Phoebe was in good health and that she and baby Wilford "shall not want any thing that I can bestow & may God hold it as an everlasting covenant between me & thee."[36] In the late fall, however, the baby came down with another attack of the ague.[37]

About that time two friends visited Phoebe and invited her to accompany them back to Scarborough, Maine, to spend the winter at her father's home and then to return to Illinois with Wilford when he arrived in the spring. She happily accepted, and by December 6 she was as far east as New York City.[38] From there she went on to Scarborough.

---

[34]Ibid., October 26, 1840, 1:541–42.
[35]Ibid.
[36]Ibid., November 5, 1840, 1:545.
[37]Ibid., January 4, 1841, 2:22.
[38]Ibid., January 13, 1841, 2:28–29.

Before Wilford left England he purchased several things Phoebe needed, including a clock for the house, shawls, linen, flannel, silk, sewing thread, stockings, handkerchief, a dress pattern, and a trunk. Friends also gave him similar things as gifts, and after he arrived in New York City on May 20, he shipped some of them to her. Nothing could have been more satisfying, however, than what happened in Scarborough on June 2. Wilford had remained in New York for a few days on Church business, but on June 1 he took a train to Boston and then an overnight steamer to Portland, Maine. The next morning he took a stage for Scarborough and that afternoon, he wrote in his journal, "I . . . was once more permitted to *embrace my Wife* & also a *son* which I had not before seen. This after being seperated from my family almost two years. It was truly a happy interview not ownly with my wife & Child but with the whole household."[39]

BATHSHEBA W. BIGLER

Bathsheba W. Bigler met George A. Smith when he was on his first mission, and he was there when she was baptized in Shinnsten, Virginia (now in West Virginia), on August 21, 1837. Her mother was baptized the same day, one sister had been baptized three days earlier, and her father and other family members united with the Church shortly thereafter. The Biglers soon joined the Saints in Missouri, where young Bathsheba and George met again, fell in love, and, on January 21, 1838, agreed to be married exactly three years from then.[40] The mission of the Twelve, of course, made that impossible.

The tragic Mormon exodus from Missouri took Bathsheba's family to Quincy, Illinois, and there, shortly after George A. left for his mission, her father succumbed to the devastating epidemic of the ague that killed many Saints. In the spring of 1840 the family moved to Nauvoo, where Bathsheba's brother Jacob built a house.[41]

Bathsheba eagerly awaited every letter from her missionary beau, but,

---

[39]Ibid., June 2, 1841, 2:105.

[40]George A. Smith to Bathsheba W. Bigler, January 14, 18, 1841, George A. Smith Collection (Appendix B, Document 20). Very little information is available on the early life of Bathsheba and particularly on the years George was away. A sensitive overview of her life, however, is found in Watt, "Bathsheba Bigler Smith." See also Godfrey, Godfrey, and Derr, "Bathsheba Wilson Bigler Smith."

[41]George A.'s father wrote to him that "Jacob Bigler has built an house a few hund[red] yard[s] to the north of where we were when you left home on a five acre lot and lives thare with the family." John Smith to George A. Smith, June 17, 1840, George A. Smith Collection.

Bathsheba W. Bigler Smith
Courtesy Special Collections
Department, University of Utah
Libraries

she recalled later, by January 1840 she still "had not heard from the man I loved." She had sent news to him, nevertheless, via Lorenzo Snow. Not long after that a neighbor came to the house with a letter addressed to her and postmarked Liverpool. But the neighbor was a tease and held the letter out of reach as she "danced and sang for joy," knowing who it was from. Her pleading finally softened him, even drawing a few tears, and he gave her the long-awaited communication. Before George A. returned the following year, she had six such letters tucked away among her most "precious belongings."[42]

On July 25, 1841, about six weeks after he arrived in Nauvoo, Bathsheba and George were married. She was nineteen years old; he was twenty-four.

JENNETTA RICHARDS RICHARDS

Willard Richards, also a bachelor when he went to England, married before returning home. The bittersweet story of his courtship of Jennetta

---

[42]Smith, "Autobiography of Bathsheba W. Bigler," 8. See also Appendix B, Documents 19 and 20.

Jennetta Richards Richards
Courtesy LDS Church Archives

Nancy Marinda Johnson Hyde
Courtesy LDS Church Archives

Richards, their marriage, and their subsequent life together in England is such an integral part of the mission that it has already been told.

NANCY MARINDA JOHNSON HYDE

Nancy Marinda Johnson married Orson Hyde in 1834. A year later her husband, along with her brothers Luke and Lyman, became members of the newly formed Quorum of the Twelve Apostles. Like Vilate Kimball, Marinda was a "missionary widow" twice while her husband traveled abroad, and the circumstances surrounding the earlier mission proved especially challenging. During the Kirtland crisis of 1837, Marinda saw both her husband and her brothers become disaffected. Orson was quickly reconciled, however, and in June he accompanied Heber C. Kimball on the first mission to England. Marinda remained in Kirtland to care for her three-week-old baby girl and face family turmoil alone. (Although Luke Johnson later returned to the Church, Lyman never did.)

Orson returned to Kirtland, Ohio, in May 1838, just in time to gather up his family and join the general exodus to northern Missouri. Soon after their summer arrival, Marinda once again was forced to assume primary responsibility for the family after Orson became ill with a "bilious fever" that incapacitated him for several months. Still very sick during the dissent and mobbings that erupted in the fall, Orson again became disaffected, further adding to Marinda's burdens. The Hydes remained behind when the Saints were driven from Missouri.

By the time Orson had spiritually and physically recovered enough to move his family to Illinois in mid 1839, his fellow apostles were already preparing to leave for England. His late arrival and renewed illness kept him in Nauvoo when his quorum departed, so Orson was with Marinda in December for the birth of their second daughter. Subsequently, however, Marinda was left to manage alone longer than any of the other apostles' wives. In April 1840, Orson left Nauvoo to fill a special mission to Palestine with John E. Page. He spent nearly ten months traveling to the east coast, preaching, raising money, and waiting for Elder Page until finally, in February 1841, he set sail without Page. After meeting briefly with the other apostles in England, he resumed his journey to Palestine at the same time most of the Twelve sailed for America.

Though details are not known, clearly Marinda faced daunting challenges at home. In December 1841, a few months after the other apostles had returned from their mission, the Prophet Joseph Smith by revelation asked the Ebenezer Robinson family to care for Sister Hyde and her children "that she should have a better place prepared for her ... in order that her life may be spared."[43] In December 1842 Elder Hyde finally returned to Marinda and his two daughters in Nauvoo.

CONCLUSION

Too often the lives and struggles of the women of the Church have been left unsung, and that is true of the lives of those who waited, prayed, and suffered while their apostle-husbands were in England. But it was not just their waiting and suffering that mattered, so far as the history of the Church is concerned. These steadfast women were very much a part of the struggling community of Saints, growing daily, who helped turn the uninviting swamplands of Commerce and vicinity into the beginnings of "Nauvoo the Beautiful" that their husbands saw when they returned two years later. While the apostles were building the kingdom of God in Great Britain, their wives and sweethearts were struggling to build a new gathering place and a new temple-city in America. In some ways their task was the more difficult and their success perhaps the more remarkable.

---

[43]*History of the Church* 4:467.

Chapter 12

THE APOSTLES RETURN TO AMERICA

The apostles were prepared to stay in Great Britain as long as Joseph Smith deemed necessary, but they also longed for home and, at times, allowed themselves the luxury of thinking they might leave soon. Heber C. Kimball even told Vilate in August 1840 that they might return that fall, if the Lord willed, but hastened to add that he did not yet feel at liberty to do so. "When I dow," he emphasized, "I shall come home as quick as wind and steam will carry me. So be of good cheer my dear Vilate we shall soon see each other."[1] The apostles wrote to Joseph Smith, asking about returning in the spring, and by early 1841, even before they had an answer, that had become their plan.

In Nauvoo, meanwhile, their wives contended with rumor and heresay that the Twelve would soon return. As early as July 1840, some even heard rumors that Joseph had been visited by a Nephite[2] who had been in England and told him that the work would be short and successful there, that great troubles were about to commence, and that great things would be accomplished within twelve months. About the same time, Mary Ann Young went to talk to Joseph Smith about a rumor that "the Presidency are about to send for the Elders to come home." He quickly squelched the gossip and, as Mary Ann reported to Brigham Young, "he said there was no such thing as sending for you." As for herself, she told her husband, she felt "as though

---

[1] Heber C. Kimball to Vilate Kimball, August 19, 1840, Heber C. Kimball Collection.

[2] The Book of Mormon reports that three of the twelve Nephite disciples chosen by Christ to lead his Church on the American continent were promised that they would never taste of death but should "behold all the doings of the Father unto the children of men" and finally "be changed in the twinkling of an eye from mortality to immortality" at the Second Coming of Christ (3 Nephi 28: 6–8). This has given rise to the belief among the Mormons that, at times, one or more of these prophets have been seen by and given messages to someone in the Church.

I would rather do any way than have you come home until you have done the will of God."[3]

Parley P. Pratt and Willard Richards had their families with them, but as the year 1840 drew to a close, the other six apostles were sometimes cruelly torn between their yearning for home and their urge to continue in Britain, for they truly exulted in the work. "You ask me what I think about going home but I will assure you that it is a hard question," Orson Pratt responded to Wilford Woodruff and George A. Smith on November 2. "I hardly know how to answer it for I am in a strait betwixt not only two but many things for I am exceedingly anxious to see my family & I am exceedingly anxious to continue labouring in the vinyard." Musing that he sometimes thought of going to get his family, he turned the question back to his two colleagues by asking what they intended to do.[4] But whenever they left, he observed later in the month, he thought they should all leave together.[5]

Orson even joked about his dilemma. He expected to see home sometime that century, he quipped to George A. Smith in December,[6] and several weeks later he found himself jovial enough to play word tricks in his correspondence. Instead of signing a February 1 letter to Elder Smith with his name or his initials, he playfully spelled out his initials: "I am as ever *Oh! Pea*."[7] A week later he wrote again, signing the letter the same way but also telling George A. that he had definitely decided to preach his farewell sermon on March 28, go to Manchester for the April conference, and then "the first good ship that sails from Liverpool for N. York I intend shall carry me & all this if the Lord will." He pressed George A. to make up his mind, too, telling him that without question Brigham Young and others were going. "Come Bro. Geo. put on your thinking cap," he prodded his young colleague.[8] His letter of March 20 carried more wry humor. "My health is good, and my spirits is up, my mind is much set upon going home, which fills me with a longing disire for the time to come when I

---

[3]Willard Richards to Brigham Young, October 24, 1840, Brigham Young Papers; Willard Richards to Brigham Young, August 22, 1840. Willard had opened Mary Ann's letter to Brigham because Brigham was in Preston when the letter came to Manchester. The quotation comes from Willard's report to Brigham.

[4]Orson Pratt to George A. Smith and Wilford Woodruff, November 2, 1840 (Appendix B, Document 16).

[5]Orson Pratt to George A. Smith, November 23, 1840, George A. Smith Collection.

[6]George D. Watt and Orson Pratt to George A. Smith, December 22, 1840, George A. Smith Collection.

[7]Orson Pratt to George A. Smith, February 1, 1841, George A. Smith Collection.

[8]Orson Pratt to George A. Smith, February 8, 1841, George A. Smith Collection (Appendix B, Document 24).

shall set sail," he said. He closed with an amusing play on what would have been simply "To G. A. S." from "O. P." Instead, the augmented initials read "Give, All, Some Oatmeal Pancakes."[9] Thinking seriously of going home clearly put Orson Pratt in a merry mood.

By November John Taylor was thinking he might return to the "western praries" in the spring,[10] and when he wrote to Leonora in February, he, too, was in a playful mood. After he and his companions arrived in Pittsburgh, he teased, they would not only inquire the way to Nauvoo but also ask if there were any women who wanted husbands. "If we meet with any we shall probably get married for a while." The humor, of course, was an effort to reassure his wife that he would not leave again for some time to come. "You know," he continued, "the law of the Israelites was that when a young man married he was not to leave home or go to war for twelve months & surely the Law of Israel should be as binding as the laws of the Medes and Persians."[11]

Other missionaries, too, were homesick, and John Taylor must have smiled when he received a letter in January from Elder Reuben Hedlock hinting that he was anxious to go home but still not willing to admit that he was sitting on his trunk. "I expect to spend many months in this City [Glasgow]," Hedlock wrote, "yet I may see home sometime in 1841 but if not I have strong hopes of arriving before the close of the nineteenth century."[12]

Brigham Young wrote to Mary Ann in October that scarcely a night went by that he did not dream of America and his friends.[13] On January 15 he wrote her that the Twelve planned to meet with other Church officers on April 6 to arrange the affairs of the Church so they could leave. "I think we shall start for home then," he said, "and make ouer way as fast as we can."[14] He then wrote his fellow apostles confirming the decision. With many branches established, local leadership firmly in place, dozens of missionaries in the field, the publishing program nearly complete, and Parley P. Pratt returned with his family to oversee the mission, there was little to keep the rest of the Quorum of the Twelve in Britain.

[9]Orson Pratt to George A. Smith, March 20, 1841, George A. Smith Collection.

[10]Orson Pratt to George A. Smith, November 23, 1840. Along the edge of the page, Taylor commented that some of them might start for Nauvoo in April.

[11]John Taylor to Leonora Taylor, February 13, 1841, John Taylor Collection.

[12]Quoted in John Taylor to George A. Smith, January 14, 1841, George A. Smith Collection.

[13]Brigham Young to Mary Ann Young, October 16, 1840.

[14]Brigham Young to Mary Ann Young, January 15, 1840.

Joseph Smith, meanwhile, after considering the inquiries he had received from the Twelve, wrote a long letter on December 15 calling them home. Though they did not receive the letter for more than two months, they received other confirmation that their plans were in accord with the Prophet's. Early in February they learned from a December 25 letter from Brigham Young's wife that Joseph Smith was writing the Twelve, telling them to hold a conference in the spring, ordain whatever missionaries they thought wise, and then return to Nauvoo.[15]

Apprehension over a possible war also affected the apostles' thoughts of leaving. On February 15 Heber C. Kimball received a letter from Vilate, dated December 30, saying that Joseph Smith had written for the Twelve to come home immediately for their own safety, for great judgments were at the door. In commenting on Vilate's letter, Wilford Woodruff expressed his own foreboding that troubles might soon arise between England and America.[16] When Joseph's letter finally arrived the apostles read the following:

I have reflected upon the subject some time, and am of the opinion that it would be wisdom in you to make preparations to leave the scene of your labours in the spring. Having carried the testimony to that land, and numbers having received it; consequently the leaven can now spread without you being obliged to stay—another thing, there has been some whisperings of the spirit that there will be some agitations, some excitements, and some trouble in the land in which you are now labouring. I would therefore say in the mean time, be diligent, organize the churches and let every one stand in his proper place, so that those who cannot come with you in the spring, may not be left as sheep without a shepherd.[17]

Tension had been brewing between the United States and England for nearly three years. During a small uprising of Canadians against the British in 1837, William Alexander MacKenzie recruited a number of sympathetic Americans and hired an American-owned steamboat, the *Caroline*, to carry supplies from New York. Canadian authorities decided to prevent such use of the boat and, on December 29, sent out fifty men under the command of a naval officer with orders to destroy it. The *Caroline*, however, was not in Canadian waters but tied up to a dock on the New York side

---

[15]The letter arrived in London on February 6, but since Brigham Young was not there Elder Woodruff read it. Woodruff, *Journal*, February 6, 1841, 2:39.

[16]Ibid., February 6, 1841, 2:39 and February 15, 1841, 2:47.

[17]Joseph Smith to the Twelve, December 15, 1840, as cited in *Millennial Star* 1 (March 1841): 266. Wilford Woodruff apparently did not read the letter until March 25, when he saw it published in the *Star*. Woodruff, *Journal*, March 25, 1841, 2:72–73.

of the Niagara River. Nevertheless, the Canadians raided it, killed one American and wounded several others, set fire to the boat, and towed it out into the river to sink.

Americans were outraged, and Secretary of State John Forsythe demanded redress. The British government replied that the raiders were merely acting in self-defense, for they had a right to prevent the *Caroline* from being used against them. The problem smoldered, along with other tensions between the two countries, for more than two years. Then, on November 12, 1840, Alexander McCloud was arrested by New York authorities and charged with the murder of the American on the *Caroline*. British authorities angrily demanded McCloud's release on the grounds that those who raided the *Caroline* did so under orders, recognized in international law, and that as an individual McCloud could not be held responsible. American authorities refused to accept any such argument, and for most of 1841 feelings ran high, with people on both sides of the Atlantic calling for war. McCloud was finally tried and acquitted in a New York court.

The apostles took seriously the possibility of war. In a letter to George A. Smith dated February 12, 1841, Wilford Woodruff referred to "great excitement" in Parliament and throughout London because of McCloud's arrest. The people of New York, he said, were determined to hang McCloud, but if that should happen, then England was determined "to have redress at the cannon mouth." In that case, he opined, "America will learn by experience that it is no Joke to have a war with England."[18] In London, meanwhile, Lorenzo Snow observed, "It is believed by many in this city that a war is about to break out between England and America."[19]

Joseph's letter confirmed the plans the apostles already had made for returning home in April, and also reflected his complete satisfaction with all the Twelve had accomplished: "It is, likewise, very satisfactory to my mind that there has been such a good understanding between you, and that the Saints have so cheerfully hearkened to counsel and vied with each other in this labour of love, and in the promotion of truth and righteousness; this is as it should be in the church of Jesus Christ; unity is strength."[20]

Parley P. Pratt, meanwhile, was delighted at the prospect of remaining

---

[18]Wilford Woodruff to George A. Smith, February 12, 1841, George A. Smith Collection.

[19]Lorenzo Snow to George A. Smith, February 17, 1841.

[20]Joseph Smith to the Twelve, December 15, 1840, as cited in *Millennial Star* 1 (March 1841): 266. See also *Times and Seasons* 2 (January 1, 1841): 258.

in England. As he wrote to Sidney Rigdon in January: "I often feel as though I should like to be in the midst of our old friends in the west, but when it will be my lot I know not. I am resigned to the kind of life I am now living; I can truly say that I was never more contented, or more happy than of late."[21]

THE LAST FEW WEEKS

Heber C. Kimball and Wilford Woodruff spent their last few weeks in London strengthening the Saints, taking care of last-minute details, and buying gifts and gadgets for home. As noted earlier, they also secured a British copyright for the Book of Mormon and published their *Address to the Citizens of London*. After they sat several times to have their portraits painted, James Albion made gilt frames for the 20 × 20-1/4-inch canvases and presented them as gifts to the apostles.[22] On February 16 Heber and Wilford had their last official meeting with the London Saints. "It was a melting time," wrote Woodruff. The next day a group of Saints filled their sitting room, bringing gifts of money and presents for the apostles' wives and children.

Heber left London on February 20. He spent a week in Bedford, preaching every night, and was "thronged all the time" with Saints. There he found the Reverend Timothy Matthews, brother-in-law to Joseph Fielding, stirring up confusion and trouble. His encounter with the elders in 1837 had convinced Matthews of the necessity of baptism by immersion, but he had refused to receive baptism at their hands and eventually simply baptized himself. Now he was calling himself a Latter-day Saint and preaching the "first principles" of the Gospel much as the elders did. Outraged by his "abominations and deceptions," Heber spoke out publicly against him. Leaving the town "in an uproar," he made his way to Birmingham, where he held a conference, and then to Staffordshire, where he worked with George A. Smith. On March 6 he went on to Manchester and, five days later, to Liverpool.[23]

After Heber C. Kimball left, Wilford Woodruff remained another few days with the London Saints, preached one last time on February 25, and then departed the next day. He traveled 120 miles to Bristol, where he had a pleasant reunion with Thomas Kington and his family.

---

[21]Parley P. Pratt to Sidney Rigdon, January 8, 1841, *Times and Seasons* 2 (April 1, 1841): 364–65.
[22]Woodruff, *Journal*, February 2, 1841, 2:35–36.
[23]Heber C. Kimball to Vilate Kimball, March 14, 1841, Heber C. Kimball Collection.

George A. Smith, preparing to leave the Potteries, wrote to Bathsheba on March 6 of his plans. Still not sure where his financial support would come from, he quipped, "When I get to New York I Expect to have to Preach my pasage home."[24] He spent the next three weeks writing letters, holding conferences, appointing and ordaining more Church officers, and making final visits to the various towns where he had so many friends. Some of them gave him presents, and when he took leave of the Saints at Leek on March 22, most were in tears. Three days later Elder Woodruff joined him at Hanley, and on March 27 the two met with the local Church council which, among other things, raised £4 to help George A. get home. The next day the two apostles conducted a conference where they were given letters of recommendation, "manifesting that the Church in this region accept of their labours & considered that they have filled their mission with honour & Dignity."[25] On March 30 they took a coach to Manchester.

In a final letter to the Saints, dated April 11, George A. Smith no doubt reflected the feeling of all the apostles as they recalled the year gone by:

Although I have suffered much bodily affliction during the past year, the Lord has blessed my labours abundantly, and I can say I never enjoyed myself better in the discharge of my duty, than I have on this mission. Among the greatest blessings I have enjoyed, has been the privilege of attending four general conferences, and meeting in council with the 12. I can assure you that a meeting with those in whose company I have suffered so much tribulation for the gospels sake, both at home and abroad, by land and sea, is to me a privilege indeed.[26]

In Edinburgh, Orson Pratt looked back with well-deserved satisfaction on all that had happened since the day he knelt on Arthur's Seat and prayed for two hundred converts. "The work of the Lord is rolling on in this City," he happily proclaimed on March 20. A little over a week earlier he had baptized a Campbellite preacher, and during that week he had baptized eight more people, bringing his total to 186.[27] He preached his farewell sermon to the Scottish Saints on March 28,[28] and two days later he left. At

---

[24]George A. Smith to Bathsheba W. Bigler, March 6, 1841, George A. Smith Collection.

[25]Woodruff, *Journal*, March 28, 1841, 2:74–76; Smith, "History," March 22–28, 1841. George A. Smith's letter read: "This is to certify that Elder G. A. Smith has faithfully laboured among us in all humility and meekness; and that we feel grateful to the Lord for his goodness in sending him among us. And we hereby recommend him as a Faithful Minister of the Gospel of Jesus Christ and a Shining Ornament to his Profession" (Certificate found in George A. Smith Collection).

[26]George A. Smith to the Editor, April 11, 1840, *Millennial Star* 1 (April 1841): 306.

[27]Orson Pratt to George A. Smith, March 20, 1841.

[28]Reuben Hedlock to George A. Smith, February 12, 1841, George A. Smith Collection.

the Manchester conference on April 6 he reported 203 members in Edinburgh.[29]

Wilford Woodruff spent the month of March slowly making his way to Manchester via various branches of the Church. In Bristol he discovered that Thomas Kington had founded a branch of some thirteen converts. He stayed there nearly a week, preaching three times and baptizing one person, then went on to Wales, where he preached at Monmouth and attended a meeting of the Garway Conference. On March 9 he arrived in Herefordshire, where generous Saints not only welcomed him warmly but also contributed money to help him along the way.

Leaving Herefordshire was particularly difficult for Wilford Woodruff. After the Gadfield Elm conference on March 15, the Saints crowded around him for hours seeking all kinds of advice and direction, and tears filled their eyes as they parted. The same thing happened a week later at the Standley Hill conference, where "I spent about three hours in shaking hands with the Saints healing the sick, giving council concerning a thousand questions & things that were presented before me by the multitude which surrounded me. Many were in tears as they parted from me." On March 25 he was in the Staffordshire Potteries, where he and George A. Smith attended another conference and baptized seven people. On March 30 the two went on to Manchester.[30]

On Thursday, March 4, Joseph Fielding left Preston for Liverpool, on his way to the Isle of Man. As he was crossing over into Burlington Street he said to himself, "Now if Br. Hyde were here how pleased I should be." Orson Hyde, Fielding knew, would be passing through England on his way to Jerusalem. It seemed an answer to Fielding's prayers when he stopped at 72 Burlington Street and was told that Elder Hyde indeed had come, along with George J. Adams. They had arrived the day before and were attending a meeting at the Arrington home, where Peter Melling was giving patriarchal blessings. Fielding hurried there and found them, postponed his trip to the Isle of Man, and accompanied them to Preston the next day. The Saints remembered well Elder Hyde's 1837–38 mission among them and were elated at his return.[31]

---

[29]*Millennial Star* 1 (April 1841): 302.

[30]Woodruff, *Journal*, February 26–March 30, 1841, 2:52–76; Wilford Woodruff to the Editor, April 1, 1841, *Millennial Star* 1 (April 1841): 305–6.

[31]Fielding, Diary, 104–5.

CONFERENCE WEEK

April 1, 1841, began a week of both reunion and farewell. That day the apostles converged in Manchester to begin their final councils in England and to say good-bye to the Saints in conference. Brigham was "much rejoiced," he noted in his diary, to see all his brethren, but especially Elder Hyde.[32] It was a fitting climax to the mission of the Twelve to Britain when, the first week in April, all nine apostles—the largest number to meet together since the days of Kirtland—met in council.[33] Unified as they had never been before, they no doubt each felt much as Wilford Woodruff felt:

> To meet once more in council after a long seperation and having passed through many sore and grievous trials exposing our lives & our characters to the slander and violence of wicked & murderous men, caused our hearts to swell with gratitude to God for his providential care over us.[34]

In its broader setting, their year of labor had caused only a little extra turbulence in the agitated waters of British religious history. They had neither overturned the churches nor shocked the nation. From the perspective of Latter-day Saint history, however, their mission had been momentous. Building on a small but solid foundation, in a remarkably short time they had erected an impressive religious structure, including an organization for emigration that would endure for more than fifty years. Some of their converts would desert them, but more would remain. Many would follow them to a new life in the New World. In all this they left an established pattern for more missionaries, more converts, more emigrants.

The apostles met in formal council on April 2, 3, and 5, though Orson Pratt arrived only in time for the second day's meeting. Among other things, they accepted the labors of Brigham Young and the publication committee and agreed that Parley P. Pratt, who would remain in England, should manage the *Millennial Star* and do additional publishing if needed. They

---

[32]Young, Diary, April 1, 1841. When Young was informed in early March of the arrival of Hyde and George J. Adams, his next thought was "but whare is Elder Page." Page never left America. Not certain Hyde would remain in England long, Young asked Richards to let him know where Hyde would be and how long: "let me know for I due not want to mis of him. . . . if nessary I will come emeditly" (Brigham Young to Willard Richards, March 5, 1841, Brigham Young Papers).

[33]John E. Page and William Smith, it will be remembered, had failed to respond to the call to preach abroad, and the vacancy created by the death of David W. Patten was only then being filled in Nauvoo. Lyman Wight, called to the Quorum in early 1841, was ordained by Joseph Smith in Nauvoo on April 8, 1841.

[34]Woodruff, *Journal*, April 2, 1841 (inserted after April 5), 2:78.

appointed Amos Fielding to superintend emigration and set April 17 as the day to sail for home.

The Twelve also made an important procedural decision with respect to the conference to be held on Tuesday, April 6. Rather than opening the meeting to business from the floor, the Twelve decided that the Quorum itself would make whatever proposals were deemed necessary and then call upon the conference for a sustaining vote. Conference members could vote either way, but this combination of authoritative direction from the Twelve with an opportunity for democratic acceptance or rejection, already tried in previous local conferences in Britain, soon became the general pattern for conducting Church business.

"We had a good time," Wilford Woodruff observed at the end of the first day of Quorum meetings. "Unity prevailed."[35] By April 5 he was even more delighted with the harmony of his quorum. "Perfect union & harmony prevailed in all the deliberations of our councils for the last four days."[36]

On Sunday, April 4, the apostles met with the Manchester Saints, and all nine bore fervent testimonies of the authenticity of the Bible, the Book of Mormon, and the prophetic calling of Joseph Smith.

The general conference of April 6 was the happy culmination of all the Twelve had worked for since their first official meeting in England just a year before. Conducting and presiding, President Brigham Young organized the conference, opened with prayer, and then called for membership reports from the various representatives of the Church throughout Britain. The tally showed a total of 5,864 members, an increase of nearly 2,200 since the last conference and more than 4,300 since the previous

---

[35]Woodruff, *Journal*, April 2, 1841, 2:77. As he had in October, Young prepared himself a brief agenda of "busness for the councel of the twelve ... a peace prapared for the Star for to govern the getherin of the saints from Urop — an agent at L. pool for to conduct the saints — another Patrick [patriarch] ordained. ... the Elders are not Fathers but midwifes high Preast[s] to be ordained." See Young, Diary, entry just before March 31, 1841, Brigham Young Papers. All of these items were taken care of between April 2 and 15, 1841.

[36]Ibid., April 5, 1841, 2:78. The "perfect union & harmony" noted here was the ideal, of course, but not always achieved. These were strong-willed and independent men and occasional clashes or tension were to be expected. For example, see the hint of this in Brigham Young to Willard Richards and Wilford Woodruff, May 24, 1840, Brigham Young Papers, or Young's brief reference to Richards, March 1, 1841, Brigham Young Papers, that "br Pratt and famely are well he has got over all his feelings about Books."

Such things were quickly resolved, however, and all of the Twelve who comment on this period stress the unusual degree of harmony that prevailed. See, for example, John Taylor to Joseph Smith, February 3, 1841, in *Times and Seasons* 2 (May 1, 1841): 401. For George A. Smith's feelings about his fellow apostles, see his letter of April 11, 1841, in *Millennial Star* 1 (April 1841): 306. For Heber C. Kimball's personal commitment to and desire for unity among the Twelve, see Kimball, Diary, January 1, 1841.

April.[37] There were also several priesthood ordinations, including that of a second patriarch for England, and the farewell addresses of several of the Twelve. Most important, the Council organized all the churches in Great Britain into conferences and appointed presiding elders over them,[38] and then placed Parley P. Pratt to preside over the whole.

A large, beautifully decorated cake graced the evening meeting where hymns and "a powerful and general feeling of delight" animated the seven hundred in attendance. Joseph Fielding thought the cake, a gift sent to the Twelve from New York, a fitting symbol "of the good things of that land from whence it came, and from whence they had received the fulness of the gospel." After Brigham Young and William Miller sang the hymn, "Adieu my dear brethren," President Young blessed the congregation and dismissed it.[39]

HOME AGAIN

The apostles spent another twelve days in Manchester, visiting with the Saints, preaching on the Sabbath, and attending to final matters of business. On April 7 they unitedly blessed Orson Hyde for his mission to Palestine.[40] They also completed for publication in the *Star* "An Epistle of the Twelve" to the Saints throughout Great Britain. There they expressed thanks for the diligence of the Saints and warned them to remember "that which we have ever taught . . . both by precept and example . . . to beware of an aspiring spirit."[41] The epistle also announced the appointments of Levi Richards and Lorenzo Snow as traveling counselors to assist Elder Pratt and instructed the Saints in detail about the gathering and emigration. Their work concluded, the apostles took the train for Liverpool on April

---

[37]These totals are from the representations in the minutes published in the *Star*, figures that Young and others include in their published histories. In addition, approximately eight hundred had emigrated and were not counted here for a total membership present and emigrated of 6,614 plus 50 not in branches, or 6,664. Subtracting from that the first representation of 1,541 leaves an increase in one year of 5,133 while the apostles often talked of "between 6 and 7,000." Part of this discrepancy may be accounted for by tallying those substantial numbers baptized by Taylor and Woodruff before April 1840; no doubt there were also many dozens if not hundreds cut off during the year, although no totals are available. It would seem that the total number of converts was closer to 6,000 than 7,000.

[38]Minutes in *Millennial Star* 1 (April 1841): 301–5.

[39]Minutes, April 6, 1841, *Millennial Star* 1 (April 1841): 304–5.

[40]Woodruff, *Journal*, April 7, 1841, 2:86.

[41]*Millennial Star* 1 (April 1841): 309–12. No doubt thinking of their own experiences in Kirtland and Missouri, they defined such a spirit as one "which introduces rebellion, confusion, misrule, and disunion, and would, if suffered to exist among us, destroy" the union and spirit and power which are associated with the priesthood and can only exist with the humble and meek.

15, arriving just in time to join with two hundred Saints in a "tea meeting" in the Music Hall.

Parting was difficult for the Saints as well as for the apostles. The year had changed all their lives, nurtured their personal development, and forged lasting bonds of love and respect. William Miller expressed the conviction of thousands when he said to Brigham Young and Heber C. Kimball: "I know that you are his [God's] servants to minister salvation to the nations of the earth."[42] The influence of the apostles had been profound, and the throngs that gathered round them as they left smothered them with the tearful farewells reserved only for the most beloved of friends.

The apostles were not the only Latter-day Saints preparing to embark from Liverpool, for some 120 converts were also there, ready to emigrate. Clearly, the Mormon emigration set in motion by the Twelve had the potential of providing a lucrative business for shippers, and the owners of the *Rochester*, one of the fastest ships plying the Atlantic, had already profited from it. Therefore, when the apostles approached them on April 16 saying that they could not leave for another five days, the owners were happy to oblige. They even gave the Twelve a special rate and reserved for them the use of the aft quarterdeck.[43]

The apostles spent Sunday and Monday, April 18 and 19, preparing to leave and giving instructions to some of the Saints and priesthood leaders in Liverpool. Grateful Saints continued to shower them with presents. One of Wilford Woodruff's converts, a man who had already helped many British Saints migrate, gave him a purse containing £50 in gold, or about $250. Characteristically, he shared it, giving £5 each to Elders Young, Richards, and Smith.[44] None of the Quorum left England with empty pockets.

Finally, on Tuesday, the apostles and the emigrating Saints loaded their baggage and provisions aboard ship. With them, too, were Jennetta Richards and little Heber John. While Parley P. Pratt, Orson Hyde, Joseph Fielding, and a "multitude of Saints" ashore waved good-bye, the *Rochester* moved

---

[42]William Miller to Brigham Young and Heber C. Kimball, August 15, 1841, in *Times and Seasons* 3 (November 15, 1841): 598.

[43]Woodruff, *Journal*, April 15–16, 1841, 2:88–90; Willard Richards, Diary, April 20, 1841; Smith, "History," April 16, 1841. Young's later reminiscent account of this has the ship waiting even longer, and Smith says that originally it was to sail on April 12. Young also adds that the "agents of the vessel said such a thing had never been done before, but they were urgent and anxious to oblige us" because of past business and future prospects. See Discourse by Brigham Young, July 17, 1870, *Journal of Discourses* 13:212.

[44]Woodruff, *Journal*, April 19, 1841, 2:90–92.

out into the River Mersey and dropped anchor. The ship was like a beehive that afternoon and the next morning, with everyone busily stowing baggage and nailing or lashing it down in preparation for the ocean crossing. At noon on Wednesday the sails were unfurled, and the *Rochester* glided majestically out to sea.[45]

To the apostles, the contrast between their arrival in England and their departure was remarkable. A year earlier they were penniless, poorly dressed, and most of them strangers in a foreign land. When they left, Wilford Woodruff wrote by way of comparison, they were with "a ship load of Saints & all that we need of this worlds goods to make us comfortable, & having an influence sufficient to detain a ship a day or two on our account. Truly the Lord hath blessed us in a manner not looked for."[46]

Any expectation the Saints might have had for a calm and pleasant voyage to America were quickly put to rest. Contrary winds blew daily, and at midnight on April 24 they increased to gale strength and blew off the fore topsail. The next day the sea seemed "mountains high," and as the monstrous waves battered the *Rochester,* nearly all the passengers became ill. On the 28th, the storm became so severe that bunks crashed down and baggage broke loose, threatening to crush the emigrants before it could be lashed down again. After everyone scurried to put things back in order, the exhausted apostles unitedly sought the intervention of the Lord. The next day they had bright sun and a fair wind for the first time since leaving Liverpool. This was not the last storm they encountered, but after this one passed, the winds at least blew in the right direction. Brigham Young confided in his diary that he could not endure many more such voyages and "ware it not for the power of god & his tendere mercy I should despare."[47]

The *Rochester* arrived in New York on May 20, and three days later, on Sunday, the Twelve met with a "large congregation of citizens." There Elders Young, Kimball, Pratt and Woodruff gave an account of their mission.

The apostles then separated to take various routes home. Elders Young, Kimball, and Taylor left New York on June 4 and arrived in Nauvoo on

---

[45]Ibid., April 19–21, 1841 2:90–93; Fielding, Diary, 110. Having labored faithfully in Britain since 1837, Fielding remained several more months and then in the fall emigrated with his wife to Nauvoo.

[46]Woodruff, *Journal,* April 16, 1841, 2:89–90. In a discourse of December 12, 1869, *Journal of Discourses* 13:160, Woodruff said they baptized "something like seven thousand people." For Young's reminiscent overviews of this mission, see discourses of July 17, 1870, *Journal of Discourses* 13:211–12 and August 31, 1856, *Journal of Discourses* 4:35–36.

[47]Woodruff, *Journal,* April 24–29, 1841, 2:93–96; Young, Diary, entries around May 5, 1841.

ere has ben som
sickness on bord sin
ce we started sister
Erikken child and
sister Greene child
has ben sick —
the Bretheren and
Sisters apere to
feele well this
morning though
som have felt to
grumble som what
we have ben on our
journey —

when the winds
ware contry the br
a great to humble
them selves before
the Lord and ask him
to turn the breese
& give us a fair
wind, we did so &
the wind soudent
changed an from
that time to this
it has belone in
our faver

we had 8 days contry
wind & 9 wind changd
had fare wind and a
plesent sale for 4 days
then the wind fell we
be calmed on the Ban
ks of new found Land
I was verry sick &
destresed in my hed
& stomick I felt as
though I could not
endure meney such
voige' as I had indur
ed for 2 years or sen
ce I started on my

mision and ware
it not for the pow
er of god & his tend
er mercy I shoul
d despare but the
Lord is my strength
this is the 5 day
of May 1841 it is
a fine plesent day
yesterday was the
first day that looke
like an american day
for the pureness of
the atmist here —

Excerpt from Brigham Young's diary, describing conditions on the voyage home
Courtesy LDS Church Archives

Pencil sketch of Nauvoo, 1848, by Seth Eastman
Courtesy LDS Church Museum

July 1.[48] Elder Richards, Jennetta, and their baby remained for a time in the East, visiting among the Saints and doing missionary work. They arrived in Nauvoo at dawn on August 16. Elder Woodruff, his wife already in the East with relatives, also preached and visited in the East for several weeks. He and his family returned to Nauvoo on October 6. Orson Pratt remained in New York long enough to reprint *Remarkable Visions* and then returned to Nauvoo in mid July. George A. Smith proceeded homeward as best he could, but he did not have the means to go to Nauvoo immediately. In Philadelphia he met the two members of his Quorum who, two years earlier, had seen too many obstacles in the way of accepting their foreign mission call. They continued to feel the same. He preached with William Smith for several days, and he urged John E. Page to leave immediately and overtake Orson Hyde in Europe. Even though he apparently had means enough, Page still declined. George A. finally arrived in Nauvoo on July

---

[48]Young, "History of Brigham Young," 2. Less than a week after parting, Young wrote a short letter to Richards telling him the least expensive way to travel on the canal and otherwise providing travel advice and information. He closed with the phrase he and Richards had used in their September 5, 1840, letter to Joseph and which had indeed become something of a motto for them in England: "I am as ever your Br. in the N[ew] Covenets and *I say goe ahead*" (Brigham Young to Willard Richards, June 9, 1841, Brigham Young Papers, emphasis added).

14 and immediately went to visit Bathsheba. The two were married six weeks later.[49]

Though no contemporary description of their various Nauvoo reunions is extant, it is easy to imagine tears of joy, long hours of conversation and renewal of acquaintance, and expressions of thanksgiving—all of which soon gave way to labors on house and farm. In later years Brigham Young recounted his feelings to the Saints. He was overjoyed, he said, to be with Mary Ann again and with their young ones—little Emma, the twins Brigham and Mary Ann, his son Joseph A.—and with his two older daughters Vilate and Elizabeth. At last he could do more than pray for their welfare. To the Prophet's inquiry about how he would live, Brigham answered directly: "I will go to work and get a living." But not yet. He had enough money left to buy one barrel of flour. He would work on the cabin, improve the garden, and sit amidst his family eating bread until the barrel was empty. That would be soon enough to go out and find work.[50]

Joseph Smith visited Brigham Young at his home a few days after his return to Nauvoo. While there, he delivered the word of the Lord:

> Dear and well-beloved brother, Brigham Young, verily thus saith the Lord unto you: My servant Brigham, it is no more required at your hand to leave your family as in times past, for your offering is acceptable to me.
>
> I have seen your labor and toil in journeyings for my name.
>
> I therefore command you to *send* my work abroad, and take especial care of your family from this time, henceforth and forever. Amen.[51]

From England Brigham had written Mary Ann of his longing to return home and spend a "seson ... with my famely ocaisonly."[52] Now he and Mary Ann could take comfort in knowing that their labor and sacrifice was acceptable and that they could enjoy as a family the longed-for season of peace—even if that season was brief.

Orson Hyde, meanwhile, continued on to Palestine and then returned to Nauvoo in December, 1842. In England Parley P. Pratt continued publishing, preaching, and directing emigration. Early in 1842 he moved his office to Liverpool. In October he chartered a ship, the *Emerald*, for the passage to America of some 250 emigrating Saints, including his family and

---

[49]Woodruff, *Journal*, May 23 to June 4, 1841, 2:103–5; Smith, "History"; and Smith, *History of the Church* 4:372.

[50]Discourse by Brigham Young, July 24, 1854, *Journal of Discourses* 2:19.

[51]D&C 126 (July 9, 1841), emphasis added. Compare Young, "History of Brigham Young," 2.

[52]Brigham Young to Mary Ann Young, June 12, 1840.

himself. They embarked October 29, leaving Thomas Ward, Lorenzo Snow, and Hiram Clark as the presidency of the mission. Sometime during the first week in February 1843, after eight days on horseback, Parley arrived in Nauvoo and set about preparing for his family's arrival. By mid April they had joined him in the city of the Saints. He was delighted with the Prophet's welcome: "God bless you, Bro. Parley." The last of the missionary-apostles was home.[53]

---

[53]P. Pratt, *Autobiography*, 315–29.

Chapter 13

CONSEQUENCES

Two vital themes ran through the instructions given to the apostles when the Quorum of the Twelve was organized in the year 1835. First, though the Twelve were "equal in authority and power" to the First Presidency of the Church, their specific mission was to "build up the church, and regulate all the affairs of the same in all nations."[1] Oliver Cowdery advised them to prepare for long periods away from home, for it was their duty to unlock the kingdom of heaven in foreign nations.[2] "No man can do that thing but yourselves," Joseph Smith told them, and each of them had "the same authority in other nations that I have in this nation."[3]

The second theme was personal humility and quorum unity. The Twelve must be one, "equal in bearing the keys of the Kingdom to all nations," Oliver Cowdery emphasized, and each must pray for the other. Unity and humility were necessary for their success, and the bonds of brotherhood should prevail above all else.[4] Until the mission to England, however, the Quorum had seldom fulfilled this charge.[5] Under Thomas Marsh it had often been contentious and divided and sometimes more concerned about prerogatives than about service. By 1841 that situation had changed dramatically, and the apostles returned from the British Isles stronger, more unified, and better prepared for new responsibilities. They had learned to rely on their God and on each other. They had increased in self-reliance and in confidence in one another. They had proved that they could work together in harmony. It was no coincidence that the nine apostles who first met as a quorum in Manchester in April 1841 soon

---

[1]D&C 107:24, 33

[2]Smith, *History of the Church* 2:193–98; Record of the Twelve, February 27, 1835, Church Archives.

[3]As quoted in Esplin, "Emergence of Brigham Young," 157.

[4]Smith, *History of the Church* 2:195–97.

[5]For further comment on this, see Esplin, "Development of the Quorum of the Twelve," 72–73.

became Joseph Smith's right hand in Nauvoo and eventually, as his successors, led the Latter-day Saint migration to the Great Basin. Thereafter these men remained unalterably united behind Joseph and his teachings, while those who refused to accept the foreign mission call eventually fell away. Like a refiner's fire, the mission abroad had molded them into a strong, cohesive body, admirably prepared for its new role in general Church leadership and administration. John Taylor, who came into the Quorum after Marsh's departure but knew of the discord and had even seen it during his early visit to Kirtland, was struck by the great harmony of the Twelve in England. "I am happy to state," he wrote to Joseph Smith on February 3, 1841, "that we have been united in our councils to the present time; that there has been no discordant feeling, nor jarring string."[6]

In addition to this newfound unity, there were many long-range consequences of the mission to the British Isles, but two results of special significance warrant discussion here: (1) the effect of their publishing program, and (2) the effect of the mission on the future of the Quorum of the Twelve and its role in Church administration.

To the Corners of the Earth: The Publishing Legacy of the 1840–41 Mission

The publishing efforts of the Twelve in 1840 and 1841 were vital to their extraordinary success as missionaries. Converts came so rapidly after 1837 that they could not print literature fast enough to keep pace with the demand. One missionary in England wrote that the pamphlets he distributed had to be retrieved a short time later so they could be used again. Beyond that, however, the publishing begun in England had important consequences for the Church. Because they were both effective and the best available, Parley P. Pratt's pamphlets influenced much subsequent Latter-day Saint literature, especially that of his brother Orson, whose own pamphlets were printed in great numbers in the late 1840s and the 1850s. Once a strong foothold was established in England, missionary work spread into Wales, where Dan Jones and John Davis issued more than one hundred items in Welsh, some of which were reprints of items published earlier by the Twelve.[7] Missionary work also spread onto the European continent and, through the international routes and bases of the British Empire, to

[6]John Taylor to Joseph Smith, February 3, 1841, in *Times and Seasons* 2 (May 1, 1841): 401.
[7]See Dennis, *Welsh Mormon Writings*.

South Africa, India, Australia, and Asia—literally, to the four corners of the earth.[8] Much of the literature taken by the missionaries to these far-flung places originated during the mission of the Twelve to England.

Another consequence of the publishing begun by the apostles was the rise of Liverpool as a center for Latter-day Saint publishing. Since it was the port of embarkation for emigration, in April 1842 Parley P. Pratt moved his office there, so that emigration and publication could be more easily coordinated. The growth of missions outside England after 1845 placed a steady demand on Liverpool to supply printed matter. By 1852 Liverpool was the book supply depot for Mormonism throughout the world, supplying not only the needs of the British mission but also handling orders from missionaries in such places as New York, St. Louis, Salt Lake City, San Francisco, Hawaii, Australia, India, and South Africa.

One reason Liverpool became so important for publications was that publishing costs were much lower in England than in America. Also, as headquarters for the British Mission and, after 1849, for the Perpetual Emigration Fund Company, Liverpool had the leadership and the capital to be the center of LDS publishing. Both the *Millennial Star* and the British Mission president assumed great influence in the publishing business. The *Star* announced new publications, and many were first excerpted or printed whole in its pages. The *Star* also regularly gave details on the value of the press in missionary work. By the 1850s catalogues of LDS publications were being separately printed—a further witness to the standardization and centralization of the Latter-day Saint press in England.[9]

Another evidence of the significance of the foundation laid by the Twelve in 1840 and 1841 is seen in the great importance of the *Latter-day Saints' Millennial Star* in Mormon history and thought. It became the longest-running periodical in LDS history, ceasing publication only in 1970.[10] Without it the history of the LDS British Mission, of other foreign

---

[8]For more detail see Whittaker, "Early Mormon Pamphleteering," 256–320.

[9]The earliest lists were those Parley included on the last page of various issues of the *Star* or on the wrappers of each issue. The first such list was published in July 1841. See the *Star* 2 (July 1841): 48. In his July 6, 1840, letter to his wife Mary Ann, Parley spoke of his total immersion in the publishing business: "I am confined entirely at home as Editor of the 'Star' and publisher of the Hymn Book, B. of Mormon, and all our other Books.... [I] employ 3 women in my Back Room as folders." Parley said he had not left his house for more than twenty-four hours in three months! A list of early book agents in England for American LDS publications is in *Times and Seasons* 2 (April 15, 1841): 390.

[10]The *Star* was issued monthly from May 1840 until June 1845 when it became semimonthly. In 1852 it began to appear weekly. In 1943 it became monthly again; and in 1970 it was discontinued when the Church consolidated all magazines. The larger impact is discussed in Crawley and Whittaker, *Mormon Imprints*, 1–13.

missions in the nineteenth century, or even of the Church itself simply could not be written. It regularly provided the informational and inspirational glue to cement together the Church in Europe and other parts of the world. The spirit of Parley P. Pratt, and especially his missionary fervor, continued in its pages for decades after he left England.

Throughout the nineteenth century, the official editions of the hymnal and the standard works descended from their earlier British editions. The *Pearl of Great Price*, canonized in 1880 as the fourth of the standard works of the Church, was first published in England in 1851. The first Latter-day Saint biography, Lucy Mack Smith's *Biographical Sketches of Joseph Smith the Prophet and His Progenitors for Many Generations* was published there in 1853, and numerous other important LDS works came from the British press over the years, all attesting to the significance of the foundation the apostles laid.

Another important legacy of early Mormon publications in Britain was in developing a standard way to present distinctive Latter-day Saint beliefs and, ultimately, in establishing a more standard theology. Believing in a revealed religion based on an expanding body of scripture, Latter-day Saints have very little official theology. Certain principles are clearly enunciated in the standard works, and official pronouncements by the First Presidency address a few other doctrinal issues, but there is nothing in the LDS Church comparable to the Westminster Confession of Faith or the Augsburg Confession. Indeed, Mormonism began with a hostility toward formal creeds. The preface of the 1835 edition of the Doctrine and Covenants, for example, refers to the aversion some members of the Church had even to printing Joseph Smith's revelations for fear they would become too confining theologically, and Joseph Smith himself commented on the importance of avoiding anything like the formal creeds of other churches. When Elders Kimball and Hyde and their fellow missionaries sailed for England in 1837, there were few LDS books and very few discussions in print of what are usually considered the distinctive aspects of Latter-day Saint belief.[11] This situation changed, however, with the multiplicity of books and pamphlets that appeared under the Twelve in Britain.

Usually a particular concept first appeared in print in some unofficial tract; then, as it was repeatedly attacked and defended, it became cemented

---

[11]See Crawley, "Passage of Mormon Primitivism." Much of the discussion here is based on Crawley and Whittaker, *Mormon Imprints*, 11–13.

in the minds of Latter-day Saints as part of an informal body of belief. In the 1840s and 1850s, prominent LDS leaders began to publish the first great synthetic works,[12] moving Mormon theology from a folk level to a more formal, though still unofficial, level. There, for the most part, it has remained. Almost none of it has been officially canonized, and little of it has been officially commented upon by the highest quorums of the Church. Subsequent LDS writers have produced their own books that restate and reinterpret the tenets of Mormonism for their particular generations, but the arguments, the defenses, and the ideas themselves remain essentially as they were written by the first generation. And that first generation drew its inspiration, in large part, from the publications of the Twelve in England.

CONSEQUENCES FOR THE QUORUM OF THE TWELVE AND THE CHURCH

On Monday, July 19, 1841, the five apostles then in Nauvoo—Brigham Young, Heber C. Kimball, Orson Pratt, John Taylor, and George A. Smith— gathered at Brigham Young's home, joined for a time by Joseph Smith and Sidney Rigdon, to meet with former apostle Lyman E. Johnson. There is no record of what happened, but there is reason to believe that Johnson felt remorse for some of his actions and had come to seek resolution.[13] Apparently they had no other important meetings or Church responsibilities for the rest of the month, and they happily attended to farm and family. The Prophet, however, already had new assignments in mind for them, which made the interlude all too brief.

In the apostles' absence, Joseph Smith's many responsibilities had become even more numerous and increasingly burdensome. Besides all his obligations as Church leader, he shouldered a multitude of temporal responsibilities, including buying and selling land, establishing civil government, promoting a huge building program, preparing for immigrants, and encouraging the Saints in the myriad economic activities necessary to create a new community. This combination of ecclesiastical and civic activity

---

[12]Spencer, *Most Prominent Doctrines*; O. Pratt, *A Series of Pamphlets*; O. Pratt, *Seer*; P. Pratt, *Science of Theology*; O. Pratt, *[Tracts] by Orson Pratt*; and Richards, *Compendium of the Faith and Doctrines of the Church*.

[13]See Young, "History of Brigham Young"; Smith, *History of the Church* 4:389. In company with former apostle John F. Boynton, Johnson had traveled to Nauvoo earlier while the Twelve were still in England. See Kimball, Diary, January 28, 1841, where Kimball wrote after receiving a December 8, 1840, letter from his wife: "the tidings was good. and we felt to rejoice much to hear that John Boyington and Lymon [no doubt Lyman Johnson] and menny other pressious things." The entry is imperfect and the letter giving more details has not been located. Presumably these discussions helped heal feelings, although Lyman, unlike his brother Luke, never returned to the Church.

left little time for the more important aspects of his prophetic calling. As early as June 1840, he revealed his frustration in a memorial to the Nauvoo High Council. As a result of all the recent problems, he wrote,

your Memorialist had necessarily to engage in the temporalities of the Church.... [But] your Memorialist feels it a duty which he owes to God, as well as to the Church, to give his attention more particularly to those things connected with the spiritual welfare of the Saints.... The time has now come, when he should devote himself exclusively to those things which relate to the spiritualities of the Church, and commence the work of translating the Egyptian records, the Bible, and wait upon the Lord for such revelations as may be suited to the conditions and circumstances of the Church.[14]

He petitioned the council for relief from some of his temporal responsibilities, but relief was not immediately forthcoming.

As a result of the mission to England, the Quorum of the Twelve Apostles came of age precisely at the time its support and strength were needed most. Under Brigham Young's direction the Twelve had achieved unprecedented proselyting success and, for the first time, had become an effective agency of ecclesiastical administration. Joseph Smith immediately recognized what had happened, including the fact that with this maturity the Quorum of the Twelve was prepared to take on its full responsibilities.

It seems probable that the Nauvoo Saints, too, looked upon the apostles with more esteem as a result of their English mission. Even while they were away, news of their amazing success circulated in Nauvoo, enhancing their prominence as leading elders in the Church. Nor did it hurt their stature among the Saints to be preceded by several hundred English converts who were devoted to them and singing their praises.

Given these circumstances, it is not surprising that there were dramatic changes in the role of the Twelve soon after their return. These changes began on August 10 when, in a private council meeting, Joseph charged them with the responsibility of supervising "the business of the church in Nauvoo." This was the first time that the Quorum had been given formal administrative authority over a fully organized and functioning stake of Zion.[15] This new authority to oversee the affairs of the stakes marked an important departure from the earlier division of responsibility between "standing high councils," or stake high councils, and the "traveling high council," or the Twelve. Several of the apostles' new responsibilities were,

---

[14]Smith, *History of the Church* 4:137.

[15]Young, "History." Although this is a reminiscent account, contemporary accounts corroborate it.

of course, natural extensions of traditional ones. They were to call and appoint missionaries, for example, and they were responsible for settling the gathered Saints once they arrived in Nauvoo. Nonetheless, the scope of their jurisdiction and responsibility was significantly expanded.

Rather than wait six weeks for general conference, Joseph Smith called a special conference for August 16 to explain this significant change to the Saints. Six apostles were in Nauvoo on the day of the conference: Brigham Young, Heber C. Kimball, John Taylor, George A. Smith, Orson Pratt, and Willard Richards (who had arrived by riverboat at dawn).[16] Because of the death of one of his children, Joseph was unable to attend the first session of the conference. Significantly, that left Brigham Young, president of the Twelve, to call the meeting to order. The Prophet had called the conference, he explained, to transact business that could not wait until the October conference: specifically, calling missionaries and providing for immigrants. He explained that the Twelve would have responsibility for these tasks. Brigham seemed uncomfortably aware, however, that the responsibility for directing such affairs within organized stakes had not previously been associated with his own calling as an apostle and that the Saints might feel that the Quorum of the Twelve was overstepping its bounds. Sensitive to such feelings, he made it clear that he did not covet the new responsibilities placed on the Twelve and that he hoped no one would think that he and his brethren were aspiring to anything. Nothing could be further from their minds, he assured the Saints, than to interfere with Church affairs in the stakes. Missionary work was his first love, and he had been in the "vineyard" for so long and become so attached to foreign missions that nothing could induce him to retire but a sense of duty or the revelations of God, "to which he would always submit, be the consequence what it might." "Amen," responded the brethren of his quorum.[17]

Elder Young then read a list of prospective missionaries and another list of cities needing elders, and "by nomination" the conference began to designate who would go where. At that point Bishop Vinson Knight suggested that to expedite things the Twelve should make the assignments and simply present them to the conference. The conference agreed, which

---

[16]Orson Hyde was on his way to the Holy Land, Parley P. Pratt presided in England, and John E. Page, Wilford Woodruff, and William Smith remained in the East. In April Lyman Wight had been selected to fill the vacancy in the Twelve, but there is no mention of his being present this day.

[17]Smith, *History of the Church* 4:402–4; Young, "History." This explanation appears only in the published minutes. Compare with Nauvoo Minutes, August 16, 1841.

meant, in effect, that the Twelve would conduct the business just as they had done in their last conference in England—as a quorum rather than by the conference.

Helping the Nauvoo Saints understand the expanded assignment of the Twelve was so important to the Prophet that, despite his bereavement, he went to the afternoon meeting and dramatically expanded on Elder Young's cautious remarks. The time had come, he publicly proclaimed, "when the Twelve should be called upon to stand in their place next to the First Presidency, and attend to the settling of emigrants and the business of the Church at the stakes, and assist to bear off the kingdom victoriously to the nations." This arrangement was sustained by the vote of the conference.[18] Later, a motion that the conference accept the missionary assignments made by the Twelve allowed Joseph Smith to further clarify the implications of the change. Because the conference had already sanctioned the doings of the Twelve, he said, a further vote was unnecessary, and transacting such business with the approval of the Presidency was, in fact, among the apostles' official duties. The Twelve had authority to administer the affairs of the Church wherever and whenever the First Presidency directed. Willard Richards summed up their new authority in a brief but notable diary entry: "Conference: business of the Church given to the Twelve."[19]

This was only the beginning. From that time on, the Twelve drew even closer to the Prophet, as he carefully prepared them for what was to come. Joseph increasingly relied on them not only to manage the day-to-day affairs of the Church but also to be his private advisers.[20] Because Brigham Young stood at the head of the Twelve, his appeal to the Saints at the death

---

[18]Smith, *History of the Church* 4:403. This is a fleshed out version of the unpublished minutes, which simply say that Joseph Smith indicated "that the twelve should be authorized to assist in managing the affairs of the Kingdom in this place [Nauvoo, church headquarters]. which he said was the duties of their office &c. Motioned seconded and carried that the quorum of the twelve be authorized to act in accordance with the instructions given by president Joseph Smith in regulating and superintending the affairs of the Church." See Nauvoo Minutes, August 16, 1841. This was the order suggested in the March 28, 1835, revelation to the Twelve but by assignment not implemented until this time. See D&C 107, especially verses 21–24.

[19]Richards, Diary, expanded version, August 16, 1841. After Wilford Woodruff arrived in Nauvoo nearly two months later, he, too, wrote of the new responsibilities, though he emphasized their temporal aspects: "The temporal business of the Church is laid upon the hands of the Twelve" (Woodruff, *Journal*, October 8, 1841, 2:132–33).

[20]For an overview of the enlarged role of the Twelve, see Esplin, "Joseph, Brigham and the Twelve," especially pp. 310–20.

of Joseph Smith was not a personal one of "follow me" but a plea that the Church recognize the legitimate authority of the Quorum of the Twelve Apostles, which, by then, had become well established.[21]

After this shift of assignment in August 1841, the growing significance of the Twelve was underscored not just by their public activities but also by the many ways that the Prophet took them into his personal confidence. In contrast to his Kirtland practice, he now met with them frequently in quorum meetings and invited them to meet with him in important private councils. In 1839 Joseph had written from Liberty Jail that he had never had the opportunity to give to the Saints all that God had revealed to him.[22] From the perspective of Joseph Smith and the Twelve, the months of private tutoring in Nauvoo finally provided that chance. Instructions to the Twelve included clarification of the doctrines Joseph Smith began to teach while they were away in England: such doctrines as baptism for the dead, eternal marriage, and plural marriage. The apostles accepted the teachings and, as he instructed them, perpetuated them after his death. Also, as they repeatedly affirmed later, the Prophet bestowed upon them additional priesthood keys—the "fulness of the priesthood" they sometimes called it—completing their authority to preside.

While all this was happening, the Saints struggled to complete the Nauvoo Temple. There, the Prophet promised, all the faithful could share in additional sacred ordinances and instructions. In preparation for the presentation of the temple "endowment" to all the Saints, Joseph chose a small group of men and women to receive the ordinances and instructions privately. Brigham Young and Heber C. Kimball were among the first to receive the ordinances, in May 1842, and those nine apostles who had fulfilled their foreign missions formed the core of those so honored. Eventually, nearly seventy men and women received the temple endowment before the Prophet's death. Under the direction of the Twelve, the same ordinances were presented to thousands of other faithful Saints in the Nauvoo Temple after the Prophet's death.[23]

---

[21]For a review of the public involvements of the Twelve in Nauvoo, see Lyon, "Nauvoo and the Council of the Twelve," 167–205.

[22]Joseph Smith to Mrs. Norman Buel, March 15, 1839, in Smith, *History of the Church* 3:286.

[23]For a discussion of Joseph Smith's private introduction of these sacred things to a select group, see Quinn, "Latter-day Saint Prayer Circles," especially pages 83–96. For a discussion of the relationship of the introduction of temple ordinances to the succession of the Twelve, see Ehat, "Joseph Smith's Introduction of Temple Ordinances." See also letter of Orson Hyde to Ebenezer Robinson, 19 September 1844, in *The Return* 2 (April 1890): 253.

Only three years after the apostles returned from Britain, Joseph Smith died a martyr. During that time he did all he could to teach the apostles more of the kingdom of God and to prepare them to build on the foundation he had begun. "From time to time," Parley P. Pratt explained a few months after the martyrdom, Joseph called the Twelve together to "instruct them in all things pertaining to the kingdom, ordinances and government of God." Once he had committed to the Twelve "all things for the building of the kingdom according to the heavenly vision, and the pattern shown [him] from heaven," he told them that he had finished his work and the labor was theirs. "The chaos of materials prepared by him must now be placed in order in the building," Pratt continued. "The laws revealed by him must now be administered in all their strictness and beauty. The measures commenced by him must now be carried into successful operation."[24]

This was the setting for the dramatic meeting of August 8, 1844, six weeks after the martyrdom of Joseph, when Brigham Young stood before a special conference in Nauvoo. The Prophet, he affirmed, had given the Twelve all the keys and power he held, and now, for the first time, they could "see the necessity of the Apostleship." "For the first time in my life," he said, "for the first time in the kingdom of God do I step forth to act in my capacity in connexion with the quorum of the Twelve as Apostles of Jesus Christ unto the People and to bear of[f] the keys of the Kingdom of God in all the world." Joseph had laid the foundation for a great work, Brigham assured the Saints that day, "and we will build upon it."[25]

The eight apostles whose lives and perspectives were refined by the crucible of the British mission, along with Orson Hyde, who had joined them in England and then filled his own mission to Palestine equally well, dedicated themselves to carrying out all of Joseph Smith's plans. They would lead the Church as Joseph would have, Brigham Young reported to his daughter following the vote of the Saints to sustain them, for that was their inescapable duty.[26] That they could do this successfully as a powerful and united quorum was, in no small measure, a consequence of their mission to Britain in 1840 and 1841.

[24]P. Pratt, "Proclamation," in *Millennial Star* 5 (March 1845): 149–53.
[25]Woodruff, *Journal*, August 8, 1844, 2:435–36. See also Nauvoo Minutes, August 8, 1844.
[26]Brigham Young to Vilate Young, August 11, 1844, Brigham Young Papers.

EPILOGUE

The eight members of the Quorum of the Twelve who served together during the momentous mission to the British Isles and Orson Hyde, who joined them in England en route to Palestine, provided the Church with its top leaders for the next fifty-eight years (sixty-one years, if we include Lorenzo Snow, who served with the apostles but was not yet a member of the Twelve).

It is no coincidence that the apostles who failed to share the mission also failed to achieve further distinction in the Church. Rather, all of them were gone from it within a few years. William B. Smith had been a member of the Twelve since 1835. Volatile and often at odds with his brother Joseph or the Twelve, he pleaded poverty and ill health even after his reconciliation in May 1839. With the death of the Prophet in 1844, William at first accepted the leadership of his quorum and the right of Brigham Young to preside, but, strong-minded and independent as ever, he soon went his own way and was excommunicated in 1845. He died in Iowa in 1893. John E. Page was ordained an apostle in 1838, at the same time as John Taylor. After the Missouri difficulties he, like William Smith, had more excuses than faith. Only irregularly involved with his quorum during the 1840s, he drifted from the Church after Joseph Smith's death and was excommunicated in 1846. He died in Illinois in 1867. Lyman Wight's ordination as an apostle in Nauvoo during the same week in April 1841 that nine of the Twelve met for their last conference in England brought the quorum to its full complement. Elder Wight thus did not serve in Britain with the Twelve, and in Nauvoo, he was very little involved in their work. No doubt his not experiencing the sacrifice and growth that bonded the apostles in Britain was a factor in that. Soon after the death of Joseph Smith in 1844, Elder Wight left the body of the Saints and led a colony to Texas, according to

319

an earlier assignment given him by the Prophet. When he declined to rejoin the Saints by 1848, he was excommunicated. He died in Texas in 1858.

The sequel for the eight who served in England, and for Orson Hyde, was totally different. After the death of Joseph Smith, Brigham Young presided over the Church as president of the Twelve until 1847 and then as the head of a new First Presidency from 1847 to 1877. During that time, the body of the Church moved from Illinois to the Great Basin, and more than four hundred colonies were established there. As president, he saw Church membership nearly triple to reach approximately 115,000 at his death. Much of the growth came from British immigration.

Legendary for his steadfast loyalty to Joseph Smith, Heber C. Kimball was equally faithful to his long-time friend and associate Brigham Young, with whom he served as first counselor in the First Presidency from 1847 until his death in 1868. Elder Kimball was noted for his plainspokenness and common sense and for his gift of prophecy. He was among the first to receive the temple ordinances under the direction of Joseph Smith in 1842, and for many years he had responsibility for ordinance work in the Endowment House in Salt Lake City.

After meeting with his brethren of the Quorum of the Twelve in England in 1841, Orson Hyde went on to Palestine, where he dedicated that land for the return of the Jews. He returned to Nauvoo in December 1842. During the exodus in 1846, he presided over Nauvoo and oversaw the finishing and final dedication of the Nauvoo Temple in May. He then returned to England, in the company of Parley P. Pratt and John Taylor, where he presided for a year. Between 1847 and 1852, he presided over the Saints in the Midwest and in the 1850s presided over settlements in what became Wyoming, in Carson Valley, Nevada, and finally in central Utah. He served as president of the Twelve from 1849 to 1875. Because John Taylor had been brought into the Quorum of the Twelve while Hyde was out of the Church in 1838, in 1875 Brigham Young placed John Taylor ahead of him in seniority. Orson Hyde died in 1878.

Parley P. Pratt continued to write treatises important both for missionary work and for the education of Latter-day Saints. After the death of Joseph Smith, he presided for a time over the branches in the eastern United States, where he published another periodical, *The Prophet*, and in 1846 he was one of three apostles who returned to manage affairs in England. In the 1850s he published the first LDS tract in Spanish and headed a mission to Chile, the first to Latin America. In 1857 he was murdered while traveling in Arkansas.

Orson Pratt returned to the British Mission in 1848 to serve a two-year term as president. During that time membership in the British Isles increased from 18,000 to about 31,000, and he dispatched twenty ships loaded with emigrants for Utah. He published fifteen pamphlets and increased the circulation of the *Millennial Star* from less than four thousand to nearly twenty-three thousand. In the 1850s he presided for a time in Washington, D.C., where he published *The Seer*, and twice more during his lifetime he resided in England to oversee work in Great Britain. Altogether, he crossed the ocean sixteen times in his years of Church service. A skilled surveyor, mathematician, and scholar, he played an important role in colonizing Utah and in its intellectual life. He often defended the Church publicly in speech and in print. Because he was out of the Church briefly in 1843, Brigham Young's rearrangement of seniority in the Twelve in 1875 placed John Taylor ahead of him. When he died in 1881, Elder Pratt was serving as Church historian and general Church recorder.

In 1842 John Taylor became associate editor to Joseph Smith of Nauvoo's important *Times and Seasons*, and the following year, when the Prophet's duties made it impossible for him to continue, Elder Taylor became the editor. Friend and confidant of Joseph Smith, John Taylor accompanied him to Carthage Jail and was seriously wounded by the mob that killed the Prophet and his brother. In 1846 he accompanied Parley P. Pratt and Orson Hyde back to England. In the 1850s he presided in continental Europe, where he published a periodical in France and another in Germany. He also presided in New York City, where he published *The Mormon*. John Taylor became president of the Twelve in 1875, and he presided over the Church in that capacity from 1877 to 1880. From 1880 until his death in 1887 he was the head of the First Presidency. Although the Church suffered from the federal government's antipolygamy campaign during the entire decade of his presidency and he himself often administered Church affairs from seclusion, under President Taylor's direction dozens of new colonies were established and Church membership increased from 115,000 to nearly 173,000.

Even before the mission to Great Britain, Wilford Woodruff had established himself as an exemplary missionary and outstanding diarist, activities that distinguished his Church service for more than half a century. Because he recorded so many vital events and preserved so many of Joseph

Smith's teachings, his diary was the basis for many entries in Joseph Smith's *History of the Church* and is a major source of early Church history. After the murder of Joseph Smith, Wilford Woodruff returned to Britain, where he presided over the mission until 1846. Back in Utah, he served as an assistant Church historian after 1856, and as Church historian and general Church recorder from 1883 until 1887. Temple work was close to his heart, and in 1877 he became the first president of the Saint George Temple, the first temple completed after the Saints left Nauvoo. He became president of the Quorum of the Twelve in 1880 and, in that capacity, presided over the Church from 1887 to 1889. In 1889 the First Presidency was reorganized, and Wilford Woodruff served as president of the Church from then until his death in 1898. He received many significant dreams and revelations, including the revelation in 1890 that led the Church to discontinue the practice of plural marriage. He also oversaw the achievement of a goal that had been sought since the exodus to the West: the winning of statehood for Utah. During his administration, Church membership grew from about 173,000 to more than 265,000. President Woodruff was the last living witness of the crucial events experienced by the Quorum of the Twelve during Joseph Smith's lifetime.

George A. Smith continued his devotion to missionary work, and it was said that in 1843 alone he traveled six thousand miles in that capacity. He too continued to be a leader among the Saints. In 1850 and 1851, he led the first colonizing mission to southern Utah and became known as the father of southern Utah settlements: Saint George, Utah, was named in his honor. After the death of Willard Richards in 1854, George A. became Church historian, and, with Wilford Woodruff, he helped complete for publication the history of Joseph Smith. After the death of Heber C. Kimball in 1868, Elder Smith became first counselor to Brigham Young in the First Presidency, an office he held until he died in 1875.

A talented recorder, scribe, and clerk, Willard Richards became Joseph Smith's assistant in Nauvoo, keeping the Prophet's journal, assisting with his history, and drafting his correspondence. He went with Joseph Smith to Carthage in June 1844 and was the only companion not wounded when the mob stormed the jail. After the Prophet's murder, Elder Richards continued as clerk and Church historian, drafting many official communications of Brigham Young and the Quorum of the Twelve. When the First Presidency was reorganized in 1847, Willard Richards was named as second counselor to Brigham Young, which office he filled until his death in 1854.

Appendix A

"THE FIELD IS WHITE ALREADY TO HARVEST"

By Malcolm R. Thorp

Authors' note: We invited Malcolm R. Thorp, professor of history at Brigham Young University, to write this essay because of his special expertise in British social and religious history. We appreciate his willingness to do so and his thorough, interesting, and scholarly treatment of the subject. Understanding the religious traditions and the religious groups from which the early Latter-day Saints converts came is extremely valuable to understanding those converts themselves and what may have helped attract them to Mormonism. It is also important, we feel, for Latter-day Saints to appreciate how the Spirit may have been operating over many years and in diverse ways to prepare the people for the message of the Restoration when it came. In addition, we see as highly significant the comparisons of the social and economic status of the Mormons with those of the members of other churches.

"For behold, the field is white already to harvest" is the best-known metaphor in Latter-day Saint scripture describing a society ready to receive the gospel.[1] Many people in Britain were indeed ripe for the harvest not only during the years of the apostolic mission but for many years thereafter, and between 1837 and 1852 the total number of conversions reached 57,000.[2] As one historian commented, the Mormons reaped the "most spectacular harvest of souls since [John] Wesley's time."[3] So impressive was Latter-day Saint growth that Horace Mann, editor of the official British religious census for 1851, remarked that the "Mormonite" movement (as

---

[1]D&C 4:4. This metaphor is used six more times in the Doctrine and Covenants and it is always used as a message to missionaries, along with the injunction to thrust in their sickles and reap. Cf. John 4:35.

[2]Evans, *Century of "Mormonism,"* 244.

[3]Armytage, *Heavens Below*, 260.

it was frequently called) represented a "New Mohammedanism" on the religious scene.

The field was white because ground was prepared and seeds were planted and nurtured long before the missionary-apostles arrived. Changing political, economic, and social conditions contributed toward creating an environment conducive to Mormon missionary work. So, too, did the religious circumstances of the times, and all these elements intertwined to help create definable social and religious groups, or what has been called an "external constituency," among which the remarkable Mormon harvest occurred.[4] In this essay we attempt to identify and explore just what groups, especially religious groups, Latter-day Saint converts came from. We will also see how conversions were related to favorable conditions in society that allowed for open proselyting.

POLITICS, NONCONFORMITY, AND THE ESTABLISHED CHURCH

When Heber C. Kimball and his companions began their missionary work in Preston in 1837, they experienced their first glimpses of the new industrial society in Britain and became aware of the process of political change as the country was making the transition from the reign of William IV to that of Victoria. No doubt they also learned of the unpopular image of monarchy. The reputations of the two previous kings were tarnished in the popular mind by their social and political conservativism as well as by images of needless extravagance and moral laxity, and at Victoria's accession the popularity of monarchy was at its lowest ebb. To many, who saw it as a bastion of privilege and archconservativism in a country crying for social and political change, monarchy was irrelevant to the common people. There was even a strong republican tradition actively soliciting support for the abolition of this ancient institution. Both Heber C. Kimball and Wilford Woodruff commented, at the occasion of a royal procession, on the extravagance of the pageantry in a country with so much economic distress.

The first Mormon missionaries arrived in Preston at the beginning of a parliamentary election made necessary by the accession of the new queen. This was one of the first elections since the 1832 Reform Bill, a measure

---

[4] "A church does not recruit the whole population of a country, but only that external constituency disposed toward membership of it," say sociologists of religion. Currie, Gilbert, and Horsley, *Churches and Church Goers*, 64.

that gave the upper middle class men the right to vote. In a town such as Preston this class comprised the prosperous cotton manufacturers, the wealthier shopkeepers, and the professional classes. Because a man had to own real property worth £10 in order to vote, however, the bill increased the electoral list by only 1 percent, or sixty-one voters. Most Preston citizens still could not vote, and the election of 1837 must have been of only marginal concern to them. Indeed, antipathy for such an exclusive political establishment helped stoke Chartist political dissent in Preston. Most political questions of the early Victorian period had religious implications, and the connection between Chartism and popular evangelism can be seen in the lines of one of the most famous Chartist hymns, "Jesus Christ was the first Chartist."[5]

Some have asserted that Mormon success was related to the collapse of such popular political movements as the Chartists, a "reflex of despair" triggered by despondency over failures, but there is little evidence to support such a conclusion. The apostles' mission was to the working people, and though a smattering of former Chartists, such as John Freeman, joined the LDS church,[6] there is a paucity of reflections on political concerns in early Mormon journals, letters, and reminiscences. There are occasional recollections of trade union activities and complaints about low wages and hard times, but there is virtually nothing in these sources that indicates a significant pattern of political involvement.

More important was the economic depression of the late 1830s and early 1840s, a hardship on the common people that produced religious conditions that contributed to LDS successes. Studies of the evangelical Nonconformist congregations[7] (Protestant groups that did not conform to

---

[5]Gash, *Aristocracy and People*, 202. The best study on the religious and anti-clerical elements in Chartism is Yeo, "Christianity."

[6]Freeman, Journal.

[7]Evangelicalism was a nondenominational movement that permeated the Established Church, as well as Nonconformity. The main tenets of evangelicalism were emphasis on personal salvation and the vital elements of Christianity that led to a change of heart. There was emphasis on good works, especially philanthropic endeavors. Evangelicals tended to be less interested in organizational modes and ecclesiastical politics. The important element within Nonconformity that is significant to this study is the denominations of New Dissent. Churches such as the Methodists, Congregationalists, and Particular and General Baptist denominations emerged out of the religious awakening of the eighteenth century. Especially in the early history of these movements, there were active attempts to appeal to the unconverted masses through camp meetings and street preaching in the new industrial towns and villages. For New Dissent, see Gilbert, *Religion and Society*, 37–39. Gilbert's book is a seminal study that is important for social questions of religion. Perhaps the most comprehensive study of religion is Chadwick, *Victorian Church*. Chadwick, however, writes with little sympathetic understanding for the numerous religious sects, including the Mormons. See pages 436–39.

the Church of England) suggest that these churches were losing members at the same time the Mormon church was experiencing its initial growth.[8] Significantly, the losses came mainly from the working classes, a pattern that accelerated during hard times. Thus the Baptists, Congregationalists, and Methodists were all affected by significant defections of working-class worshipers. By the end of the 1840s evangelical Nonconformity had lost its earlier working-class appeal and was becoming bourgeois, or middle-class, in membership and social outlook.[9]

The Methodists were particularly hard hit by defections into reform movements and into other religious sects that perhaps displayed greater social concern for the plight of the laboring classes. Jabez Bunting, leader of the main body of Methodists, adamantly disassociated that church from secular working-class political movements.[10] Indeed, by the 1830s and 1840s, Methodism had changed its recruiting strategies in such a way that most Methodist denominations no longer made appreciable contact with common people. The mainline Methodist churches, for example, shunned association with the revivalist technique of camp meetings and other forms of popular preaching that in an earlier age had brought them conversions from such occupational groups as miners, iron workers, weavers, skilled artisans, and day laborers in the new industrial towns. At the same time, tension was created between the ministry and the laity as Methodism moved from earlier popular participation in church affairs to ministerial domination over the congregation. The increased professionalization of the ministry combined with diminished opportunities for lay participation further lessened Methodist appeal among the working class.[11]

These institutional changes also led to a splintering of the Methodists into various bodies, the most important of which, for our study, was the Primitive Methodist movement. From its inception around 1806, this splinter group continued the tradition of the popular religious revival.[12] The

---

[8]Ward, *Religion and Society*, 266, 276; Gilbert, *Religion and Society*, 30.

[9]"The pretentiously middle class ethos of the emerging Victorian Nonconformity, the preoccupation with order, respectability, and style, reinforced the external societal pressures cutting Methodist, Congregational, and Baptist communities adrift from the lower sections of the social constituency on which they had relied during the early industrial age. While Walter Wilson had complained early in the nineteenth century that 'large accessions of numbers' had been lowering the social 'quality' of Nonconformity, in 1849 [Edward] Mial was worried about the 'preference of quality over numbers' characteristic of his contemporaries" (Gilbert, *Religion and Society*, 162).

[10]Ingliss, *Churches and the Working Classes*, 16; Davies, George, and Rupp, *Methodist Church* 2:270–71.

[11]Gilbert, *Religion and Society*, 162.

[12]Werner, *Primitive Methodist Connection*.

Primitive Methodists recruited successfully among miners, artisans, factory workers, and farm laborers, and the practice of allowing common people to participate in chapels as lay preachers and group leaders as well as missionaries was a strong attraction. In addition, unlike the more middle-class Methodist denominations, the "Ranters," as they were commonly called, often demonstrated sympathy for radical political movements and other forms of social protest. With beliefs in witches, "physical manifestations of the Devil, miraculous healings and special providences," Primitive Methodism also fit better, ideologically, into the prevailing common culture.[13]

Both obvious differences and important similarities between Primitive Methodist beliefs and those of the Latter-day Saints help account for the rivalry that developed between them. The similarities, especially the appeal of both churches to biblical primitivism (i.e., the idea that they were teaching the same gospel as the primitive Christian church), help explain the significant number of conversions to the Latter-day Saints during the early years of Mormon activity in Britain.[14] Indeed, many who emerged as local LDS leaders were formerly Primitive Methodist preachers.

Recognizing that the Mormon missionaries were formidable rivals with a message that likewise had popular appeal, Primitive Methodist clergy took a conspicuous part in the various anti-Mormon disturbances during this pèriod. Fear of losing "sheep" motivated such activities, for the ministers knew that in the fluid religious environment of the time, converts from earlier religious revivals could turn to new religious experiences as quickly as they had embraced the old.

While the denominations of evangelical nonconformity were increasingly narrowing their social appeal, the established church was attempting to widen its influence. But the Church of England faced image problems. Until as recently as 1828 it was allied with the state in trying to preserve political and social values and to curb the influence of nonconformity. By the 1830s, however, the secular state had turned on its erstwhile ally, and there were several attempts through parliamentary commissions to bring about far-reaching administrative reforms within the church.[15] That was only the beginning of a long political battle over church reform — a struggle that resulted in the diminution of Anglican influence. "Gradual disestablish-

[13]McLeod, Religion and the Working Class, 27; Obelkevich, Religion and Rural Society.
[14]Phillips, Sectarian Spirit, 53.
[15]Thompson, Bureaucracy, 26–55.

ment" was a long process that stretched beyond Victorian Britain. But in the 1830s alone, the Church of England's power was curbed by parliamentary statutes that secularized the registration of vital statistics and legally recognized nonconformist marriages.[16]

The established church eventually awakened to the realities of the new industrial society. By the late 1830s it demonstrated a renewed vitality by building new parish churches in the industrialized cities and expanding educational facilities throughout the country.[17] Despite this new vibrancy, however, the social conservativism of the clergy continued to be a barrier to popular appeal. The bishops were vocal opponents of political change during the debates over the Reform Bill of 1832, a point repeatedly emphasized by radicals. The church in the 1830s was in the process of losing the heated battle over the payment of church rates, an obligation often imposed on non-Anglicans in many local communities.[18] There was likewise much complaint about the system of pew rents in the local parish church.

Working-class criticisms of the established church continued to be commonplace. One newspaper, for example, blamed Mormon successes in the West Midlands in the early 1840s on the negligence of the Bishop of Gloucester and his "tithe-fattened clergy."[19] An early Mormon convert, John Spiers, said that he left the established church because of the "character of her ministers [rather] than her doctrines."[20] William Lang, a young farm laborer who joined the Latter-day Saints, asserted that he had attended the Anglican Church "about as much for fashion or form as anything else," but when he first heard a Mormon elder preach, he reflected: "What a contrast! instead of long robed Gentleman preaching sprinkling of Infants, Hell and damnation &c I saw a man [who] looked like a farmer in plain attire quoting from the Holy Scriptures and preaching the Gospel of Christ in its ancient purity."[21]

Anticlerical hostility can also be seen in the career of John Simons, vicar of Dymock, Gloucestershire, whose bitter opposition to the Latter-day Saints, ironically, only added to the hostility. In 1840 several of his parishioners joined the LDS faith. Simons was so disturbed by their de-

---

[16]See Gilbert, *Religion and Society*, 163 for a summary of Victorian "disestablishment" legislation.
[17]Norman, *Church and Society*, 123–66.
[18]Ward, *Religion and Society*, 178 and passim.
[19]Joseph Smith, *History of the Church* 4:236.
[20]Whitney, *History of Utah* 4:396.
[21]Lang, Autobiography, 1–2.

fections that he launched a crusade against Mormonism that included the writing of two pamphlets and the organization of local ruffians who "hooted," howled, and threw rocks at missionaries. But because of his alleged neglect of pastoral cares, Simons had problems retaining the loyalty of his parishioners. Upon his death in 1866, one of them wrote a poem in which he mocked the late clergyman's crusading zeal against the Mormons by juxtaposing it with Simons's frequent absenteeism and neglect of the congregation during his years in service.[22] In all fairness, however, Simons's misconduct did not represent the norm. Modern research has dispelled rumors of widespread clerical corruption, and there is evidence of improvement in the clergy's performance throughout the Victorian era.[23] It is also obvious that these changes were too little and too late to ease the popular image of an indifferent clerical establishment that was more concerned with financial remuneration than with the temporal well-being of its flocks.[24]

PREVIOUS RELIGIOUS AFFILIATION

An interesting question relating to Latter-day Saint success in Britain has to do with the previous religious affiliations of early converts. It has been argued that they tended to come from "splinter groups" who had earlier broken away from mainline nonconformist churches,[25] and even though, as demonstrated later, most converts actually came from mainline churches, in the early years of the British Mission some of the most dramatic successes did come from among such small defecting congregations. Heber C. Kimball's first conversions in 1837 came from Reverend James Fielding's Primitive Episcopal church in Preston, which was connected with an obscure religious movement in Bedford headed by his brother-in-law, the Reverend Timothy Matthews.[26] The Mormons were likewise successful in

---

[22][Anonymous], *He is gone* . . . .

[23]Norman, *Church and Society*, 123–66.

[24]Ibid., 135–36. Norman's defense of the clerical establishment, however, does not fully explain the widespread criticism that goes beyond the radicals and the intellectuals. For extreme examples of such hostility, see Yeo, "Christianity," 123–37.

[25]P. Taylor, *Expectations Westward*, 37–38.

[26]The Reverend James Fielding came from a Methodist background in St. Neats, Huntingtonshire. He was a local businessman until he was persuaded by his brother-in-law, the Reverend Timothy Matthews, to go to Preston and establish a Primitive Episcopal congregation. See Fielding, Diary, 88. For a recent discussion that fundamentally alters the traditional story found in LDS accounts concerning Fielding's church in Preston and its connection with Matthews's Primitive Episcopal Church in Bedford, see Thorp, "Early Mormon Confrontations."

converting a number of Primitive Methodists from the Preston chapels on Vauxhall and Laurel streets as well as in the nearby town of Longton.[27] Joseph Beecroft, a convert from Bradford, Yorkshire, recorded that prior to his joining Mormonism he had belonged to the Methodist New Connection but had then followed his minister into a "new society."[28]

At Bedford, the early missionary successes occurred in the church of the Reverend Timothy Matthews, who had earlier separated from the Church of England and taught such doctrines as the restoration of spiritual gifts and premillennialism.[29] Other such groups represented in the previous religious backgrounds of Mormons include the Wroites, Irvingites, and Swedenborgians, although these groups were not as prominent as splinter Methodist sects.[30]

The Aitkenites, or the New Christian Society, constituted another splinter group of some significance to early Mormon successes. Founded by Robert Aitken in the 1830s, this group had churches in many of the major towns of the north, including Liverpool, Manchester, and the Staffordshire Potteries. In 1823 Aitken was a deacon in the Church of England, but he became dissatisfied with the established church's position on ecclesiastical polity. He was strongly influenced by Methodism and its emphasis on individual conversion, but he was denied entrance into the Methodist ministry. He then founded his own movement and soon attracted a considerable following. Through his ministerial charisma, Aitken became one of the most popular revivalist preachers of the 1830s. Thomas Whittaker, an important "teetotal" preacher, averred that Aitken was the most powerful preacher he ever heard.[31] Even Wilford Woodruff, who usually had little positive to say about ministers, was impressed by the power of Aitken's

[27]Phillips, *Sectarian Spirit*, 49.

[28]Beecroft, Journal, 2–3.

[29]Whitney, *Life of Heber C. Kimball*, 148; Thorp, "Early Mormon Confrontations," 51–54.

[30]The Wroites were followers of the millenarian prophet, John Wroe, who claimed heavenly revelations concerning the restoration of Israel and organized his followers according to Judaic customs, including breakdown into Twelve Tribes. They formed a community in Ashton-under-Lyne in the Potteries. A group from this community evidently joined the Mormons. See Harrison, *The Second Coming*, 138–60. The Swedenborgians originated from the eighteenth-century teachings of Emanuel Swedenborg (1688–1772), who was convinced of fresh revelations coming to him from Jesus Christ. The Swedenborgians were known as the New Church, and they had small congregations scattered throughout the northern industrial towns. Like the Mormons, they preached teetotalism and health codes. The Irvingites were of a higher social class than the Mormons, but they had many similar theological doctrines, especially the emphasis on spiritual gifts (including prophecy), the coming millennium, and the need for a modern group of twelve apostles. Their liturgical practices, based on primitivism, were of special significance and were often emulated. For comparison with Mormonism, see Lively, "Catholic Apostolic Church."

[31]Whittaker, *Life's Battles*, 245.

sermons delivered to overflowing crowds at Zion's Chapel, Waterloo Road, in London.[32]

Aitken's theology was an eclectic synthesis of ideas borrowed from the Methodists and the Church of England (especially the Tractarians). His ideas on personal salvation were similar to those in Methodism, but his notions of sacramental authority were in accordance with the Anglican High Church tradition. Aitken also preached temperance and the doctrine of the millennium. Alfred Cordon, an early convert who became president of the Staffordshire Conference, belonged to the Aitkenites before joining the Latter-day Saints, and it was he who converted a number of Aitkenites in Doncaster, Yorkshire.[33] Heber Kimball noted that after such successes among the Aitkenites there was

considerable ill feeling and opposition among the ministers belonging to that sect.

Having lost quite a number, and seeing that many more were on the eve of being baptized, one of the ministers [Robert Aitken] came to Preston and announced that he was going to put down "Mormonism," expose the doctrines and overthrow the Book of Mormon.[34]

In 1840, however, Aitken became disenchanted with his own religious society and he returned to the Church of England, accepting a vicarage in Cornwall.[35]

The most spectacular success among the defecting Methodist sects was Wilford Woodruff's conversion of United Brethren in the rural regions around Ledbury, Herefordshire, in the spring of 1840. Under the leadership of a dynamic Primitive Methodist circuit preacher, Thomas Kington, the group had separated from Methodism, probably in late 1832.[36] Kington

---

[32]Woodruff records: "Mr. Akens said in his sermon that the gentiles with all their present glory would soon be glad to take hold of the skirt of a Jew & say let us go with you. He also says that most are ignorant of the meaning & fulfillment of the Bible & will remain so untill it is revealed by the spirit of God. But notwithstanding Mr Akins has sum sublime truths yet he is building a great house without any foundation by rejecting the first principles of the gospel." That evening Woodruff returned to hear Aitken preach a second sermon: "He presented some of the most sublime truths that I ever herd delivered by a sectarian priest. Also he whiped the present religionist of the day at a tremendous rate. He said they would go to Hell as a body for their religion was ownly a cloke to cover adulterers and evry evil work. He said the judgments of God would spedily overtake them. . . . He wept over the present state of things" (Woodruff, *Journal*, August 23, 1840, 1:498).

[33]Alfred Cordon to Parley P. Pratt, December 2, 1841, *Millennial Star* 2 (December 1841): 126.

[34]Kimball, *Journal*, 38; Whitney, *Life of Heber C. Kimball*, 163–64.

[35]*The Dictionary of National Biography* 1:206.

[36]Great Britain. Register General's Office [London]. RG 31/2, Places of Religious Worship, Returns, Vol. 2. On December 12, 1832, the house occupied by John Benbow at Castle Froome was licensed, as well as that of Thomas Clark (who also became a prominent United Brethren preacher) at Bromyard. (Hereford

taught that the dead weight of formal religion was insufficient for salvation, and his favorite text was "except ye repent, ye shall all likewise perish."[37] His successes as a circuit preacher in camp meetings around Froomes Hill, Herefordshire, were recorded in the *Primitive Methodist Magazine*, and the following year an article appeared describing Kington's role in the faith healing of an elderly woman named Sarah Harding.[38] But Kington evidently ran into difficulties with fellow preachers, for he "stirred up his hearers and annoyed the more formal and better paid preachers of that denomination." As a result of this dispute (seemingly over institutional formalities), Kington was expelled.[39] Soon thereafter he was instrumental in forming the United Brethren and became the superintendent of that body. It grew to include thirty-eight meeting places, organized into two circuits, with a membership of about seven hundred believers, mostly recruited from the ranks of the "poor."[40] The church believed in spiritual gifts, and its members were primitive restorationists awaiting divine direction and further religious insight when Wilford Woodruff began his mission in Herefordshire.[41] From Woodruff's journal, it would appear that more than half of the United Brethren Church joined the Mormons, including Kington.[42] The Saints then adopted the intact circuit structure as their own.

During the earliest years of the LDS Church in Britain, chapels of various denominations were often given over to the elders for preaching, the ministers seeing the new religion as but another revivalist movement from America.[43] As the tenets of Mormonism became better known, however, and as sectarian rivalry developed, chapels were closed to the missionaries. Hence, the number of conversions from the various splinter group sects declined, and the Mormons were forced to rely on street

Diocese, #519, #567). On April 19, 1833, Kington licensed houses at Brooms Green and Dymock for worship. (Diocese of Gloucester, p. 26. See also pp. 27 and 29 for other houses licensed between 1835–39). The late 1832 date for the organization of the United Brethren fits all the available evidence, although this is only a tentative assertion.

[37]Smith, "United Brethren," 819.

[38]*Primitive Methodist Magazine* (1832): 113; (1833): 64–65.

[39]Smith, "United Brethren," 819. Smith states that the expulsion occurred before 1830, but this does not fit with the above evidence.

[40]"United Brethren Preachers' Plan."

[41]Smith, "United Brethren," 823.

[42]Woodruff, *Journal*, August 2, 1840, 1:488–89. Not all of the converts were United Brethren, for Woodruff asserts that they came from "The Church of England & all other Protestant Churches."

[43]Kimball, *Journal*, 18, 25, 34–35. For the American influence on revivalism in Britain, see Thistlewaite, *Anglo-American Connection*; Cardwardine, *Trans-Atlantic Revivalism*; Wilson, "American Religion."

Table I
Last Prior Religious Affiliation
of 280 Mormon Converts

	Total	%
Methodist	70	25.0
Church of England	58	20.7
Religiously Inclined but Not Specifically Affiliated	41	14.6
"Splinter Groups" and Other Minor Sects	36	12.9
Baptists	31	11.1
Primitive Methodists	31	11.1
Independents	17	6.1
Presbyterians	13	4.6
Not Religiously Inclined	4	1.4
Infidels	3	1.1
Catholics	2	0.1
Teetotallers	2	0.1
Total	280	100

meetings and occasional camp meetings, where there was a wider religious spectrum present. This change in missionary approach undoubtedly brought the Saints into visible contact with more people from the mainline religious movements, and the religious backgrounds of converts tended to reflect the new missionary tactics.

The most comprehensive study yet of the religious backgrounds of Mormon converts between 1837 and 1852 used 280 diaries, journals, reminiscences, and family histories to determine prior religious affiliations.[44] It was found (see Table I) that the converts tended to come from such major religious denominations as the Methodists, the Church of England, and the congregations of Old Dissent (Presbyterians, Baptists, and Independents).

Many early Mormon converts were religious seekers, that is, individuals who drifted from one denomination to another while searching for absolute authority and for teachings that conformed to their interpretations of the Bible. Of the 280 converts studied, 104, or nearly 37 percent, clearly were in that category.[45] But because many were vague in their descriptions of previous religious life, it appears likely that 40 percent or more had been seekers before conversion. Some belonged to six or more religious bodies before joining the LDS Church.

The experience of William Lee, who joined the Saints at West Bromwich in 1846, is typical. As a small boy, Lee was apprenticed to a tinsmith at

---

[44]Thorp, "Religious Backgrounds."
[45]Ibid., 54.

Stourport but, upon completion of the apprenticeship, he moved to West Bromwich and worked in the glass-blowing trade. He attended Sunday school because his father could not send him to day school. At age fourteen William became affiliated with the Methodists, and when he was seventeen he was appointed a local preacher. He later recorded that "great numbers came to hear me." Soon, however, he became dissatisfied with the Methodists and went from one church to another in his search for truth. "In reading the New Testament," he stated, "I perceived the doctrine of Methodists was not in accordance with the teachings of Jesus Christ and his Apostles. Neither in all my search amongst other sects could I find any who taught the true principals of the Gospel." Lee was evidently searching for a pattern of authority that conformed with his interpretation of the scriptures, for he was impressed with the Catholic doctrine of apostolic succession and was about to join that church when he found a copy of Parley P. Pratt's influential pamphlet, *Voice of Warning*. He later recalled the impression it had on him: "I read the book with much interest. It was a source of light. It was the very thing I was so anxious to find." He then sought out the Saints. "It was noised abroad that an Apostle of the Church of Jesus Christ of Latter Day Saints was in town. This startled me. For I had not learned that Apostles lived in our day." "The first sermon he [William Lee] heard was preached by . . . John Taylor, the text being Revelation, Chap 14, verse 6 'and I saw another angel etc.' This made such an impression."[46]

The experience of Thomas Day is also instructive because of his experience as a seeker and also for what it reveals about his working-class background. He was born in 1814 at Epnoll Lane, near Wolverhampton. As a young boy, he worked for a "machine company." When Thomas was thirteen his father died, and Thomas helped his mother and three young sisters on a meager wage of four shillings per week, though he soon improved his economic condition by moving to Kidiminster, where he worked in a carpet factory. But the factory owner reduced the workers' wages, precipitating a sixteen-week strike. "At the end of this time, the men returned to work reduced to dire poverty and completely conquered." On another occasion, he worked in the "rope-yards" from three in the morning until late at night. He then moved to Bronsgrove, where he found employment in a button factory and later in a needle factory.

Before moving to Bronsgrove, Day led a life similar to that of most

---

[46]Lee, Diary.

men of his class: he was not affiliated with any denomination, and he probably was not religiously inclined. But then a crisis occurred in his life. "While in Bronsgrove . . . I had taken a turn for a rather wayward life and wild companions," he later recalled. One evening, when he was detained at home, his companions were involved in some prankish mischief that ended in their being sent to prison. "I began to think, deserted my rude companions, forsook whiskey and tobacco entirely and searched among the different religions for something on which to pin my faith." In 1833 he joined the "Arminian Methodists" and soon rose to the position of exhorter and, later, local preacher. When he left that group he became a Primitive Methodist local preacher. In 1838 he changed Methodist denominations yet again, this time becoming an Association Methodist. For four years he was a class leader, but all that time he was disturbed by the disorders in meeting "which they have not the means of preventing." At that point Thomas heard the Mormon elders. He was impressed by "simplicity and unassuming manners and the authority and assurance with which they spoke together with the Plainness in which they proved their principles from the Bible." Despite his favorable initial impression, he still worried that the Saints might only be deceiving the people, and it was some time (September 1842) before he joined them.[47]

As one commentator on Victorian religion asserted, common people did "not regard public worship as an essential of religion, but only an optional accessory."[48] Early Victorian working people were religious in that they tended to believe in the ethical dimensions of religion, and most undoubtedly thought themselves to be Christian. But without the compulsion that had typified the earlier centuries of British religious life, they generally shunned membership in organized religious institutions.[49] Even those churches that conscientiously lowered social barriers in an effort to attract converts were only marginally successful among the common people. That 58 of the 280 Mormon converts studied (20.7 percent) were formerly Church of England members can be explained in part by the fact that many had been baptized in infancy, but their reminiscences seldom reveal deep commitment to that faith. It seems that Anglicanism was often more a family tradition than a source of spiritual satisfaction.

Only 4 of the 280 Mormon converts studied (1.4 percent) claimed that

---

[47]Day, Journal and Reminiscence.

[48]Thomas Wright, Our New Masters (1873), as quoted in Kent, "Feelings and Festivals," 860.

[49]Ingliss, Churches and the Working Classes, 1–2 and passim.

they were not religiously inclined before baptism, and only 3 (1.1 percent) openly professed secularism as their belief. These statistics suggest that LDS missionaries made little headway with the people "of the world." On the other hand, the number of Saints recruited from the religiously inclined but not institutionally affiliated (41 individuals, or 14.6 percent) suggests that the Latter-day Saint message appealed overwhelmingly to the "churched" Christian population rather than to the "unchurched" majority. Indeed, the archetypical Saint was usually young (sixteen to twenty-four years of age), had a background in either the Anglican or the Methodist denominations (sometimes both), and was most impressed by the "primitive simplicity" (conformity to the New Testament pattern) of the Mormon message as well as gifts of the Spirit that were found in Latter-day Saint meetings.[50] All of this attests to their other-worldly aspirations both before and after baptism.

Of course, beyond all these factors that affected people in their religious choices was a deeply personal element in the conversion experience. Many among the new converts attested, as did John Bennion, that conversion was a matter of right religious reasoning—that the message was "too plain and scriptural for me to reject."[51] For others, conversion accompanied religious experiences. George Morris, for example, borrowed a copy of the Book of Mormon and, he reported, "I had not read far before the spirit of the Lord bore testimony to me that it was the Truth of heaven." Thus convinced, he walked eight miles to Manchester to attend a fast meeting. He discovered in this meeting "the gift of Tongues, the interpretation of Tongues, and the spirit of prophecy was poured out richly upon the Saints and they sang the sweet songs of Zion." Shortly thereafter, on June 28, 1841, he was baptized.[52] Charles Miller, a convert of 1839, wrote of his experience:

> Long had I served the Lord according to the light Enjoyed by all sects, till truth so dencely bright Shone in my precious soul unfolding to my mind Messiahs only plan to save poor lost mankind. I now saw that the way of truth was plain. . . . Long did I halt in mind, but I decided Even while on my knees. Then I was baptized Rejoicing I remember what [William] Clayton was then teaching Being filled with the spirit while he to us was preaching About Christs second coming and Zions happy land.[53]

---

[50]Thorp, "Religious Backgrounds," 63.
[51]Barker, "John Bennion."
[52]Morris, Autobiography.
[53]Miller, Diary.

While doctrinal similarities with other Victorian sects existed, the restored gospel was distinctively different from the dogmas of the Saints' religious past. Conversion accounts reveal, whether through the logic of the "plainness of the truth" or through spiritual manifestations, there was conviction that religious illumination had taken place, allowing the converts to see new patterns of harmony in the scriptures and a new vision of the purpose of life.

RELIGION AND SOCIAL CLASS

That most Latter-day Saint converts came from the working classes is significant because of the relationship between social class and religion in British society.[54] That relationship helped create the "external constituency" prepared to hear the message of the apostles from America.

Most of the early Victorian British converts came from the working class, but, significantly, of the 410 converts in one study, nearly one-third (31.2 percent) were artisans (carpenters, tailors, shoemakers, etc.).[55] (See Table II.) Generally better off than others of the working class, artisans were the most prominent group of common people in the Victorian nonconformist chapels. Conversely, the number of agricultural laborers among the Saints was insignificant, even though as late as 1850 agriculture was still the largest employer in the country. No doubt many of the United Brethren converted by Wilford Woodruff were either farm laborers or craftsmen connected with West Midlands agriculture, but they were not typical of most British converts. Except for Heber C. Kimball in 1837 and Wilford Woodruff in Herefordshire, Mormon missionaries usually did not do well in rural areas, where old traditions and social allegiances remained

---

[54]See chapter 1.

[55]Thorp, "Social and Religious Origins." This study is based on 410 diaries, journals, and other literary sources. The statistical tabulations (pp. 10–12) have been somewhat altered for purposes of this essay. The most complete study of the social composition of Mormonism is that by P. A. M. Taylor, in which he tabulated occupational data of emigrating Saints from ship registers for the years 1841–1869. Taylor's figures reveal that 11.49 percent of the emigrants for this period were middle class, and that over 80 percent were from working-class occupations. Taylor's figures are the best available, and certainly within these broad categories his findings are correct. It must be remembered, though, that while Taylor's sample was 8,491 emigrating Mormons, at least half of the converts who joined the Church stayed behind, either as the remnant of remaining British Saints or as those who eventually left the Church. We might presume that some of the very poor Saints did not have the means to go to America, even with Church programs that provided assistance such as the Perpetual Emigration Fund. Thus, if anything, it would appear that the working-class composition of the Church might have been even slightly higher than indicated by Taylor. One other problem with his figures is that they do not indicate the percentage of Mormons who were skilled artisans. The present study does not significantly modify Taylor's general findings, but it adds some perspectives. See Taylor, *Expectations Westward*, 149–51.

Table II
LDS Occupational Structure

	Total	%
Artisans	128	31.2
Laborers	85	20.7
Shopkeepers and Professionals	41	10.0
Colliers, Miners, etc.	38	9.3
Laborers (farm)	22	5.4
Domestic Servants	14	3.4
Farmers	12	2.9
Merchants and Manufacturers	1	0.02
Other Occupations	69	16.8
Total	410	100.0

strong. Nor were there many converts from the large ranks of Victorian domestic servants—only 14 of 410 converts studied were in this group, and were perhaps as few as 1 percent of all the converts. Farm workers and household servants tended to be dominated by the values of their employers, who may have looked upon conversion to Mormonism as undesirable.

Interesting comparisons can be made between the occupations of the Mormons and those of the members of major British denominations.[56] The Mormons were appreciably lower in social class than any other denomination except the Primitive Methodists. Mormons and Primitive Methodists were roughly similar in social composition, though the Mormons had a slightly higher proportion of shopkeepers. Perhaps more significant is the higher proportion of artisans in the Primitive Methodist Church than among the Latter-day Saints (47.7 percent to 31.2 percent). This proportion suggests that the LDS Church was rather distinctive in its working-class appeal, a factor that becomes even more significant in light of the diminishing appeal of the churches of New Dissent to the common people in the 1840s.

Historians generally agree that industrialism, the movement of populations into the growing cities, the breakdown of paternalism, and the intensification of class antagonisms all contributed in some measure to the creation of early nineteenth-century evangelical nonconformity. These same ingredients may also have contributed something to Mormon missionary successes, as accelerating class antagonisms continued to drive

[56]See Gilbert, *Religion and Society*, 63. Gilbert compiled statistics for a slightly earlier period (1800–37), and the categories in Table II were made to parallel his as closely as possible. It must be observed that this sample is not random in the scientific sense but is based on recorded occupational information from Mormon diaries and journals, as well as compiled biographical materials. This table is meant to be an approximate cross-section that is suggestive rather than definitive.

socially and religiously alienated Christians away from their old congregations and into Mormon meetings. As Hugh McLeod has written about working people of this time, "Conscious of an inferior status in the eyes of his social superiors," individuals would often react against those above them socially by behaving in ways condemned by their superiors. Hence, "If... Nonconformity often represented a middle-class rejection of the politics and cultural values of the gentry, working men frequently signalled their rejection of both upper class and middle class values by Secularism or by simple indifference."[57] Another way of showing alienation would have been to adopt the religion of a group such as the Mormons, a group that was viewed by many social superiors with disdain. Indeed, it was commonly asserted by persons of the middle and upper classes that only the "deluded" and "simple minded" would join such a church as the Latter-day Saints.

If factors such as these helped create interest in Mormonism, they also tested the mettle of those who joined. Fellowship with the Saints was often followed by social ostracism and even dismissal from employment. Robert Campbell, a Mormon missionary, wrote in 1843: "The people here are bound down by their tyrannical employers.... They [the laboring people] are afraid of joining for their work's sake as their masters are much endowed with the Spirit of aristocracy and they have to crouch beneath their opinions as semislaves."[58] The amazing thing about the Mormon converts was that despite such difficulties so many ceased their seeking: at last they had found their permanent religious home.

It was mainly among the working classes, then, that the LDS apostles and their companions thrust in their sickles and reaped their harvest. The message they brought, moreover, could not have appealed more readily to the people among whom they worked. Many religious leaders of the time carefully refrained from criticizing conditions in the new industrial society,[59] but the Mormons boldly characterized that society as "Babylon," rejected deferential social conventions, and decried the maldistribution of

[57]McLeod, "Class, Community and Region," 34–35.

[58]Campbell, Diary, 15–16.

[59]In an earlier study, Paul T. Phillips wrote that Mormons shared with other sect groups the same "withdrawal syndrome": "they made no criticism of the state of industrial society," and they failed to stir up people against the existing order. See Phillips, Sectarian Spirit, 18. The evidence here presented modifies that conclusion.

wealth. Instead of making accommodations with it, they preached the building of Zion in America.[60]

This rejection of the British "Babylon" also applied to many features of working-class popular culture. Latter-day Saints shunned the pub and found much in common with preachers of teetotalism.[61] They looked upon the use of alcoholic beverages as a major cause of social distress, and teetotalism offered a remedy for the alleviation of social misery. Some Church leaders appeared as speakers on the teetotal platform, for the national movement was ecumenical in spirit and did not prohibit Mormons from appearing as lecturers, so long as they confined their remarks to abolition of strong drink.[62] The Saints also rejected some forms of popular dancing as well as "black art magic" (crystal ball gazing), and there is no indication from contemporary sources that the Mormons condoned popular amusements and sporting activities.[63] Church leaders even counseled members against participating in various friendship societies, teaching them instead to live as frugally as possible to save for the goal of emigrating to Zion.

Opposition in Perspective

For decades before the arrival of the first LDS missionaries, the compact between church and state that dominated the eighteenth century was breaking asunder, allowing an almost laissez-faire marketplace for the interchange of religious ideas without fear of legal interference. Landmarks in the breakup of the church-state compact were the repeal of the Five Mile and Conventicle Acts in 1812 and the Test and Corporation Acts in 1828, which eliminated the last remaining disabilities for Protestant Nonconformists. These measures were followed by the Catholic Emancipation Act of 1829, which allowed Catholics the same political freedoms as their Protestant counterparts. In Parliament, from the 1830s onwards, there was little sustained interest in promoting the enforcement of religious dogmas except in the case of atheism. As long as preachers such as Mormon missionaries complied with the law and obtained the required license, there was no state interference.

---

[60]One early convert, James Bywater, for example, stated that after a decade of "the hateful labors of factory life," he saw emigration as the only alternative to "white slavery" in English factories. Valentine, *Trio's Pilgrimage*, 8.

[61]Billington, "Popular Religion," 272 and passim; Whitney, *Life of Heber C. Kimball*, 152.

[62]Harrison, *Drink and the Victorians*, 31.

[63]Miller, Diary, 12.

The removal of legal disabilities was accompanied by a change in the public attitude toward freedom of religion. Although interest in formal concepts of toleration had waned by the 1830s and 1840s, there was a general consensus in favor of making toleration part of ethical Christian practices and a mark of true religion. Such "peace and meekness texts" as "whatsoever ye would that men should do to you, do ye even so unto them" became the norm.[64] There were frequent breaches in this norm, but intolerance never reached the excesses of former times.

The arrival of Mormonism was accompanied by bitter sectarian denunciations of the newcomers, but anti-Mormon writers also acknowledged boundaries to these attacks. One of the first pamphleteers, H. Stevenson, warned Anglicans, dissenters, Primitives, and Wesleyans at Alston that a common enemy had appeared in their midst, "one that aims at the destruction of them all." Yet Stevenson spoke against physical violence:

> I do not mean that the Mormons should be pelted with stones; they should rather be pitied, and prayed for.... I do not mean ... that the Book of Mormon should be committed to the flames, although it richly deserves such a fate; yet I would preserve it as an ill-written novel, and as a monument of human folly.[65]

Thomas Taylor, another anti-Mormon pamphleteer, reminded his readers of the public guarantees of freedom to worship:

> It cannot but afford unspeakable pleasure to every reflecting mind, to consider that we live at a period, and have our existence in a country, where the right of private judgment in matters both of a civil and religious character, is acknowledged and protected by the laws of our land. But while it is the duty of every man to regard these privileges as sacred, and use all constitutional means to ... support them, it is equally incumbent upon him to keep a watchful [eye] upon the cunning craftiness of the unprincipled demagogue, and the impious, self-interested religious impostor, whose energies are exerted to beguile the unsuspecting, and ingratiate himself into the confidence of the credulous, in order to raise his own popularity, and enrich himself at the expense of his dupes.[66]

Although the Mormons were denounced as "vile hypocrites" and deceivers who were engaged in "wicked practices" that were "sufficient to lay half the world in ruins, and to bind the other half in chains," there

---

[64]Henriques, *Religious Toleration*, 268.
[65]Stevenson, *A Lecture on Mormonism*, 31, 27–28.
[66]Taylor, *An Account of the Complete Failure*, 1.

was an underlying recognition of the need to tolerate even the most unacceptable of religious dogmas.[67]

Nevertheless, despite the changes in the civil law and theories of toleration that produced a climate more conducive to freedom of religious expression than ever before, tranquillity was often disturbed by bitter denominational rivalry. In the 1830s and 1840s, for example, political and social questions, including the heated debate over the payment of church rates by non-Anglicans, tended to be fought along denominational lines, creating ill-will among various sects.[68] Often these rivalries produced both verbal and physical abuse. As W. R. Ward has written:

> Uniting in-groups by anathematising out-groups converted social tension into the denominational warfare which formed the main substance of politics in the 'thirties and 'forties; it raised controversy to a deplorable level, and provoked a degree of physical violence now difficult to conceive.[69]

In early Victorian Britain, the habits of public order and obedience to law, virtues often associated with the English character, were not fully developed, and a tradition of violence associated with religious revivals and unpopular movements affected the Mormons as well. At the outset of Heber C. Kimball's mission in Preston, it was necessary for the town corporation to give him police protection. Still, while he experienced modest degrees of opposition from time to time, the first mission to England encountered verbal denunciations rather than physical violence.[70]

The 1840–41 mission also was occasionally marred by sectarian violence.[71] It was not uncommon for the missionaries to be "hooted" and shouted down or for services to be interrupted by showers of stones, rotten eggs, vegetables, and manure. Such incidents were perpetrated with the conscious design of heaping ridicule on the Mormons rather than committing bodily harm, which might have brought in the police. Ridicule was a serious matter of public humiliation in the nineteenth-century community, and such mob actions were meant to unify the community against the outsider.[72]

There is little evidence that early Mormon persecutions in Britain,

---

[67]Palmer, *External Evidence*, 27.

[68]Ward, *Religion and Society*, 177–92.

[69]Ibid., 3–4.

[70]Kimball frequently complained of "opposition," but his journal does not reveal incidence of violence. See Kimball, *Journal*, 27–47.

[71]Thorp, "Sectarian Violence."

[72]Storch, " 'Please to Remember,' " 83.

unlike those in America, were ever intended to go beyond public humiliation. Yet, occasionally, mob activities posed danger to both the victims and the perpetrators. In January 1842, for example, attempts to shout down the Mormon elders at Lightwood Green, Shropshire, led to a fistfight in which a Brother Richard Ashley was struck in the mouth and "4 or 5" of the anti-Mormons had to be physically removed from the Saints' meetinghouse. In retaliation for this setback, an angry mob surrounded the building and threw stones (one of which, hurled through the window, injured a sister). The mob then attempted to beat down the door with sticks. The severity of the situation prompted Joseph Horton, a sympathetic non-Mormon, to fire a loaded gun over the heads of the angry crowd as a warning. This action had its desired effect and the mob withdrew. But, Elder Charles Smith reported, that did not end the harassment, for the Saints' meetings in this region were constantly disturbed by mob actions.[73]

Despite sporadic hostilities, however, there were few recorded instances of serious injuries or loss of life during the early years of the LDS Church in Britain.[74] Mob violence was not an unusual phenomenon for revivalist preachers of the period, and the experiences encountered by the Mormons were similar to those of the Primitive Methodists, Bible Christians, and even teetotal preachers.[75] Nor were they as severe as the anti-Mormon activities a decade later (1854–57), when sectarian opposition created a series of violent disturbances in Birmingham, Bath, Bristol, and other towns in the West Midlands.[76] The missionaries were free to preach the gospel without interference and to travel into remote country regions successfully without purse or scrip. A tradition of public debate on religion allowed for the interchange of religious information and required listeners to remain silent until the message had been delivered, at which time they were free to make inquiries. Oftentimes rabble-rousers intent on disruption would themselves be shouted down by observers who wanted to hear the message and judge for themselves.

Mormonism's impressive successes attest both to the power of the

---

[73]Charles Smith, Journal, 4–5.

[74]Mary Ann Weston Maughan claimed that her first husband, John Davis, was badly beaten by a mob at Tirely, Gloucestershire, on December 23, 1840, and that he later died of complications that were related to this attack. The evidence that his death was a result of the internal injuries he received on this occasion is complicated and inconclusive. This appears to be, however, the most serious personal injury received during the anti-Mormon hostility of this period. See Maughan, "Journal of Mary Ann Weston Maughan."

[75]Billington, "Popular Religion," 268.

[76]Cotterill, "Midland Saints," 322–31.

message and to the empathy displayed by the missionaries toward the common people. This message, which included a warning to the faithful to withdraw from "Babylon" and the hope that they could help build Zion in a new land, was a powerful motive that provided converts with a vision of the future not to be found in other Victorian sects. As one missionary cogently stated: "Oh! Lord hasten the day when the poor Saints that are faithful shall be gathered home to Zion and delivered from the power of the Tyrant."[77]

---

[77]Haight, Biographical Sketch, 100–101.

SELECTED DOCUMENTS OF THE MISSIONARY APOSTLES

Each of the following documents opens a direct window on the past. Unrehearsed, written amid the exigencies of the moment to communicate with family and friends, each conveys a sense of immediacy that helps recreate a world now gone. For the most part, the writers lacked formal education and refinements; spelling, for example, was often by the ear, not by the book—"creative" by modern standards. The same might be said of grammar and punctuation. Such idiosyncracies, however, do not prevent the letters from communicating across the years; indeed, they help provide an authentic sense of time and place. These missives, selected from a large and rich treasure trove, preserve emotion and drama and illustrate the spirit that accompanied these pioneering missionary-apostles.

Letters for which we have no holograph are reproduced here as they were originally printed in contemporary journals. With minor exceptions we have transcribed all of the documents as faithfully as possible, including retaining original spelling and grammar. We have silently omitted inadvertent repetitions and the author's deletions, except in those few cases where the deleted material conveys useful information. Where the author added material between the lines, we have simply inserted it so that it reads as the writer intended. To improve readability, we have added a minimum of punctuation and paragraphing and have supplied capitalization, where missing, both at the beginning of sentences and for the names of people and places. Terminal dashes have been converted to periods. We have placed in brackets editorial insertions that supply missing or unintelligible text (our best guess about an illegible word). Editorial comments that are not part of the original text are italicized within brackets.

1

ORSON HYDE TO MARINDA HYDE, SEPTEMBER 14, 1837

I labor in the vineyard night and day and the Lord labors with me

Two months after Heber C. Kimball and Orson Hyde arrived on the first apostolic mission to England, Elder Hyde penned the following powerful and tender letter to his wife. It reveals his deep feelings about his calling, his views on his new surroundings, his attitude toward the people he was working with, and his longing for home and family—a fitting introduction to this pivotal mission. Midway through the letter, Elder Hyde filled his large sheet of paper then, because he wanted to say more, he began writing perpendicularly across the lines he had already written. Source: *Elders' Journal* 1 (1838): 19–22.

Preston, Eng. Sept. 14, 1837.

MY DEAR MARINDA: —

I have been and procured a large sheet of paper which will give me ample room to redeem the promise I made to you in a few lines which I addressed to you in Bro. Kimball's letter to his wife. Through the favor of the Lord, I am in good health and spirits, and so are all the brethren. I read your letter with peculiar interest and have but one fault to find, and that is, there was not quite enough of it. I should like to have heard how the brethren are getting along, but I know you could not think of every thing. I never wanted to see you more than I do at this time: But in this I cannot be gratified at present. There are about four thousand and two hundred *long miles* which separate us, and the mighty ocean rolling between. Since I came to this place I have been down by the water side and looked westward over the surface of the deep as far as the eye could extend, fancy painting to my imagination the prospect of catching a glimpse of my native shore through the glass of great desire and intense anxiety, but, alas! the greatness of the distance blasted the prospect, and the fleet and extended imagination returned within its own native borders. Again I looked as the sun was fast reclining in the western sky, leaving his golden beams in the mirror of waters, and descried a proud and lofty billow bending its course towards the shore, as if to say, I have brought tidings from your home, *your* dear native home: But O! how I was disappointed again on seeing this false messenger sink by its own gravity to rise no more. This much is the result of one view of the sea shore.

I labor in the vineyard night and day and the Lord labors with me.

There has been between one and two hundred baptized in this place since we came; and Elder Kimball is now a laboring about 15 miles from this place where he has raised a small church, and I do not know but that it is a large one by this time. The Lord is with him, and he can preach so loud and so fast that the Catholics call him a noisy devil. Bro. Goodson has this day returned from Bedford and says that he left thirteen baptized into the new covenant there, and bro. Richards is left with them. Bro. Goodson will remain in this place with me for a season. Brother Snider has returned from the borders of Scotland where he and bro. Russel went to labor, and Bros. Fielding and Snider left this place yesterday to go out into the country on a mission, and will go from house to house. Bro. Russel has not baptized any as yet but he will soon I think.

Those who have been baptized, are mostly manufacturers and some other mechanics. They know how to do but little else than to spin and weave cotton, and make cambrick, mull and lace, and what they would do in Kirtland or the city "Far West," I cannot say. They are extremely poor, most of them not having a change of clothes decent to be baptized in, but they have open hearts and strong faith. We have taught them nothing about the gathering for they have no means to bring them to America, let alone procuring them a place to live after they get there. We all pay 2 english shillings per week for our lodging which is nearly 50 cents, and then we buy our own provisions at the market and it is cooked for us. The brethren will frequently divide the last loaf with us, and will do all in their power for us. If it had not been for brother Goodson's books, I know not how we should have lived. They are very kind to us where we are, but their circumstances will not allow them to do much for us without pay. I have frequently seen the tender and delicate females with their old pails or baskets in the streets gathering up fresh horse dung with their naked hands, and then go and sell it and get a penny or two's worth of bread for themselves and hungary children. Marinda, how would you like to follow that business? I pray God that such may not be your lot. Tell the brethren if it would be a pleasure to them to see their wives carrying on such or a similar branch of business for a living, to bring them along with them when they come to old England to preach the gospel. Whoever comes here for loaves and fishes will realize their expectations as much as our Kirtland *speculators*.

If brother Joseph never advised correctly before, he *certainly* did when he advised the brethren to leave their women at home. My humble advice is, that if they have any compassion on their wives, let them for God's sake and for their wive's sake leave them at home. It is of no use for any to come into this country to preach the gospel unless they are able to defend it like a man of God. For unless they have a pretty powerful gift, they cannot live. Not so at home, if a preacher has but a small gift there, he can get what he wants to eat &c. because there are none so distressedly poor there and they will keep him over night free, but this is not the custom in this country. The people expect pay for what they do; and in fact, that people who will receive the gospel, are not able to do it without pay. Now if there are any elders or preachers in the church of Latter Day Saints in America who have faith to brook all these difficulties, let them come to Old England. We want them. We must have such men, and we say to them "come over into Macedonia and *help* us." We do believe that Kirtland affords some such men, men who are willing to forsake wife and children for Christ's sake and the gospel's, and look forward for their recompense at the resurrection of the just. It would be altogether better for the brethren to see us before they commence their labors in this country, for we can tell them many things respecting the customs of the people, and the laws of the land respecting preaching the gospel, that will be of great service to them. I understand that brother Pratt has gone East with his wife to spend the winter, and meet some other brethren in N. Y. in May next to come to England: But he had better wait and see us in Kirtland before he starts, or any one else; for we can tell them things that will prove to their advantage and to the advantage of the cause if they will do so. We shall probably sail for N. York about the first of March next, at least some of us, if not all: And we hope to be in Kirtland about the first of May next.

My dear wife, I never wanted to see you more than I do at this time, yet I am glad you are where you are, and that I am where I am. But the time will be when we shall meet again and rejoice before the Lord. I can truly say that I never before preached with that power and Spirit that I have since I come to this place. In fact, I am surprized at myself many times. The priests all fear and tremble and Babel's towers begin to fall. The priests talked of putting me in prison for preaching without a liscence from under this government. I made application to the Clerk of the *peace* for a liscence, but he informed that I could not obtain one until the court of quarter sessions which would be in October. I thought it would not answer for me to be idle until that time, therefore I continue preaching in houses, and in the streets, and on the public grounds, and in the market places, and am liable to be taken & thrust into prison any day when informed against: But the priests dare not really do this for fear of the people, for all men, almost, consider us to be prophets of God. Thus by the power and goodness of God we still continue to preach Jesus Christ and him crucified.

We are now occupying a large and spacious building in town owned by a *general philanthropist*, but does not belong to any church. The place will accommodate towards eight hundred people, and we have it free of charge. The priests have been to him telling him that he was encouraging false doctrine by letting us have the house &c. His reply to them is, "You are at liberty to go and contest the point with them; and if you think their doctrine incorrect, go and expose them.—You shall have your turn in the use of the house:" This shuts their mouths and puts them in rather an awkward position. The people here are quite anxious to build a chappel for themselves by laying aside sixpence a week out of their scanty earnings, but we shall advise them upon this subject to do differently.

We have not said a hard word against the priests since we came here, neither have we spoken against any sect, yet they say all manner of evil against us. The people have discovered this difference between us, and they are most agreeably surprised, and it gives us unbounded influence. We tell them that God has not sent us to judge and condemn another man's servant: But he has sent us to preach the kingdom of God. The short experience that I have had here, causes me to regret that all the elders have not observed the same course. I am *quite* satisfied that the *great* and *frequent* anathemas pronounced by many of our elders upon people who do not believe their testimony, are not by the Spirit of God: neither do I think it wisdom to be clubing the sects always: but let them alone, and preach Jesus Christ.

My dear wife:

I take the liberty to write a few more words across the lines which I hope you will be able to read: I feel that I have given myself wholy to the Lord and to the work of the ministry. I feel that I am far from home and no arm to lean upon but the arm of the Almighty. In him do I put my trust; and to him do I look for every blessing that I need. I know that in me there is no goodness, that is, in my flesh, For when I view my past course, I am ready to say, O Lord deliver thy servant from vanity—Cleanse

349

his heart from all unholy desires. Let the virtue of thy blood wash him and make him fit for an inheritance with the Saints in light. Let him be sanctified, a vesel of honor to bare glad tidings to those who sit in darkness, and call upon poor wandering prodigals to return to their father's house. Give him prosperity in the promulgation of thy words; and let the enemies of the cross be confounded and put to shame before the sublimity and power of his arguments. Let him raise the standard of the cross in every land and nation where he shall go; and let the simple and broken hearted flock unto it and rejoice beneath its heavenly banner. Before the light which he shall hold forth, let error, ignorance, and superstition fall like Dagon before the ark of God, or flee like the shades of night before the rising glory of the king of day. Let his heart become the storehouse of charity and good will to men, and his body the temple of the Holy Ghost. Let his tongue be armed with truth supplied from the rich and flowing fountain of the heart.

O Lord, remember the partner of all my joys and sorrows; and when she reads this epistle from her dear and affectionate husband, Bless, O bless her with the same love and joy that now inspire my bosom. Let her enjoy health of body and peace of mind. When she is sick, do thou heal her: When she is cast down, do thou raise her up. When she is sorrowful do thou comfort her, when the tear of deep affection steels down her cheeks, do thou cheer her mind with the prospect of once more seeing the object of her earthly hopes; and with open arms embracing her nearest and dearest friend. And now O Lord, have thou respect unto the little babe which thou hast given us. Take it not from us, but let it remain as a source of comfort unto its parents. Give her health and prosperity and may she grow like thine own plants and let the blessings of heaven rest upon her. Let the babe and her mother be faithfully preserved until thy servant shall return to his home. Let these, the humble petitions of thy servant be answered, for I ask them in the name of Jesus Christ thy Son, Amen.

> Now farewell for a little season
> Until I come and bring a reason,
> Why I left my all behind,
> To go and warn all mankind.
>
> For lo! the time is drawing nigh,
> When Christ will take us up on high;

No more to part, no more to sorrow,
The time is nigh 'twill be *tomorrow*.

I am as ever your
affectionate husband
ORSON HYDE.

MARINDA HYDE.

2

THE PROPHET'S ADDRESS TO THE TWELVE, JULY 2, 1839

And let the Twelve be humble

During the summer of 1839, as they were trying to settle their families and at the same time prepare for their mission, the Twelve received many instructions from the Prophet Joseph Smith. On the afternoon of Tuesday, July 2, a particularly important meeting was held in which Joseph gave pointed advice to the Twelve and other missionaries respecting the attitudes they should have and how they should behave. We here reproduce those timeless instructions as they appear in Joseph Smith's *History*, though that entry is based largely on Wilford Woodruff's journal and the last paragraph is based on Willard Richards's "Pocket Companion." This is an exception to our general policy but since there is no original from Joseph Smith himself, we reproduce the best edited version. Source: Joseph Smith, *History of the Church*, 3:383–85. Cf. Wilford Woodruff, *Journal*, July 2, 1839, 1:342–44. See also Ehat and Cook, *The Words of Joseph Smith*, 6–8, 17, 413–14.

[Wilford Woodruff began his diary account with this preface: "Then Joseph arose & presented some precious things of the kingdom unto us in the power of the Holy Ghost, yea precious principles that ought to be engraven upon our hearts & practiced in our lives, some of which are as follows":]

Ever keep in exercise the principle of mercy, and be ready to forgive our brother on the first intimations of repentance, and asking forgiveness; and should we even forgive our brother, or even our enemy, before he repent or ask forgiveness, our heavenly Father would be equally as merciful unto us.

Again, let the Twelve and all Saints be willing to confess all their sins, and not keep back a part; and let the Twelve be humble, and not be exalted, and beware of pride, and not seek to excel one above another, but act for each other's good, and pray for one another, and honor our brother or make honorable mention of his name, and not backbite and devour our

351

brother. Why will not man learn wisdom by precept at this late age of the world, when we have such a cloud of witnesses and examples before us, and not be obliged to learn by sad experience everything we know? Must the new ones that are chosen to fill the places of those that are fallen, of the quorum of the Twelve, begin to exalt themselves, until they exalt themselves so high that they will soon tumble over and have a great fall, and go wallowing through the mud and mire and darkness, Judas like, to the buffetings of Satan, as several of the quorum have done, or will they learn wisdom and be wise? O God! give them wisdom, and keep them humble, I pray.

When the Twelve or any other witnesses stand before the congregations of the earth, and they preach in the power and demonstration of the Spirit of God, and the people are astonished and confounded at the doctrine, and say, "That man has preached a powerful discourse, a great sermon," then let that man or those men take care that they do not ascribe the glory unto themselves, but be careful that they are humble, and ascribe the praise and glory to God and the Lamb; for it is by the power of the Holy Priesthood and the Holy Ghost that they have power thus to speak. What art thou, O man, but dust? And from whom receivest thou thy power and blessings, but from God?

Then, O ye Twelve! notice this *Key,* and be wise for Christ's sake, and your own soul's sake. Ye are not sent out to be taught, but to teach. Let every word be seasoned with grace. Be vigilant; be sober. It is a day of warning, and not of many words. Act honestly before God and man. Beware of Gentile sophistry; such as bowing and scraping unto men in whom you have no confidence. Be honest, open, and frank in all your intercourse with mankind.

O ye Twelve! and all Saints! profit by this important *Key* — that in all your trials, troubles, temptations, afflictions, bonds, imprisonments and death, see to it, that you do not betray heaven; that you do not betray Jesus Christ; that you do not betray the brethren; that you do not betray the revelations of God, whether in the Bible, Book of Mormon, or Doctrine and Covenants, or any other that ever was or ever will be given and revealed unto man in this world or that which is to come. Yea, in all your kicking and flounderings, see to it that you do not this thing, lest innocent blood be found upon your skirts, and you go down to hell. All other sins are not to be compared to sinning against the Holy Ghost, and proving a traitor to the brethren.

I will give you one of the *Keys* of the mysteries of the Kingdom. It is an eternal principle, that has existed with God from all eternity: That man who rises up to condemn others, finding fault with the Church, saying that they are out of the way, while he himself is righteous, then know assuredly, that that man is in the high road to apostasy; and if he does not repent, will apostatize, as God lives. The principle is as correct as the one that Jesus put forth in saying that he who seeketh a sign is an adulterous person; and that principle is eternal, undeviating, and firm as the pillars of heaven; for whenever you see a man seeking after a sign, you may set it down that he is an adulterous man.

3

JOHN TAYLOR TO LEONORA TAYLOR, SEPTEMBER 19, 1839

If he took me I felt that it would be well. He has spared me, & it is better

When the apostles left Commerce, soon to be Nauvoo, Illinois, most were ill and penniless, making their overland journey to New York City one of the most difficult times of their entire mission. Here, describing a portion of his trip, John Taylor reveals his hardships, his faith, and his deep concern for his family (see photograph, p. 69). Source: John Taylor Collection, Church Archives. Previously published in Ronald K. Esplin, ed., "Sickness and Faith, Nauvoo Letters," *BYU Studies* 15 (Summer 1975): 431–33.

Germantown Ia Sept
19, 1839

My George   MY DEAR NORA   My Mary Ann
      My Joseph

To you may grace be added   and peace from God
our Father & from Our   Lord Jesus Christ Amen

I thank my heavenly Father through our Lord Jesus Christ that I have this oppertunity of addressing you. When I last wrote to you I did not know what was laying before me. You will probably recollect me remarking that I had a slight indisposition. That was a cold which seated in my bones & brought on a violent fever which nearly terminated my existence.

The next day after I wrote the letter I felt very unwell & went to bed as soon as we got to the Tavern that night & took a sweat. We started off early next morning & travelled 14 or 15 miles before breakfast when we stayed I felt unwell & before we started again I fainted away. I however

353

soon recovered & travelled 40 miles that day. In the Evening we got into the neighborhood where we lived in Indianna. (I called upon Esqr. Jenkins saw Dr. Wilson who was very freindly & Mrs. Zimmerman. She is strong in the faith & wanted your address. I gave it to her. She said that she would write. I also saw Eatons people who were glad to see me. I am told they are now doing well & bear a good character. I also saw Mr. Hoffman who was glad to see me. He is living in the house that we did. I did not see Br. Anderson, but am told that he is doing well & preaching around the country.) That night I stayed at Mr. Combs. They were glad to see me & treated us well. I felt middling well & stayed talking with them till ten O Clock at night. I went to bed but took no rest. I was not in pain but my nervous system was in some way affected so that it deprived me of rest.

Next morning I partook very hearty of milk which I think curdled on my stomach. I had not gone above two or three miles before I was very ill. The waggon had to stay near Indianapolis. I got out about a mile on this side & told them to drive on & I would come up. When I got out of the waggon, I was very sick, vomited but with extreme difficulty. I then after some time made out to stagger on to the waggon, & when I got there I fainted away in the road. I took something to refresh me & drove on through Indianapolis about two miles & could go no further. I got onto a bed in a house & had a raging fever & a bilious affection at the same time. Father Coltron learned we were not far from Br. Eldredge, he who wanted me to go into that neighborhood when we lived at Mr. Millers. He gave me a lobelia emetic & I t[ook] medicine by wholesale for near two hours. It produced however a beneficial effect. I purged, vomited & prespired violently & felt myself better but weak in the morning &, as Father Coltron was in a hurry to proceed I started with him next morning & we travelled 40 miles that day but I found it was too much for me. I got no sleep at night & next morning soon after we started, I thought I should have died. I again fainted away. We travelled about 12 miles & I could go no further so we stayed at a tavern. They waited a day & a half for me. When I saw that there was no prospect of me continuing my journey, I told them that they had better proceed. They did so.

I have a very good Tavern to stay at. The Landlord & Landlady treated me as their own. I placed myself under the care of a Docter who did all that he could for me & now, near three weeks after my arrival, I have got clear of my fever & am fast recovering. I[t] brought me however to the gates of death. Several times. It laid hold of me like a strong man armed

& I was led to quail beneath the power of the adversary, for I believe his hand was in it.

You may ask me how I am going to prosecute my journey, with my trunk a distance of 300 miles or upwards by land, without means. I do not know but one thing I do know, that there is a being who clothes the lillies of the valley & feeds the ravens & he has given me to understand that all these things shall be added & that is all I want to know. He laid me on a bed of sickness & I was satisfied, he has raised me from it again & I am thankful. He stopped me on my road & I am content. When my way is open to proceed I shall go on my way rejoicing. If he took me I felt that it would be well. He has spared me, & it is better. The Lord does all things well. Bless his holy name Oh my soul & forget not all his mercies.

I left $4 worth of papers for Br. Eldridge to sell. He will let you have the amount of it in boots or shoes. You can tell him that I did not get anything from Father Colt[on] [*illegible word*] shall I as he is gone on perhaps Br. Eldridge may be there when this reaches you. You can tell him what I say if you see him. When you write if anything particular has taken place in the church let me know. Tell who of the twelve have started &c. If this reaches you in a week from this date send me a few lines directed to Daton Ohio. If I get them well, if not they will do no hurt.

I am as ever your Affectionate husband

John Taylor

A little letter to my Son George

George your Father has been sick but God has made him well. Your Father prays for you that you may not be sick. George be a good boy. Do what your Mother tells you & God will love you & I will love you & your Mother Amen.

John Taylor

A little letter to my Daughter

Mary Ann

Mary Ann the Lord has healed your Father from being sick. your Father prayes that you & your mother & Baby may not be sick. Mary Ann do not leave your Mother when she tells you to stay at home. Be a good girl. God Bless you Amen.

John Taylor

[*Written between the above letters:*]
A kiss for Joseph & Mother

[*Written on the margin:*] You can write to Daton. If I get it well if not there is no harm done but I shall expect a letter at New York.

4

VILATE KIMBALL TO HEBER C. KIMBALL,
SEPTEMBER 21, 1839

I have got a trial of my faith as I never had before

Heber C. Kimball, like several of the apostles, left his wife both ill and destitute, trusting only in God, and in Joseph Smith's promise that his family would be cared for. This letter, written only three days after Heber left Nauvoo, reflects the suffering and the trials of the women who remained behind. Vilate suggests that unless her health improves, she will be unable to keep the promise Heber exacted from her to write once a week. Source: Heber C. Kimball Collection, Church Archives.

September 21 friday eve [*1839*]

My very Dear Husband

with a weak and trembleing hand I attempt to write a few lines, agreable to your request to let you know how we do; which is very poorly I can assure you. As to my feelings I dont know but I am perfectly reconciled to your going. But I must say I have got a trial of my faith as I never had before.

The day you left home, was as sick a one as I ever experianced, the pain in my back and head was almost intolerable. No doubt the pain in my head was worse on the account of my much weeping. But I did not weep any after you left, for my distress was so great I could think of not much els. William moaned and cried about all day, and had a chill in the evening. Sister Bently staid with me through the day. She was sick, but she did all she could for me. Fanny Dort came over and stayed all night with me. I was a lone a little while before she came. I then cralled out of bed, and bowed before the Lord and pled with him to give us a good nights rest and he did so, and be assured I did not forget to pray for you.

The next morning I felt free from pain; [*but I was so light*] headed that I could not walk without staggering. William and Helen was not able to do any thing so I was obliged to crall round and do my chores, and wash a little for the babe; no one to help me but little Heber P. I soon got over done and brought on my chill and fever, so that I had a very sick afternoon, and did not rest but little last night.

To day I have not ben able to do any thing. I was taken early this morning with a shake, and shook about an hour and a half as hard as I ever saw any body in my life, and then weltered under a fever and extream pain until almost night. William has just had the hardest chill that he has had in a number of days. Br Rogors has ben here and left more pills for him, and he has taken them up, but they dont seem to do him any good. He offered to leave some for me, but I told him I would try what virtue there was in bone set first. But it has not done me any good. And what to [do I] dont k[n]ow. I have no one to get any thing for me, or to do any thing for my comfort. Br Bently has moved in here, but sister Ann is very feble hardly able to do her own work. She is very kind and would be glad to doctor us if she was able. Helen is complaining all the time, but is able to do some chores to day.

Now I have given you a statement of our situation, not to make you feel bad, but because you requested it of me. Thus you see I have got a trial of my weak faith as I said before. But all that I can ask of you is to pray that I may have patience to endure to the end whether it be long or short. I feel as though if you ever see your famaly all alive again it will be through your faith.

Saterday morning, dear Heber we are all alive and tolerable comfortable this morning. Would to God we could remain so through the day. We will hope for the best. Mother Bemon stayed with me last night. She said I [must] tell you she had slept with your little Prophet. I must draw to a close for Br George is waiting. Unless my health should improve I shall not be able to write next week as you requested, for im groing weak every day. You had better enquire for a letter at New York, perhaps I shall direct there. So fare you well my dear Heber. I pray that it may be well with you. [*Signature clipped out.*]

Sister Ann send love to you.

The children all send love to you.

5

HEBER C. KIMBALL TO VILATE KIMBALL, OCTOBER 24, 1839

I have told you the truth. . . . now do the same to me, then we will be even

When Heber C. Kimball wrote the following letter from Pleasant Garden, Illinois, he apparently had not yet received Vilate's letter of September 21. The letters are appropriate companion pieces, for both Heber and Vilate were longing to see each other, worried about each other's health, and having serious illnesses and financial problems. They had promised faithfully to write and, equally important, to be honest with each other about their respective well-being. Like Vilate's letter, Heber's account of his illness and arduous journey reflects that honesty, along with the anxious desire that the troubles it revealed would not worry his companion needlessly. "Don't be concerned about me," he pleaded, "for I am in the hands of God." Heber concludes with an inquiry about a pamphlet—an account of his 1837 mission to Britain, which was published as the *Journal of Heber C. Kimball* in 1840, while he was on his second British mission. Source: Heber C. Kimball Collection, Church Archives.

Plesant Garden   Oct the 24   1839

My verry dear Companion, through the goodness of God I am permited this morning to set down to rite a few lines to you that you may no how I guit a long upon my journey. I will ashure you that it is with trembling limbs that I do it. But to fulfill my word that I made to you, I procede in the name of the Lord.

I left Winchester on the day that I stated to you in my last, with your father & Br. Brigham went six miles to misters Bares. Stade all night. The next day Br Lorenso car[ri]ed us to Jaksonvill stade all night. The next day Brother Babcock got a buggy and careed us to Springfield being 35 miles. Went it in half a day. Stood it well my self; Br B was taken sick. Not able to travel or to set up much, he went threw with a can of medison by Br Cones.

We remained thare one week. I spent my time in going from hous to hous amongst the brethren strengthing and teaching them the things of the kingdom, and preached on the Sabath to them. Thare was a great feeling of love shone to us. They went and got a two hors waggon and harnis for us which they paid 55 dollars, and made up 35 dollars in money for the company. Here was great liberal felings and they shall in no wise lose thare reward seth the Lord. Judge Adams tock me home with him and made welcom to his hous. I stade with him three nits and most part of three days. He was asking questions all the time. When I left him he gave me five dollars. He is judge of the Suprem Cort. He will come in to the Church soon I think.

We put the three horses before the waggon and started on friday Evning went 8 miles and stade at old mister drapers being quite late in the [*day*] when we got thare then found them sick, our living slim quite. So, next day went on our journey. Travled all day till night when we put up. I went [on] foot part of the way being [all sick]. Got su[p]per. I slept in the waggon with your father and Br Hadlock. I got cold. The next morning they would not guit us anny vitles to eat because we was Mormons. Went on our journey.

Got to a brothers hous about 10 oclock. They got us sumthing to eat about noon and this was corn dodger and transparant pork. By this time I began to fail our waggon began to fail brock down [*illegible word*] and the chiles came on to me again, about two in the afternoon, and hold me till night. Then the fever hold me all night. This continued for three days. I had lost my apetite not having anny thing betwixt meals to eat. The third chill that I had it seam to me as tho I could not live till night my distress was so great. I got to Doctter Modsett about dusk. I made out to guit in to the hous with helpe. I was made welcom by the Docter and his wife. I throde my self on to the bed laid a short time got up set a spell and began to grow faint. I then told them that I must go to bed. The Docter and B Sprung to helpe me and I fainted and fell my hole length on the flower. Thare was hardly a breth of life in my body. I laid on the flore fore a long time before I could be taken up. When I was put on to the bed it tock the docter and his wife and Br Brigham all nite to keep a breth of life in my body. This continued till about ten in the morning when I felt better. Thare was cold sweat that Rolled out of me all night, which swet the deseas out of me; and I have had no chills since. I got to the Docters thursday night.

The next morning the brethren twock the team and went on and left Br B with me his helth being very power. When they left me they wep like children aspechly your father for he thought I should not live. Mondy nite brother Babbit and Docter Niter came to see me if I was a live. The next morning I felt to start on my journy. The Docter twock his carrage and carred me with in fore miles of Plesent Gardens whare brother Babbet was laboring. Br Babbit tok me into his waggon and car[ri]ed me to Br Crosby. I have made my home thare and at Docter Niter. He is one of B Babbits children. He is [in] a verry eminet pasition a man of great welth. Brother Almon has begun a good work in this place and in the Regions Round about. He has suffered sum percicution, they have ingered his waggon some. His wife is with him. He has baptised five [and there are] some more that have presented them selvs for baptism.

We expect we shall start from here to morrow if the Lord will. Brother Babbit ses he will take us on our journy leven miles. We have sent on our trunk. We expect thare is a brother that will take us to the capital [of] Indiany, then I expect we shall have to take stage to Columbus [if] then we shall have to take the canall, after we leave this plase I dont [object]. My courage is good at this time and has ben [*since*] I left home. My helth is increasing verry fast at present. Dont be concerned about me for I am in the hands of God.

Now my dear Companion do not feel bad becaus I have told you the truth, for this I agreede to do when I left home, now do the same to me, then w[e] w[ill] b[e] even. I heard from you by the way of Brother [*word torn*] an [*2-3 words torn*]. They left thare about [4] days ago sed your helth w[as] [*improved, which*] was glad tidings to me of great joy. But I [*3-4 words torn*] when I recieve a leter from your own ha[nd] [*2-3 words torn*] have under gon more in my feelings in my life [*2-3 words torn*] I left home, about the Children and your self, I am going to trye to be more of a man than I have been. Tell me all about the children how they guit a long. Tell William and Hellen I think of them all the time that I pray for them, and I wont they should for me. Tell litle F to be a good boy Kiss litle D for me. Take good care of your Self and be prudent my dear Vilate. Give my love to all my friends. Tell me what Brother Thomson is doing with the pamphlet. Now I bid you fare well Vilate for a litle Season

Heber C Kimball

6

JOHN TAYLOR TO LEONORA TAYLOR, JANUARY 30, 1840

O that this people were in possession of the same glorious principles that we possess

This lengthy letter from John Taylor to his wife is especially significant because his diaries are not available. Here, copying from his diary, he reports in detail his voyage, his arrival, and his earliest missionary activities in Preston and Liverpool. (The dates from the diary are often wrong, usually by one day.) He warns future travelers of the impositions practiced by so-called shipping agents in New York and provides interesting information about the postal system. An Englishman returned home, he notes visits with family and friends, including the baptism of George Cannon, brother to his wife Leonora, with whom he lived in Liverpool. He also recounts his warm reunion with Joseph Fielding, a fellow Englishmen who emigrated in the 1830s, joined the Church with him in Canada, and became his first missionary companion in Britain. Source: John Taylor Collection, Church Archives.

Mr. George Cannons No. 43 Norfolk St Liverpool Jany 30, 1840
O My Dear Leonora

  After waiting impatiently for a long time in hopes of hearing from you I at length sit down to write to you. I have never received any intelligence from you since your two first letters both of which I received on my arrival at New York, which were wrote I believe before Elders Young & Kimball left Commerce or soon after. How to account for this I know not. I am sure that My Nora never would forget to write to me she knows that I feel anxious about her welfare & that of the children. They must have miscarried. I have peculiar feelings about you my dear. I last night dreamed that I saw you in some difficulty & I am fearful that you are. I have prayed to my heavenly Father to bless you protect & deliver you & I beleive that he will. Do not be afraid of communicating to me all your feelings & all about your situation & perhaps I can administer unto you comfort & relief. Meanwhile I say unto you that others shall. Inasmuch as you are patient humble & faithful you shall be blessed & provided for in the name of Jesus Christ Amen.

I beleive the P. O. regulations are that letters must be paid to the lines c/e to New York, which will be I think 25 cents. If this is not done I think that they will not come. I wish it were otherwise because I know that you have not too much money. When you or any of the Sisters direct to Preston it will be necessary to write on the direction the number of the house, the name of the Street, as well as of the person otherwise the P. O. Regulations are that they keep them eight days & afterwards send them to the dead letter office in London from whence I expect it would be difficult to obtain them. Liverpool however is an exception to that. They have a strangers letter office the same as they have in New York & other parts of the U. S. I have however made some arrangements with the P. O. in Preston so that if letters should come addressed to me at the above named place I might have some prospect of obtaining them, but when you write again direct as on the top of this letter.

I now commence to give you some account of my proceedings & the delings of the Lord with me since I last wrote to you from New York. I extract from my journals.

Dec 19 Left New York Dock on the Ship Oxford a liner in Company with Elder Woodruff & Turley for Liverpool. Paid $15 for our Passage in the Steerage. There was no second cabin in the vessel. I write the following for the benefit of others who may come.

There is a great deal of imposition practised by those who are proffessed Agents for those Vessels but who in reality have no commission. They will advertize certain Vessels the time of their departure together with their names & place of residence, & passengers are frequently deceived by going to these offices as everything is plausible about them. They have bills for shipping passengers with the owners signatures printed. They will receive & give reciepts for passengers money on those bills & then if the legalized Agents should not have a sufficient number of passengers to fill the Steerage there may be a chance for those obtaining a berth — but if the Legal Agents have filled the Berths then the passengers shipped by the other have to wait till another boat sails, go with a transient vessel or lose their passage money which is not unfrequently the case.

There is another imposition practised by those Agents or Owners or Captain or All together. When you go to examine the Vessel to choose a berth you are sheon a number of berths standing which you are told by the Agents are all that there will be & if you have your berth regular there will the number of your berth marked on your ticket or receipt. But it was the case on our vessel that there were 5 marked for 1 Berth instead of two & there were numbers shipped that had no berths at all so that instead of 40 passengers, which we were told there would be, there was 63 passengers in the Steerage, which altered the conditions of the passengers very much as there had to be a number of extra berths put up & [illegible word] to contain 4 men. 4 were stuck into the place where the chains are. A woman & a man had no berth at all but were obliged to lay on the Boxes [on] the floor or where they could.

There is also another difficulty. When you arrive on board as soon as you leave the pier you can obtain no redress. You are told by the Captain or Mate that they know nothing of the affairs of the Merchants or Brokers, that you are under their control & must be subject to their government. Therefore it is best for every one fully to understand their own business before they go on board if possible — get their tickets at the boat & their numbers marked on their tickets &c.

We sailed on the 20th at 12 O. Clock fair wind. 21 fair wind. 22 unfavourable. 23 Unfavourable. 24 Stormy unfavourable. 25 Half calm Half of the day stormy. 26 Fair wind rough. 27 Fair wind. 28 2 points of[f] course 1200 m[ile]s from N.Y. 29 – 2 Points off Stormy. 30 Very Stormy. 31 Rough near the course. 1 June 1840 Stormy 2 Points of[f] course. Jun 2 calm till 6 O clock then fair wind. 3 Fair wind. 4 wind aft. 5 Fair wind. 6 calm. 7 Calm. 8 Close to the wind. 9 Fair wind. 10 Saw Cape Clear. 11 Passed Hollyhead. Took in a Pilot & were informed that we were before the Steam Ship Liverpool that set sail 5 days before us & the Ship Independence that sailed 11 days before us had only just arrived. Hauled into the Princes Dock the same [day].

12th On Sunday I saw your Br. George, took Dinner with him. I found him to be an inteligent man & a Gentleman. He & his his wife used me well. They made me think of My Nora. I unfolded briefly the first principles of the Gospel to them & left a Book of M & Voice of Warning with them. 13 Cleared the Custom House paid 6 per lb on American Books.

Left Liverpool in the Rail Road Cars. Started from Lime St at 1/4 before 5 O Clock. Your Br. George saw us off. Arrived in Preston Lancashire same night. Saw Br. Richards & many other brethren who crouded in, being rejoiced to see us. It gave me peculiar feelings to meet with the Saints in England. I was much pleased & edified at the kindness & love manifested by the bretheren & Sisters & with their simple unadorned manner. Took dinner with Br. John Parkman & had peculiar feelings at seeing his wife after dinner leave the house, her husband (a shoemaker) & children to work in a factory (a practice very prevalent in this & other manufacturing towns) thus breaking up those social endearments that unite the family. It makes my heart bleed to see these things. When will the earth cease to mourn. In the Evening I had the pleasure of seeing Br. Clark. He rejoiced to see me & I to see him. It gives us peculiar feelings to meet our friends in another country.

(14) I found my Uncle George Hodgson, visited him & family. He is doing a very good business in partnership with his son John who is a very accomplished & intelligent young man. Cousin Betsy had been Dead 3 Years. My Uncle & Aunt look much the same only a little older & more care worn. Uncle & John had upwards of 20 men at work. Their address is—I have forgot the addresses but direct George & John Hodgson Plumbers Painters & Glaziers [Fishergate] Preston, it will find him. 15th Called upon and took dinner with Uncle James Hodgson. He & Aunt Mary were well but he looks much older then he did. I saw Cousins James & Robert Atkinson. James is married & has I think 3 Children. He is following his business, Cabinet Maker. Robert is also married, has I think 3 Children. He is foreman for Uncle George in the Plumbing Glazing & Painting business. I wish my dear that you would communicate this last intelligence to my Father (direct to Mr. James Taylor Mr. Arrowsmiths Springvale in care of J. N. Rust & Co Oquawke Warren Co Ill.) with my kindest love to Father & Mother & all my Friends. Tell them to be faithful & to pray for me as I do for them.

16th I saw my old Friend Elder Fielding & was rejoiced to see him as he was also to see me. I thank God that he has preserved him & given him wisdom for the arduous duties devolving upon him. We felt something like Jonathan & David after an absence of 3 Years. 18th held council with those of the bretheren that had just come about the best way to dispose of ourselves until the rest of the Quorum of the Twelve should come. We did not feel disposed to interfere with any body's business but our own — but were rejoiced to see the order & amity that prevailed in the Church. Er. Feilding Presided. It was Resolved that I should go to Liverpool & Elder Feilding accompany me — that Er. Clark go to Manchester that Elder Wilford Woodruff & Er. Turley go to the Potterries from thence to Birmingham as they should deem prudent.

17 — Elders Woodruff Clark & Turley left Preston for the places of their destination. We took the parting hand with them at the railroad after having blessed them & they us. 18 S Preached to the Saints in Preston. 19 — Went in Co[mpany] with Ers. Richards & Feilding to Penwortham. Preached at Br. Moons house on Pauls declaration "I am not ashamed of the Gospel of Christ &c". 20 Visited my uncle Georges, told them about my mission & promised when I came again to visit them get all my friends together & preach the gospel to them. 21 Left Preston in Co[mpany] with Er Feilding Preached in Longton on the Angel Flying in the midst of Heaven &c. 22 we pursued our course to Orms Park but had no opening for preaching so we pursued our course to Liverpool the same night. Called at Wm. Armstrongs Tailors he received us kindly. We took tea with him & I stayed at your Br Georges.

23 Called upon Wm. Batemans. Took tea with him. Called upon a Mr. Kent a Preacher & a beleiver in the personal Reighn of Christ. We told him our mission, he did not reject it. A Gentlemen who had been ordained a Church of England Minister from Plymouth came in while we were conversing with Mr. Kent. We delivered our testimony to him but he rejected it. We warned him in the name of The Lord & told him that if he opposed these things that portion of the spirit which he had received should leave him that he would be brought into darkness & the concerns in which he was engaged would not prosper. Br. Feilding told him this & I sanctioned it & warned him against baptizing any more as he was without authourity. He is connected with a church in Stafford I beleive of the Same order of Mr. Wm. Millerd in Canada, beleives in baptism & the Personal Reighn of Christ. He was a learned & highly polished man, his words were

smoother than oil but the poison of asps was under his toungue. He said our work was from hell &c. We washed our feet & bore testimony before the Lord—Saying Oh Lord our Heavenly Father we thy servants have bore testimony of the truth of those things that thou hast revealed to Mr. Steward & he has rejected our testimonys. Oh Father thou knowest that we have no hard feelings towards the man. If thou canst forgive him & lead him to the truth do, we pray the[e] Oh Father. We do this that we may fulfill thy word & bear this testimony before thee according to thy command & now O Father we leave him in Thy hand praying thee to guide us into all truth & fulfill all Righteousness in the name of Jesus Christ Amen.

26th Went in the morning to Mr. Aitkens Chapel, a place where Mr. Matthews Er. Feildings Br. in Law is the preacher. He however was not there but we heard a young man preach who seemed very devoted. Lamented over the state of the professing Church, prayed for the blessing of the Holy Ghost & looked for the coming Kingdom of Christ &c. &c. I had peculiar feelings when I heard him & saw the situation of the people & felt Oh that I could have an opportunity of unfolding to them the glorious things of the Gospel. O that this people were in possession of the same glorious principles that we possess. Br. Feilding felt the same.

After meeting was over I desired an opportunity of speaking a few words saying that I was much interested in the things that I heard. I was told that I had better go into the vestry & that they would there speak to me. Accordingly Br Feilding and I were introduced into the company of from 16 to 20 Class Leaders & Preachers & they then wanted to know what sect I was of or what was my profession? I then addressed them.

"Gentlemen friends & bretheren—I have listened with deep interest to the things that I have heard this morning. I have observed with peculiar emotions the deep anxiety the fervent prayer & the strong solicitude that is manifested by you for the obtaining of the Gift of the Holy Ghost. I have been pleased with the correct veiws that you entertain in regard to the situation of the Church & of the World & as you beleive in these things so do we & as we hear that you beleive in baptism & laying on of hands (for Mr. Mathews had not only baptized since our bretheren came & got that from our bretheren but he had asked Br. Feilding how he laid on hands & had attended to that with out authourity. The people however were not to blame for that but were sincere in what they did)—so do we. Bretheren & friends we are the humble followers of Jesus Christ & are from America. I have lately arrived in this place, have come a distance of

2000 miles without purse or scrip & testify to you bretheren that the Lord has revealed himself from Heaven & put us in possession of those things that you are so anxiously looking for & praying that you may receive. (Glory to God was shouted by many present & great emotion manifested.) That thing has taken place which is spoken of by John in the revelations & I saw another angel flying in the midst of Heaven having the everlasting gospel to preach &c. Rev. 14 This gospel has got to be proclaimed to every nation kindred people & tongue & we the Servants of God are come to this City to warn the inhabitants of their approaching danger & to call upon them to repent & be baptized in the name of Jesus Christ for the remission of sins & they shall receive the Gift of the Holy Ghost. Bretheren & Friends I feel an anxious desire to deliver this testimony. I feel the word of the Lord like fire in my bones & am desirous to have an opportunity of proclaiming to you these blessings that you are looking for, that you may rejoice with us in those great & glorious things which God has revealed for the salvation of the world in these last days & if it would be consistent with your feelings I should be glad of an opportunity of speaking in your Chapel this afternoon next week or any time when it would be convenient for you.

Many present rejoiced others wept some were jealous & angry. They then asked what society we belonged to enquired if we did not belong to the Mormons. I said no we belong to the Church of Jesus Christ of Latter Day Saints known in some instances by the name of Mormons. One said we have heard an unfavorable opinon of you by our Pastors Mr. Matthews & Aitkens. Mr. Matthews says that the thing is from Hell. They however had no authourity about the meeting unless Mr. Matthews was here. Some felt anxious about it. Br Feilding told them that he was Mr. Matthews Brother in Law. One of them asked if we could not in a few words put them in the way of obtaining the Holy Ghost. I told them no but if they would wait for two hours as the thing was of importance I would wait & explain it to them.

In the Afternoon we went to a Baptists Meeting, told our errand was invited home by a Gentleman & introduced to the Rev Mr. Creasy, a rigid Calvenistic Baptist. Mr. Creasy however did not love the truth. The Gentleman at whose house we were was very frank & invited us to call again but said as to their people he knew they were so rigid that if we were to preach in their place they would not hear us out. I am afraid that the religion of this Generation will sink them to hell. They have so much religion that they have no time to listen to the truths of God. In the Evening we again went to Mr. Aitkins Chapel. All eyes were upon us. There are many honest hearted among them but like others they are under the influence of Preists. After Meeting one of their Leaders invited us home. His name is Mr. Mitchell. He & his wife received the word with gladness.

27 Went in the Evening to Visit a Captain Gile was introduced by Mrs. Cannon. Captain Gile was not at home but there was another Captain a Cousin of his by the name of Philip Gile (I think you wont know him) A young gentleman a Methodist Mrs Gile a Miss Collister & another Lady. I preached the gospel to them & we delivered our testimony. Mrs. Gile invited us to call again. We have several times since that & Mrs. Gile & Miss Collester are very much beleiving.

28 Attended an appointment that we had at Mr. Mitchells. The Elders of Mr. Aitkins Church had been very much excited in consequence of our being here & would not give him rest till they made him promise that we should not preach in his house. He however said that he would talk with us. His wife had been to tell the neighbours & freinds of the meeting but gave them back word. In spite of this however the house was near full. I talked with them a little on the Scriptures. His heart was overjoyed. Others were pleased with what they heard & thus in spite of all the influence that can be brought to bear they "can do nothing against the truth but for the truth."

29 — This morning we were waited upon by a woman who stated that she never had such feelings before as when I arose in the Chapel. She beleived that we were men of God as soon as she saw us. She & some others sent us some money. By this shall ye know that they are my deciples if the[y] feed you & clothe you &c. 31 — Met a few at Mr. Mitchells. Br. Feilding spoke. After he had got through a Methodist Preacher wanted to know if we could heal the sick. I told him that we had not come to testify of ourselves but to the truth that if he beleived the scriptures he must beleive these things. He wanted to have a sighn. I gave him to understand in a spirit of meekness that a wicked & adulterous generation seeketh after a sighn. He thought that there was not much error in the churches. After a few remarks I prayed that the matter might drop & that at least we might have no more contention. There were several different orders present. We said no more but they soon fell out among themselves thus proving that they had not the spirit to lead them into all truth.

2 S Went to a Floting Chapel on the Kings Dock heard a preacher of

the New Association a sort of Methodists. His Text was "go ye into all the world & preach the gospel to every creature." There was much darkness manifested & I thought Oh that generation would receive the truth & that the servants of God might have an opportunity of proclaiming it to them. After service was over we waited upon the minister who introduced us to Captain Hudson a Gentleman who has the principal charge of & preaches on the floating Chapel. I told him who we were, that I had lately come from America & that I wanted an opportunity of preaching in some place in town & hearing that differrent orders preached on that place I thought that I would make application. He invited us to call upon him at his house. We did so a day or two afterwards but he was too good a man to do anything, too wise to be instructed & too holy to be made righteous.

In the evening we attended a place that we had hired as a preaching room that would hold about 300 people lighted with Gas & although we had been very still & said little the room was nearly full of people who joined in singing & gave good attention. I preached from Jude upon the faith that was once delivered to the Saints. I spoke upon the desire that had been manifested by men in differrent ages to reform – that Luther Malancthon, Calvin Wesley Whitfeild & others since them had tried to bring about the ancient order of things & that however laudible their attempts might have been they had failed – that there was neither the love, unity power nor blessings now in existence that existed among the Ancient Saints, that many had it in their hearts to pray for the ancient order & wished they had ancient Methodism Presbyteranism &c. but we would now see what kind of Gospel the ancients Saints had & be governed by it. I then shewed what the gospel was as presented by Peter Paul Phillip &c. Began at the day of Pentecost &c. Spoke of the Order Spirit Doctrines Ordinances Gifts, Blessings &c. of the gospel & shewed that if it was true then it was true now, that if it was the privilege to enjoy these thing it was ours now to possess as great blessings through the same gospel – that as many of them had been praying for the ancient faith the Lord had answerd their prayers & sent us his servants to testify to them that God had restored these things – that he had sent the Angel according to the testimony of John having the everlasting Gospel to preach &c. We were witnesses of it & had come to unfold the same glorious things to them that they might rejoice with us, that I had left my family & come a distance of 2000 miles without purse or scrip for this purpose that they might rejoice in the same glorious things that God had revealed to us. I said this is glorious intelligence & asked is it not. Yes was responded by many & praise the Lord. Br. Feilding then made a few remarks & bore testimony to what I had said. I then said that the Lord had sent us to baptize & called upon them to repent & be baptized in the name of Jesus Christ &c. That we his servants stood ready to administer in this ordinance that if any wanted to be baptized they may make it known to us.

After the congregation was dismissed there was great emotion in the meeting. Many wept others rejoiced & praised the Lord. The spirit of the Lord indeed was with us & bore testimony to what we said & I plainly saw that it was the power of God & not the wisdom of man – that I could do nothing unless the spirit of God bore testimony to that word. After the meeting a young man came to me & told me that the Lord had showed these things to him in a vision. He rejoiced & said that he would be baptized. A young woman come to me & wept & said that she knew it was the truth, the power of God & the word of God. Several said that they beleive we were the Servants of God & wanted to obey the Gospel. It caused our hearts to rejoice. Mr. Mitchell spoke to many of his class who were present & told them that these things were of God & that he could not resist, them that he would obey the gospel & hoped that they would consider seriously about it. We appointed Teusdy at 3 O Clock to baptize & went on our way rejoicing thanking God that he bore Testimony by his spirit to those things that he had comissioned us to impart. On Tuesday ten ca[me] forward in baptism. This was after the first preaching.

I must now pass over many things & hasten to tell you that the week following I baptized 4. Will it not cause the heart of My Leonora to rejoice when I tell her Br. George & his Wife made two of this number & they now stand in a nearer relationship than kindred flesh. They are brother & sister in Jesus Christ. They have manifested to us the greatest kindness since we came & we have made thier house our stopping place. I believe the Lord has many people in this town. I pray that he may role on his work.

I have just received a letter from Er. Woodruff. He is well & doing well. Br. Turley is gone to Birmingham. Br. Woodruff expects soon to join him there. I received a letter from Er. Clark two days ago, he had got a letter from Sister Clark. He is well & he begins to get his [mouth of]. He has baptized several. There is nothing in the letter about you or sister Woodruff. Er's Wright & Mulliner are in Scotland & have commenced baptizing. Elder Feilding is well, has a daughter, desires to be remembered to you & his Sisters. He & I are like David & Jonathan. The Latest accounts from Er. Richards were that he was not very well. Ers Kimball Young Smith P.P. Pratt O Pratt nor Hadlock have not yet arrived. We are looking for some of them daily.

I called upon your old friend Mrs. Porter she was glad to see & asked why I did not bring you along. I saw Mr. Tubman Your Uncle. Your Aunt is dead. He is married again & keeps the railroad tavern. Ann Tubman is married to a man from London. Ann Crawford is married to A Mr. Kidd Clark in the [*illegible word*]. I saw Mr. & Mrs Clark they are well. I called upon Mrs. Crane Ann Neil. Nora Vale is well. I saw her Stepmother. Your Sister Elleoners Husband is dead & 2 Children. The first Husband freinds keep one since his death. Elleoner is well. I have seen her two or three times. John is with David in Sidney. I have seen one of his letters & some of David's. John Laments Leaving England without seeing you. David is steady & expects to return with something that will do him good in a few years. I saw Mrs Crawford from Ramsy. Thomas is dead.   J.T.

[*Change of handwriting. The following is a note written by George Cannon, Leonora's brother.*] Dear Sister I hope you and your little ones are well. You may imagine how surprized I was to see Mr. Taylor. I should have been happy if you had been along with him, I believe that the Lord had a hand in sending him to England and shewing me in what a dangerous state I lived without even the form of religion but with the assistance of Gods Holy spirit we — that is Ann and I are determined to lead a new life and shew a better example to our children. Dear Sister I wish you were here. There are many things I could talk to you about that I am ashamed to let others know I am ignorant of, but I am in hopes that I shall see you and your dear little ones before I die. Death has taken one little one from us. John was 3 1/2 years old when he died and only eight days illness, a brain fever. I mean to write you a long letter soon dear Sister remember me in your prayers. Seldom as I went on my knees, I always prayed for you and my brothers. God has promised to hear us when we are gathered together in his name. Our prayers may ascend the same time to the throne of grace, for what is distance in the sight of God.   G. Cannon

[*The remaining section is written by John Taylor.*]

I must now my dear bring this communication to a close. Tell George & Mary Ann that Father is going to get a Mansion a glorious inheritance a fortune & that if they are good Father & Mother & George & Mary Anne & Joseph will soon live together with God & with the holy Angels. Accept of the kindest love my Dear from your distant John & 100 kisses each for the Children.

I hope that more of your friends may yet embrace the gospel. Your sister Ann has introduced us to many of them. She is a complete missionary & happy in the Lord. George & Mary want to be baptized. Give my kindest love to all the Brethren Brs. Joseph & Sidney if returned from Washington, Br. & Sister Hyrum Smith Br. & Sister Thompson Father & Mother Smith Bishops Partrige Whitney & Knight Ripley Br. Miller & all the Saints. I pray for you & for them & ask an interest in the prayers of my bretheren & I know that you will not forget me. I should be glad if Georges schooling could be attended to.

I feel thankful my dear that I have never lacked any good thing since I left home. The Lord has been & is with me. I have realized the truth of this, that the God that feeds the ravens & clothes the lillies numbers the hairs of my head. I have nothing to say about myself, my intelligence virtue or perseverance but I have much to say about the goodness of God. I feel that while the Lord takes care of me I am rich. Praise the Lord Oh my soul praise him Nora & my children praise him his saints praise the Lord put your trust in him my dear & he will take care of you till I return. I bless you & the children in the name of the Lord Jesus Christ Amen & remain as ever Your Affectionate Husband for ever & ever Amen— —John Taylor

A letter has just come to Er. Hadlock

He has not arrived [*two words illegible*]

Lean upon the Lord my dear & he will remember you [*and*] yours. God bless you.

7

WILFORD WOODRUFF TO WILLARD RICHARDS, 25 MARCH 1840

The Lord of Hosts is with me in power & some of the time the Devil to

Written about three weeks after his arrival in Herefordshire, this letter includes fascinating details of his astonishing success in that area. His personality and his deep and abiding faith come through these pages. An avid fisherman, Wilford calls his Herefordshire success "the strongest fishing ever I have done," and notes that such "rapid work" had gathered in some who would not and should not stay. In the last half of the letter, responding to Willard's request for prayers and advice regarding the trials facing him and his ailing wife Jennetta, Wilford offers tender council and inspired blessings. Source: Willard Richards Collection, Church Archives.

Hill farm, Froomes Hill, Ledbury, Herefordshire, March 25th 1840

Elder W. Richards

Dear Brother. May grace, peace, strength, faith & victory rest upon you & Sister Richards from God our father & our Lord Jesus Christ. Dear Brother it is amid peculiar feelings that I take up my pen to address you this morning. I have so many things in my mind at this time that I wish to communicat & so little time & room to do it in that I hardly know where to begin or how to end. I feel that there never was a store House ten story high filled from top to bottom with Merchentdize that canst have more of a variety in it than I have in my mind at this time. & I hardly know how to go to work to give you a description of my situation but I will try to do it by parible, figure, similee or sumthing or other. I am far from feeling vane or like trifling but I take the Liberty of making expressions to you that I would not to the world that you may ketch my view of the situation of things here. In the first place permit me to say that I never before witnessed such a scenery as I am experiencing here neither did I ever expect to in my generation. The Lord of Hosts is with me in power & some of the time the Devil to. I have had some mighty Battles with the devil [several] in [*illegible word*] since I have been here & God has enabled me to give him a deadly wound and routed him out of his camp & he has fled from me wounded & roaring like a Lion & I can hear the sound of his roar about ten miles off & I expect him to return for another Battle by & by for you are aware that an enemies camp cannot be broak up without some noise & so you can form sumthing of an Idea of it from the following description.

I have been here 21 days preached 20 times & Baptized Mr Thomas Kington the superintendant of the preachers of the United Brethren, a branch of or broke off from the Methodist Church & with Mr Kington I Baptized 23 preachers of the same order that was under his superintendance & also I Baptized 46 of the members of the same Church making 70 in all. This scenery has committed into my hands & charge & my controll mostly 45 established places of preaching most of which are licensed according to Law & also 48 Preachers 24 of which I have already Baptized & most of the rest are ready as soon as they can have an opportunity. As I said before I say again their will be a mighty harvest here, for all the churches which these preachers are over are ready to recieve the word. Should I judge from outward appearances I should think their would spedily be 500 Baptized in this region & probably more still I don't wish to count chickens before they are hatched. I am now Baptizing about 10 daily, day before yesterday 12 & yesterday 9. Some days I have to go to the water 3 time a day. I Baptized 6 preachers yesterday & I have a number to Baptize to day. Yesterday 3 preachers came in a charriot or gig to visit me. They never had herd me preach at all. I had on wet clothes & going to the pool to Baptize. I testified of Jesus Christ unto them. The power of God rested upon us & they kneeled down and weept & prayed & their gig stood still & they all went down into the pool the same hour and I Baptized them & they went their way rejoicing & praising God. Mr. Kington is an humble man. I have Ordained him an Elder & I ordained five priest. Their will be many worthy labourers raised up in this country.

You see by this time Brother Richards I am not Idle but have much to do & need much wisdom from God to do it well, for it is the strongest fishing ever I have done & I don't expect any thing els but while gathering the salmon I will get among them some ells & snakes for their has already been some after they were Baptized that would pitch & Bound like a porpose or jump & roll like a hen with their head cut off manifesting any kind of spirit but that of order & if ever an Elder had any triming to do I expect to have my share of it by & by for in doing such a rapid work as this I have to become all things to all men for I cannot get time to do much triming as yet. In fact some have before I was aware of it bounded into the water to me stark naked excepting a loose cloth around their legs but I put a stop to all disorder as fast as possible. & again I am Having a mighty struggle against this [illegible word] power of falling down like a dead man stiff as a Stake which is in some of the preachers as well as the people. I have to handle all these things in wisdom.

Among the number that I have & are Baptizing are some large farmers having 3 or 400 acres of land. I have Baptized some constables as well as preachers. There is a Merchant in Hanly that we Baptized that trade is so bad that he is winding up business & wants to go to Zion with the Saints. I have Baptized most of his relatives here severel Brothers & Sisters here. He has come down to visit them. He has said sumthing to them about it. & they all want to [illegible word] up business here & move with the Saints in the U.S.A. & in fact most all the Saints are getting the same spirit here without my preaching it. I do wish the Twelve would spedily come to England that we might hold a council somewhere about these & many other things. When you next write to me say a word to me what your mind is about this. The farmers here feel like this that bad times are coming & the sooner they can turn their property into gold the better & in fact with the view I have of the times I cannot advise them as yet to the contrarey.

You begin to see Brother Richards that I must have much to occupy my mind at present considering what I have to do. & in addition to this I have just recieved a Letter from Elder Cordon at Burslem. Stating that Elder Turley is taken with a *States warrent* & put into Stafferd *Jail*. It was done by a man in Birmingham for an old Debt that Brother Turley contracted 15 years ago before he left England. Or in other words Turley was in partnership with a man & when they dissolved Turley gave up the Stock into his hands to sell & he supposed it was all Settled but now the man claims that he did not sell the Stock for as much as he expected & that he has still claims on Turley. John Jones in Burslem was connected in taking him. It is merely a trick of the Devil to stop his preaching but I believe the Lord will overturn it for good. How long he will be confined in prison I do not know. The whole Labour at the Potteries is now flung upon Elder Cordon & when he wrote me he was some out of health. & should their be any faithful labourer at liberty would they not do well to go into that part of the vineyard & assist. And again in addition to this care I have a Certain Brother Richards whome I love of a truth for the truths sake that dwelleth in him. & I pray God that it may be with him forever & he asks an interest in my progress in his behalf & his companions that the Lord may manifest his will concerning them.

I will now say Dear Brother I will gladly comply with your request the first leasure moments I can get, in fact I have attemped two or three times since I recieved your two Letters upon the subject to lay the case before the Lord but no sooner than I would begin to pray some one would be wraping at my door for me to go & baptize them or for sumthing els. In fact since I recieved your letters I have had no spare time hardly to pray for any thing, for you see how things are with me & of course can judge how my time is taken up. I scarcely pass a pool of water but what sumbody is waiting there for me to baptize them. & in fact if John had more Baptizing to do when all Judea & Jerrusalem went unto him to be Baptized, than I have had for a few days past he certainly had his hands full. But do not think dear Brother that I shall close this letter without answering the questions you have asked me & expressing my feelings unto you. No God forbid not withstanding I have not had time to lay your case before the Lord as I could wish. Yet I have a word to express upon the subject. In the first place I wish to say I recieved your two letters & have read them over several times. & you speak my mind perfectly with regard to any other persons opening any of our letters excepting our own Quorum. & when I gave permission for a letter to be opened should one come before my returned, I did not then expect to be gone but very few days before my return & it was under the impression that if I had a letter at all during my absence it would be from Brother Clayton in Manchester, & as they wanted to hear from him I gave them that privilege with a charge to say nothing concerning the contents if their was anything that the church should not know. But being gone longer than I expected your letter arived & was opened by Brother Turley. But I have sent orders for no more letters to be opened that are sent to me. And with regard to the question you asked me on the scrap of paper. (I say yes let them eat or drink what they will in such cases). I would be pleased Brother Richards to hear from you often & give me all the news you [hear] from any quarter. I was pleased to hear of doors being opened in Scotland. Tell me where I can direct a Letter to Elder Mullenner in Scotland. Also inform me of any information you get from any of the Twelve. I wonder why they tarry so long in America may the Lord hasten them to this country. Also inform me concerning Sister Richards health from time to time give my love to her & tell her I would be exceding glad to see her but when I shall get out of this part of the vineyard I cannot tell. Pray for me Brother Richards that I may be meek & humble that I may fully overcome any speces of pride & self wrighteousness that I may feel my dependence on God in all things, & that I may know the mind of God concerning me in all things.

A word concerning you & Sister Richards. But what am I that I should teach or instruct thee or inquire the will of the Lord concerning thee. O that I was more worthy that I might speak thee the desire of thy heart in this thing & that I might more fully know the mind of God concerning myself & all things that are required at my hand that I might be more fully prepared to greant thee thy request. But if you can receive it at my hands I say unto you thus saith the Lord let not my servant Willard Richards litely essteam his calling or Station for I have called him & he is a chosen vessel unto me & no man shall ever do his work or take his crown. For he is humble & seeks my will. His afflictions shall work together for his good in the end. Let him be not weary in committing his case unto the Lord or trusting in my name & I will bring it to pass & the darkness shall pass away & the light shall come. & I [shall] breck the bands that bind him &

lift him from those under his charge for they [are] not worthy & some are under condemnation for litely essteeming the priesthood & him whome God has set over them. Let him still call upon me in Mighty prayer & be not weary committing his companion & all his ways into my hands & I will work out his deliverance in a way that I have prepared. & he shall yet have many souls as Seals of his ministry, & be mighty in council, & much beloved by his brethern the Twelve.

Thus Dear Brother is the voice of the spirit concerning you & I would say to Sister Richards, by way of council to try not to be discouraged nor desire to die but to live. Though your afflictions may be great for a time yet consider what Jesus has bourn. Commit all yours ways unto the Lord you will ere long enter that rest that remains for the people of God. Then your morning will be turned into joy & will be satisfyed with the goodness of the Lord. I feel as though the Lord will open a door whereby you will be liberated before many days. I will pray for you before God that your faith fail not & that you may have grace & strength according to your day. Whatever is manifested unto me I will endeavour to communicate it unto you from time to time. Write me soon Brother Richards & dont be discouraged God will be your friend. I would be glad to see the second No of the Times & Seasons should you get one please send it to me at Ledbury. Any thing you may have upon your mind pleas communicate freely. It will meet a welcome reception.

W Woodruff

Excuse my scribling I dont have time to write very plain.

8

HEBER C. KIMBALL TO VILATE KIMBALL, APRIL 3, 1840

The waves rolled mountains high . . .
it seam[ed] as tho the sea would swallow us up

While the second contingent of apostles was still aboard ship, Heber C. Kimball began a letter to Vilate describing his departure from New York and the unpleasant ocean crossing. Full of interesting detail about provisions and life aboard ship, this account nonetheless emphasizes the difficulties of the voyage — a contrast to the unusually fast and smooth crossing he enjoyed in 1837. Compare this letter with Parley P. Pratt's account of the same voyage, which follows. Source: Heber C. Kimball Collection, Church Archives.

3 April 1840

In the english channel too hundred miles from Liverpoll beeting against the wind. Now my dear Vilate I will begin back at New York. and let you [k]now how things went with us, since I Rote last from York. I stade thare about fore weeks in the time, I was going from hous to hous teaching them the Gospell of Salvation, and also in publick while thare, thare was about forty Baptised in to the Church. menny more that was just Redy to go forward. And beter Saints I never saw before. They fed us and gave us clothes and money and such things as we had need of as much as it was in thare power as they ware verry pooer. Thare was one Georg Adams a Tailor that made me a pare of Pantaloons and a vest. The vest did not suit me and I gaive it to Brigham for it fittid him. This mister Adams was a Medthodist Teacher. He claimed me as his Spiritual Father in the gospell before we left he was ordained an Elder. He had been in the Church only a week.

The Patrick Henry did not sail on 7th of March as she did not guit Redy. We sailed on the 9 about 12 Oclock and before night we was out of sight of land. We had not been out but a short time before we was all sick. It continued so for three or fore days then began to guit ove[r] it. Those that had been sick with the chill fever suffered the most. I was very sick but I could not vomit. This made it still wors for me. I canot describe the seen. Suffise it to say that it was a great deal worse than it was when you and I went up the Lake. Our apitit[e]s did not surve us at first. The brethren put up evry thing that was good to eat. I will tell you what we had. Potatoes gren Aples, dried Aples, dride Prunes dried Plumes; Preserves quince, Plum, Peach; dride Beef, Ham, Pork, Cod fish, swet bread, bakers Bread, common bread, Crackers, Wrice, Chogar [sugar], Buter, Peper, mustard Salt, Horsh Redish Pickles lemmons Rasons, Pies.

We had Straw ticks and two Blankets and Coverled and Pillows. Br. Adams gave us thre[e] pare of sheets but we did not euse them, and twelve or forteen towels and sope. They gave us money to pay our passage, over the Sea. We had to pay 18.00 a peas which was two dollars less then others, the Reasson was becaus, one Mr Cresson came from Pheladelph[i]a. He went and got our pasage, being a quainted with the Agent he got it cheper, and telling him that we was Ministers. Let me tell you that most of the means was made out by those that was converted after I got thare, and some given by those of the world. One man gave ten dollars and a barrel of Bread. So my Dear companion how the Lord works in these Last days. Some of our brethren in Kirtland would not give us, for they did not believe the Lord had not sent us to preach the Gospel becaus we was sick. These ware those that colds them selves Saints. They will have thare Reword. When I see you I will tell you who they are. So you see if one will not an other will, for the Lord has the harts of all men.

Sartaday the 4 this morning sit my self down by our chest, the ship about half turned over, with a hard head wind, about 60 miles from Liverpoll. From N Y to this place we had a head wind. We had a heavy gale yes two of them that lasted sevrel days. The ~~Mountain rolled~~ waves rolled mountains high. I am not able to discribe. It seam as tho the sea would swallow us up some times. We ware driven before the wind to the Rate of ten miles an [h]our with all sail taken in, not a peas out as big as your Apron. It Rained and hailed and Snowed and thundered and Litned. The offersers and sailors said they had not seen such a time in fifteen years. The Captain is a verry carfull man so that no accident has hapen to the ship as yet or at anny one bord of it.

I relate one thing that will give you some idea of this storm. When Brigham and my Self lay in our berth we could look out of the Ha[t]ch way and see the Mountains of water. From the place whare we lay to the top of the Bulk works is [116] feet. Now you m[a]y think this to been strang[e]. It would been the sam[e] as to take and cut a hole three feet Square out Ridg of your Hous in the Center and lay in your bed and look out of this hole and see these Mountins. This would bee when we was in the vallies. One night thare was some of the bull works washed a way and much damage. Thare was but a few days but what the sea would beet over the bull works and come down the Ha[t]ch in torrants. Some days the pasengers and Sailors would bee as wet as tho they had been taken out of the sea. This would last sevrel days at a time. Now five to go to we had to lay a beed the most of the time, some times seam as thos I should freeze. I See Br. Orson [Pratt] seting on a bale of Cotten the water came on Deck so that the Cotten S[w]iming with him on it. My helth is quite good this day only I had to lay a beed most of the day. it is so cold.

The brethren all injoy good helth and thare courage is good. We have had perfect peas among our selves. Br. Hadlock has been cheaf coock. I have been coock [and] I have made good menny Pies and turn overs. and menny others good things. Sum times I think the Sea had brocken over its bounds, for it seems as far again as it did when I went before. We could not have gon in [a] worse time in the whole year for head winds. I bid you g[ood] evning. I have more to say to you tomorrow, good night.

[*On address page, different hand:*]

Have arrived and B Young, PP. Pratt. O. Pratt Hadlock G.A. Smith, H.C. Kimble. When you write always give an account of all the Elders familys as to their health &c. I mean those Elders that are here. & you had better tell the other Sisters to do the same & then we might all of us know about the health of our families &c.

Direct to No. 43 Norfolk St. Liverpool England care of John Taylor
I am as ever your own Heber Kimble

Vilate Kimble

Commerce Hancok Co Ill

United States

9

PARLEY P. PRATT TO MARY ANN PRATT, APRIL 6, 1840

We had fiddling, fluiting, dancing, singing . . . togather with Blasphemy, Swearing, Contending, Laughing, Courting and Vomiting

On April 6, 1840, almost as soon as he stepped ashore in Liverpool, Parley P. Pratt wrote to Mary Ann. Although, like Heber C. Kimball, he provided her a wonderfully descriptive account of the ocean voyage, it is interesting to note the different details the two men decided to report. Parley devoted considerable space to telling Mary Ann how anxious he was to have her and the children join him in England — perhaps the reason that he emphasized the more positive side of the voyage. Source: Parley P. Pratt Collection, Church Archives.

Liverpool, Eng. April 6th, 1840

Mrs. Pratt,

We all arrived in safety this morning, 28 days from N.Y. We are all well, for which we thank God. I will now proceed to give you some account of our passage. There were about 50 or 60 stearage passengers. Some 6 women and 10 children. Some Irish, some English, some Scotch and some Americans, and some of the filthyest, Lousyest caractors I ever saw. But all very generous and kind to us, and mostly to each other. We had fiddling, fluiting, dancing, singing, (mostly Love or war songs, some Religious) to-gather with Blasphemy, Swearing, Contending, Laughing, Courting and vomiting, as well as Cooking, Eating, drinking, sleeping and reading; and I had like to have said preaching, for the mate sometimes delivered us a Negro Sermon.

After Eld Foster left us in N York Bay, we sailed with a fine breese, till we saw the sun set behind a distant Island, soon after which being rather quamish we went in to our filthy dungeon and retired to rest. By this time the vessel tossed very much and we were all quite sick and some began to vommit. Next morning I arose first and went on deck. The wind was still fare, the sea rough and nothing in sight but the distant Heavens, and the wide expance of ocean. We all continued sea-sick for 3 days mostly confind to our beds, for we did not feel half as sick wen Lying down as when seting up.

It soon came on a heavy gale of wind, mingled with storm, which drove us perhaps ten miles per hour with out having up any sail. This lasted two or 3 days, and the mate said he had not seen such a gale in 13 years. The sea Looked like mountains and vallies. Sometimes the ship would be on the top of a wave as high as a three story building, and the next moment it would plunge into a yawning gulf, where the water would be perhaps thirty feet higher than the vessel on every side, and Every few minits a mountain wave would dash over the deck and drench the sailors and Every thing in sea water. The waves frequently broke over the uper deck where you stood when we viseted the vessel. After five days, the wind turned into the east and Blew against us hard for four days, during which we were exeedingly tost; all the sailors wet to the skin and many of the passengers wet as often as they went upon deck, and even Barrels of water dashed into the hole and wet some of the women in their Births. No one could stand or walk with out holding on, and the dish would frequently run a way with the spoon. Everything had to be Lashed to its place with ropes, and several nights we Lay awake rolling in our births and holding on to keep from being thrown out.

After four days head wind there came a perfect calm and the vessel stood still for some hours. The wind then blew Lightly in our favour, for a few hours, and then turned eastward again, and blew hard for some days, then another calm, and after it a light breese in our favour for a few hours and then more heavy winds against us, and so on till the second of April, when at the seting of the sun we saw land, like a distant Cloud. It was a part of Ireland. The first we had seen for 23 days. We were then 200 miles from Liverpool and the wind still ahead insomuch that it took us four days to get in to port. We wasted, gave away or eat up all our provisions so that we had to buy one or two meals towards the Last. But if we had antisipated so long a passage we could have been more prudent and it would have been sufficient for a much longer voyage. Our passage was 8 or 10 days Longer than usual. There was but little sea sickness after 3 days.

The passage seemed very Dreary for it was so cold and wet that there was no comfort to be taken on Deck, and it was wet and crowded, and Dark and filthy to be below. But much of the suffering would be dispensed with if one would come over in a warm pleasant time in the season; but After all, the Women and Children seemed to stand it very well, the Little ones two or 3 years old were frequently playing on the Deck. One man had 4 children about the age of ours, the youngest a babe, he had no person but himself to take care of them. One woman had a Little babe 3 weeks old. She got a long very well. The Child was not sea sick at all.

On the passage I would allways be dreeming when asleep, and not one night passed in the whole voyage without my seeing you and the children in my dream.

Yesterday we passed the day in plain view of the mountains of Wales besprinkled with houses and farms, and this morning we found the ship at anchor in a view like it was when you saw it last; while on one side was Liverpool, like N York, and on the other it looked like Brooklyn. We 3 of us took a little boat and landed early in the morning. As we jumped ashore Br Young gave a Shout and Br Kimball and myself thought Amen. We took Board and Lodgings at Mrs Beals, No. 8 Union Street, where I now sit writing. 3 Oclock pm, O[rson] P[ratt], R[euben] H[edlock], and G[eorge] S[mith] have just Landed and Sat down to dinner at our Boarding house. G. S. Sais thank God, we all think amen.

So here we are in a new world to us, and yet the very world of our fore fathers, and a world where we hope soon to have thousands of Children in the Gospel. The faces I have seen here look nothin different from Americans. The Buildings more ancient and durible. The houses are more stout, large and Beautiful; the ladies I have seen are not as Beautiful as ours; But the Carts 3 times as large, and Begers more in earnest, Manners some what different, and Little or no timber in any direction; and yet upon the whole it seems much like our own country.

I have now given you a sketch of our journey, and I would now Inform you that when the sun rises here and we arise, it is only a bout 2 oclock in N.Y. and you lye sleeping for four or five hours longer, and when we go to rest here at 9 in the evening it is about half past four in the afternoon with you. As to house rent in this country I am in formed it is not one half as dear as in N.Y. and as to fewel it will not probably cost one third as much as in N.Y. and as to provision it is as cheep, and merchandise of every kind nothing like as dear here as there. Upon the whole I do not think it will cost us much to live in this country as in that.

Here all the kingdoms of Europe are before us on every side. Here is a boundless harvest for the next 15 or 20 years, or as long as God holds forth the arm of mercy: and here if the Lord will I expect to spend five or ten years at least. Time with me is to precious, money to scarce, and comfort to dear, to be thrown away in crossing the ocean every few months. Therefore in view of all these things I wish you as soon as you get this letter, to sell every thing except beding and wearing apparrel, and fill two chests and a trunk, and get ready to come to England the first oppertunity, with Br Hyde, Br John Page, Br Winchester and Lady, or whoever comes first.

Do not Bring a new feather Bed, nor any Books, nor more dishes than you need nor any article unmade up; if you do the duties will be more than to buy them here. Collect all that is due for Books; sell all you can, Pay the seventy five dollars to the printer, Mr Harrison; and Leave the Book Buisness with Eld Foster [let] him sell them whole sale and retale and Pay the money in, to Mr Shipman as he gets more Bound: and so till they are all Bound: or till I write to him on the subjet. I will allow Eld Foster a good percent For his trouble, if he will take Charge of this Buisiness. And now I say to you and to him in particular Do not let the Books go without the pay in hand, for they have cost me much money and I owe for them; and I need the remainder after the debt is paid, to support my family.

If you are careful in making a bargain you can get yourself and Children a passage to Liverpool. I [count] whole 1 passage and one half. If you can get a passage in the 2d cabbin in stead of the Stearage. It will only Cost a few dollars more, say 4 or 5 and it will not be so crouded with filthy vagrants of the rougher sort. The Cook will Cook your provisions and wash your dishes all the way for a dollar or two, although you will have to prepare it and cary it to him. And as to milk, they had a cow on board and gave the children and women plenty of milk, and very frequently others got it also.

If you get this Letter in one month after date I Shall begin to look for you the Latter part of june. If you think you cannot stand it to come any other way, perhaps some good friend will help you to money by loan or otherwise; if so then take cabbin passage, which by takeing pains can be got for you and the children for 150 dollars. You will then be in a clean, warm, well firnished place, everything foud you, and a Chambermaid to wait upon you. If you take cabbin passage you need not wait for any of the Elders to come with you, for it will be conveniant to come alone, as much so as to go to Boston. Women cros the sea a Lone as often as any other way, Bothe in the sterage and in the cabbin. [*two illegible words*] passage takes from 18 to 20 days. Then you Land in Liverpool, order a carriage to Mrs Beals, Union Street, No 8, she keeps a boarding house. You can then stay there, and send a line to me, to Preston, Pole St, No 21, which is 30 miles distant or you can take passage and come out to Preston in about 3 hours. And depend upon it, If my life and Liberty is spared I will be found in Preston waiting for you whether in June or July.

Courage, Mrs Pratt, you have performed more difficult journeys than this, and if you will take hold with courage the Lord will bless and prosper you and our Little ones and Bring you over in Safety. I must now close. Bless the Children for me. My Love to all the Saints. God Bless you all Amen. The Brethren send their Love Both to you and all the friends, with many good wishes.

	I remain your faithful
Mary Ann Pratt	Husband P.P. Pratt

Direct your Letters to Preston, Lancashire, Eng. Pole Street, No. 21.

It may be some of us will be preaching in Liverpool when you land. and perhaps there will be Saints there. If so we will leave written directions with Mrs Beal No. 8 Union Street so that by enquiring for me you will find us.

10

WILLARD RICHARDS TO BRIGHAM YOUNG, JUNE 15, 1840

It seems I ought to see my wife

Though Willard Richards begins and ends this short letter with information about his ministerial labors, the continuing illness of his wife Jennetta weighs heavily upon him. Here a discouraged Willard, writing from Dymock, seeks additional advice from friend and quorum president Brigham Young, Manchester, who had earlier suggested that the Richards family move to Manchester where Willard could help his wife and still serve. Jennetta declined, however, and explained why in a letter that Willard here shares. A Thompsonian or herbal doctor, Willard has used his medical skills on her behalf but to no avail, nor have prayers and faith yet prevailed. What is God's will? Source: Brigham Young Papers, Church Archives.

Dymock June 15 1840

To Bro B. Young,

After walking from Turkey Hall almost melted. I sit down to tell you we had a good meeting yesterday at the chapel, full house, men women & Devils. I have not time to tell you porticulars, only I told them I would never attend another meeting in that place if they did not take take care of those Rascols — though the Lord helped me to scare the Devil pretty well till after conference, but more porticuler hireafter.

In the midst of the meeting I received a letter from Jennetta — Dated June 9th Walkerfold. I will copy a few lines:

"Yours of the first instant I received this morn, which I will attempt to answer if it be only a few words for I am very poorly. Have only just got out of bed, can sit up but little at a time, never free from pain a moment. No not one moment. I can assure you that Death would be a friend at present, would my heavenly father take me to himself, but his will be done. I do not know what he intends doing with me — but let him do as seameth him good only some one in his kingdom with all his chosen ones. Have been very poorly ever since I wrote you last. I have taken the medicine (Thomsonian) while I could take it no longer, & have given it up — & will leave myself in the hands of the Lord, & say with Paul to live is Christ & to die is gain. [*Philippians 1:21*] With respect to my going to Manchester it will be almost impossible as things are, though I should be very happy to me[e]t you & all the Elders there & when you write to Bro Young give my kind Love to him. Tell him I thank him for his kind invitation." & [etc.]

Now you see we have much to do here next sabbath, & all the way to Manchester Conference. & as things are it seems I ought to see my wife. Now is not the Lord willing to hear prayers in her behalf, & let me stay in the vineyard till conference? If so get me an answer from the Lord at Manchester I beseech of you, for I have enquired & we have called upon God here — but no answer either, by dream, or vision, or Revelation. Does God want to Destroy her, or Does the Devil, or why is it her life must be a continual burden — & I be taken from the vineyard to take care of her? The heavens are brass here — & I wish you could get an answer from the Lord to these things & write me at Ledbury, [*illegible word*] friday next — & what the Lord says I will do.

The work is still progressing — have had no chance yet to enquire about more money — heard from Bro Benbows to day all well. We go to Lugwarden, Marsden Thacknell Hill, Stanley Hill conference & start for Potteries monday next. I am sorry to hear that John Moon has gone to America. He has lost a blessing.

Will it be necessary to return the pay for the Star from this region to Manchester & may it be [appopriated] to the payment of Sister Pitt (Kington)? The Star were between 4 & 5 shilling each bunch & we have not been able to find the Van (baggage waggon) office at Manchester yet. It wont do to pay so much for cartage if we don't [have all] this month.

Bro. Woodruff has gone 9 miles to attend meeting his eve — well — I am in great haste.

Yours forever

Willard R.

I have just written to Sister Richards to encourage her to get faith & come to Manchester yet. [*Illegible word*] all things are posible for God that [need] to [*illegible word*] — & I want to know his will in this Matter.

[*Written on the side of the address page:*]
Shall not be able to distribute all the Stars instantly
Calls keep increasing the only way to sell is to keep them on hand and they will all be wanted hear in time.

11

BRIGHAM YOUNG TO WILLARD RICHARDS, JUNE 17, 1840

I percive more than words in your letter

As senior member of the Quorum of the Twelve Apostles, Brigham Young provided the administrative direction and nurtured the brotherly bonds that helped focus and unify the mission. By letter when he could not do it in person, he encouraged, counseled, and kept informed the apostles serving with him. Though usually short, his letters document his wisdom and good humor, along with the friendship and love he shared with his fellow servants. This letter to Willard Richards, answering the urgent pleas in the letter that precedes it in this collection, illustrates the style of leadership that helped make the mission so successful (see photograph of address side of letter, p. 156). Willard and Jennetta did move to Manchester, as Brigham counseled, where Willard was able to assist his wife and still serve as a missionary. Source: Willard Richards Collection, Church Archives.

Manchester June 17 1840

Brother

Beloved Willard Richards,

I now set down to wright a fue lines to you. I have jest recived yours of the 15th. I am allways glad to here from my Broth[ren] but I sory to here that Sister Jane is not well. I percive more than words in your letter but how to ancer the dezire manefested I know not. I can ancer concerning the papers; all the monny recived for papers we expected to pay in for the borod monny in that place, ether to Brother Kington or Br. Benbow, after the expences was paid. I said somthing to you in my other letter concerning Br. Benbow's going to America before we pay him his monny, if Brother and Sister Benbow are amind to doe so, it would favor us for we can not get the Hym Book out till in to july and then they will have to be bound before they can be sold. If they goe as soon [*as*] july which likely they will, they will need to start as soon as the last of july or in augast in order to goe through in the plesent part of the year. There will be a nother company going from here about that time and I think some one of the American Br. will acompany them.

A verry little knews[:] we have agreed for the printing of the Book of Mormon this day have bargaind for the paper (190 reems demi which amounts to £ 111 18 03). We have hired the capender's hall for to Preach in, a large fine place for meetings it will hold about 2000 people. Last week was wisen weak. The Brotherin wanted somthing good so we told them to aske fore the blessings of the Lord and get the gifts. On frida[y] night we met together, by sunday there was plenty to rise up in the name of the Lord and speak with other tongues, and provisy in the name of Jesus. There are menny that have the power of God so upon them they can not work—and I tell you the Devel is close by and he has grate power. The second No of the Star is out. We are geting along finely with the hym Book thou[gh] my labor has been such that I am quite unwell, but I keepe doing with all my might.

I want to see the Brothern in that contry [*Herefordshire*]. I shall never forget my little mision in that contry with Brother Woodruff and with Br. Richards after he arived there. Br. P. P[ratt] has had a letter from O. Pratt. He is in Edenburge in Scotland, he has ben there som time. He hired a hall had perty large congr[eg]ations at first. He now has a bout one doson or 15 herears non[e] Baptized yet but the work is going finely in that contry round about. The Church is in cresing in Liverpool and about here. Give my love to Br. and Sister Kington and all the rest of them.

Now as to the other question about Jennet, thus saith the scripter[:] he that provideth not fore his own house hold [*1 Timothy 5:8*] has—but perhaps he has no hous, well has he got a famely[?] Yes, he has got a wife. Then let him see that she is taken care of and her hart comforted. But stop say som, why doe you not takcare of your family[?] I doe when circumstances doe not renderit otherwise. There is a difference betwene 3 months jorny and afue [h]ours ride. Now I say to ancer my own feelings com as soon as you can leve things there. This is not by revelation nor by commandment so put it not with the anapistles of the new testament but Brigham sayes come and see your wife.

To W. Richards I am yours in the N[ew] C[ovenant]. Brigham Young.

[Squeezed in upside down at the top of the page:]

A word to Brother Woodruff, I am rejoiced to here from you and of your prosperity in the work. When you are climing over sties remember me. M[a]y the Lord bless you and B[ro]. W[illard]. Give my love to the B[rethre]n that enquire after [*me*].

I am y[ours] in n[ew] c[ovenant], B. Y[oung]

[Postscript folded inside near address:]

Excuse erours and mestakes you must remember its from me. Elizabeth Havens is maried to J. Barlow.

387

12

BRIGHAM YOUNG AND WILLARD RICHARDS TO THE FIRST PRESIDENCY, SEPTEMBER 5, 1840

In a land of strangers . . . we feel our own
weakness & insufficiency for the great work

Five months after the full contingent of the Twelve arrived in Britain, Brigham Young and Willard Richards, on behalf of their quorum, wrote a lengthy and interesting report to the First Presidency in Nauvoo. Expressions of love and humble appeals for council begin and end the letter, but graphic descriptions of the distressing social conditions fill most of the pages. After describing how economic dislocation and pervasive taxation multiplied the misery of the poor, the apostles revealed that they had obtained credit in their own names so that more of the poor could escape to the land of Zion. Source: Joseph Smith Collection, Church Archives; also published in Ronald Walker, ed., "The Willard Richards and Brigham Young 5 September 1840 Letter from England to Nauvoo," *BYU Studies* 18 (Spring 1978): 466–75.

Star Office, 149 Oldham Road
Manchester, End.
Sept. 5th 1840

To the first Presidency of the church of Jesus Christ of Latter Day Saints, viz, Joseph Smith Jun, Sidney Ridgon & Hyrum Smith,

Beloved of the Lord and of his saints;

We esteem it a great privilege to be permitted to address you on paper, while we are far separated from you in a land of strangers, or perhaps we might say with propriety, the land of our forefathers: but be this as it may, it, is, indeed, a land of strangers to us, only so far as we have began to become acquainted with the inhabitants by a few months or years travels among them. The time of our acquaintance is but Short at the longest, but when we contemplate our absence from our homes & kindred, & especially from the Society of those who are over us in the Lord, whose faces we delight to look upon, & whose councils we are ever glad to receive, & rejoice in following, the time seems to be prolonged; & while we remain in this situation we hope you will not think us burdensome, if we trouble you occasionally to read our thoughts, & answer us a few questions, or many, even as many as is wisdom in God you should answer, for if we ask those which are improper it shall be on account of our ignorance, therefore we pray you forgive us. We desire not to council you in any, but to be counseled by you, for it is the desire of our hearts to do the will of God in all things, & we feel our own weekness & insufficiency for the great work which is committed to us, & feel to place all our hope, strength, & confidence in Israel's God, who is sufficient for all things, & not do as many who profess to love the Lord, & at the same time live in neglect of his commandments & his ordinances & despise the order of his council & government. No. We rejoice that the Church has a *Moses* in these last days (and an *Aaron* by his side) of whom the Saints may Enquire, as in days of old, & know the mind of the Lord.

We by no means suppose you ignorant of our situation or the situation of the people here, or our proceedings, & yet as is common among men we presume it will not be unacceptable to you to read something from us also, concerning the circumstances by which we are surrounded. There are some things which we expect to find common amongst men of different nations, such as a disposition to believe error instead of truth, & love Sin instead of holiness; also, a disposition, among a few of the honest in heart to believe the truth & rejoice in it when it is brought within their reach; & yet, such are the attendant circumstances with which people of different nations are surrounded & individuals of the same nations, but of different neighborhoods, that they require very different treatment or address in order to induce them to receive the truth, & even then will require very different degrees of time to accomplish or bring into exercise the same amount of faith. The man who has only read the histories of the people of England, which we had seen before we left America, is liable to meet with some disappointments, at least, when he comes to make his introduction amongst them. This may in part be owing to the historian, for it is generally the case that what we find in history relates more particularly to the higher classes, in the nations, for England, unlike America, is divided into classes; many indeed, but they may all be comprised in three, so far as we need designate at this time, (viz) Lords, Tradesmen, & mechanics or laborers, or, in other words, the highest, middle, & lowest classes, each of which have their particular customs, & manners but the histories we refer to, have more generaly treated of those of the higher order, or, at least, we find on acquaintance that those histories are now more applicable to the higher & middle classes than any other. But, perhaps a part may be owing to the great changes which have taken place in the nation, within a few years, with regard to money matters, which has caused a mighty revolution, in the affairs of the common people.

A few years since, and almost every family had their garden, their cow on the common & their pig in the Stye, which added greatly to the comforts of the household; but now we seldom find either Garden, Cow or Pig.

As we pass around among the country cottages & see the stone walls which are thrown down, but more commonly the hedges in a decaying & mutilated state, it is very naturally for us to inquire what have you here? & what the cause of this destruction? & we generally get but one answer, "A few years ago I had a flourishing garden on the spot you now see, & it was surrounded with this hedge which was planted by my own hand; I had a cow of my own which fed on yonder common. I labored on my masters farm, & had plenty of time, morning and evenings, to till my garden, in which I raised sauce Enough for my family, & every year I had a good pig, plenty to eat, & we were happy. But our Lords & masters have become more avaricious, & are trying to get all they can themselves, & will hardly let the poor live. You see my landlord has made my garden into a meadow, & feeds his own cattle upon it; the Lord of the manner fenced in the common, so that I had no place to keep my cow & I was obliged to sell her; I killed my pig to prevent its starving. The small farms are united & made into large ones, so we could get nothing to do on the land. I have been obliged to go into the factory, with my wife & children, to get a morsel of bread;" or, "I have taken to hand loom weaving, to keep my wife & little one from starvation."

By this brief sketch you will easily discover that the histories, which we refer to, were much more applicable to the times for which they were written, than for the present time, so that it is no wonder foreigners should be disappointed in visiting England at the present time, who may not have seen some very recent histories. It cannot be expected that we should give any thing like a history of all the changes in Old England, in one brief communication, & that in the midst of much confusion, arising from the preparation for the departure of the brethren, the getting up of the Star &c, &c, which is now crowding us, but you will see at a glance that the few changes we have hinted at would prove the cause of a multitude of effects.

Manufacturing is the business of England. The cotton mills are the most numerous, the weevers will get from 6 to 10 shillings per week, the spinners something more. The handloom weevers have to work hard to get 6 shillings per week. Now after paying 2 or 3 shillings rent per week — 1 shilling for coal, beside taxes of *every kind*, we might say, for smoke must not go up chimney in England without a tax, Light must not come in at the window without paying duties, many must pay from 1 penny to 6 pence per week for water, & if we should attempt to tell all we should want a government list. After paying all taxes what think you will a family have left for bread stuff? Add to this the tax on corn, which is a great share of the expense of the article, & what is left but starvation, leaving out of account all seasonings such as Peppers, Spices, &c which by taxation is four times the value it is in the United States. So you may well suppose that the poor are not troubled much with these things. The poor are not able to keep dogs, & if they were they would have to pay from 8 shilling to 1 £ per head per annum, tax. There are taxes for living & taxes for dying, insomuch that it is very difficult for the poor to get buried any how, & a man may emigrate to America & find a grave, for less money, than he can get a decent burial for in Old England. We scarce recollect an article without tax except cats, mice & fleas.

After what we have written we scarce need tell you that England is filled with beggars. They call at our doors, from [1/2] a Dozen to a Dozen per day. If we go in the streets they gather round us and it is hard to get rid of them without a penny, indeed, we do not try, so long as we can get a penny by buying or begging, for we remember that the measure we meet shall be measured to us again. Hunger & Rags are no curiousity here, & while things remain as they are what can we expect but theft, robery, murder which now fill the land—Leaving out of the account, both as cause & effect the drunkeness & gambling, sweering & debauching—which are common on every hand?

It will readily be discovered that the people have enough to do, to keep from dying with hunger without taking much thought for the im- provement of the mind. Many of the people cannot read, & a great many cannot write, children are admitted into the factories at 8 years old, working a part of the day & attending school a part till they are 14 years old, & then work continually, though as yet we have been able to discover but very little benefit from the factory school, it is by Parliament compulsion on the part of the masters, & not of free will, of course the easier got over the better, the cheaper the master, the more money remains in the pocket.

A few years since the spinners & weavers had "Turn outs" (as they now sometimes have in America) when their masters displeased them— but trade is now so dull, the masters care little for their manufactures, & have reduced their workmens wages to, almost, the lowest extremity, & if their hands should turn out for more wages, they have nothing before them but destruction for there [are] thousands & tens of thousands who cannot get one days work in a month, or six months, so they continue to labor 12 hours in a day for almost nothing rather than starve at once. Their miserable pittance is mostly oatmeal & water boiled together, & they would be quite conten[t]ed if they could get enough of that, with sometimes a little Treacle, which is blood & molasses, or a little rancid butter, or skim milk made of whiting & water to a great extent if we mistake not, although they have to give from 3 to 4 pence per quart for it. Buttermilk is also a treat to the poor people and is easily increased in quantity by whiting & water. There is no scheme which can be devised left unimproved to grind the face of the poor & thus [illegible word] & we feel that the time has nearly come for the words of James to be fulfilled[:] go to now ye rich men weep & howl for the misaries which are come upon you & [et]c. [James 5:1]

Much has been said in history of the learning & neetness of the English people. Of the latter subject we have neither time nor disposition to say much, although we are not short of matter, but simply ask how can it be expected that neatness should be a very prominent trait in the habits of a people who are obliged to improve every moment to get a morsel of bread? And as to learning such a thing as a news-paper is scarcely to be found among the common people, & if it was the English papers are filled with little else than "cold blooded murder," "Horrid Tragedies" "Roberies" "Thefts" "Fires" "Notice of the Que[en]s Dinner" or "Prince Alburts Ride out," or ["]visit to the Theatre," or ["]Rail Road accident;" "Hunting excursions["] &c, &c, &c, which is calculated to harden the heart & prepare it for far still greater wretchedness. Such is the poverty of the people that but few of the Saints can afford to take the Star we are publishing once a month, price 6 pence.

Neither have the priests much more information than the people, indeed there are many of the common people whom they dare not meet in argument, although they have their livings, thousands upon thousands, & some of them own whole townships or parishes, & will tell their parishioners & tenants if they allow any one to preach in their houses they will be turned out of doors, or if they are baptized they will fare no better, & thus many simple souls who believe our message dare not be baptized, because they have not faith sufficient to screen them from the threats of an insolent priest or factory master knowing they will worry them to the utmost if they displease him, our hearts mourn for such. It is apparently starvation on one hand & domination on the other. The Lord have mercy upon them—Amen.

We find the people of this land much more ready to receive the gospel than those of America, so far as they do receive it, for they have not that speculative inteligence, or prejudice, or prepossession, or false learning, call it what you please, which they have there. Consequently we have not to labor with a people month after month to break down their old notions, for their Priests have taught them but little, & much of that is so foolish as to be detected at a glance. Viewing the subject in this light we find ignorance a blessing, for the more ignorant of false notions the more readily they sense truth. The greatest opposition we meet with is from the Methodist. The Church of England would fain make themselves believe they are on the rock and cannot be shaken, therefore they trouble themselves little about these things, as yet, the more is to come.

Thus while we have not the learning and prejudice of the people to contend against as in America we have the influence of the monied *monopolizing* Priests & factory masters, & yet after all their influence, those who have received the word have generally received it very readily & the trouble of keeping up church discipline here has been small compared with our native country. But how those who receive the word so readily will stand in the day of trial remains yet to be proved, as there has been nothing in this land as yet which need try the faith of any one. But of this we confidently hope that many have already received the word which will endure unto the end.

We have many things we would gladly say to you did time permit, & were we not afraid of wearying your patience, but, brethren, bear with us a little further, we beseech of you, for we want to tell you a little of what we have done, & ask a few questions. & for your patience you shall have our feeble prayers that our heavenly father will multiply his blessings unto you.

According to council we have gathered from different parts of England & Scotland a company of the Brethren & sisters who are now in Liverpool ready to sail for America on Monday next. Most of them are very poor; Those who had money have given most of it to help those who had need, & as this was not sufficient; *we*, seeing the poverty & distress of some families, *have made* use of *our own credit*, among the *brethren* to carry them along with the rest. It was the decision of the Council in July that Elder Turly should lead this company to Zion, & he goes accordingly.

Brethren, our hearts are pained with the poverty & misery of this people, & we have done all we could to help as many off as possible, to a land where they may get a morsel of bread, & serve God according to his appointment; & we have done it cheerfully as unto the Lord. & we desire to ask you have we done right? Or is it a right principle, for us to act upon, to involve ourselves, to help the poor Saints to Zion?

We have heard by the bye that Brothers Joseph & Hyrum ~~Smith~~ are coming to England next season. Is this good news true? May we look for you?

Shall we gather up all the saints we can & come over with them next spring?

Have we done right in Printing a hymn book?

Are we doing right in Printing the book of Mormon?

Are we doing right in staying here & leaving our families to be a burden to the C[hurch]?

We have sent some of our papers to America, is this Right?

When the Book of Mormon is completed, will it be best for any one to carry any of them to America?

Shall we print the Doctrine & Covenants here or not? or will the D. & C. be printed & go to the nations, as it now is or not? or will it be reviewed & printed for the nations?

Shall we send all we can to America next season & stay here ourselves?

What is the Lords will concerning Bro. Richards? Shall he take his family to America next season? or shall he tary here with them awhile longer? what shall he do?

We have lately visited a museum where we saw an E[gyptian] mummy. On the head stone &c are many ancient & curious characters, & we asked the privilege of copying them, but have not received an answer, yet.

Shall we copy them & send them to you for translation?

Finally, Brothers, how long must we be deprived [of] the company of our Dear Brethren whom we Love for this works sake, & we feel that it is our privilege to love those who are willing to lay down their lives for the Brethren.

We need not say we send our love to you for that is always with you. Should you doubt it time & works must declare it. We hope you will favor us with a letter, for we exceedingly desire council in these matters, & all others, which the Lord may have in store for us.

We would rejoice to see you in this country, & although your hearts would be pained with the poverty & wretchedness that prevails – you would see many things which would interest you, such as the ancient & curious workmanship of the churches, cathedrals, monuments &c which have stood, some of them a 1000 years or more & are now in a good state of preservation.

We remember the observation of Bro Joseph, "that we should hardly get over the nation before the Judgments of God would overtake the people," & we fully believe it & are trying to do what we can to send forth the Gospel. One of our elders has gone to South Australia, one to the East Indies, & we expect one to start for Hamburgh in Holland this week. We want council & wisdom, & any thing that is good. Our motto is *go ahead*. Go ahead – & *ahead* we are determined to go – till we have conquered every foe. So come life or come death we'll go ahead, but tell us if we are going wrong & we will right it.

Your Brethren in the Everlasting Lord

B. Young

W. Richards

13

ORSON PRATT TO GEORGE A. SMITH, SEPTEMBER 24, 1840

I keep hammering & pounding away perhaps the stone will break by and by

Orson Pratt and George A. Smith enjoyed a particularly warm correspondence with each other. In this letter Elder Pratt tries to encourage his younger colleague, who is having a difficult time in London. Somewhat discouraged with his own work, Pratt seems to be telling George A. that neither one of them should be discouraged or "let go." Note also Orson's description of *Interesting Account of Several Remarkable Visions*, his pamphlet containing the first published account of Joseph Smith's First Vision. Source: George A. Smith Collection, Church Archives.

Edinburgh Sept 24th 1840

Dear Brother

Yours of the 22nd came to hand this morning. I was happy to hear from you & think that you have been prospered for I laboured a number of weeks faithfully in this city before I could baptise any one. Indeed I was not as much favored as you for I could not get the Priests out to hear as you have done: and notwithstanding I have been here upwards of 4 months & have held 5 or 6 meetings per week yet I cannot awake the attention of the people so as to get them out to hear. Only a very few attends the meeting but I keep hammering & pounding away perhaps the stone will break by and by. I have baptized only 40 & ordained 2 Priests. I think there is nothing like perseverance in any place. Therefore I hope you will hold on to the Londonites for it is an important station & will give us great advantages over the enemy. If you cannot turn the London world upside down perhaps you can weaken its foundations.

I shall be at conference on the 6th of Oct. if the Lord will. I shall bring about 2000 pamphlets with me which are now in the press. It contains 24 pages with a cover & the title page reads as follows "An interesting account of several remarkable visions and the late discovery of Ancient American Records which unfold the history of that continent from the earliest ages after the flood to the beginning of the fifth century of the Christian era; with a sketch of the rise, faith & doctrine of the church of Jesus Christ of Latter Day Saints." Price 4d. single copy or 25 shillings per hundred. Brother Mullener will be at conference after which he will go immediately home. If you wish to send any thing home you can send it by him. Do not fail of being at the conference If you can come conveniently as I want to see how you look for we have been seperated So long that I dont know but we should be strangers almost. I intend to return to Edinburgh immediately after conference if the Lord will & I am in hopes yet to prevail in this city. Elder Hedlock will be at conference. Give my love to Elder Kimball. I hope you will not be so backward about writing hereafter as you have now learned where to direct your letters. I now close by subscribing myself your brother in the bonds of the everlasting Covenant.

O. Pratt

To George A. Smith

14

RICHARD RUSHTON, JR., TO GEORGE A. SMITH, SEPTEMBER 25, 1840

We can never repay your kindness

The Rushton family of Leek were among George A. Smith's greatest admirers and best friends in England. Richard Rushton Jr. began doing missionary work almost immediately after his baptism. Here he reports to George A. Smith, who is preaching in London, on several happenings in Staffordshire, including instances of speaking in tongues. This letter illustrates the warm bonds which developed between the missionary apostles and the British Saints. Source: George A. Smith Collection, Church archives.

Leek 25 Septem 1840

Dear Brother Smith,

I received your kind Letter yesterday, and was happy to hear that you are in good health and Spirits, and that Elder Kimball is recover'd from his Ilness. We are Sorry to hear that the people are so harden'd in their hearts against the truth. We feel Somewhat disappointed that you cannot attend the Pottery Conference yet we Submit to your judgment and to the will of God.

Dear Brother we have had a many blessings in our church at Leek Since Last Sunday. Sister Mary Wych came over from the Potteries and at the meeting the Gifts of tongues fell upon many of our Sisters. Sister Mary and Fanny have the gift of tongues, Sister Plant and her two Daughters, Sister Wardle and Sister Harriet Wardle, Sister Alcock and Sister Maryann Tatton and Sister Mycock have all got the gift of tongues. These things of course cause great opposition from the Sectarians. Our room is crowded every Meeting. We Baptised four Last Wednesday Evening Namly Brother Edwin, and Brother Fredricks wife, Brother Knights wife and Brother Hudsons wife and the Saint[s] are in better Spirits and more united now than I have ever seen them before. Thay all join in Love to you and Brother Kimball. These things took Place when I was at the Potteries warning the people in that region.

Dear Brother you said in your Last Letter that the oftener I Stood up before the people, to warn them the greater Blessings I Should receive and you[r] words have been verified for I receive greater blessings and Power every time I get up to Speak even so as to astonish myself. Sister Wych has visited Several of the hireling Priests in Leek and confound[ed] and caused them to tremble at the Power of the Gospel. She sends her Love to you with her Prayer for your wellfare. We have taken another room more up in the town. My Father and Mother Sister Mary and Fanny and all the rest of our Family Send their Love to you and [are] Praying for the time to come when we Shall all meet together to rejoice in the fulness of Gods Blessings. Their is some more ready to be Baptised and the Spirit of enquiry is very great.

We are happy to hear you have commenced Baptising and ordaining in London. May God Bless your Labours in that great and wicked City, and give you many Souls as Seals of your Ministry. Dear Brother I cannot discribe the Love and gratitude I feel towards you for the great Blessings you have been instrumental in the hands of God of bringing upon our Family and Neibourhood. We can never repay your kindness towards us. But God will Bless you for your Labour. Dear Brother we Shoud be happy to see you again soon, and we hope the time is not far distant when we Shall all meet together to converse on the things of Christ and his kingdom. We continue to keep up good Spirits and warn the people to repent of their Sins and Be Baptized for the remission of them. I am Sorry I cannot write oftener to you But I am not at home Long together. Brother Knight and Brother Jackson are begining to Speak boldly before the people warning them to repent and also Brother John Wardle is doing the duties of his office and now Dear Brother farewell for the present and may the peace of God rest upon you for evermore is the fervent Prayer of your faithfull and affectionate Brother in the Gospel

Rich. Rushton

Canal Street Leek 25th Sept 1840

15

BRIGHAM YOUNG TO MARY ANN YOUNG, OCTOBER 16–30, 1840

How I long to see my wife and children

Brigham Young began this lengthy letter on October 16 in Manchester and continued it on the 20th and the 30th. Here he freely expressed his longings and concern for his family, and also his confidence that they would be alright. Along with news and inquiries for news, he includes a heart-felt testimony of Joseph Smith, "our Moses that the Lord has given us," and an expression of hope that the Church might more faithfully follow his counsel. All this and an interesting note to his brother Joseph Young is written on a single large sheet folded once to provide four writing pages. Source: Luna Young Thatcher Collection, Church Archives; this letter was previously published in Ronald K. Esplin, "Inside Brigham Young: Abrahamic Tests As a Preparation for Leadership," *BYU Studies* 20 (Spring 1980): 300–10.

Manchester oct 16 1840   No 1 Chapman Street

Once more I take my pen to wright to you. It is about five weaks sence I wrote; it was by Brother Turley who saled from Liverpool the 7 of september with about 200 of the Brethren. We have not hered from them yet, but think we shall before long. Brother P. P. Pratt, that left here the first of July for New York for to bring his famely, we have not hered a word from him. We have hered of O. Hyde & J.E. Pages starting for Jerusalem but have not seene them yet; We hope we shall before we leve England. They doe not apear to progress in there jorny much faster then we did. I am verry ancious to have them arive here for I long to see them. Brother Levi Richards wrote from Richmond July the 18th if I reculect right, he stated in his letter that a bout 10 of the Bretherin would start from New York the first of September. I hope they will be here soon for we want help in the vinyard. The work is grate in this contry—and to all apperence it will be verry short for nothing but destruction awates this Nation. It will spedily be upon them. I have not herd who is acoming but I trust they will be good men that will be sent, for churely it requires men of strong mind and determined persistence to due all things right, & then due nothing more.

I find I am not in America althou there is [s]carsly a night but what I dreme of being in my own native contry with som of my old frends. Brother O Pratt received a letter from his wife and one from Dr. Foster dated September. They boath stated that the families of the Bretherin ware all well, which gave me feelings of joy, to here from my wife and children while in a far contry; I am rejoiced to here that you are this side the missicippy River, I hope you and the rest of the Bretherin will have the priveledge of staying their till we returne and could wish that we might still have the prevelige of staying their and makeing our selves comfortble. I trust within one year from this time I shall have the priveledge [of] injoying the society of my famely; I feel as though their faceses would look and voices sound better than ever before. How I long to see my wife and children. When I let my mind meditate upon past scenes and the triels we have past through to gether, I feele as thou I could not concent to be so far from them, and whare I cannot administer to their comfort. But so it is, and I must be content. One thing I have to say prase God for it: I have wanted for nothing but what I could get, all of my wants have ben suplied. There has ben an efectual dore opened for us sence we left home. Could I be sure that my famely fared as well as I due, I would be happy. Still I have not ben concerned about them, for the Lord said by the mouth of Brother Joseph, that they should be provided for, and I believed it, and through the goodness of God I have ben anabled to send some little help to you, which I hope you have injoyed the good of in a degree.

We have past through scenes that when I think of it causes my hart

[to] greve and morn, your scenes in Kirtland and goin; up to Mos. [Missouri], your sickness the summer we ware there, and fortugue [fatigue] comming out of the State—I never want you to moove agan unless I am with you, if it can be so, but I trust I shall be reconciled to all things, knowing that all shall worke to gether for good especily to them that love the Lord [*Romans 8:28*]. and I think we have grate reson to love and serve him. To think that we have the priveledge of seeing and knowing what we doe in these last days, while thousands are in midnight darkeness.

Sence we have ben in Manchester We have don all that we posably could to spread this work. We have succeeded in makeing the priest mad, so that they rave like demonds. We keepe Baptiseing every weak which causes much per[se]cution. We have Baptised som of the old Westl[y]ans, which makes they feele verry uneasy.

I am with Brother Richards at Present. His wife sister Jennette has got a fine Boy. His name is Hebor John. He was born last Sabath the 11 of oct about 10 c-a.m. Brother and Sister Richards talks much about you. He thinks he has got the best woman for his wife that there is in the world, excep you. Their is non better in his eye then coson Mary Ann. Brother Kimball is with me. We are agoing to leve here soon for Preston and Liverpool on som buysness concerning the Book of Mormon. When we get through with our busyness in this part of contry we expect to g[o] to London to [*spend*] the Winter or the most of it their. I think it will be an advantage to my helth. I doe not enjoy good heth in this place though my helth is much better then it was. I trust I shall regain my heth agan by a nother year if [*I*] could be in a warm country it would be better for me.

I som expect som to goe in to Hamburgh Germany befor I return home. We have one Elder there, I hope there will be a church there before we leve this contry; their is a smal branch in Ireland. Brother Theodoah Curtis from New York is laboring their. Brothers Taylor and Clark is on the Ile is man, the work takes grate hold their.

[*October*] 20—yesterday about 2 oclock in after noon Brother P.P. Pratt, his wife, wife['s] sister and children arived here in Manchester. Brothers Kimball & Richards and my self had jest recieved two letters, one from Orson Hyde. He was in Pheledelphy Brother Page was not with him. He thought he should come with Brother Pratt. The other letter was from Father John smith to George Smith. We ware jest rejoycing for the knews from America when P.P. and famely arived. I know [now] am at liberty to goe to other places to Preach and attend to buisness. Br. P. Pratt had a long jorney, 37 days going to New York, 34 on there return to Liverpool, but they are all well and in good spirits, but I think they will get enuph of old England before one year roles around. I am glad that my famely is in America and if it was the will of the Lord I should be willing to be their my self though I am contented here at present.

How much I think of [*the*] children, I want them to be [*good?*] children. I pray for you all continualy that God will preserve you from all evel from sickness and from sin. My daughter Elizabeth be a good girl, love and serve the Lord with all your hart, stay at home, goe not into company unless it is among humble ones, let your mother direct you in all things. I pray the Lord to preserve you and the rest of the children. I have sent you som presents, but I have one for you and Vilate that I keep till I com home and bring it to you my self. Elizabeth doe not run about anny but take good care of your heth and take care of the little children and mind your mother. I want my daughter Vilate to be a good girl and mind your mother. Spend all the time you can get in stud[y]ing your book and instructing the little children.

Oct 30 I jest arrived in Liverpool with Brother Kimball. There was a letter here fore him from his wife. It gave us good knews from our famelys except the sickness of Elizabeth and Vilate which I hope is over by this time. I aske my Hevenly Father to preserve my famely till I returne home. How I long to see my famely or know they are well and provided for so that they doe not suffer for food and rament, and I know that the Church is poor and it is as much as they can doe to attend to without doing enything for my famely. I know they woul[d] [*have*] done if they could but th[e]y cannot. Sister Kimball states in hir letter that you boath had recieved a present we sent you. I am thankful that I had it in my power to send you som assistence, and be fore this I hope you have recived som things from Br Turly which will cause you to rejoice I think.

Last weak Brother Kimball and my self left Manchester for Preston and Liverpool on buisness about the Book of Mormon. Last Monday a letter came to Preston, from Br Richards. Stated that Br Lorenzo Snow had arived from Nauvoo, had brought a letter from you [*and*] one from Presedent Joseph Smith in ancer to mine to him. We wrote to Manchester to have Br Richards to keep all the letters till we returne to that place. When I com to your letter I expect I shall want to wright agane but I doe not know what the knews will be but hope it will [*be*] good. The worke of the Lord is roling on in this contry, the Elders are going in every direction to preach, the people are reciving there testemony and they are building up churches in meny parts of the Land. The Book of Mormon will not be out of press as soon as we expec[te]d but we shall get it to the People as soon as we can.

I feele to say [a] fue words of what past yesterdy. We ware in South Port at the house of Sister Dickson. Brother Peter Mellen [Melling] the Patriarch was there. He was fild with the holy Spirit of the Lord was upon him. He Proveside [prophesied] concerning things which caused my hart to rej[oi]ce in the Lord—I feele to say no more about it at present but may hereaf[t]er.

Sister Kimball stated in hir letter there had ben about 50 deths this seson. This gives pane of hart but still I feele they are better of[f] then they are here. Nawvoo is a sickely place. I think the mob will not truble them selves about the saints while they are in Nawvoo. I expect I should hardly know the Place if [I were] to come home now, and my Children will grow out of my knowledge so things will apear strange to me no dout when I doe come. I hope and pray you will not have so much trial to pass through as to alter you so I shall not know you. Sister Vilate says your house could hardly be caud [called] a shelter this makes me fee[l] bad but I will doe [all] I can for you to help you to make you and the Children comfortable while I am in the vinyard.

Doe tell mee somthing about T. B. Marsh when you wright agan if you can and tell me about [him], I have som dreams about him and others. Sister Kimball all so states that Br. Joseph Smith was agoing to send for som of the Elders to come home and takcare of their famelies, perhaps I am one of them. I have not seene his letter yet. I think we shall get home jestebout the right time. I want the Lord to conduct the hol matter, for I doe not feele as though I could doe enny thing with out him. The Lord must guide me or I shall goe rong.

How doe the church feele about Br. Joseph Smith at [this time?]. Is there feelings agan[s]t him. I have ben informed he has said the Brotherin would for sake him and som of them would secke his life and he would have to swim the Missi[ssip]p[i] River to get out of their hands. I shall be glad when church understand things and Lern that the Lord is God and he will takcare of his own work, and Moses will doe the work the Lord tells him to doe. May the Lord preserve us from provoking him as the Children of Isreal did the Lord and Moses in there day. I aske one thing of the Lord God the Eternall Father in [the] name of Jesus Christ that is that our Moses that the Lord has given us, may live to see the winding up scene of this generation, sin and inetquity destroyed from the face of the earth and Jesus come to raign with is people on the Earth and he go into the promist Caneneon [Canaan].

To Brother Joseph Young. We wis[h] you and your Br[ethre]n the Presidents of the 70ts woul[d] send som faithfull Elders that are men of judgment and that is capable of buylding up the Church—and managen things in the Church. and also see the Presedent of the Hy Priest Quorum and send som high preast. We have hered their is som on the way but we have seene non. L. Snow is in Manchester. We want menny. Brothers Hadlock and Clark will soon be gone over with companys. The Saints have got a start for to gether to America and goe they will, and nothing can stop them, and it is ne[ce]ssary to send some one of the America Brotherin with them. But for Heven sake due not send me here that is to big to be counsled. We doe not want men to leve there families to suffer for we can see enupth of poverty here with out here [hearing] of it from home. Among the Church there.

Some have sa[iled] for New orleans. Brother Mulner and some famelies from Scotland they have been gone about 2 weaks. We expect a company to start about the first of february provibly Br. Hadlock will goe with them. A nother company in spring early as posable and so[o]n they have so much of the spirit of getherin that they would goe if they knew they would die as soon as they got there or if they knew that the mob would be upon and drive them as so[o]n as they got there. They have the spirit of the times here as well as the Church there. They get the spirit of Provisi [prophecy] upon them and they tell many things that is about so and all we can due is to laugh at them a little and so pass it off. There will be a grate menny comming next seson.

I wish you would get councel from Br. Joseph Smith and doe acordinly. We will not ask you to send more Elders to us then we send to you. Change of Pasters [pastures] makes fat calves, so it is in comparson with the Elders, they due better in a strange contry then in there own as a general thing.

Give my love to Jane and the children and to all my frend[s], I have not time and paper to mechen names—I remember all of them—I am your Br. in the New Cv[Covenant] Brigham Young

Mary I shall not have time and room to say much more to you at present. I shall wright agan soon as I trust you will be anabled to take letters out of the office. I dremed last night of seeing the house whare you live. I [*illegible word*] it looked very open and cold, I feele for you. Tel Brs. of the first Presedent my love to them. I want you to see Br. Truman Angel for me and if you can due enny thing for him due it for me or my sake. Give my love to Mother Angel and Careoline. I am glad that you have not come a way from that contry. I trust I shall have plashier of seeing that contry agan. I am rejoiced to here that the Brotherin are settin up west and north. Take good care of the little Children. I have sent som presents to the Children. I am your husben and frend in E[verlasting] C[ovenant] Brigham Young

[*The letter was addressed* Mrs. Mary A. Young, Nauvoo Post Office, Hancock County, State of Illinoce, North America. *The notation* Single Sheet *reminded the postmaster that the large folded letter required only the lowest rate. It was to go* Via steam ship Packet to Halifacks and Boston. *Brigham Young penned the following postscripts in the address quarter of the large sheet, the last one added after the letter was sealed:*]

Mary take no concern about me for I am duing as well as I can and fare as well as I can ask. The Brotherin and Sisters would pluck out there eyes for me if it ware ne[ce]ssary. They due all they can for my comfort. They feed me and give me close and monny. They wash my feet and wate upon me as they would a little child, and may the Lord bless them for it and he will and they shall stand upon Mount Zion.

The climet dos not agree with me in this contry. I expect to try London this winter to see how that place will agree with me though my helth is a grate deal better then it was when I first came here. The helth of all the Bretheren is better. Be of good chere, the time will soon come when we shall meet agan and rejoice to gether. I supose the time seemes long to you and the Children that I am gon; it would seeme longer ware it not the will of Lord. When I think how diligant you are and how faithful to my famely and willing to suffer for the sake of my going to preach the gospel, you must be blest and blest you shall be. I pray the Lord to Bless you and I Bles you and all the faithful sisters—so farewell.

I am now in Liverpool but shall goe to Manchester to morrow or next day. Shall see Br Snow and find out more about things. I want to here from Br. Rigdon and know how he is and Br. G. Roberson. Give my love to them. Tell my Br[others] acording to the flesh to not come here till I returne home. May the Lord bless you and the Children and preserve your lives and helthes. I am as ever

Br Kimball sends his love to you and the children and all the frends.

[*Written in a box on the first page:*]
Mr. Brigham Young
52 Iron Monngor Row St. Luke Church London
in care of Henry Connor
Direct all of your letters to me [*there*] after you receive this as a bove stated as I expect to spend the winter their. B. Young

16

ORSON PRATT TO GEORGE A. SMITH AND WILFORD WOODRUFF, NOVEMBER 2, 1840

I presume we could do more good in Edinburgh & London
if we could bring the enemy into open combat

Inevitably Orson Pratt compared his slow progress in Scotland with reports of John Taylor's success on the Isle of Man and similar successes elsewhere. Reflecting on this, he concluded that opposition is often important to success. While fellow-quorum members met active opposition, in Scotland his strenuous efforts had so far generated insufficient interest *or* opposition for broad success. Note also Orson's early thoughts and mixed feelings about returning home. Source: George A. Smith Collection, Church Archives.

No 40 North Richmond St. Edinburgh
November 2nd—40
Dear brethren Smith & Woodruff
Yours of October 31st came to hand this morning. I cannot forbear tendering to you my thanks for the interesting news which it gave of the success & triumph of truth in Birmingham, Potteries, Preston, Glasgow, Paisley, Belfast, Hillsborough &c. It seems that the work of the Lord is truly triumphing among the nations. I was much pleased with the contents of the letter you enclosed; from it we can see that the truth is rapidly spreading in our native land. It seems that our persecutions have given it a fresh impulse.

This morning I received the "Manx Liberal" from the "Isle of man"; It contained a lengthy reply by Er Taylor to the Rev. Hey's second Address. Er Taylor has cut up Hey into fine fodder. The same paper contains Dr J.

405

Curran's conclusion against Mormonism It also contains a sad & laughable lamentation over the dying struggles of Methodistism by some person signing himself "A Staunch Wesleyan["] who probably had seen the folly of Mr. Hay. The probability is that the controversial war will continue a short time at least long enough to gether out the honest in heart. Er Taylor understands weilding the weapons of truth to a very good advantage & he has a very good good opportunity of doing it.

I presume we could do more good in Edinburgh & London if we could bring the enemy into open combat but in this place I can hardly get a dog to move his tongue. Indeed they are so effectually secured behind the bulwarks of Priest Craft that they are as careless as the Babylonians were when surrounded by Cyrus's army.

You ask me what I think about going home but I will assure you that it is a hard question & I hardly know how to answer it for I am in a strait betwixt not only two but many things for I am exceedingly anxious to see my family & I am exceedingly anxious to continue labouring in the vinyard. Sometimes I think about returning to stay with & visit them for a season & sometimes I think of sending for them & sometimes I think of going after them but as yet I am altogether undetermined relative to these matters. If you have entered into any determinations relative to going home &c. please inform me in your next.

[*At the bottom of the address page:*]
I have baptized none since my last. No news from any quarter by letter except from London therefore none to write. I am as ever

O. Pratt

To Ers Woodruf & Smith

17

HENRY CONNOR, JR., TO GEORGE A. SMITH, NOVEMBER 11, 1840

All the affection of A brother

Among George A. Smith's contacts and friends in London was Henry Connor, Jr., son of the first London convert. Although young Connor had a difficult time accepting the teachings of the American apostles, he was genuinely touched by George A. and the two apparently spent much time together discussing the scriptures. Only a day after the apostle left, Henry Jr. wrote his friend this poignant letter. Just a month later, on December 16, young Connor was baptized. Source: George A. Smith Collection, Church Archives.

Nov 11th — 40

My Dear Friend

I take up my pen to address you for beleave me I have all the feelings of A friend and A brother towards you. I hope you arived safe at your journeys end and that this letter will find you in good health and spirits. It is true that I cannot see the scriptures in the same lite as you yet I beleave the Lord has blesst me with some degree of Christian charity and I extend to you and all around the hand of friendship. I wish you success with all my heart in doing good to the sons of men for when I look around me I see little else but sin and wickedness. I am but A young beginner in the way of richiousness and as yet but little expearienced yet my trust is in God and I can say from my heart I am sincear in all I do and say. I shall feel it my boundend duty as A Christian to do all I can to assist you in any way that I can.

I must confess that I was loath to part with you for I feel for you all the affection of A brother. I pray that the Lord may [speed] you if you are wright and convince me that I am wrong. May you have faviour in the eyes of the people and do all the good you can to the perishing souls of men awaken the [cairless] and the ardend sinner encourage those that seek the Lord and do good unto all men and if my Dear Brother I should never again meet you to take you by the hand in this life may I meet you in A better place.

My Father is getting quite well and able to attend to his work. There is not any one knows that I have writen to you but W Woodruff. I was obliged to get your address from him or I should not have told him. If you can find time I shall be happy to hear from you till then fairwell

I Remain Yours Sincearly
H. C. Connor Junr

18

HEBER C. KIMBALL TO GEORGE A. SMITH, DECEMBER 12, 1840

You Say the Devle is mad. This makes me glad,
and I Shall not try to pleas him

Along with a commitment to keep each other informed about the work and to buoy each other up, the apostles shared a deep friendship that further motivated them to keep in touch. This letter, from Heber in London to George A. in Leek (but recently in London), is representative of the letters that traveled back and forth. Source: George A. Smith Collection, Church Archives.

London December the 12 1840

No 40 Iron Mongor Row Saints Luks Church London

Dear Brorather Smith I Recieved your last Leter with pleasure. Glad to hear of the prosperity of the work in that part of the Land. You Say the Devle is mad. This maks me glad, and I Shall not try to pleas him. I know that your disposition is some like mine on this Subjet. I have great love fore the Saints in that part of the Land. When I think of thare poverty it gives me Some Strong feelings. I Say in my heart O Lord Rowl on thy work and cut it chort in Richousness, that thy Saints may dwewll in peas whare poverty will be done away, when we can See face to fase, when we can have the prevledg of building and inhabit plant and Eat the frieut of the Same with out being driven frome the Same as we have Suffered in America. Dear Brother the day will Soon come So we will press forward to the prise which lais at the end of the Rase, when we will not have to Suffer as we do at this time.

The 13 this morning I feel to rite a few more lines that you may know how we guit a long here in London. Things go Slow here in this City. I baptised Sisters Cop[e]land Sister. Since I came here. She is the one that came and hurd when you and myself was here. I think Mr Morgan and his wife well go forward Soon. Thare are Sevrel others that believe. Last Sunday we had the Hous nearly full, both after noon and Evning on week days nights. Thare is only fore or five that comes in to hear besids the Church.

Elder Young left here on the 10 for Heritfordshier. He was here 9 or 10 days Spent his time mostly in looking at thing[s] in london. I Expected to Have gon with him to those Confrences but I thought I would Stay a chort time. The Br[ethren] Seam to think it was best. I have a bad cold and travling goes Hard with me. my lungs are very bad. I am not able to Speak much in publick or in privit. The are [air] is very dence, the weather Cold, the Smok So bad that they have to lite up thare Lamps, and we have to write by candle some time in the midle of the day. It makes me like a hors that has got the Heaves. Elder young felt quite porly while here. Br Robart Williams is here. He has no home only what we make fore him. He has a Father here but he dosenot go Home. on the acount of his Step mother. His Father Came to hear once. He Seames to hear and Recieve.

The Brethren and Sisters are all well at present. and feel well. Preas [*Priest*] Copen is by my Side this morning, thank God. When we guit threw with the duties of the day I will tell you more that is if thare is more to Say.

Good morning. 14 this morning we are Still alive. I have got a bad cold in my lungs which gives me a bad coff. I feel well at Hart and in good Spirrits. You know this is the main point. On the Sabath, In the after noon we had a hous full. We administerd the Sacrament at the Chappel. Before meting. All of the Saints present Except Mother Copen. After we got threw we then gave them a chort discours. Had a good time. Our Evning meting was not So full as the after noon. Mr Morgan and wife and Harrit Have Set the time to be baptised, on wensday Evning next. Harrit is on well with the Leprosy. Thare is Sevrel others that beliey.

I have just Recieved a leter from Elder Young. He had got to Chatten-ham. He Ses the prospect is good thare at present. [*Word*] from Elder O Pratt Stating that he had got one leter from his wife one from the quater master General he had got two numbers of the times and Seasons. Sept. and Oct. numbers. Gives the tidings of thare last confrance. Not much news in the leters. Elder Woodruff is well. We have Recieved a leter from Mrs [Songivannt]. She longs to guit with us to be baptised. She inquired fore you. I think I have told all of the news that I have to tell at present. Now dear Brother give my love to all of the Saints in that part. I cannot mention names fore I donot know them. May God bless you and them fore Ever. Elder Woodruff Sends His love. I am as Ever your Br in Christ

H C Kimball

[*Written on both sides of the address page, in Wilford Woodruff's hand:*]
Elder G. A. Smith

Dear Brothr, I have Receivet two Letters from [you] which I have not answered for the want of time one Dated Nov 30th the other Dec 3d. I was truly Glad to get them both. As Broth Kimball has told you the knews I shall not say much now. I shall be glad to hear from you at any time.

Give my love to all the Saints & take agood Share yourself. My Wife Sends her respects to you in her last letter & Said some of your Fathers family had been Sick but had got better. The work is prospering rapidly in America. Which makes me rejoice. Milton Holmes thinks of comeing to England this winter. Yours in the kingdom of patience

W Woodruff

19

GEORGE A. SMITH TO BATHSHEBA W. BIGLER, DECEMBER 5, 1840

*I am determined Never to take another Mission
across the Ocean without Leaveing a* Rib *at home*

While his fellow missionaries thought often of their wives and children, George A., the only unmarried apostle, thought of his sweetheart and bride-to-be, Bathsheba W. Bigler. George and Bathsheba made an agreement in 1838 to marry in three years thence. Though Bathsheba and their plans were much on his mind, George A.'s illness and his uncertainty about her address kept him from writing for months. Awkward and untutored but full of tender feelings, this letter breaks the silence. Source: George A. Smith Collection, Church Archives; part of a letter, same date, to Josiah Fleming.

Stoke Upon Trent Staffordshire   Dec 5th 1840
Dearest Sister Bathsheba

I take the Liberty to inform you in my Letter to Br Josiah, that you are Not Forgoten. I keep you Still in Memory and the Pleasante hours which I have Spent in your Society are also Remembered. I Should be very happy in the Enjoyment of A Privelege which I often anticipate of once more Enjoying your Society Which Was always vary Pleasant. And the Lord willing We Shall See Each other again & talk Over Matters. I am Determined Never to take another Mission across the Ocean without Leaveing a *Rib* at home unless the Lord So orders it. If you Look at the Motto on the Chain it Reads be ye Clean that Bear the vessels of the Lord. This Motto was my Choice when I was Called to My Lords Work and I am determined to Live up to it. I know that if the Power of Satan Does N[ot] Entirely Blind my understanding I Shall be faithfull to [*two illegible words*]. I told you that if I thought I Should Get A Companion For Life in England I would Make the Choice before I Left home but I Shall Never take any Such Step while you are the Choice of My Heart which is the Case at Present.

I have Not Writen to you as I ought to have Done. Will you Pleas forgive Me. I Expe[c]t Some Litters have been Lost. I heard your Family had Moved away after your Fathers Death and I Rote to America For their adress and for Eight Months after I Left Home I Could Not Write any and most all thought I Should not Recover of my Sickness & Blindness which I then had which Delay an[d] My hurt Must have kept you 12 Months without hearing from Me. Truly if you and I Come to gather it will be because we were Each others in Eternity. I Remain your Most Faithfull

Friend in a Distant Land   Geo. A Smith   to Bathsheba Bigler   Pleas write to Me as Soon as you Get this

20

GEORGE A. SMITH TO BATHSHEBA W. BIGLER, JANUARY 14, 18, 1841

*If I could Enjoy your Society I Should be Well Satisfied
but the Lord called and I have to Obey*

This second letter from George A. Smith to Bathsheba W. Bigler bears an inside address of January 14, but the letter itself suggests that the body was begun on January 18, just three days before the marriage date they had agreed to in 1838. The plan now, with George thousands of miles away? "We agreed to Attend to these Matters as Soon as Convenient after the time which had been appointed."

Burslem Staffordshire England January 14th
1841

Dearest Bathsheba as the time apointed for our trial of the Game of Choosing as we first agreed in the Month of January 1838 has almost Gone and we acording to that arangement Should be Maried on the 21st day of this Month and it is Now the 18th and I am Nearly 6000 Miles from you and 3 Days to the time appointed I Remember it Well and Shall Not forget it for years to Come. And as we agreed to Attend to these Matters as Soon as Convenient after the time which had been appointed we Shall Let [it] Rest till then. I am Certin that you have yet A Sure Confidence in Me if you Still Retain your Integrity. As you know I Love Integrity and those Who Possess it and I am A true friend and do not think it Prudent for me to forsake *A tried friend* for A New One as my father['s] advise to me Was to Not Go far from home after A Wife.

Dear Sister you Will Please Excuse me as I am thinking the time will come When We Shall be One. The Lord knows and Will mak known in Due time. I am Enjoying Comfortable heath for Which I feel thankfull. I am Not Strong but Comfortable and as happy as I Could. If I could Enjoy your Society I Should be Well Satisfied but the Lord called and I have to Obey. I shall have to Leave of[f] Writing and Go to Meeting as I have Writen three Letters to Day one to G W Gee one to H C Kimball one to J Taylor.

After taking Some Supper of tost and Cold Water And Looking at the time I find I have Nearly one hour before Meeting and So I finish my Letter. It Will be as Good half an hours conversation. Perhaps I Shall Send

A Number of Letters to you by Elder Clark Who is Going to Start for Home in A Few Days and as it is the only Chance we have to Convers I feel to impose. I Received the Letter you Wrote and have answered it as it Was Jacobs Letter. I Directed it to him. It may Cause A Laugh at my Expense if Not at yours as I Wrote Some things that Were Laughable and hope the Letter Will Reach you Safely. I Was Much Pleased With the Letter you Sent me and Read it over many times and Would be Glad to See you and talk it over as I Read it over and Over again. I Will Write By the Next Steam Packet Which you Will get before you Do this and hope you Will Give me Another Letter as soon as Convenient. Give my love to your Mother and Jacob Sarah and Malisa and Caleb Lyons and Josiah Fleming Sister Nancy and Br and Sister Martin all Our Virginia friends as if I wrote their Names And take A Large Share to yourself.

The work of the Lord Prospers in all Parts of this Kingdom. The Elders are Well and Doing Well. Elder Hadlock is Enjoying better health than he has been and Elder Kimball is Well. Sends his Love to you. Also Elder Woodruff. They are in London and doing Well. Now Dear Sister all I can Say is to again advise you to Remember the Principle of Pure and undefiled Religion and *the Golden Rule* and all Will bee Rite. I Must Confess I think the Advise Needless but it Will do No hurt. But the Cry is its Meeting time. I must Ley Down my pen and Go So I Bid you Good Night.

Jan 19th. On Looking over my Sheet this morning I feel Most Ashamed of it but as you know how to Look over my faults I shall Let it Go. I had A Good Meeting Preached to A Crowded Asembly Ordained one Elder and Confirmed one A Member. Had the Best Liberty to Preach that I have Enjoyed for Some time. My heath is geting better that is my Lungs. But my Sheet is full I must Close by Saying my hearts Desire and Prayer to God is for your Preservation Welfare and happiness and I Remain Sincrely your Most faithfull friend   George A. Smith To Bathsheba Bigler

January 19th 1841

Will you Please Remember Me to Sister Kimball and family to all the Young Gentleman And Ladies Who Enquire after me. You will also Please Give my Love to My Father['s] Family and Espetialy my Sister Caraline. Tell her I am in firs[t] Rate Spirits And think if I Do Not Get home in 1841 I have Strong hopes of Geting there in the 19th Century. The Lords Will be Done   G A S
Success to T G Bishop and Charles Shermand & Eliza

21

JOSEPH SMITH TO THE TWELVE, DECEMBER 15, 1840

I have great confidence in your united wisdom.

The following letter demonstrates Joseph Smith's awareness of the Twelve's labors in Britain and his full satisfaction with them. No doubt this was especially important to the Twelve since they had received so little official communication from the Presidency. (For the first six months they received none; in late fall Lorenzo Snow arrived with their first letter from Joseph Smith, and this, which arrived midwinter, would have been the second.) Among business items in the letter was the Prophet's approval of their plans to return home in the spring, and among the news from Nauvoo was Joseph Smith's own explanation of the newly revealed doctrine of baptism for the dead. Source: the hard-to-read original is in the Joseph Smith Collection, Church Archives, but we have relied on the transcription in Dean C. Jessee, ed., *The Personal Writings of Joseph Smith*, 480–87. A major excerpt from the letter, undated, appeared in *Times and Seasons* 1 (January 1, 1841): 258–61; and a slightly edited version can be found in Joseph Smith's *History* 4:226–32, but it is misdated as if it had been written in October 1840.

Nauvoo Hancock Co, Ills. Decr. 15. 1840

Beloved Brethren.

May Grace, Mercy, and Peace rest upon you, from God the Father and the Lord Jesus Christ.

Having several communications laying before me, from my Brethren the "Twelve" some of which ere this merited a reply, but from the multiplicity of business which necessarily engages my attention I have delayed communicating to them, to the present time. Be assured my beloved brethren, that I am no disinterested observer of the things which are transpiring on the face of the whole earth and amidst the general movements which are in progress, none is of more importance, than the glorious work in which you are now engaged, and consequently, I feel some anxiety on your account, that you may, by your virtue, faith, diligence, and charity, commend yourselves to one another, to the Church of Christ and to your Father which is in heaven, by whose grace you have been called to so holy a calling, and be enabled to perform the great and responsible duties which rest upon you. And I can assure you, that from the information I have received; I feel satisfied, that you have not been remiss in your duty but that your diligence and faithfulness have been such as must secure you the smiles of that God, whose servants you are, and the good will of the saints throughout the world.

The spread of truth throughout England is certainly pleasing; the contemplation of which, cannot but afford feelings of no ordinary kind in the bosoms of those who have had to bear the heat and burthen of the day, and who were its firm supporters, and strenuous advocates in infancy, while surrounded with circumstances the most unpropitious, and its destruction threatened on all hands. But like the gallant Bark, that has braved the storm unhurt, spreads her canvass to the breese, and nobly cuts her way through the yielding wave, more conscious than ever of the strength of her timbers and the experience and capabilities of her Captain, Pilate and crew.

It is likewise very satisfactory to my mind, that there has been such a good understanding existing between you, and that the saints have so cheerfully, hearkened to council and vied with each other in their labors of love; and in the promotion of truth and righteousness; this is as it should be in the Church of Jesus Christ. Unity is strength. "How pleasant it is for brethren to dwell together in Unity &c." Let the saints of the most high, ever cultivate this principle, and the most glorious blessings must result, not only to them individually but to the whole church — The order of the kingdom will be maintained — Its officers respected, and its requirements readily and cheerfully obeyed. Love is one of the leading characteristics of Deity, and ou[gh]t to be manifested by those who aspire to be the sons of God. A man filled with the love of God, is not content with blessing his family alone but ranges through the world, anxious to bless the whole of the human family. This has been your feelings and caused you to forego the pleasures of home, that you might be a blessing to others, who are candidates for immortality but who were strangers to the principals of truth and for so doing I pray that Heavens' choicest blessings may rest upon you.

Being requested to give my advice respecting the propriety of your returning in the spring, I will do so willingly. I have reflected on the subject some time and am of the opinion that it would be wisdom in you to make preparations to leave the scene of your labors in the spring. Having carried the testimony to that land, and numbers having received it, consequently the leaven can now spread, without your being obliged to stay. Another thing, there has been some whisperings of the spirit; that there will be some agitation, some excitement, and some trouble in the land in which you are now laboring. I would therefore say in the mean time be diligent, organize the churches and let every one stand in his proper place, so that those who cannot come with you in the spring may not be left as sheep without shepherds.

I would likewise observe that inasmuch as this place has been appointed for the gathering of the saints, it is necessary that it should be attended to, in the order which the Lord intends it should; to this end I would say that as there are great numbers of the saints in England, who are extremely poor and not accustomed to the farming business, who must have certain preparations made for them before they can support themselves in this country, therefore to prevent confusion and disappointment when they arrive here, let those men who are accustomed to making machinery and those who can command a capital even if it be but small, come here as soon as convenient and put up machinery and make such other preparations as may be necessary, so that when the poor come on they may have employment to come to. This place has advantages for manufacturing and commercial purposes which but very few can boast of; and by establishing Cotton Factories, Founderies, Potteries &c &c would be the means of bringing in wealth and raising it to a very important elevation. I need not occupy more space on this subject as its reasonableness must be obvious to every mind. In my former epistle I told you my mind respecting the printing of the Book of Mormon, Hymn Book &c &c. I have been favored by receiving a Hymn Book from you and as far as I have examined it I highly approve of it and think it to be a very valuable collection. I am informed that the Book of Mormon is likewise printed which I am glad to hear, and should be pleased to hear that it was printed in all the different languages of the earth. You can use your own pleasure respecting printing the Book of Doctrine & Covenants, if there is a great demand for them, I have not any objections, but would rather encourage it.

I am happy to say, that as far as I have been made aquainted with your movements, I have been perfectly satisfied that they have been in wisdom, and I have no doubt but the spirit of the Lord has directed you and this proves to my mind that you have been humble, and your desires have been for the salvation of your fellow man, and not your own agrandizement and selfish interest. As long as the saints manifest such a disposition their council will be approved of, and their exertions crowned with success. There are many things of minor importance, on which you ask council, but which I think you will be perfectly able to decide upon as you are more conversant with the peculiar circumstances than I am, and I feel great confidence in your united wisdom, therefore you will excuse me for not entering into detail. If I should see any thing that was wrong I should take the priviledge of making known my mind to you and pointing out the evil.

If Elder Parley Pratt should wish to remain in England for some time longer than the rest of the Twelve, he will feel himself at liberty to do so; as his family are with him consequently his circumstances are somewhat different to the rest, and likewise it is necessary that some one should remain who is conversant with the rules, regulations &c &c of the church and continue the paper which is published; consequently taking all these things into consideration I would not press upon Brother Pratt to return in the spring.

I am happy to inform you that we are prospering in this place, and that the saints are more healthy than formerly, and from the decrease of sickness this season, when compared with the last, I am led to the conclusion that this must eventually become a healthy place.

There are at present about 3000 inhabitants in Nauvoo, and numbers are flocking in daily; several stakes have been set off in different parts of the country, which are in prospering circumstances. Provisions are much lower than when you left. Flour is worth about four dollars per barrel, corn 25 cents per bushel: pottatoes about 20 cents and other things in abou[t] the same proportion. There has been a very plentiful harvest indeed, throughout the Union.

You will observe by the "Times & Season" that we are about building a Temple for the worship of our God in this place: preparations are now making, every tenth day is devoted by the brethren for quarrying rock &c &c. We have secured one of the most lovely sites for it that there is in this region of country. It is expected to be considerably larger and on a more magnificent scale than the one in Kirtland and which will undoubtedly attract the attention of the great men of the earth. We have a bill before the Legislature for the incorporation of the City of Nauvoo for the establishment of a Seminary and other purposes, which I expect will pass in a short time.

You will also have received intelligence of the death of my Father, which event altho painful to the family and to the church generally, yet the sealing testimony of the truth of the work of the Lord was indeed satisfactory; the particulars of his death &c you will find in the Sep. number of the "Times and Seasons." Brother Hyrum succeeds him as patriarch of the Church, according to his last directions and benedictions.

Several persons of emmine[n]ce and distinction in society, have joined the Church, and become obedient to the faith, and I am happy to inform you that the work is spreading very fast on this continent. Some of the Brethren are now in New Orleans, and we expect to have a large gathering from the South.

I have had the pleasure of welcoming about one hundred of the Brethren from England who came with Elder Turley, the remainder I am informed stoped in Kirtland, not having means to get any further. I think those that came here did not take the best possible rout or the least expensive. Most of the brethren have obtained employment of one kind or another and appear tolerably well contented and seem disposed to hearken to council. Brothers Robinson & Smith lately had a letter from Elders Kimball, Smith & Woodruff in London which gave us information of the commencement of the work of the Lord in that City, which I was glad to hear. I am likewise informed that Elders have gone to Austrailia & to the East Indies I feel desireous that every providential opening of that kind should be filled, and that you should, prior to your leaving England, send the gospel into as many parts as you possibly can.

Beloved brethren, you must be aware in some measure of my feelings when I contemplate the great work which is now rolling on, and the relationship which I sustain to it; while it is extending to distant lands, and islands, and thousands are embracing it, I realize in some measure my responsibility and the need I have of support from above, and wisdom from on high; that I may be able to teach this people, which have now become a great people, the principles of righteousness, and lead them agreeably to the will of heaven so that they may be perfected and prepared to meet the Lord Jesus Christ, when he shall appear in great glory. Can I rely on your prayers to your heavenly Father in my behalf? and on the prayers of all my brethren & sisters in England? (whom having not seen yet I love) that I may be enabled to escape every stra[ta]gem of satan, surmount every difficulty, and bring this people, to the enjoyment of those blessings, which are reserved for the righteous. I ask this at your and their hands in the name of Jesus Christ.

Let the saints remember that great things depend on their individual exertion, and that they are called to be co-workers with us and with the holy spirit in accomplishing the great works of the last days, and in consideration of the extent, the blessings, and the glories of the same let every selfish feeling be not only buried, but anihalated, and let love to God and man, predominate and reign triumphant in every mind, that their hearts may become like unto Enoch's of old so that they may comprehend all things, present, past, and future, and "come behind in no gift waiting for the coming of the Lord Jesus Christ." The work in which we are unitedly engaged in, is one of no ordinary kind, the enemies we have to contend against are subtle and well skilled in manuvering. It behoves us then to be on the alert, to concentrate our energies, and that the best feelings should exist in our midst, and then by the help of the Almighty we shall go on from victory to victory and from conquest unto conquest, our evil passions will be subdued, our prejudices depart, we shall find no room in our bosoms for hatred, vice will hide its deformed head, and we shall stand approved in the sight of heaven and be acknowledged "the sons of God." Let us realize that we are not to live to ourselves but to God. By so doing the greatest blessings will rest upon us both in time and in Eternity.

I presume the doctrine of "Baptism for the dead" has ere this reached your ears, and may have raised some inquiries in your mind respecting the same. I cannot in this letter give you all the information you may desire on the subject, but aside from my knowledge independant of the Bible, I would say, that this was certainly practised by the antient Churches and St Paul endeavours to prove the doctrine of the ressurrection from the same, and says "else what shall they do who are baptised for the dead["] &c &c. I first mentioned the doctrine in public while preaching the funeral sermon of Bro Brunson, and have since then given general instructions to the Church on the subject. The saints have the priviledge of being baptized for those of their relatives who are dead, who they feel to believe would have embraced the gospel if they had been priviledged with hearing it, and who have received the gospel in the spirit through the instrumentality of those who may have been commissioned to preach to them while in prison. Without enlarging on the subject you will undoubtedly see its consistancy, and reasonableness, and [it] presents the the gospel of Christ in probably a more enlarged scale than some have viewed it. But as the performance of this right is more particularly confined to this place it will not be necessary to enter into particulars, at the same time I allways feel glad to give all the information in my power, but my space will not allow me to do it.

We had a letter from Elder Hyde a few days ago, who is in New Jersey, and is expecting to leave for England as soon as Elder Page reaches him. He requested to know in his letter if converted Jews are to go to Jerusalem or to come to Zion. I therefore wish you to inform him that converted Jews must come here. If Elder Hydes & Pages testimony to the Jews at Jerusalem should be received then they may know "that the set time hath come": I will write more particular instructions to them afterwards.

Your families are well and generally in good spirits, and bear their privations with christian fortitude and patience.

Brother Richards' question respecting coming in the spring is answered. I shall be very happy to see him & his family & likewise Brother Fielding. Tell him that Bro Thompson is making preparations for his coming.

With respect to the rout best to be taken I think you will be better able to give advise than myself. But I would not advise coming round by the lakes. And it would not be prudent to come via New Orleans in the sickly season, but in the spring or fall or winter it might do. Give my kind love to all the brethren, and sisters, and tell them I should have been pleased to have come over to England to see them, but am afraid that I shall be under the necessity of remaining here for some time, therefore I give them a pressing invitation to come and see me.

I am D[ea]r Brethren yours, affectionately
Joseph Smith

To the Travelling High Council and Elders of the Church of Jesus Christ of LDS in Great Britain

To The "Twelve"

Do not understand me to say that all the Elders are to come with you, as it will be necessary for some to stay. J.

22

GEORGE A. SMITH TO JOHN LYMAN SMITH, JANUARY 8, 1841

*Think how foolish it makes me feel
to be looked up to with so much Earnestness*

This touching letter to a younger brother reveals a good deal about George A. Smith's personality, including his thoughtful concern for parents and siblings with whom he clearly maintained strong bonds. He thought often of family, knew they thought often of him, and tried to reassure them about his own precarious health. George A. urges Lyman to "spare no pains" in assisting their parents, but also to attend to his studies—a point reinforced by his description of how he feels about teaching people he sees as more learned and experienced than himself. Source: George A. Smith Collection, Church Archives.

Stafford St Longton Staffordshire Eng.
Janaury [8] 1841

Dear Brother Lyman this Cold Weather Makes me think of you as I have to Sleep alone and find it vary Cold. But I have A good Bed and Plenty of Cloths to keep me warm and the Night Passes vary Comfortably as I Seldom go to Bed before 12 o Clock and vary often Lay till 2 o clock in the Morning. This Comes from my having Somany Who Come to hear me talk and Recive instruction from me. You may well think I have to be A teacher of good Principles to them that Recieve my testimony, and you Cannot think how foolish it makes me feel to Be Looked up to with So much Earnestness by Persons Who have been Professers of Religon and Preachers of the Different Sects. I thank the Lord for the Wisdom he has given me and the Success I have had in the teaching thes Men for thire is Now in this District No less than 84 88 official Members in the Church and they all Look to me for instruction as Children to A Father and this Makes me feel vary Small indeed and Causes me to Cry unto my father Who is in heaven for Wisdom and Paetence to do my fathers Work and Sound his Gospel to the World Which may the Lord Grant.

Now Lyman as I am a Long way from home and do not know how things are Going I Want you Should keep a Good Look out and See that Father and Mother are taken Good Care of in my absence. Spare No Paines to Mane [make] them [comforatable] and hapy and When you Get this Letter Please to Write and Let me [*know*] how you Get along for food and Clothing and how you Get along Sleeping alone this Cold Winter and how you Get along Studying Geography and Learning to Write and Read and do Not Neglect to Spell all your Words Correctly. I want to know about your Progress in School. Do you keep the Old White Mare yet Old Cheese (the old Pied Cow that Was Gone So long What is be come of her)[?] Do you have Milk this Winter & Pleanty of hoe cake and [transp] Pork to Live on[?] I am in the Land of Englishmen but Get Plenty to Eat While thousands are Suffering for food and fire.

Last Sabbath there Was A Storme of thunder and Rain which Was So

Dreadfull at Birmingham that the People thought the Saviour Was Coming. The Church of St Peter Was Struck with Lightning at Wolverhampton and Set on fire and Greatly Damaged. It Was Built in the year 866 966 the Oldest Church in this Part of the Kingdom. The Pulpit is Cut Out of A Solid Rock and Display Great knowlede of the Archatects of the 10th Century.

Remember Me to all our Cousins and All the Friends and tell them to Pray for me. I Cannot tell When I Shall Come home or how long I Shall See you but hope it Will be Soon for I think Much of you and Caroline. I am in as Good health as Could be Expected for me as you know how bad I was when I Left home and how Much I have had to Encounter. I am not Strong but feel very well. My Eyes are So I can Write with A Strong Light and Not by A Candle. I Do Not Read but Little. How are Mothers Eyes[?] I Shall try to Get her Some Glasses when [I] leave for home in New York. Whi[le] I was in London I had Not the Meanes. I [should] Like to know how her Eyes are as I Can Judge better. Can she See with any Glasses better than Without? I use A Pair of old ones to Write in as my Eyes Seem too Dim to Do without but I will Lay them of and Write that you may See the diffrent Hand) I Expect to Send by Elder Clark to you and Menny others as Every Letter here Costs me 20 Cints or one Shiling English. You will pleas to Write as Soon as you Get this and tell me how you Get on in the World

I Remain your Brother George A. Smith

To John Lyman Smith

[*Written on the side of the last page:*]
Be a Good Lad and Do Good to all and mind your Parents Give my Love to Father & Mother Caraline and the Children

[*Written on the side of the first page:*]
Direct to G. A Smith at Mr. Players Stafford Street Longton Staffordshire England and I Shall Get it if it Crosses the Pond.

[*George scribbled several additional notes on the address page, including one that confirms the letter was* "Writen to Send by Elder Clark" *in order to save postage.* "The Weather is More Mild and Damp this Past Week here" *says another, perhaps a boon to George A., who noted that* "my health is as good as it has been since I Left home." *Still another note urged Lyman to* "be a Good Boy [and] Study and Mind your father and Mother and Pray for me as your Brother."]

23

PARLEY P. PRATT TO SIDNEY RIGDON, JANUARY 8, 1841

A little news from this part of the vineyard

The following is an extract from a letter sent by Parley P. Pratt to Sidney Rigdon, First Counselor to Joseph Smith in the First Presidency of the Church. While it is typical of the newsy letters the apostles sent in order to keep the Presidency informed, its report of British Campbellites gives it special interest. Before he became a Latter-day Saint, Sidney Rigdon had been an associate of Alexander Campbell in Ohio where, later, he was also a spiritual mentor to Parley. After Parley encountered the Book of Mormon, the tables were turned: it was he who introduced his friend Sidney to the glad tidings. Sidney also accepted, and both then had missionary success among people Campbell had taught to look for a restoration. Here Parley tells Sidney of the first baptisms in Britain from among the Campbellites, a harbinger, he hopes, of things to come. Source: *Times and Seasons* 2 (April 1, 1841): 364–65; brackets are in the original.

Manchester, Jan. 8th, 1841.

Pres't S. Rigdon:

Dear Brother,

I take this opportunity to address you, hoping these lines will find you alive, and recovered from that lingering sickness which has so long prayed upon your system. We are well; that is, myself, wife, and children, and the brethren generally, with whom you are acquainted. We have just received a few numbers of the Times and Seasons, [Sept. and Oct. Nos.,] from which we learn that Gadianton [Lilburn] has sent a demand for some of us to come back to Mo. in order to have a trial. Say to him and his band, that I for one, will be there quite as soon as he will wish to see me, and that when I come it will be to have a trial, and a just one too! therefore in his patience let him possess his soul; in the mean time I will be gathering up witnesses, for I only left the dungeon to be gathering up witnesses whom he had dispersed, and thus prepare for trial. Tell Missouri to fear not, for we will never forsake her.

I must now give you a little news from this part of the vineyard. In the first place, we have had one snow this winter of some 3 inches deep. The weather is now so cold that it is in danger of freezing potatoes in the chamber: it is the coldest we have had.

It is somewhat sickly with scarlet and other fevers. One family of Saints burried 3 children at a time.

Peace is declared between the allied powers and Egypt. Palestine is in the hands of Turkey. The Jews have as much libery there as the United States Government guarantees to its citizens.

As to the progress of the work of God in this country it is increasing at every step. It is now prospering in Ireland, and in Wales, as well as in Scotland and England. It is spreading into various new places in England. We have several hundred faithful preachers; and the spirit of enquiry seems to be generally awakened. The Clergy of the church of England, the Methodist priests, and the Baptist ministers, and Unitarians, etc. are all in arms, as it were, against the Saints.

The country is flooded with pamphlets, tracts, papers &c. published against us. Some of them have *bear & wolf* stories in them, some of them, have *snake* stories, and others *gander* stories. I must say that "Jonathan" is far behind "John Bull" in ingenuity in regard to inventing lies; all the foolishness ever published in the United States against the truth, would be considered sober earnest, compared to the follies which are being made manifest here, but I will forbear with a promise to send you a few specimens when our next emigrants sail for your place.

I must now inform you of the fact, that we have rept the first fruits of Campbellism in England. A few societies have been formed in England upon that principle for some years, but have made but little progress. One society of one hundred members exists about seventy miles from Manchester, at a place called Nothingham. They discovered about 2 years ago that they had been baptized for the remission, of sins without authority, and that they had not obtained remission, nor the gifts of the Spirit. From that time till now, many of them have been seeking and praying for the Lord to send officers and raise up his own church. At length, some of our writings fell into some of their hands, which soon brought two of their number to Manchester to enquire. They attended our meeting in the hall of Manchester, were well pleased, and called at our office next morning: after spending the day in enquiring, etc. one of them purchased 3 Voices of Warning and returned home; the other, (an inteligent gentleman,) staid two or three days, enquired diligently, and at length was baptized and confirmed, and went home to tell the glad tidings; this was a week or two ago. We expect to hear from them soon, and go out and baptize and organize a church there. Tell friend Campbell to go ahead and prepare the way, the Saints will follow him up and gather the fruits. The work of the Lord in this country rolled on unnoticed for some years except by the few. It was almost exclusively confined to the poor, and what they would call the lower classes; the editors, priests, and public in general hardly knew of its existence: but at length they began to "smell the rat," and since that time it has blazed forth like a flame which had been smothered. Many of its opposers who were very violent against it have become preachers of it; and at this time a general spirit of enquiry is beginning to be awakened among all classes.

I often feel as though I should like to be in the midst of our old friends in the west, but when it will be my lot I know not, I am resigned to the kind of life I am now living; I can truly say that I was never more contented, or more happy than of late. It does us much good to hear from Nauvoo, and I hope the presidency, and others will favor us with frequent communications. Say to President Smith that I want to see his essay on the priesthood very much. Br. Rigdon, be sure to write to me when you receive this. Our latest news from Nauvoo is Nov. 12, or when the two Englishmen left there — they have just arrived safe with letters. &c. this is January 13th.

Yours &c.

P. P. Pratt

24

ORSON PRATT TO GEORGE A. SMITH, FEBRUARY 8, 1841

Come Bro. Geo. put on your thinking cap

By early 1841 all the apostles were thinking of going home, a prospect they discussed freely in their letters. Here Orson Pratt writes to George A. Smith about the possiblities, and the letter seems to indicate some indecision on the part of George A. This letter also demonstrates that these two apostles had a sense of humor. Note Orson's play on his initials at the close. Source: George A. Smith Collection, Church Archives.

40 North Richmond St. Edinburgh   Feb 8th 1841

Dear Brother George:

Your letter of the 6th came duly to hand this morning. I rejoice to hear from you but am sorry to hear of your ill health. But I feel in hopes bro. George that you will gain your health again. A good hearty strong constitution is an excellent qualification in the midst of a land of wretchedness & want. I suppose that 250 or 300 saints are now swiftly sailing between Old England & Ireland bound for Joseph's land. Dear Bro. Geo. you have often wished to know what I thought about going home. I think I can now give you a decided answer. I intend to preach my farewell discourse on Sunday the 28th of March, & on monday morning the 29th of March I intend to leave Edinburgh for Liverpool, & from the first of April until Wednesday morning the 7th of April I intend to be with all of our Quorum that meet in Manchester & then the first good ship that sails from Liverpool for N. York I intend shall carry me & all this if the Lord will.

And now brother George I have told you my calculations without joking. What say you? Will you go too? come let me have a decided answer. Er Young says he intends going immediately after the conference on the 6th of April. Er Hedlock's calculations were the same the last news. Er H. Clark is already pitching & diving towards the promised land. I think the most if not all the 12 will be going. Come Bro. Geo. put on your thinking cap & think out the time you will go & write me the results or conclusions of your mind on this subject.

The sea was so rough last week that I did not baptize any although I set 2 different evenings to attend to baptism. If the wind & waves will permit I shall probably baptize some to night. I have no late news from Er Hedlock. Please write immediately for it is necessary to keep the mail & letter carries busy this cold weather

Yours &c Oh! Pea!

To G.A.S.

25

EPISTLE OF THE QUORUM OF THE TWELVE TO THE BRITISH SAINTS, APRIL 15, 1841

*Feeling anxious for your welfare and happiness
in time and in eternity*

Early in April, 1841, the eight apostles serving in Britain met in Manchester before all but Parley P. Pratt departed for America. The addition of Orson Hyde, passing through en route to fulfill his special mission to Palestine, brought to nine the number of apostles meeting that April—the most to meet together as a quorum since the spring of 1836 when the Kirtland Temple was dedicated! Among their last official acts as a quorum in Britain, these nine completed and signed their final farewell and counsel to the British Saints, and its publication closed volume one of the *Star*, the periodical they had launched the April before. Source: *Millennial Star* 1 (April 1841): 309–312.

AN

EPISTLE OF THE TWELVE

To the Church of Jesus Christ of Latter-Day Saints in England, Scotland, Ireland, Wales, and the Isle of Man, Greeting:-

Beloved Brethren, —Inasmuch as we have been labouring for some time in this country, and most of us are about to depart for the land of our nativity; and feeling anxious for your welfare and happiness in time and in eternity, we cheerfully offer you our counsel in the closing number of the first volume of the Star, hoping you will peruse it when we are far away, and profit by the same.

First of all, we would express our joy and thanksgiving to Him who rules and knows the hearts of men, for the heed and diligence with which the Saints in this country have hearkened to the counsel of those whom God has seen fit to send among them, and who hold the keys of this ministry. By this means a spirit of *union,* and consequently of *power,* has been generally cultivated among you.

And now let the Saints remember that which we have ever taught them, both by precept and example, viz: to beware of an aspiring spirit, which would lift you up one above another: to seek to be the *greatest* in the kingdom of God. This is that spirit which hurled down the angels— it is that spirit which actuates all the churches of the sectarian world, and most of the civil and military movements of the men of the world—it is that spirit which introduces rebellion, confusion, misrule, and disunion, and would, if suffered to exist among us, destroy our *union,* and consequently our *power,* which flows from the spirit, through the priesthood— which *spirit,* and *power,* and priesthood, can only exist with the humble and meek of the earth.

Therefore beware, O ye priests of the Most High! lest ye are overcome by that spirit which would exalt you above your fellow- labourers, and thus hurl you down to perdition, or do much injury to the cause of God. Be careful to respect, not the eloquence—not the smooth speeches—not the multitude of words—not the talents of men: but be careful to respect the offices which God has placed in the church. Let the members hearken to their officers, let the priests, teachers, and deacons hearken to the elders, and let the elders hearken to the presiding officers of each church or conference. And let all the churches and conferences hearken to the counsel of those who are still left in this country to superintend the affairs of the church; and by so doing, a spirit of union will be preserved, and peace and prosperity will attend the people of God.

We have seen fit to appoint our beloved brethren and fellow-labourers, Levi Richards and Lorenzo Snow, to travel from conference to conference, and to assist brother Pratt in the general superintendence of the church in this country. These are men of experience and sound[n]ess of principle, in whose counsel the church may place entire confidence, so long as they uphold them by the prayer of faith.

The spirit of emigration has actuated the children of men from the time our first parents were expelled from the garden until now; it was this spirit that first peopled the plains of Shinar, and all other places; yes, it was emigration that first broke upon the deathlike silence and loneliness of an empty earth, and caused the desolate land to team with life, and the desert to smile with joy. It was emigration that first peopled England, — once a desolate island, on which the foot of man had never trod, but now abounding in towns and cities. It was emigration that turned the wiles of America into a fruitful field, and besprinkled the wilderness with flourishing towns and cities, where a few years since the war whoop of the savage, or the howl of wild beasts was heard in the distance. In short, it is emigration that is the only effectual remedy for the evils which now afflict the over-peopled countries of Europe. With this view of the subject, the saints, as well as thousands of others, seem to be actuated with the spirit of enterprise and emigration, and as some of them are calculating to emigrate to America, and settle in colonies of our brethren, we would here impart a few words of counsel on the subject of emigration.

It will be necessary, in the first place for men of capital to go on first and make large purchases of land, and erect mills, machinery, manufac-tories, &c., so that the poor who go from this country can find employment. Therefore it is not wisdom for the poor to flock to that place extensively, until the necessary preparations are made. Neither is it wisdom for those who feel a spirit of benevolence to expend all their means in helping others to emigrate, and thus all arrive in a new country empty handed. In all settlements there must be capital and labour united in order to flourish. The brethren will recollect that they are not going to enter upon cities already built up, but are going to "*build* cities and inhabit them." Building cities cannot be done without *means* and *labour*.

On this subject we would call the particular attention of the Saints to the epistle, and also to the proclamation, signed by the first presidency of the church, published in the eleventh number of this work; and would earnestly exhort them to observe the order and instructions there given. We would also exhort the Saints not to go in haste, nor by flight, but to prepare all things in a proper manner before they emigrate; and especially in regard to their dealing with the world, let them be careful to settle everything honestly as becometh Saints, as far as lies in their power, and not go away in debt, so far as they have the means to pay. And if any go away in debt, because they have not means to pay, let it be with the design of paying as industry shall put it in their power, so that the cause of truth be not evil spoken of.

We have found that there are so many "pick-pockets," and so many that will take every possible advantage of strangers, in Liverpool, that we have appointed Elder Amos Fielding, as the agent of the church, to superintend the fitting out of the Saints from Liverpool to America. Whatever information the Saints may want about the preparations for a voyage, they are advised to call on Elder Fielding, at Liverpool, as their first movement, when they arrive there as emigrants. There are some brethren who have felt themselves competent to do their own business in these matters, and rather despising the counsel of their friends, have been robbed and cheated out of nearly all they had. A word of caution to the wise is sufficient. It is also a great saving to go in companies, instead of going individually. First, a company can charter a vessel, so as to make the passage much cheaper than otherwise. Secondly, provisions can be purchased at wholesale for a company much cheaper than otherwise. Thirdly, this will avoid bad company on the passage. Fourthly, when a company arrives in New Orleans they can charter a steam-boat so as to reduce the passage near one- half. This measure will save some hundreds of pounds on each ship load. Fifthly, a man of experience can go as leader of each company, who will know how to avoid rogues and knaves.

Sovereigns are more profitable than silver or any other money in emigrating to America; and the brethren are also cautioned against the American money, when they arrive in that country. Let them not venture to take *paper* money of that country until they become well informed in regard to the different banks; for very few of them will pass current very far from the place where they are issued, and banks are breaking almost daily. It is much cheaper going by New Orleans than by New York. But it will never do for emigrants to go by New Orleans in the Summer on account of the heat and sickness of the climate. It is, therefore, advisable for the Saints to emigrate in Autumn, Winter, or Spring. Let the Saints be careful also to obtain a letter of recommendation, from the Elders where they are acquainted, to the brethren where they are going, certifying their membership, and let the elders be careful not to recommend any who do not conduct themselves as Saints; and especially those who would go with a design to defraud their creditors.

In regard to ordaining and licensing officers, each conference is now organised, under the care of their respective presidents, who, with the voice of the church, may ordain, according to the gifts and callings of God, by the holy spirit, and under the general superintendance of Elders Pratt, Richards, and Snow. Licenses should be signed by the presiding officers.

There are many other items of importance, which we would gladly mention, had we time and space sufficient, but this must suffice for the present; and may the God of our fathers bless you all with wisdom and grace, to act each your part in the great work which lies before us, that the world may be warned, and thousands brought to the knowledge of the truth; and may he bless and preserve you blameless until the day of his coming. Brethren and sisters pray for us. We remain your brethren in the new and everlasting covenant,

> BRIGHAM YOUNG,
> HEBER C. KIMBALL,
> ORSON HYDE,
> P. P. PRATT,
> ORSON PRATT,
> WILLARD RICHARDS,
> WILFORD WOODRUFF,
> JOHN TAYLOR,
> G. A. SMITH.

Manchester, April 15th, 1841

BIBLIOGRAPHY

Most of the rich manuscript material on which this book is based is housed in the Church Archives, Historical Department, The Church of Jesus Christ of Latter-day Saints, Salt Lake City, Utah, cited below as well as in the text as Church Archives. In addition to the material specifically cited in the footnotes, there are other published and unpublished materials that the reader may find of great value. We have also listed some of them below. The reader will be interested, for example, in noting that in later years members of the Quorum of the Twelve prepared personal "histories" that were published in the *Deseret News* and the *Latter-day Saints' Millennial Star* (cited as *Millennial Star*). A more detailed guide to topics addressed in this volume is David J. Whittaker, "Mormonism in Victorian Britain: A Bibliography," in *Mormonism in Early Victorian Britain*, ed. Richard L. Jensen and Malcolm R. Thorp, 258–71. A valuable guide to primary sources of Mormon history is Davis Bitton, comp., *A Guide to Mormon Diaries and Autobiographies* (Provo, Utah: Brigham Young University Press, 1976). An excellent guide to the published works on Mormonism during the first 100 years is Chad J. Flake, comp., *A Mormon Bibliography, 1830–1930* (Salt Lake City: University of Utah Press, 1978). A ten-year supplement by Chad J. Flake and Larry W. Draper appeared in 1989.

JOURNALS, DIARIES, AND PERSONAL HISTORIES OF THE TWELVE, PUBLISHED AND UNPUBLISHED

ORSON HYDE

Hyde, Orson. Autobiography (1804–1842). Holograph and typescript, Church Archives.
———. "History of Orson Hyde." Published serially in the *Deseret News* 8 (May 5–May 12, 1858) and again in the *Millennial Star* 26 (November 19–December 10, 1864).

HEBER C. KIMBALL

Kimball, Heber C. Autobiography. Ms. Heber C. Kimball Collection, Church Archives.
———. Diary. Heber C. Kimball Collection, Church Archives.
———. *Journal of Heber C. Kimball.* Nauvoo, Ill.: Robinson & Smith, 1840.
———. *President Heber C. Kimball's Journal.* Salt Lake City: Juvenile Instructor Office, 1882.
———. "Synopsis of the History of Heber Chase Kimball." Published serially in the *Deseret News* 8 (March 31–April 28, 1858) and again in the *Millennial Star* 26 (July 16–November 12, 1864).

Kimball, Stanley B., ed. *On the Potter's Wheel: The Diaries of Heber C. Kimball*. Salt Lake City: Signature Books, 1987.

ORSON PRATT

Pratt, Orson. "History of Orson Pratt." Published serially in the *Deseret News* 8 (June 2 – June 9, 1858) and again in the *Millennial Star* 27 (January 14 – February 11, 1865).

———. *The Orson Pratt Journals*. Comp. and ed. Elden J. Watson. Salt Lake City: Elden J. Watson, 1975.

PARLEY P. PRATT

Pratt, Parley P. *Autobiography of Parley Parker Pratt*. (1874) 5th ed. Ed. Parley P. Pratt, Jr. Salt Lake City: Deseret Book Co., 1961.

———. "History of Parley P. Pratt." Published in the *Deseret News* 8 (May 19, 1858) and again in the *Millennial Star* 26 (December 24, 1864).

WILLARD RICHARDS

Richards, Willard. Diary. Holograph and typescript, Willard Richards Collection, Church Archives. (In addition to the small holograph diary kept in England, there is a typescript of another version apparently expanded by Richards later. Both versions have been used, and the distinction is made in the footnotes.)

———. "History of Willard Richards." Published serially in the *Deseret News* 8 (June 23 – June 30, 1858) and again in the *Millennial Star* 27 (February 25 – March 18, 1865).

GEORGE A. SMITH

Smith, George A. "History of George Albert Smith." Typescript, George A. Smith Collection, Church Archives. This typescript is based on "Memoirs of Geo. A. Smith," ms., George Albert Smith Collection, which, in turn, is based on "History of George Albert Smith by himself," ms., George A. Smith Collection. The last item is an expanded version of the Journal listed below.

———. Journal. George A. Smith Collection, Church Archives.

———. "My Journal." Published serially in *The Instructor* 81–84 (1946–1949).

———. "Sketch of the Auto-Biography of George Albert Smith." Published serially in the *Deseret News* 8 (August 11–August 18, 1858) and again in the *Millennial Star* 27 (July 1– July 15, 1865).

JOHN TAYLOR

The "History of John Taylor" was never published, and no contemporary diaries, journals, or personal histories are currently available. A scrapbook containing contemporary newspaper accounts of his Isle of Man mission is in Church Archives.

WILFORD WOODRUFF

Cowley, Matthias F., ed. *Wilford Woodruff Fourth President of the Church of Jesus Christ of Latter-day Saints. History of His Life and Labors as Recorded in His Daily Journals*. Prepared for publication by Matthias F. Cowley. 1909. Reprint. Salt Lake City: Bookcraft, 1964.

Woodruff, Wilford. "History of Wilford Woodruff." Published serially in the *Deseret News* 8 (July 7–August 4, 1858) and again in the *Millennial Star* 27 (March 18–June 24, 1865).
———. Journal. Wilford Woodruff Collection, Church Archives. For the sake of convenience, we have used and quoted from *Wilford Woodruff's Journal, 1833–1898*. Typescript. 9 vols. Ed. Scott G. Kenney. Midvale, Utah: Signature Books, 1983–1985.
———. *Leaves from My Journal*. Salt Lake City: Juvenile Instructor, 1881. 2nd ed., 1882. Reprinted in *Three Mormon Classics*, comp. Preston Nibley. Salt Lake City: Bookcraft, 1944.

BRIGHAM YOUNG

Young, Brigham. Diary. Brigham Young Papers, Church Archives.
———. "History of Brigham Young." Ms. Church Historian's Office Collection, Church Archives. Three manuscripts preliminary to the *Deseret News* history below.
———. "History of Brigham Young." Published serially in the *Deseret News* 7–8 (January 27– March 24, 1858) and again in the *Millennial Star* 25–26 (May 9, 1863–June 4, 1864).
———. *Manuscript History of Brigham Young 1801–1844*. Ed. Elden J. Watson. Salt Lake City: Elden J. Watson, 1968.

OTHER DIARIES, JOURNALS, AND MANUSCRIPT COLLECTIONS, PUBLISHED AND UNPUBLISHED

Allen, James B. and Thomas G. Alexander, eds. *Manchester Mormons: The Journal of William Clayton, 1840 to 1842*. Santa Barbara: Peregrine Smith, Inc., 1974. The original of this journal is in the Harold B. Lee Library, Brigham Young University, Provo, Utah.
Beecroft, John. Journal. Church Archives
Blair, Phillip. Collection. J. Willard Marriott Library, University of Utah, Salt Lake City, Utah.
Campbell, Robert Lang. Diary. Original and typescript. Harold B. Lee Library, Brigham Young University, Provo, Utah.
Clayton, William. Collection. Church Archives.
Cordon, Alfred. Journal. Church Archives.
Day, Thomas. Journal and Reminiscence. Harold B. Lee Library, Brigham Young University, Provo, Utah.
Fielding, Joseph. Collection. Harold B. Lee Library, Brigham Young University, Provo, Utah.
———. Collection. Church Archives.
———. Diary (holograph and typescript; for convenience, since dates are difficult to find in the holograph, we have referred to page numbers in the typescript). Church Archives.
Fleming, Helen Bourne. Collection. Church Archives.
Freeman, John. Journal. Church Archives.
Haight, Isaac Chauncy. Biographical Sketch and Diary. Typescript. Church Archives.
Hyde, Orson. Collection. Church Archives.
The Journal History of the Church of Jesus Christ of Latter-day Saints. Church Archives.
Kimball, Heber C. Collection. Church Archives.
Lang, William. Autobiography. Typescript. Harold B. Lee Library, Brigham Young University, Provo, Utah.

Lee, William. Diary, 1820–1895. Typescript. Harold B. Lee Library, Brigham Young University, Provo, Utah.

"Manuscript History of the British Mission." 48 vols., 1837–1962. Church Archives.

Maughan, Mary Ann Weston. "Journal of Mary Ann Weston Maughan." *Our Pioneer Heritage.* 20 vols. Ed. Kate B. Carter. Salt Lake City: Daughters of Utah Pioneers, 1958–1977. 2:354–55.

Miller, Charles M. Diary. Typescript. Harold B. Lee Library, Brigham Young University, Provo, Utah.

Minutes of Conferences and Councils. Church Archives.

Morris, George. Autobiography. Typescript. Harold B. Lee Library, Brigham Young University, Provo, Utah.

Nauvoo Minutes. Church Archives.

Pratt, Orson. Collection. Church Archives.

Pratt, Parley P. Collection. Church Archives.

Richards, Willard. Collection. Church Archives.

Russell, Isaac. Collection. Harold B. Lee Library, Brigham Young University, Provo, Utah.

Smith, Bathsheba W. Bigler. "Autobiography of Bathsheba W. Bigler." Typescript. Ed. Alice Merrill Horne. Copy in possession of Harriet Horne Arrington.

——. Collection. Church Archives.

Smith, Charles. Journal. Church Archives.

Smith, George A. Collection. Church Archives.

——. Family Papers. J. Willard Marriott Library, University of Utah, Salt Lake City, Utah.

Smith, Joseph. Collection. Church Archives.

Snow, Lorenzo. Collection. Church Archives.

——. Journal. Church Archives.

——. Notebook. Church Archives.

Taylor, John. Collection. Church Archives.

Thatcher, Luna Young. Collection. Church Archives.

Thomas, Wanda Clayton. Collection. J. Willard Marriott Library. University of Utah, Salt Lake City, Utah.

Turley, Theodore. "Theodore Turley Mission Journal 1839–40." Ed. Richard Eyring Turley, Jr. Senior honors project, Brigham Young University, 1982. Original journal in Harold B. Lee Library, Brigham Young University, Provo, Utah.

"United Brethren Preacher's Plan of the Frooms Hill Circuit, 1840." Broadside. Church Archives.

Woodruff, Wilford. Collection. Church Archives.

Young, Brigham. Papers. Church Archives

CONTEMPORARY PUBLICATIONS

Copies of these rare works are available in the Church Archives or Harold B. Lee Library, Brigham Young University, Provo, Utah.

[Anonymous]. *He is gone . . .* Dymock, England, 1866. Photocopy of poem, Church Archives.

Adams, George J. *A Letter to His Excellency John Tyler, President of the United States,*

Touching the Signs of the Times, and the Political Destiny of the World. New York: C. A. Calhoun, 1844.

Bennett, Samuel. *A Few Remarks by way of Reply to an Anonymous Scribbler, Calling Himself a Philanthropist, Disabusing the Church of Jesus Christ of Latter-day Saints of the Slanders and Falsehoods Which he has Attempted to Fasten upon it.* Philadelphia: Brown, Bicking & Guilbert, 1840.

The Book of Mormon: an Account Written by the Hand of Mormon, Upon Plates Taken From the Plates of Nephi... Translated by Joseph Smith, Jr. Kirtland, Ohio: Printed by O. Cowdery and Co., for P. P. Pratt and J. Goodson, 1837.

The Book of Mormon: an Account Written by the Hand of Mormon Upon the Plates Taken From the Plates of Nephi... Translated by Joseph Smith, Jr. First European Edition, From the Second American Edition. Liverpool: Printed by J. Tompkins for B. Young, H. C. Kimball and P. P. Pratt, 1841.

A Collection of Sacred Hymns For the Church of Jesus Christ of Latter-day Saints in Europe, Selected by Brigham Young, Parley P. Pratt, and John Taylor. Published by Order of a General Conference, and for Sale at 124 Oldham Road, Manchester, and by Agents Throughout England. Manchester: Printed by W. R. Thomas, 1840.

Doctrine and Covenants of the Church of the Latter-day Saints: Carefully Selected From the Revelations of God, and Compiled by Joseph Smith, Junior, Oliver Cowdery, Sidney Rigdon, Frederick G. Williams [Presiding Elders of said Church] Proprietors. Kirtland, Ohio: Printed by F. G. Williams and Co. for the Proprietors, 1835.

Elders' Journal of the Church of Latter Day Saints. Kirtland, Ohio, and Far West, Missouri, October 1837 – August 1838.

Haining, Samuel. *Mormonism Weighed in the Balances, of the Sanctuary, and Found Wanting; The Substance of Four Lectures.* Douglas, Isle of Man: Robert Fargher, 1840.

Hewitt, William. *Exposition of the Errors and Fallacies of the Self-named "Latter-day Saints." In Which the Author exposes the Fallacies of the L.D.S. by Publishing His Sentiments.* Lane-End, England: C. Watts, 1840.

Howe, Eber D. *Mormonism Unvailed: or, A Faithful Account of That Singular Imposition and Delusion, From its Rise to the Present Time. With Sketches of the Characters of its Propagators, and a Full Detail of the Manner in Which the Famous Golden Bible was Brought Before the World. To Which Are Added, Inquiries Into the Probability That the Historical Part of the Said Bible was Written by One Solomon Spalding [sic], More Than Twenty Years Ago, and by Him Intended to Have Been Published as a Romance.* Painesville, Ohio: Published by the author, 1834. Reprinted in 1840 under the title *History of Mormonism....*

Hyde, Orson. *A Timely Warning to the People of England of Every Sect and Denomination, and to Every Individual Into Whose Hands it May Fall, by an Elder of the Church of Latter Day Saints.* Broadside. Manchester: W. R. Thomas, 1840. The first version of this broadside was entitled *A Prophetic Warning To all the Churches...*, and was printed in Toronto, Canada, August 1836. It was revised and printed under the current title in Preston, in 1837, and later reprinted in Manchester.

The Imposture Unmasked; or, A Complete Exposure of the Mormon Fraud; Being a Critical Review of the Book of Mormon, and an Expose of the Character of Joseph Smith,

Sidney Rigdon, Martin Harris, Parley Pratt, and Other Leading Actors in the Latter-Day Saint Delusion. 2d ed. Douglas, Isle of Man: Reprinted from the Mona's Herald and Central Advertiser for the British Empire, by R. Fargher, 1841.

Latter Day Saints' Messenger and Advocate. Kirtland, Ohio, October 1834 — September 1837.

The Latter-day Saints' Millennial Star. Liverpool, England. 1840–1970.

Lewis, Samuel. *Topographical Dictionary of England.* 4 vols. 7th ed. London: S. Lewis and Co., 1848.

Livesey, Joseph. *Reminiscences of Early Teetotalism.* Preston, n.d.

Livesey, Richard. *An Exposure of Mormonism, Being a Statement of Facts Relating to the Self-styled "Latter-day Saints," and the Origin of the Book of Mormon.* Preston: J. Livesey, 1838. 2d edition, Manchester: William Shackleton and Son, 1840.

Palmer, William. *The External Evidence of the Book of Mormon Examined.* London: Arthur Hall and Co., Briscoe, Printer, [1849?].

Pratt, Orson. *Absurdities of Immaterialism; or, A Reply to T. W. P. Taylor's Pamphlet, Entitled: "The Materialism of the Mormons or Latter-day Saints Examined and Exposed."* Liverpool: R. James, 1849.

——. *[An] Interesting Account of Several Remarkable Visions, and of the Late Discovery of Ancient American Records.* Edinburgh: Ballantyne and Hughes, 1840.

——. *The Seer.* Washington, D.C., and Liverpool, January 1853-August 1854.

——. *A Series of Pamphlets by Orson Pratt, One of the Twelve Apostles of the Church of Jesus Christ of Latter-day Saints . . . .* (Fifteen pamphlets.) Liverpool: Franklin D. Richards, 1851.

——. *[Tracts] by Orson Pratt, One of the Twelve Apostles of the Church of Jesus Christ of Latter-day Saints and President of Said Church Throughout Great Britain and all European Countries.* (Eight pamphlets.) London: L.D.S. Book and Star Depot, August 25, 1856 — March 15, 1857.

Pratt, Parley P. *An Address by a Minister of the Church of Jesus Christ of Latter-day Saints, to the People of England.* Manchester: W. R. Thomas, 1840.

——. *An Address by Judge [Elias] Higbee and Parley P. Pratt, Ministers of the Gospel of the Church of Jesus Christ of "Latter-day Saints," to the Citizens of Washington, and to the Public in General.* [Washington, D.C.?]: 1840.

——. *An Answer to Mr. William Hewitt's Tract Against the Latter-day Saints.* Manchester: W. R. Thomas, 1840.

——. *Dialogue Between a Latter-day Saint and an Enquirer After Truth. (Reprinted From the Star of January 1) To Which is Added, A Solemn Warning to the Methodists. By One Who was Formerly a Preacher Among Them.* Manchester: Parley P. Pratt, 1842.

——. *An Epistle of Demetrius, the Silversmith, to the Workmen of Like Occupation and all Others to Whom it May Concern, — Greeting: Showing the Best Way to Preserve our Craft and to Put Down the Latter-day Saints.* Manchester: W. Shackleton and Son [1842].

——. *History of the Late Persecution Inflicted by the State of Missouri Upon the Mormons, in Which Ten Thousand American Citizens Were Robbed, Plundered, and Driven From the State, and Many Other Imprisoned, Martyred, &c., for Their Religion, and all This by Military Force, by Order of the Executive.* Detroit: Dawson & Bates, 1839. Reprinted with additions under the title *Late Persecution of the Church of Jesus Christ of Latter-Day*

Saints. Ten Thousand Citizens Robbed, Plundered, and Banished; Others Imprisoned, and Others Martyred for their Religion. With a Sketch of Their Rise, Progress and Doctrine. New York: J. W. Harrison, 1840.

——. *Key to the Science of Theology: Designed as an Introduction to the First Principles of Spiritual Philosophy; Religion; Law and Government; as Delivered by the Ancients, and as Restored in This Age, for the Final Development of Universal Peace, Truth and Knowledge.* Liverpool: F. D. Richards, 1855.

——. *A Letter to the Queen Touching the Signs of the Times and the Political Destiny of the World.* Manchester: Printed and Published by P. P. Pratt, 1841.

——. *The Millennium, a Poem. To Which is Added Hymns and Songs on Various Subjects New and Interesting, Adapted to the Dispensation of the Fulness of Times.* Boston: Parley P. Pratt, 1835.

——. *The Millennium and Other Poems: To Which is Annexed, A Treatise on the Regeneration and Eternal Nature of Matter.* New York: W. Molineux, 1840.

——. *Mormonism Unveiled: Zion's Watchman Unmasked, and its Editor, Mr. L. R. Sunderland, Exposed: Truth Vindicated: The Devil Mad, and Priestcraft in Danger!* New York: Parley P. Pratt, 1838.

——. *The Prophet.* New York City, May 1844-May 1845.

——. *Prospectus of the Latter-day Saints' Millennial Star.* Broadside. Manchester: W. R. Thomas, 1840.

——. *A Reply to Mr. Thomas Taylor's "Complete Failure," &c., and Mr. Richard Livesey's "Mormonism Exposed."* Manchester: W. R. Thomas, 1840.

——. *Truth Defended, or, A Reply to the "Preston Chronicle," and to Mr. J. B. Rollo's "Mormonism Exposed."* Manchester: Printed and published by Parley P. Pratt, 1841.

——. *A Voice of Warning and Instruction to All People, Containing a Declaration of the Faith and Doctrine of the Church of the Latter-day Saints, Commonly Called Mormons.* New York: W. Sandford, 1837.

Primitive Methodist Magazine.

Richards, Franklin D. *A Compendium of the Faith and Doctrines of the Church of Jesus Christ of Latter-day Saints. Compiled From the Bible, and Also From the Book of Mormon, Doctrine and Covenants, and Other Publications of the Church.* Liverpool: Orson Pratt, 1857.

Rigdon, Sidney. *An Appeal to the American People: Being an Account of the Persecutions of the Church of Latter Day Saints; and of the Barbarities Inflicted on Them by the Inhabitants of the State of Missouri.* Cincinnati: Glezen and Shepard, 1840.

Rollo, J. B. *Mormonism Exposed, From the Word of God.* South Bridge, England: Glass, Printer, [1841].

Smith, George A. *The Rise, Progress, and Travels of the Church of Jesus Christ of Latter-day Saints, Being a Series of Answers to Questions. . . .* Salt Lake City: Printed at the Deseret News Office, 1869.

Smith, Joseph. *General Smith's Views of the Powers and Policy of the Government of the United States.* Nauvoo, Ill.: John Taylor, 1844.

Spencer, Orson. *Letters Exhibiting the Most Prominent Doctrines of the Church of Jesus Christ of Latter-day Saints.* 3d ed. Liverpool: Orson Spencer, 1848.

Stevenson, H. *A Lecture on Mormonism, Delivered in the Wesleyan Methodist Chapel, Alston, December 7th, 1838*. Newcastle, England: J. Blackwell and Co., 1839.

Taylor, John. *An Answer to Some False Statements and Misrepresentations Made by the Rev. Robert Heys, Wesleyan Minister, in an Address to His Society in Douglas and its Vicinity, on the Subject of Mormonism*. Douglas, Isle of Man: Penrice and Wallace, 1840.

———. *Calumny Refuted and the Truth Defended; Being a Reply to the Second Address of the Rev. Robert Heys, Wesleyan Minister to the Wesleyan Methodist Societies in Douglas and its Vicinity*. Douglas, Isle of Man: Penrice and Wallace [1840].

———. *The Mormon*. New York City, February 1855-September 1857.

———. *A Short Account of the Murders, Roberies [sic] Burnings, Thefts, and Other Outrages Committed by a Mob & Militia of the State of Missouri, Upon the Latter Day Saints. The Persecutions They Have Endured for Their Religion, and Their Banishment From that State By the Authorities Thereof*. [Springfield, Ill.?], 1839.

———. *Truth Defended and Methodism Weighed in the Balance and Found Wanting: Being a Reply to the Third Address of the Rev. Robert Heys, Wesleyan Minister to the Wesleyan Methodist Societies in Douglas and Vicinity. And Also an Exposure of the Principles of Methodism*. Liverpool: J. Tompkins, 1840.

Taylor, Thomas. *An Account of the Complete Failure of an Ordained Priest of the "Latter-day Saints" to Establish His Pretensions to the Gift of Tongues, Which Took Place Oct. 12, 1840: With an Address to Men of Reason and Religion, Warning Them Not to be Deceived by the Craftiness of Such Low Impostures*. Manchester: Pigot and Slater, [1840].

The Times and Seasons. Nauvoo, Ill., 1839–1846.

Webster, Thomas. *Some Extracts from the Book of Doctrine and Covenants of the Church of the Latter Day Saints, to Which are Added Some Facts Tending to Show the Utter Failure of Their Pretended Prophecies and Their Unsuccessful Attempts at Working Miracles, &c. By Thomas Webster, Formerly One of the Elders of the Mormon Church*. Preston: W. Pollard, [1841?].

Winchester, Benjamin. *An Examination of a Lecture Delivered by the Rev. H. Perkins on the Religious Opinions and Faith of the Latter-day Saints and Some of the Most Prominent Errors and Mistakes Corrected*. [Philadelphia?]: 1840.

[Woodruff, Wilford, and Heber C. Kimball]. *The Word of the Lord to the Citizens of London*. London: Doudney and Scrymgour, [1841].

OTHER SECONDARY LITERATURE

Alexander, Thomas G. "The Reconstruction of Mormon Doctrine: From Joseph Smith to Progressive Theology." *Sunstone* 5 (July/August 1980): 24–33.

———. *Things in Heaven and Earth: The Life and Times of Wilford Woodruff, a Mormon Prophet*. Salt Lake City: Signature Books, 1991.

———. "Wilford Woodruff and the Changing Nature of Mormon Religious Experience." *Church History* 45 (March 1976): 50–69.

———. "The Word of Wisdom: From Principle to Requirement." *Dialogue: A Journal of Mormon Thought* 14 (Autumn 1981): 78–88.

Allen, James B. "Emergence of a Fundamental: The Expanding Role of Joseph Smith's First Vision in Mormon Religious Thought." *Journal of Mormon History* 7 (1980): 43–61.

———. "Line upon Line: Church History Reveals How the Lord Has Continually Added to His People's Knowledge and Understanding." *Ensign* 9 (July 1979): 32–39.

———. "The Significance of Joseph Smith's 'First Vision' in Mormon Thought." *Dialogue: A Journal of Mormon Thought* 1 (Autumn 1966): 29–45.

———. *Trials of Discipleship: The Story of William Clayton, a Mormon*. Urbana: University of Illinois Press, 1987.

———, ed. " 'We Had a Very Hard Voyage for the Season': John Moon's Account of the First Emigrant Company of British Saints." *Brigham Young University Studies* 17 (Spring 1977): 339–41.

———, and Glen M. Leonard. *The Story of the Latter-day Saints*. Salt Lake City: Deseret Book Co., 1976.

———, and Malcolm R. Thorp. "The Mission of the Twelve to England, 1840–41: Mormon Apostles and the Working Classes." *Brigham Young University Studies* 15 (Summer 1975): 499–526.

Armytage, W. H. G. *Heavens Below: Utopian Experience in England, 1560–1960*. Toronto: University of Toronto Press, 1961.

Arrington, Leonard J. *Brigham Young: American Moses*. New York: Alfred Knopf, 1985.

———, and Ronald K. Esplin. "The Role of the Council of the Twelve during Brigham Young's Presidency in the Church of Jesus Christ of Latter-day Saints." *Task Papers in LDS History*, No. 31. Salt Lake City: Historical Department of The Church of Jesus Christ of Latter-day Saints, 1979.

Axon, William E. A., ed. *The Annals of Manchester: A Chronological Record from the Earliest Times to the End of 1885*. Manchester: John Heywood, 1886.

Backman, Milton V. *Joseph Smith's First Vision: The First Vision in Historical Context*. 1971. 2nd edition. Salt Lake City: Bookcraft, 1980.

———. "Joseph Smith's Recitals of the First Vision." *Ensign* 15 (January 1985): 8–17.

Banks, J. A. "The Contagion of Numbers." In *The Victorian City: Images and Reality*, 2 vols., ed. H. J. Dyos and Michael Wolff, 1:105–22. London: Routledge & Kegan Paul, 1973.

Barker, Helen Bennion. "John Bennion." In *Our Pioneer Heritage*, 20 vols., ed. Kate B. Carter. Salt Lake City: Daughters of Utah Pioneers, 1958–1977. 13:408–10.

Barlow, Brent A. "History of the Church of Jesus Christ of Latter-day Saints in Ireland Since 1840." Master's thesis, Brigham Young University, 1968.

———. "The Irish Experience." In *Truth Will Prevail: The Rise of The Church of Jesus Christ of Latter-day Saints in the British Isles 1837–1987*, ed. V. Ben Bloxham, James R. Moss, and Larry C. Porter, 299–331. Solihull, England: The Church of Jesus Christ of Latter-day Saints, 1987.

Barron, Howard H. *Orson Hyde: Missionary, Apostle, Colonizer*. Bountiful, Utah: Horizon Publishers, 1977.

Billington, Louis. "Popular Religion and Social Reform: A Study of Revivalism and Teetotalism, 1830–50." *Journal of Religious History* 10 (June 1979): 266–93.

Bitton, Davis. "The Waning of Mormon Kirtland." *Brigham Young University Studies* 12 (Summer 1972): 455–64.

Bloxham, V. Ben. "The Apostolic Foundations, 1840–1841." In *Truth Will Prevail: The Rise of The Church of Jesus Christ of Latter-day Saints in the British Isles 1837–1987*, ed. V.

Ben Bloxham, James R. Moss, and Larry C. Porter, 121–62. Solihull, England: The Church of Jesus Christ of Latter-day Saints, 1987.

———. "The Call of the Apostles to the British Isles." In *Truth Will Prevail: The Rise of The Church of Jesus Christ of Latter-day Saints in the British Isles 1837–1987*, ed. V. Ben Bloxham, James R. Moss, and Larry C. Porter, 104–20. Solihull, England: The Church of Jesus Christ of Latter-day Saints, 1987.

Briggs, Asa. *The Making of Modern England 1784–1867: The Age of Improvement*. New York: Harper & Row, 1959.

Buchanan, Frederick S. "The Ebb and Flow of the Church in Scotland." In *Truth Will Prevail: The Rise of The Church of Jesus Christ of Latter-day Saints in the British Isles 1837–1987*, ed. V. Ben Bloxham, James R. Moss, and Larry C. Porter, 268–98. Solihull, England: The Church of Jesus Christ of Latter-day Saints, 1987.

———. "The Ebb and Flow of Mormonism in Scotland, 1840–1900." *Brigham Young University Studies* 27 (Spring 1987): 27–52.

Bush, Lester E., Jr. "The Spaulding Theory, Then and Now." *Dialogue: A Journal of Mormon Thought* 10 (Autumn 1977): 40–69.

———. "The Word of Wisdom in Early Nineteenth Century Perspective." *Dialogue: A Journal of Mormon Thought* 14 (Autumn 1981): 46–65.

Cannon, M. Hamlin. "Migration of English Mormons to America." *American Historical Review* 52 (April 1947): 436–55.

Cardwardine, Richard. *Trans-Atlantic Revivalism, Popular Evangelicalism in Britain and America, 1790–1865*. Westport, Conn.: Greenwood Press, 1978.

Carter, Kate B., ed. *Heart Throbs of the West*. 20 vols. Salt Lake City: Daughters of Utah Pioneers, 1958–77.

Chadwick, Owen. *The Victorian Church*, Part I. New York: Oxford University Press, 1966.

Cook, Lyndon W. *Joseph Smith and the Law of Consecration*. Provo, Utah: Grandin Book Co., 1985.

———, and Donald Q. Cannon, eds. *Far West Record: Minutes of The Church of Jesus Christ of Latter-day Saints, 1830–44*. Salt Lake City: Deseret Book Co., 1983.

Cotterill, John. "Midland Saints: The Mormon Mission in the West Midlands, 1837–77." Ph.D. thesis, University of Keele, 1985.

Crawley, Peter. "A Bibliography of The Church of Jesus Christ of Latter-day Saints in New York, Ohio, and Missouri." *Brigham Young University Studies* 12 (Summer 1972): 465–537.

———. "A Descriptive Bibliography of the Mormon Church, 1830–1847." (Unpublished manuscript.)

———. "Parley P. Pratt: Father of Mormon Pamphleteering." *Dialogue: A Journal of Mormon Thought* 15 (Autumn 1982): 13–26.

———. "The Passage of Mormon Primitivism." *Dialogue: A Journal of Mormon Thought* 13 (Winter 1980): 26–37.

———, and Richard Lloyd Anderson. "The Political and Social Realities of Zion's Camp." *Brigham Young University Studies* 14 (Summer 1974): 406–20.

———, and David J. Whittaker. *Mormon Imprints in Great Britain and the Empire, 1836–1857*. Friends of the BYU Library Newsletter No. 30. Provo, Utah: Friends of the Brigham Young University Library, 1987.

Currie, Robert, Alan Gilbert, and Lee Horsley. *Churches and Church Goers: Patterns of Church Growth in the British Isles Since 1700*. Oxford: Clarendon Press, 1977.

Curtis, N. F. R. "Economic Growth and the Standard of Living." Chapter 5 of *British Economic Growth During the Industrial Revolution*. Oxford: Clarendon Press, 1985.

Davies, Rupert, A. Raymond George, and Gordon Rupp, eds. *A History of the Methodist Church in Great Britain*. 3 vols. London: Epworth Press, 1978.

Dennis, Ronald D. *Welsh Mormon Writings from 1844 to 1862, A Historical Bibliography*. Provo, Utah: Brigham Young University Religious Studies Center, Special Monograph Series, vol. 4, 1988.

The Dictionary of National Biography. 22 vols. London: Oxford University Press, 1917.

Dyos, H. J., and Michael Wolff, eds. *The Victorian City: Images and Realities*. 2 vols. London: Routledge & Kegan Paul, 1973.

Ehat, Andrew F. "Joseph Smith's Introduction of Temple Ordinances and the 1844 Mormon Succession Question." Master's thesis, Brigham Young University, 1982.

———. and Lyndon W. Cook, eds. *The Words of Joseph Smith: The Contemporary Accounts of the Nauvoo Discourses of the Prophet Joseph Smith*. Provo, Utah: Brigham Young University Religious Studies Center, 1980.

Eliade, Mircea, ed. *The Encyclopedia of Religion*, 16 vols. New York: Macmillan, 1987.

Ellsworth, S. George. "A History of Mormon Missions in The United States and Canada, 1830–1860." Ph.D. dissertation, University of California at Berkeley, 1951.

England, Breck. "Gospel Seeds in Scottish Soil." *Ensign* 17 (February 1987): 26–31.

———. *The Life and Thought of Orson Pratt*. Salt Lake City: University of Utah Press, 1985.

Esplin, Ronald K. "Brigham Young in England." *The Ensign* 17 (June 1987): 28–33.

———. "The 1840–41 Mission to England and the Development of the Quorum of the Twelve." In *Mormons in Early Victorian Britain*, ed. Richard L. Jensen and Malcolm R. Thorp, 70–91. Salt Lake City: University of Utah Press, 1989.

———. "The Emergence of Brigham Young and the Twelve to Mormon Leadership, 1830–1841." Ph.D. dissertation, Brigham Young University, 1981.

———. "Inside Brigham Young: Abrahamic Tests As a Preparation for Leadership," *Brigham Young University Studies* 20 (Spring 1980): 300–310.

———. "Joseph, Brigham and the Twelve: A Succession of Continuity." *Brigham Young University Studies* 21 (Summer 1981): 301–41.

———. "Sickness and Faith, Nauvoo Letters." *Brigham Young University Studies* 15 (Summer 1975): 425–34.

Evans, Richard L. *A Century of "Mormonism" in Great Britain*. 1937; reprint, Salt Lake City: Bookcraft, 1984.

Fales, Susan. "Artisans, Millhands, and Laborers: The Mormons of Leeds and Their Nonconformist Neighbors." In *Mormons in Early Victorian Britain*, ed. Richard L. Jensen and Malcolm R. Thorp, 156–78. Salt Lake City: University of Utah Press, 1989.

———. "The Nonconformists of Leeds in the Early Victorian Era: A Study in Social Composition." Master's thesis, Brigham Young University, 1984.

Foster, Craig L., "Anti-Mormon Pamphleteering in Great Britain, 1837–1860." Master's thesis, Brigham Young University, 1989.

Fussell, G. E., and K. R. Fussell. *The English Countryman: His Life and Work from Tudor Times to the Victorian Age*. London: Orbis Publishing, 1981.

——. *The English Countrywoman: A Farmhouse Social History* A.D. 1500–1900. 1953: Reprint. New York: Benjamin Blom, 1971.

Gash, Norman. *Aristocracy and People: Britain 1815–1865*. London: Edward Arnold, 1979.

Gilbert, Alan D. *Religion and Society in Industrial England*. London: Longman, 1976.

Girouard, Mark. *Cities & People: A Social and Architectural History*. New Haven, Conn.: Yale University Press, 1985.

Godfrey, Kenneth W., Audrey M. Godfrey, and Jill Mulvay Derr, "Bathsheba Wilson Bigler Smith (1822–1910)." In *Women's Voices: An Untold History of the Latter-day Saints 1830– 1900*, 121–33. Salt Lake City: Deseret Book Co., 1985.

Hammond, J. L. and Barbara Hammond. *The Age of the Chartists 1832–1854: A Study of Discontent*. 1930; reprint, New York: Augustus M. Kelley, 1967.

Hardwick, Charles. *History of the Borough of Preston and its Environs, in the County of Lancaster*. Preston: Worthington & Co., 1857.

Harris, Jan G. "Mormons in Victorian England." Master's thesis, Brigham Young University, 1987.

——. "Mormons in Victorian Manchester." *Brigham Young University Studies* 27 (Winter 1987): 47–56.

Harrison, Brian. *Drink and the Victorians*. London: Faber and Faber, 1971.

Harrison, J. F. C. "The Popular History of Early Victorian Britain: A Mormon Contribution." *Journal of Mormon History* 14 (1988): 3–15.

——. *The Second Coming: Popular Millenarianism 1780–1850*. New Brunswick, N.J.: Rutgers University Press, 1979.

Hastings, James, ed. *Encyclopedia of Religion and Ethics*. 13 vols. New York: Charles Scribner's Sons, 1951.

Henriques, Ursula. *Religious Toleration in England 1787–1833*. Toronto: University of Toronto Press, 1961.

Hicks, Michael. *Mormonism and Music: A History*. Urbana: University of Illinois Press, 1989.

Hill, Marvin S. "An Historical Study of the Life of Orson Hyde, Early Mormon Missionary and Apostle 1805–1852." Master's thesis, Brigham Young University, 1955.

Hobsbawm, E. J. "The British Standard of Living, 1790–1850." *Economic History Review*, Second Series, 10 (1957): 53–54.

Hopkins, James K. *A Woman to Deliver Her People: Joanna Southcott and English Millenarianism in an Era of Revolution*. Austin: University of Texas Press, 1981.

Hoskins, W. G. *The Making of the English Landscape*. Hammondsworth: Penguin Books, 1933.

Ingliss, Keith S. *Churches and the Working Classes in Victorian England*. London: Routledge & Kegan Paul, 1963.

Jackson, J. Hampden. *England Since the Industrial Revolution 1815–1948*. Westport, Conn.: Greenwood Press, 1975.

Jensen, Richard L. "The British Gathering to Zion." In *Truth Will Prevail: The Rise of The Church of Jesus Christ of Latter-day Saints in the British Isles 1837–1987*, ed. V. Ben Bloxham, James R. Moss, and Larry C. Porter, 165–98. Solihull, England: The Church of Jesus Christ of Latter-day Saints, 1987.

——. "The John Taylor Family." *Ensign* 10 (February 1980): 50–56.

——, and Malcolm R. Thorp, eds. *Mormons in Early Victorian Britain*. Salt Lake City: University of Utah Press, 1989.

Jessee, Dean C. "The Early Accounts of Joseph Smith's First Vision." *Brigham Young University Studies* 9 (Spring 1969): 275–94.

———. "Wilford Woodruff." In *The Presidents of the Church*, ed. Leonard J. Arrington, 117–43. Salt Lake City: Deseret Book Co., 1986.

———. "The Writings of Brigham Young." *Western Historical Quarterly* 4 (July 1973): 273–94.

———, ed. "Joseph Smith's 19 July 1840 Discourse." *Brigham Young University Studies* 19 (Spring 1979): 390–94.

———, ed. *Letters of Brigham Young to His Sons*. Salt Lake City: Deseret Book Co., 1974.

———, ed. *The Personal Writings of Joseph Smith*. Salt Lake City: Deseret Book Co., 1984.

Jones, Garth N. "Who Came in Second?" *Dialogue: A Journal of Mormon Thought* 21 (Summer 1988): 149–54.

Jorgensen, Lynn Watkins. "The First London Mormons: 1840–1845. 'What Am I And My Brethren Here For?' " Master's thesis, Brigham Young University, 1988.

Journal of Discourses. 26 vols. London: Latter-day Saints' Book Depot, 1854–1886; reprint, Salt Lake City, 1967.

Kent, John. "Feeling and Festivals: An Interpretation of Some Working Class Religious Attitudes." In *The Victorian City: Images and Reality*, 2 vols., ed. H. J. Dyos and Michael Wolff, 2:855–71. London: Routledge & Kegan Paul, 1973.

Kimball, Stanley B. "Brigham and Heber." *Brigham Young University Studies* 18 (Spring 1978): 396–409.

———. "Heber C. Kimball and Family, the Nauvoo Years." *Brigham Young University Studies* 15 (Summer 1975): 447–79.

———. *Heber C. Kimball: Mormon Patriarch and Pioneer*. Urbana: University of Illinois Press, 1981.

Lewis, Samuel. *Topographical Dictionary of England*. 7th ed. 4 vols. London: S. Lewis and Co., 1848.

Lively, Robert L. "The Catholic Apostolic Church and The Church of Jesus Christ of Latter-day Saints: A Comparative Study of Two Minority Millenarian Groups in Nineteenth Century England." Ph.D. dissertation, Oxford University, 1977.

Lyon, T. Edgar. "Nauvoo and the Council of the Twelve." In *The Restoration Movement: Essays in Mormon History*, ed. F. Mark McKiernan, Alma R. Blair, and Paul M. Edwards, 167–205. Lawrence, Kansas: Coronado Press, 1973.

———. "Orson Pratt: Early Mormon Leader." Master's thesis, University of Chicago, 1932.

Marcus, Steven. "Reading the Illegible." In *The Victorian City: Images and Reality*, 2 vols., ed. H. J. Dyos and Michael Wolff, 1:257–76. London: Routledge & Kegan Paul, 1973.

McKay, John P., Bennett D. Hill, and John Buckler. *A History of World Societies*. Boston: Houghton Mifflin Co., 1984.

McLeod, Hugh. "Class, Community and Region: The Religious Geography of Nineteenth-Century England." In *A Sociological Yearbook of Religion in Britain*, ed. Michael Hill, 6:29–72. London: SCM, 1973.

———. *Religion and the Working Class in Nineteenth-Century Britain*. London: Macmillan, 1984.

"Missionary Sketches." *Juvenile Instructor* 5 (October 15, 1870): 166–67.

Mitchell, B. R. *Abstract of British Historical Statistics*. Cambridge: Cambridge University Press, 1962.

Moore, Richard G. "A History of Mormon Periodicals from 1830 to 1838." Master's thesis, Brigham Young University, 1983.

Moss, James R. "The Gospel Restored to England." In *Truth Will Prevail: The Rise of The Church of Jesus Christ of Latter-day Saints in the British Isles 1837–1987*, ed. V. Ben Bloxham, James R. Moss, and Larry C. Porter, 71–103. Solihull, England: The Church of Jesus Christ of Latter-day Saints, 1987.

———, and Lavell Moss. *Historic Sites of The Church of Jesus Christ of Latter-day Saints in the British Isles*. Salt Lake City: Publisher's Press for The Church of Jesus Christ of Latter-day Saints, 1987.

Noall, Claire. *Intimate Disciple: Portrait of Willard Richards*. Salt Lake City: University of Utah Press, 1957.

Norman, Edward R. *Church and Society in England 1770–1970*. Oxford: Clarendon Press, 1976.

Obelkevich, James. *Religion and Rural Society in South Lindsey, 1825–1875*. Oxford: Clarendon Press, 1976.

Perkes, William Evans. *History of Richard Rushton Sr. and Family*. Alhambra, California: Published privately by the Rushton Family Organization, 1977.

Peterson, Paul H. "An Historical Analysis of the Word of Wisdom." Master's thesis, Brigham Young University, 1972.

Petrie, Sir Charles. *The Victorians*. Westport, Conn.: Greenwood Press, 1960.

Phillips, Paul T. *The Sectarian Spirit: Sectarianism, Society, and Politics in Victorian Cotton Towns*. Toronto: University of Toronto Press, 1982.

Pickup, David M.W. *"The Pick and Flower of England": The Story of the Mormons in Victorian Lancashire*. Burnley, Lancashire, England: Living Legend, 1991.

Pierce, J. *Joseph Livesey as Reformer and Teacher*. N.p., 1885.

Pike, E. Royston. *"Hard Times": Human Documents of the Industrial Revolution*. New York: Frederick A. Praeger, 1966.

Pusey, Merlo. *Builders of the Kingdom: George A. Smith, John Henry Smith, George Albert Smith*. Provo, Utah: Brigham Young University Press, 1981.

Quinn, D. Michael. "Latter-day Saint Prayer Circles." *Brigham Young University Studies* 19 (Fall 1978): 79–105.

Roberts, B. H. *A Comprehensive History of the Church*. 6 vols. Salt Lake City: Deseret News Press, 1930.

———. *The Life of John Taylor*. 1892. Reprint. Salt Lake City: Bookcraft, 1963.

Sekers, David. *The Potteries*. Great Britain: Shire Publications Ltd., 1981.

Sheppard, Francis. *London 1808–1870: The Infernal Wen*. London: Secker & Warburg, 1971.

Shepperson, Wilbur S. "The Place of the Mormons in the Religious Emigration of Britain." *Church History* 20 (July 1952): 207–18.

Simpson, J. A., and E. S. C. Weiner, eds. *The Oxford English Dictionary*. 20 vols. Oxford: Clarendon Press, 1989.

Smart, Paul F. "The History of the Early Members of The Church of Jesus Christ of Latter-day Saints in Preston, Lancashire, England [1837–c.1851]. Master's thesis, Brigham Young University, 1989.

Smith, Job. "The United Brethren." *Improvement Era* 13 (July 1910): 818–23.

Smith, Joseph, Jr. *History of The Church of Jesus Christ of Latter-day Saints.* Ed. B. H. Roberts. 2d ed. rev. 7 vols. Salt Lake City: The Church of Jesus Christ of Latter-day Saints, Deseret Book Co., 1971.

Smith, Paul Thomas. "Among Family and Friends: John Taylor's Mission to the British Isles." *The Ensign* 17 (March 1987): 36–41.

——. "John Taylor." In *The Presidents of the Church*, ed. Leonard J. Arrington, 75–114. Salt Lake City: Deseret Book Co., 1986.

Sonne, Conway B. *Saints on the Seas: A Maritime History of Mormon Migration, 1830–1890.* Salt Lake City: University of Utah Press, 1983.

——. *Ships, Saints, and Mariners: A Maritime Encyclopedia of Mormon Migration, 1830–1930.* Salt Lake City: University of Utah Press, 1987.

Stock, Hugh. "The Book of Mormon, 1830–1879, A Publishing History." Master's thesis, University of California at Los Angeles, 1979.

Storch, Robert D. " 'Please to Remember the Fifth of November': Conflict, Solidarity and Public Order in Southern England, 1815–1900." Chapter 4 of *Popular Culture and Custom in Nineteenth-Century England*, ed. Robert D. Storch. London: St. Martin's Press, 1982.

Stott, G. St. John. "John Taylor's Religious Preparation." *Dialogue: A Journal of Mormon Thought* 19 (Spring 1986): 123–28.

Taylor, Arthur J., ed. *The Standard of Living in Britain in the Industrial Revolution.* London: Methuen & Co. Ltd., 1975.

Taylor, P. A. M. *Expectations Westward: The Mormons and the Emigration of their British Converts in the Nineteenth Century.* Edinburgh: Oliver and Boyd, 1965.

Taylor, Samuel W. *The Kingdom or Nothing: The Life of John Taylor, Militant Mormon.* New York: Macmillan, 1976.

Thistlewaite, Frank. *The Anglo-American Connection in the Early Nineteenth Century.* Philadelphia: University of Pennsylvania Press, 1959.

Thompson, F. M. L. *The Rise of Respectable Society: A Social History of Victorian Britain, 1830–1900.* Cambridge: Harvard University Press, 1988.

Thompson, Kenneth A. *Bureaucracy and Church Reform.* Oxford: Clarendon Press, 1970.

Thorp, Malcolm R. "Early Mormon Confrontations with Sectarianism, 1837–40." In *Mormons in Early Victorian Britain*, ed. Richard L. Jensen and Malcolm R. Thorp, 46–69. Salt Lake City: University of Utah Press, 1989.

——. "The Religious Backgrounds of Mormon Converts in Britain, 1837–52." *Journal of Mormon History* 4 (1977): 51–66.

——. "Sectarian Violence in Early Victorian Britain: The Mormon Experience, 1837–1860." *Bulletin of the John Rylands University Library of Manchester* 70 (Autumn 1988): 135–47.

——. "Social and Religious Origins of Early English Mormons." *World Conference on Records*, Series 444, August 12–15, 1980. Salt Lake City: Corporation of the President of The Church of Jesus Christ of Latter-day Saints, 1980.

Underwood, Grant R. "The Millenarian World of Early Mormonism." Ph.D. dissertation, University of California at Los Angeles, 1988.

Valentine, Hyrum W. *The Trio's Pilgrimage.* N.p., 1947.

Van Wagoner, Richard S. "Sarah M. Pratt: The Shaping of an Apostate." *Dialogue: A Journal of Mormon Thought* 19 (Summer 1986): 69–99.

Walker, Ronald W. "Cradling Mormonism: The Rise of the Gospel in Early Victorian England." *Brigham Young University Studies* 27 (Winter 1987): 25–36.

———, ed. "The Willard Richards and Brigham Young 5 September 1840 Letter from England to Nauvoo." *Brigham Young University Studies* 18 (Spring 1978): 466–75.

Ward, W. R. *Religion and Society in England 1790–1850.* London: B. T. Batsford Ltd., 1972.

Watt, Barbara Fluckiger. "Bathsheba Bigler Smith: Woman of Faith and Courage." In *Sister Saints*, ed. Vicky Burgess-Olsen, 201–21. Provo, Utah: Brigham Young University Press, 1978.

Weber, Adna Ferrin. *The Growth of Cities in the Nineteenth Century: A Study in Statistics.* Ithaca, N.Y.: Cornell University Press, 1965.

Weinreb, Ben, and Christopher Hibbert. *The London Encyclopedia.* London: Macmillan, 1984.

Wells, Emmeline B. "Biography of Mary Ann Young." *The Juvenile Instructor* 26 (June 15, 1891): 56–57.

Werner, Julia Stewart. *The Primitive Methodist Connection: Its Background and Early History.* Madison: University of Wisconsin Press, 1984.

Whitney, Helen Mar. "Scenes in Nauvoo." *Woman's Exponent* 10 (August 1, 1881): 34.

Whitney, Orson F. *History of Utah.* 4 vols. Salt Lake City: George Q. Cannon & Sons, 1904.

———. *Life of Heber C. Kimball.* 1888. 3d ed. Salt Lake City: Bookcraft, 1967.

Whittaker, David J. "The 'Articles of Faith' in Early Mormon Literature and Thought." In *New Views of Mormon History: Essays in Honor of Leonard J. Arrington*, ed. Davis Bitton and Maureen Ursenbach Beecher, 63–92. Salt Lake City: University of Utah Press, 1987.

———. "The Bone in the Throat: Orson Pratt and the Public Announcement of Plural Marriage." *Western Historical Quarterly* 18 (July 1987): 193–314.

———. "Early Mormon Pamphleteering." Ph.D. dissertation, Brigham Young University, 1982.

———. "Harvest in Herefordshire." *Ensign* 17 (January 1987): 46–51.

———. "Orson Pratt, Prolific Pamphleteer." *Dialogue: A Journal of Mormon Thought* 15 (Autumn 1982): 27–41.

Whittaker, Thomas. *Life's Battles in Temperance Armour.* London: Hodder and Stoughton, 1884.

Willson, David Harris, and Stuart E. Prall. *A History of England*, 3d ed. New York: Holt, Rhinehart and Winston, 1984.

Wilson, Brian R. "American Religion: Its Impact on Britain." In *Contagious Conflict: The Impact of American Dissent on European Life*, ed. A. N. J. Den Hollander, 233–63. Leiden: E. J. Brill, 1973.

Yeo, Eileen. "Christianity in Chartist Struggle 1838–1842." *Past and Present*, no. 91 (May 1981): 109–39.

INDEX

447

Cold weather, brings misery, hampers work, 197, 208, 208 n. 10, 224
Collection boxes, passed in meetings, 102
Coltrin, John, 68
Commerce, Illinois. *See* Nauvoo
Conferences: definition of, 102; organized at Bran Green, Gadfield Elm, and Froome's Hill, 153
Conferences, general: of 1840, 135, 201; of 1841, 168, 301
Confirmation, first, in England, 38–39
Congregationalists, 325 n. 7, 326
Connor, Henry, Jr.: baptism of, 221–22; letter from, to George A. Smith, 406–7
Connor, Henry, Sr.,: watchmaker in London, 191; conversion of, 192
Converts: previous religious affiliation of, 329–37; social class of, 337–40
Copeland, William, Dr.: prominent convert, 18; entertains apostles in London, 221, 222; baptism of, 224
Cordon, Alfred: debates with John Berry, 203; early convert from Aitkenites, 331
Cottage workers, demise of, 13
Cowdery, Oliver, advises Twelve, 309
Cowley, Charles and Ann, 179
Cry from the Wilderness, by Orson Hyde, 263–64

Davis, John, 343 n. 74
Dawson, Ann: hospitality of, to elders, 36; confirmations performed in her home, 39
Day, Thomas, conversion of, 334–35
Demographics of Church members in England, 18, 323–44
Devils: appear to Heber C. Kimball, 33–34; key to detect, 59; annoy George A. Smith at London, 196; confrontation of, with Wilford Woodruff, 214, 224
Disease, afflicts apostles and their families, 58, 72, 218
Downham, village of, success of Heber C. Kimball in, 49–51
Draper, Father, 72
Dreams: of fishes and missionary success in Liverpool, 118; of fishing, 199, 214, 221; of home and America, 294
Drunkenness: in England, 10; forbidden to

Church members, 103; public, on Whit Monday, 144
Dust, shaken off feet as testimony, 88, 111

Echo, emigrant ship, 232
Economic conditions, in England, 107
Edinburgh: "Athens of the North," 163; intellectual climate in, 165
Education, formal, of apostles, 4
Emerald, emigration ship, 307
Emigration: affected by economic conditions in England, 18; spirit of, in England, 19; apostles discuss policies of, 135; spirit of, strong in British Saints, 135, 232; Joseph Fielding's apprehensions about, 136; item of business in council of apostles, 136; rich to aid poor in, 136, 230; Parley P. Pratt leads discussion of, 136; John Moon leads first group, 137; first group sails on *Britannia*, 144; financed by John and Jane Benbow, 181; departure of various companies in, 232; Joseph Smith on, 233; organization for, 300; conditions on sailing ships described, 377–81. *See also* Gathering
Enclosure movement, 19
England: description of, in 1840, 10, 324, 389–93; society in, 12; suffrage in, 12; economics in, 13; industrial revolution in, 13; sanitation in, 15; hunger in, 15; pollution in, 16; unemployment in, 16; average age of death in, 16, 16 n. 21; child labor in, 17; report of Brigham Young and Willard Richards on, to the First Presidency, 10, 12, 389–95
Epistle of Demetrius . . . , as satirical attack on clergy by Parley P. Pratt, 258
Eternal marriage, 317
Evangelicalism, 325–26
Evening and the Morning Star, 237
Everlasting covenant, 101

Far West, Missouri: place of departure for second mission to England, 54; danger to Twelve at, 56; site of "early morning meeting," 8, 57; cornerstone laid at, 57
Fielding, Amos, Church emigration agent, 235

of Saint George Temple, 322; issues Manifesto, 322; letter from, to Willard Richards, 371–76; letter to, from Orson Pratt, 405–6

Word of Wisdom: taught in England, 47; taught to temperance societies, 89, 340; early interpretation of, 103–4, 137, 224

World Turned Upside Down, or Heaven on Earth, The, by Parley P. Pratt, 259

Wright, Alexander: mission of, to Scotland, 130; receives fatherly advice from Wilford Woodruff, 131; in Scotland, 162

Wroe, John, 330 n. 30

Young, Brigham: senior apostle, 6, 55; vocations of, 6; education of, 6; report of, on conditions in England, 10; on Zion's Camp, 21; directs exodus from Missouri, 55; emerges as strong leader, 55; illness of, on departure for England, 70–71; feeds George A. Smith during illness, 76; arrival of, in Liverpool, 83; sustained as president of the Twelve, 89, 134; orders fine watch, 98–99; longs for home, 99; sends presents home, 100; seeks Joseph Smith's approval of British agenda, 135; denies John Taylor's request to bring family to England, 147; labors of, in Herefordshire, 147–52; quiets antagonists at Gadfield Elm, 150; preaches to the United Brethren, 150; commences work on publishing Book of Mormon and hymnal, 150; excuses Willard Richards to care for wife, 155; administrative duties of, 157; works on hymnal, 157; weaknesses as editor and publisher, 157–58; sense of humor, 158; determined to eliminate practice of "greeting" kiss, 170; writes agenda for conference meetings, 201; agonizes over poverty of members, 206; goes to Wales, 207; indexes and publishes Book of Mormon, 207; organizes emigration, 229; advice of, on emigration, 234; on publishing committee, 245, 250; proceeds with publications without authorization, 245–46; to help select hymns for hymnal, 247; raises funds for publishing, 248; recalls beneficial effect of publishing, 265; concern of, for family, 271–72; dreams of home and family, 294; sings at Manchester conference, 301; revelation to, regarding future service, 307; statement of, on not aspiring to power, 315; legitimate authority of, to lead Church, 317; receives endowments, 317; comprehends office of apostleship, 318; history of service of, 320; letter to, from Willard Richards, 384–85; letter to Willard Richards, from, 386–87; letter from, to the First Presidency, 388–95; letter from, to Mary Ann Young, 398–405

Young, Joseph, 275

Young, Mary Ann Angell: hardships of, 270–72; uncomplaining nature of, 270; crosses Mississippi River in open boat, 270–71; builds house in husband's absence, 272; inquires of Joseph Smith about return of apostles, 292; letter to, from husband, 398–405

Zion: site of, designated, 20; North and South America identified as, 87–88

Zion's Camp, 9, 21